The War on Terror Encyclopedia

The War on Terror Encyclopedia

FROM THE RISE OF AL-QAEDA TO 9/11 AND BEYOND

Jan Goldman, Editor

A B C ✦ C L I O

Santa Barbara, California • Denver, Colorado • Oxford, England

Library of Congress Cataloging-in-Publication Data
The war on terror encyclopedia : from the rise of Al-Qaeda to 9/11 and beyond / Jan Goldman, editor.
     pages cm
   Includes bibliographical references and index.
   ISBN 978-1-61069-510-7 (alk. paper) — ISBN 978-1-61069-511-4 (ebook) 1. War on Terrorism, 2001–2009—Encyclopedias. 2. Terrorism—United States—History—21st century—Encyclopedias. 3. Terrorism—History—21st century—Encyclopedias. I. Goldman, Jan.
   HV6432.W37185 2014
   363.32503—dc23   2014014854

ISBN: 978-1-61069-510-7
EISBN: 978-1-61069-511-4

18 17 16 15 14   1 2 3 4 5

This book is also available on the World Wide Web as an eBook.
Visit www.abc-clio.com for details.

ABC-CLIO, LLC
130 Cremona Drive, P.O. Box 1911
Santa Barbara, California 93116-1911

This book is printed on acid-free paper ∞
Manufactured in the United States of America

All statements of fact, opinion, or analysis expressed are those of the authors and do not reflect the official position or views of any U.S. government agency. Nothing in the contents should be construed as asserting or implying U.S. government authentication of information or endorsement of the authors' views.

To those individuals affected by terrorism, and their resilience to persevere, protect, and promote democratic ideals.

Morality is contraband in war.
—Mahatma Gandi

Contents

List of Entries

Preface

Everyone is aware of international terrorism. Death and destruction are usually the result of such an action. Unfortunately, terrorism is not limited to any particular region; acts of terrorism can occur in almost every country, from any country. Reportedly, the United States is a target less than 10 percent of the time when an act of international terrorism occurs. However, when it does occur, military and diplomatic personnel are mostly targets. Although international terrorism has existed long before that fateful day on September 11, 2001, to most people those attacks were the turning point in American history. The war on terror was no longer limited to distant locations overseas or government officials; terrorism arrived on American soil.

This encyclopedia seeks to put acts of terrorism, specifically against the United States and its citizens, within the context of policies, politics, culture, economics, and individuals that were either victims or perpetrators of these actions. Of course, some people may not see the "war on terror" as a war.

The word "terror" is a noun that creates fear. However, when used in the proper context, "terror" describes a violent or destructive act committed by a group to intimidate a population or government. In contrast to the term "Cold War," which attributed with an adjective a relationship between the United States and Soviet Union, how do you characterize a war with a noun? In other words, how do you go to war with something that describes an action?

First, this is not a book about the general nature of "terror" or "terrorism." This is a book about the "*war*" on terror as viewed from the American perspective. Without a doubt, this country has the resources to fight conventional wars, but what happens when the enemy is not a nation-state?

It is the goal of this encyclopedia to focus on the conflict between the United States and groups that seek to commit acts of terror against Americans and their allies. This encyclopedia will focus on the actions, events, and people involved in this "war on terror" from both sides. Additionally, this book seeks to look at acts of terrorism against the United States from an objective perspective, rarely wandering from the facts or from what are widely believed to be the facts by academics. On the other hand, this book will focus on terrorism from a policy perspective, as portrayed on the global battlefield.

It is hoped that by providing a factual basis from both sides, the reader is in a better position to develop an opinion and will use this encyclopedia as a foundation for additional research. All of the contributors to this encyclopedia are experts who have been studying and writing on terrorism and what it means to fight a war on terror. I hope the reader will be able to use this knowledge to become a more informed citizen and student.

Jan Goldman, EdD
Washington, D.C.

Introduction

Jan Goldman

After the terrorist attacks of September 11, 2001, the Bush administration declared a worldwide "war on terror," involving open and covert military operations, new security legislation, efforts to block the financing of terrorism, and more. Washington called on other nations to join in the fight against terrorism, asserting, "[E]ither you are with us, or you are with the terrorists."[1]

Almost a decade later, the war is over. The United States is no longer engaged in a "war on terrorism." Neither is it fighting "jihadists" or involved in a "global war." President Obama's top homeland security and counterterrorism official took all three terms off the list of acceptable words inside the White House during a speech given by Secretary of State Hillary Clinton. According to Clinton, the administration was no longer using the term "war on terror." There was no specific directive from the White House, and Mr. Obama had not used the term "war on terror" since January 23, 2012, his fourth day as president.[2]

Officially, the term "war on terror" may no longer be in vogue, but the reality is that the United States remains involved in a war with no end in sight. Dismissing the term or label does not equate to dismissing the action. Of course, this begs the question: How does a country go to war against terror and when do we know the war has ended? Can we ever determine if the United States won or lost the war on terror?

First, let us be clear that "terror" is not a country or sovereign nation, but rather an emotion of an intense feeling of fear. According to most standard definitions, terror is caused by violent or destructive acts committed by groups in order to intimidate a population or government for specific objectives or goals. Terror on a massive scale can translate into different forms of terrorism. Those different forms can include "state terrorism," when a nation supports terrorist actions or groups to conduct such actions; "bioterrorism," the use of chemical or biological diseases to affect a population's health; "cyberterrorism," the use of technology to attack critical infrastructure or databases; and "nuclear terrorism," the dispersal of highly deadly radioactive material. These are only a few tactics used to inflict terror on a population—acts of terror caused by terrorists.

Although we are fighting a "war against terror," it is a war against terrorists. As long as the American citizens are targets for terrorists, we rely on the United States government to marshal national security resources to protect its citizens and interests. In the past, battles were fought after a country officially declared "war" upon another country or when it became apparent that a country had declared war after a "surprise attack" (i.e., an undeclared war on an adversary before notifying that adversary they were officially at war). According to some definitions, the military can only fight a war when a declaration of war has been formally announced by one nation against another. This declaration is usually provided in a formal announcement by the senior leadership in the government. This is what happened in World War II.

Historians cite the United States' "unofficial" entry into World War II at 7:48 a.m. (Hawaiian time) on December 7, 1941. At that time, the first of over 4,000 bombs fell from the sky from Japanese aircraft. On that earth-shattering day, almost 3,000 military and civilians were killed in Japan's attack on the U.S. Naval Base at Pearl Harbor, in Hawaii. Officially, the United States did not enter World War II *when* the attack occurred at Pearl Harbor. The next day, Congress held a vote to officially enter the war against Japan. On December 11, 1941, Congress would "officially" declare war on Germany and Italy. That same day, Germany and Italy would declare war on the United States. Almost six months later, on June 5, 1942, the United States would officially declare war on Bulgaria, Hungary, and Romania. This would be the last time the United States would officially declare war on a country.

Rhetorically, that would not prevent the United States from using the term "war" in support of a policy. In 1971, President Richard Nixon would popularize the term "war on drugs," declaring drug abuse as "public enemy number one." (Of course, this is a mixed metaphor, since an "enemy list" was mostly popularized by the FBI in capturing criminals as displaying a "top 10 most wanted list"; in effect, the United States was declaring a war on an object that was neither a country or a person.) In 2009, the U.S. Office of National Drug Control Policy signaled that it would no longer use the term "war on drugs." In 1964, President Lyndon B. Johnson unofficially declared a "war on poverty" as a part of his belief in expanding the government's concern in terms of education and health care for the poor. Today in the United States, more people are living in poverty than 60 years ago, with no truce with poverty in sight.

According to former CBS News anchor Katie Couric, "The war on terror began with the September 11 attacks on the United States. Similarly, NBC News anchor Brian Williams declared that we are a nation at war because of what happened in New York."[3] Although there is no official and exact determination of when the United States became involved in the "war on terror," we may have an idea of when this nation's involvement began, down to the minute, assuming you consider the "war on terror" began on this day.

At 8:14 a.m. on September 11, 2001, the United States was attacked in the opening salvo in the "war on terror." At that exact time, two hijackers stabbed two flight attendants on American Airlines Flight 11 bound for Los Angeles, California, from Boston, Massachusetts. On board were 81 passengers and 11 crew members. Just over 30 minutes later, at 8:45 a.m., and traveling at over 450 miles per hour, the plane slammed into World Trade Center Tower #1, between the floors 93 and 99 in New York City. About 15 minutes later, another plane slammed into the adjoining tower between floors 77 and 85. Within an hour, another hijacked aircraft was deliberately crashed into the Pentagon, while another plane would crash in an open field in Pennsylvania, reportedly never reaching its intended target, either the White House or the U.S. Capitol, both in Washington, D.C. On that fateful day, over 3,000 American citizens were killed in four coordinated terrorist attacks. The war on terror between the United States and terrorists began at that time . . . or did it?

If you look at the timeline in this book, you will see that the United States was fighting a war on terror many, many years before September 11, 2001. Whether the fact was recognized by the media, the government, or citizens, the United States was under attack before 9/11. Terrorist attacks occurred on U.S. property, killing many of the nation's citizens, and in almost every continent around the world, including locations in Kenya, Tanzania, Lebanon, Iraq, Iran, Libya, Philippines, Saudi Arabia, United Kingdom, Persian Gulf, Germany, and Italy, to list a few.

It is not unusual to use death as the starting point for major conflicts. However, according to Article 1, Section 8, of the United States Constitution, only Congress shall have power to declare war. Although the number of deaths are very similar (roughly 3,000) in both the attack on December 7, 1941, and the one on September 11, 2001, there is a huge difference between the two attacks. Although Congress did declare war on Japan, it did not, nor could it, officially declare war on terror, terrorism, or terrorists. Terrorism is a transnational threat—that is, it transcends politically sovereign territory. Congress may have come closest to declaring "war on terror" on August 22, 1998, when U.S. government officials declared a "long-term battle" against terrorists in Afghanistan and Sudan.

For purposes of clarity, terrorist acts against the United States conducted overseas by external groups are referred to as "international terrorism," and those committed within the territorial jurisdiction of the United States by internal groups are called "domestic terrorism." Since the attacks of 9/11, the United States has been using both military and law enforcement organizations to fight both international and domestic terrorism. This book takes the "war on terror" at face value.

This publication looks at the political, social, and economic policies, as well as the tactical operations, involved in fighting terrorism. This book also includes some of the major individuals on both sides of this war. Unlike the "war on drugs" or the "war on poverty," this war involves kidnapping, murder, destruction, and violent acts to human life that violate federal or state law with the sole purpose of intimidating or coercing the American population and influencing U.S. policy makers.

Although the "war on terror" can be used figuratively in speech, there is some truth behind this concept. War kills people and it seeks to destroy or severely hamper governments from operating in a standard (i.e., normal) manner. War can include the destruction of property. The war on terror includes death and destruction on both sides. The war on terror has taken lives in Pakistan, Afghanistan, Spain, Somalia, the United Kingdom—indeed, in almost every country on earth.

Nevertheless, the focus of this book is to systematically, categorically focus the war on terror as a war against a known entity. This requires identifying such topics as people, strategy, financial costs, advanced technological weaponry, propaganda, policy, ships, aircraft, and the men and women on both sides of the battlefield. Unfortunately, the battlefield includes shopping centers, schools, and movie theaters. Fighting terrorists rarely occurs under the moonlit sky of an empty pasture with the sound of gunfire, but rather in the daylight under a traffic light in the middle of a crowded street with the explosion of a car bomb. And because the war on terror has ill-defined boundaries, measuring progress in defeating this enemy is all the more difficult.

Notes

1. President George Bush's Joint Session of Congress, September 20, 2001, http://georgewbush-whitehouse.archives.gov/news/releases/2001/09/20010920-8.html.

2. Jay Solomon, "U.S. Drops 'War on Terror' Phrase, Clinton Says," March 31, 2009, *Wall Street Journal*, http://online.wsj.com/news/articles/SB123845123690371231#printMode.

3. Stephen D. Reese and Seth C. Lewis, "Framing the War on Terror: The Internalization of Policy in the U.S. Press," *Journalism: Theory, Practice and Criticism* 10, no. 6: 777–97.

A

Abdel-Rahman, Omar (aka the Blind Sheikh)

(1938–)

Omar Abdel-Rahman was born in Fayyum, Egypt, on May 3, 1938. He suffered from childhood diabetes, which resulted in blindness when he was 10 months old. By age 11, he had memorized the Koran and devoted himself to preaching the Muslim faith. He graduated in Koranic studies from Al-Azhar University in Cairo. As a professor at the Theological College in Asyut, he gained a large militant following in Cairo's southern slums and villages after speaking out against the government's violations of traditional Islamic sharia laws. Abdel-Rahman became the spiritual leader of the loosely knit, highly militant al-Gama'a al-Islamiyya (Islamic Group) umbrella organization and the Egyptian Islamic Jihad. Both organizations opposed the Egyptian government's policies and preached militant jihad. Islamic Jihad was responsible for the 1981 assassination of Egyptian president Anwar Sadat.

In 1981, Abdel-Rahman and 23 other Islamic militants were arrested in connection with Sadat's assassination. Abdel-Rahman spent three years in Egyptian jails, where he was tortured. Although acquitted of conspiracy in the assassination of Sadat, Abdel-Rahman was expelled from Egypt and went to Afghanistan, where he reportedly made contact with Al-Qaeda leader Osama bin Laden. Abdel-Rahman then traveled widely, recruiting mujahideen to fight in Afghanistan against the Soviet Union. Returning to Egypt, he was again arrested in 1989 for inciting antigovernment clashes in Fayyum but was again acquitted.

Abdel-Rahman fled Egypt after being linked to further terrorist attacks on Coptic Christians in northern Egypt, and illegally entered the United States in 1990 on a tourist visa obtained in Sudan. He gained permanent U.S. residency as a religious worker in 1991, an action that the U.S. Immigration and Naturalization Service (INS) now says was erroneous. However, Abdel-Rahman's marriage to an American Muslim convert enabled him to avoid deportation despite Egypt's calls for his extradition and his status as a prominent figure on the official U.S. terrorist list.

In January 1993, Abdel-Rahman was discovered to be actively preaching militant Islamic fundamentalist sermons to thousands of Egyptian, Yemeni, Sudanese, and other Muslim immigrants in New York's mosques. The sheikh's messages, secretly recorded on tape cassettes and funneled to his followers in the Egyptian underground, advocated "the eradication of all those who stand in the way of Islam" because "the laws of God have been usurped by Crusaders' laws. The hand of a thief is not cut off,

Sheikh Omar Abdel-Rahman is an Egyptian the-ologian who went into self-exile in the United States in 1990 to escape trial in Cairo for his sus-pected involvement in several terrorist attacks on Coptic Christians in northern Egypt. He is the ru-mored spiritual leader of the loosely knit, highly militant al-Gama'a al-Islamiyya (Islamic Group) umbrella organization. (AP Photo/Mark Lennihan)

the drinker of liquor is not whipped, the adulterer is not stoned. Islamic holy law should be followed to the letter."

Abdel-Rahman was arrested in the United States in July 1993 for his sus-pected involvement in the World Trade Center bombing, but insufficient evidence forced the INS to initially hold him on lesser charges of illegal immigration and polygamy. He was held in a U.S. federal prison while he appealed the deportation order against him and was awarded lim-ited preferential treatment because of his ill health and blindness.

On October 1, 1995, in the largest ter-rorism trial up to that point in U.S. history,

Abdel-Rahman was convicted of 48 of 50 charges, including seditious conspiracy, for leading a four-year terrorist campaign of bombings and assassinations intended to destroy the United Nations building and other landmarks in the New York area. He was also convicted of conspiring to assas-sinate Egyptian president Hosni Mubarak and of solicitation to attack U.S. military installations. Abdel-Rahman was sen-tenced to life imprisonment on January 17, 1996. He is currently serving his life sen-tence at the Federal Administrative Maxi-mum Penitentiary Hospital in Florence, Colorado. Abdel-Rahman is also believed to have ordered the November 1990 as-sassination in New York of militant Zion-ist leader Rabbi Meir Kahane. In 2005, members of Rahman's legal team, includ-ing lawyer Lynne Stewart, were convicted of facilitating communication between the imprisoned sheikh and members of the ter-rorist organization al-Gama'a al-Islamiyya in Egypt. They received long federal prison sentences based on their violated obligation to keep the sheikh incommunicado while providing him with legal counsel. In 2012, it was rumored that Egypt's new president, Mohamed Morsi, had begun negotiations with the United States to have the sheikh extradited to Egypt, but Morsi's ouster in July 2013 likely put an end to such efforts.

Spencer C. Tucker

See also: World Trade Center Bombing; Yousef, Ramzi Ahmed

Further Reading

Fried, Joseph P. "Sheik Sentenced to Life in Prison in Bombing Plot." *New York Times*, January 18, 1996.

Hedges, Chris. "A Cry of Islamic Fury Tape in Brooklyn for Cairo." *New York Times*, Janu-ary 7, 1993.

Kohlmann, Evan F. *Al-Qaida's Jihad in Europe.* London: Berg Publishers/Bloomsbury Academic, 2004.

Lance, Peter. *1000 Years for Revenge: International Terrorism and the FBI.* New York: Harper-Collins, 2003.

Macfarquhar, Neil. "In Jail or Out, Sheik Preaches Views of Islam." *New York Times,* October 2, 1995.

Able Danger

A highly classified U.S. military intelligence program whose leaders have claimed to have identified Muhammad Atta and three other members of the plot to hijack U.S. airliners and use them as weapons well before the September 11, 2001, terror attacks. General Hugh Shelton, chairman of the Joint Chiefs of Staff, issued a directive in early October 1999 to establish an intelligence program under the command of the U.S. Special Operations Command (SOCOM) of the Department of Defense to be directed specifically against the Al-Qaeda terrorist organization and its operatives. The commander of Able Danger was navy captain Scott Philpott, who headed a unit of 20 military intelligence specialists and a support staff. The chief analyst of Able Danger was Dr. Eileen Priesser.

The purpose of Able Danger was to identify Al-Qaeda members and neutralize them before they could initiate operations against the United States. The data-mining center was located at the Land Information Warfare Activity (LIWA)/Information Dominance Center at Fort Belvoir, Virginia. In the summer of 2000, the LIWA was transferred to Garland, Texas.

Members of this unit began intelligence operations seeking to identify Al-Qaeda operatives both in the United States and abroad. Its computer analysts set up a complex computer analysis system that searched public databases and the Internet for possible terrorist cells. One of the terrorist cells so identified contained the name of Mohamed Atta and three others who were later implicated in the September 11 plot. Atta's name was supposedly placed, along with those of the others, on a chart of Al-Qaeda operatives. Lieutenant Colonel Anthony Shaffer, a reserve officer attached to the Pentagon, and Able Danger's liaison with the Defense Intelligence Agency (DIA), as well as others, decided to inform the FBI about the threat posed by the Al-Qaeda operatives. Three potential meetings with the FBI were postponed because of opposition from military lawyers in the Pentagon. The apparent reason for the opposition from SOCOM was fear of controversy that might arise if it were made public that a military intelligence unit had violated the privacy of civilians legally residing in the United States. Another possible reason was that the lawyers believed that the program might be violating the Posse Comitatus Act, which prohibits employing the military to enforce civil laws.

The leaders of Able Danger then decided to work their way up the military chain of command. In January 2001, the leadership of Able Danger briefed General Hugh Shelton, still the chairman of the Joint Chiefs of Staff, on its findings. Shortly afterward, the Able Danger unit was disbanded, its operations ceasing in April 2001. Defense Department lawyers had determined that the activities of Able Danger violated President Ronald Reagan's Executive Order 12333, intended to prevent the Pentagon from storing data about U.S. citizens. A direct order came from the Defense Department to destroy the database; as a result, 2.4 terabytes of information about possible Al-Qaeda terrorist activities were destroyed in the summer of 2001. A chart identifying four hijackers, including Mohamed Atta, was produced by Able Danger and presented to the Deputy National Security Advisor, Jim Steinberg, but nothing came of it.

Able Danger was a classified program until its story surfaced shortly after the National Commission on Terrorist Attacks upon the United States, or the 9/11 Commission, issued its report, which stated categorically that the U.S. government had no prior knowledge about the conspiracy that led to the September 11 attacks. Keith Phucas, a reporter for the *Norristown Times Herald* in Pennsylvania, broke the story of Able Danger on June 19, 2005, in an article titled "Missed Chance on Way to 9/11."

When the story about Able Danger became public, it erupted into a political controversy. On June 27, 2005, Representative Curt Weldon (R-PA), the vice chairman of the House Armed Services and House Homeland Security committees, brought the Able Danger issue into the national limelight. In a speech before the House of Representatives, Weldon accused the U.S. government of negligence in its failure to heed the information gathered by Able Danger.

Despite some lapses of information (and a tendency to blame the Bill Clinton administration for the lapses), Weldon summarized many of the features of Able Danger without disclosing its nature as a secret military intelligence initiative run from within the Department of Defense. Weldon also disclosed that the information about Able Danger had been reported to the staff of the 9/11 Commission.

Members of the 9/11 Commission responded to these charges with a series of denials. Lee H. Hamilton, former vice chair of the 9/11 Commission, admitted learning about the Able Danger program, but denied hearing anything credible about a possible identification of Atta or other skyjackers in the 9/11 plot. This argument contradicted the testimony of Shaffer that he had communicated Able Danger's findings about Atta in a meeting with the commission's executive director, Philip Zelikov, at Bagram Air Base, Afghanistan, in late 2003. Leaders of the commission then requested and obtained information about Able Danger from the Defense Department, but there had been nothing about Atta in the information provided. They also admitted that Captain Philpott had mentioned something about Atta only days before the final report came out.

This denial of prior knowledge by members of the 9/11 Commission drew the attention of Lieutenant Colonel Shaffer. In an interview on August 15, 2005, Shaffer told the story of Able Danger, and he indicated that he had been at the "point of near insubordination" over the refusal to pursue the information about Atta. Furthermore, Shaffer insisted that he had talked to the staff of the 9/11 investigation in October 2003 in Afghanistan, where his next tour of duty had taken him. Captain Philpott and civilian contractor J. D. Smith confirmed Shaffer's claim about Able Danger's awareness of Atta.

The controversy has continued because the participants were felt left out of the investigation of the events surrounding September 11. Many of them have placed their careers in jeopardy by countering the government's version. Shaffer had his security clearance revoked by the Defense Intelligence Agency (DIA) and his personal records of Able Danger destroyed. In September 2006, the Defense Department's inspector general issued a report denying that Able Danger had identified Atta by calling the testimony of witnesses inconsistent.

Weldon criticized the report and investigation as incomplete. Although Weldon was an effective spokesperson in Congress who kept the story alive, his defeat in the 2006 elections deprived him of that important forum. A lengthy report released by the U.S. Senate Intelligence Committee in December 2006 confirmed that neither Atta nor any other September 11 conspirator or participant had ever been identified by Able Danger. That report, however, has failed to silence some skeptics.

Stephen E. Atkins

See also: Atta, Mohamed el-Amir Awad el-Sayed; National Commission on Terrorist Attacks upon the United States

Further Reading

Lance, Peter. *Triple Cross: How Bin Laden's Master Spy Penetrated the CIA, the Green Berets, and the FBI—and Why Patrick Fitzgerald Failed to Stop Him.* New York: ReganBooks, 2006.

McCarthy, Andrew C. "It's Time to Investigate Able Danger and the 9/11 Commission." *National Review* (December 8, 2005): 1.

Rosen, James. "Able Danger Operatives Sue Pentagon." *News Tribune* (Tacoma, WA), March 4, 2006, 6.

Abouhalima, Mahmud

(1959–)

Mahmud Abouhalima was one of the principal conspirators in the 1993 World Trade Center bombing. He was a devoted follower of the militant Islamist imam Sheikh Omar Abdel-Rahman, serving as his guide and driver. When Ramzi Yousef took charge of the plot to bomb the World Trade Center, Abouhalima, his friend, became his chief assistant.

Abouhalima never fit into any community he lived in until he became an Islamist. Born in 1959 in the small town of Kafr Dawar, about 15 miles south of Alexandria, Egypt, he was unhappy about his lack of career prospects in Egypt and left school early, emigrating to Munich, West Germany. There he lived among fellow Arabs, working first as a dishwasher and later in the meat department of a grocery store. Although he disliked Germany, he married a German woman. When his German visa expired, Abouhalima decided to move his family to the United States.

Abouhalima and his wife arrived in the United States in 1986. Soon after arriving in New York City, he found a job as a taxicab driver. His career as a cabbie had its ups and downs. Because he drove his taxi without license or registration, Abouhalima was often in trouble with police because of traffic violations; his most common offense was running red lights. However, his income allowed him to live in Brooklyn with his wife and four children.

Abouhalima became a convert to the extremist theology of Islamists while in the United States. He left New York City in the late 1980s to travel to Afghanistan to fight against the Soviets. Besides gaining combat experience, he received a strong dose of Islamist propaganda that culminated in his conversion to radical Islam. While in Afghanistan, he became friendly with expert bomb maker Ramzi Yousef. Abouhalima then returned to the United States, determined to carry the religious fight to the secular West.

The arrival of Abdel-Rahman in July 1990 gave Abouhalima a spiritual mentor. Most of Abouhalima's nonwork activities revolved around the al-Farouq Mosque and the al-Kifah Refugee Center. Abouhalima became Abdel-Rahman's principal guide and driver. When the militants began to plan terrorist operations, Abouhalima participated in discussions and volunteered his services. When El Sayyid Nosair decided to assassinate the Israeli extremist Meir Kahane, Abouhalima was to provide his escape transportation. However, a mistake kept Abouhalima and his transportation from arriving. Nosair shot Kahane and tried to escape but was wounded in the throat and captured. Abouhalima's role in this conspiracy was not discovered by the police until much later.

Abouhalima played a major role in the 1993 World Trade Center bombing, helping Yousef build the bomb. On February 23, 1993, Abouhalima drove a car escorting the bomb van. After the terrorists parked the Ryder van in the underground garage of the World Trade Center, Abouhalima and the others awaited the results of the explosion but were disappointed when the North Tower failed to collapse and fall into the South Tower. The day after the bombing, Abouhalima flew to Saudi Arabia. After a brief stay, he decided to visit family in Egypt, but on entering the country in March 1993, he was arrested and turned over to Egyptian interrogators. Abouhalima soon confessed to his role in the World Trade Center bombing.

Egyptian authorities turned Abouhalima over to American authorities for trial. Despite evidence of a large terrorist conspiracy, Abouhalima and his fellow plotters were tried as criminals rather than as national security concerns or as conspirators in an intelligence matter, in keeping with FBI policy. After five months of testimony, on March 4, 1994, Abouhalima was found guilty on all counts. Abouhalima and his three codefendants each received a sentence of 240 years; Abouhalima is now serving his sentence at a maximum

security federal prison. Unfortunately, this bombing was only the first salvo in a continuing war by Islamist terrorists against the United States.

Stephen E. Atkins

See also: Abdel-Rahman, Omar (aka the Blind Sheikh); World Trade Center Bombing; Yousef, Ramzi Ahmed

Further Reading

Bell, J. Bowyer. *Murders on the Nile: The World Trade Center and Global Terrorism.* San Francisco: Encounter Books, 2003.

Reeve, Simon. *The New Jackals: Ramzi Yousef, Osama Bin Laden and the Future of Terrorism.* Boston: Northeastern University Press, 1999.

Abu Ghraib

Abu Ghraib is a prison facility located about 20 miles west of the Iraqi capital of Baghdad. Known during the regime of Saddam Hussein as an infamous place of torture and execution, the prison later drew international attention when photographs of inmate abuse and reports of torture at the hands of coalition troops were made public in 2004.

Officially called the Baghdad Central Confinement Facility (BCCF) under the Hussein regime, Abu Ghraib was built by British contractors hired by the Iraqi government in the 1960s. Covering an area of about one square mile, the prison housed five different types of prisoners during the Hussein regime: those with long sentences, those with short sentences, those imprisoned for capital crimes, those imprisoned for so-called special offenses, and foreign detainees. Cells about 51 square feet in area held as many as 40 people each.

During the 1980–1988 Iran-Iraq War, the Iraqi Baathist regime used the facility to imprison political dissidents and members of ethnic or religious groups seen as threats to the central government. In particular, hundreds of Arab and Kurdish Shiites and Iraqis of Iranian heritage were arrested and housed in the BCCF; torture and executions became routine. Among the tactics used by prison guards was the feeding of shredded plastic to inmates, and it has been speculated that prisoners were used as guinea pigs for Hussein's biological and chemical weapons. Although the Iraqi government kept its actions within the complex secret from Iraqi citizens and the international community alike, Amnesty International reported several specific incidents, including the 1996 execution of hundreds of political dissidents and the 1998 execution of many people who had been involved in the 1991 Shiite revolt. The prison, which contained thousands of inmates who were completely cut off from outside communication and held without having been convicted of crimes, was also used to house coalition prisoners of war during the Persian Gulf War.

With the 2003 U.S.-led Iraq War and subsequent fall of the Hussein government in Iraq, coalition troops took control of Abu Ghraib prison. The U.S. military used the complex for holding Iraqi insurgents and terrorists accused of anti-U.S. attacks, although by 2004 it had released several hundred prisoners and shared use of the facility with the Iraqi government. Because of the disarray in the Iraqi criminal system, many common criminals uninvolved in the war were held at the facility as well. Abu Ghraib became a household name in April 2004, when the television program *60 Minutes II* aired photographs of prisoner abuse at the hands of coalition troops. Just two days later, the photographs were posted online with Seymour Hersch's

article in *The New Yorker* magazine. The photos, which showed prisoners wearing black hoods attached to wires with which they were threatened with electrocution and placed in humiliating sexual positions, sparked worldwide outrage and calls for the investigation and conviction of the military personnel involved.

The abuse was immediately decried by U.S. president George W. Bush and Defense Secretary Donald Rumsfeld, who on May 7, 2004, took responsibility for the acts occurring during his tenure. The Pentagon, which had been investigating reports of abuse since 2003, launched a further investigation into the acts documented by the photographs. Previously, detainee abuse had been investigated by U.S. Army major general Antonio Taguba, who had been given digital images of the abuse by Sergeant Joseph Darby in January 2004. Major General Taguba concluded in his 53-page report that U.S. military personnel had violated international law. More than a dozen U.S. soldiers and officers were removed from the prison as a result of the internal investigation.

More details emerged following the *60 Minutes II* broadcast. Photographs that the U.S. government would not allow to be released earlier were circulated in 2006. Most importantly, it appeared that the senior U.S. military officer, Lieutenant General Ricardo Sanchez, had authorized treatment "close to" torture, such as the use of military dogs, temperature extremes, and sensory and sleep deprivation, thus making it more difficult to locate responsibility for the general environment leading to abuse. However, in addition to charging certain troops and contractors with torture, the United States made an effort to reduce the number of detainees—estimated at 7,000 prior to the scandal's outbreak—by several

A U.S. soldier restrains a dog before a handcuffed Abu Ghraib detainee. Photos like this were given to the U.S. Army Criminal Investigation Command in January 2004 by Sergeant Joseph Darby, a military policeman. The photos came to public attention in April of that year. (AP Photo)

thousand. However, many argued that the measures taken were not harsh enough to fit the crime, and some demanded Rumsfeld's resignation. Meanwhile, in August 2004, a military panel confirmed 44 cases of prisoner abuse at the facility and identified 23 soldiers as being responsible. The so-called ringleader of the operation, Army Specialist Charles Graner, was convicted and sentenced to 10 years in prison in January 2005. Since that time, Abu Ghraib has twice been attacked by insurgents, who have attempted to undermine U.S. security at the facility and set prisoners free.

The United States continued to hold detainees in the portion of the prison known as "Camp Redemption," built in 2004, but in September 2006, the United States handed over control of Abu Ghraib to the Iraqi government. The Iraqi government held convicted criminals in the older area known as the "Hard Site," but closed the facility in 2007. In 2009, Abu Ghraib was reopened and renamed Baghdad Central Prison. By 2010, it was expanded and designed to hold as many as 15,000 prisoners. In July 2013, some 500 prisoners—many of whom were Al-Qaeda operatives—escaped from the facility.

Jessica Britt

See also: Bush Administration; Bush Doctrine; Iraqi Freedom, Operation; Rumsfeld, Donald Henry; Torture of Prisoners

Further Reading

Danner, Mark. *Torture and Truth: America, Abu Ghraib, and the War on Terror.* New York: New York Review Books, 2004.

Graveline, Christopher, and Michael Clemens. *The Secrets of Abu Ghraib Revealed.* Dulles, VA: Potomac Books, 2010.

Greenberg, Karen J., and Joshua L. Dratel, eds. *The Torture Papers: The Road to Abu Ghraib.* Cambridge, MA: Cambridge University Press, 2005.

Strasser, Steven, ed. *The Abu Ghraib Investigations: The Official Independent Panel and Pentagon Reports on the Shocking Prisoner Abuse in Iraq.* New York: Public Affairs, 2004.

Achille Lauro Hijacking

(October 7, 1985–October 10, 1985)

The *Achille Lauro* was an Italian passenger liner hijacked by Palestinian terrorists in the eastern Mediterranean on October 7, 1985. Construction of the ship began at Vlissingen in the Netherlands in 1939 but was interrupted by World War II. Launched in 1946, the ship entered service in late 1947 as the *Willum Ruys.* Sold to the Italian Lauro Line in 1964, the ship was rebuilt, modernized, and returned to service in 1966, named for the former mayor of Naples. Displacing about 21,100 tons, the *Achille Lauro* could accommodate 900 passengers.

The terrorists had been surprised by a crew member and were forced to act prematurely, but they demanded that the *Achille Lauro* steam to Tartus, Syria, and threatened to blow up the ship if Israel did not release 50 Palestinian prisoners held in Israel. The sole casualty of the affair was U.S.-born Jewish passenger Leon Klinghoffer, who was confined to a wheelchair. Reportedly, he confronted the hijackers and was shot by them, and his body was thrown overboard.

Syrian authorities refused to allow the ship to dock, and it returned to Port Said.

Following two days of negotiations, the terrorists agreed to release the ship and its passengers in return for safe conduct aboard an Egyptian airliner to Tunis. On October 10, U.S. aircraft intercepted the Egyptian plane and forced it to fly to a North Atlantic Treaty Organization (NATO) base in Sicily. Disregarding U.S. government appeals, Italian authorities released the passengers, reportedly including Abu Abbas, although he was subsequently sentenced in absentia by an Italian court to life in prison.

Some sources state that it was the close relationship between Abu Abbas and the Palestine Liberation Organization (PLO) that caused the U.S. government to deny a visa to PLO chairman Yasser Arafat to enter the United States in order to speak to the United Nations (UN) General Assembly in November 1988. Abu Abbas had been a member of the PLO Executive Committee during 1984–1991. Arrested in Iraq following the U.S.-led invasion of that country in 2003, he died, reportedly of natural causes, while in U.S. custody on March 8, 2004. The other three hijackers served varying terms in Italian prisons.

On November 29, 1994, the reflagged *Achille Lauro* was steaming off the coast of Somalia when a fire broke out. All 1,090 passengers and crew abandoned ship. Other ships were soon on the scene, but two people died in the lifeboat transfers. The fire totally consumed the ship, and it sank on December 2.

On January 19, 1996, the PLO agreed to provide an undisclosed sum to finance the Leon and Marilyn Klinghoffer Memorial Foundation of the U.S. Anti-Defamation League. The foundation is dedicated to combating terrorism through peaceful means. In return, Klinghoffer's daughters dropped a lawsuit brought against the PLO. The *Achille Lauro* hijacking has been the subject of a 1990 television docudrama and an opera, *The Death of Klinghoffer* (1991), which appeared as a film version in 2003.

Spencer C. Tucker

See also: Terrorism

Further Reading

Bohn, Michael K. *The Achille Lauro Hijacking: Lessons in the Politics and Prejudice of Terrorism.* Dulles, VA: Potomac Books, 2004.

Cassese, Antonio. *Terrorism, Politics and Law: The Achille Lauro Affair.* Princeton, NJ: Princeton University Press, 1989.

Afghanistan War. *See* Enduring Freedom, Operation

African Embassy Bombings

(1998)

The biggest and most lethal Al-Qaeda operation against the United States before September 11, 2001, was the 1998 embassy bombings in Africa. As early as 1993, Osama bin Laden had his military commanders study the feasibility of a major terrorist act in Africa. The Egyptian American soldier, Ali Mohamed, scouted out targets in Nairobi, Kenya, for Al-Qaeda. Mohamed surveyed American, British, French, and Israeli embassies as potential targets and reported to bin Laden that the best target was the American embassy in Nairobi. Bin Laden, then living in Khartoum, Sudan, agreed in a personal report. Reluctant at that time to approve a bombing mission in Africa with retaliation so close at hand, he kept the operation under advisement.

Several years later, bin Laden decided to give permission to carry out the bombings of the American embassies in Nairobi, Kenya, and Dar es Salaam, Tanzania. In the meantime, Al-Qaeda operatives assisted the Saudi group Hezbollah al-Hijaz in carrying out the bombing of the Khobar Towers on June 25, 1996, in Dhahran, Saudi Arabia, killing 19 American servicemen and wounding hundreds of others. Bin Laden denied direct participation, but American authorities did not believe his statement. After issuing his declaration of jihad in 1998 against Americans for occupying sacred Saudi soil, bin Laden proceeded with preparations for the African embassy bombings as previously planned.

Al-Qaeda prepared methodically. Early in 1995, agents had been sent to Kenya and Tanzania to establish cells. The mastermind of the operation was Abdullah Ahmed Abdullah. Mohamed Odeh arrived in Mombasa, Kenya, where he set up a fishing business as a cover. To maintain further cover, he married a Kenyan woman. He was soon followed by Al-Qaeda's military commander, Abu Ubaidal al-Banshiri, who died in a ferry accident on Lake Victoria in the spring of 1996. Al-Banshiri's successor was Haroun Fazil, who stayed with bin Laden's former secretary, Wadih el-Hage. Fazil rented a villa in Nairobi, where the bomb was assembled, and a Nissan truck was purchased to carry the bomb.

One of the two men selected for martyrdom in Nairobi was Mohamed Rashed al-Owhali. Al-Owhali was born in 1977 in Liverpool, England, but he never cared for English life. In 1996, he traveled to Afghanistan, where he underwent Al-Qaeda training and was selected for the martyrdom mission in Nairobi, Kenya. Al-Owhali arrived in Nairobi on August

Devastation from the August 7, 1998, blast adjacent to the U.S. embassy in Nairobi, Kenya. This attack, as well as a near-simultaneous explosion at the U.S. embassy in Dar es Salaam, Tanzania, was the work of the Al-Qaeda terrorist organization and prompted a U.S. military response two weeks later. (AP Photo/Sayyid Azim)

2, 1998, just five days before the mission. Al-Qaeda's Egyptian bomb expert, Sheikh Ahmed Salim, had already built the bomb. Leaders of the Kenyan cell were already leaving for Afghanistan at the time of his arrival. conspirator Mohamed Rashed Al-Owhali soon met his fellow martyr, a Saudi named Azzam. On August 5, 1998, they scouted out the embassy target.

The Nairobi bombing was scheduled for Friday, August 7, 1998. The explosion was timed to take place before 11:00 a.m., when observant Muslims would be at prayer. Azzam was to be the driver, and al-Owhali's job was to persuade the guards to let them close to the embassy. Unable to persuade the gate guard, he threw a homemade stun grenade and ran away before exploding the bomb. The bomb, which was large, exploded at 10:30 a.m. on a workday, producing horrible casualties.

The Nairobi embassy building sustained considerable damage. Prudence Bushnell, the American ambassador to Kenya, had previously written to and cabled Madeleine Albright, then secretary of state, and the State Department about the vulnerability of the embassy in its location on a busy thoroughfare in the middle of Nairobi, close to the street. Twelve Americans and 201 Kenyans were killed. Four thousand others were wounded—some seriously.

Nine minutes after the Nairobi bombing, a bomb exploded at the American embassy in Dar es Salaam, Tanzania. Less is known about this operation; indeed, what little is known comes from a low-level Al-Qaeda operative, Khalfan Khamis Mohamed, who was trained in an Al-Qaeda training camp and was then sent back to his home in Dar es Salaam. An Al-Qaeda leader approached him several years later to help find a place to build a bomb and a way to transport it to the target. Al-Qaeda's Egyptian bomb expert, Abdel-Rahman, built this bomb also. Mohamed's sole responsibility was to guide the bomb's driver, Hamden Khalif Allah Awad—also called Ahmed the German—to the target, leaving before the bomb went off. The bomb exploded at exactly 10:39 a.m.

The bombing at the Dar es Salaam embassy caused less damage and fewer casualties than the Nairobi bombing. Because the embassy was better protected, the bomb did less structural damage to the embassy. No Americans were killed, but 11 Tanzanians died—most of them Muslims.

American intelligence had been following an Al-Qaeda cell in Kenya for over a year before the bombings, but agents were caught by surprise by the plot—astounding in light of the warning of an Egyptian defector from Al-Qaeda, Mustafa Mahmoud Said Ahmed, who informed Nairobi embassy intelligence officers of a plot to bomb the embassy, using stun grenades to allow a truck loaded with a bomb close to the embassy. This warning was given nine months before the bombing, but nothing was done by the American agents to guard against such an event.

One of the leaders of the African bombing plot, Odeh, was arrested in the Karachi airport when returning from Africa. Odeh was detained because of discrepancies in his passport, but soon Pakistani officials suspected him of participation in the African embassy bombings. They turned Odeh over to Pakistani intelligence, and he soon confessed to his role in the bombings. Another member of the plot, Khalfan Khamis Mohamed, was arrested in Cape Town, South Africa, in October 1999.

Another break for American intelligence was the arrest of al-Owhali while he was

receiving medical treatment for injuries sustained at the bombing. His wounds were all in his back, causing speculation that he had been running away from the bomb explosion. Kenyan officials arrested him on August 12, 1998, and immediately turned him over to American intelligence officials. It took only a few days for al-Owhali to confess to his role in the Nairobi embassy bombing.

Once it was established that the African embassy bombings were an Al-Qaeda operation, President Bill Clinton authorized retaliatory attacks on alleged Al-Qaeda targets in Afghanistan and Sudan. Tomahawk cruise missiles were fired with limited effect at six Al Qaeda base camps around Khost, Afghanistan, and at an alleged chemical weapons al-Shifa plant in Khartoum, Sudan. Al-Qaeda leaders had been expecting retaliation and made preparations, but an additional warning about the date gleaned from Pakistani intelligence made certain that damage to Al-Qaeda would be minimal. The death toll at the Khost was lessened further because two of the cruise missiles failed to explode.

At the time of the missile attacks, the movie *Wag the Dog* portrayed a president who started a war to mitigate the effects of a sex scandal. Critics of the Clinton administration seized upon the theme of this movie and accused him of misjudgments in his fight against terror. This criticism seemed to make Clinton less aggressive in his operations against bin Laden and Al-Qaeda during the remainder of his administration.

Those arrested in Kenya, Pakistan, and Tanzania were extradited to the United States for trial as terrorists. Four members of the African embassy bombing plot— Wadih el-Hage, Mohamed Rashed Daoud al-Owhali, Khalfan Khamis Mohamed, and Mohammed Saddiq Odeh—were tried before a Manhattan federal court beginning February 5, 2001. Al-Owhali and Mohamed faced the death penalty, but Odeh and El-Hage faced life in prison. A jury of seven women and five men declared the men guilty in May 2001. At a July 2001 death penalty hearing, however, the jury refused to bow to prosecutors' demands for death sentences for Odeh and Mohamed. All four men were sentenced to life imprisonment without parole on October 18, 2001, only weeks after the September 11 attacks. Jurors later explained that they didn't want to risk portraying al-Owhali and Mohamed as martyrs.

Stephen E. Atkins

See also: Al-Qaeda; Bin Laden, Osama; Clinton Administration; Terrorism

Further Reading

Bergen, Peter L. *Holy War: Inside the Secret World of Osama bin Laden.* New York: Free Press, 2001.

Weiser, Benjamin. "A Jury Torn and Fearful in 2001 Terrorism Trial." *New York Times*, January 5, 2003, 1.

Weiser, Benjamin. "Going on Trial: U.S. Accusations of a Global Plot; Embassy Bombings Case." *New York Times*, February 4, 2001, 29.

Aircraft, September 11, 2001, Attack. *See* American Airlines Flight 11; American Airlines Flight 77; United Airlines Flight 93; United Airlines Flight 175

Alec Station

U.S. government-sanctioned Central Intelligence Agency (CIA) unit charged with the mission of hunting down and capturing or killing Al-Qaeda leader Osama bin Laden. In late 1995, two members of the Bill Clinton administration, National Security Advisor Anthony (Tony) Lake and National Coordinator for Counterterrorism Richard Clarke, met with the head of the CIA's Counterterrorism Center (CTC) to discuss the need for a unit to concentrate solely on bin Laden. Soon afterward, CIA director George Tenet approved just such a unit. The plan called for Alec Station to run for only a couple of years before merging completely with the CTC, but as bin Laden became a greater and greater threat, Alec Station continued its operations for more than a decade.

When the CIA began Alec Station on January 8, 1996, bin Laden was mostly known as a financier of terrorism. Soon afterward, it became apparent that he had declared open warfare against the United States and its allies, and the campaign against bin Laden was stepped up. Michael Scheuer, a veteran CIA agent, was placed in charge of the program when it was founded. Although the formal title of the program was the Usama Bin Laden Issue Station (UBL), it soon took the name Alec Station, after Scheuer's adopted Korean son, Alec.

Alec Station functioned as a subunit of the CIA's CTC. Sponsors of this program set it up as an interagency unit running agents from both the CIA and the Federal Bureau of Investigation (FBI). The plan was for this unit to fuse intelligence disciplines into one office that included operations, analysis, signals intercepts, overhead photography, and covert action.

As the unit developed, its strength lay in analysis. It began as a small unit with a staff of only about 15 analysts, mostly young women. Alec Station, not considered a choice assignment, was a low-profile operation and was at first housed outside Langley, Virginia, until it moved to the CTC.

By 1998, Scheuer was convinced that bin Laden posed an ongoing danger to the United States but had difficulty convincing his superiors, partly because of his difficult personality; he managed to alienate even those who agreed with him. After learning that bin Laden had attempted to acquire nuclear materials, Scheuer had difficulty convincing his superiors to accept the information and use it to inform others in the government. Scheuer, believing that bin Laden constituted a clear and present danger, became increasingly frustrated by the lack of action taken toward bin Laden.

Scheuer also had difficulties with the FBI. Although Alec Station had been set up as an interagency operation, the FBI often refused to share information with the CIA. The most intransigent member of the FBI in this regard was John O'Neill, the FBI's top counterterrorism expert. O'Neill possessed a notebook captured from an Al-Qaeda operative that he refused for a year to turn over to Alec Station. In another instance, an FBI agent was caught raiding CIA files with the intent of taking their contents back to the FBI. Scheuer claimed that Alec Station sent 700 to 800 requests for information to the FBI but never received answers to any of them.

Alec Station planned to capture bin Laden after he moved to Afghanistan in May 1996. For the first time, the CIA knew where bin Laden and his family lived, in the Tarnak Farm compound 12 miles outside Kandahar. Beginning in 1997, plans were made with Afghan tribal leaders to kidnap bin Laden and take him to an Arab country or the United States for trial. The CIA even staged four rehearsals for the operation in late 1997 and early 1998. Then,

on May 29, 1998, Tenet, the head of the CIA, called off the operation. Scheuer's reaction was swift. He complained that the CIA had enough intelligence against bin Laden and Al-Qaeda to eliminate both, and he could not understand why the U.S. government had failed to take the chance to do so. The Clinton administration responded that it feared collateral damage and any negative publicity that might follow a less-than-perfect operation.

It was only after the bombings on August 7, 1998, of the two U.S. embassies in Tanzania and Kenya that the attention of the Clinton administration was redirected toward bin Laden. This resulted in the August 20, 1998, U.S. missile attacks on an Al-Qaeda training camp in Afghanistan near Khost and on the El Shifa pharmaceutical plant in Khartoum, Sudan, in which 79 Tomahawk cruise missiles were fired from U.S. Navy ships in the Arabian Sea. However, warnings from Pakistani sources likely made certain that bin Laden escaped the missiles, and the Sudanese plant proved to be a harmless pharmaceutical factory. Several other plans were made to either capture or kill bin Laden, but they were cancelled each time because of one difficulty or another. Most cancellations were caused by a lack of confidence in intelligence sources and information.

The most promising opportunity came in February 1999. CIA agents learned that bin Laden was going to join a number of sheikhs from the United Arab Emirates at a desert hunting camp in Helmand Province, Afghanistan. Satellite pictures identified the camp on February 9. CIA operatives confirmed bin Laden's presence and requested a missile strike. Over the next several days, the Clinton administration debated a missile strike before learning that members of the United Arab Emirates royal family were also present at the camp. Because of foreign policy complications with the United Arab Emirates (a provider of gas and oil supplies), nothing happened, and Scheuer was furious. His e-mails expressing his unhappiness traveled around government circles.

Tenet removed Scheuer from his position as head of Alec Station in the spring of 1999. The CIA claimed that Scheuer's inability to work with superiors and the FBI led to his dismissal. His critics within the agency claimed that he had a vendetta against bin Laden. CIA analysts at Alec Station blamed O'Neill for the firing of Scheuer because the dispute had reached the level of the agency heads of the CIA and FBI. Scheuer's replacement was a key assistant on Tenet's staff and a Middle East specialist, but he lacked Scheuer's drive. By this time, Alec Station had grown from 12 analysts to 25. Most of these analysts were women, something that hurt their credibility in the male-dominated CIA. There was also a feeling in the CTC that others in the CIA ridiculed members of the Alec Station for their zeal in tracing the actions of bin Laden.

The status of Alec Station became more precarious after September 11, 2001. Some of the criticism directed against the CIA for failing to uncover the September 11 plot descended on Alec Station, and Scheuer reappeared as a senior analyst at the station after September 11. Members of Alec Station adamantly insisted that little if any connection existed between Iraqi dictator Saddam Hussein and Al-Qaeda, something they communicated to Tenet. However, this stance made them enemies in the George W. Bush administration, which wanted the CIA to provide justification for the invasion of Iraq and the overthrow of Hussein. Those in the CIA who opposed the invasion became administration enemies. Per-

sonnel were transferred out of Alec Station until only 12 analysts remained. Scheuer protested this action, resigning from the CIA on November 12, 2004. Not long afterward, the CIA disbanded Alec Station entirely. Bin Laden was eventually killed on May 2, 2011, nearly 10 years after the September 11 attacks, by a U.S. Naval Special Warfare Group in a residential compound in Pakistan.

Stephen E. Atkins

See also: Al-Qaeda; Bin Laden, Osama; Bush Doctrine; Central Intelligence Agency; Clinton Administration; Counterterrorism Strategy; Tenet, George

Further Reading

Anonymous. *Imperial Hubris: Why the West Is Losing the War on Terror.* New York: Brassey's, 2004.

Coll, Steve. *Ghost Wars: The Secret History of the CIA, Afghanistan, and Bin Laden, from the Soviet Invasion to September 10, 2001.* New York: Penguin, 2004.

Tenet, George. *At the Center of the Storm: My Years at the CIA.* New York: HarperCollins, 2007.

Wright, Lawrence. *The Looming Tower: Al-Qaeda and the Road to 9/11.* New York: Vintage Books, 2007.

Al-Ittihad al-Islami (also Al-Itihaad al-Islamiya) (AIAI)

Al-Ittihad al-Islami (AIAI, or Islamic Unity) was the precursor to the later Somali Islamic Courts Union and the current Islamist al-Shabaab movement. Indeed, it has been shown that AIAI, which was alleged to have had links to Al-Qaeda, provided the basis for the wider network of violent Islamists currently active in the Horn of Africa and East Africa.

The AIAI developed during the 1980s as a loose movement of generally educated Somalis, many of whom had worked or studied in the Middle East, and who opposed the repression and control of the regime of Siad Barre, then president of Somalia. They believed the only way to rid the country of its endemic corruption and clan factionalism was through the institution of a rigid theocratic order based on a strict interpretation of Islamism.

Following the collapse of the Barre regime in 1991, Osama bin Laden is thought to have funded and supported the AIAI as a conduit through which to gain an operational foothold in the Horn of Africa. Some experts continue to believe that the 1993 killings of Belgian, Pakistani, and U.S. military personnel associated with the United Nations Operation in Somalia (UNOSOM) II mission in Somalia had nothing to do with warlord General Mohammad Farah Aideed but were in fact the work of Al-Qaeda and AIAI.

By the mid-1990s, along with a power base in Bosaaso and the Puntland region of Somalia, AIAI had also become active among the Somali population in the Ogaden region of eastern Ethiopia and the wider Somali diaspora in Kenya. At its height, it is believed that the group had around 1,000 active members. Despite attending a February 1995 peace conference for the Somali nation, AIAI was later linked to a number of terrorist attacks, including two hotel bombings in Ethiopia and the attempted assassination of Ethiopian minister of transport and communications Abdul Majid Hussein in 1996. In 1999, the group was implicated in the murder of an American aid worker near the Kenyan-Somali border. Perhaps more significantly, U.S. officials have claimed that elements of AIAI cooperated with the Al-Qaeda cell responsible for the August 1998 twin suicide bombings of the U.S. embassies in Nairobi, Kenya, and Dar es Salaam, Tanzania. At the time, these attacks were some of the most lethal directed against American interests, leaving 224 people dead and thousands of others wounded.

In the aftermath of the September 11, 2001, terror attacks, AIAI's finances, together with those of the group's leaders, Hassan Dahir Aweys and Hassan al-Turki, were sanctioned under U.S. Executive Order 13224. The action was justified on account of the group's suspected links to Al-Qaeda, which purportedly included the establishment of joint training camps in various parts of Somalia. Following the onset of Operation Enduring Freedom (OEF) and the U.S.-led global war on terror, many AIAI members dispersed across the Gulf of Aden to the tribal areas of Yemen. Even so, AIAI's legacy continued to have a significant bearing on events in Somalia. One of the main leaders of the Islamic Courts Union, which seized the capital city of Mogadishu in June 2006, was Hassan Aweys. More important was the "career" trajectory of al-Turki, who went on to lead al-Shabaab—then the youth movement of the Islamic Courts Union and one of the main terrorist-insurgent threats in the country. After 2006, rumors abounded that the AIAI was dissolved, although it is quite possible that it was folded into another group or reorganized under a different name.

Richard Warnes

See also: Al-Qaeda; Enduring Freedom, Operation

Further Reading

Gunaratna, Rohan. *Inside Al-Qaeda*. New York: Columbia University Press, 2002.

Rabasa, Angel. *Radical Islam in East Africa*. Santa Monica, CA: RAND, 2009.

Rotberg, Robert, ed. *Battling Terrorism in the Horn of Africa*. Washington, DC: Brookings Institution Press, 2005.

Al-Qaeda

Al-Qaeda is an international radical Islamic organization, the hallmark of which is the perpetration of terrorist attacks against local governments or Western interests in the name of Islam. In the late 1980s, members of Tanzim al-Qaida (Arabic for "base" or "foundation") fought with the mujahideen against the Soviet occupation of Afghanistan.

Al-Qaeda, a salafi Sunni organization, was established around 1987–1988 by Sheikh Abdullah Azzam, a mentor to Osama bin Laden. Azzam was a professor at King Abdul Aziz University in Jeddah, Saudi Arabia. Bin Laden attended that university, where he met and was strongly influenced by Azzam.

Al-Qaeda developed from the Mujahideen Services Bureau that Azzam established in Peshawar, Afghanistan. Bin Laden funded the organization and was considered the deputy director. This organization recruited, trained, and transported Muslim volunteers from any Muslim nation into Afghanistan to fight the jihad (holy war) against the Soviet armies in the 1980s.

Other elements in Al-Qaeda arrived with members of radical groups from other countries, such as a faction of Egyptian Islamic Jihad, some of the members of which had been indicted and had fled Egypt. The credo of Al-Qaeda came from its beliefs, based on ideas by many radical Islamist thinkers, including the practice of *takfir* (declaring that Muslim leaders who colluded with non-Muslim interests were apostates). Azzam adopted and expanded on these arguments, and bin Laden applied them to the government of Saudi Arabia, which he believed was too closely allied with the West. He proposed armed struggle to combat the far enemy as well as the near enemy in order to create a new Islamic society.

Following the mysterious death of Sheikh Azzam in November 1989, perhaps at bin Laden's behest, bin Laden took over the leadership of Al-Qaeda. He continued to work toward Azzam's goal of creating an international organization comprised of mujahideen who will fight the oppression of Muslims throughout the world. Al-Qaeda aims to establish an authentic Islamic form of government, to fight against any government viewed as contrary to the ideals of Islamic law and religion, and to aid Islamic groups trying to establish an Islamic form of government in their countries.

No attacks by Al-Qaeda are known to have occurred against Israel. The most damaging Al-Qaeda attack by far has been the September 11, 2001, attack on the United States. The genesis of Al-Qaeda's great antipathy toward the West—in particular the United States—can be traced back to the 1991 Persian Gulf War, precipitated by the Iraqi invasion of Kuwait on August 2, 1990. Bin Laden, originally a well-to-do Saudi Arabian, allegedly offered to commit Al-Qaeda mujahideen to the defense of Saudi Arabia in case of an Iraqi invasion of that nation. The Saudi government declined the offer and permitted the stationing of hundreds of thou-

Osama bin Laden (second from left) and his top lieutenant, Ayman al-Zawahiri (second from right), are shown at an undisclosed location with two unidentified men in this image, which was broadcast by Al Jazeera on October 7, 2001. As the leader of Al-Qaeda, bin Laden established the basic principles of the 9/11 attacks, although more detailed planning of the operation was handled by other Al-Qaeda operatives. (AP Photo/Al Jazeera)

sands of U.S. and coalition soldiers in Saudi Arabia during the run-up to the war (Operation Desert Shield). This move enraged bin Laden, who perceived the presence of foreign troops in Saudi Arabia as a blatant acknowledgment of the political linkage between his government and the United States. He also portrayed this as a religious failing, for Saudi Arabia is home to both Mecca and Medina, the holiest of places in all of Islam, and the members of the Saudi royal family are the guardians of these sites.

Once in Sudan, bin Laden began training Al-Qaeda fighters, and is believed to have carried out an abortive assassination attempt against Egyptian president Hosni Mubarak in 1994. Under intense international pressure led by the United States, Sudan expelled bin Laden and Al-Qaeda leadership in late 1996. From Sudan they traveled directly to Afghanistan, where the Islamic fundamentalist Taliban regime had already ensconced itself. The Taliban not only protected Al-Qaeda but also in all probability helped arm it, and by doing so gave to it an air of legitimacy, at least in Afghanistan. In 1998, bin Laden joined forces with leaders from the Egyptian Islamic Jihad, such as Ayman al-Zawahiri, and several other radical organizations, all of whom vowed to wage a holy war against Israel and its allies. In August of that year, Al-Qaeda carried out what is thought to be its first overseas attack against Western interests. That month saw the bombings of the U.S. embassies in Dar es Salaam, Tanzania, and Nairobi, Kenya. More than 200 people died in the attacks, and another 4,000 were wounded. In October 2000, Al-Qaeda also carried out an attack on the U.S. Navy guided missile destroyer *Cole* in the Yemeni port of Aden in which 17 U.S. sailors perished.

The organization of Al-Qaeda has a *majlis al-shura*, or consultative council. The *amir al-mu'minin* (commander of the faithful) was bin Laden, followed by several other generals and then additional leaders of related groups. Some sources say that there are 24 related groups as part of the consultative council. The council consists of four committees: military, religious-legal, finance, and media. Each leader of these committees was selected personally by bin Laden and reported directly to him. All levels of Al-Qaeda are highly compartmentalized, and secrecy is the key to all operations.

Al-Qaeda's ideology has appealed to both Middle Eastern and non–Middle Eastern Muslim groups. There are also a number of radical Islamic terrorist groups, such as al-Qa'ida fi Bilad al-Rafhidayn ("in the land of the two rivers," meaning Iraq) and al-Qa'ida fi Jazirat al-Arabiyya ("of the Arabian Peninsula"), that initiated an association with Al-Qaeda via public declarations. Nevertheless, Al-Qaeda continues to be the central force of world terrorism because of the media attention given to its occasional pronouncements and the September 11 attacks.

Al-Qaeda's most horrific deed has undoubtedly been the September 11, 2001, attacks on the United States. The attacks, which killed an estimated 2,976 people, were carried out by the hijacking of four commercial jetliners, two of which were flown into New York City's World Trade Center, destroying both towers. A third jetliner was crashed into the Pentagon outside Washington, D.C., while a fourth, supposedly bound for the White House or the U.S. Capitol, crashed in a western Pennsylvania field, killing all on board. However, many Muslims and others demanded proof of a direct connection between bin Laden and the perpetrators of 9/11 and were unsatisfied with the results of the investigation into the terrorist attacks, believing instead that the event may have been staged.

It has been alleged that Al-Qaeda inspired the March 2004 Madrid train bombings that killed nearly 200 and the July 2005 London subway bombings that killed 52. Although Al-Qaeda took responsibility for the latter, there is no irrefutable evidence linking Al-Qaeda to either attack; however, it is believed that the perpetrators borrowed Al-Qaeda tactics to pull them off.

The global war on terror, initiated since the September 11 attacks, resulted in an invasion of Afghanistan and the toppling of the Taliban in late 2001 (Operation Enduring Freedom). Since the 2003 Anglo-American invasion of Iraq, Al-Qaeda was thought to have supported the growing insurgency in Iraq, which became a virtual full-blown civil war during 2006. Since 2007, U.S. and coalition forces have enjoyed some success in purging Iraq of Al-Qaeda operatives. While most Arab and Muslim governments have tried to distance themselves from Al-Qaeda and its operations, there can be little doubt that the group enjoys support among significant elements of the populations of these countries. Pakistan is home to the largest number of al-Qaeda affiliates, with 12, followed by Afghanistan with five.[1]

Bin Laden was able to put most of the radical Islamic terrorist groups under the umbrella of Al-Qaeda. Indeed, its leadership has spread throughout the world, and its influence penetrates many religious, social, and economical structures in most Muslim communities. Today, the upper-echelon leadership of Al-Qaeda continues to elude American intelligence and Western armies in Afghanistan and Pakistan. The membership of Al-Qaeda remains difficult to determine because of its decentralized organizational structure. By early 2005, U.S. officials claimed to have killed or taken prisoner two-thirds of the Al-Qaeda leaders behind the September 11 attacks. However, some of these prisoners have been shown to have had no direct connection with the attacks.

Although Al-Qaeda continues to periodically release audio recordings and videotapes, since the death of bin Laden, the organization has released fewer of them. Most of the recordings were on current issues, exhort followers to keep up the fight, and to prove to Western governments that it is still a force to be reckoned with. In the summer of 2013, the United States closed 20 embassies across the Middle East and part of Africa amid increased Al-Qaeda activity in the region of possible attacks. Despite the decimation of Al-Qaeda's core leadership in Afghanistan and Pakistan, it continues to be a major threat. According to experts, the organization moved from a centralized organization to a series of local-actor organizations forming a terrorist network. Al-Qaeda in Iraq was decimated by the end of the Iraq War in 2009, but regained control of many of its former staging areas and the ability to launch weekly waves of multiple car bomb attacks.

On May 1, 2011, bin Laden was killed. President Obama called the killing of bin Laden the "most significant achievement to date" in the effort to defeat Al-Qaeda. Bin Laden was located at a compound in Abbottabad, Pakistan, and after a firefight, U.S. Special Forces killed bin Laden and took custody of his body. DNA testing confirmed that it was bin Laden.

In July 2013, more than 1,000 people were killed in Iraq, the highest monthly death toll in five years. Most of the attacks were led by Al-Qaeda. That same year, in Syria, Al-Qaeda affiliate Jabhat al Nusra fought with some success in several battles against the regime of Syrian dictator Assad, which accounted for most of the deaths. The force reports directly to Al-Qaeda. Between 2009 and 2013, Al-Qaeda-affiliated terror groups in Libya were blamed for the September 11, 2012, attack on the U.S. consulate in Benghazi. That attack left the U.S. ambassador and three other Americans dead. Al-Qaeda leaders in strongholds in the south of Yemen have not been vanquished by a Yemen military—backed by U.S. forces and drone strikes. Al-Qaeda affiliates in Iraq, Syria, Yemen, and West Africa have dramatically expanded their operating areas and capabilities during that time and appear poised to continue their expansion.

Harry Raymond Hueston II

See also: Al-Qaeda in Iraq; Al-Qaeda in the Arabian Peninsula; Al-Qaeda in the Islamic Maghreb; Bin Laden, Osama; Taliban; Terrorism

Note

1. Nikhil Sonnad, "Countries with al-Qaeda Affiliates Now Includes Nigeria, Quartz," http://qz.com/213501/this-map-of-countries-with-al-qaeda-affiliates-now-includes-nigeria/#/h/71753,1/.

Further Reading

Bergen, Peter L. *Holy War, Inc.: Inside the Secret World of Osama bin Laden.* New York: Touchstone, 2002.

Gunaratna, Rohan. *Inside Al-Qaeda: Global Network of Terror.* New York: Berkley Publishing Group, 2003.

Hueston, Harry R., and B. Vizzin. *Terrorism 101.* 2nd ed. Ann Arbor, MI: XanEdu, 2004.

Zuhur, Sherifa. *A Hundred Osamas: Islamist Threats and the Further of Counterinsurgency.* Carlisle Barracks, PA: Strategic Studies Institute, U.S. Army War College, 2006.

Al-Qaeda in Iraq

Al-Qaeda in Iraq (al-Qa'ida fi Bilad al-Rafhidayn, AQI) is a violent Sunni jihadist organization that has taken root in Iraq since the 2003 Anglo-American–led invasion of that nation. The U.S. government has characterized AQI, sometimes referred to as Al-Qaeda in Mesopotamia, as the most deadly Sunni jihadist insurgent force now in Iraq. Other sources and experts argue that this designation is exaggerated, as the group is merely 1 of more than 40 similar organizations, and that the claim was made symbolically to rationalize the idea that coalition forces are fighting terrorism in Iraq and thus should not withdraw precipitously.

Opponents of the continuing U.S. presence in Iraq have argued that the 2003 invasion sparked the growth of salafi jihadism and suicide terrorism in Iraq and its export to other parts of the Islamic world. AQI first formed following the invasion and toppling of the Iraq regime, under the name Jama'at al-Tawhid wa-l Jihad (Group of Monotheism and Jihad) under Abu Musab al-Zarqawi.

Zarqawi had fought in Afghanistan in the 1980s and 1990s, and upon traveling to Jordan he organized a group called Bayt al-Imam with the noted Islamist ideologue Abu Muhammad al-Maqdisi (Muhammad Tahir al-Barqawi) and other veterans of the war in Afghanistan. Zarqawi was arrested and imprisoned but was released in 1999. Returning again to Afghanistan and setting up camp in Herat, he reportedly took charge of certain Islamist factions in Kurdistan, from there moving into Iraq and sometimes into Syria. Once Mullah Krekar, the leader of the Kurdish group Islamist Ansar al-Islam, was deported to the Netherlands in 2003, certain sources claim that Zarqawi led some 600 Arab fighters in Syria.

Tawhid wa-l Jihad was blamed for, or took credit for, numerous attacks, including bombings of the Jordanian embassy, the Canal Hotel (which killed 23 at the United Nations [UN] headquarters), and the Imam Ali mosque in Najaf. It is also credited with the killing of Italian paramilitary police and civilians at Nasiriyah and numerous suicide attacks that continued through 2005. The group also seized hostages and beheaded them. A video of the savage execution of U.S. businessman Nicholas Berg, murdered in Iraq on May 7, 2004, reportedly by Zarqawi himself, was followed by other killings of civilians.

The group has targeted Iraqi governmental and military personnel and police because of their cooperation with the American occupying force. AQI's recruitment videos have highlighted American attacks and home searches of defenseless Iraqis, and promise martyrdom. Estimates of AQI members have ranged from 850 to several thousand. Also under dispute have been the numbers of foreign fighters in relation to Iraqi fighters. Foreign fighters' roles were first emphasized, but it became clear that a much higher percentage (probably 90 percent) of fighters were Iraqi: members of the salafist jihadist, or quasi-nationalist jihadist, groups.

In October 2004, Zarqawi's group issued a statement acknowledging the leadership of Al-Qaeda under Osama bin Laden and adopted the name al-Qa'ida fi Bilad al-Rafhidayn. The Iraqi city of Fallujah, in western Anbar Province, became an AQI stronghold. U.S. forces twice tried to capture the city, first in the prematurely terminated Operation Vigilant Resolve from April 4 to May 1, 2004. The Fallujah Guard then controlled the city. U.S. military and Iraqi forces conquered the city in Operation Phantom Fury (code-named Operation al-Fajr) from November 7 to December 23, 2004, in extremely bloody fighting.

Zarqawi formed relationships with other salafist jihad organizations, announcing an umbrella group, the Mujahideen Shura Council, in 2006. After Zarqawi was reportedly at a safe house in June 2006, the new AQI leader, Abu Ayyub al-Masri, announced a new coalition, the Islamic State of Iraq, which included the Mujahideen Shura Council.

Al-Qaeda, along with other Sunni salafist and nationalist groups, strongly resisted Iraqi and coalition forces in Baghdad, Ramadi, and Baqubah and continued staging damaging attacks into 2007. However, by mid-2008, U.S. commanders claimed dominance over these areas. Nevertheless, AQI was acknowledged to still be operative southeast of Baghdad in Jabour, Mosul, Samarra, Hawijah, and Miqdadiyah. AQI has strongly influenced other jihadist groups and actors, particularly through its Internet presence. In sparking intersectarian strife in Iraq, the group has also damaged Iraq's postwar reconstruction efforts, and it has tapped into the intolerance of many salafi groups as well as other Sunni Iraqis and Sunni Muslims outside of Iraq who have been threatened by the emergence of Shia political parties and institutions that had suffered under the Baathist regime of Saddam Hussein. Iraq's Al-Qaeda affiliate claimed responsibility for the July 23, 2013, jailbreak from the infamous Abu Ghraib prison that unleashed 500 to 600 militants into an already unstable region and boosted the group's resurgent fortunes in Iraq and Syria. The prisoners were freed in two coordinated assaults in which fighters used suicide bombs and mortars to storm the two top security prisons on Baghdad's outskirts at Abu Ghraib and Taji. Both were once run by the U.S. military and housed the country's most senior Al-Qaeda detainees. At least 26 members of the Iraqi security forces and more than a dozen prisoners were killed. The scale of the attacks against the heavily guarded facilities reinforced an impression building among many Iraqis that their security forces were struggling to cope with a resurgent Al-Qaeda since U.S. forces withdrew in 2011, taking with them much of the expertise and technology that had been used to hold extremists at bay. Iraqis' fears about the resurgent Al-Qaeda were further vindicated as the group had taken control of most—if not all—of Fallujah by January 2014. Meanwhile, car bombings, kidnappings, and other violence perpetrated by Al-Qaeda and allied groups accelerated rapidly during 2013 and into 2014.

Sherifa Zuhur

See also: Al-Qaeda; Bin Laden, Osama; Iraq War

Further Reading

Associated Press. "In Motley Array of Iraqi Foes, Why Does U.S. Spotlight al-Qaida?" *International Herald Tribune*, June 8, 2007.

Brisard, Jean-Charles, in collaboration with Damien Martinez. *Zarqawi: The New Face of al-Qaeda*. New York: Other Press, 2005.

Burns, John, and Melissa Rubin. "U.S. Arming Sunnis in Iraq to Battle Old Qaeda Allies." *New York Times*, June 11, 2007.

Congressional Research Service, Report to Congress. *Iraq: Post-Saddam Governance and Security, September 6, 2007*. Washington, DC: U.S. Government Printing Office, 2007.

Al-Qaeda in the Arabian Peninsula

Al-Qaeda in the Arabian Peninsula (al-Qaida fi Jazirat al-Arabiyya, AQAP) is an underground Muslim militant group based in Saudi Arabia that is loosely affiliated with the transnational Al-Qaeda network. It was organized in 2001–2002 and emerged publicly in 2003 when it carried out a series of deadly bombings against the Saudi government and expatriate residences in the kingdom's major cities, including the capital city of Riyadh and the key Red Sea port city of Jeddah. The group came under attack in 2004 and 2005 during a series of arrests and shootouts with Saudi police and soldiers. These shootouts resulted in the deaths of several top AQAP leaders and operatives, including its founder, Yusuf Salah Fahd al-Uyayri (Ayiri) and his two successors, Abd al-Aziz bin Issa bin Abd al-Muhsin al-Muqrin and Salah al-Alawi al-Awfi.

AQAP's primary goal was to overthrow the House of Saud, the kingdom's ruling family, which is seen as corrupt and anathema to the "pure" society that the group's members and other unaffiliated and non-militant opponents of the monarchy seek to establish. The monarchy is harshly criticized by both the opposition and many of its own supporters among the ranks of the kingdom's official religious scholars (*ulama*) as being too closely aligned with foreign powers, such as the United States, to the detriment of Saudi interests and social values. AQAP members proved to be adept users of the Internet, creating Web sites and widely read online publications such as the Web magazine *Sawt al-Jihad* (Voice of Jihad).

Despite a series of small-scale attacks on Europeans and Americans in the kingdom during 2002 and early 2003, Saudi authorities did not acknowledge the existence of AQAP as a fully operational group until May 12, 2003. On that day, the group carried out three simultaneous suicide vehicle bombings at the Hamra, Vinnell, and Jedewahl housing compounds used by foreign (mainly Western) expatriates. The attacks killed 35 people, including 9 of the terrorists, and wounded 200 others. According to senior U.S. diplomats and Saudi intellectuals, this attack drove home to Crown Prince Abdullah (now King Abdullah) the need to vigorously combat homegrown Saudi radicalism.

In response to the attacks, hundreds of suspects were arrested by Saudi authorities, many of them with ties to AQAP and to the resistance in Iraq, although many were also probably figures from the non-militant religious opposition whom the authorities wished to silence under the guise of combating terrorism. Al-Uyayri (or Ayiri), AQAP's founder and first leader, was killed in June 2003 at the height of this sweep by Saudi authorities. He was succeeded by Abd al-Aziz al-Muqrin.

On November 3, 2003, Saudi security forces had a shootout with AQAP operatives in the city of Mecca, the location of the Kaba, Islam's holiest shrine, that resulted in the deaths of two militants and the capture of a large weapons cache. Five days later, AQAP launched a successful suicide bombing attack against the Muhayya housing complex in Riyadh, which was home to many non-Saudi Arab expatriate workers; the attack killed 18 people and wounded scores of others.

The group continued to launch attacks on Saudi and foreign targets, including a Riyadh government building on April 21, 2004, and an oil company office in Yanbu on May 1 that resulted in the killing of five Western workers. AQAP suffered another setback on March 15, 2004, when Khalid Ali bin Ali al-Haj, a Yemeni national and senior AQAP leader, was killed in a shootout with Saudi police along with his companion, AQAP member Ibrahim al-Muzayni. The group retaliated with a host of deadly attacks on expatriates, killing Herman Dengel (a German) on May 22, 2004, BBC cameraman Simon Cumbers on June 6, Robert Jacob (an American) on June 8, Kenneth Scroggs (an American) on June 12, Irish engineer Tony Christopher on August 3, British engineer Edward Muirhead-Smith on September 15, and Laurent Barbot (a French citizen) on September 26.

The most widely publicized attack, however, was the June 12, 2004, kidnapping and June 18 beheading of Paul M. Johnson, Jr., an American employee of U.S. defense contractor Lockheed Martin. His kidnappers demanded the release of all detainees held by Saudi authorities, which was denied. The beheading was filmed and released on Web sites associated with and sympathetic to AQAP. That same day, Muqrin was killed by Saudi security forces during a raid on an AQAP safe house. Meanwhile, on May 29, the group succeeded again in

successfully carrying out attacks on three targets in the city of Khobar, taking hostages in oil business offices and housing complexes associated with foreign companies. Saudi police and soldiers stormed the buildings the next day and rescued many of the hostages, but not before the attackers had killed 22 others. Shortly after this attack, the U.S. Department of State issued a statement urging U.S. citizens to leave the kingdom. The year was capped off with a massive December 6 attack on the U.S. consulate in Jeddah, in which five consulate employees, four Saudi national guardsmen, and three AQAP members were killed. The Saudi government waged a successful campaign against AQAP throughout 2004 and into 2005, killing dozens of the group's members and nearly wiping out its senior leadership. In April 2005, several senior operatives were killed in a shootout in Rass, and in August, Saudi security forces killed Muqrin's successor and AQAP leader Salah al-Alawi al-Awfi in the holy city of Medina. Other members of the group were arrested. After suffering dramatic setbacks, AQAP continued to organize and plan attacks through 2008.

The group's members remain at large, and Saudi and foreign intelligence agencies continue to warn that AQAP poses a threat. The Saudi government has responded with antiterrorist measures such as conferences and public pronouncements, a highly structured in-prison counseling program designed to de-radicalize detainees, and the Sakinah program that analyzes and engages Internet postings. In 2007 and 2008, Saudi security forces detained and imprisoned hundreds of people, some of them suspected militants, in a variety of incidents, including planning an attack during the hajj, the annual religious pilgrimage.

On September 30, 2011, a U.S. drone attack in Yemen resulted in the death of Anwar al-Awlaki, one of the group's leaders, and Samir Khan, the editor of *Inspire*, its English-language magazine. Both were U.S. citizens. AQAP claimed responsibility for the May 21, 2012, suicide attack at a parade rehearsal for Yemen's Unity Day that killed over 120 people and injured 200 more. The attack was the deadliest in Yemeni history. The pace of U.S. drone attacks quickened significantly in 2012, with over 20 strikes in the first five months of the year, compared to 10 strikes during the course of 2011. During 2013, targeted killings by U.S. drones and Special Forces increased in number, thanks in part to the erection of secret U.S. bases in the Horn of Africa and the Arabian Peninsula. In the summer of 2013, in response to news that AQAP was planning an offensive against U.S. diplomatic posts abroad, the American government temporarily closed more than two dozen embassies and legations as a precaution. This corresponded with an uptick in U.S. drone attacks, which now began to target lower-level AQAP members and other militant Jihadists. On October 4, 2012, the United Nations 1267/1989 Al-Qaida Sanctions Committee and the U.S. State Department designated Ansar al-Sharia as an alias for Al-Qaeda in the Arabian Peninsula.

Christopher Anzalone

See also: Al-Qaeda; Global War on Terror; Terrorism

Further Reading

Al-Rasheed, Madawi. *Contesting the Saudi State: Islamic Voices from a New Generation.* Cambridge: Cambridge University Press, 2006.

Cordesman, Anthony H., and Nawaf Obaid. *Al-Qaeda in Saudi Arabia: Asymmetric Threats and Islamist Extremists.* Washington, DC: Center for Strategic and International Studies, 2005.

Johnsen, Gregory. *The Last Refuge: Yemen, al-Qaeda, and America's War in Arabia.* Melbourne, AU: Scribe, 2012.

Murphy, Caryle. "Saudi Arabia Indicts 991 Suspected Al-Qaeda Militants." *Christian Science Monitor*, October 22, 2008. http://www.csmonitor.com/World/Middle-East/2008/1022/p04s01-wome.html.

Riedel, Bruce, and Bilal Y. Saab. "Al-Qaeda's Third Front: Saudi Arabia." *Washington Quarterly* 21 (2008): 33–46.

Zuhur, Sherifa. "Decreasing Violence in Saudi Arabia and Beyond." In *Home Grown Terrorism: Understanding and Addressing the Root Causes of Radicalisation among Groups with an Immigrant Heritage in Europe*, Vol. 60, edited by Thamas M. Pick, Anne Speckard, and B. Jacuch, 74–98. NATO Science for Peace and Security Series. Amsterdam: IOS Press, 2010.

Al-Qaeda in the Islamic Maghreb

Al-Qaeda in the Islamic Maghreb (Tanzim al-Qaida fi Bilad al-Maghrib al-Islamiyya, QIM) is an Algeria-based clandestine jihadi organization founded on January 24, 2007, that employs terrorist tactics in support of Islamist ideology. It symbolizes Algeria's continuing political instability, North Africa's increasing vulnerability to militant Islam, and Al-Qaeda's little-discussed ability to expand not by diffusing or splintering into local cells but rather by skillfully drawing established organizations into its sphere of influence.

QIM's origins lie in Algeria's modern history. The French-Algerian War (1954–1962) freed Algeria from French colonialism and led to rule under the wartime resistance movement, the National Liberation Front (Front de Libération Nationale, or FLN). In 1989, however, militant Muslim opponents of the FLN regime formed the Islamic Salvation Front (Front Islamique du Salut, or FIS). In the early 1990s, the FLN manipulated and canceled elections to prevent the FIS from ascending to power, sparking a bloody civil war. This conflict radicalized and fragmented the opposition, with extremists gathering in the Armed Islamic Group (Groupe Islamique Armé, or GIA), a faction bent on utterly destroying the FLN regime and installing a Muslim state under sharia (Islamic law) through indiscriminate terrorist attacks against moderates and foreigners. The FLN weathered the storm, and as the civil war reached a horrendously violent stalemate, a new Islamist group—the Salafist Group for Preaching and Combat (Groupe Salafiste pour la Prédication et le Combat, or GSPC)—superseded the GIA by denouncing the widely detested violence against civilians. Founded in 1998, the GSPC would adopt the Al-Qaeda moniker a decade later.

The journey from GSPC to QIM was the result of a political dilemma facing Algerian Islamists combined with deft diplomacy by Al-Qaeda operatives. The GSPC's first leader, Hassan Hattab (aka Abu Hamza), kept the popular promise to attack only government officials and forces, hoping to regain the far-reaching support for Muslim militancy enjoyed by the FIS. But building a broad backing was slow going, and over time it was determined by some of his followers that the FLN could withstand a conventional insurgency. Impatient elements within the GSPC forced Hattab's resignation in 2004. His successor, Nabil Sahraoui (aka Abu Ibrahim Mustafa), enjoyed only a brief reign before Algerian soldiers located and eliminated him in June 2004. Abdel-

malek Droukdal (aka Abu Musab Abd al-Wadoud) has run the organization since, overseeing its radicalization, renaming, and return to GIA tactics.

Al-Qaeda worked to influence the GSPC from its very inception. It helped to fund Muslim militants in Algeria in the early 1990s but refused to fully endorse the GIA despite experiences that so-called Afghan Arabs in the two organizations shared while fighting the Soviets in Afghanistan in the 1980s. In 1998, Al-Qaeda leader Osama bin Laden welcomed the advent of the GSPC, a group manned in part by Al-Qaeda trainees who tied their renunciation of terrorism to an international Jihadi agenda.

The new ideology harnessed the GSPC to Al-Qaeda, and 12 days after the terror attacks of September 11, 2001, U.S. president George W. Bush labeled the GSPC a terrorist organization and froze its assets. This confrontation with the West—along with defections after 2000 of the halfhearted adherents, thanks to the Algerian government's amnesties for repentant civil war insurgents—further sharpened the GSPC's anti-Western extremist edge.

In 2002, Al-Qaeda sent an emissary to Algeria for meetings with sympathetic figures within the GSPC. Two years later, Chadian forces captured a key GSPC regional commander moving through the Sahara, and his colleagues decided to pressure Chad's ally, France, for his release. They reached out to Al-Qaeda for assistance, and an obliging Abu Musab al-Zarqawi, head of Al-Qaeda in Mesopotamia (Iraq), agreed to support the GSPC by kidnapping French citizens as bargaining chips. The plan did not materialize, but the congenial link remained, and after 2004, the GSPC's new hard-line leaders ultimately developed the link. Al-Qaeda, for its part, grew increasingly interested in the GSPC after 2005, when the attempt to forge an affiliate terrorist network in Morocco had failed. Al-Qaeda's strategists came to recognize that within North Africa, a critical region supplying long-standing Muslim immigrant communities to nearby Western Europe, only Algeria lacked a pervasive security apparatus capable of rooting out terrorist cells. The two organizations issued cordial statements throughout 2005, and by late 2006, a formal merger between Al-Qaeda and the GSPC was announced, with the latter's name change coming the following year.

Since this merger, QIM has grown more powerful and dangerous. Al-Qaeda is probably funneling resources into QIM, supplementing funds that the Algerian organization can gather on its own through the European financial network it inherited from the GIA. In return, QIM is internationalizing its purview. Some fear that it could make Europe an area of operations, and it has already forgone expansion—remaining at several hundred active members—in order to send newly trained North African recruits to fight in Iraq. The Al-Qaeda—QIM alliance has been most pronounced in terms of tactics. The GSPC initially acquired conventional weaponry for guerrilla ambushes, false checkpoints, and truck bombs against military and government targets. With Al-Qaeda's help and encouragement, QIM now executes significant terrorist attacks including suicide bombers and civilian casualties. Since December 2006, QIM has bombed not only the Algerian prime minister's office and an army outpost, but also foreign oil-services contractors and United Nations (UN) staff.

On January 22, 2009, Edwin Dyer was one of four Westerners who were kidnapped when their convoy was ambushed near the border between Niger and Mali by an African terrorist group calling itself Al-Qaeda in the Islamic Maghreb. The group demanded that the British government release Abu Qatada, the Jordanian known as Osama bin Laden's right-hand man in Europe, or Dyer would face execution. On May 31, 2009, the terrorist group released a statement on a known terrorist Web site claiming to have executed Dyer. His death was confirmed by the prime minister of the United Kingdom Gordon Brown on June 3, 2009, after reports on an Islamist Web site that he had been killed. Prime Minister Gordon Brown condemned what he called an "appalling and barbaric act of terrorism."

Al-Qaeda in the Islamic Maghreb continues to remain one of the richest and best-armed jihadi terrorist organizations in the Middle East. Much of its funding comes from Western governments and international organizations, which pay hefty ransoms for individuals kidnapped by the organization or its allied groups. In turn, some of that money is funneled to other jihadi groups. In September 2010, jihadists associated with Al-Qaeda in Islamic Maghreb kidnapped four European tourists in Timbuktu (Mali); one died, and the fate of the others is unknown. In December 2011, the group abducted five Europeans, and in September 2013, it claimed responsibility for a car bombing that resulted in two civilian deaths in Timbuktu.

Benjamin P. Nickels

See also: Al-Qaeda; Al-Qaeda in Iraq; Bin Laden, Osama; Global War on Terror

Further Reading

Gunaratna, Rohan. *Inside Al-Qaeda: Global Network of Terror.* New York: Berkley Publishing Group, 2003.

Hansen, Andrew, and Lauren Vriens. "Al-Qaeda in the Islamic Maghreb (AQIM) or L'Organisation Al-Qaïda au Maghreb Islamique (Formerly Salafist Group for Preaching and Combat or Groupe Salafiste pour la Prédication et le Combat)." Council on Foreign Relations, Backgrounder, updated July 31, 2008. Available online at www.cfr.org/publication/12717.

Hunt, Emily. "Islamist Terrorism in Northwestern Africa: A 'Thorn in the Neck' of the United States?" Washington, DC: The Washington Institute for Near East Policy, Policy Focus #65, February 2007, www.washingtoninstitute.org/templateC04.php?CID=266.

Ibrahim, Raymond. *The Al-Qaeda Reader.* New York: Doubleday, 2007.

Stora, Benjamin. *Algeria: A Short History.* Ithaca, NY: Cornell University Press, 2004.

Al-Quds Mosque

Al-Quds Mosque was the mosque in Hamburg, Germany, where leaders of the September 11, 2001, terror operation worshipped, and where they planned the attack. It was located on Steindamm Street, in a poorer section of Hamburg. The mosque was situated above a bodybuilding gym near Hamburg's central railway station. This location, close to cheap transportation, made it attractive to expatriate Muslims. Al-Quds was one of the few Arab Sunni mosques; most of others in Hamburg were Shiite or Turkish Sunni. It was small, holding at most 150 people at prayer time. These small mosques were good places for Islamist extremists to cultivate and recruit members.

Al-Quds was an extremist mosque because of the preaching of its leading cleric, Mohammed al-Fazazi. The founders of the mosque had been Moroccans, and most of its clerics were Moroccans—including al-Fazazi. He preached there constantly. Al-Fazazi believed Western civilization was the enemy of the Muslim world, and he believed in martyrdom. He was quoted in 2000 as saying that "who[ever] participates in the war against Islam with ideas or thoughts or a song or a television show to befoul Islam is an infidel on war footing that shall be killed, no matter if it's a man, a woman, or a child." It was these ideas that attracted Mohamed Atta to Islamist extremism and later to Al-Qaeda. Al-Fazazi spent considerable time with the young men in his congregation talking with them about jihad, holy war, and martyrdom. Later, al-Fazazi's involvement in bombings in Morocco and Spain landed him a 30-year prison sentence in Morocco.

The al-Quds Mosque remained a place where it was possible to recruit others susceptible to the appeal of al-Fazazi and, later, Al-Qaeda. Atta taught religious classes at al-Quds Mosque, but his hardline position alienated all but those who thought as he did. All of the members of the Hamburg Cell were recruited at the al-Quds Mosque, including Marwan al-Shehhi and Ramzi bin al-Shibh. In August 2010, growing concerns that the site was again serving as a gathering place for Islamic extremists led German security officials to close the mosque.

Stephen E. Atkins

See also: Atta, Mohamed el-Amir Awad el-Sayed; Hamburg Cell

Further Reading

Corbin, Jane. *Al-Qaeda: The Terror Network That Threatens the World.* New York: Thunder's Mouth, 2002.

McDermott, Terry. *Perfect Soldiers: The 9/11 Hijackers: Who They Were, Why They Did It*. New York: HarperCollins, 2005.

Vidino, Lorenzo. *Al-Qaeda in Europe: The New Battleground of International Jihad*. Amherst, NY: Prometheus Books, 2006.

American Airlines Flight 11

American Airlines Flight 11 was a Boeing 767-223ER that was the first aircraft to crash into the North Tower of the World Trade Center complex in New York City on September 11, 2001. The pilot of the aircraft was John Ogonowski, a 52-year-old Vietnam veteran from Massachusetts, and its first officer was Thomas McGuinness. Flight 11 departed from Boston's Logan International Airport nearly 14 minutes late, at 7:59 a.m., bound for Los Angeles International Airport. It carried slightly more than half its capacity of 158 passengers and a crew of 11, and had a full load of 23,980 gallons of aviation fuel at takeoff, which was routine.

The leader of the terrorist team, and its designated pilot on board Flight 11, was Mohamed Atta. Atta and other members of the hijack team—Satam al-Suqami, Waleed al-Shehri, Wail al-Shehri, and Abdul Aziz al-Omari—had bought first-class seats, which research conducted on other flights convinced them gave them the best opportunity to seize the cockpit and gain control of the aircraft. Two of the hijackers sat near the cockpit and two near the passenger section. Atta sat in 8D, from whence he could command both teams.

The hijackers had little trouble passing through checkpoint security. American Airlines' security checkpoints at Logan International Airport were operated by a private company, Globe Security, which operated these checkpoints under a contract with American Airlines. Because American Airlines' desire was for passengers to be harassed at checkpoints as little as possible, the hijackers had no difficulty in passing through the checkpoints carrying box cutters and mace.

Instructions had been given by Al-Qaeda trainers to the hijackers to seize the aircraft by force within 15 minutes of takeoff. Around 8:14 a.m., they did so, killing two attendants and a passenger, Daniel Lewin, immediately. Lewin, formerly an officer in the elite Sayeret Matkal unit of the Israeli military, was seen as a threat. The hijackers, who had apparently identified him as a potential air marshal, killed him as soon as possible. To allay suspicions, the hijackers lulled the passengers and crew into a false sense of hope by giving the impression that the plane would land safely and that the passengers would be used as hostages, a successful tactic of hijackers in the past.

Air traffic controllers received information from the cockpit via Ogonowski's radio, over which they heard a conversation between the pilot and a hijacker in the cockpit that made it evident that a hijacking was in progress. More ominously, they also learned from a hijacker's comment about plans to seize control of other aircraft. This information was the first indication of a plot to hijack numerous aircraft in flight.

The first concrete information about the hijacking came from Betty Ong, a flight attendant on Fight 11, who contacted the American Airlines Flight Center in Fort Worth, Texas, and related that two flight attendants had been stabbed and that another was on oxygen. A passenger, she said, had been killed, and the hijackers had gained access to the cockpit, using some type of mace-like spray to neutralize the crew.

Once the hijackers gained control of the aircraft, they took precautions to control the passengers, securing the first-class section by intimidation, mace and pepper spray, and threats to detonate a bomb. The rest of the passengers, in coach, were led to believe that a medical emergency had occurred in the first-class section. The hijackers also told the passengers that the aircraft was returning to the airport. Another attendant, Madeleine Sweeney, contacted authorities and confirmed Ong's earlier message to the American Flight Services Office in Boston. She re-established communication and was in fact on the line as the aircraft approached the North Tower of the World Trade Center. By the time the passengers realized what was happening, it was too late to do anything. Many hurriedly called their loved ones and said goodbye either by talking with them or by leaving messages.

The aircraft crashed at about 378 miles per hour between the 94th and 98th floors of the North Tower. The crew, passengers, and hijackers all died instantly from the force of the explosion and the fire that accompanied it. The force of the explosion alone shattered the aluminum wings and fuselage of the aircraft into pieces the size of a human fist.

The impact of the crash and the prolonged burning of aviation fuel weakened the structure of the North Tower, trapping those people above the 98th floor, who had no chance of escape. Those threatened by fire and smoke began to jump from the building. The North Tower collapsed on itself shortly after the South Tower fell.

Stephen E. Atkins

See also: American Airlines Flight 77; Pentagon Attack; United Airlines Flight 93; United Airlines Flight 175; World Trade Center, September 11, 2001

Further Reading

Aust, Stefan, et al. *Inside 9/11: What Really Happened*. New York: St. Martin's, 2001.

Bernstein, Richard. *Out of the Blue: The Story of September 11, 2001, from Jihad to Ground Zero*. New York: Times Books, 2002.

Craig, Olga. "At 8:46 AM, the World Changed in a Moment." *Sunday Telegraph* (London), September 16, 2001, 14.

9/11 Commission. *The 9/11 Commission Report: Final Report of the National Commission on Terrorist Attacks Upon the United States*. New York: Norton, 2004.

Trento, Susan B., and Joseph J. Trento. *Unsafe at Any Altitude: Failed Terrorism Investigations, Scapegoating 9/11, and the Shocking Truth about Aviation Security Today*. Hanover, NH: Steerforth, 2006.

American Airlines Flight 77

American Airlines Flight 77, a Boeing 757-223, was the third aircraft seized by hijackers on September 11, 2001. It left Dulles International Airport, near Washington, D.C., at 8:20 a.m., bound for Los Angeles International Airport with 58 passengers and a crew of six. The pilot was Charles Burlingame and the first officer was David Charlebois. Because of problems at the security gate, the flight was 10 minutes late taking off. The security checkpoint at Dulles International Airport was operated by Argenbright Security under a contract with United Airlines.

Passenger screeners at Dulles International Airport were 87 percent foreign-born and mostly Muslim. Three of the hijackers failed the metal detector test, but, after passing hand-wand screening, were permitted to enter the aircraft. There was no indication that any of them were carrying prohibited weapons.

The five-person terrorist team was led by Hani Hanjour, who was also the team's designated pilot. Other members of his team were Nawaf al-Hazmi, Salem al-Hazmi, Khalid al-Mihdhar, and Majed Moqued, who had all bought first-class tickets to gain better access to the aircraft's cockpit. The hijackers used knives and box cutters to gain control of the cockpit sometime between 8:51 and 8:54 a.m., after which Hanjour turned the aircraft around and headed for Washington, D.C. Like the hijackers of American Airlines Flight 11, the hijackers of Flight 77 calmed passengers by convincing them that the plane would land, after which they would be used as hostages.

Although by this time it was known that other aircraft had been seized and turned into flying bombs, authorities in Washington, D.C, were slow to respond. Two passengers, Renee May and Barbara K. Olson, the wife of U.S. solicitor general Theodore Olson, made phone calls reporting the hijacking. She made two calls to her husband, giving him details of the hijacking. He told her the news of the two aircraft crashing into the World Trade Center.

By this time, the Dulles air controllers were aware of an approaching unauthorized aircraft coming at high speed toward Washington, D.C. They had been able to obtain a visual confirmation from a military transport, a C-141, as the hijacked aircraft headed toward the Pentagon. Between 9:37 and 9:40 a.m., Flight 77 crashed at 530 miles per hour into the ground at the base of the west side of the Pentagon, killing all passengers. Although much of the crash site contained recently renovated, unoccupied offices, the explosion and the resulting collapse of parts of the five-story building killed 125 people. The explosion did its greatest damage to the three outer rings of the Pentagon, but the two inner rings sustained damage as well.

Stephen E. Atkins

See also: American Airlines Flight 11; Pentagon Attack; United Airlines Flight 93; United Airlines Flight 175; World Trade Center, September 11, 2001

Further Reading

Aust, Stefan, et al. *Inside 9/11: What Really Happened.* New York: St. Martin's, 2001.

Bernstein, Richard. *Out of the Blue: The Story of September 11, 2001, from Jihad to Ground Zero.* New York: Times Books, 2002.

9/11 Commission. *The 9/11 Commission Report: Final Report of the National Commission on Terrorist Attacks upon the United States.* New York: Norton, 2004.

Trento, Susan B., and Joseph J. Trento. *Unsafe at Any Altitude: Failed Terrorism Investigations, Scapegoating 9/11, and the Shocking Truth about Aviation Security Today.* Hanover, NH: Steerforth, 2006.

Amman Hotel Bombings

On November 9, 2005, a trio of Iraqi suicide bombers detonated devices at three separate hotels in Amman, Jordan. The attacks, organized by Abu Musab's al-Zarqawi's Tanzom Qa'idat al-Jihadi Bilad al-Rafidyan (QJBR, or Al-Qaeda in Iraq [AQI]), resulted in the deaths of 62 people and the reported wounding of 115 others. The most deadly explosion occurred at the Radisson SAS, where one of the terrorists detonated himself in the middle of a wedding celebration attended by Jordanians and Palestinians. The bombings produced a major backlash against AQI within

Jordan, and to some extent the larger Middle East, depriving the group of much of its earlier popularity.

Prior to the November 2005 bombings, al-Zarqawi had been linked to several unsuccessful plots in Jordan. In 1999, he was implicated in the failed "millennium plot" that was to have targeted the Radisson SAS and various other tourist sites in the country. In August 2005, he was tied to another unsuccessful strike, this time a rocket attack in Aqaba. Overall, Jordan's General Intelligence Department (GID) believed al-Zarqawi had been behind at least a dozen attempted acts of terrorism, although some security officials gave numbers as high as 150. The Amman bombings dramatically broke this pattern and were generally seen as indicative of

a change in targeting away from fortified strategic buildings toward "soft" civilian-centric venues. AQI itself claimed the hotels had been selected because they were frequented by the intelligence services who were coordinating activities against the mujahideen in Iraq, by North Atlantic Treaty Organization (NATO) commanders, by Shia militias, and by Jewish and Christian tourists. The group also asserted that the properties were centers of vice and prostitution.

There is no indication that Al-Qaeda's central command had any role in planning the attacks. Indeed, in July 2005, Ayman al-Zawahiri, then Osama bin Laden's second in command, had advised al-Zarqawi to focus on expelling American forces from Iraq and consolidating the establishment

A Jordanian policeman stands guard in the damaged lobby of the Grand Hyatt hotel in Amman, Jordan, November 10, 2005. Al-Qaeda issued an Internet claim of responsibility for three suicide bomb attacks on Western hotels that killed at least 56 people. (AP Photo/Hussein Malla)

of an Islamic state before attempting to export the jihad to neighboring countries.

Perhaps indicative of Al-Qaeda's non-involvement, actual preattack preparations appeared to be minimal. On November 5, 2005, four members of AQI—Ali Hussein al-Shumari, 35, and his wife, Sajida Mubarak al-Rishawi, 35; Rawad Jassem Muhammad Abed, 23; and Safaa Muhammad Ali, 23—crossed the border from Iraq to Jordan with fraudulent passports. The terrorists then rented an apartment in a neighborhood of Amman and hired a car. According to the GID, once the team had crossed the border into the country, all communications with the AQI leadership were cut.

It is unclear whether the bombers assembled their suicide belts once in Amman or whether the devices were smuggled in separately. An AQI statement issued on the Internet two days after the bombings asserted that that the attackers conducted "one month" of surveillance before carrying out their mission. However, this is clearly contradicted by the date the bombers entered the country, only three days prior to the explosions. In fact, several witnesses claimed to have seen two men canvassing one of the targeted properties, the Days Inn, just one day before it was hit.

On the evening of September 9, the suicide bombers traveled to their respective hotels: al-Rishawi and al-Shumari to the Radisson SAS; Muhammed Abed to the Grand Hyatt; and Muhammad Ali to the Days Inn. At approximately 8:50 p.m., the attacks were launched.

At the Raddison SAS, al-Rishawi failed to detonate her suicide belt due to technical difficulties and fled the scene. Her husband then reportedly jumped on a table in the center of the room and triggered his device. The ensuing blast was the most lethal

of the three, as it took place in the middle of a wedding reception.

The attack at the Grand Hyatt took place in the lobby, resulting in the death of several Palestinian officials, including the head of military intelligence for the West Bank, Major General Bashir Nayef. American-Syrian filmmaker Mustafa Akkad and his daughter were also among those killed. The explosion at the Days Inn occurred immediately outside the hotel and was initially thought to have been the result of a car bomb. However, it was later determined that the perpetrator had merely detonated his suicide belt inside the vehicle. Three members of a Chinese military delegation were among the fatalities.

The day after the bombings, a statement claiming responsibility in the name of "Al-Baraa bin Balik Brigade" was posted on a Web site often used by AQI. A second communiqué clarifying the reasons behind the attacks was issued shortly thereafter, apparently in an attempt to ameliorate the condemnation already building within the Arab media and on the streets of Jordan. A third message appeared on Friday, November 11, providing more details about the operation and confirming that the bombers were all Iraqis and included three males and one female. It is not clear whether the GID was aware at this time that al-Rishawi had been involved or whether the statement alerted them that she was still at large.

Following the attacks, the border with Iraq was immediately closed, and a heavy security dragnet was instituted across the capital. Over the next couple of days, 120 suspects were rounded up in what was described as the country's largest manhunt in history. Al-Rishawi was eventually traced to Salt, a town northwest of Amman, where she had taken refuge in a house owned by a local family.

There is well-documented evidence that before the bombings, the majority of the population of Jordan was sympathetic to AQI and believed that suicide bombings could be legitimate if carried out to defend Muslim lives. These attitudes changed dramatically following the attacks. According to surveys conducted by the Pew Research Center, whereas 57 percent of respondents had declared militant martyrdom as sometimes or often justified in early 2005, only 29 percent did so in 2006. Confidence in bin Laden and Al-Qaeda affiliates similarly plummeted, from 61 percent in 2005 to 24 percent in 2006. Even Internet polling of jihadis showed a high level of discomfort with the Amman bombings.

Condemnation of the attacks was visibly reflected in mass public protests that sprang up in Amman, with some gatherings numbering as many as 200,000 people. Demonstrators berated AQI and vocally reaffirmed their support for and loyalty to the Jordanian government, then a key U.S. ally in the so-called global war on terror. Arguably more significantly, al-Zarqawi's own clan, the al-Khalaliyah, published advertisements in local newspapers denouncing the attacks, disowning the AQI leader and pledging allegiance to the king.

The overwhelming public narrative surrounding the bombings was that they mindlessly targeted civilians. The images and stories from the attack on the wedding at the Radisson SAS triggered a particularly dramatic backlash, not least because it had resulted in the indiscriminate slaughter of innocent Jordanian and Palestinian Muslims. Ashraf al-Khalid, the groom at the celebration, later became a public activist against terrorism and cofounded the global survivors' network.

Despite the overwhelming revulsion the bombings caused, conspiracy theories fueled stories among a small minority that the attacks were legitimately aimed at foreign intelligence agencies and that intended Jewish targets had received advanced notice of the impending strikes. The activities of the head of West Bank intelligence, Major General Bashir Nayef, and the Chinese military delegation that died in the explosion at the Days Inn attacks remain largely unexplained. Furthermore, *Haaretz* reported that Israeli citizens were escorted out of the Raddison SAS shortly before the attacks and alleged that an advisory warning against travel to Jordan had been posted before the bombings occurred.

Gregory Wyatt

See also: Millennium Plots; Zawahiri, Ayman al-

Further Reading

Blumenkrantz, Zhoar, and Yoav Stern. "Scores Dead in Three Amman Hotel Bombings; Israelis Evacuated before Attack." *Haaretz,* November 10, 2005. http://www.haaretz .com/print-edition/news/scores-dead-in -three-amman-hotel-bombings-israelis -evacuated-before-attack-1.173770.

"JTIC Exclusive Interview: Major-General Samih Asfoura, Director, Jordanian General Intelligence Department." Jane's Terrorism and Insurgency Center, December 22, 2005. Accessed January 31, 2012. http://jtic .janes.com.

Phillips, James. "Zarqawi's Amman Bombings: Jordan's 9/11." Heritage Foundation, Washington DC, November 18, 2005. Accessed January 31, 2012. http://www .heritage.org/research/reports/2005/11/ zarqawis-amman-bombings-jordans-9-11.

"Suicide Bombers Hit Amman Hotels." Jane's Terrorism and Insurgency Center, November 10, 2005. Accessed January 31, 2012. http://jtic.janes.com.

"Unfavorable Views of Jews and Muslims on the Increase in Europe." Pew Research

Center, Washington D.C., September 17, 2008. Accessed January 31, 2012. http:// www.pewglobal.org/2008/09/17/chapter-3 -muslim-views-on-extremism-and-conflict/.

Anglo-American Alliance

This is one of the most potent and enduring strategic partnerships of modern times, which evolved into a multifaceted strategic relationship based on the solid foundation of common heritage, culture, and language, as well as shared values, vision, and interests. Because of its paramount strategic importance, the Middle East played an extremely important role in the evolution of the Anglo-American alliance. Despite sporadic disagreements, most notoriously during the 1956 Suez Crisis and the Yom Kippur (Ramadan) War of 1973 when American and British priorities diverged in the overall course of the Cold War and beyond, Anglo-American relations were generally harmonious, and both powers complemented each other's role in the region. This trend only gained momentum in the post–Cold War world, when new major challenges and threats, particularly the risk of the proliferation of the weapons of mass destruction and international terrorism, stimulated common Anglo-American security concerns and mutual recognition of the need for close strategic cooperation in the region.

There were also several other important factors dealing with the American and British postures in the Middle East and U.S.-UK relations that contributed to the further development of the alliance. Politically and diplomatically, the two powers needed each other in the Middle East. For the United States, the solid and stable alliance with Britain had a special value in this volatile and unpredictable region where changing calculations of self-interest too often motivated many other American partners. Also, the alliance with Britain—one of the major powers and a permanent member of the United Nations (UN) Security Council—enhanced U.S. global leadership and gave American interests in the Middle East an additional international legitimacy. Moreover, despite their withdrawal from empire in the 1950s, 1960s, and 1970s, the British still retained close contacts with many regimes in the Middle East, and their expertise in local culture and traditions was of great advantage in dealing with Muslim countries, particularly during the 1991 Persian Gulf War, the global war on terror, the Afghanistan War (beginning in 2001), and the Iraq War (beginning in 2003). These connections allowed a division of labor within the alliance: the British were indispensable at international coalition-building efforts, while the Americans could concentrate more on strategic and military planning and preparations.

Militarily, the alliance provided the British with critically important access to American high technology, particularly in reconnaissance and surveillance. At the same time, Britain's experiences of providing a long-term military presence in the Middle East, particularly in special operations, counterinsurgency, urban warfare, and pacification of hostile populations, were made available for the Americans.

Intelligence was another area of particularly fruitful cooperation between the United States and the United Kingdom. The degree of intelligence sharing and reciprocity in intelligence-gathering operations is unlikely equaled between any other two countries in the world. Recently, the intelligence services of both countries have been actively involved into gathering information about terrorist activities, particularly Al-Qaeda, and the risk of the proliferation of weapons of mass destruction in the Middle East.

The close personal relations between American presidents and British prime ministers, who as a rule came to depend on each other, have also been of much importance for the development of the Anglo-American alliance. Many British prime ministers, particularly Margaret Thatcher and Tony Blair, kept extraordinarily high profiles in Washington, frequently setting the very agenda of the alliance with much eloquence and persuasiveness and even personifying the alliance internationally. For example, just prior to the 1991 Persian Gulf War, Thatcher convinced President George H. W. Bush that he must not shy away from using military force if Iraqi president Saddam Hussein did not leave Kuwait within the time span set by the UN.

There was also a strong inclination in both capitals to reassert and solidify the special relationship in any international turmoil, including in the Middle East, on the basis of an almost axiomatic assumption that in case of crisis and/or war, both partners must stand shoulder to shoulder. On the British side, that trend is frequently supplemented by the belief that a firm commitment to sharing military burdens with the United States and providing Washington with open-ended unqualified support will make Britain the most trusted American ally. In so doing, London believes that it can influence the way in which America exercises its might, and this elevates Britain to the status of pivotal global power, greatly multiplying its real weight in international affairs.

The removal of the Taliban from power in Afghanistan in late 2001 and the rapid military overthrow of the Saddam Hussein regime in Iraq in 2003 signified the culmination of the ongoing Anglo-American strategy in the Middle East, which included the victory in the Persian Gulf War and cooperation in policing of the no-fly zones in the Iraqi sky in its aftermath as well as military collaboration in Operation Desert Fox in 1998. Diplomatically, the U.S.-UK partnership was instrumental in securing UN backing for the occupation and rebuilding of Iraq, in the promotion of the two-state solution for the Israeli-Palestinian problem, and in Libya's renunciation of its weapons of mass destruction program.

At the same time, the evolution of the Afghanistan War and the Iraq War into protracted insurgencies revealed some underlying problems and complexities in the Anglo-American alliance. Once more, these demonstrated the power asymmetry between the partners, where close security ties are of much more importance for London than for Washington. There are also differences in the decision-making process and in implementation of security policies in the two countries, as well as differences in the command and control systems and structures of their respective militaries. Moreover, the British Army found itself underequipped and overstretched by deployments in two very complex combat zones. Furthermore, the British public was not enamored of the alliance and protested their nation's involvement in Iraq, while Tony Blair was exceedingly unpopular in most parts of the Middle East because of his close ties with American president George W. Bush.

Turning to the specific issues of the Anglo-American partnership, there were also some initial strategic disagreements between the parties on the priorities of the global war on terror. For example, the United States sought a military defeat of the terrorists and the states that support and harbor them, while Britain sought a more strategic approach by continuing a dialogue to an active search for the resolution of the Arab-Israeli conflict, which it believed was fanning the flames of terrorist sentiment. In setting the aims of the Iraq War, Britain's primary concern was to prevent Saddam Hussein from acquiring weapons of mass destruction, while the United States was also seeking immediate regime change in the country. The British also paid much more attention than the United States did to the efforts to secure UN sanctioning of the Iraq War and the Iraqi occupation and reconstruction efforts in the country. The British, concerned about the threat of chaos in Iraq after the victory, did not support the U.S.-promoted de-Baathification program.

In Afghanistan, the British supported the anti-Taliban factions among the dominating Pashtun tribes, while the United States supported the rival Northern Alliance. Additionally, there was a growing critique on the part of the U.S. military of British combat performance against the insurgencies in Iraq and Afghanistan. These included complaints about the institutional arrogance of the British military command, its overconfidence in its own counter-insurgency experiences, and its general inflexibility.

The aforementioned trends and developments have complicated the achievement of stability in the Middle East and within the alliance. Emphasizing Britain's modest military resources and its strong desire to achieve a UN mandate for military action, the most active proponents of interventions in Afghanistan and Iraq in

the George W. Bush administration—Vice President Dick Cheney, Secretary of Defense Donald Rumsfeld, and Undersecretary of Defense Paul Wolfowitz—were rather skeptical about the values of British contributions to Afghanistan and Iraq. On the British side, there was wide and sustained popular and political criticism about following the American lead, particularly in Iraq. Indeed, the Iraq War was hugely unpopular. Critics emphasized that the war isolated Britain from other European countries, damaged its international stance, and instead of providing Britain with a voice in American decisions, turned the country into a de facto silent vassal and strategic hostage of the United States. In this atmosphere, Tony Blair nevertheless maintained his desire to stay with America until the end, risking his own political future.

Blair resigned in 2007, suffering from historically low approval ratings. He was succeeded by Labour Party leader Gordon Brown, who was less comfortable with coddling the Americans. Nevertheless, he and President Barack Obama, who took office in January 2009, enjoyed a relatively cordial relationship, as both men agreed on the need to wind down the war in Iraq as quickly as possible. By July 21, 2009, all but 400 British servicemen had been withdrawn from Iraq, and the Brown government announced across-the-board decreases in defense spending amid the building economic recession that had begun in 2008. In 2009, three Londoners, Tanvir Hussain, Assad Sarwar, and Ahmed Abdullah Ali, were convicted of conspiring to detonate bombs disguised as soft drinks on seven airplanes bound for Canada and the United States. The massively complex police and MI5 investigation of the plot involved more than a year of surveillance work conducted by over 200 officers in both countries.

In May 2010, Brown was succeeded as prime minister by David Cameron, leader of the Conservative Party. This change slightly strained Anglo-American relations, chiefly because Obama and Cameron were on opposite sides of the political divide. This strain became more apparent after the Wikileaks scandal that began in 2011. In May 2011, Obama made his first official state visit to Great Britain, during which he praised the British government and reaffirmed the Anglo-American alliance. In 2013, the Americans and British closed ranks after leaks by former U.S. defense contractor Edward Snowden revealed that their two countries had jointly engaged in widespread spying against mutual allies. Regardless of these issues of contention, the British have proven to be an unfailing partner with the United States. Indeed, in all three conflicts—the Persian Gulf War, the Afghanistan War, and the Iraq War—Britain provided far more troops than any other nation besides the United States.

Peter J. Rainow

See also: Arab-Israeli Conflict, Overview; Bush Administration; Obama Administration

Further Reading

Coughlin, Con. *American Ally: Tony Blair and the War on Terror.* New York: Ecco, 2006.

Dumbrell, John. *A Special Relationship: Anglo-American Relations from the Cold War to Iraq.* New York: Palgrave Macmillan, 2006.

Naughtie, James. *The Accidental American: Tony Blair and the Presidency.* New York: PublicAffairs, 2004.

Shawcross, William. *Allies: The U.S., Britain, and Europe in the Aftermath of the Iraq War.* New York: PublicAffairs, 2005.

Anthrax Attacks (United States)

On September 18, 2001, just one week after the terrorist attacks of September 11, five letters contaminated with anthrax bacteria were mailed in the United States to five media outlets. Over the next month, two more letters were sent. Altogether, the anthrax letters (which were mailed from a postal box in New Jersey) resulted in the deaths of 5 people and the infections of 17 more.

The anthrax-laced letters originally sent on September 18 were sent to the offices of ABC News, CBS News, NBC News, the *New York Post*, and the *National Enquirer*. Nearly a month later, two more letters were sent to Democratic senators Tom Daschle and Patrick Leahy at the Senate building in Washington, D.C. The postal service misdirected Leahy's letter, but the letter addressed to Daschle was opened by an aide, who became infected. Unlike the earlier letters, the second set of letters contained higher-quality weapons-grade anthrax capable of infecting victims with greater lethality.

In response to the attacks, thousands of people who came in contact with or were near the envelopes began taking strong doses of ciprofloxacin ("cipro"), an antibiotic capable of preventing anthrax infections. In addition, the federal government began radiation treatment of all incoming mail to defuse any possible anthrax inside. Post office employees began wearing gloves and masks and warned all Americans to carefully examine their mail and report any suspicious letters or packages.

Five people died from the anthrax infection: one employee at the *National Enquirer*, two post office employees, and two other unconnected people whose mail was likely cross-contaminated by the anthrax letters. Government officials began an investigation immediately after discovering the anthrax letters. Following a variety of leads, the investigators profiled the suspect as a chemical or biological engineer in the United States who had likely worked at government facilities in the past. Some microbiologist experts who examined the anthrax stated that its quality was likely greater than that of the anthrax found in either U.S. or Russian stockpiles and thus was likely created in recent government anthrax programs.

The Federal Bureau of Investigation eventually concluded that Dr. Bruce Ivins, a microbiologist working at the U.S. Army's Bio-Defense Laboratory in Maryland, was responsible for the attacks. To this day, however, questions remain about his guilt, and there continues to be speculation that the true perpetrator is still on the loose. Ivins committed suicide in 2008, before any formal charges could be brought against him.

Peter Chalk

See also: Impact of 9/11 on U.S. Public Opinion; Terrorism

Further Reading

"American Anthrax Outbreak of 2001." University of California at Los Angeles (UCLA) Department of Epidemiology, August 24, 2008. http://www.ph.ucla.edu/epi/bioter/detect/antdect_intro.html.

Croddy, Eric A., and James Wirtz. *Weapons of Mass Destruction.* Santa Barbara, CA: ABC-CLIO, 2005.

Shane, Scott. "Colleague Rebuts Idea That Suspect's Lab Made Anthrax in Attacks." *New York Times,* April 23, 2010.

"Troubled Scientist's Anthrax Attack May Have Been Misguided Attempt to Test Cure." Associated Press, August 1, 2008.

Arab-Israeli Conflict, Overview

The Arab-Israeli conflict has been going on at varying levels of intensity for almost 60 years, but its roots extend back for centuries. The current incarnation of this conflict can be traced to the establishment of the State of Israel. A key set of documents was instrumental in the creation of Israel. These documents (including the Basle Declaration, the Sykes-Picot Agreement, the Balfour Declaration, the British Mandate for Palestine of 1920, and the Israelis' Proclamation of Independence in 1948) increased tensions in the region by establishing and recognizing on a global stage the State of Israel, carved out from the lands of Palestine.

From its beginning in 1948 (which Israel considered a "rebirth" rather than an initial founding), the new Jewish state has been able to prevail over various combinations of Arab opponents. The founding members of Israel vowed that there would never be another Holocaust. They decided that the Jewish state would spend unlimited effort and money on the Israeli armed forces to prevent an Arab victory, which they believed could only end in another, final Holocaust. The Arabs, united in their opposition to Israel, remained divided along nationalist, tribal, and familial lines. Despite their tremendous advantages in geography, population, and resources, the Arabs have never been able to match Israel's military prowess, although they nearly did so in 1973.

Both the Arabs and the Israelis have received help from other nations. In the early stages, Israel received assistance from Great Britain and France in the form of diplomatic recognition and a supply of

Israeli troops in armored vehicles advance against Egyptian troops near Rafah, Gaza Strip, at the start of the "Six-Day War" on June 5, 1967. Also known as the "Arab-Israeli War of 1967," the Six-Day War pitted Israel against the Arab nations of Egypt, Jordan, and Syria. The war ended with the Israeli occupation of the Sinai and Gaza Strip, the Golan Heights, and the West Bank. (Getty Images)

arms. It also received financial assistance from private individuals in Europe and the United States, which made possible the purchase of sophisticated technology from weapons-exporting states. The lower technological levels of military forces in the Middle East made the use of surplus equipment left over from World War II sufficient to meet the needs of the belligerents for more than a decade after the declaration of Israeli independence. After the Suez Crisis fiasco of 1956, Israel turned to the United States, which had always backed it diplomatically and now began to supply it with weapons. The Arab world reached out to the Soviet Union. This aid also helped the Soviet Union achieve its long-sought goal of a military presence in the Mediterranean.

Below is a general overview of the major conflicts.

The Israeli War of Independence, 1948

From a population of 600,000, Israel fielded 30,000 for local defense and 15,000 as a field force. The return of personnel from World War II, particularly those who had served in the British military, as well as the existence of Jewish militias created before the war, allowed Israel to quickly field a unified command of veteran fighters. Israel quickly defeated the local Palestinian contingents. Then, in a war characterized by a series of truces followed by a series of battles, the Israel Defense Forces (IDF) grew in strength as a result of foreign volunteers and the purchase of equipment. Intervention by Egypt, Jordan, Lebanon, and Syria, with support from Iraq and Saudi Arabia, was poorly coordinated, and the Israeli forces were able to defeat them piecemeal, utilizing the advantage of interior lines to shift forces to whichever front faced the most imminent threat. The Israeli War of Independence culminated in a series of individual armistice agreements in 1949, which defined Israel's borders but never led to a treaty of peace.

The Sinai Campaign, 1956

The Arab world was humiliated by its defeat in 1949 and formally expressed its determination never to make peace with Israel and to eradicate it as a nation. Discontent with the undeniable fact of Israel's existence led to a long series of assassinations of Arab leaders. A result of one of these assassinations was the rise to power of the charismatic Gamal Abdel Nasser in Egypt. Nasser, proclaiming his intention of destroying Israel, rearmed Egypt with massive supplies of modern equipment from Czechoslovakia, then a Soviet satellite. Nasser supported Arab revolutionary movements throughout the Arab world and gained great prestige by seizing and nationalizing the Suez Canal.

France and Great Britain reacted to this violation of the Anglo-Egyptian Treaty by planning an invasion of Egypt. Israel, already concerned about Nasser's repeated threats, was planning an invasion of its own. It readily accepted an Anglo-French invitation to participate, gaining an influx of French arms. The Anglo-French-Israeli alliance counted on the United States and the Soviet Union not intervening because of the current tensions over Hungary and Poland.

Israeli forces conquered the Sinai Peninsula in what military historians have termed "a work of art." However, muddling by the British and French leadership and the surprisingly vehement disapproval of the United States and the Soviet Union resulted in a complete fiasco. The French and British forces, late in arriving, were forced to withdraw. Israel had to give up the territory it had conquered in the Sinai Campaign in return for promises of free passage of its shipping in certain Arab waters. Curiously, Nasser, despite the overwhelming defeat of his forces at the hands of the Israelis, gained even greater stature as a result of his defiance of France and England. Israel realized through the Sinai Campaign that it could not rely on foreign assistance to achieve its own security. The machinations of the superpowers would always take precedence over any guarantees to the fledgling Jewish state. As such, Israel embarked on a massive effort to develop its own weapons industry, military education system, and compulsory service for its citizenry.

The Six-Day War, 1967

Hostilities continued after 1956 with border clashes and a perpetuation of the long cycle of violence. Revolution and assassinations were common, with Iraq coming under Soviet influence and a civil war breaking out in once-peaceful Lebanon. During 1967, Egypt mobilized forces on Israel's borders, as did Jordan and Iraq. Other Arab states sent volunteer forces to participate in Nasser's oft-threatened invasion. France cut off its supply of weapons to Israel, seeking to curry favor with the Arab nations. Israel responded with a brilliant campaign that saw the Israeli Air Force (IAF) carry out a successful surprise attack on Arab air forces on the ground, essentially destroying them in the first two days of the conflict. After that, Israeli air superiority ensured the serial defeat of Egyptian, Syrian, Jordanian, and Iraqi forces. The Arab nations accepted a cease-fire proposed by the United Nations (UN) on June 10, ending the Six-Day War. Israel had seized large amounts of Arab territory during the conflict, including the West Bank and East Jerusalem from Jordan, the Sinai Peninsula and Gaza Strip from Egypt, and the Golan Heights from Syria. While the seizures and subsequent occupations created a more defensible perimeter for Israel, they also virtually guaranteed a future conflict and transformed the international perception of Israel from a state on the defensive seeking to protect its own territory to a regional conqueror, aggressively expanding its national borders.

The War of Attrition, 1967–1970

The undeclared War of Attrition did not receive much attention outside of the Middle East but was a proclamation of the Arab world's intent to reclaim all the territory it had lost during the Six-Day War. In the process, the conduct of warfare in the Middle East was totally revised with the introduction of modern weapons, including surface-to-air missiles (SAMs), sophisticated radar defenses, and much more. Further, it introduced the Cold War directly into the Middle East, where, for the first time, the results of an Arab-Israeli conflict had the potential to escalate into a nuclear exchange between the superpowers. The Soviet Union sent thousands of personnel to teach the Egyptian forces Soviet tactics and supplied thousands of tanks, artillery, and aircraft. Israel was supplied with modern arms by the United States and built up a series of fortifications along the Suez Canal known as the Bar-Lev Line. These defenses were to serve as a tripwire to allow Israel sufficient time to call up its reserves and then defeat any Arab incursion.

Israeli leaders began to assume a permanent superiority over any Arab military forces, and this arrogance led to a gradual decline in the equipment and readiness of IDF personnel.

The Yom Kippur War, 1973

Evidence indicates that Nasser intended to invade Israel again in 1970, but a fatal heart attack in September forestalled this plan. His successor, Anwar Sadat, was widely discounted as a leader yet proved to be a man of exceptional vision. Sadat felt that all he had to do was seize some of the land that Israel had conquered in 1967 and hold it until the UN began hearings. He believed those hearings would force Israel to leave the Arab territory it occupied. He masterfully disguised his intentions, even while obtaining Syria's agreement to go to war against Israel in October 1973. To counter Israeli air superiority, so amply demonstrated in the Six-Day War, Sadat negotiated for the construction of a massive Soviet air defense network, including radar installations, mobile command centers, and a dense concentration of surface-to-air missiles (SAMs), including man-portable weapons. Likewise, Syrian president Hafez al-Assad accepted Soviet assistance in the form of antitank weapons to counter Israeli armor superiority. The Israeli leaders, intoxicated by their previous successes, allowed hubris to cloud their judgment. As a result, the well-coordinated Egyptian and Syrian attack was a complete surprise and came very close to defeating Israel. The IDF just managed to hold on while the United States and the Soviet Union bristled with misunderstandings that almost escalated to a nuclear exchange. U.S. secretary of state Henry Kissinger was able to assuage Soviet fears while also mediating the armistice talks between the Arabs and Israelis.

Eventually, the IDF prevailed in the Yom Kippur War (also known as the October War and the Ramadan War), but only by the narrowest margin and thanks in great part to a massive resupply effort by the United States code-named Operation Nickel Grass.

Since 1973, conflict has continued at varying levels, from suicide bombers to the massacre of Israeli athletes at the 1972 Munich Olympics to Israel's 1982 invasion of southern Lebanon. There have been peaceful high points as well, including the unprecedented visit by Sadat to Jerusalem in 1977; the Camp David Accords of 1978 and the subsequent Jewish withdrawal from the Sinai; and the Oslo Agreement of 1993, in which Israel and the Palestinian Authority (PA) formally recognized each other. Israel showed unusual restraint during the 1991 Persian Gulf War, when Iraqi leader Saddam Hussein authorized the firing of missiles against Israel. Diplomatic pressure from the United States, as well as the transfer of Patriot antiballistic missile (ABM) systems, convinced the Israelis to withhold retaliatory strikes. The likely consequence of any such strike would have been the disintegration of Arab participation in the coalition against Iraq, as no Arab state would deliberately side with Israel against a fellow Islamic government. On a number of occasions, Israeli air forces have since bombed neighboring territory, typically in response to missile or mortar strikes on Jewish settlements within Israel.

More recently, Israel launched another invasion of southern Lebanon in the summer of 2006, with the goal of eradicating Hezbollah guerrilla sites near the Israeli border. In September 2007, Israeli planes bombed a suspected nuclear site in Syria.

In May 2010, Israeli naval assets intercepted an international humanitarian flotilla in the Mediterranean Sea, bound for the Gaza Strip. The Israelis suspected that the flotilla contained contraband goods, and the raid precipitated strong protests from the international community. In the fall of 2013, during the Syrian civil war, Israeli warplanes attacked a missile site in Latakia that housed Russian-made missiles that the Israelis feared would fall into the hands of Hezbollah militants operating in Syria. Meanwhile, fighting between Hamas, operating in the Gaza Strip, and Israel has continued sporadically, punctuated by at least two shaky ceasefires. Since 2010, efforts to revive the flagging Israeli-Palestinian peace process have resulted in a number of terror attacks sponsored by Hamas and designed to torpedo the negotiations. After U.S. secretary of state John Kerry took office in February 2013, he made the peace process a major part of his diplomatic plans. While talks have since been reopened, there has been no concrete progress toward achieving a lasting peace.

Walter Boyne and Paul Joseph Springer

See also: Anglo-American Alliance; Cold War Peace Dividend, U.S. Troop/Force Structure Reductions

Further Reading

Barker, A. J. *Arab-Israeli Wars.* New York: Hippocrene, 1980.

Hammel, Eric. *Six Days in June: How Israel Won the 1967 Arab-Israeli War.* New York: Scribner, 1992.

Herzog, Chaim. *The Arab-Israeli Wars: War and Peace in the Middle East from the War of Independence to Lebanon.* Westminster, MD: Random House, 1984.

Oren, Michael B. *Six Days of War: June 1967 and the Making of the Modern Middle East.* Novato, CA: Presidio, 2003.

Taylor, Alan R. *The Superpowers and the Middle East.* Syracuse, NY: Syracuse University Press, 1991.

Atef, Mohammad

(1944–2001)

Mohammad Atef was Al-Qaeda's head of military operations during the planning and implementation of the September 11, 2001, terror attacks against the United States. At that time Atef was number three in the Al-Qaeda hierarchy, behind Osama bin Laden and Ayman al-Zawahiri. Atef made decisions about the events of September 11 from the beginning, assisting Khalid Sheikh Mohammed in the final stages of the plot.

Atef converted to Islamist extremism early in his career. Born in 1944 in Menoufya, Egypt, in the Nile Delta, about 35 miles north of Cairo, he was named Sobhi Abu Sitta. After graduating from high school, he served his required two years of military service in the Egyptian Army. Reports that Atef was a policeman in Egypt have been denied by the Egyptian government. In the late 1970s, Atef joined an Egyptian terrorist organization, the Egyptian Islamic Jihad. Evidently a low-ranking member, he did not meet with its leader, al-Zawahiri, while both were in Egypt. Despite his involvement in this group, he escaped arrest after the crackdown on extremists that followed the assassination of President Anwar Sadat in 1981. In 1983, Atef left Egypt for Afghanistan to fight with the mujahideen against Soviet forces; here, he first met al-Zawahiri, who then introduced him to bin Laden. Atef and bin Laden became close friends. Atef also became acquainted with Abdullah Azzam and admired him greatly, but in the subsequent battle between Azzam and al-Zawahiri for bin Laden's support, Atef supported al-Zawahiri. In 1999, Egyptian authorities sentenced Atef to a seven-year prison term in absentia for his membership in the Egyptian Islam Jihad, but Atef never returned to Egypt.

Atef's close personal relationship with bin Laden made him an important member of Al-Qaeda. When bin Laden founded Al-Qaeda, Atef was a charter member. Ubaidah al-Banshiri was Al-Qaeda's head of military operations, and Atef assisted him. He was active in organizing Somali resistance to American military presence in 1992, but some evidence suggests that his stay there was not entirely successful. Atef also served as bin Laden's chief of personal security. Al-Banshiri's death in a boat accident in Africa allowed Atef to replace him in 1996. From then until his death in 2001, Atef was in charge of military operations for Al-Qaeda. All military operation came under his oversight, but he remained subordinate to bin Laden even after bin Laden's eldest son married one of Atef's daughters in January 2001.

Atef was aware of the September 11 plot from its beginning. Khalid Sheikh Mohammed outlined the plan to bin Laden and Atef as early as 1996. Bin Laden finally agreed on the basics of the plot in 1998. It was Atef's job to search Al-Qaeda's training camps for suitable candidates for a martyrdom mission that required operatives to live unnoticed in the United States.

Al-Qaeda avoided having its leaders at a single site except for particularly special occasions, a policy prompted by fears of American assassination of Al-Qaeda's leaders. Bin Laden announced that in case of his death or capture, Atef would succeed him as head of Al-Qaeda. Once the

United States began military operations against the Taliban and Al-Qaeda in Afghanistan, it became even more important for Al-Qaeda's leaders to be at separate locations. Atef was at a gathering in Kabul on November 18, 2001, when a Predator unmanned aerial vehicle fired Hellfire missiles, killing Atef and those with him—something for which the United States had been offering a $5 million reward. The loss of Atef was a blow to Al-Qaeda, but he was soon replaced as military commander by Abu Zubaydah.

Stephen E. Atkins

See also: Al-Qaeda; Atta, Mohamed el-Amir Awad el-Sayed; Bin Laden, Osama; Hamburg Cell

Further Reading

Dawoud, Khaled. "Mohammed Atef; Egyptian Militant Who Rose to the Top of the al-Qaida Hierarchy." *Guardian* (London), November 19, 2001, 1.

MATP. "Iron Fist Reaches from Far Side of the Globe." *Australian* (Sydney), November 19, 2001, 8.

Atta, Mohamed el-Amir Awad el-Sayed

Commander of the Al-Qaeda terrorist team that hijacked four American jetliners that were then used to attack the United States on September 11, 2001. Muhammad al-Amir Awad al-Sayyid Atta was born on September 1, 1968, in the village of Kafr el-Sheikh in the Egyptian Delta and had a strict family upbringing. His father was a middle-class lawyer with ties to the fundamentalist Muslim Brotherhood. Atta's family moved to the Abdin District of Cairo in 1978 when he was 10. His father,

who had a dominating personality, insisted that his children study, not play; thus Atta's family life allowed him few friends.

After attending high school, Atta enrolled in the Cairo University in 1986. At his graduation in 1990, his grades were not good enough to admit him to graduate school. On the recommendation of his father, he planned to study urban planning in Germany. In the meantime, he worked for a Cairo engineering firm.

Atta traveled to Hamburg, Germany, in July 1992 to begin studies there. During his courses he interacted very little with fellow students, earning a reputation as a loner. His classmates also noted his strong religious orientation. He traveled to Turkey and Syria in 1994 to study old Muslim quarters. After receiving a German grant, Atta and two fellow students visited Egypt to study the old section of Cairo, called the Old City. Up to this point in his life, Atta appeared to be an academic preparing for a career as a teacher at a university. In 1995, however, Atta became active in Muslim extremist politics. After a pilgrimage to Mecca, he initiated contact with Al-Qaeda recruiters. Atta was just the type of individual sought by Al-Qaeda: intelligent and dedicated.

After returning to Hamburg to continue his studies, Atta attended the al-Quds Mosque, where his final recruitment to radical Islam took place. There Atta met radical clerics who steered him toward an Al-Qaeda recruiter. Muhammad Haydar Zammar, a Syrian recruiter for Al-Qaeda, convinced Atta to join that organization. Several of his friends, Ramzi Muhammad Abdallah ibn al-Shibh, Marwan al-Shehhi, and Ziyad al-Jarrah, also joined Al-Qaeda at this time. Atta became the leader of the so-called Hamburg cell of radical Islamists.

In 1998, Atta left for Kandahar, Afghanistan, to receive military and terrorist training at the Al-Qaeda training camp at Khaldan. He so distinguished himself during the training that Al-Qaeda leaders decided to recruit him for a suicide mission. Atta ranked high in all the attributes of an Al-Qaeda operative—intelligence, religious devotion, patience, and willingness to sacrifice. Atta, Jarrah, and Shehhi met and talked with Osama bin Laden in Kandahar. Bin Laden asked them to pledge loyalty to him and accept a suicide mission. They agreed, and Muhammad Atef, Al-Qaeda's military chief, briefed them on the general outlines of the September 11 operation. Then Atta and the others returned to Germany to finish their academic training.

Atta was a complex individual, deeply affected psychologically by a fragile outlook of society in general. He held the typical conservative Muslim view that relations with the opposite sex should not be permitted outside of marriage. Atta also held strong anti-American views, disturbed as he was by the Americanization of Egyptian society.

After Atta finished his degree in 1999, Al-Qaeda's leaders assigned him the martyrdom mission in the United States, a mission planned by Khalid Sheikh Mohammed. Atta arrived in the United States on June 2, 2000. His orders placed him in charge of a large cell, but he, Jarrah, and Shehhi were the only members of it who knew the details of his mission. Several times Atta flew back and forth between the United States and Germany and Spain to coordinate the mission. Members of his cell arrived in the United States at various times. Atta and key members of the cell received orders to take pilot lessons to fly large commercial aircraft.

Most of Atta's time was spent in pilot lessons in Florida. Before he could qualify for training on large commercial aircraft, Atta had to learn to fly small planes. Most of his flying instruction took place at Huffman Aviation in Sarasota, Florida. Next, he began to use simulators and manuals to train himself to fly the larger aircraft.

Atta gathered most of the members of his cell together in Florida for the first time in early June 2001. He organized the cell into four teams, each of which included a trained pilot. Throughout the summer of 2001, each team rode as passengers on test flights in which they studied the efficiency of airline security and the best times to hijack an aircraft. They discovered that airline security was weakest at Boston's Logan International Airport and decided that the best day for hijacking would be a Tuesday. They also decided that first-class seats would give them better access to cockpits. Although the teams tried to remain inconspicuous, the film actor James Woods reported suspicious behavior by one of the teams on a flight. He reported his suspicions to the pilot and a flight attendant, who passed them on to the Federal Aviation Administration (FAA), but nothing came of his report.

Atta selected two airlines—American Airlines and United Airlines—that flew Boeing 757s and 767s, aircraft that hold the most aviation fuel because they are used for long flights. These aircraft were also equipped with up-to-date avionics, making them easier to fly.

Atta called for a leadership meeting in Las Vegas, Nevada, in late June 2001. Atta, Ziyad Jarrah, Hani Hanjour, and Nawaf al-Hazmi then completed plans for the September 11 operation. Atta and Jarrah used a local Cyberzone Internet Café to send e-mails to Al-Qaeda leaders abroad.

Atta then traveled to Spain via Zurich, Switzerland, to update his handlers on his final plans and receive last-minute instructions. He met with Al-Qaeda representatives in the resort town of Salou on July 8, 2001, receiving his final authorization for the September 11 mission. Atta was given final authority to determine the targets and date of the operation. Several times bin Laden had attempted to push the plan forward, but Atta had refused to carry out the mission before he was ready and was backed by Khalid Sheikh Mohammed in this decision. Atta flew back to the United States, and, despite an expired visa, had no trouble getting into the country.

Atta issued final instructions about the mission on the night of September 10, 2001. One-way tickets for flights on September 11 had been bought with credit cards in late August. Atta had made arrangements to have the cell's excess funds transferred back to Al-Qaeda on September 4. He traveled to Portland, Maine, with Abd al-Aziz al-Umari, and they stayed in South Portland. They caught a 5:45 a.m. flight out of Portland International Airport, but Atta's luggage arrived too late to make American Airlines Flight 11 from Logan International Airport. At 7:45 a.m., Atta and Umari boarded American Airlines Flight 11. Soon afterward, Atta phoned Marwan al-Shehhi, on board United Airlines Flight 175—also at Logan International Airport—to make sure everything was on schedule.

Atta commanded the first team. Approximately 15 minutes after takeoff, his team seized control of the aircraft using box cutters as weapons. Atta redirected the aircraft toward New York City and the World Trade Center complex, where it crashed into the North Tower of the World Trade Center at about 8:45 a.m. Members of the other teams carried out their attacks successfully, except for the one flight lost in western Pennsylvania, where the passengers—informed of what had happened with the other three hijacked airplanes—fought the hijackers. Atta, along with the plane's entire crew and all passengers, died instantly when the airliner slammed into the North Tower of the World Trade Center. The North Tower collapsed less than two hours later.

Stephen E. Atkins

See also: Bin Laden, Osama; Hamburg Cell; Pentagon Attack; World Trade Center, September 11, 2001

Further Reading

Fouda, Yosri, and Nick Fielding. *Masterminds of Terror: The Truth behind the Most Devastating Terrorist Attack the World Has Ever Seen.* New York: Arcade, 2003.

McDermott, Terry. *Perfect Soldiers: The 9/11 Hijackers: Who They Were, Why They Did It.* New York: HarperCollins, 2005.

Miller, John, Michael Stone, and Chris Mitchell. *The Cell: Inside the 9/11 Plot, and Why the FBI and CIA Failed to Stop It.* New York: Hyperion, 2002.

Sageman, Marc. *Understanding Terror Networks.* Philadelphia: University of Pennsylvania Press, 2004.

Australian Embassy (Jakarta) Bombing

On September 9, 2004, a bomb hidden in a white Daihatsu minivan detonated in front of the Australian embassy in Jakarta, Indonesia. The attack took place at approximately 10:30 a.m. and killed 9, wounding another 161. The diplomatic mission was badly damaged, as were surrounding

Australian Federal Police officers confer at the site where a bomb went off outside the Australian embassy in Jakarta, Indonesia, September 10, 2004. Muslim militants purportedly claimed responsibility for a car bomb that exploded outside the embassy, killing nine people and wounding 173 in a bloody strike at a key U.S. ally in the war in Iraq. (AP Photo/Dita Alangkara)

buildings in the Kunigan business district. Although serious, the incident could have been far worse had the vehicle transporting the explosives exploded inside the embassy's perimeter walls; as it was, no one inside the building was killed, and the majority of those wounded sustained only minor injuries. Virtually all of the casualties were Indonesian nationals, many of them Muslim.

Jemaah Islamiyah (JI), an Islamic militant organization with alleged ties to Al-Qaeda, claimed responsibility for the bombing. The group had carried out several previous attacks in Indonesia, including strikes against tourist venues in Bali in 2002 (which left 191 people dead) and the J.W. Marriott in Jakarta the following year.

Authorities believed the 2004 incident was the work of a highly militant JI faction that apparently believed the group's goal of a Southeast Asian caliphate could be "fast-tracked" through an indiscriminate campaign of mass-casualty terrorism.

The device used in the attack was based on potassium chlorate and contained between 200 kilograms (400 pounds) and one ton (2,204 pounds) of explosives. The bomb-manufacturing techniques of JI had evolved only marginally since the 2002 Bali atrocity. Experts believed that this was partly due to more effective counterterrorism strategies in Indonesia, which had denied the group a secure safe haven in which to test, refine, and improve explosives and their delivery systems.

In line with many of JI's attacks, the bombing took the form of a suicide operation. Subsequent investigations identified two people as the chief bomb makers: a former university lecturer, Dr. Azahari bin Husin (Azhari Husin); and an electronics expert, Dulmatin (also known as Joko Pitono and Genius). Both were also believed to have been involved in the manufacture of the explosives used in the 2002 Bali attack and to be key players in JI's militant faction. Husin, who had earned a doctorate from the University of Reading in Great Britain, was later killed in a police raid in November 2005; five years later authorities also fatally shot Dulmatin after tracing him to a hideout in Jakarta.

The actual perpetrator was an Islamist militant by the name of Heri Golun. Oddly enough, even though the weapon of choice was a truck bomb, he did not know how to drive. It has since been alleged that the inexperienced Golun was given some basic training on how to operate a van and was assisted in guiding the attack vehicle through the midmorning rush hour by an accomplice before he was allowed to take over. If true, this could explain why the van did not crash through the gates of the embassy in the more dramatic fashion of previous suicide vehicle bombers but detonated in the street in front of the embassy after having emerged from a side street.

Following the bombing, Indonesian police arrested six suspected JI members. Among them was Iwan Darmawan (also known as Rios), who was alleged to have been the chief planner for the attack. He was detained with two other militants on the main island of Java. According to authorities the trio were all wearing explosive belts but did not have time to detonate them before they were seized.

Rios later confessed his involvement in the bombing. He claimed that Al-Qaeda had financed the operation through an intermediary based in Malaysia. There is also evidence to suggest that additional monies were needed to cover the cost of the attack and that these were raised through donations, illegal gold trafficking, and criminal activities that targeted non-Muslims.

On September 13, 2005, Rios was sentenced to death for his participation in the event, after which he recanted his previous confession, saying, "I'm innocent and I wasn't involved in this." Although the sentence was appealed, it was upheld by the Indonesian High Court the following December. At the time of this writing, Rios had yet to be executed and remained in prison. Another accomplice, Irun Hidayat, was charged with providing housing and money to the perpetrators. He was convicted on July 21, 2005, and sentenced to three years for his role in the attack. Hidayat had been inducted into Darul Islam by Kang Jaja in 1987 at age 15. He was a close friend of Rios and was the local head of the religious council of the Indonesian Muslim Workers Union (Perserikatan Pekerja Muslim Indonesia [PPIM]).

There was some speculation that the attack was designed to influence the upcoming September 20 elections in Indonesia. Others believed it was in commemoration of 9/11, given that it occurred just two days before the attacks in New York and Washington. Still others speculated that the attack could have been prompted by Canberra's support for the U.S.-led global war on terror and participation in the 2003 invasion of Iraq.

Following the bombing, Australian prime minister John Howard announced that he would be setting up a fund to assist the victims of the attack and that his government would make an initial kick-off contribution. He also encouraged the public to donate, saying that "it is the least that this country can do as a measure, not only of our respect for them, our compassion for their families, but also as a practical help to people who will need help in this very tragic situation."

Donna Bassett

See also: Al-Qaeda; Bali Bombings

Further Reading

Chalk, Peter, Angel Rabasa, William Rosenau, and Leanne Piggott. *The Evolving Terrorist Threat to Southeast Asia: A Net Assessment.* Santa Monica, CA: RAND, 2009.

International Crisis Group. *Terrorism in Indonesia: Noordin's Networks.* Asia Report no. 114, May 5, 2006.

Jackson, Brian, John Baker, Kim Cragin, John Parachini, Horacio Trujillo, and Peter Chalk. *Aptitude for Destruction.* Vol. 2, *Case Studies of Organizational Learning in Five Terrorist Groups.* Santa Monica, CA: RAND, 2005.

Sidel, John. *Riots, Pogroms, Jihad: Religious Violence in Indonesia.* Ithaca, NY: Cornell University Press, 2006.

"Axis of Evil"

A term coined by President George W. Bush in his January 29, 2002, State of the Union address to describe regimes that sponsor terrorism. Specifically, he identified the axis as consisting of Iran, Iraq, and North Korea, all of which he believed threatened the security of the United States. Conceived by presidential speechwriter David Frum, the phrase "axis of evil" was originally intended to justify the invasion of Iraq, but it came to be used by political neoconservatives to criticize

Secretary of State Colin Powell's position on the Bush Doctrine. That doctrine, arising after the September 11, 2001, terror attacks, modified U.S. military policy to allow for a preemptive war against terrorists, unilateral military action against rogue states, and American measures to remain the sole military superpower in the world.

The origin of the phrase "axis of evil" can be traced to December 2001, when head speechwriter Mike Gerson tasked David Frum with articulating the case for ousting the government of Saddam Hussein in a few sentences, which were to be included in the 2002 State of the Union address. Frum originally intended to use the phrase "axis of hatred," but changed it to "axis of evil" to match the "theological" tone adopted by President Bush after September 11, 2001. Expecting his speech to be edited, Frum was surprised when his "axis of evil" was actually included, and the text of the speech was read nearly verbatim by President Bush, a controversial move that was seen in some quarters to be dangerously undiplomatic. Certainly, that speech, and particularly the term "axis of evil," was not well received in many of the world's capitals.

The usage of the phrase "axis of evil" was ultimately meant to suggest links between terrorists and nations that, according to neoconservatives, threatened the United States and its allies. Criteria for inclusion in the "axis of evil" were that the included nations be "rogue states," or that they allegedly support terrorist groups that sought to attack the United States or its allies, potentially with weapons of mass destruction.

President Bush's 2002 speech shocked people in many nations, but it was also viewed with considerable trepidation by

America's stalwart allies. Not surprisingly, Iraqi president Saddam Hussein mocked and dismissed the talk as needless bluster. In Tehran, the fundamentalist regime there sharply denounced its inclusion in the "axis of evil." North Korean spokesmen bitterly rebuked Bush and his speech and vowed that any aggression toward North Korea would be met with withering military counterforce. In the longer term, Bush's incendiary language may have had the opposite effect intended; it likely induced Pyongyang and Tehran to be even less compliant with international rules of behavior.

Keith A. Leitich

See also: Bush Doctrine; Powell, Colin Luther; Terrorism

Further Reading

Cha, Victor D. "Korea's Place in the Axis." *Foreign Affairs*, 81, no. 3 (May/June 2002): 79–92.

Frum, David. *The Right Man: The Surprise Presidency of George W. Bush*. New York: Random House, 2003.

Woodward, Bob. *Bush at War*. New York: Simon and Schuster, 2002.

Azzam, Sheikh Abdullah Yussuf

Sheikh Abdullah Yussuf Azzam was one of the spiritual leaders of the international radical Islamist movement. His ideas of jihad inspired the September 11, 2001, terrorists. Before his death he traveled around Europe, the Middle East, and the United States advocating religious warfare against the West.

A Palestinian by birth, Azzam devoted his life to building the Islamist movement. He was born in 1941 in the small village of Selat al-Harithis, near Jenin, Palestine.

Most of his early schooling took place in Jordanian religious schools. After graduating from Khadorri College, he taught in the village of Adder in South Jordan. In the early 1960s, he attended the Sharia College of Damascus. Azzam fought with the Palestinians in the Six-Day War in 1967 but left the Palestinian resistance movement because he considered it "a political cause insufficiently rooted in Islam." In 1967, he moved to Egypt, where he worked toward a master's degree in Islamic law at Cairo's famous al-Azhar University. Among his acquaintances was Omar Abdel-Rahman, with whom he often talked about the creation of an Islamist state. After graduation, Azzam taught for a couple years before returning to al-Azhar University to study for a PhD in Islamic jurisprudence. Azzam received his doctorate in 1971, after which he took a teaching job at the University of Jordan. In 1980, he was dismissed from the university because of his activity with the Palestinian movement. He found a job leading prayers at the school mosque at King Abdul Aziz University in Jeddah, Saudi Arabia. Among his students there was Osama bin Laden. Azzam refused to return to Palestine because of his continued unhappiness with the secularism of the Palestine Liberation Organization (PLO). Later his views crystallized, and he helped start Hamas in December 1987 to serve as a counterweight to the PLO.

Azzam was a proponent of the use of holy war, or jihad, to liberate the Muslim world from what he considered the tyranny of the secular West. He wanted to reestablish the caliphate by any means possible. J. Boyer Bell described Azzam's tactics as use of "jihad and the rifle alone; no negotiations, no conferences, no dialogues." Azzam taught this doctrine of jihad at every turn at King Abdul Aziz University. Although his teachings made the Saudi government nervous, authorities left him alone. After the invasion of Afghanistan by the Soviet Army in 1979, Azzam decided to place his Islamist doctrine and himself at the service of the Afghan fighters. At the same time, Saudi authorities expelled him from his teaching post. In November 1981, he found a position teaching Arabic and the Koran at the International Islamic University in Islamabad, Pakistan, but he soon found the war in Afghanistan more important than his teaching.

Azzam moved to Peshawar, Pakistan, to organize the mujahideen fighters in their operations against the Soviets. He traveled throughout the Arab world—and even Europe and the United States—recruiting fighters and raising money. His former student, bin Laden, who was also in Pakistan, began working with him. They founded the Mujahideen Services Bureau (MSB) in 1984, with Azzam providing the inspiration and theology and bin Laden the funding (from his personal fortune). It was also in 1984 that Azzam issued a fatwa making it obligatory for every able-bodied Muslim to fight against the Soviets in Afghanistan. Azzam made frequent trips into Afghanistan to preach global jihad, but he avoided the fighting. His sermons and other discourses reached most of the 16,000 to 20,000 Afghan War veterans. He also made several trips to the United State looking for money and recruits for the war. While in the United States, he established branches of the MSB. Both abroad and in Pakistan he constantly preached the necessity of jihad, expressing himself best in his own works explaining his doctrine of jihad.

Azzam's ideas became more radical as the war in Afghanistan progressed. He became convinced of a conspiracy on the part of Pakistan and the United States to weaken the Islamist cause. In 1987, he conceptualized an Islamist vanguard, or al-Qaeda al-Sulbah (the Solid Base), to carry the creation of a purified Islamist society. It was this concept of an Islamist base organization that bin Laden later developed into Al-Qaeda.

Azzam and bin Laden's relationship deteriorated because they disagreed over the strategy of exporting terror. Azzam first wanted to concentrate on building an Islamist society in Afghanistan. He opposed launching a terrorist campaign against Arab regimes before consolidating affairs in Afghanistan and Pakistan. Azzam was not adverse to the idea of rolling back Christian encroachment on formerly Muslim lands, but he opposed internal Muslim infighting. In contrast, bin Laden aimed to liberate the Muslim community everywhere—including in Muslim countries. Ayman al-Zawahiri, who was even more radical in his views than bin Laden, used his close contacts with bin Laden to undermine Azzam. This open disagreement between Azzam and bin Laden led the latter to break with Azzam in 1987, something partly caused by Azzam's increasing closeness with Ahmad Shah Massoud. Azzam believed that Massoud was a possible leader of an Islamic Afghanistan. Bin Laden and al-Zawahiri violently disagreed with Azzam over this. Azzam's career ended abruptly on November 24, 1989, when a bomb exploded under his car in Peshawar, killing him, two of his sons, and a companion. He was killed shortly after a meeting where he had been forced to justify his spending on Islamist operations. At first, suspicion centered on Pakistani security forces as the killers, but there is no satisfactory evidence of who planted the bomb—although the person who benefited most was al-Zawahiri. Regardless of the intent of the assassins, Azzam's stature in the Islamist movement remains strong because his backers have continued to advance his cause.

Stephen E. Atkins

See also: Abdel-Rahman, Omar (aka the Blind Sheikh); Bin Laden, Osama; Zawahiri, Ayman al-

Further Reading

Boyer Bell, J. *Murders on the Nile: The World Trade Center and Global Terror.* San Francisco: Encounter Books, 2003.

Gunaratna, Rohan. *Inside Al-Qaeda.* New York: Columbia University Press, 2002.

Sageman, Marc. *Understanding Terror Networks.* Philadelphia: University of Pennsylvania Press, 2004.

Wright, Lawrence. *The Looming Tower: Al-Qaeda and the Road to 9/11.* New York: Knopf, 2006.

B

Baghdad Ministry of Justice and Provincial Council Building Bombings

On October 25, 2009, two suicide bombings near the center of Baghdad, Iraq, killed some 160 people and wounded more than 720 others. The attacks occurred within 15 minutes of each other (at 10:15 and 10:30 a.m.) and targeted the Justice Ministry, the Ministry of Municipalities and Public Works, and the Provincial Council; the blasts also destroyed the medical clinic that was part of the only Anglican Church in Iraq. They occurred at the height of a Sunni Muslim terrorist campaign that was primarily designed to show the Iraqi population two things: first, that the Shiite Muslim–led government of Prime Minister Nouri al-Maliki could not provide public safety as American military forces withdrew from the country; and second, that his administration did not have the required sense of direction in the face of the January 2010 national elections.

The strikes cost roughly $120,000 and took the form of vehicle-borne improvised explosive devices (VBIEDs) that consisted of a minivan and a 26-seat day care bus. The operation itself was both strategically and tactically significant. Not only were the devices constructed and deployed in the most secure part of Iraq—the heavily fortified Green Zone—

but the bombings were also executed at a time when it had become increasingly difficult to conduct any type of attack. Overall, it was the deadliest act of terrorism in the country since a series of VBIEDs had killed 500 people in northern Iraq in August 2007.

The mastermind behind the operation was Manuf al-Rawl. He had already been implicated in a series of explosions on August 19, 2009, that struck Iraq's finance and foreign ministries and left 122 people dead. He was captured in a raid on March 11, 2010, and later confessed that the October bombings were designed to compound the destabilizing effects of the earlier ones. In the end, however, the withdrawal of U.S. troops continued unabated, and al-Maliki, who had staked his political future on a pledge to bring peace to Iraq, was elected to a second term in January 2010.

Indeed, the attacks probably did more to hurt the Sunni cause than to advance it. One of the government buildings hit was the Justice Ministry. At the time it was attempting to reduce the number of inmates in Iraq's chronically overcrowded prisons. The attacks halted this process and served to further backlog outstanding criminal cases. Both aspects generated considerable dissatisfaction among the Sunnis, who make up only 20 percent of the population but 80 percent of those in jail.

The day after the explosions, Al-Qaeda in Iraq (AQI) posted a message on the Internet taking credit for the attacks. The group is a Sunni umbrella association of semiautonomous terrorist organizations made up mostly of Iraqis. It was forged in the aftermath of the 2003 American invasion to overthrow Saddam Hussein, and according to U.S. intelligence sources, has a largely foreign leadership. At the zenith of the Iraqi insurgency, AQI effectively governed large parts of the country, and in common with the Taliban in Afghanistan, was able to operate, recruit members, and raise funds openly. By 2010, however, nearly three-quarters of the group's top commanders had been eliminated, and as a result of its brutality and indiscriminate violence it had lost much of its original internal backing.

Donna Bassett

See also: Al-Qaeda; Al-Qaeda in Iraq; Taliban

Further Reading

Atwan, Abdel Bari. *The Secret History of al Qaeda*. Berkeley: University of California Press, 2008.

Forest, James, ed. *Teaching Terror: Strategic and Tactical Learning in the Terrorist World*. Lanham, MD: Rowman & Littlefield, 2006.

Hafez, Mohammed. *Suicide Bombers in Iraq: The Strategy and Ideology of Martyrdom*. Washington, DC: U.S. Institute of Peace Press, 2007.

Pirnie, Bruce, and Edward O'Connell. *Counterinsurgency in Iraq (2003–2006) RAND Counterinsurgency Study*. Vol. 2. Santa Monica, CA: RAND, 2008.

Bali Bombings

On October 12, 2002, the Indonesian island of Bali was rocked by devastating suicide bombings. The attacks, carried out by the Al-Qaeda–linked group Jemaah Islamiyah, were the deadliest in Indonesian history and the first major terrorist action after the September 11, 2001, attacks on the United States.

About an hour before midnight on October 12, a suicide bomber walked into Paddy's Bar in the resort town of Kuta and detonated an explosive device hidden in his backpack. Half a minute later, another suicide bomber triggered a much larger bomb rigged to a van parked across the street at the Sari Club. A third, significantly smaller device was also detonated at the U.S. consulate in the nearby city of Denpassar, although it caused only minor injuries and minimal property damage.

The attacks in Kuta killed 202 individuals, including 88 Australians, 38 Indonesians, 24 Britons, and 7 Americans. Another 240 people were injured, many with severe burns. The local hospital was soon overwhelmed, and many of the wounded had to be flown to Australia for extensive burn treatment. Two days later, the United Nations (UN) Security Council unanimously passed Resolution 1438, condemning the attacks.

Although Jemaah Islamiyah, a Southeast Asian Islamist organization, was immediately suspected, its leader, Abu Bakar Bashir, quickly denied the group's involvement, instead blaming the United States for the attacks. Several days after the bombings, the Arab news network Al Jazeera released an audio recording from Al-Qaeda leader Osama bin Laden, who claimed that the attacks were conducted in retaliation for the U.S.-led war on terror and Australia's involvement in securing East Timor's independence from Indonesia in 1999. Jemaah Islamiyah and Al-Qaeda have been closely linked since the Soviet occupation of Afghanistan in

A police officer stands guard at the area of the ruins of a nightclub after a bomb blast destroyed the club, killing more than 180 people and injuring hundreds others in Denpasar, Bali, Indonesia, October 12, 2002. (AP Photo/Itsuo Inouye)

the 1980s, and the two groups frequently share recruiting, training, and financial resources.

Legal proceedings against those suspected of masterminding the attacks began on April 30, 2003. Three men were sentenced to death: Amrozi bin Haji Nurhasyim on August 8, Imam Samudra on September 10, and Ali Ghufron on October 1. The executions of all three were carried out by firing squad on November 9, 2008. A fourth individual, Ali Imron, who reportedly showed remorse for his role in orchestrating the attacks, received a sentence of life imprisonment on September 18, 2003. On October 15, 2004, Bashir was charged with involvement in the Bali bombings as part of a larger indictment for a 2003 bombing in Jakarta, Indonesia. Although acquitted of the 2003 bombing, Bashir was convicted of conspiracy in relation to the Bali attacks and sentenced to two and a half years in prison (although he served only a small portion of this sentence before being released). A number of other individuals with ties to Jemaah Islamiyah were also convicted, but later appealed and had their convictions overturned. Others involved in the bombings may still be at large.

A memorial to the victims of the attacks was dedicated on October 12, 2004—the second anniversary of the bombings—at the site of the explosions in Kuta. Other memorials have been erected in Melbourne, Sydney, Perth, and London. The bombings are also remembered through the 2007 Indonesian film *Long Road to Heaven,* directed by Enison Sinaro, which chronicles the planning and execution of the attacks, as well as the sentencing of the suspects.

On October 1, 2005, Kuta was again the site of a series of suicide bombings. Although considerably smaller than the 2002 attacks, the explosions resulted in 26 deaths and more than 100 injuries.

Spencer C. Tucker

See also: Al-Qaeda; Bin Laden, Osama; Global War on Terror

Further Reading

"Bali Death Toll Set at 202." *BBC News*, February 19, 2003.

"Bin Laden Voices New Threat to Australia." *Age*, November 14, 2002.

Firdaus, Irwan. "Indonesia Executes Bali Bombers." *Jakarta Post*, November 9, 2008.

Benghazi Attacks

(September 11–12, 2012)

On September 11–12, 2012, as many as 150 people stormed the U.S. compound for the U.S. diplomatic mission at Benghazi, Libya. Armed with rocket-propelled grenades, machine guns, hand grenades, and other weapons, the mob breached the main gates of the compound and later fired mortars at a nearby consular annex, where staff had taken refuge. Four Americans were killed in the incident: U.S. ambassador to Libya J. Christopher Stevens; security personnel Tyrone S. Woods and Glen Doherty, both former Navy SEALs; and foreign service officer Sean Smith.

While many details of the attacks remain mysterious, it was captured by surveillance cameras and witnessed by the surviving guards.

The causes and motives of the attackers are murky. Initially, the attacks were said to be a spontaneous response to an anti-Muslim film created in the United States. The film had already led to protests in Benghazi and Cairo. However, the attacks were later described as intentional and preplanned. In the investigation that followed, the State Department reported that the attacks were carried out by a North African branch of Al-Qaeda as well as an extremist militia called Ansar al-Shariah. In the meantime, as the November 6 presidential election approached, Republicans sharply criticized the Barack Obama administration for its handling of the attacks.

The Arab Spring and Instability in Libya

In late 2010 and well into 2011, popular uprisings throughout the Arab world overthrew governments in Egypt, Libya, Yemen, and Tunisia. In Libya, Muammar Gaddafi lost power in late 2011 to rebel forces aided by the North Atlantic Treaty Organization (NATO). Western forces hoped the new leadership in Libya would bring in a new democratic government. However, after the overthrow, Libya remained unstable despite having an interim government and parliament.

After the fall of the Gaddafi government, the Obama administration approved reopening the U.S. embassy in Tripoli. However, in the months prior to the attack, intelligence had reportedly reached the Obama administration that security in Libya was faltering. Extremist groups connected to Al-Qaeda were training in

Burnt house and car inside the U.S. embassy compound in Benghazi following an overnight attack on the building, September 12, 2012. (AFP/Getty Images)

the mountains near Tripoli, and there had been attacks on a British diplomatic motorcade and the Red Cross. In an e-mail, Stevens told Washington officials that he was nervous about a lack of security in Benghazi. In the week before the attacks, in fact, there was a car bombing in Benghazi, and the Libyan government issued security warnings. The State Department responded to these warnings by increasing the fortification of the U.S. compound in Benghazi, but it is not clear that the government received direct warnings of a specific threat. Stevens's e-mail was later cited by Republicans who criticized the Obama administration's handling of the security threats in Libya.

Ansar al-Shariah, the militant group that has taken credit for the attacks, was training openly near Benghazi. The group's location was so well known that local citizens stormed it in protest after the attacks. U.S. intelligence and even Libyan intelli-

gence reported that there was a certain loss of control over these areas.

The Benghazi Attacks

The U.S. compound in Benghazi is a collection of buildings surrounded by walls. Security at the compound included five diplomatic security officers and four members of a local militia provided by the Libyan government. A rapid response team was housed at an annex facility approximately a mile away. The timeline of events, according to the State Department, shows that the attacks took place over a very short period of time on September 11 and 12.

Sometime around 9:40 p.m. on September 11, 2012, security agents reported hearing loud noises and gunfire at the front gate of the compound, and cameras showed an armed group entering it. Calls were made to officials at the U.S. embassy in Tripoli as well as officials in Washington and Libya, and the quick reaction force at the nearby annex was also contacted.

Armed security personnel took Stevens and Smith to a safe room inside the compound's main residence building. Attackers stormed this building. The attackers were unable to break into the room Stevens and Smith were hiding in, so they lit fires around it with diesel fuel. The smoke made breathing nearly impossible. Other members of the U.S. security team returned and pulled Smith out, but he had died from smoke inhalation. They were not able to find Stevens in the smoke-filled building. With security forces unable to hold the perimeter, the decision was made to evacuate the compound and retreat to the annex facility.

Between 4:00 and 5:00 a.m. on September 12, a six-man security team from the embassy in Tripoli arrived at the annex, after being told that a search for Stevens at the compound would be futile. The annex was hit by mortar fire around this time, killing Woods and Doherty. After the mortar attacks, the decision was made to evacuate all remaining personnel to Tripoli, with the last plane leaving around 10:00 a.m.

In the hours after the initial attack on the compound, locals found Stevens, who had tried to escape the smoke, and took him to the closest medical center. There he was pronounced dead due to asphyxiation.

Response to the Attacks

On September 12, Obama used the word "terror" to describe the attacks in his first public statement, but did not specifically label the incident as terrorist attacks. Republican presidential candidate Mitt Romney argued that the failure to do so immediately showed weakness and that the situation was mishandled.

On September 16, U.S. ambassador to the United Nations Susan Rice stated on several talk shows that the events at the compound were the result of spontaneous protests. However, at the same time, new intelligence reports stated this was not the case. In her remarks, Rice was using the Obama administration's talking points based on preliminary intelligence assessments, but because the administration also conveyed what it learned from the newer intelligence reports, it seemed to shift its explanation of the attacks. This led to severe criticisms from congressional Republicans and Romney in what many described as a political attack.

Congressional Republicans called for an investigation into the Obama administration's handling of the event. They questioned why the attacks were not immediately labeled as terrorism and why the administration allegedly ignored calls for increased security at the consulate in Benghazi.

On September 26, Secretary of State Hillary Rodham Clinton announced that the attacks were planned by militant groups with Al-Qaeda ties. The events in Benghazi showed that Libya was still very unstable and that the government did not have complete control of the country.

On October 10, Charlene Lamb of the State Department said that she did not approve increased security for Benghazi despite the increased violence because she wanted local Libyan forces to be trained for security purposes. On October 15, Clinton officially took the blame for the security oversights. At a Senate hearing in mid-December, Sen. John Kerry (D-MA) said Congress also must accept blame for the attacks as it had not approved increased funding for embassy security.

In January 2013, Clinton was called to the Senate to testify about the Obama administration's handling of the attacks. The White House and intelligence officials have maintained that they are searching for answers and the people behind the attacks. The one person held in connection to the attacks was picked up at an airport in Turkey and was sent to his native Tunisia, where he was later released due to a general lack of evidence.

The Benghazi attacks have led to an ongoing internal investigation as well as congressional testimony from top State Department officials. While some say the investigations and attacks from Republicans are merely political, others say the investigation is necessary not only for understanding what went wrong and how to improve security, but also for understanding the instability caused by the Arab Spring. In early June 2014, the alleged mastermind of the attack, Ahmed Abu Khatallah, was watched by U.S. Army Delta Force commandos, FBI and CIA officials for days before his capture on June 15. No shots were fired when the manhunt was successfully completed. His arrest was the first one in connection with the attack in Benghazi, Libya. After extensive questioning of Khatallah, he will face charges for his role in the attack. Abu Khatallah is one of several people under indictment, but he is the only one captured. If convicted, Khatallah could face the death penalty.

Daniel Katz

See also: Al-Qaeda; Central Intelligence Agency; Obama Administration

Further Reading

"Briefing by Senior Administration Officials to Update Recent Events in Libya." U.S. State Department, September 12, 2012. http://www.state.gov.

Kirkpatrick, David. "Election-Year Stakes Overshadow Nuances of Libya Investigation." *New York Times*, October 16, 2012.

Margasak, Larry. "Timeline of Events, Comments Surrounding Benghazi." BigStory.AP.org, October 19, 2012.

Times Topics: Libya—The Benghazi Attacks. *New York Times*, January 8, 2013.

"U.S. Confirms Its Libya Ambassador Killed in Benghazi." *BBC, Africa*, September 12, 2012.

Bin Laden, Osama

Osama bin Laden was an Islamist extremist and, as head of Al-Qaeda, the world's most notorious terrorist leader until his

Osama bin Laden was undoubtedly the world's most notorious terrorist. He was widely held to be responsible for approving the September 11, 2001, terrorist attacks on the United States as well as many other acts of terrorism in the Middle East and elsewhere in the world. (AP/Wide World Photos)

death in 2011. He was directly linked to the notorious September 11, 2001, suicide attacks on the United States as well as numerous other acts of terrorism across the globe.

Born on March 10, 1957, in Riyadh, Saudi Arabia, Usamah bin Muhammad bin Awa bin Ladin was most usually known as Osama bin Laden. His father, Muhammad bin Awdah bin Laden, was a highly successful and immensely wealthy construction manager from Yemen who was closely linked to the Saudi royal family and whose business ventures included the development of major highways and the reconstruction of the Muslim holy cities of Medina and Mecca. Bin Laden, Sr., who was strongly opposed to Israel, reportedly had 21 wives and fathered 54 children. Osama was the 17th son and only child of his father's 10th wife, Hamida al-Attas. Bin Laden, Sr., died in a plane crash in 1967, leaving behind an estate reported at $11 billion. Of this, an estimated $40 to $50 million went to Osama.

The family moved a number of times but settled in Jeddah, Saudi Arabia. There, bin Laden attended al-Thagr, the city's top school. He had some exposure to the West through vacations in Sweden and a summer program in English at Oxford University. At age 17, bin Laden married a 14-year-old cousin of his mother and in 1977 enrolled at King Abdulaziz University (now King Abdul Aziz University) in Jeddah, where he majored in economics and business management. Bin Laden was an indifferent student, but this was at least in part because of time spent in the family construction business. He left school altogether in 1979, evidently planning to work in the family's Saudi Binladen Group that then employed 37,000 people and was valued at some $5 billion. This plan was apparently blocked by his older brothers.

As a boy, bin Laden had received religious training in Sunni Islam, but around 1973, he began developing a more fundamentalist bent and interest in the Muslim Brotherhood (MB). This orientation, which was apparently strong enough to alarm other family members, was strongly reinforced by the influence of two key individuals: Muhammad Qutb, brother of the MB's martyred leader Sayyid Qutb and his mentor in religious study at the university, and Sheikh Abdullah Yussuf Azzam, a proponent of jihad (holy war).

Two events were also to have a profound impact on bin Laden. The first was the seizure of the Grand Mosque in Mecca by Islamists led by Juhayman ibn-Muhammad-ibn Sayf al-Otaibi and the subsequent martyrdom of the group. The incident impressed on bin Laden that those who truly believed in their religious convictions were not only imbued with qualities of absolute loyalty but, more tellingly, were willing to contemplate self-sacrifice if circumstances required it. The second, and arguably more significant, event was the Soviet Union's invasion and subsequent occupation of Afghanistan between 1979 and 1989. It is safe to say that this episode marked probably the most important turning point in bin Laden's life.

Following Moscow's incursion into Afghanistan in 1979, bin Laden traveled to Pakistan, where he met with Afghan leaders Burhanuddin Rabbani and Abdul Rasul Sayyaf. He then returned to Saudi Arabia, where he recruited some 10,000 volunteers to form the bedrock of a resistance movement—the mujahideen (freedom fighters, holy warriors)—dedicated to driving the Soviets out of Afghanistan. Bin Laden also procured a wide array of construction equipment to build roads, tunnels, shelters, hospitals, and other infrastructure for assisting the rebel campaign.

Bin Laden's organizational skills and financial assets were probably his most important contribution to the Afghan resistance, however. He worked actively with Sheikh Abdullah Yussuf Azzam to train mujahideen recruits, providing much of the funding for this from his personal fortune as well as supplemental financial contacts he tapped in Saudi Arabia. A centerpiece of this mobilization effort was the Mujahideen Services Bureau, which he and Azzam established in conjunction with Pakistan's Inter-Services Intelligence (ISI) Directorate. Between 1985 and 1989, approximately 150,000 soldiers entered Afghanistan after "graduating" from camps run by the bureau.

In 1986, bin Laden, now having relocated to Peshawar, Pakistan, joined a mujahideen field unit and took part in actual combat. Notably, this included the 1987 Battle of the Lion's Den near Jaji. This experience helped to greatly enhance bin Laden's prestige and standing among jihadis fighting in Afghanistan.

The mysterious assassination of Azzam on November 14, 1989, opened the way for bin Laden to assume a greater role in extremist Islamic politics. While he agreed with Azzam about the need for jihad against the enemies of Islam, bin Laden carried this philosophy a step further in insisting that it should be extended to a holy war on behalf of Muslims around the world. It was this objective that was to define the ideology and subsequent direction of the Al-Qaeda ("the Base") movement that he had founded with Azzam in the fall of 1989 (and that he now exclusively led after the death of the latter).

With the end of the Soviet-Afghan War, bin Laden returned to Saudi Arabia, where he was universally acclaimed as a hero by both the people and the government. Bin Laden subsequently approached Prince Turki al-Faisal, head of the Saudi intelligence services, offering to lead a guerrilla war to overthrow the Marxist government of South Yemen. Turki, however, rejected the suggestion, after which bin Laden settled in Jeddah and worked in the family construction business. All this changed after Saddam Hussein sent his army into Kuwait in August 1990.

The Iraqi military takeover of Kuwait directly threatened Saudi Arabia, and bin Laden once again offered his services to the government—this time with an entreaty to recruit as many as 12,000 men to defend the kingdom. As before, Riyadh rebuffed his overture and instead turned to the United States and other allied powers to liberate Kuwait using Saudi Arabia as a base from which to launch a counteroffensive. Incensed at both the rejection of his services and the injection of hundreds of thousands of infidels into his homeland, bin Laden bitterly denounced the Saudi regime and demanded that all foreign troops leave at once. His vocal opposition to Riyadh brought him a brief period of house arrest.

Following the end of the Gulf War, bin Laden left Saudi Arabia and together with his family moved first to Pakistan and then to Sudan, where he owned property around Khartoum. He also transferred a considerable degree of money to the East African country, investing in a series of successful business ventures, including a road-building company, which added considerably to his personal fortune.

From Sudan, bin Laden mounted increasingly acerbic attacks on the Saudi royal family and the kingdom's religious leadership, accusing them of being false Muslims. These verbal assaults eventually led Riyadh to strip him of his citizenship (April 1994) in addition to freezing those financial assets he still retained in the kingdom (by now his share of the family business was estimated to be about $7 million).

It was at this time that bin Laden started to concertedly organize the terrorist activities of Al-Qaeda and exhort Muslims from around the world to join in a defensive jihad directed against the West and tyrannical secular Islamic governments. Bin Laden established a jihadist training camp at Soba, north of Khartoum; sent advisors and equipment to assist rebels fighting Western peacekeeping troops that had been dispatched to Somalia following the fall of the Siad Barre dictatorship in 1991; and commenced terrorist activities against American interests in Saudi Arabia. As part of the latter endeavor, he orchestrated a car bombing in Riyadh on November 13, 1995, that killed 5 Americans and 1 Saudi and wounded 60 others. Other similar actions followed.

Largely as a result of mounting Saudi and U.S. pressure, the Sudanese government asked bin Laden to leave the country in 1996, after which he relocated to Afghanistan. The South Asian state was a natural choice from which to base his activities. The Islamic fundamentalist Taliban had come to power, and bin Laden had forged a close relationship with its head, Mullah Mohammad Omar. Although there was some unease among certain elements within the Taliban leadership over the possible consequences of hosting a by now internationally acknowledged terrorist, scruples were quickly overcome by bin Laden's promises of financial assistance and contacts in the Arab world. The Taliban subsequently permitted him to establish a network of training camps across the country. The alliance was sealed when bin Laden ordered Al-Qaeda to assist Omar's regime in repelling the Northern Alliance (NA) forces of General Ahmed Shah Massoud.

Now firmly ensconced in Afghanistan, bin Laden began planning a series of attacks against the perceived worldwide enemies of Islam. His principal target was the United States, and on August 23, 1996, he issued a call for jihad against the Americans for their presence in Saudi Arabia. Two years later, he broadened this message in the now-infamous "Khost fatwa" that urged Muslims worldwide to kill Americans and Jews whenever and wherever they were able. The double suicide bombings of Washington's embassies in Kenya and Tanzania, which collectively killed over 200 and injured 4,000 others, followed in August of that year.

It is thought that arrangements for the September 11, 2001, or 9/11, strikes on the United States also started around this time. The plan, which was to involve the simultaneous hijacking of several commercial airliners that would then be flown into prominent buildings in New York City, northern Virginia, and Washington, D.C., was hatched by Khalid Sheikh Mohammed and marked the zenith of Al-Qaeda aggression against America.

Bin Laden approved the 9/11 operation in the expectation that, if successful, it would trigger a vigorous and unconstrained U.S. response that would, in turn, produce an outpouring of support for his cause from within the Arab world. The first assumption proved correct. Following the attacks on the World Trade Center and

Pentagon, Washington demanded that the Taliban turn over bin Laden and take action against Al-Qaeda. When Omar and his co-leaders refused, U.S. forces, assisted by an international coalition made up largely (but not exclusively) of other Western nations, invaded Afghanistan, joined with the Northern Alliance, and drove the Taliban from power. The second assumption, however—that a forceful American response would bring a Muslim backlash—proved false, and indeed, for a certain period of time, the United States enjoyed an unprecedented degree of support and sympathy from Islamic and non-Islamic states alike.

After the fall of the Taliban, bin Laden retreated into his stronghold in Tora Bora, a cave complex in the White Mountains of eastern Afghanistan, where he remained until December 2001. U.S.-led efforts to capture him and his followers were botched, and he fled the country along with his second in command, Ayman al-Zawahiri. Despite a reward of $50 million for his capture—dead or alive—bin Laden continued to thwart efforts to bring him to justice for a decade. He was eventually tracked to a compound at Abbottabad, just outside the Pakistani capital. On May 2, 2011, American commandos from the elite Sea, Air, and Land (SEAL) Team Six stormed the complex and shot bin Laden in the head; his body was seized and later buried at sea. It remains unclear whether the Al-Qaeda chief was deliberately executed or killed in an exchange of fire.

Although bin Laden's death was welcomed around the world, it severely strained Washington's relations with the Pakistani government, which, because it had been given no advance notice of the operation, saw the raid as an unacceptable violation of national sovereignty. Further fueling tensions has been widespread speculation that bin Laden had been living in Abbottabad with the knowledge, if not the direct protection, of the Pakistani government. Al-Zawahiri was appointed the new leader of Al-Qaeda in June 2011.

Harry Raymond Hueston II and
Spencer C. Tucker

See also: Al-Qaeda; Pentagon Attack; Taliban; Terrorism; World Trade Center, September 11, 2001; Zawahiri, Ayman al-

Further Reading

Bergen, Peter L. *Manhunt: The Ten-Year Search for Bin Laden: From 9/11 to Abbottabad.* New York: Random House, 2012.

Bergen, Peter L. *The Osama bin Laden I Know: An Oral History of al Qaeda's Leader.* New York: Free Press, 2006.

Randal, Jonathan. *Osama: The Making of a Terrorist.* New York: Knopf, 2004.

Scheuer, Michael. *Through Our Enemies' Eyes: Osama bin Laden, Radical Islam and the Future of America.* Dulles, VA: Brassey's, 2006.

Zuhur, Sherifa. *A Hundred Osamas: Islamist Threats and the Future of Counterinsurgency.* Carlisle Barracks, PA: Strategic Studies Institute, U.S. Army War College, 2006.

Blackwater (Academi)

Blackwater USA (known as Academi since 2011) is a private U.S.-based security firm involved in military security operations in Afghanistan and Iraq. It is one of a number of private security firms hired by the U.S. government to aid in security operations in Afghanistan and Iraq. The company was founded in 1997 by Erik D. Prince, a former Navy SEAL, wealthy heir to an auto parts fortune, and staunch supporter of the

Republican Party. He served as the firm's chief executive officer (CEO) until 2010, at which time he sold it to a group of private investors, who renamed the company. Prince no longer has any direct connection with the company. The firm was initially named for the brackish swampy waters surrounding its 6,000-plus acre headquarters and training facilities located in northeastern North Carolina's Dismal Swamp.

Details of the privately held company are shrouded in mystery, and the precise number of paid employees is not publicly known. Unconfirmed reports stated a good number of its employees were not U.S. citizens. At its peak of operations, Blackwater trained upwards of 40,000 people per year in military and security tactics, interdiction, and counterinsurgency operations. Many of its trainees were military, law enforcement, or civilian government employees, mostly American, but foreign government employees were also trained at the Blackwater facility. The company claimed that its training facilities were the largest of their kind in the world at the time. By 2007, nearly 90 percent of the company's revenues were derived from government contracts, many of which were no-bid contracts. It is estimated that between 2002 and 2009, Blackwater garnered U.S. government contracts in excess of $1 billion.

Following the successful ouster of the Taliban regime in Afghanistan in late 2001, Blackwater was among the first firms to be hired by the U.S. government to aid in security and law enforcement operations there. In 2003, after coalition forces ousted the regime of Iraqi president Saddam Hussein, Blackwater began extensive operations in the war-ravaged country. Its first major operation here included a $21 million no-bid contract to provide security services for the Coalition Provisional Authority and its chief, L. Paul Bremmer. Blackwater subsequently received contracts for several hundred million dollars more to provide a wide array of security and paramilitary services in Iraq. Some critics—including a number of congressional representatives and senators—took issue with the centrality of Blackwater in Iraq, arguing that its founder's connections to the Republican Party had helped it secure huge no-bid contracts.

Although such information has not been positively verified by either Blackwater or the U.S. government, it is believed that at least 30,000 private security contractors were in Iraq by 2007; some estimates claim as high as 100,000. Of that number, a majority were employees or subcontractors of Blackwater. The State Department and the Pentagon, which have both negotiated lucrative contracts with Blackwater, contend that neither one could have functioned in Iraq without resorting to the use of private security firms. Indeed, the use of such contractors helped keep down the need for even greater numbers of U.S. troops in Iraq and Afghanistan. After Hurricane Katrina smashed the U.S. Gulf Coast in 2005, the U.S. government contracted with Blackwater to provide security, law enforcement, and humanitarian services in southern Louisiana and Mississippi.

In the course of the Iraqi insurgency that began in 2003, numerous Blackwater employees were injured or killed in ambushes, attacks, and suicide bombings. Because of the instability in Iraq and the oftentimes chaotic circumstances, some Blackwater personnel found themselves in circumstances in which they felt threatened and had to protect themselves by force. This led to numerous cases in which they were criticized, terminated, or worse for their actions. Because they were not members of the U.S. military, such individuals often fell into a gray area, which sometimes elicited demands for retribution either by the American government or Iraqi officials.

Loose oversight of Blackwater's operations led to several serious cases of alleged abuse on the part of Blackwater employees. One of the most infamous examples of this occurred in Baghdad on September 16, 2007. While escorting a diplomatic convoy through the streets of the city, a well-armed security detail comprised of Blackwater and Iraqi police mistakenly opened fire on a civilian car that it claimed had not obeyed instructions to stop. Once the gunfire began, other forces in the area opened fire. When the shooting stopped, 17 Iraqi civilians lay dead, including all of the car's occupants. Included among the dead was a young couple and their infant child. At first there were wildly diverging accounts of what happened, and Blackwater contended that the car contained a suicide bomber who had detonated an explosive device, which was entirely untrue. The Iraqi government, however, faulted Blackwater for the incident, and U.S. Army officials backed up the Iraqi claims. Later reports state that the Blackwater guards fired on the vehicle with no provocation.

The Baghdad shootings caused an uproar in both Iraq and the United States. The Iraqi government suspended Blackwater's Iraqi operations and demanded that Blackwater be banned from the country. It also sought to try the shooters in an Iraqi court. Because some of the guards involved were not Americans and the others were working for the U.S. State Department, they were not subject to criminal prosecution.

In the U.S. Congress, angry lawmakers demanded a full accounting of the incident and sought more detailed information on Blackwater and its security operations. To make matters worse, just a few days after the shootings, federal prosecutors announced that they were investigating allegations that some Blackwater personnel had illegally imported weapons into Iraq that were then being supplied to the Kurdistan Workers' Party, which had been designated by the United States as a terrorist organization.

These incendiary allegations prompted a formal congressional inquiry, and in October 2007, Erik Prince, Blackwater's CEO, was compelled to testify in front of the House Committee on Oversight and Government Reform. Prince did neither himself nor his company much good when he stonewalled the committee and told them that Blackwater's financial information was beyond the purview of the government. He later retracted this statement, saying that such information would be provided upon a "written request." Blackwater then struggled under a pall of suspicion, and multiple investigations were soon under way involving the incident in Iraq, incidents in Afghanistan, and the allegations of illegal weapons smuggling by company employees. In the meantime, Congress considered legislation that would significantly tighten government control and oversight of private contractors, especially those involved in sensitive areas such as military security.

In February 2009, Blackwater officials announced that the company would now operate under the name Xe, noting that the new name reflected a "change in company focus away from the business of providing private security." There was no meaning in the new name, which was decided upon after a year-long internal search. Prince abruptly announced his resignation as CEO and left the company in December 2010, at which time its ownership and management was taken over by an unnamed group of private investors. The investors substantially reorganized the company, changed its name to Academi, and drastically changed its mission. It largely divested itself of overseas private security programs and added a division that deals strictly with corporate governance and ethics issues.

In June 2009, the Central Intelligence Agency (CIA) disclosed to Congress that in 2004, it had hired members of Blackwater as part of a secret effort to locate and assassinate top Al-Qaeda operatives. Reportedly, Blackwater employees assisted with planning, training, and surveillance, but no members of Al-Qaeda were captured or killed by them. By 2008, most Blackwater employees had left Iraq; U.S. troops were withdrawn from the country in December 2011. Blackwater continues to operate in Afghanistan, but in much reduced numbers and with a much lower profile.

Paul G. Pierpaoli, Jr.

See also: Central Intelligence Agency; Global War on Terror; SEAL Teams, U.S. Navy

Further Reading

Buzzell, Colby. *My War: Killing Time in Iraq.* New York: Putnam, 2005.

Engbrecht, Shawn. *America's Covert Warriors: Inside the World of Private Military Contractors.* Dulles, VA: Potomac Books, 2010.

U.S. Congress. *Private Security Firms: Standards, Cooperation, and Coordination on the Battlefield: Congressional Hearing.* Darby, PA: Diane Publishing, 2007.

Bojinka, Operation

The Bojinka plot (also known as the Manila air plot) was a conspiracy engineered by Khalid Sheikh Mohammed and his nephew Ramzi Yousef. The plan was primarily aimed at bombing 12 U.S. airliners as they crossed the Pacific Ocean but also included other goals, such as assassinating President Bill Clinton and Pope John Paul II during their respective visits to Manila in November 1994 and January 1995.

Mohammed and Yousef began planning Bojinka in 1994 when both men rented an apartment in the capital and started gathering the necessary chemicals and equipment for the plane bombs. They were later joined by a third man, Abdul Hakim Murad, who had undergone terrorist training in Pakistan; Murad's role was to help purchase explosives and timing devices in the Philippines.

The aviation part of the plan called for the targeting of U.S.-flagged airlines that served routes in East or Southeast Asia. Five individuals were envisaged to carry out the attacks. Each would board one leg of the flight, assemble and place the bomb, and then exit the aircraft during the first layover. The bombs were timed to detonate as the airplane proceeded across the Pacific Ocean toward the United States. Most of the targeted flights were bound for Honolulu, Los Angeles, San Francisco, or New York. Four of the five bombers were to return to Karachi, Pakistan, while the fifth would return to Doha, Qatar. Mohammed left the Philippines for Pakistan in September 1994, and later Yousef met him in Karachi, where both men enlisted a fourth man, Wali Khan Amin Shah (also known as Usama Asmurai). Yousef and Shah returned to the Philippines to continue preparations for the operation.

Yousef decided to conduct at least two trial runs for their improvised explosive device, detonating one in a Manila movie theater on December 1, 1994, and a second one 10 days later on an actual airline flight. For the airline test, Yousef chose a Philippine Airlines 747 aircraft that was scheduled to fly from Manila to Tokyo, via Cebu. Yousef boarded the aircraft in Manila, during which time he positioned the explosive device under a passenger seat. Upon landing in Cebu, Yousef disembarked from the jet, which flew back to Manila before heading to Japan. While the Philippine Airlines aircraft was roughly 190 miles east of Okinawa, the bomb exploded, killing a 24-year-old Japanese national and injuring eight others. The pilot was able to maintain control of the aircraft and land it in nearby Naha, Okinawa.

Soon after, the Philippines-based Abu Sayyaf Group (ASG) called an Associated Press office in Manila and claimed it had conducted the attack. Authorities learned about (and hence disrupted) the Bojinka/Manila air plot on January 7, 1995, when volatile explosive compounds ignited a fire in the apartment that Yousef and Murad were renting. Neighbors who witnessed smoke coming out of the unit quickly alerted security personnel, who after being denied entry called the police and fire department. Investigators subsequently discovered an assortment of items suggesting criminal behavior, including cartons of chemicals, Casio timers, and juice bottles with unknown substances inside. In addition, they found photographs of Pope John Paul II, Bibles, and confessional materials, which would later be linked to the assassination plot. Realizing their plan had been disrupted, Yousef and Murad attempted to flee the area.

Although the police quickly detained the latter (who was apprehended while attempting to retrieve a laptop computer that had been left in the apartment), the former managed to escape to Pakistan. However, soon after he arrived in that country U.S. embassy officials in Islamabad received a tip that Yousef was hiding somewhere in the city; he was subsequently discovered at a guest house, where he was arrested on February 7, 1995.

In 1995, Yousef, Murad, and Shah (who had fled to Malaysia) were extradited to the United States. They were charged with various terrorism-related offenses related to the Bojinka plot and prosecuted in a federal court in Manhattan. The men's trial lasted more than three months, and the jury heard from more than 50 witnesses and viewed over 1,000 exhibits. A critical part of the U.S. government's case involved the contents of the laptop that was seized in the Manila apartment in 1994; it contained airline schedules, photographs, evidence of money transfers, and a threat letter that warned of further attacks on American interests by the "Fifth Division of the Liberation Army."

Ultimately, a federal jury in New York convicted the three men for their role in the Bojinka plot. Yousef was also convicted on a separate count for his role in bombing the Philippine Airlines 747 jet. The significance of the Manila/Bojinka air plot is that it would provide a conceptual blueprint for subsequent aviation plots, including the September 11, 2001, attacks in the United States and the liquid-explosives airline plot that was disrupted in the United Kingdom (August 2006). It has also been speculated that Bojinka may have provided the inspiration for other major attempted airline attacks, including those carried out by Richard Reid (the "shoe bomber") in December 2001 and Umar Farouk Abdulmutallab (who attempted to detonate explosives hidden in his underwear on Christmas Day 2009).

Paul Smith

See also: Terrorism; Yousef, Ramzi Ahmed

Further Reading

Bonner, Raymond. "Echoes of Early Design to Use Chemicals to Blow Up Airlines." *New York Times*, August 11, 2006.

Elegant, Simon. "Asia's Own Osama." *Time*, April 1, 2002.

McDermott, Terry. "The Plot." *Los Angeles Times*, September 1, 2002.

McKinley, James. "Suspected Bombing Leader Indicted on Broader Charges." *New York Times*, April 1, 1995. http://www.nytimes.com/1995/04/14/nyregion/suspected-bombing-leader-indicted-on-broader-charges.html.

Ressa, Maria. "Philippines: U.S. Missed 9/11 Clues Years Ago." *CNN.com*, July 26, 2003. http://www.cnn.com/2003/WORLD/asiapcf/southeast/07/26/khalid.confession/index.html.

Spaeth, Anthony. "Rumbles in the Jungle." *Time*, March 4, 2002.

Boston Marathon Bombing

(April 15, 2013)

The Boston Marathon bombing was a terrorist attack perpetrated in Boston, Massachusetts, during the 117th running of the Boston Marathon on April 15, 2013. The marathon included 23,336 competitors from the United States and 92 foreign nations. The attack resulted in the deaths of three people—Krystle Campbell, Lu Lingzi, and Martin Richard—and more than 200 people injured.

At 2:49 p.m., two bombs detonated near the marathon's finish line, about 13 seconds and 180 yards apart. At that point, there were still some 5,500 marathoners who had yet to cross the finish line. The explosions occurred on Bolyston Street near Copley Square, on the edge of Boston's Back Bay. The area is in a densely populated commercial and residential part of the city. Three people died from the explosions, and more than 200 were reported wounded, some with life-threatening injuries. The bombings touched off a massive manhunt in Boston and its suburbs that brought the city to a virtual halt for several days. The manhunt ended on April 19, with one suspect dead and the other captured but seriously injured.

The blasts did not cause structural damage to nearby buildings, but they did blow out windows. Officials determined that the bombs were relatively crude devices, with low-yield explosives contained in enclosed pressure cookers and detonated remotely with a hand-held device. They were packed with metal shards, perhaps ball bearings and nails, to increase their lethality. The area had twice been swept for bombs by police and K-9 units, but the perpetrators had planted the bombs after the second sweep.

Police immediately sealed off the area and instructed hundreds of spectators to leave out of fear that more bombs might be set off. At the same time, city and state law enforcement authorities immediately contacted the Federal Bureau of Investigation (FBI), which termed the bombings an act of terror and mounted a massive search for evidence as well as the bombers themselves. Footage from nearby commercial surveillance cameras revealed two suspects carrying large backpacks but leaving the area without the packs.

Emergency personnel carry a wounded person away from the scene of an explosion at the Boston Marathon in Boston on April 15, 2013. Two explosions shattered the euphoria at the marathon finish line, sending authorities out on the course to carry off the injured while other runners were rerouted away from the smoking site of the blasts. (AP Photo/Kenshin Okubo)

One of the backpacks could also be seen from media footage of the race; it had been placed near the edge of the sidewalk where many spectators were watching the event, and it seemed to match one of the backpacks seen in the surveillance footage. Authorities quickly zeroed in on the two young men with the backpacks, releasing the surveillance images to the media, and received numerous calls from individuals who either knew the suspects personally, or who had seen them in the area of the explosions. Eventually, the manhunt and investigation included local and state officials, the FBI, the Bureau of Alcohol, Tobacco, Firearms and Explosives (ATF), the Drug Enforcement Agency (DEA),

the Central Intelligence Agency (CIA), and the National Counterterrorism Center (NCTC).

Many Americans, especially Bostonians, remained on edge, not knowing if the bombings were part of a larger conspiracy. By April 18, officials had positively identified the two suspects—26-year-old Tamerlan Tsarnaev and his 19-year-old brother Dzhokhar. Both were ethnic Chechens; Tamerlan was a legal alien, while Dzhokhar had become a U.S. citizen in 2012. Late on the evening of April 18, the suspects allegedly assaulted and killed security officer Sean Collier at the Massachusetts Institute of Technology (MIT) in Cambridge. After that, they allegedly carjacked a Mercedes SUV, also in Cambridge. The man whose car was stolen told police that the two men had told him they were the bombers. Police were able to track the SUV because the owner's cell phone was left in the car.

In the very early morning hours of April 19, police in Watertown, Massachusetts, and law enforcement officials cornered the two suspects—one was in the SUV, and the other in a Honda. Tamerlan was killed during an ensuing firefight and attempt to flee. His younger brother, however, escaped and sped from the scene, in one of the stolen cars and then on foot. Authorities locked down Watertown and began a house-to-house search for the remaining suspect. Eventually, Dzhokhar was found hiding under a canvas covering a boat in the backyard of a Watertown home. He was taken into custody at 8:42 p.m. on April 19, seriously wounded and bleeding badly.

Dzhokhar was formally charged on April 22; at that time, he had been hospitalized since his capture with wounds suffered in a shootout and getaway attempt. He faces 30 federal charges, including using a weapon of mass destruction to kill. Dzhokhar could get the death penalty if prosecutors choose to pursue it. In the summer of 2014, Dzhokhar's lawyers were seeking to move the trial out of Boston, with a decision expected by the end of the year.

Paul G. Pierpaoli, Jr.

See also: Terrorism

Further Reading

CNN. "Terrorism Strikes Boston Marathon as Bombs Kill 3; Scores Wounded." http://www.cnn.com/2013/04/15/us/boston-marathon-explosions.

The Guardian. "Dzohkhar Tsarnaev Charged with Boston Marathon Bombings." http://www.guardian.com.uk/world/2013/apr/22/boston-bombings-one-week-suspect-dzohkhar-tsarnaev-live.

Brooklyn Bridge Bomb Plot

On May 1, 2003, a Columbus, Ohio, trucker named Iyman Faris (alias Mohammad Rauf) pleaded guilty to plotting to destroy the Brooklyn Bridge (in New York) and launch a simultaneous attack designed to derail trains near Washington, D.C. The plot was allegedly to have been carried out with direct Al-Qaeda sanction and support.

Faris, born on June 4, 1969, in Pakistan-occupied Kashmir, entered the United States in 1994 on a student visa. He married Geneva Bowling in 1995 while he was working at H&M Auto in Columbus, Ohio, and obtained U.S. citizenship in 1999. He allegedly returned to Pakistan the following year. The couple divorced amicably in April 2000.

According to court documents, Faris's first contact with Al-Qaeda occurred in late 2000, when he traveled from Pakistan to Afghanistan with a longtime friend who was already an operative in the terror group. During a series of subsequent visits, Faris was apparently introduced to Osama bin Laden and at least one senior operational leader (identified only as C-2 but thought to be number 3 in Al-Qaeda), who allegedly instructed Faris to assess the feasibility of conducting attacks in New York and Washington, D.C., when he returned to the United States.

While continuing his job as an independent trucker, Faris conducted surveillance in New York City to ascertain the feasibility of destroying a major bridge by cutting the suspension cables with gas cutters. He also procured equipment to conduct a second, simultaneous attack aimed at derailing a train in the Washington, D.C., area. In communications with Al-Qaeda, Faris referred to the gas cutters as "gas stations" and tools for the strike on the train as "mechanics shops."

In coded messages sent to his handlers in Afghanistan via an unnamed third party in the United States, Faris said he was still trying to obtain "gas stations" and rent "mechanics shops" and was continuing to work on the project. After scouting the Brooklyn Bridge and deciding its security and structure meant the plot was unlikely to succeed, he passed along a message to Al-Qaeda in early 2003 that simply said, "The weather is too hot."

In addition to scouting for the New York and Washington, D.C., attacks, Faris also carried out several other tasks for Al-Qaeda. These included acting as a cash courier, providing information about ultralight aircraft as potential getaway vehicles, ordering 2,000 sleeping bags for militants based along the Afghan-Pakistani border, obtaining extensions for six airline tickets for jihadists traveling to Yemen, and delivering cell phones to Khalid Sheikh Mohammed. It was the latter who, after he was captured in early 2003, provided information on Faris and his various activities.

On March 19, 2003, two agents from the Federal Bureau of Investigation (FBI) and one antiterror officer visited Faris and confronted him with Mohammed's testimony and voice recordings intercepted from telephone calls as part of the National Security Agency's secret eavesdropping program. Faced with overwhelming evidence, Faris agreed to work as a double agent, reporting to the FBI and cooperating with ongoing federal investigations into Al-Qaeda. He was ordered to leave his home in Columbus and stay at a safe house in Virginia, from which he would continue to engage in discussions with his contacts and handlers. This cooperation continued until May 1, 2003, when Faris pleaded guilty to the New York and Washington, D.C., plots. He was eventually convicted on October 28, 2003, and sentenced to 20 years in prison for conspiracy to provide material support to terrorism.

Donna Bassett

See also: Al-Qaeda; Mohammed, Khalid Sheikh

Further Reading

Emerson, Steven. *Jihad Incorporated: A Guide to Militant Islam in the US*. Amherst, NY: Prometheus Books, 2006.

Bush Administration

President George W. Bush showed considerable interest in the activities of Osama bin Laden and Al-Qaeda during the early days of his administration; the rest of his administration less so. Although they criticized the Bill Clinton administration for its failure to end the Al-Qaeda threat, most high-ranking officials in the Bush administration had other priorities. These were a missile defense system, military reform, China, and Iraq. Most of these priorities were intended to enhance the ambitions of President Bush and his chief administrators. Even those who knew something about Afghanistan—and they were few indeed—had ties to Pakistan. Pakistan was a supporter of the Taliban, who in turn was protecting bin Laden. Briefings about the importance of terrorism and bin Laden given by the existing Clinton administration to the incoming Bush administration were largely ignored.

Perhaps the least enthusiastic member of the Bush administration vis-à-vis Al-Qaeda was Attorney General John Ashcroft. Ashcroft had higher priorities for the Department of Justice—guns, drugs, and civil rights. He made counterterrorism a third-tier issue. Meanwhile, requests for increased funding for counterterrorism were turned down. Efforts to talk to Ashcroft about counterterrorism proved futile. A Federal Bureau of Investigation (FBI) request for an increase to its counterterrorism budget by $58 million had been turned down by Ashcroft on September 10, 2001. This proposal had called for 149 new counterterrorism field agents, 200 additional analysts, and 54 extra translators. Ashcroft's refusal to consider counterterrorism as a priority changed dramatically after the terror attacks of September 11, 2001.

Secretary of Defense Donald Rumsfeld was no more enthusiastic about bin Laden and Al-Qaeda than Ashcroft. Rumsfeld had been briefed on counterterrorism activities in the Defense Department by outgoing Secretary of Defense William Cohen, but he has since stated that he remembered little of this briefing. Responsibility for counterterrorism in the Defense Department was given to the Assistant Secretary of Defense for Special Operations and Low-Intensity Conflict (SOLIC). This post had not even been filled by September 11, 2001. Rumsfeld's major concern upon taking office had been the building of a missile defense system and development of an advanced weapons system. For this reason a request to allocate $800 million more to counterterrorism was turned down by Rumsfeld, and the funds were diverted

to missile defense. Counterterrorism was simply not a part of Rumsfeld's agenda. This is also why a weapon useful against Al-Qaeda, the Predator unmanned aircraft and its Hellfire missile system, was allowed to languish behind other projects.

Another leading figure in the Bush administration who showed little interest in Osama bin Laden and Al-Qaeda prior to September 11 was Condoleezza Rice, Bush's national security advisor in 2001. In an article in *Foreign Affairs* published before she took office, Rice criticized the Clinton administration for focusing on terrorism rather than on the few great powers that she considered dangerous to peace. It was her thesis that American power and prestige had been frittered away by the concentration on issues like terrorism. Richard Clarke, the holdover counterterrorism expert, tried to persuade Rice of the danger posed by bin Laden and Al-Qaeda in a January 2001 memorandum, but Rice took no action. In a meeting on July 10, 2001, George Tenet, the head of the Central Intelligence Agency (CIA), warned Rice of the strong likelihood of an Al-Qaeda strike against the United States, possibly within the United States. Rice listened to Tenet's arguments, but several times afterward when Tenet brought up the subject she was unable to recall either the meeting or the subject of the meeting. It was only in October 2006 that this meeting and its subject matter surfaced in Bob Woodward's book *State of Denial.* Even then Rice stated that she had difficulty remembering the meeting.

Bush's neoconservative advisers were much more attracted to overthrowing Saddam Hussein in Iraq than to Osama bin Laden and Al-Qaeda. Paul Wolfowitz, the deputy secretary of defense, complained that too much attention had been devoted to the activities of bin Laden. In his view, bin Laden was overrated as a threat. Bin Laden was far down on the neoconservatives' list of priorities. Only President Bush showed curiosity about bin Laden and Al-Qaeda, ordering intelligence reports sent to him daily about Al-Qaeda's activities.

Opposition to Clinton administration policies also extended to economic matters. The previous administration had attempted to control the flow of money to Osama bin Laden. Efforts were made to embarrass those countries with loose banking regulations into tightening them up. More than 30 countries were participating in this effort when the Bush administration assumed office. The Clinton administration had also proposed the creation of the National Terrorist Asset Tracking Center as part of this campaign. Paul O'Neill, the new secretary of the treasury, disapproved of any attempt to interfere in the banking industry, even as regards banks and financial institutions that were supporting terrorist activities. Consequently, O'Neill shut down anti–money-laundering operations, and the National Terrorist Asset Tracking Center was dismantled because of lack of funding.

After September 11, 2001, the Bush administration made a complete reversal, and resources now poured into counterintelligence. It also created a sprawling and wide-reaching national security apparatus and championed the passage of the October 2001 PATRIOT Act. Many Americans, however, were ambivalent toward some of these measures, fearing that they would trample civil liberties. President Bush gave the CIA complete authority to carry out covert operations against terrorists and terrorist organizations. Once it became apparent that Pakistan's Taliban regime

would not give up Osama bin Laden, an American-sponsored war was unleashed to overthrow it. This was accomplished by year's end, but the work in Afghanistan was only beginning. Soon, however, the desire to overthrow Iraqi dictator Saddam Hussein became paramount, and this diverted the Bush administration's focus away from bin Laden, Al-Qaeda, and Afghanistan.

The invasion of Iraq began on March 19, 2003. It was predicated on the premise that Hussein possessed weapons of mass destruction (WMD) and was involved in— or at least supportive of—international terrorism. Neither of these premises turned out to be true, however. The attack on Iraq was also predicated on the 2002 Bush Doctrine, which embraced the concept of preemptive war to punish or destroy regimes that were a potential threat to the United States. After the invasion phase, which ended on May 1 and during which the Hussein regime was promptly overthrown, the Iraq War soon devolved into a bloody insurgency and sectarian-ethnic civil conflict that threatened to swamp the United States and its limited international coalition in Iraq. That phase of the war lasted until December 2011, when virtually all U.S. troops were withdrawn from Iraq. The war in Iraq became highly unpopular at home as well as abroad, and Bush's popularity began to plummet. Indeed, far more troops died during the insurgency than had died during the invasion phase of the war. Bush nevertheless won reelection in 2004.

In 2005–2006, the Bush administration endured a number of setbacks. It botched relief efforts after Hurricane Katrina in September 2005, and in November 2006 the Republicans lost control of both houses of Congress, which was largely interpreted as a rebuke of Bush's domestic and foreign policies. Just six weeks later, Bush was forced to fire his controversial defense secretary, Donald Rumsfeld. Meanwhile, in January 2005, Secretary of State Colin Powell resigned because of his reservations over Bush's foreign policy and his handling of the war on terror. In 2007, the situation in Iraq became even worse, while Bush's ballooning budget deficits were beginning to exert a heavy drag on the economy.

In January 2007, Bush announced a "troop surge" that sent another 40,000 troops to Iraq in order to arrest the insurgency and bring stability to the war-torn nation. In Afghanistan, however, years of neglect had the fanned the flames of a growing insurgency sponsored by the Taliban and its allies, including Al-Qaeda. Many Bush detractors, including some Republicans, now began to assert that America's quagmire in Iraq had needlessly undermined U.S. policies in Afghanistan. By now, Bush had stretched U.S. armed forces so thinly that he was hard-pressed to dispatch more troops to Afghanistan. In 2008, the Bush administration was pressured to admit that "coercive interrogation techniques" had been used on some enemy combatants and terror suspects since 2001, although the White House insisted that techniques like waterboarding did not constitute torture.

By mid-2008, Bush's troop surge in Iraq had largely stemmed the worst of the insurgency there, and the situation had improved enough for the White House and Pentagon to consider drawing down troop deployments, which began in 2009. In the last two years of the Bush administration, with most of the dogmatic neoconservatives gone, American foreign policy became more circumspect, and Secretary of State Condoleeza Rice began the process of repairing America's tarnished image on the world stage. In Afghanistan, however, the Taliban-led insurgency grew worse, but Bush decided to leave that legacy to his successor, Barack Obama.

The U.S. economy became increasingly unstable in early 2008, and in the fall a massive series of bank, investment house, and insurance company failures pushed the economy into a tailspin. Meanwhile, budget deficits run up over the eight years of the Bush administration meant that the federal government had far fewer tools with which to battle the downturn. In the last quarter of 2008, unemployment began to rise dramatically, and consumer spending contracted significantly. The looming economic recession, the worst in at least 35 years, enabled the election of Democrat Barack Obama to the presidency in November 2008. He faced the daunting prospects of stabilizing the sinking economy, withdrawing all U.S. troops from Iraq, and reinvigorating the war in Afghanistan with an eye toward an American withdrawal from that country as quickly as possible.

Stephen E. Atkins

See also: Al-Qaeda; Bin Laden, Osama; Clinton Administration; Enduring Freedom, Operation; Global War on Terror; Iraqi Freedom, Operation; Obama Administration; Powell, Colin Luther; Rumsfeld, Donald Henry

Further Reading

Coll, Steve. *Ghost Wars: The Secret History of the CIA, Afghanistan, and bin Laden, from the Soviet Invasion to September 10, 2001.* New York: Penguin, 2004.

Risen, James. *State of War: The Secret History of the CIA and the Bush Administration.* New York: Free Press, 2006.

Woodward, Bob. *State of Denial: Bush at War, Part III*. New York: Simon and Schuster, 2006.

Woodward, Bob. *Bush at War*. New York: Simon and Schuster, 2002.

Bush Doctrine

The Bush Doctrine is the foreign/national security policy articulated by President George W. Bush in a series of speeches following the September 11, 2001, terrorist attacks on the United States. The Bush Doctrine identified three threats against U.S. interests: terrorist organizations; weak states that harbor and assist such terrorist organizations; and so-called rogue states. The centerpiece of the Bush Doctrine was that the United States had the right to use preemptive military force against any state that is seen as hostile or that makes moves to acquire weapons of mass destruction, be they nuclear, biological, or chemical. In addition, the United States would "make no distinction between the terrorists who commit these acts and those who harbor them."

The Bush Doctrine represented a major shift in American foreign policy from the policies of deterrence and containment that characterized the Cold War and the brief period between the collapse of the Soviet Union in 1991 and the events of 2001. This new foreign policy and security strategy emphasized the strategic doctrine of preemption. The right of self-defense would be extended to use of preemptive attacks against potential enemies, attacking them before they were deemed capable of launching strikes against the United States. Under the doctrine, furthermore, the United States reserved the right to pursue unilateral military action if multilateral solutions cannot be found. The Bush Doctrine also represented the realities of international politics in the post–Cold War period; that is, that the United States was the sole superpower and that it aimed to ensure American hegemony.

A secondary goal of the Bush Doctrine was the promotion of freedom and democracy around the world, a precept that dates to at least the days of President Woodrow Wilson. In his speech to the graduating class at West Point on June 1, 2002, Bush declared that "America has no empire to extend or utopia to establish. We wish for others only what we wish for ourselves— safety from violence, the rewards of liberty, and the hope for a better life."

President George W. Bush delivers his first State of the Union address to a joint session of Congress at the U.S. Capitol Building on January 29, 2002. In his speech, Bush outlined his plan to fight the Global War on Terror and characterized the nations of Iran, Iraq, and North Korea as forming an "axis of evil." (AP Photo/Doug Mills)

The immediate application of the Bush Doctrine was the invasion of Afghanistan in early October 2001 (Operation Enduring Freedom). Although the Taliban-controlled government of Afghanistan offered to hand over Al-Qaeda leader Osama bin Laden if it was shown tangible proof that he was responsible for the September 11 attacks and also offered to extradite bin Laden to Pakistan where he would be tried under Islamic law, its refusal to extradite him to the United States with no preconditions was considered justification for the invasion.

The administration also applied the Bush Doctrine as justification for the Iraq War, beginning in March 2003 (Operation Iraqi Freedom). The Bush administration did not wish to wait for conclusive proof of Saddam Hussein's alleged weapons of mass destruction (WMDs), so in a series of speeches, administration officials laid out the argument for invading Iraq. To wait any longer was to run the risk of having Hussein employ or transfer the alleged WMDs. Thus, despite the lack of any evidence of an operational relationship between Iraq and Al-Qaeda, the United States, supported by Britain and a few other nations, launched an invasion of Iraq. As it turned out, despite a multiyear search for WMDs in postinvasion Iraq, no such items were found.

The use of the Bush Doctrine as justification for the invasion of Iraq led to increasing friction between the United States and it allies, as the Bush Doctrine repudiated the core idea of the United Nations (UN) Charter. The charter prohibits any use of international force that is not undertaken in self-defense after the occurrence of an armed attack across an international boundary or pursuant to a decision by the UN Security Council. Even more vexing, the distinct limitations and pitfalls of the Bush Doctrine were abundantly evident in the inability of the United States to quell sectarian violence and political turmoil in Iraq. The doctrine did not place parameters on the extent of American commitments, and it viewed the consequences of preemptory military strikes as a mere afterthought.

The advent of the Barack Obama administration in 2009 marked a significant shift away from the Bush Doctrine. The new administration's foreign and military postures became far more cautious and stressed the need for multinational, multilateral action in the face of foreign threats. The concept of preemptive war seemed to have faded into the background. America's new international policies now stressed patience, negotiation, and international agreements in lieu of blunt military force. Some critics of this approach, however, have asserted that Obama's policies have resulted, in some instances, in a weak and rudderless reaction to international threats.

Keith A. Leitich

See also: Bush Administration; Cheney, Richard Bruce; Coercive Interrogation Techniques; Enduring Freedom, Operation; Feith, Douglas; Iraqi Freedom, Operation; Obama Administration; Powell, Colin Luther; Tenet, George

Further Reading

Buckley, Mary E., and Robert Singh. *The Bush Doctrine and the War on Terrorism: Global Responses, Global Consequences.* London: Routledge, 2006.

Dolan, Chris J. *In War We Trust: The Bush Doctrine and the Pursuit Of Just War.* Burlington, VT: Ashgate, 2005.

Gurtov, Melvin. *Superpower on Crusade: The Bush Doctrine in U.S. Foreign Policy.* Boulder, CO: Lynne Rienner, 2006.

Heisbourg, François. "Work in Progress: The Bush Doctrine and Its Consequences." *Washington Quarterly* 6, no. 22 (Spring 2003): 75–88.

Jervis, Robert. *American Foreign Policy in a New Era*. New York: Routledge, 2005.

Schlesinger, Arthur M. *War and the American Presidency*. New York: Norton, 2004.

C

Carter Doctrine

U.S. foreign policy precept enunciated by President James "Jimmy" Carter in 1980 that pledged the nation to protect American and Allied interests in the Persian Gulf. By 1980, the Carter administration, which had been engaged in an ongoing debate over the direction of U.S. foreign policy as détente faded, declared its determination to use any means necessary, including military force, to protect American interests in the Persian Gulf. These interests mainly involved Persian Gulf oil and regional shipping lanes.

On January 23, 1980, Carter, in his State of the Union message, declared that "an attempt by any outside force to gain control of the Persian Gulf region will be regarded as an assault on the vital interests of the United States of America, and such an assault will be repelled by any means necessary, including military force." This emphasis on American military power marked a fundamental reorientation in Carter's foreign policy. Since 1977, in response to public disillusionment with the Vietnam War and disgust over the Watergate scandal, Carter had attempted to fight the Cold War with different weapons. While not ignoring the Soviet Union, he determined that U.S.-Soviet relations would not be allowed to dominate foreign policy formulation, a stance that he saw as having led to the costly containment policy and the tragedy of Vietnam. Instead, other nations, especially those in the developing world, would be considered in a regional rather than a global context. Additionally, the United States would assert its international predominance by emphasizing moral rather than military superiority by focusing on human rights and related humanitarian concerns.

By January 1980, however, the international climate had changed drastically. The Islamic Revolution in Iran had displaced America's longtime ally, Mohammad Reza Shah Pahlavi. On November 4, 1979, Iranian students seized the American embassy in Tehran and took 70 Americans hostage. This precipitated a 444-day crisis during which the Carter administration could do little to free the hostages. Also, on December 26, 1979, the Soviet Union invaded Afghanistan, sparking a bloody nine-year war there. Faced with these twin crises—religious fundamentalist terrorism and communist advancement by military force—during an election year, Carter reoriented his foreign policy. Although he did not abandon his commitment to human rights, the issue was accorded a much lower priority in policy formulation and was no longer used as a major weapon with which to wage the Cold War. Instead, the administration's official posture reflected a more customary Cold War policy that emphasized the projection of military power and communist containment. In addition, a globalist perspective began to supplant the regionalist outlook, with increased emphasis on East-West issues. These trends were accelerated considerably under President Ronald Reagan, Carter's successor. The Carter Doctrine is still operative in American foreign policy, more than three decades after it was enunciated. Indeed, it was used as a partial justification for the 1991 Persian Gulf War and the 2003 invasion of Iraq.

Donna R. Jackson

See also: Bush Administration; Clinton Administration; Iraqi Freedom, Operation; Obama Administration; Persian Gulf War

Further Reading

Brzezinski, Zbigniew. *Power and Principle: Memoirs of the National Security Adviser, 1977–1981.* New York: Farrar, Straus and Giroux, 1985.

Carter, Jimmy. *Keeping Faith: Memoirs of a President.* Fayetteville: University of Arkansas Press, 1982.

Vance, Cyrus. *Hard Choices: Critical Years in America's Foreign Policy.* New York: Simon and Schuster, 1983.

Centennial Olympic Park Bombing

On July 27, 1996, during the 1996 Summer Olympics, an improvised explosive device (IED) bomb hidden in a knapsack detonated at the Centennial Olympic Park in Atlanta, Georgia, killing 2 people and wounding 111 others. The fatalities were Alice Hawthorne, who died in the cross-blast, and a Turkish cameraman, Melih Uzunyol, who had a heart attack while running to film the devastation. Among those injured were six state troopers and one Georgia Bureau of Investigation agent.

Bomb experts said the crudely made device, filled with masonry nails that served as shrapnel, was designed to kill. The pack used a steel plate to direct the blast and could have done more damage, but it had tipped over at some point. It was the largest pipe bomb in U.S. history, weighing in excess of 40 pounds.

Initial suspicions centered around Richard Jewell, a contract guard with AT&T who brought the bomb to the attention of the authorities. The Justice Department formally declared on October 26, however, that he was not a target of investigation. On December 9, the Federal Bureau of Investigation (FBI) asked for any photographs or videotapes taken in the park on the night of the bombing and offered a $500,000 reward. The bureau also released a tape of a 911 call warning of the impending attack.

On February 21, 1997, a dynamite bomb exploded at the Otherside Lounge, a gay/lesbian bar in Atlanta's Piedmont Road neighborhood, injuring five people. A second device was found in the parking lot the next morning, where it was defused. Both were similar to an IED used to attack abortion clinics in Atlanta and Birmingham the month before, and all four bore a strong resemblance to the Centennial Park bomb.

On May 5, 1998, the FBI charged Eric Rudolph with the Birmingham clinic bombing and linked it to the Centennial Park incident, saying that the two IEDs employed in the attacks were very similar in design. The bureau offered a $1 million reward for information leading to Rudolph's arrest and placed him on the 10 Most Wanted Fugitives list. Five months later, Attorney General Janet Reno and FBI Director Louis Freeh jointly announced that Rudolph was the chief suspect in four unsolved acts of terror—the Centennial Park attack and the 1997 bombings of the Otherside Lounge and the Atlanta and Birmingham abortion clinics.

Rudolph was eventually captured on May 31, 2003. As part of a deal, Rudolph provided authorities with the location of more than 250 pounds of dynamite buried in the mountains of North Carolina. FBI agents and officers with the Alcohol, Tobacco and Firearms Bureau subsequently found the massive stash in three different locations near populated areas.

Rudolph's justification for the Centennial Park bombing was political. In a statement made on April 13, 2005, he asserted, "In the summer of 1996, the world converged upon Atlanta for the Olympic Games. Under the protection and auspices of the regime in Washington millions of people came to celebrate the ideals of global socialism. . . . The purpose of the attack on July 27 was to confound, anger, and embarrass the Washington government in the eyes of the world for its abominable sanctioning of abortion on demand."

Rudolph later claimed that he had intended to carry out a much larger bombing campaign at the Atlanta Games site, involving five IEDs detonated over several days. He maintained that he intended to make phone calls well in advance of each explosion, leaving only armed uniformed government personnel exposed to potential injury. When asked why he had not proceeded with the more elaborate attack, Rudolph responded that poor planning on his part made it impossible.

On August 21, 2005, after years on the run, Rudolph was sentenced by a federal judge to four consecutive life sentences plus $2.3 million in damages for the Centennial Park, Otherside Lounge, and Atlanta and Birmingham abortion clinic bombings. Before he was sentenced, he

apologized to the victims of the Olympic Games attack. Rudolph was sent to the ADX Florence Supermax federal prison, where he spends 22-½ hours per day alone in his 80-square-foot cell.

Donna Bassett

See also: Alec Station; Terrorism

Further Reading

Hillard, Robert L., and Michael C. Keith. *Waves of Rancor: Tuning In the Radical Right.* Armonk, NY: M. E. Sharpe, 1999.

Schuster, Henry (with Charles Stone). *Hunting Eric Rudolph.* New York: Penguin, 2005.

Central Intelligence Agency

The Central Intelligence Agency (CIA) record prior to September 11, 2001, was emblematic of the pressures placed upon it in a changing, post–Cold War world. Its central problem was the transition from the Cold War to international terrorism, and then to stateless terrorism that could strike the United States at any time. Surveillance against terrorism in the continental United States was the responsibility of the Federal Bureau of Investigation (FBI), but the CIA had responsibility for international intelligence gathering. In any case, its record was found to be lacking in terms of defending against international terrorism.

Over a period of years, the leaders of the CIA had limited human intelligence assets. In the early and mid-1990s, the CIA had reduced its human intelligence capability through a staff reduction of 20 percent. By the late 1990s, the agency lacked the agents, the language skills, and the organizational flexibility to spot a conspiracy in the making. Instead, the CIA depended on intelligence reports from friendly intelligence services and political departments. Even when it had a human intelligence source, the CIA was slow to react to warnings coming from that source. A case in point is that the CIA had an aggressive agent in Germany monitoring the activities of the Hamburg Cell, but no additional resources were placed at his disposal.

Bureaucracy often threatened the efficiency of CIA operations. Its agents were reluctant to share information with the FBI for fear of losing control of the case. Part of this fear was an incompatibility of function between the two institutions. The FBI had the task of bringing lawbreakers to justice. That organization approached a case by accumulating evidence that could stand up in a court of law. CIA agents were less interested in prosecuting than intelligence gathering. They wanted to follow the leads to see where they would go. This meant that the CIA was unwilling to share crucial information because such sharing might compromise intelligence sources.

The decision by John Deutch, director of the CIA from 1995 to 1996, to call for prior approval from CIA headquarters before recruiting any person with a criminal or human rights problem as an intelligence asset made it difficult for the CIA to recruit intelligence agents. This decision came after a controversy involving the CIA's employment of a paid informant in Guatemala who had been involved in the murders of an American innkeeper and the Guatemalan husband of an American lawyer. Hundreds of paid informants were dismissed from the rolls of the CIA. Almost all of the human intelligence assets in the Middle East were terminated in this purge. This restriction was still in place on September 11, 2001.

The CIA had been monitoring the activities of Osama bin Laden and Al-Qaeda through its Counterterrorism Center. CIA agents had been able to recruit 30 Afghans operating under the codeword GE/SENIORS to monitor bin Laden's activities in Afghanistan since 1998. They each received $10,000 a month for this mission. Numerous times during the Bill Clinton administration, analysts in the Counterterrorism Center and its Alec Station unit proposed operations to neutralize bin Laden using Afghan agents or missile attacks, but none of these operations received approval. Part of the problem was that bin Laden was so elusive, traveling at irregular times. There was also the fear of collateral damage that would outrage domestic and international public opinion and compromise secrecy. The Clinton administration became paralyzed by indecision caused by its lack of confidence in CIA intelligence and the ongoing political difficulties of President Clinton's Monica Lewinsky scandal.

George Tenet, who succeeded Deutch, was able to make the transition from the Clinton administration to the George W. Bush administration. He had been constantly warning both administrations about the danger of bin Laden and Al-Qaeda. Although the Clinton administration came to recognize the truth of the terrorism threat, the Bush administration was slow to accept it until September 11, 2001. Tenet had been able to establish a good working relationship with President Bush, but he was unable to get him to act quickly on Al-Qaeda. After September 11, however, the Bush administration left nothing to chance in fighting terrorism. According to Seymour Hersh in *Chain of Command*, it unleashed the CIA to undertake covert action against terrorists with no restrictions, but deniability for the president. The support for the Northern Alliance led to the overthrow of the Taliban regime in Afghanistan and ended safe sanctuary for bin Laden and the other leaders of Al-Qaeda. But bin Laden and most of Al-Qaeda's and the Taliban's leaders were able to escape. Part of the reason for the escape was the reluctance of the Bush administration to commit American forces until it was too late.

In the middle of the hunt for bin Laden and the wiping out of Al-Qaeda's leadership, the Bush administration decided that Saddam Hussein and his alleged weapons of mass destruction were greater threats. Even prior to September 11, it was known in the CIA that the Bush administration was eager to overthrow Saddam Hussein. Its reasoning was that deposing Hussein and establishing a favorable, democratic government in Iraq would produce a base of support in the Middle East for the United States, because it was apparent that there was no solution to the Israeli-Palestinian conflict.

Extreme pressure from the neoconservatives in the Bush administration, led by Vice President Dick Cheney, for the CIA to produce intelligence justification to go to war with Iraq resulted in widespread dissatisfaction among CIA analysts. Many of them believed that an Iraqi war would hinder the hunt for bin Laden and other Al-Qaeda leaders and lead to a degeneration of the continuing war in Aghanistan. They believed that the United States should concentrate exclusively on Afghanistan and the Al-Qaeda network. Those analysts who were too vocal with their dissatisfaction were fired, transferred, or severely criticized. Despite warnings from these CIA analysts about the lack of concrete intelligence, Tenet assured President Bush

and his advisers that Iraq had weapons of mass destruction. The ultimate failure to find these weapons of mass destruction ended Bush's confidence in Tenet. In the meantime, the rank and file of the CIA had become critical of the Bush administration. These individuals issued a series of intelligence reports that contradicted or were critical of the premises of the Bush administration's invasion and occupation of Iraq. Many of these reports were leaked to the news media, with devastating results for the Bush White House.

After Tenet's resignation in July 2004, Bush appointed former Florida congressman Porter Goss to head the CIA. He had worked for the CIA in the 1960s, but most of his knowledge of the CIA came from his seven years as chairman of the House Permanent Select Committee on Intelligence. President Bush gave Goss a mandate to bring the CIA back to Bush's political team. A short time after Goss arrived at Langley headquarters, senior CIA officials began to leave in droves. In April 2005, the CIA inspector general's report surfaced that presented detailed criticism of the performance of more than a dozen former and current CIA officials. Goss quashed the recommendation that there be accountability boards to recommend personnel actions against those charged in the report. Despite this action, the clash between Goss's team and CIA veterans reached epic proportions. In the long run, however, it was Goss's inability to work with his nominal boss, John Negroponte, the director of national intelligence, that led to his demise. President Bush asked for and received Goss's resignation on May 5, 2006. His successor was U.S. Air Force four-star general Michael Hayden, the former head of the National Security Agency (NSA) and the number two person under Negroponte. In February 2009, following Barack Obama's inauguration as president, Hayden was replaced by Leon Panetta.

The CIA played the central role in gathering the intelligence that led to the raid on the Abbottabad compound that resulted in bin Laden's death on May 1, 2011 (which was May 2, Pakistani local time). Beginning in August 2010, CIA operatives spent months tracking a lead that eventually allowed them to positively identify one of bin Laden's couriers, who in turn led them to suspect the compound, located in a suburb of the Pakistani capital of Islamabad, as bin Laden's likely hiding place. With Obama's final approval in late April 2011 and under the direction of Panetta, the CIA organized and oversaw the raid on the compound, which was carried out by elements of the U.S. Navy SEALs. Panetta left the CIA in July 2011 to become defense secretary. He was succeeded as permanent CIA director by former General David Petraeus, who was forced to resign in November 2012 after acknowledging an inappropriate extramarital affair. John O. Brennan became Petraeus's permanent replacement in March 2013.

On May 22, 2013, the Obama administration outlined a new plan in which the CIA's Counterterrorism Center would, over time, cease to be the hub of America's targeted killing operations against terrorists in Pakistan, Yemen, and other places. It was widely seen as a move to shift the CIA's focus from covert warfare back toward traditional spying and strategic analysis.

Stephen E. Atkins

See also: Alec Station; Counterterrorism Center; Counterterrorism Strategy; Hamburg Cell; Tenet, George

Further Reading

Drumheller, Tyler, and Elaine Monaghan. *On the Brink: An Insider's Account of How the White House Compromised American Intelligence*. New York: Carroll and Graf, 2006.

Hersh, Seymour M. *Chain of Command: The Road from 9/11 to Abu Ghraib*. New York: HarperCollins, 2004.

Miller, John, Michael Stone, and Chris Mitchell. *The Cell: Inside the 9/11 Plot and Why the FBI and CIA Failed to Stop It*. New York: Hyperion, 2002.

Naftali, Timothy. *Blind Spot: The Secret History of American Counterterrorism*. New York: Basic Books, 2005.

Risen, James. *State of War: The Secret History of the CIA and the Bush Administration*. New York: Free Press, 2006.

Tenet, George, and Bill Harlow. *At the Center of the Storm: My Years at the CIA*. New York: HarperCollins, 2007.

Cheney, Richard Bruce

(January 30, 1941–)

Politician, businessman, secretary of defense (1989–1993), and vice president (2001–2009). Richard Bruce "Dick" Cheney was born on January 30, 1941, in Lincoln, Nebraska. He grew up in Casper, Wyoming, and was educated at the University of Wyoming, earning a BA in 1965 and an MA in political science in 1966. He completed advanced graduate study there and was a PhD candidate in 1968.

Cheney acquired his first governmental position in 1969 when he became the special assistant to the director of the Office of Economic Opportunity. He served as a White House staff assistant in 1970 and 1971 and as assistant director of the Cost of Living Council from 1971 to 1973. He briefly worked in the private sector as the vice

Richard Cheney served as secretary of defense during the 1991 Persian Gulf War. A highly controversial, yet powerful, vice president of the United States during 2001–2009, he was a prime mover behind the decision to invade Iraq in 2003. (White House)

president of an investment advisory firm. In 1974, Republican Richard Cheney served as secretary of defense during the 1991 Persian Gulf War. A highly controversial yet powerful vice president of the United States from 2001 to 2009, he was a prime mover behind the decision to invade Iraq in 2003.

In 1975, President Gerald R. Ford appointed Cheney as his deputy assistant, later rising to the level of White House chief of staff. In 1978, Cheney was elected to the U.S. House of Representatives, serving six terms. He was elected House minority whip in December 1988. Cheney was known for his conservative votes: he opposed gun control, environmental laws, and funding for Head Start.

Cheney became secretary of defense on March 21, 1989, in the George H. W. Bush administration. In this position, Cheney significantly reduced U.S. military budgets and canceled several major weapons programs. In addition, in the wake of the Cold War he was deeply involved in the politically volatile task of reducing the size of the American military force throughout the world. Cheney also recommended closing or reducing in size many U.S. military installations, despite intense criticism from elected officials whose districts would be adversely impacted by the closures.

As secretary of defense, Cheney also provided strong leadership in several international military engagements, including the December 1989 Panama invasion and the humanitarian mission to Somalia in early 1992. It was Cheney who secured the appointment of General Colin Powell as chairman of the Joint Chiefs of Staff in 1989.

Cheney's most difficult military challenge came during the 1991 Persian Gulf War. He secured Saudi permission to begin a military buildup there that would include a United Nations (UN) international coalition of troops. The buildup proceeded in the autumn of 1990 as Operation Desert Shield. When economic sanctions and other measures failed to remove the Iraqis from Kuwait, the Persian Gulf War commenced with Operation Desert Storm on January 16, 1991. A five-week air offensive was followed by the movement of ground forces into Kuwait and Iraq on February 24, 1991. Within four days, the UN coalition had liberated Kuwait. Cheney continued as secretary of defense until January 20, 1993, when Democrat Bill Clinton took office.

Upon leaving the Pentagon, Cheney joined the American Enterprise Institute as a senior fellow. He also became president and chief executive officer of the Halliburton Company in October 1995 and chairman of its board in February 2000.

Only months later, Republican presidential candidate George W. Bush chose Cheney as his vice presidential running mate. After a hard-fought campaign, the Bush-Cheney ticket won the White House in December 2000, although only after a court fight and having lost the popular vote.

Arguably one of the more powerful vice presidents in U.S. history, Cheney endured much criticism for his hawkish views (he is believed to have strongly promoted the 2003 Iraq War) and his connections to the oil industry (Halliburton won several contracts for work in postwar Iraq). He also raised eyebrows by refusing to make public the records of the national energy task force he established to form the administration's energy initiatives.

Many people who knew Cheney personally have asserted that he became a changed man after the September 11 terrorist attacks. He became, they say, far more secretive, more hawkish than ever before, and, some say, even paranoid, seeing terrorists everywhere. As one of the principal promoters of the U.S. invasion of Iraq (Operation Iraqi Freedom), which began in March 2003, Cheney was well placed to receive the burden of criticism when the war began to go badly in 2004. As the subsequent Iraqi insurgency increased in size, scope, and violence, Cheney's popularity plummeted. Following the 2006 midterm elections, which caused the Republicans to lose control of Congress principally because of the war in Iraq, Cheney took a far lower profile.

When his fellow neoconservative Donald Rumsfeld, the secretary of defense, resigned in the election's aftermath, Cheney was increasingly perceived as a liability to the Bush White House, which was under intense pressure to change course in Iraq or quit it altogether.

Cheney did not help his approval ratings when he accidentally shot a friend during a hunting trip in February 2006 and the information about the incident was slow to be released. Even more damaging to Cheney was the indictment and conviction of his chief of staff, I. Lewis "Scooter" Libby, for his involvement in the Valerie Plame–Joseph Wilson CIA leak case. Some alleged that it was Cheney who first leaked the classified information to Libby and perhaps others, who in turn leaked it to the press. Cheney continued to keep a remarkably low profile. Beginning in 2007, a small group of Democrats in the House attempted to introduce impeachment proceedings against Cheney, but such efforts did not make it out of committee. After leaving office, Cheney became a frequent critic of the Obama administration's policies, especially those related to national security and international affairs.

Paul G. Pierpaoli, Jr.

See also: Bush Administration; Bush Doctrine; Iraqi Freedom, Operation; Persian Gulf War; Rumsfeld, Donald Henry; World Trade Center, September 11, 2001

Further Reading

Nichols, John. *The Rise and Rise of Richard B. Cheney: Unlocking the Mysteries of the Most Powerful Vice President in American History.* New York: New Press, 2005.

Woodward, Bob. *State of Denial: Bush at War, Part III.* New York: Simon and Schuster, 2006.

Woodward, Bob. *Plan of Attack*. New York: Simon and Schuster, 2004.

Woodward, Bob. *Bush at War*. New York: Simon and Schuster, 2002.

Chomsky, Noam

(December 7, 1928–)

Noam Chomsky has long been an active critic of the U.S. government and its policies, and his views on the events surrounding September 11, 2001, resonate in radical left circles in the United States. A distinguished academic in the field of linguistics, he has spent much of his career as a self-appointed commentator on the failures of the American government. Chomsky is not an advocate of conspiracy theories, but he has a unique perspective that sometimes gets him into political difficulty. Chomsky belongs to no political party, and his critiques have been equally harsh on both sides of the political spectrum.

Chomsky is the product of an anti-Zionist Jewish background. He was born December 7, 1928, in Philadelphia, Pennsylvania. His father was a Hebrew scholar and a member of the radical labor union International Workers of the World (IWW). Both parents were from Russia: his father from the Ukraine and his mother from Belarus. Chomsky grew up immersed in Hebrew culture and literature. He attended and then graduated from Central High School in Philadelphia in 1945.

That same year he started studying philosophy and linguistics at the University of Pennsylvania. Shortly after graduation from the University of Pennsylvania, he married fellow linguist Carol Schatz. Chomsky continued graduate work in linguistics, receiving his PhD in 1955. During the period from 1951 to 1955, he was a Harvard Junior Fellow working on his dissertation. Soon after graduation, he found a teaching position at the Massachusetts Institute of Technology (MIT). His 1957 book *Syntactic Structures* began to revolutionize the study of linguistics. His growing renown led to his appointment in 1961 as full professor in MIT's department of modern languages and linguistics. In 1966, he was appointed to the Ferrari P. Ward Professorship of Modern Languages and Linguistics, a position he held until 1976. He remained a professor at MIT until his retirement. He is now a professor emeritus of linguistics at MIT.

Chomsky was famous worldwide for his contributions to theories on linguistics, but he began a lifelong involvement with politics in the 1960s. His first engagement in politics was as a vocal critic of the Vietnam War. After the Vietnam War ended, Chomsky continued his critique of the U.S. government. He asserts that the foreign policy of the United States promotes a double standard by preaching democracy and freedom for all but at the same time supporting and allying itself with nondemocratic and repressive states and political groups. He has also been critical of the American capitalist system and big business. His political views can be loosely defined as libertarian socialist. Although he is opposed to most wars, Chomsky is not a pacifist: he has stated that he thought World War II was a just war.

In his comments on the September 11 attacks, Chomsky acknowledged that it was an Al-Qaeda operation, but he still questions government actions taken before September 11. He considers September 11 an atrocity, but he is more concerned about the reasons for the attack. He has chronicled a series of missteps by the U.S. government in the last 30 years that led to the attack on the United States. It is his contention that the United States is a terrorist state, and it should not be surprising that the American government should be so hated in the Muslim world.

Chomsky warned that the George W. Bush administration would take advantage of the September 11 attacks to embrace an adventurous foreign policy. He was critical of the invasion of Afghanistan, but the invasion of Iraq in 2003 has brought forth a barrage of articles and talks highly critical of this action. Chomsky did not defend Iraqi dictator Saddam Hussein, but he noted that most of the atrocities of Hussein's regime were committed when he was an ally of the United States. Chomsky believes that the United States has overextended itself in these countries and that American actions there have been both illegal and immoral.

Chomsky frequently agitated right-wing supporters of the Bush administration. They called him a traitor and a madman. He has also been highly critical of the Barack Obama administration, asserting that Obama has committed a number of war crimes, including targeted assassinations. His biographer, Robert F. Barsky, has commented that Chomsky's ideas have "led people to idolize him, debate about him, arrest him, utter slanderous comments about him, and censor his work." Chomsky responds to his critics in the same way that he addresses his supporters—by careful reasoning and citing facts. It is interesting to note that in a poll conducted by the British magazine *Prospect*, Chomsky was ranked as "the world's greatest intellectual." Chomsky is more modest than this, but he does confess

to holding the United States to a higher standard of conduct because it is a free society.

Stephen E. Atkins

See also: Bush Administration; Enduring Freedom, Operation; Iraqi Freedom, Operation; Obama Administration; Pentagon Attack; World Trade Center, September 11, 2001

Further Reading

Barsamian, David. "The United States Is a Leading Terrorist State." *Monthly Review* 53, no. 6 (November 2001): 1.

Barsky, Robert F. *Noam Chomsky: A Life of Dissent.* Cambridge, MA: MIT Press, 1997.

Blackburn, Robin, and Oliver Kamm. "For and against Chomsky." *Prospect* (London), October 20, 2005, 1.

Chomsky, Noam. *9/11.* New York: Seven Stories, 2001.

Hegarty, Shane. "Lighthouse of the Left." *Irish Times* (Dublin), January 14, 2006, 5.

Christmas Day (2009) Airline Terror Plot

On December 25, 2009, Nigerian citizen Umar Farouk Abdulmutallab unsuccessfully attempted to bomb Northwest Airlines Flight 253 from Amsterdam to Detroit as it approached its final destination. The device, which consisted of a six-inch packet of powdered PETN (which becomes a plastic explosive when mixed with triacetone triperoxide/TAPN) sewn into his underwear and a syringe of liquid acid, ignited a small fire that was promptly put out by a passenger and flight crew members. After the incident, officials discovered that Abdulmutallab had been in regular communication with Anwar al-Awlaki, an American-born Islamist widely believed to be the chief ideologue of

Al-Qaeda in the Arabian Peninsula (AQAP) in Yemen.

Public responses included a barrage of criticism aimed at the U.S. national security and intelligence organizations for not preventing the attempted bombing, especially given the billions of dollars that had been invested to improve aviation security since September 11, 2001. Of particular concern was the fact that U.S. officials had received a warning from Abdulmutallab's father in November 2009, who was concerned over his son's increasingly extremist views. Although the 23-year-old Nigerian had been put on watch lists and even denied a visa renewal by Britain in May 2009, his name was apparently lost among thousands of others and not flagged. Critics also asked why X-ray checks had failed to detect the explosive materials he carried.

Three days after the attempted attack, President Barack Obama publicly addressed the incident while on vacation in Hawaii, receiving some criticism that he showed a lack of concern for Americans' fear for their safety. He mandated a thorough investigation of the event, which he officially blamed on AQAP a week later. A declassified report subsequently released to the public in January 2010 detailed the intelligence and defense agencies' failures to streamline their information and "connect the dots." The president ordered further reforms to fix these weak links and also instigated heightened security measures at airports, including the installation of whole-body scanners in airports and delaying the release of Yemeni prisoners at Guantánamo Bay. He also announced that he would more than double the $70 million in security aid that Washington had sent to Yemen in 2009 and, along with the United Kingdom, would jointly finance a new counterterrorism unit in the country.

Abdulmutallab was taken into custody on December 26, 2009, and charged with eight felonies, including the attempted use of a weapon of mass destruction and the attempted murder of 289 civilians. He was found guilty of all eight counts and sentenced to life imprisonment with no parole on February 16, 2012.

Peter Chalk

See also: Al-Qaeda; Al-Qaeda in the Arabian Peninsula; Christmas Eve (2000) Bombings

Further Reading

Baker, Peter. "Obama Says Al-Qaeda in Yemen Planned Bombing Plot, and He Vows Retribution." *New York Times*, January 3, 2010.

Borzou, Daragahi. "Bin Laden Takes Responsibility for Christmas Day Bombing Attempt." *New York Times*, January 24, 2010.

Margasak, Larry, Lara Jakes, and Jim Irwin. "Man Cites Orders from al-Qaeda in Failed Bid to Blow Up Plane." *Globe and Mail* (Canada), December 26, 2011.

Savage, Charlie. "Nigerian Indicted in Terrorist Plot." *New York Times*, January 6, 2010.

"'Underwear Bomber' Abdulmutallab Pleads Guilty." *BBC News*, October 12, 2011. http://www.bbc.co.uk/news/world-us-canada-15278483.

Christmas Eve (2000) Bombings

On December 24, 2000, Islamic militants carried out a series of coordinated bombing attacks in Indonesia, targeting Christians and Christian-owned properties. They deployed 34 improvised explosive devices (IEDs), most left in cars parked outside selected venues, of which an estimated 19 detonated as planned. An additional 15 bombs were found before they detonated.

Most, but not all, were successfully defused. In total, 10 cities in three provinces were hit: 6 in Java (Jakarta, Bekasi, Bandung, Sukabumi, Ciamis, and Mojokerto), 3 in Sumatra (Medan, Pematang and Sinatar), and 1 in Lombuk (Mataram). The combined attacks left 19 people dead and another 120 wounded, and are thought to have cost around $47,000.

Because the bombings took place over such a large area and were highly coordinated, the press speculated that rogue elements of the Indonesian military might have been involved, accusing them of trying to manipulate religious conflict in an effort to shore up the army's influence, which had been abruptly curtailed following the fall of the Suharto regime in 1998. President Abdurrahman Wahid, who was under pressure to resign because of worsening political and economic conditions at the time of the explosions, accused his opponents of complicity, claiming they were trying to discredit him by creating fear and panic.

Several Islamist entities denied any responsibility for the attacks. The paramilitary organization Laskar Jihad issued a statement denouncing the bombings as "immoral and politically motivated." Gerakan Aceh Merdeka (GAM, or the Free Aceh Movement) similarly distanced itself from the incidents, with the group's spokesman, Teungku Amni bi Marzuki, affirming, "We have no connection with the bombings in several places in Indonesia because the conflict in Aceh is not a religious conflict."

On December 26, it was announced that two people had been arrested in connection with the attacks—one of whom (Dedi Mulyadi) later claimed to have received training in Afghanistan during the early 1990s. They were detained at a house in the Antapani area of Bandung after an IED exploded prematurely during the construction process. Both men were seriously injured in the blast, which killed three additional suspects and 10 civilians and injured at least 95 others. Authorities also announced that documents had been found in the course of the detentions implicating Jemaah Islamiyah (JI) field commander Nurjaman Riduan Isamuddin (Hambali) in the bombings. Abu Bakar Bashir (Abu Bakar Ba'asyir, also known as Abdus Samad), the spiritual leader of the group, was later tried for his alleged involvement but found not guilty. During the course of his trial, it was alleged that the attacks were part of a campaign of terror aimed at tilting the religious balance in Southeast Asia in order to create a pan-regional caliphate that was to include Indonesia, the southern Philippines, the Malay Muslim provinces of Thailand, and Brunei.

It is now known that the first planning meeting for the operation took place in Kuala Lumpur in October 2000. It was here that cities were selected for attack and arrangements made for the procurement of explosives; the latter material was sourced out of Manila with the help of JI's representative in Singapore, Faiz bin Abubakatheafana. At a subsequent gathering held on or around December 15, principal team members were identified, provided with money, and given basic instruction in bomb-making techniques. They were also told to place the IEDs in different churches and that, if a suitable venue was not available, other "infidel" or Chinese-owned properties should be targeted.

On January 25, 2011, JI leader and explosives expert Umar Patek, also known as Pak Taek, Abu Syekh, and Zachy, was arrested in Pakistan. Like Al-Qaeda leader

Osama bin Laden, he had been hiding in Abbottabad. He was extradited to Indonesia the following August and under interrogation admitted his complicity in the Christmas Eve explosions as well as the 2002 attacks in Bali. Patek's capture was a major blow to JI's so-called pro-bombing faction and removed arguably the most dangerous terrorist in Southeast Asia from circulation.

Donna Bassett

See also: Al-Qaeda; Al-Qaeda in the Arabian Peninsula; Bali Bombings; Christmas Day (2009) Airline Terror Plot

Further Reading

Abuza, Zachary. *Militant Islam in Southeast Asia: Crucible of Terror.* Boulder, CO: Lynne Rienner, 2003.

Chalk, Peter, Angel Rabasa, William Rosenau, and Leanne Piggott. *The Evolving Terrorist Threat to Southeast Asia: A Net Assessment.* Santa Monica, CA: RAND, 2009.

Sidel, John T. *Riots, Pogroms, Jihad: Religious Violence in Indonesia.* Ithaca, NY: Cornell University Press, 2006.

Turnbull, Wayne. "A Tangled Web of Southeast Asian Islamic Terrorism: The Jemaah Islamiya Terrorist Network." Monterey, CA: Monterey Institute of International Studies, July 31, 2003. Available online at http://www.terrorismcentral.com/Library/terroristgroups/JemaahIslamiyah/JITerror/WJ2000.htm.

Clarke, Richard A.

(1950–)

Richard A. Clarke was the chief counterterrorism adviser on the U.S. National Security Council on September 11, 2001. He was a career specialist in intelligence and counterterrorism. Clarke was one of the few carryovers from the Bill Clinton administration that the George W. Bush administration had retained, but he had difficulty in making the case that Al-Qaeda posed a major danger to the United States prior to the September 11, 2001, attacks.

Clarke's entire career was in government service. He was born in 1950 in Boston, Massachusetts. His father was a blue-collar factory worker at a Boston chocolate factory, and his mother was a nurse. After a divorce, Clarke was raised by his mother. He won a competitive exam to attend the prestigious Boston Latin School, from which he graduated in 1969. He earned his undergraduate degree from the University of Pennsylvania in 1972. He then attended the Massachusetts Institute of Technology (MIT), where he earned a degree in management. His first job, beginning in 1973, was with the U.S. Department of Defense as a defense analyst counting Soviet nuclear warheads. After a series of appointments, he was promoted in 1985 to assistant secretary of state for intelligence in the Reagan administration. By this time, Steve Coll asserts, he had earned a reputation as being a "blunt instrument, a bully, and occasionally abusive." He continued to work with the George H. W. Bush administration and helped on security affairs during the 1990–1991 Persian Gulf War. In 1992, James Baker, the U.S. secretary of state, fired him for his apparent defense of Israel's transfer of U.S. technology to the People's Republic of China. Clarke then moved to the National Security Council in the White House, where he began to specialize in counterterrorism. Clarke was also held over in the Clinton administration, continuing as a member of the National Security Council from 1992 to 2003.

Clarke's preoccupation was counterintelligence. Among his contentions was that

Osama bin Laden's Al-Qaeda was a growing threat to the United States. President Clinton agreed with this assessment, but he was engaged in a series of controversies that distracted him and his administration and did not entirely trust the Central Intelligence Agency (CIA). Clarke lobbied for a Counterterrorism Security Group to be chaired by a new national security official, the National Coordinator for Infrastructure Protection and Counterterrorism. President Clinton approved this office, signing Presidential Decision Directive 62 on May 22, 1998.

Clarke presided over a working group that included the counterterrorism heads of the Central Intelligence Agency (CIA), Federal Bureau of Investigation (FBI), Joint Chiefs of Staff (JCS), the Defense Department, the Justice Department, and State Department. But the National Coordinator for Infrastructure Protection and Counterterrorism had a limited staff of 12 and no budget; moreover, operational decision making could come only from the departments and agencies of the intelligence community. As Clarke has pointed out, he had the "appearance of responsibility for counterterrorism, but none of the tools or authority to get the job done." Nevertheless, Clarke was in the middle of several counterterrorism operations. He was involved in the decision making about the CIA's snatch operation against Osama bin Laden in 1998. An Afghan team was to capture bin Laden at his residence at Tarnak Farms near Kandahar. This raid was called off because there was a lack of confidence among CIA leadership, the White House, and Clarke that it would succeed.

Clarke continued his position on the National Security Council during the early years of the Bush administration. He proposed a plan to combat Al-Qaeda that included covert aid to the Afghan leader of the Northern Alliance, Ahmad Shah Massoud, spy flights of the new Predator drone, and new ways to eliminate bin Laden as a threat to the United States, but there was little enthusiasm for this report within the Bush administration. Becoming frustrated, Clarke decided to resign from government work in November 2001. In the interval, the events of September 11, 2001, transpired, changing the American political landscape. On September 12, President Bush instructed him to try to find evidence that Iraqi dictator Saddam Hussein was connected to September 11. Clarke sent a report to the White House stating categorically that Hussein had nothing to do with these terrorist attacks, but there is no evidence indicating whether or not President Bush read the report. The report was sent back to be updated and resubmitted, but nothing came of it.

Clarke left government service in 2003. He then became an outspoken critic of the Bush administration and its policies prior to September 11. This led the White House to engage in a character assassination campaign against him. Clarke testified for 20 hours during the 9/11 Commission hearings in 2003 and 2004. He made national headlines for his apology stating that the government had failed to prevent the September 11 attacks. In March 2004, in the middle of the 9/11 Commission hearings, Clarke published his book *Against All Enemies: Inside America's War on Terror*, which gives his side of the controversy.

In his book, Clarke was especially critical of the Bush administration's invasion of Iraq. Most of his criticism stems from his belief that, by redirecting attention away from bin Laden and Al-Qaeda, the Bush administration has allowed Al-Qaeda to reconstitute itself into an ongoing threat to the United States. In his eyes, the invasion of Afghanistan was so halfhearted in its commitment of American forces that bin Laden and nearly all of the Al-Qaeda and Taliban leaders easily escaped. By not committing the necessary resources to rebuild Afghanistan, Clarke wrote, the Bush administration allowed both Al-Qaeda and the Taliban to threaten the pro-American Afghanistan state—all to depose Saddam Hussein.

Also in 2004, Clarke released *Defeating the Jihadists: A Blueprint for Action*, in which he outlined his idea for a more effective counterterrorism strategy. His other works include *Your Government Failed You: Breaking the Cycle of National Security Disasters* (2008) and *Cyber War: The Next Threat to National Security and What to Do about It* (2010), as well as two novels. Clarke is also a frequent guest on news programs, writes newspaper and magazine articles, and occasionally delivers speeches on national security topics.

Stephen E. Atkins

See also: Al-Qaeda; Bin Laden, Osama; Bush Administration; Central Intelligence Agency; Clinton Administration; Terrorism

Further Reading

Benjamin, Daniel, and Steven Simon. *The Age of Sacred Terror*. New York: Random House, 2002.

Clarke, Richard A. *Against All Enemies: Inside America's War on Terror*. New York: Free Press, 2004.

Coll, Steve. *Ghost Wars: The Secret History of the CIA, Afghanistan, and Bin Laden, from the Soviet Invasion to September 10, 2001*. New York: Penguin, 2004.

Naftali, Timothy. *Blind Spot: The Secret History of American Counterterrorism*. Basic Books, 2005.

Clinton Administration

Although the Bill Clinton administration was no longer in power when the events of September 11, 2001, unfolded, some of its policies nevertheless played a role in setting the stage for the attacks. It was during President Clinton's eight years in office that Osama bin Laden and Al-Qaeda emerged as a threat to the United States. Bin Laden twice, in 1996 and again in 1998, issued declarations of hostilities against the United States. President Clinton had priorities other than terrorism, such as health care, education, the North American Free Trade Agreement (NAFTA), gays in the military, instability in Russia, the Israeli-Palestinian conflict, and the policies of rogue states. Early in his administration, President Clinton dealt with foreign policy issues as they became crises: Bosnia, Haiti, and Somalia. Despite these other issues, bin Laden made the Clinton administration pay attention with attacks against Americans around the world.

The lack of attention to terrorism by the Clinton administration led to the weakening of the intelligence capability of the Central Intelligence Agency (CIA), as weak CIA directors were appointed. First, Clinton appointed James Woolsey as the director of the CIA. This appointment was in keeping with Clinton's pattern of maintaining his distance from the CIA, which has been described by Steve Coll as "distant, mutually ill-informed, and strangely nonchalant." Woolsey was more interested in scientific and technical programs, particularly spy satellites, than in human intelligence. Consequently, the CIA came to depend on scientific/technical programs and deemphasized human intelligence gathering. It was not all Woolsey's fault; President Clinton held only two semiprivate meetings with Woolsey in his two years as CIA director. The CIA had hindered the Federal Bureau of Investigation (FBI) on the Aldrich Ames spy case, and this case had long-term negative impact on CIA-FBI relations. Ames, a veteran CIA agent, had been caught spying for the Soviet Union and had betrayed more than 100 CIA agents before being caught in 1994. There had been indicators that Ames was a spy, but the CIA had refused to pass on the information to the FBI. In the course of nearly two years, Woolsey had alienated Clinton, the FBI, Congressional leaders, and the CIA's rank and file. He resigned on December 26, 1994.

Next, Clinton appointed John Deutch as director of the CIA. Deutch did not want the job because he was content in his position as deputy secretary of defense, but Clinton persuaded him to take it anyway. Even more so than Woolsey, Deutch was a champion of scientific and technical intelligence collection. He belittled the need for human intelligence, and by telling this to the CIA's analysts, he promptly alienated them. The CIA budget shrank under his watch and veteran CIA administrators and analysts were encouraged to retire. Deutch lasted only 19 controversial months before Clinton fired him in December 1996.

Several events in 1995 had made the Clinton administration aware of the rising dangers of terrorism. One was the sarin gas attack in the Tokyo subway system by the Aum Shinrikyo sect on March 25, 1995. The vocal anti-Americanism of this sect of 50,000 members worried counterterrorism officials. The next event was the Oklahoma City bombing on April 19, 1995, by Timothy McVeigh and associ-

ates. It showed how easily terrorists could acquire bomb-making materials.

In February 1995, the Clinton administration had already introduced the Omnibus Counter-Terrorism Act in an attempt to bypass some of the limitations placed on intelligence operations. But even after the Oklahoma bombing, the Republican-controlled House of Representatives refused to bring it to a vote. Disbelieving that a major terrorist threat was on the horizon, Republicans decided to sacrifice any efforts at counterterrorism and instead criticize the Clinton administration for its failures. In 1996, Congress did pass the Antiterrorism and Effective Death Penalty Act of 1996, but many of the original provisions involving firearms control were eliminated because of the objections of the gun lobby. Two important provisions were retained: chemical markers on high explosives and legal authority to bar terrorists from entering the United States (Alien Terrorist Removal Court).

During his second term in office, Clinton and his administration became more aware of the threat of both domestic and foreign terrorism. His appointment of George Tenet to the CIA directorship helped stabilize that organization, but Clinton still had reservations about the reliability of intelligence coming from the CIA. The presence of Richard A. Clarke, National Coordinator for Security, Infrastructure Protection, and Counter-Terrorism in the White House, brought counterterrorism to the forefront of the president's agenda. Bombings of U.S. embassies at Nairobi and Dar-es-Salaam in August 1998 were rude wake-up calls. President Clinton authorized cruise missile attacks on an Al-Qaeda training camp and on a factory in Sudan. A large meeting of Al-Qaeda leaders was scheduled to be held at the Zawhar

Kili training camp complex near Khost, in eastern Afghanistan, on August 20, 1998. Osama bin Laden was supposed to be at this meeting. Seventy-five cruise missiles hit the complex, killing at least 20 and wounding scores of others. This attack proved to be a failure, probably because Pakistani security Inter-Services Intelligence (ISI) warned Al-Qaeda about the attack. (At least this is alleged by Steve Coll in his book *Ghost Wars*.) The other cruise missile attack, at the al-Shifa plant in Sudan, was no more successful. Indeed, a controversy erupted over that because the al-Shifa plant turned out to be a pharmaceutical factory and not a chemical factory producing chemicals for Al-Qaeda.

Several times, the Clinton administration proposed special operations to be conducted by the military against terrorist targets. Each time, senior generals in the Pentagon were reluctant to undertake special operations against terrorism suspects. Yet Richard Clarke reported that these senior generals were eager to let the word spread down through the ranks that the politicians in the While House were reluctant to act. They also communicated this to members of Congress and the media.

Hostile criticism about the missile attacks in 1998 from Republicans cooled the Clinton administration's ardor for further efforts to capture or kill bin Laden. Yet both the CIA and FBI reported intelligence to the Clinton administration that Al-Qaeda was planning terrorist activities within the United States. With these warnings still fresh, the Clinton administration slowly closed down any operations against bin Laden.

After the 1998 embassy attacks, the Clinton administration did attempt to disrupt Al-Qaeda's financing. It took legal steps to freeze $240 million in Al-Qaeda and Taliban assets in American bank accounts. Assets of Afghanistan's national airline, Ariana Afghan, were also frozen. These actions were inconvenient for Al-Qaeda and made it shift its assets into commodities—diamonds and blue tanzanite—and led to the creation or use of Islamic charities to raise funds. Hindering the Clinton administration was the weakness of the international money-laundering laws. These laws were particularly weak in Kuwait, Dubai, United Arab Emirates (UAE), Bahrain, and Lebanon. Also, the traditional Islamic banking system, the hawala, heavily used in Afghanistan and Pakistan, was cash based, leaving no written or electronic records. These factors brought limited success to the Clinton administration's efforts to restrict the flow of funds to Al-Qaeda. But the incoming George W. Bush administration seemed even less interested in Al-Qaeda and terrorism in general, even after its officials were warned by outgoing Clinton appointees of the potential dangers.

Stephen E. Atkins

See also: African Embassy Bombings; Al-Qaeda; Bin Laden, Osama; Bush Administration; Central Intelligence Agency; Clarke, Richard A.

Further Reading

Benjamin, Daniel, and Steven Simon. *The Age of Sacred Terror.* New York: Random House, 2002.

Bernstein, Richard. *Out of the Blue: The Story of September 11, 2001, from Jihad to Ground Zero.* New York: Times Books, 2002.

Clinton, Bill. *My Life.* New York: Vintage Books, 2005.

Coll, Steve. *Ghost Wars: The Secret History of the CIA, Afghanistan, and Bin Laden, from the Soviet Invasion to September 10, 2001.* New York: Penguin, 2004.

Naftali, Timothy. *Blind Spot: The Secret History of American Counterterrorism.* New York: Basic Books, 2005.

Posner, Gerald. *Why America Slept: The Failure to Prevent 9/11.* New York: Ballantine, 2003.

Coercive Interrogation Techniques

Methods of interrogation meant to compel a person to behave in an involuntary way or reveal information by use of threat, intimidation, or physical force or abuse. In particular, coercive interrogation has been used during the recent U.S. Middle East wars and the global war on terror to obtain information from prisoners, especially those being held as terrorists. Coercive interrogation has been labeled by numerous individuals and organizations as inhumane torture and as war crimes that violate international law. In addition, coercive interrogation has been criticized by many for being ineffective; critics contend that it leads to false confessions.

There are various techniques of interrogation that can be described as coercive, including, but not limited to, sleep deprivation, food deprivation, ceaseless noise, sexual abuse, forced nakedness, cultural humiliation, exposure to extreme cold, prolonged isolation, painful postures, beating, and waterboarding. Waterboarding, a highly controversial interrogation method, involves positioning victims on their backs, with the head in a downward position, while pouring water over the face and head. Soon, as water enters the nasal passages and mouth, the victim believes that drowning is imminent. Waterboarding is a favored interrogation technique because it leaves no visible marks on the victim and can be very effective in extracting confessions.

During the 1991 Persian Gulf War, records indicate that the U.S. military generally abided by international law concerning treatment of civilian and military detainees. However, there is ample evidence that Iraqis tortured American prisoners of war (POWs) by employing numerous coercive interrogation techniques. Coercive interrogation became a much larger issue during the George W. Bush administration after the global war on terror began in 2001. Although many international agreements signed by the United States forbid torture, President Bush and Vice President Richard Cheney and the Bush administration as a whole supported the use of coercive interrogation in the global war on terror, the Afghanistan War, and the Iraq War. After the September 11, 2001, terrorist attacks on the United States, the Bush administration acknowledged a need for new interrogation techniques.

Shortly after the September 11 attacks, the Bush administration worked to gain support for coercive interrogation techniques and began to change the definition of torture to better suit its needs. Numerous senior officials believed that the Central Intelligence Agency (CIA) had to employ coercive interrogation techniques to deal with Al-Qaeda suspects and other terrorists. The administration now began to devise arguments for going against prevailing prescriptions vis-à-vis torture. First, Bush believed that as commander in chief he could use the inherent powers given to him in the U.S. Constitution to stretch U.S. policy to best protect the citizens of the United States. The administration had argued repeatedly that terrorism is a major threat that cannot be fought with conventional means. Also, the White

House repeatedly stated that coercive interrogation is not torture in the strict sense of the word. Most legal scholars on the subject disagree with this assessment.

Beginning in 2004, accounts surfaced of Iraqi prisoners being abused by U.S. soldiers in the Abu Ghraib Prison in Iraq. Pictures showing U.S. military personnel abusing and violating prisoners by various means proved highly incendiary. Some methods used included urinating on prisoners, punching prisoners excessively, pouring phosphoric acid on prisoners, rape, forcing prisoners to strip nude and attaching electrodes to their genitals, or photographing prisoners in compromising positions to humiliate them. Eventually, 17 soldiers and officers were removed from duty because of the Abu Ghraib scandal; some eventually faced criminal charges and trial.

The situation was compounded when the CIA was accused of having destroyed evidence of the torture of civilian detainees in 2005. There were apparently two videotapes (subsequently destroyed) that contained images of Al-Qaeda suspects being tortured. By 2007, the CIA admitted to some use of coercive interrogation. However, the agency admitted that this had happened rarely and that techniques such as waterboarding were used fewer than five times. In a television interview in December 2008, Vice President Cheney admitted that he had supported the use of waterboarding. More allegations of CIA-sponsored torture surfaced, but the Bush administration stuck to its support of coercive interrogation techniques, asserting that they were not cruel and unusual and therefore did not constitute torture. Nevertheless, under considerable pressure, Bush signed an executive order in July 2007 forbidding the use of torture against terror suspects; it did not, however, specifically ban waterboarding.

In early 2008, waterboarding was again a hot topic as Congress considered an antitorture bill designed largely to limit the CIA's use of coercive interrogation. The bill, which was passed in February 2008, would have forced the CIA to abide by the rules found in the *Army Field Manual on Interrogation* (FM 34-52). The manual forbids the use of physical force and includes a list of approved interrogation methods; waterboarding is not among them.

Arizona senator John McCain, who had been brutally tortured as a POW during the Vietnam War and had already engaged in a war of words with the Bush White House over the use of torture, voted against the bill. McCain, in defending his vote, argued that the CIA should have the ability to use techniques that are not listed in the *Army Field Manual of Interrogation*. He argued that there are other techniques available that are effective and not cruel and unusual. He continued to claim, however, that waterboarding is torture and illegal. Bush vetoed the February 2008 bill, and its proponents did not have the requisite votes to override it.

Arthur M. Holst

See also: Abu Ghraib; Al-Qaeda; Bush Administration; Central Intelligence Agency; Torture of Prisoners

Further Reading

Bellamy, Alex J. "No Pain, No Gain? Torture and Ethics in the War on Terror." *International Affairs* 82 (2006): 121–48.

Dershowitz, Alan M. *Is There a Right to Remain Silent: Coercive Interrogation and the Fifth Amendment after 9/11.* Oxford: Oxford University Press, 2008.

Guiora, Amos N. *Constitutional Limits on Coercive Interrogation.* New York: Oxford University Press, 2008.

Posner, Eric A., and Adrian Vermeule. *Terror in the Balance? Security, Liberty, and the Courts.* New York: Oxford University Press, 2007.

Cold War Peace Dividend, U.S. Troop/Force Structure Reductions

In the aftermath of the Cold War, the administrations of U.S. presidents George H. W. Bush and Bill Clinton sought to reduce military expenditures to secure a peace dividend whereby spending previously devoted to defense could be redirected to social programs, internal infrastructure improvements, etc. As early as the 1970s, U.S. officials had sought an elusive peace dividend from savings following the Vietnam War, which ended for the United States in January 1973.

In the late 1980s, as Cold War tensions eased substantially, the George H. W. Bush administration developed plans to reduce the nation's force structure while also cutting spending on advanced weaponry, including weapons of mass destruction (WMDs). The administration pursued a three-track strategy that included reductions in standing troops and the redeployment of forces, consolidation of military bases and facilities, and arms control and disarmament efforts. All three tracks were interrelated. As arms control measures such as the 1990 Treaty on Conventional Forces in Europe mandated significant cuts in standing military forces in Europe, the United States was able to redeploy and reduce troop strength and eliminate both foreign and domestic bases. The United States was also able to decommission sizable numbers of nuclear missile forces, a result of historic arms-reduction efforts

begun under Bush's predecessor, President Ronald Reagan.

Under the Bush administration, the number of active duty U.S. military personnel was reduced from 2.24 million in 1989 to 1.92 million by 1992. The number of U.S. forces deployed overseas was also reduced significantly. For example, U.S. forces in Europe declined from 300,000 in 1989 to 150,000 by 1993. U.S. military expenditures fell from 5.5 percent of gross domestic product (GDP) to 4.8 percent from 1989. Overall, defense spending fell from $303.4 billion in 1989 to $273.3 billion in 1991 before rising again to $298.4 billion in 1992 with the costs associated with the 1991 Persian Gulf War. Bush reoriented U.S. defense policy so that the nation's military was no longer mandated to be prepared to fight two major military campaigns simultaneously (for instance, a World War II–style campaign in Europe and a similar effort in Asia). Instead, the Pentagon was required to be ready to fight simultaneously two regional conflicts of the size and scale of the 1991 Persian Gulf War. The administration also initiated a series of military facility closures and consolidations under the Base Realignment and Closure Commission (BRAC). Throughout the 1990s, there were four rounds of cuts under BRAC, including the closure of 97 major domestic bases and 55 realignments. Overseas, more than 960 facilities were closed. BRAC produced $16 billion in savings during the 1990s, with annual savings thereafter of at least $6 billion.

In 1993, the Clinton administration launched the Bottom-Up Review (BUR) of U.S. defense needs and capabilities. BUR kept the requirement to fight two simultaneous regional conflicts but suggested a new approach, the win-hold-win strategy in which the country would maintain the capability to win one regional war while preventing defeat in the second (the hold strategy). After victory in the first conflict, forces would be redeployed to the second to gain victory. BUR also recommended $105 billion in defense cuts through 1999. These recommendations became the basis for the Clinton administration's defense policy.

By 2000, U.S. forces had been reduced to 1.49 million, while defense expenditures had been cut to 3 percent of GDP. Defense spending declined from 1993 through 1998, falling from $291.1 billion in 1993 to $268.5 billion in 1998; however, spending did increase in 1999 and 2000, rising to $294.5 billion the last full year Clinton was in office (2000).

A range of problems emerged with the Cold War peace dividend. The first was that the reduction in defense expenditures contributed to the 1992–1993 recession, as defense firms cut research and production and laid off approximately one-third of all their civilian workers by the late 1990s. Especially hard hit were California, Massachusetts, and Texas, which were home to significant numbers of high-tech and defense-related firms. There was also a wave of mergers and consolidations among military contractors, resulting in an industry dominated by several large firms, including Boeing, General Dynamics, Halliburton, Northrop Grumman, and Lockheed Martin. By 1998, more than 500 smaller defense firms had gone out of business or had been acquired by larger competitors.

In addition, the BRAC closings had a significant impact on many communities that had come to depend on military facilities to power the local economy. While some localities were able to re-cover quickly by using the former military facilities in new and often innovative ways, other towns and cities were hard-pressed to replace the impact of federal outlays. One result was increased political opposition to BRAC's recommendations. The cuts in military personnel were not accompanied by significant alterations in force structures in that the U.S. military continued to emphasize conventional forces designed to counter Cold War–style threats instead of transitioning to lighter, more mobile forces. Troop reductions also created further problems by increasing the reliance on military reserve units and National Guard forces. This became a major problem after 2003, when the George W. Bush administration attempted to wage two wars simultaneously—one in Afghanistan and the other in Iraq—without making any arrangements for a larger standing force. The result was a badly overstretched standing army and an increased reliance on reserve and National Guard personnel, many of whom endured multiple deployments that were greatly disruptive to them and their families.

Tom Lansford

See also: Clinton Administration; Multi-National Force—Iraq

Further Reading

Braddon, Derek. *Exploding the Myth? The Peace Dividend, Regions and Market Adjustment.* Amsterdam: Oversees Publishers Association, 2000.

Hogan, Michael J., ed. *The End of the Cold War: Its Meaning and Implications.* New York: Cambridge University Press, 1992.

Markusen, Ann, Peter Hall, Scott Campbell, and Sabrina Deitrick. *The Rise of the Gunbelt: The Military Remapping of Industrial America.* New York: Oxford University Press, 1991.

Cole, USS, Attack On. *See* USS *Cole*
Bombing

Combined Forces Command— Afghanistan

This was the highest-level U.S. military command in Afghanistan for Operation Enduring Freedom from November 2003 to February 2007. By the spring of 2003, combat operations in Afghanistan had scaled down. As a result of the relatively stable environment in the country and to conserve manpower, which was now crucial with the beginning of Operation Iraqi Freedom in March 2003, the headquarters in Afghanistan shifted from a three-star corps-level command down to that of a two-star division level, designated Combined Joint Task Force 180 (CJTF-180). Overwhelmed with too many tasks, however, the CJTF focused on issues relating directly to military operations rather than on larger political and strategic concerns.

In the summer of 2003, the commanding general of U.S. Central Command (CENTCOM), General John Abizaid, decided that Afghanistan required a different and more effective headquarters organization that could focus on political-military efforts. In September 2003, Abizaid ordered the creation of a new three star–level coalition headquarters in Afghanistan to take over high-level political, military, and strategic planning, which would permit the divisional headquarters to focus on combat operations. Newly promoted lieutenant general David W. Barno took command in October 2003.

Barno moved the new headquarters out of Bagram Air Base, which was the headquarters for CJTF-180, into the Afghan capital of Kabul. He began with a staff of six and had to borrow facilities and personnel from CJTF-180 to operate. Staff also came from active-duty personnel from all U.S. military services and from the U.S. reserve forces as individual ready reservists and individual mobilization augmentees, service members serving separately from rather than with a unit. Coalition partners also contributed personnel. Great Britain, for example, filled the deputy commander position. In early 2004, the new headquarters was designated Combined Forces Command—Afghanistan (CFC-A). By 2005, the CFC-A had grown to a staff of more than 400 personnel, about 10 percent of whom were from coalition nations including France, South Korea, and Turkey. The CFC-A provided needed continuity because rotations of the staff were staggered to keep some personnel with knowledge and experience in the command at all times; meanwhile, combat units rotating through Afghanistan stayed for a year or less and were replaced with units often unfamiliar with conditions on the ground.

The CFC-A was responsible for Afghanistan as well as southern Uzbekistan, southern Tajikistan, and Pakistan, with the exception of Jammu and Kashmir. CFC-A commanders regularly traveled and coordinated with senior leadership in these countries. During the command's duration, Afghan and Pakistani leaders met with the CFC-A commander for a quarterly conference to coordinate border security and other issues. Under Barno's command, the CFC-A also had a close working relationship with the U.S. embassy in Kabul, headed by Ambassador Zalmay Khalilzad. Taking a few staff members with him, Barno moved into an office in the embassy and lived in a trailer complex within the embassy compound. Barno and Khalilzad coordinated and integrated military and civilian efforts throughout Afghanistan.

In early 2004, Barno established regional commands, designated Regional Command East, Regional Command South, and Regional Command West. The regional commanders assumed responsibility for all military forces in their areas of operation. Before this change, military units stayed on large bases, went out into the countryside to conduct an operation for a week or two, and then returned to their bases. The new organization allowed commanders to become more familiar with their areas of operation, work in them for the duration of their tours of duty in Afghanistan, and build relationships with local Afghans as part of a counterinsurgency campaign to prevent the reemergence of the Taliban and other insurgent groups.

One of the first tasks of the CFC-A was to create a campaign plan for Afghanistan to address security, stability, and reconstruction issues. Begun by the British director of planning, this campaign plan evolved into a counterinsurgency approach supported by the U.S. embassy, the Afghan government, and the international community. It required keeping the Afghan people the central focus of the campaign rather than killing the enemy. The strategy included a broad range of activities meant to defeat terrorism and deny the enemy safe sanctuary, enable the Afghans to provide their own security, promote good local and provincial governments, and encourage reconstruction.

During his tenure, Barno had to respond to accusations that American military personnel acted too aggressively and used firepower too heavily when conducting military operations. As a result, the CFC-A created a list of guidelines for American military personnel to follow during operations in order to reduce tensions with the Afghan people. One guideline, for example, required service members to ask locals to open locked doors whenever possible instead of forcing entry.

Lieutenant General Karl W. Eikenberry took over command of the CFC-A in May 2005, shifting the emphasis of operations back to fighting enemy forces. He also moved back into the military compound located at Bagram Air Base. Eikenberry oversaw the transition of Operation Enduring Freedom from an American-led operation to an effort led by the international community. In mid-2005, the North Atlantic Treaty Organization (NATO) began to take responsibility for military operations in Afghanistan, beginning in the north and moving into the west and south. In late 2006, NATO assumed command of all operations throughout Afghanistan except for an area along the Pakistan border. With this shift in responsibility to NATO, Eikenberry supervised the closure of the CFC-A, which was deactivated in February 2007. Combined Joint Task Force 76, a division-level command based on the U.S. Army's Southern European Task Force and 173rd Airborne Brigade, both deployed from Italy, assumed responsibility for all U.S. forces in Afghanistan, while the Combined Security Transition Command—Afghanistan, another division-level command, retained the mission to train the Afghan National Army and police forces. Before the dissolution of the CFC-A, General John Abizaid presented the command with three Joint Meritorious Unit Awards.

On May 26, 2014, President Obama, announced that it was "time to turn the page on a decade in which so much of our foreign policy was focused on the wars in Afghanistan and Iraq." Under his plan, the

32,000 American troops in Afghanistan would be reduced to 9,800 at the end of the year, which would be further reduced to under 5,000 by the end of 2015, and almost all the U.S. troops removed by the end of 2016. A small force would protect the U.S. embassy in Kabul and help the Afghans with military purchases and other security matters. At the height of American involvement, in 2011, the United States had 101,000 troops in the country.

Lisa Marie Mundey

See also: U.S. Central Command; U.S. European Command; U.S. Special Operations Command

Further Reading

Barno, David W. "Fighting 'The Other War': Counterinsurgency Strategy in Afghanistan, 2003–2005." *Military Review* (September–October 2007): 32–44.

Combat Studies Institute, Contemporary Operations Study Group. *A Different Kind of War: The United States Army Operation Enduring Freedom (OEF), September 2001–September 2005.* Fort Leavenworth, KS: Combat Studies Institute Press, 2009.

Rasanayagam, Angelo. *Afghanistan: A Modern History.* London: I. B. Tauris, 2005.

Stewart, Richard W. *The United States Army in Afghanistan: Operation Enduring Freedom, October 2001–March 2002.* Washington, DC: U.S. Government Printing Office, 2003.

Conscientious Objection and Dissent in the U.S. Military

Conscientious objection—the refusal to wage war because of religious, ethical, moral, philosophical, or humanitarian convictions—is a basic human right confirmed by the Universal Declaration of Human Rights (1948) and other United Nations (UN) conventions, including the nonbinding 1998 General Assembly resolution that explicitly asserts the right for soldiers already performing military service to claim conscientious objector status. In international law, conscientious objection is complemented by Article 4 of the Nuremberg Principles established after World War II, which mandates that following orders does not relieve one from responsibility for war crimes. Although bona fide conscientious objector status has been a part of the American identity since the Revolutionary War, conscientious objection by members of the U.S. armed forces since 2001 has frequently proven controversial, with many conscientious objectors imprisoned or driven into exile. Issues surrounding conscientious objector status and dissent during the 1991 Persian Gulf War were extremely limited in scope because of the very short duration of that conflict.

The U.S. Department of Defense Directive 1300.6 (revised 2007) provides a narrowed definition of conscientious objection. Conscientious objectors may be officially recognized if claimants establish "sincere objection to participation in war in any form, or the bearing of arms, by reason of religious training and/or belief." While the Defense Department guidelines do encompass "moral and ethical beliefs" outside traditional religion, they exclude "selective" conscientious objection to specific conflicts or modes of warfare. Each armed service has regulations codifying the processing of conscientious objector claimants (e.g., chaplain and psychiatrist interviews, a hearing before an investigating officer, Defense Department review board, etc.). In accordance with inactive Selective Service guidelines for conscription, bona fide conscientious objectors

U.S. Army staff sergeant Camilo Mejia, left, and his attorney Louis Font, prepare to speak to reporters on May 19, 2004 in Fort Stewart, Georgia. Mejia was convicted in a military court of desertion. He sought to plead his case for conscientious objector status. (AP Photo/Stephen Morton)

are to be discharged from the military or reassigned to noncombatant duties.

Between 2002 and 2006, the Pentagon reported 425 requests for conscientious objector status, with 224 (53 percent) approved, covering both the Afghan War and the Iraq War. However, in September 2007, the U.S. Government Accountability Office acknowledged a potential underreporting of applicants. Meanwhile, a consortium of churches, veterans, and peace groups networked in the GI Rights Hotline has reported counseling thousands of soldiers who have experienced a crisis of conscience. Alleging that many conscientious objection claims are not represented in official figures because they never reach the Pentagon, the Center for Conscience and War has lobbied Congress for new legis-

lation that would streamline conscientious objector processing and recognize the "selective" objection encompassed by UN guidelines and many religious doctrines. At the same time, dissenting soldiers have continued to manifest objection to the wars in Afghanistan and Iraq in other ways.

Echoing similar actions by the GI Movement against the Vietnam War, these demonstrations of opposition to U.S. war policies are rooted in isolated acts of individual conscience. However, the current all-volunteer U.S. armed forces means that today's conscientious objectors are in an entirely different situation than those in the Vietnam War era, when the draft brought hundreds of thousands into the armed forces involuntarily. Because today's conscientious objectors volunteered to join the armed forces, implying their willingness at least at the time of enlistment to engage in combat, the Defense Department understandably carefully examines each petition for conscientious objector status today.

The first soldier to publicly oppose Operation Iraqi Freedom was Marine Reserve lance corporal Stephen Funk, who learned of the possibility of claiming conscientious objector status just before his unit was activated in February 2003, a month before the war began. After missing deployment to prepare his conscientious objection claim, Funk turned himself in and explained that he went public with his claim to allow others to realize that conscientious objector status was an option. Because of his unauthorized absence, Funk's conscientious objection claim was not processed, and he was sentenced to six months' imprisonment and a bad conduct discharge.

In the months that followed, as public criticism of the George W. Bush administration's justifications for the Iraq War intensified and American occupation policies drew international censure, more U.S. service members became disillusioned. By the beginning of 2006, according to a Zogby Poll, almost 30 percent of American troops in Iraq wanted the United States to withdraw immediately, and 72 percent believed that American forces should leave the country within a year. An *Army Times* poll conducted later that same year revealed that only 41 percent of soldiers believed the war should have occurred. Press reports have noted increased alcohol and drug abuse, and one out of three combat veterans has sought psychological counseling. Also, between 2002 and 2008, the U.S. Army suicide rate nearly doubled. Although other factors related to military service, such as more frequent overseas deployments, multiple combat tours, the pressures of family separations, etc., are more likely contributing factors in the rise in the negative statistics, opposition to the war should not be ruled out.

Meanwhile, roughly 150 members of the U.S. military have publicly refused to fight, resulting in criminal charges, imprisonment, and bad conduct discharges. Some of them were declared prisoners of conscience by the human rights organization Amnesty International. The more highly publicized cases include Staff Sergeant Camilo Mejia, an army squad leader who refused to return to Iraq from leave in 2003 and was sentenced to 12 months in prison; Kevin Benderman, an army sergeant and Iraq War veteran who resisted redeployment in 2005 and was sentenced to 15 months in prison; U.S. Navy petty officer 3rd Class Pablo Paredes, who abandoned ship in 2004 and was sentenced to 3 months' hard labor without confinement; and Texas Army National Guard specialist Katherine Jashinski, who after her conscientious objector claim was denied following 18 months of processing was court-martialed in 2006 for refusing weapons training in preparation for deployment to Afghanistan and was sentenced to 120 days of confinement. These cases unfolded amid the climate of a threefold increase, between 2002 and 2006, in the number of army soldiers court-martialed for desertion, defined by the military as being absent without leave (AWOL) for more than 30 days. Most deserters were to be serving in Iraq; desertion rates for those serving in Afghanistan have been considerably lower.

While tens of thousands of service members have gone AWOL since 2001, such absences range from as short as a few hours to as long as weeks and months. It is impossible to know for certain service members' individual reasons for being AWOL; however, some 200 have sought sanctuary in Canada, where more than three dozen have formally applied for political asylum. Refusing to consider the legality of the Iraq War, the sitting Conservative government refused to grant any of the AWOL Americans official refugee status. However, on June 3, 2008, the Canadian Parliament passed a nonbinding resolution asking the prime minister to allow conscientious objectors from wars not sanctioned by the UN to become Canadian residents. Canadian courts have stayed a number of threatened deportations.

Questions concerning the Iraq War's legality as well as the limited Defense Department definition of conscientious objection have also been highlighted in the prosecution of First Lieutenant Ehren Watada, a U.S. Army infantry officer who asserted in June 2006 that it was his "command responsibility" to refuse participation in "war crimes." In February 2007, a court-martial judge declared a mistrial, ruling that the legality of Watada's deployment orders was a "nonjusticiable political question." That October, the army's attempt at another court-martial was declared unconstitutional double jeopardy by a U.S. District Court, which ruled that Watada could not be tried on three of the five counts with which he was charged. At the end of 2008, Watada remained on active duty at Fort Lewis, Washington, as the Defense Department decided whether to appeal the case further or to try him on the two remaining counts of conduct unbecoming an officer.

The contested nature of active service members' First Amendment right to free speech provided the context for another high-profile development in military dissent. Knowing that soldiers are explicitly permitted by law to contact their congres-

sional representatives, in late 2006, U.S. Navy seaman Jonathan Hutto instigated an "Appeal for Redress," an Internet statement and organizing tool that by the end of 2008 had mobilized more than 2,200 service members, including some 100 field officers, to publicly declare, "As a patriotic American proud to serve the nation in uniform, I respectfully urge my political leaders in Congress to support the prompt withdrawal of all American military forces and bases from Iraq. Staying in Iraq will not work and is not worth the price. It is time for U.S. troops to come home."

Hutto has sought assistance from and has been supported by David Cortright, a Vietnam War veteran and author of *Soldiers in Revolt*, an account of military dissent during that war; Courage to Resist, a San Francisco–based coalition of activists that originated in community support mobilized during Lance Corporal Funk's court-martial in 2003; and Iraq Veterans against the War (IVAW), the 1,200-member organization eventually joined by most of today's military objectors.

Modeled after the influential Vietnam Veterans against the War (VVAW) group established in 1967, the IVAW was founded in 2004 at the annual convention of Veterans for Peace, a national peace group encompassing all veterans who have embraced nonviolence. Like the "Appeal for Redress," these organizations have capitalized on the credibility gained by their members having served their country in uniform to legitimate their antiwar message.

The point needs to be emphasized that the vast majority of the members of the all-volunteer U.S. Armed Forces (as of 2009, this represented 1.5 million active component personnel and 850,000 in the reserve components), regardless of how they might personally have felt about the Afghanistan War and the Iraq War, continued to perform their duties as they signed on to do. Despite several high-profile instances of war resistance and of military personnel claiming conscientious objector status, the impact of such actions has apparently not had an appreciable effect on armed forces recruiting or on reenlistment rates, both of which remain high.

The Obama administration had managed to withdraw virtually all American troops from Iraq by December 2011, ending that eight-year conflict, and with it any conscientious objection to it. By 2012, Obama was also making concrete plans to extricate the United States from Afghanistan, which may occur as early as 2015 or 2016. His administration has generally continued the policies of its predecessor vis-à-vis conscientious objection and military dissent.

Jeff R. Schutts

See also: Abu Ghraib; Enduring Freedom, Operation; Iraqi Freedom, Operation; September 11 Terrorist Trial Controversy; Weapons of Mass Destruction

Further Reading

Hutto, Jonathan W., Sr. *Antiwar Soldier: How to Dissent within the Ranks of the Military.* New York: Nation Books, 2008.

Iraq Veterans against the War and Aaron Glantz. *Winter Soldier Iraq and Afghanistan: Eyewitness Accounts of the Occupations.* Chicago: Haymarket Books, 2008.

Lauffer, Peter. *Mission Rejected: U.S. Soldiers Who Say No to Iraq.* White River Junction, VT: Chelsea Green, 2006.

Cost, Global War on Terror

From 2001 to 2011, the global war on terror, which includes the wars in Afghanistan, Iraq, and Pakistan, has cost the United States an estimated 225,000 lives and approximately $4 trillion in expenditures. Among the war dead are U.S. military personnel, civilians, and private contractors working under U.S. military authority. According to the Eisenhower Research Project, a nonpartisan initiative based at Brown University's Watson Institute for International Studies, the financial costs of the war on terror will include medical care and disability payments for current and future veterans.

The Eisenhower Research Project "Costs of War" project, which includes various experts from a variety of fields, ranging from economists, political scientists, to legal experts, estimates the human and financial costs of the U.S. military response to the 9/11 attacks from 2001 to the present. This project was also crucial in finding many of the conflict's hidden costs, among them interest on war debt and benefits for veterans. Moreover, foreign aid, in the form of reconstruction projects in Iraq and Afghanistan, is also a large part of the mounting expenses.

The Eisenhower Research Project "Costs of War" found that approximately 200,000 civilians have been killed as a result of the fighting at the hands of all parties in the conflicts in Afghanistan, Iraq, and Pakistan. Moreover, the increasing amount of money spent in fighting overseas conflicts will increase as well as the increasing amount of the interest-rate that will be paid on war-related debt and expenditures. This will impact future federal budgets as more money is allocated to account for these expenses over the next several decades, particularly for benefits for veterans. The costs for veterans' medical care and disability will continue to increase as more active military personnel are discharged and apply for benefits.

Abraham O. Mendoza

See also: Economic Impact of the September 11, 2001, Attacks; International Emergency Economic Powers Act; War Powers Act

Further Reading

Eisenhower Research Project, Brown University. "Estimated Cost of Post-9/11 Wars: 225,000 Lives, up to \$4 Trillion." http://news.brown.edu/pressreleases/2011/06/warcosts.

Bilmes, Linda J., and Joseph E. Stiglitz. *The Three Trillion Dollar War: The True Cost of the Iraq Conflict.* New York: W. W. Norton, 2008.

Counterinsurgency

Counterinsurgency is a warfare strategy employed to defeat an organized rebellion or revolutionary movement aimed at bringing down and replacing established governmental authority. Among the more confusing terms relating to the practice of warfare, the term "counterinsurgency" implies both the purpose of military operations and methods selected. U.S. interest in counterinsurgency soared in 2005 as it became increasingly apparent that an insurgency was gravely undermining the efforts of the United States and its allies to establish a new regime in Iraq after the 2003 Anglo-American–led invasion and occupation. A revived Taliban movement has also hindered U.S. progress in nation building in Afghanistan, and counterinsurgency tactics are being employed there as well.

Understanding the term "counterinsurgency" requires an appreciation of its logical opposite, insurgency. Counterinsurgency originated as a conceptual response to the spread of insurgencies, particularly as carried out by anticolonialist or communist movements during the Cold War from the late 1940s to the 1980s. Insurgents typically lacked key sources of power, such as financial wealth, a professional military, or advanced weaponry, that were available to established regimes or governments. Consequently, insurgents adopted asymmetric tactics and strategies that focused on avoidance of direct combat until such time as governmental power had been gravely weakened. Instead, skillful insurgents blended an array of methods including propaganda, attacks on public institutions and infrastructure, the creation of secret support networks, and use of unconventional or guerrilla combat tactics. By these means, insurgents could whittle away the strength of existing regimes or occupying powers while slowly increasing their own capabilities.

U.S. interest in counterinsurgency, sometimes referred to as counterrevolutionary warfare, grew during the Vietnam War. Efforts to defeat the Viet Cong guerrillas in South Vietnam were considered important but more often than not took a backseat to the conduct of conventional military operations against the People's Army of Vietnam (PAVN, North Vietnamese Army). With the American withdrawal from Vietnam in 1973, however, the U.S. military resumed its focus on conventional war, and the study of counterinsurgency by the U.S. Army waned. Even with the end of the Cold War in 1991, the U.S. military did not regard the study of counterinsurgency as equally important to the mastery of conventional combat.

To many, Operation Desert Storm in Iraq in 1991 justified the American focus on conventional combat. The Persian Gulf War provided a striking demonstration of U.S. military proficiency and technology. Indeed, American dominance was so compelling that it may have dissuaded potential opponents from attempting to challenge American might on any conventional battlefield. One result may have been to encourage adversaries to attack U.S. interests by asymmetric means, such as guerrilla insurgency tactics or terror. There was also a growing perception among enemies of the United States that American politicians and military leaders were extremely uncomfortable in situations in which they could not bring superior conventional military power to bear. The deaths of 18 U.S. Army soldiers on October 3–4, 1993, during a raid against a renegade warlord in Somalia may have been the exception that proved the rule. Largely a product of events in Somalia, Bill Clinton's casualty-averse posture of U.S. forces in subsequent peacekeeping missions in Haiti, Bosnia, and Kosovo during the 1990s tended to reinforce the view that Americans were reluctant to suffer any casualties in scenarios short of unconstrained conventional combat.

Very soon, the tools of counterinsurgency would prove most relevant in Afghanistan against surviving remnants of the Taliban that found sanctuary along the Pakistani frontier. One important measure taken was the creation and deployment of Provincial Reconstruction Teams (PRTs) beginning in 2003. These combined a small number of military specialists with representatives of various U.S. or other foreign governmental agencies possessing expertise in diplomacy, policing, agriculture, and other fields relevant to the process of fostering security and development. Found to be effective in Afghanistan in extending governmental reach to remote areas, the concept soon found application in Iraq as well.

In the meantime, the invasion of Iraq in March 2003, while initially marking an-

other triumph of conventional operations, did not result in a smooth transition to a stable civilian government. Indeed, coalition forces in Iraq soon faced a formidable counterinsurgency challenge for which neither military nor civilian officials had fully prepared. In fact, many critics maintain that the early failure to establish public order, restore services, and identify local partners provided the insurgency, which Iraqis term "the resistance," with an interval of chaos that enabled it to organize and grow. Since Iraqi politics had consistently shown wave after wave of resistance, purges, and new coups, such a challenge could reasonably have been expected. Sectarian leaders and their militias began to assert influence, and Al-Qaeda fighters infiltrated key provinces in anticipation of a new struggle to come.

By 2005, spreading ethnic and religious violence in Iraq resulted in the deaths of many civilians as well as local governmental and security personnel. Suicide bombings as well as the remote detonation of improvised explosive devices (IEDs) became signature tactics of the Iraqi insurgency. Furthermore, repeated attacks on United Nations (UN) personnel and foreign relief workers caused a virtual suspension of outside aid to the Iraqi people.

Recognition of the need to focus on counterinsurgency methods led to a vitally significant effort to publish a military doctrinal manual on the subject. An initial indicator of the official shift in U.S. military thinking was the release of Department of Defense Directive 3000-05 on November 28, 2005, which specifically acknowledged responsibility for planning and carrying out so-called support and stability operations essential to any counterinsurgency campaign. Under the leadership of Lieutenant General David Petraeus during his tenure as the commander of the Combined Arms Center and commandant of the U.S. Army Command and General Staff College at Fort Leavenworth, Kansas, in 2006–2007, a team of writers and practitioners with experience in Iraq and Afghanistan undertook a crash project to draft, revise, and publish the new manual.

In his opening address to the Combat Studies Institute Military History Symposium on August 8, 2006, Petraeus set forth several points of emphasis of the soon-to-be-published U.S. Army Field Manual 3-24 (also known as U.S. Marine Warfighting Publication No. 3-33.5), titled *Counterinsurgency*. Asserting that T. E. Lawrence (of Arabia) had figured out the essentials of counterinsurgency during World War I, Petraeus contended that any prospect of success depended upon identifying capable local leaders, providing them necessary assistance without doing the hard work for them, fostering the development of public institutions, forming a partnership with existing security forces, and maintaining a flexible and patient outlook. In other words, counterinsurgency would require far more of military leaders than the performance of traditional and familiar combat tasks. Petraeus himself had practiced these principles in Iraq, where in late 2004 he served as the first commander of the Multi-National Security Transition Command—Iraq, which focused on the training of local personnel to become civilian and military leaders in Iraq.

Officially released in December 2006, *Counterinsurgency* attracted great attention in the press and conveyed the impression that the military was not stuck in an outmoded mind-set. Rather, U.S. Army and U.S. Marine Corps leaders on the ground in Afghanistan and Iraq became increasingly adaptive and creative in the search for improved solutions to the problem of combating insurgency where nation building was still very much in progress. *Counterinsurgency* devoted a majority of its eight chapters and five appendices to tasks other than war fighting. Lengthy sections also related to ethics, civilian and military cooperation, cultural analysis, linguistic support, the law of war, and ethical considerations.

Of course, the U.S. Army and the U.S. Marine Corps had not ignored the principles of counterinsurgency before the new doctrine was published. However, publication signaled to the American public and the U.S. Congress that the military was wholly committed to the implementation of counterinsurgency principles. Since the end of 2007, the implementation of this new counterinsurgency doctrine began to bear fruit, as there was a sizable diminution in violence in most parts of Iraq beginning in the fourth quarter of the year. This was also due to the Bush administration's troop surge, which also began in 2007.

In January 2007, President George W. Bush increased the number of American troops in Iraq to provide security to Baghdad and Al Anbar Province. Bush ordered the deployment of more than 20,000 soldiers to Iraq—five additional brigades—and sent the majority of them into Baghdad. He also extended the tour of most of the Army troops, and some of the marines, in the country. In 2008, according to most polls, the majority of Americans thought the troop increase was effective and successful in stabilizing the war in Iraq. After being elected president in November 2008, Obama reluctantly continued the surge until the military agreed that the situation had been turned around.

By 2010, the situation in Iraq had been substantially stabilized, allowing the incoming Obama administration to begin a drawdown of troops from that country, which was completed in December 2011. Unfortunately, however, the Iraqi government faced a resurgence of sectarian and terroristic violence during 2013, continuing into 2014. That has threatened to plunge the country into political crisis and civil war.

The situation in Afghanistan has, however, continued to deteriorate since 2009. The Taliban- and Al-Qaeda–led insurgency compelled Obama to reluctantly approve a troop surge to that nation comprised of 33,000 additional soldiers and Marines in December 2009. The success of the surge was at best mixed, but as promised, Obama withdrew those forces from Afghanistan by September 2012. There were, however, more than 60,000 troops remaining in Afghanistan at the end of 2012. The White House remained largely silent about the surge, clearly an indication that it was not terribly successful.

The surge did not work for several reasons. First, the Afghan government under Hamid Karzai never truly supported the initiative, and if anything it became less cooperative with the United States' strategy as the surge unfolded. Second, Pakistan, where many insurgents were hiding, did not crack down on insurgent strongholds along the Afghan frontier. Third, the Afghan army was neither able nor willing to control areas that had been cleared of insurgents by U.S. forces. Fourth, the surge should have been larger, and scheduled for a longer lifespan, something that the Obama administration was unwilling to do. The situation in Afghanistan remains uncertain and shaky, and the Karzai regime has done little to stabilize the country. In November 2013, the Americans and Afghans agreed on a bilateral security pact

that would allow a gradual drawdown of American troops, but would give to the United States the right to determine the exact number of forces that would remain in Afghanistan for some unspecified period of time. These troops would continue to train Afghan army and security forces and would participate in anti-terror and counterinsurgency operations against terrorist groups, including Al-Qaeda.

Robert F. Baumann

See also: Al-Qaeda; Al-Qaeda in Iraq; Enduring Freedom, Operation; Improvised Explosive Devices; Iraqi Freedom, Operation; Iraqi Insurgency; Petraeus, David Howell; Somalia, International Intervention; Taliban

Further Reading

Keegan, John. *The Iraq War: The Military Offensive, from Victory in 21 Days to the Insurgent Aftermath*. New York: Vintage, 2005.

Kitson, Frank. *Low Intensity Operations: Subversion, Insurgency and Peacekeeping*. London: Faber and Faber, 1971.

Nagl, John A. *Learning to Eat Soup with a Knife: Counterinsurgency Lessons from Malaya and Vietnam*. Chicago: University of Chicago Press, 2005.

Counterterrorism Center

In 1985, the Central Intelligence Agency (CIA) decided to create a new section to fight international terrorism. This decision came shortly after intelligence failures in Lebanon led to the deaths of 241 U.S. marines and the kidnapping and killing of CIA section chief William Buckley. President Ronald Reagan placed pressure on then director of the CIA William J. Casey to do something about terrorism. Casey approached Duane R. "Dewey"

Clarridge, a respected veteran field officer, to make a recommendation for a way that the CIA could most effectively fight terrorism. Clarridge recommended an interdisciplinary center in the CIA that had an international reach and could utilize all the capabilities of the CIA. Part of its mission was to launch covert action against known terrorists, so the Special Operations Group (SOG) was transferred to the Counterterrorism Center. It was to be a section staffed by 100 persons with representation from the Federal Bureau of Investigation (FBI). Casey accepted Clarridge's recommendation and appointed him as its head. Instead of the original plan for a staff of 100, Casey authorized it at a staffing of 250. The Counterterrorism Center became operational in February 1986.

Clarridge's first target as head of the Counterterrorism Center was the Abu Nidal Organization (ANO). In the 1970s and 1980s, the ANO, named after its leader, was the most violent terrorist group in operation and had become the number one terrorist threat. The CIA was able to recruit a source within ANO, and this source provided inside information. Much of this information was published in a State Department publication entitled *The Abu Nidal Handbook*. After this information became public, Abu Nidal became so concerned about penetration of his organization that he ordered the execution of a large number of his followers in Libya. This purge ended the effectiveness of the ANO.

The next target was Hezbollah (Party of God) in Lebanon. Hezbollah, a Shiite terrorist organization, had killed the 241 marines in Beirut and had captured a number of Western hostages. Among its victims was William Buckley, the CIA section chief in Lebanon, who died from harsh treatment. This campaign against Hezbollah was less successful because it proved impossible to find an agent able to penetrate Hezbollah's leadership. Efforts to launch covert operations were also hampered by a lack of intelligence and the reluctance of the American military to lend support.

Clarridge became frustrated by the lack of support for the Counterterrorism Center. His role in the Iran-Contra scandal also led his superiors in the CIA to question his judgment, particularly after his illness. Clarridge maintained that Oliver North had misled him regarding the exchange of hostages from Iran for weapons to be used by the Contras to fight against the Sandinista government in Nicaragua. Clarridge's goal had been to make the center a proactive force against terrorism. Instead, he found that his boss, CIA director William Webster, who had assumed control of the CIA on May 26, 1987, was averse to risk. This lack of support led Clarridge to leave the Counterterrorism Center later in 1987. In June 1988, he was forced to resign from the CIA by Webster.

Clarridge's successor, Fred Turco, picked the next target for the Counterterrorism Center, and it was Peru's Shining Path. Abimael Guzmán, a philosophy professor, had founded the Maoist terrorist group in 1970, and it had opened a war against the Peruvian government. The Counterterrorism Center provided the Peruvian police with sophisticated electronic surveillance equipment and training that enabled them to capture Guzmán in a Lima suburb in September 1992. They learned that Guzmán had a special diet and smoked a particular brand of tobacco. After briefing the Peruvian authorities on these facts, Peruvian police identified the stores that handled these items. By searching garbage, it was established where Guzmán was staying.

The Counterterrorism Center's activities assumed more importance in 1993. By this time the new head of the Counterterrorism Center was Winston Wiley, who had assumed control in November 1992. Two events mobilized this activity. First was the murder of two CIA employees in Langley by Mir Amal Kasi on January 25, 1993. Believing the CIA responsible for countless Muslim deaths, Kasi opened fire with an AK-47 assault rifle just outside of CIA headquarters, killing the employees. Kasi was from Baluchistan, and he managed to escape back to Pakistan, where he promptly disappeared. A special CIA unit was set up to locate and capture him. Kasi was finally captured on June 15, 1997.

An even bigger task was the investigation of the conspiracy behind the World Trade Center bombing on February 23, 1993. While the domestic investigation was left up to the FBI, the Counterterrorism Center established a subunit to gather intelligence about the bombing. Information was slow to surface, and at first the Counterterrorism Center suspected that it had been a state-sponsored terrorist operation with Iraq, Libya, and Iran as the prime suspects. Slowly the intelligence analysts came to realize that it was an independent operation led by Ramzi Yousef. In a combined CIA/FBI operation Yousef was captured in Islamabad on February 7, 1995.

The Counterterrorism Center continued to select terrorist groups to fight against. First under Geoff O'Connell and then under J. Cofer Black, the Counterterrorism Center planned counterterrorist operations. Black's target was Osama bin Laden and Al-Qaeda. He was also able to count on an expanded Counterterrorism Center. In 1986, the center had 20 analysts, but by early 2001 it had 340 people, of which more than a dozen were FBI agents. Despite the additions, the staffing of the Counterterrorism Center was too low to handle the volume of information flowing into it. Not surprisingly, considering the staffing, the leaders and the staff of the Counterterrorism Center were caught unawares on September 11, 2001.

American pressure on Sudan led bin Laden to move from Sudan to Afghanistan. Bin Laden, his family, and their retainers boarded an aircraft on May 18, 1996, for the trip. The staff of the Counterterrorism Center thought that this presented a golden opportunity to capture bin Laden in transit. A proposal to do so was given to President Bill Clinton, but it never received presidential approval. Members of the Counterterrorism Center were furious over this lost opportunity.

Throughout the late 1990s the analysts in the Counterterrorism Center were monitoring bin Laden's activities from sources within Afghanistan. The problem was that bin Laden was constantly moving, so that tracking him was almost impossible. Bin Laden was never in one place long enough to either capture or kill him. There was also an ongoing debate in the Clinton administration that was never resolved on whether it was legal to assassinate bin Laden. Attorney General Janet Reno made it plain to the head of the CIA, George Tenet, and then head of the Counterterrorism Center Geoff O'Connell that any attempt to kill bin Laden was illegal. All schemes involved capturing bin Laden first and killing him only in self-defense.

Another problem was the issue of collateral damage in an attack on bin Laden. Isolating bin Laden from civilians was almost impossible. Members of the

Counterterrorism Center wanted to proceed with covert action that might lead to collateral damage regardless of the consequences. They considered bin Laden too dangerous to the United States to live.

In the middle of the debate over bin Laden, the destroyer USS *Cole* was attacked in the harbor in Aden, Yemen, on October 12, 2000. A small boat filled with explosives blew up alongside the *Cole*, killing 19 American sailors and wounding scores more. This incident shocked the analysts in the Counterterrorism Center because there had been no intelligence indicating that something like this was going to happen. It took a while for the analysts to find the evidence connecting this attack with Al-Qaeda, but the evidence was found. Counterterrorism Center staffers wanted retaliation, but the American military was reluctant to undertake any operations and so advised the White House. To the leadership of the Counterterrorism Center the only option was to support the Afghan leader General Ahmad Shah Massoud and his war against the Taliban. But the Clinton administration was reluctant to back Massoud and forbade the Counterterrorism Center from increasing aid. The Clinton administration left office with the problem of bin Laden and Al-Qaeda unresolved.

The analysts of the Counterterrorism Center continued to be frustrated by the inaction of the Bush administration toward terrorism. Reports indicated increased activity by Al-Qaeda, but the problem was that there was no evidence of where or what kind of operation it was planning. A series of warnings came out of the Counterterrorism Center that Tenet took to President George W. Bush and other prominent administration figures. These warnings coincided with similar warnings from the FBI. Some of these warning even made the case

that Al-Qaeda operatives might carry out an operation in the United States. What weakened these frequent warnings was the lack of specific details. The Bush administration listened to the warnings, noted the lack of specifics, and took no action. President Bush wanted more specific intelligence before he would authorize any action.

Tenet ordered the CIA to round up suspected Al-Qaeda members to try to find information on what Al-Qaeda was planning. This tactic had two purposes: to gather intelligence and to delay Al-Qaeda missions. Several Al-Qaeda plots were uncovered, and a massive amount of intelligence material arrived at the Counterterrorism Center. The problem was that there were not enough translators and analysts to handle this mass of material. Frustration was high among the intelligence analysts because they were fearful that important information was being overlooked. In mid-July, Tenet ordered the Counterterrorism Center analysts to search back in its files and its current information on bin Laden's major plots. He was suspicious that bin Laden might be targeting the United States for a terrorism mission. Tenet took the information the Counterterrorism Center had uncovered and presented the report "Bin Laden Determined to Strike in United States" to President Bush at his Crawford, Texas, ranch on August 6, 2001. In early September, the Bush administration began to consider a plan to attack terrorism, especially bin Laden and Al-Qaeda, but there was no sense of haste.

After September 11, resources flowed into the Counterterrorism Center. By the summer of 2002, George Tenet had expanded its staff to 1,500. A staff of this size was able to handle 2,500 classified electronic communications a day, and it could produce 500 terrorist reports a month.

The Counterterrorism Center has also been given the responsibility for the interrogations of important Al-Qaeda prisoners. A series of secret interrogation centers, which have all been closed, were established in friendly countries. Top Al-Qaeda prisoners have been kept at an interrogation center, Bright Lights, the location of which even some analysts in the Counterterrorism Center had not been informed. The location, confirmed in the media on December 8, 2011, was in Bucharest, Romania. There have also been reports of CIA interrogators using questionable interrogation techniques, so the FBI wants nothing to do with these interrogations. Several news reports confirmed this information, and CIA agents were increasingly uncomfortable regarding their legal position over these interrogations. This nervousness about interrogation techniques led to controversy in December 2007, when news surfaced that the secret tapes of CIA interrogations had been destroyed in 2005. This action was defended by the head of the CIA, Michael V. Hayden. Although Bush and his successor, Barack Obama, have denied allegations that the CIA employs torture during its interrogations, many believe that the practice continues unabated. The Counterterrorism Center continues it work in Afghanistan and other areas of the world in which terroristic activity is a concern, but due to the extremely clandestine nature of its operations, it has rarely become a subject of media or press reporting.

Stephen E. Atkins

See also: Alec Station; Bin Laden, Osama; Bush Administration; Central Intelligence Agency; Clinton Administration; Coercive Interrogation Techniques; Counterterrorism Strategy; Rendition; Tenet, George; Terrorism

Further Reading

Coll, Steve. *Ghost Wars: The Secret History of the CIA, Afghanistan, and Bin Laden, from the Soviet Invasion to September 10, 2001.* New York: Penguin, 2004.

Kessler, Ronald. *The CIA at War: Inside the Secret Campaign against Terror.* New York: St. Martin's Griffin, 2003.

Miller, John, Michael Stone, and Chris Mitchell. *The Cell: Inside the 9/11 Plot and Why the FBI and CIA Failed to Stop It.* New York: Hyperion, 2002.

Naftali, Timothy. *Blind Spot: The Secret History of American Counterterrorism.* New York: Basic Books, 2005.

Posner, Gerald. *Why America Slept: The Failure to Prevent 9/11.* New York: Ballantine, 2003.

Risen, James. *State of War: The Secret History of the CIA and the Bush Administration.* New York: Free Press, 2006.

Tenet, George, and Bill Harlow. *At the Center of the Storm: My Years at the CIA.* New York: HarperCollins, 2007.

Counterterrorism Strategy

A general approach toward the struggle against terrorism that involves the selection, distribution, and application of all resources and means available to achieve the desired aims (i.e., the prevention and/or eradication of terrorism). A successful counterterrorism strategy must target the vital dimensions of terrorism; address its current and prospective trends; reflect its rapidly changing nature, complexity, and flexibility; and employ a wide array of military, political, economic, social, ideological, cultural, law enforcement, and other means in often intermingled offensive and defensive efforts.

Terrorist activity, especially from Islamic extremists based in the Middle East, has in recent years demonstrated significantly

A soldier from the 422nd Civil Affairs Battalion exchanges thumbs up with a child in a village near Najaf, Iraq, on April 2, 2003. The army unit was in the town to provide humanitarian assistance as part of Operation Iraqi Freedom. (U.S. Army)

increasing diversity and complexity. There is a wide range of participants with a diverse set of motivations, goals, structures, and strategies. Despite the destruction of the Al-Qaeda sanctuaries in Afghanistan after the September 11, 2001, terror attacks, this global terrorist clearinghouse network continues to operate and, utilizing global information technology, continues to recruit and train supporters, share experiences, coordinate activities of various widely dispersed terrorist cells, and advance its ideological and strategic goals. These include the eradication of Western influence and presence in the region and the overthrow of existing regimes that accommodate the Western powers.

More structured than Al-Qaeda, Hezbollah, headquartered in Lebanon, retains some potential for regional and even overseas terrorist activity but currently is concentrating its efforts on securing additional political influence within Lebanon and is not engaging in violence within Lebanon against Lebanese. The Palestinian terrorist organization Islamic Jihad has continued sporadic terrorist activities, mainly within the framework of the Israeli-Palestinian confrontation. Syria and Iran view support for organizations such as Hamas and Hezbollah as a means to promote their own national interests and ambitions in the region.

The successful expansion of transnational terrorism, according to American analysis under President George W. Bush, owes much to the emergence of so-called failed states such as Afghanistan, where such terrorism was able to prosper, virtually unchecked, due to the combination of political and social disintegration, fierce civil strife, and a lack of interest and support from the international community. The concept of a failed state is, however, disputed in the region, where underdevelopment and incomplete political control are commonplace. According to the Western ideas about transnational terrorists, the latter use the paramount anarchy in the failed states as well as weak governmental control over some portions of territory to obtain safe haven and to set up their training camps and communication centers, exploiting the remains of local infrastructure. In the late 1990s, Al-Qaeda managed to secure a close alliance with the Taliban in Afghanistan. The Taliban, along with Al-Qaeda, after being driven from Afghanistan in late 2001, has managed to reestablish itself in a number of areas, including the remote Afghanistan Pakistan border, and the long-term prospects of a stable, insurgent-free Afghanistan had faded considerably by 2010.

Any effective counterterrorism strategy must also take into account new developments in strategy and tactics of the terrorist actors. The terrorists have constantly tried to acquire more lethal weapons. This is particularly true with respect to weapons of mass destruction (WMDs). Until 2001, Al-Qaeda, using sanctuaries in Afghanistan, planned to launch chemical or biological attacks on U.S. and European targets. In addition to the continuous pursuit of more deadly weapons, the terrorists persistently employ suicide bombings to increase the lethality of their attacks.

Terrorist leaders have also demonstrated their ability to adjust to changing conditions. The decentralized, loose organizational structure of Al-Qaeda allowed it to continue to operate even after the loss of Afghanistan in 2001. This has been amply demonstrated in its terrorist attacks in Yemen, Tunisia, Saudi Arabia, Jordan, and Kuwait as well as in Istanbul, Madrid, and London. The U.S. government had argued that Al-Qaeda operated a network that recruited and operated in the Muslim communities of Britain, Spain, France, Germany, Italy, Spain, the Netherlands, and Belgium. Current thinking, however, sees Al-Qaeda more as an inspiration to and clearinghouse for local autonomous groups. By active participation in the Iraqi insurgency after 2003, the terrorist networks acquired experience in urban warfare and enhanced their skills in ambush tactics, assassinations, and kidnappings.

The profound transformation in both the scale and the complexity of operations that terrorists could undertake allowed powerful, well-organized, and devoted groups and associations as well as smaller groups to evade state powers and to obtain global-reach capability. These terrorists are able to endanger the international security profoundly. Because the terrorist challenge amounts to a new form of warfare, successful counterterrorism strategy must constantly realign itself with the developments of the threats. Conventional military force has played a strong role in the struggle against alleged terrorism, as the long history of Israeli military campaigns against the Palestine Liberation Organization (PLO), the Israeli-Hezbollah War of 2006, and the Gaza War of 2009 demonstrate. Israel's strategy of heavy punishment of a neighboring state for permitting and/or abetting terrorism while inflicting disproportionate loss of life and property damage does not seem to have ended terrorist activity, which its proponents regard as rightful and necessary resistance, and has led to serious criticism of the Jewish state, even from its traditional allies.

Special operations forces play an important role in the struggle against terrorism.

While capable of a global reach, military operations against terrorists need to be pinpointed and limited in scale to avoid civilian and collateral damage. This is particularly important because of the inability or reluctance of particular governments to attack the terrorist leadership and cells directly. Special operations transcend national boundaries and reflect the transnational character of the struggle against terrorism. The Israeli experience of deep-penetration commando raids and targeted assassinations of terrorist leaders reveals the ability of special operations to undermine the morale and disrupt activities of terrorist organizations and to violate state sovereignty as well as the terms of truces concluded with the enemy, although there are limits to what special operations can accomplish. Primarily, these special operations have angered the local population, making the resistance, or terrorism, that much more difficult to uproot.

Conventional military approaches retain their importance in dealing with state-sponsored terrorism, namely to wage wars against nations and achieve regime change, surely denying safe haven for the terrorists. At the same time, as the U.S.-led campaigns in Afghanistan after 2001 and Iraq after 2003 demonstrated, even victorious conventional campaigns can be complicated by ensuing insurgencies, which demand much greater flexibility on the part of the military. Here again, special operations come into play.

While the achievement of a decisive military victory remains elusive because of the dispersed and decentralized organizational structure of modern terrorism, and while the use of military means resembles an endless war of attrition, the readiness to apply overwhelming and destructive military force can work to some extent. As recent changes in the policies of the Palestinian National Authority (PNA) and Libya have suggested, providing government bodies with enticements to stop terrorist activities can also work to curb terrorist activity. These include economic, territorial, and governing incentives.

Diplomacy is another essential tool in fighting terrorism. International cooperation is vital in collecting information on terrorist cells, which includes the tracking and disrupting of financial transactions, recruitment, and propaganda activities of the terrorists. It is also of paramount importance in seeking to isolate regimes that sponsor terrorism.

Intelligence gathering is essential in any successful counterterrorist strategy. Simply gathering the information is not sufficient; it must be properly disseminated and coordinated within government agencies. The failure of the U.S. intelligence community to provide early warning about the September 11 terrorist attacks demonstrates this all too clearly.

Defensive efforts within the framework of counterterrorism strategy focus predominantly on homeland security and encompass enhanced border security. This includes monitoring and protecting likely terrorist targets (transportation, communication systems, and other elements of infrastructure as well as high-profile objects and places of significant concentration of populations) using intelligence, law enforcement, and military means. While Israel over the years has dealt with existential threats by developing comprehensive, integrated, and highly effective systems of territorial defense, the United States and European countries remain vulnerable to terrorist attacks because of porous borders and/or the ability of the Islamic terrorists to strike from inside, mobilizing militants from the Muslim diaspora, particularly in Western Europe. While the Western democracies' domestic counterterrorism strategies have improved vastly since September 11, 2001, they still remain deficient compared to those of Israel.

Comprehensive and multifaceted counterterrorism strategies must also involve political efforts to mobilize domestic support, social and cultural efforts to resist extremist propaganda efforts, and a determination to resolve problems and issues that terrorists often use for their own advantage. This is perhaps the most challenging aspect of any successful counterterrorism strategy. Political activities should include the resolution of the regional disputes, especially the Israeli-Palestinian issue; the advancement of economic development; addressing economic inequality and poverty; the promotion of democracy; high-quality governance; and the rule of law.

Peter J. Rainow

See also: Al-Qaeda; Central Intelligence Agency; Democratization and the Global War on Terror; Global War on Terror; Martyrdom; Narcoterrorism; Taliban; Terrorism

Further Reading

Berntsen, Garry. *Human Intelligence, Counterterrorism, and National Leadership: A Practical Guide.* Washington, DC: Potomac Books, 2008.

Forrest, James J. F. *Countering Terrorism and Insurgency in the 21st Century.* 3 vols. Westport, CT: Praeger Security International, 2007.

Freedman, George. *America's Secret War: Inside the Worldwide Struggle between America and Its Enemies.* New York: Broadway Books, 2004.

Guiora, Amos N. *Global Perspectives on Counterterrorism.* New York: Aspen Publishers, 2007.

Rubin, Barry, and Judith Colp Rubin, eds. *Anti-American Terrorism and the Middle East.* New York: Oxford University Press, 2002.

Cultural Imperialism, U.S.

The term cultural imperialism refers to the process of imposing cultural values onto another culture or entity, often for the purposes of assimilation and political domination or to cultivate long-term economic ties. It is also seen in policies that assume that the cultural values of the dominant country are the norm, while those of another culture are deviant, traditional, or less desirable. The ambiguity in defining this term in relation to the Middle East stems from the highly politicized attitudes of the West toward the Middle East, coupled with an almost total ignorance of the region's cultures. A similar Middle Eastern lack of sustained contact with and knowledge of the United States and distrust of its political motives in the region exists, as well as a long-standing embrace and defense of traditionalism.

Imperialism implies the extension of power over another entity for exploitative purposes. Typically, this term is used in reference to empires, colonies, nations, and states. Culture generally refers to patterns of human activities and symbolic expressions. So, while imperialism takes the forms of military hostilities, political dominance, or economic leverage, cultural imperialism is a more subtle process achieved mainly through symbolism, language, education, and meaning via consumer products, civil institutions, and the media.

Since at least the turn of the 20th century, some have labeled the United States a cultural hegemon that practices the transmittal of cultural imperialism through both government-sponsored means as well as private enterprise. Indeed, the concept of "American exceptionalism," the idea that the U.S. democratic political system represents not only the best of all systems but should stand as an example, a "shining city on a hill" for other countries to emulate, dates back to the founding of the republic. Much of this American attitude was embodied in President Woodrow Wilson's Fourteen Points, his plan to remake the post–World War I world by calling for self-determination of peoples and representative institutions. Nationalists throughout the Middle East embraced Wilson's program. At the same time, they saw no need to give up their own cultures.

Most Middle Eastern populations, while they had had little contact with Americans, had experienced extensive cultural imperialism accompanied by political manipulation at the hands of French, British, Italian, and other European nations. Thus, in the case of Egypt, everything that was native Egyptian, or *baladi*, was degraded, whereas that which was foreign, of Turko-Circassian origin or Levantine, French, or British, was prized. Those who embraced the occupying foreigners and their cultures secured special legal and economic privileges through the capitulatory treaties.

The impact of Western cultural influences in the Middle East accelerated rapidly after World War II with the advent of modern communication and transportation technologies that figuratively shrunk the world. The sheer size and dominance of the U.S. economy in the decades after World War II ensured that American cultural values would spill into all corners of the globe, mainly through the media and consumerism. In the Middle East, as in other parts of the Third World, this influence mostly impacted the upper elites, but it also coincided with new governmental policies and national pride in indigenous language, customs, traditions, and the arts. Many countries in the region sought to overcome disadvantageous balances of trade, which accompanied colonial suppression of native industries. Many people saw and wanted American products and tried to buy them whenever possible. However, these came with heavy tariffs, as certain governments, such as Syria, or Egypt until 1974, applied protective policies so as to bolster indigenous industries and agricultural products. Western foods and customs of eating more protein foods, such as red meat and chicken, often displaced local consumption patterns as Western-style one-stop supermarkets replaced traditional markets.

As far as social culture was concerned, the worlds of the Middle East and United States and other Western nations were at polar opposites. Many in the Middle East did not understand or wish to replicate American individualism and societal independence, in which people live at great distances from their relatives, may marry or not as they choose, have relationships outside of marriage without censure, and are not expected to care for their parents in old age.

Many young people in the Middle East, however, embraced American popular culture, products, and business methods. In a number of countries, the United States Information Service offered English classes and general programs about the United States and American culture, which were very popular. At the same time, however, Arab populations were in general critical of U.S. Middle East foreign policy that appeared to offer unconditional support to Israel or that, even though principally intended to counter Soviet influence in the region during the Cold War, seemed intended to secure American dominance in the region.

In the 1970s, the rise of more militant Islamist movements and groups coincided with economic changes that saw a greater influx of imported consumer goods, such as cars and electronic items, from the West, which not all could afford. Conservative and new Islamist groups were specifically critical of the way their nations' elites and youth aped Western styles and overspent to acquire the latest products. Many were highly suspicious of U.S. motives and saw American culture as antithetical to their own basic values.

This theme was the subject of a book in prerevolutionary Iran by Jalal-e Ahmad, which identified *gharbzadeghi*, or "Westoxification," as a primary problem. Islamists elsewhere complained of women dressing in Western styles, and Islamic businesses and banks responded to consumers' desire to spend where they would not be contributing to usury.

U.S. cultural imperialism in the Middle East has been most evident in political campaigns and efforts to influence Islamic beliefs and societies since both the September 11, 2001 (or 9/11) terrorist attacks against America and the commencement of the Iraq War of 2003. It has manifested itself in a battle "to win the hearts and minds" of the Muslim world, specifically in Iraq and Afghanistan, but also to pressure the broader Islamic world to refrain from and reject militant Islamic policies. In this, the so-called global war on terror was used as a vehicle for promoting American culture in the region that had given birth to the 9/11 terrorists. The basic logic of U.S. cultural imperialism suggested that if

American values could be brought to bear in radical Islamic societies, then potential terrorists would not hate America.

The official campaigns that involved winning "hearts and minds" claimed that the United States invaded Iraq in 2003 to overthrow an evil dictator and to establish democracy there. However, it was clear to most people in the Middle East that this was a war of choice, waged for other reasons, and many believed that securing Iraq's oil industry was a primary reason.

Americans had promoted democracy, although not its attendant cultural aspects, in a region historically dominated by authoritarian rulers and repressive regimes. However, in the case of key allies, U.S. foreign policy in the region had often downplayed democratization in favor of stability. Thus the United States had not promoted democracy in Saudi Arabia, nor did it insist that the Shah of Iran democratize or that the Egyptian and Syrian governments do so.

The Middle East was bombarded in the years following 2001 with Western critiques of its culture and deeply held religious beliefs. Such messages of cultural superiority were ill-timed, coming as they did after decades of programs aimed to build pride in national and religious identity.

Various U.S. organizations engaged in "information warfare," "information campaigns," or "information operations," and understood that such programs could be the strongest weapons in the global war on terror. The processes of this cultural imperialism are manifested primarily through media outlets, with the basic goal of the United States being to expunge the enemy's civil and governmental media and replace it with its own. For example, Iraqi radio and television stations were one of the first U.S. targets at the beginning of the March 2003 invasion. Iraqis laughed at many of these programs because they had extensive experience with official propaganda under Hussein's regime. The bright side was a mushrooming of many smaller news publications, even though many have been censored.

There were various tangible applications of cultural imperialism by several branches of the U.S. government. The Public Diplomacy and Public Affairs Office conceived of promoting positive images of the United States to the Arab/Muslim world after 9/11. The Office of Global Communications was also created immediately after 9/11 by the White House to synchronize official opinion among various organizations like the Central Intelligence Agency (CIA), the Department of Defense, and the State Department. The Advertising Council of America, a World War II creation, formulated positive television advertisements for the White House. As per military operations, press agencies called "Coalition Information Centers" were created in November 2001 by the U.S. government to ensure that official opinions were aired during Operation Enduring Freedom in Afghanistan.

During the Iraq War, coalition air forces dropped leaflets with the intention of warning civilians of upcoming military dangers or to threaten Iraqi military forces of the dire consequences of resisting. The U.S. Department of Defense converted all Iraqi television stations into the al-Iraqiyya Network, while the State Department created a satellite and cable network, known as 911, for promoting American-friendly programming. Many other organizations also performed information operations funded annually by the federal government.

A more extensive example of an American information operation can be seen through Radio Sawa (sawa meaning "together"). This station broadcasts in FM and medium-wave frequencies, day and night, to Middle Eastern and North African countries. It replaced the Voice of America in the region, which was never as popular as the BBC radio service. It took advantage of new rules that permitted establishment of private FM radio stations; in the past, all were state controlled. Syria and Saudi Arabia have not yet liberalized their radio station practices.

Listeners can also tune in to Radio Sawa via the Internet. Its stations are located in Washington, D.C., and Dubai, United Arab Emirates (UAE). In addition, Radio Sawa has several news centers in the region. The broadcast language is Arabic, and the content consists of information and entertainment programs friendly to American culture. It broadcasts a strange mix of Arabic, American, and Spanish-language music. It is a service of U.S. International Broadcasting, which is organized, managed, and funded by the Broadcasting Board of Governors, an agency of the State Department under supervision of the U.S. Congress. The station is meant to counterbalance the frequently anti-American Arabic news organizations. However, its impact is minimal in much of the region, where, like the decidedly unpopular American-created Alhurra (al-Hurra) television satellite channel, it is regarded as a propaganda outlet. Far more popular than Radio Sawa are many smaller radio stations, some of which focus on Arabic musical heritage and now broadcast hard-to-find recordings, more popular types of music, or controversial news programs.

Despite American efforts, positive Arab sentiments toward the United States decreased with exposure to information warfare. Prior to 9/11, the Arab world was already resentful of American financial and moral support of Israel. However, immediately after 9/11, most moderate Arabs expressed genuine sympathy for American suffering and support for the global war on terror. This did not last long, however, as antipathy toward the United States skyrocketed in the wake of the 2003 Iraq War and the occupation and pacification campaign there. In the absence of a United Nations (UN) resolution calling for armed intervention in Iraq, many in the Arab world viewed the U.S.-led war as illegal, and the mere existence of Iraq's large oil reserves created skepticism toward the motives behind the American-led invasion amid U.S. calls for democracy and freedom. When no weapons of mass destruction (WMDs) were discovered in Iraq, many Muslims became even more cynical of U.S. motives. In Iraq, impatience with the continuing presence of American troops also served to disillusion many who initially welcomed the action.

Many Arabs feared that the U.S. attempt to shape Iraq into a democracy would merely be the opening step in a U.S. effort to transform the entire region. Indeed, some U.S. officials, such as neoconservative Paul Wolfowitz, had long asserted this to be a U.S. objective. People in the region do not object to democracy; rather, they object to a pseudo-democracy set up by a foreign government by military means that imposes a particular set of foreign policies on the new government.

Many of the new political leaders in Iraq support the imposition of Islamic law rather than the Iraqi civil code. Indeed, the Iraqi constitution sets out the role of Islamic law in Iraq. With the intensely Islamist atmosphere in Afghanistan and Pakistan, many American programs, products, and movies are highly controversial and are banned by Islamist conservatives throughout the region. Tying the creation of markets to democratization tends to confuse the issue of cultural imperialism in the Middle East.

Americans tend to believe in the universality of their goods, ideas, and culture, and that deep within every Iraqi or Afghan, there is an American waiting to leap out. This is not the case.

Dylan A. Cyr and Sherifa Zuhur

See also: Bush Doctrine; Enduring Freedom, Operation; Global War on Terror; Iraqi Freedom, Operation; Television, Middle Eastern

Further Reading

Eckes, Alfred, and Thomas Zeiler. *Globalization and the American Century*. Cambridge: Cambridge University Press, 2003.

Harding, Jim. *After Iraq: War, Imperialism and Democracy*. Black Point, NS: Fernwood, 2004.

Said, Edward. *Culture and Imperialism*. New York: Knopf, 1999.

Schiller, Herbert. *Communication and Cultural Domination*. New York: M. E. Sharpe, 1976.

Tatham, Steve. *Losing Arab Hearts and Minds: The Coalition, Al-Jazeera and Muslim Public Opinion*. London: Hurst, 2006.

D

Dallas Skyscraper Plot

On September 24, 2009, Hosam Maher Husein Smadi, a 19-year-old Jordanian, was arrested and charged with attempting to bomb the Wells Fargo Bank office tower, a 60-story skyscraper near Fountain Place in downtown Dallas, Texas. The Federal Bureau of Investigation (FBI) had been monitoring his movements and activities ever since he had been discovered communicating with an online group of extremists. Between March and September, undercover agents interacted more than 60 times with the Jordanian, during which times he made clear his intention to act as a "soldier" for Osama bin Laden and conduct violent jihad.

According to sworn testimony presented in court, Smadi had initially wanted to target the Dallas/Fort Worth International Airport. However, he abandoned this plan because the facility was too strong and well protected. On July 16, he allegedly contacted one of the undercover FBI agents and said he was going to bomb the building containing the bank in order to further disrupt the economy, which was already shaken and weak, in Texas and the United States.

Eventually, Smadi and the undercover agent had a meeting where it was decided that a vehicle-borne improvised explosive device (VBIED) would be used for the attack. Federal agents then built a dummy bomb and placed it in a 2001 Ford Explorer Sport Trac. According to documents filed on September 24, 2009, Smadi knowingly took possession of the vehicle believing that it contained an active weapon of mass destruction. The indictment went on to say that he drove the Ford to Dallas, parked it at 1445 Ross Avenue (the address of the Wells Fargo Bank office tower), and activated a timer device connected to the bomb. He apparently then left the truck and departed from the scene in a car with an undercover law enforcement agent.

Smadi pleaded guilty on May 26, 2010, to one count of attempted use of a weapon of mass destruction. On October 19, 2010, U.S. District Court Judge Barbara M. G. Lynn sentenced him to 24 years in prison. Assistant Attorney General David Kris said the court's ruling should send a clear message of the serious consequences to be paid by those willing to carry out acts of violence in the United States to further the terrorist cause.

Donna Bassett

See also: Al-Qaeda; Bin Laden, Osama; Brooklyn Bridge Bomb Plot; Sears Tower Bomb Plot; Times Square Bomb Plot

Further Reading

Emerson, Steven. *Jihad Incorporated: A Guide to Militant Islam in the US*. Amherst, NY: Prometheus Books, 2006.

"Jordanian Man Pleads Guilty in Dallas Bomb Plot." *CBS News,* May 6, 2010. http://www.cbsnews.com/stories/2010/05/26/national/main6522078.shtml.

Morrow, Stacy, and Elvira Sakmari. "FBI Arrests Man in Dallas Skyscraper Bomb Plot." *NBC News*, September 25, 2009. http://www.nbcdfw.com/news/local-beat/FBI-Arrests-Man-Accused-in-Skyscraper-Bomb-Plot–61272512.html.

"Terror Plot Foiled: Inside the Smadi Case." Federal Bureau of Investigation, Washington, D.C., November 5, 2010. http://www.fbi.gov/news/stories/2010/november/terror-plot-foiled/terror-plot-foiled.

Dar es Salaam, U.S. Embassy Bombing

(August 7, 1998)

Early on the morning of August 7, 1998, Al-Qaeda operatives, using a truck bomb, attacked the U.S. embassy in Dar es Salaam, Tanzania, killing 12 people and injuring 86 others. U.S. Federal Bureau of Investigation (FBI) investigators concluded that the bomb was most likely planted in a refrigeration truck. The building suffered major damage and was deemed unusable. A year prior to the attack there had been a warning of a possible terrorist attack on the embassy, but it had been ignored because the source could not be verified.

The attack on the embassy in Dar es Salaam caused far fewer casualties than the nearly simultaneous attack on the U.S. embassy in Nairobi, Kenya, also targeted by Al-Qaeda. In fact, none of the Dar es Salaam personnel inside the building were killed in the attack. The Tanzanian embassy was located farther from the city center, which helped to minimize civilian casualties. According to reports, the truck bomber was unable to penetrate the outer wall of the embassy because a water tanker had blocked its path. When the bomb detonated, the tanker absorbed much of the blast that otherwise would undoubtedly have caused greater damage to the chancery building.

The investigators concluded that Osama bin Laden, leader of Al-Qaeda, had masterminded the embassy attacks. As a result, the U.S. government issued indictments against him and offered a $5 million dollar reward for his capture. In 2001, four men were convicted in U.S. federal courts and sentenced to life in prison for their role in the bombings of the U.S. embassies in Kenya and Tanzania.

In response to the attacks on the U.S. embassies, President Bill Clinton pledged to wage a war against international terrorism. In retaliation for the bombings, on August 20, 1998, the United States launched cruise missiles against three terrorist camps in Afghanistan and a suspected chemical weapons plant in Sudan. The operation was code-named Infinite Reach. The attacks on the camps in Afghanistan killed 24 people but failed to kill bin Laden. The attack on the plant in Sudan came under great criticism because there was no corroborating evidence to justify the attack, and many believe that the plant produced pharmaceuticals rather than chemical weapons. That attack killed the night watchmen at the plant.

In the United States, some cynics accused President Clinton of mounting the retaliatory attacks to distract the public's attention from the still-unfolding Monica Lewinsky scandal. The cruise missile attacks precipitated massive protests around the world, mostly in Muslim countries. In addition, bin Laden pledged to strike the United States again, a threat that he made good on with the devastating attacks in New York and Washington, D.C., on September 11, 2001.

Daniel W. Kuthy

See also: Al-Qaeda; Bin Laden, Osama; Clinton Administration; Nairobi, Kenya, Bombing of U.S. Embassy

Further Reading

Ferguson, Amanda. *The Attack against the U.S. Embassies in Kenya and Tanzania.* New York: Rosen Publication Group, 2003.

Labévière, Richard. *Dollars for Terror: The United States and Islam.* New York: Algora Publishing, 2000.

Obwogo, Subiri. *The Bombs That Shook Nairobi & Dar es Salaam: A Story of Pain and Betrayal.* Nairobi: Obwogo and Family, 1999.

Defense Intelligence Agency

Formally established at the direction of Secretary of Defense Robert McNamara on October 1, 1961, the Defense Intelligence Agency (DIA) is the leading intelligence agency for the Department of Defense. The DIA is directly responsible for meeting the intelligence requirements of the secretary of defense, the Joint Chiefs of Staff (JCS), and each of the Combatant Commands. Prior to the agency's establishment, each of the military services collected and analyzed its own intelligence separately and disseminated the intelligence to its own service chiefs, components, and the Unified and Specific Commands (now called Combatant Commands).

The Defense Reorganization Act of 1958, which gave birth to the DIA, sought to reduce the duplication and uncoordinated efforts that derived from those separate efforts. It also hoped to provide integrated intelligence analysis and support to the JCS and secretary of defense. The DIA acquired the mandate for all aspects and phases of the Defense Department's intelligence production except those intelligence-collection platforms and activities specifically assigned to the individual military services.

The 1962 Cuban Missile Crisis was the first major test for the DIA. That crisis was followed almost immediately by the Berlin Crisis. For a new agency, the DIA performed surprisingly well in both instances.

The Vietnam War saw the DIA become the primary authority and coordinating agency for military intelligence related to facilities and infrastructure. In the late 1970s, the DIA also became the coordinating agency for any Defense Department relationships with foreign military intelligence organizations. By the 1980s, the DIA became the Defense Department's coordinating agency for national collection assets as well as its spokesman before Congress on budgeting and national intelligence production priorities.

Driven by the lessons learned from the Persian Gulf War (Operation Desert Storm, 1991), the DIA's authority and mission expanded in consonance with America's increasing integration of its military forces into a joint structure and operations. Combatant Command intelligence centers now report their production requirements to and acquire their operating funds from the DIA. Although dissenting intelligence analysis is included in the DIA's coordinated national intelligence assessments, the DIA's assessment has become the dominant one.

The September 11, 2001, terror attacks on the United States perpetrated by Al-Qaeda and the sequelae from these have placed a spotlight on the DIA and its activities. The September 11 Commission, charged with evaluating America's response to the 9/11 attacks, was critical of the DIA's inability to thwart them and called into question its ability to effectively compile and disseminate intelligence information to prevent another such terrorist attack.

Similarly, the DIA has been criticized by the Weapons of Mass Destruction (WMD) Commission for its role in the faulty intelligence surrounding Iraq's alleged WMD program prior to the Anglo-American invasion of Iraq in March 2003. The George W. Bush administration was later embarrassed when no WMDs were found in Iraq. Their presence had been one of the key justifications for the invasion. Indeed, both commissions cited the DIA's failure to use open-source and human intelligence sources effectively. In all fairness, however, other intelligence agencies were criticized in similar fashion. The intelligence-gathering reforms based on the commission's recommendations began in 2005 but were not fully implemented until the end of the decade. In 2005, a new cabinet-level intelligence position was created: director of national intelligence. The director serves as the president's chief intelligence adviser and also serves as principal adviser to the National Security Council and the Department of Homeland Security. As such, the post calls upon the director to coordinate information from the DIA and other intelligence-gathering agencies.

Carl Otis Schuster

See also: Bush Administration; Central Intelligence Agency; Iraqi Freedom, Operation; National Security Agency; Weapons of Mass Destruction

Further Reading

Richelson, Jeffrey T. *The U.S. Intelligence Community.* 4th ed. Boulder, CO: Westview, 1999.

Roberts, Pat, ed. *Report on U.S. Intelligence Community's Prewar Intelligence Assessments on Iraq: Conclusions.* Washington, DC: Diane Publishing, 2004.

United States. *21st Century Complete Guide to American Intelligence Agencies.* Washington, DC: U.S. Government Printing Office, 2002.

Democratization and the Global War on Terror

The link between democratization and the global war on terror has been one of the most controversial elements of post–September 11, 2001, U.S. foreign policy. However, democratization has also been a consistent plank of U.S. foreign policy, especially in the Middle East, although more often stated than fully supported. Democratization is the complex process whereby a democracy replaces a nondemocratic political regime or pluralism is increased. Free elections for government control, the participation of a legal opposition or multiple parties, the application of equal rights, and the extension of liberal rules of citizenship and laws are typically considered minimum requirements of democratization. In turn, the term "global war on terror" may take either of two meanings. First, it may refer to a general state of conflict against violent radicalism, broadly defined. In this sense, the George W. Bush administration contended that democratization was the key to winning the global war on terror, especially in the Middle East. Second, the term may refer to a bundle of unilateralist and often forceful security strategies initiated by the United States after the September 11 terror attacks. This interpretation of the global war on terror is also closely associated with an assertive promotion of democracy, including by military imposition, as seen in the U.S.-led invasions of Afghanistan (2001) and Iraq (2003). This entry focuses on the second meaning of the term.

The notion that democratization enhances national and global security is deeply rooted in the study of international relations as well as U.S. foreign policy. The liberal (sometimes called idealist) approach to international relations views nondemocratic governments as a primary cause of war. Eighteenth-century German philosopher Immanuel Kant proposed that "perpetual peace" requires an alliance of liberal states. Such governments, he reasoned, need the consent of citizens who are averse to the risks of war. In 1917, President Woodrow Wilson justified the U.S. intervention in World War I by condemning traditional balance-of-power politics as the undemocratic "old and evil order" that pushed nations toward war. Future world peace, Wilson asserted, must be founded upon political liberty. When he spelled out U.S. war aims in his Fourteen Points speech of January 8, 1918, Wilson made an international organization of nations one of them. The representatives at the Paris Peace Conference of 1919 set up the League of Nations called for by Wilson, and its covenant was very much along the lines he proposed. While the U.S. Senate failed to ratify the treaty that would have brought U.S. membership in the League of Nations—and indeed the United States never joined that organization—liberal Wilsonian internationalism continues to influence U.S. foreign policy. President Franklin Roosevelt was a firm believer in Wilsonian principles and continued this approach. Roosevelt was an ardent champion of the successor to the League of Nations, the United Nations (UN), which came into being after World War II.

In recent years, scholars have turned to historical evidence to test whether or not democracies are indeed more pacific than undemocratic regimes. Proponents of the democratic peace theory argue that similar liberal institutions, cultures, laws, and linked economies make democracies especially unwilling to fight each other. Consequently, Michael Doyle argues that liberal democracies have reached a separate peace among themselves, although they remain insecure and conflict-prone toward nations that are not democratic.

Liberal theorists therefore expect that an increase in the number of democracies will expand existing zones of the democratic peace. Not all agree, however, on the full implications to the world system. For example, John Owen argues that a peaceful union of liberal countries would still need nondemocratic states against which to define themselves.

Many notable scholars, particularly those working in the dominant realist tradition of international relations, vigorously dispute the premises of democratic peace theory. They maintain, for example, that the theory neglects how peace among Western democracies during the Cold War was induced by a shared Soviet threat. Moreover, Edward Mansfield and Jack Snyder conclude that emerging democracies are historically more, not less, war-prone than other states.

Such criticisms aside, democratic peace theory's impact on U.S. policy makers since the 1980s is hard to exaggerate. Proponents, including both Republican and Democratic presidents, presented the 1989 fall of the Berlin Wall, the 1991 collapse of the Soviet Union, and a roughly concurrent rise in the global number of democracies as bellwethers of a freer, more secure international order. Political theorist Francis Fukuyama's famous thesis on the emergence of Western liberal democracy (*The*

End of History and the Last Man) as "the final form of government" captured liberalism's optimistic, even triumphal, spirit at the start of the post–Cold War era.

Complicating the picture, however, was the distinctive neoconservative political philosophy that also gained influence in the 1980s, especially within the Republican Party. With the Soviet collapse, neoconservatives contend that the proper role of the United States as the sole remaining superpower is to forge and maintain a benevolent world order. Neoconservatives share liberals' confidence that democracies do not fight each other, but they depart from traditional liberalism by arguing that the United States should shun reliance on international organizations—including the UN, toward which they have much antipathy—in promoting democracy overseas. Rather, the United States should be willing to use unilateral force if necessary to bring democracy to steadfastly nondemocratic states and regions.

Significantly, a public letter from associates of the neoconservative think tank Project for the New American Century urged President Bill Clinton to consider removing Iraqi dictator Saddam Hussein militarily more than three years before the 2001 terror attacks. The 1998 letter was signed by numerous individuals who would go on to occupy top foreign and national security policy posts in the first and second George W. Bush administrations, including Secretary of Defense Donald Rumsfeld, Deputy Secretary of Defense Paul Wolfowitz, Undersecretary of Defense for Policy Douglas Feith, and U.S. Representative to the UN John Bolton.

Neoconservative influence became most pronounced after September 11, which the Bush administration framed as an attack on liberal democracy around the world. Shortly after the invasion of Afghanistan, neoconservative speechwriter David J. Frum coined the phrase "axis of evil" to describe undemocratic Iran, Iraq, and North Korea for the president's January 2002 State of the Union address. This address was widely seen as setting the stage for further U.S. military action overseas. Other aspects of the global war on terror strategy reflect neoconservative precepts, including the Bush Doctrine of preemptive war, the decision to invade Iraq despite strong international and UN opposition, the belief that a lack of democracy in the Middle East fosters terrorism, and the argument that democratization justifies military action.

The ideas of Israeli politician and former Soviet dissident Natan Sharansky also align with neoconservative priorities. In 2005, President Bush praised Sharansky's recent work, which argues that the United States must lead the drive for democratization, as "a great book" that validated his own policies. However, observers noted a decline in the more forceful aspects of the administration's prodemocracy rhetoric after Egyptian Islamists made notable gains in 2005 parliamentary elections and the armed Hamas movement won the Palestinian parliamentary elections in January 2006.

Policy makers continue to debate both the desirability of an alliance of democracies and the U.S. role in promoting democracy abroad. Critics of the current strategy linking democratization to national security and the global war on terror reflect a number of ideological and theoretical approaches and include former Bush administration officials. They can be divided into three major camps, with frequent overlap.

One camp emphasizes pragmatism and feasibility. These critics see efforts to propel democracy via military invasion and occupation as unworkable, fed by false analogies to post–World War II Germany and Japan. They may also judge the strategy counterproductive, arguing that it heightens anti-Americanism and hurts the legitimacy of local prodemocracy groups in target countries. A second camp is rooted in ethical or nationalistic concerns. While some critics label the democratization strategy hypocritical in light of close American ties to Saudi Arabia and other undemocratic states, others assert that neoconservatives in the Bush administration have crafted a global war on terror strategy that privileges Israeli over U.S. security concerns. A third camp argues that the global war on terror is a veiled and fundamentally antidemocratic attempt to enhance U.S. power in regions rich in important natural resources, such as oil.

The difficulty of installing stable, workable, and effective governments in Afghanistan and Iraq offer a prime example of the problems associated with linking democratization to the global war on terror. In nations that have no history of democratic organizations, imposing democracy—even by use of force—is rife with difficulties and contradictions. Furthermore, in nations in which the economic system was either nonexistent (such as Afghanistan) or badly damaged (such as Iraq), the cultivation of democracy is not as important as survival for the great majority of the citizenry. Democracy and widespread poverty and economic and social inequalities do not often go together very well.

Ranjit Singh

See also: "Axis of Evil"; Bush Doctrine; Failed States and the Global War on Terror; Feith, Douglas; Global War on Terror; Rumsfeld, Donald Henry; Terrorism

Further Reading

Doyle, Michael W. "Liberalism and World Politics." *American Political Science Review* 80 (December 1986): 1151–1169.

Fukuyama, Francis. *The End of History and the Last Man*. New York: Free Press, 1992.

Kant, Immanuel. *Perpetual Peace, and Other Essays on Politics, History, and Morals*. Translated by Ted Humphrey. Indianapolis: Hackett, 1983.

Mansfield, Edward D., and Jack Snyder. *Electing to Fight: Why Emerging Democracies Go to War*. Cambridge, MA: MIT Press, 2005.

Owen, John M., IV. *Liberal Peace, Liberal War: American Politics and International Security*. Ithaca, NY: Cornell University Press, 1997.

Sharansky, Natan, and Ron Dermer. *The Case for Democracy: The Power of Freedom to Overcome Tyranny and Terror*. New York: PublicAffairs, 2004.

Woodward, Bob. *State of Denial: Bush at War, Part III*. New York: Simon and Schuster, 2006.

Dozier (James) Kidnapping

On December 17, 1981, the Italian Brigate Rosse (BR, or Red Brigade), considered one of Europe's most ruthless and violent terrorist organizations, kidnapped American General James Lee Dozier, who at the time was deputy chief of staff for logistics and administration at NATO's headquarters in southern Europe. Dozier was a graduate of West Point and had received the Silver Star due to his service in Vietnam. Friends would describe Dozier as a "soldier's soldier" who was "low key and efficient." The kidnapping was particularly notable in that it was the first time the BR had targeted a prominent non-Italian.

Dozier's kidnappers accessed the general's apartment (in Verona, Italy) by posing as plumbers who claimed they needed to fix a leak. As they entered, one of the terrorists struck Dozier on the head with a pistol butt; his wife was subsequently seized and then tied up, her eyes and mouth fastened with adhesive tape. The kidnappers placed the general in a small refrigerator box, dragged him out of the apartment, and put him into a van. They then drove 50 miles to a safe house on the outskirts of Padua.

For roughly six weeks, Dozier was kept in a single location, chained to a steel cot positioned under a small tent. He was forced to endure constant lighting and to listen to loud music, which he would later blame for hearing loss. While Dozier was held captive, the BR aired various statements to the public that detailed their demands or particular grievances. The first communiqué, issued only days after the kidnapping, made no specific reference to a ransom but rather addressed particular matters of interest to the BR and paid tribute to a fellow red terrorist organization, the German Red Army Faction (Rote Armee Fraktion, or RAF).

Other communiqués followed, which again were notable for their lack of specific demands (monetary or otherwise) for Dozier's release. By this time, however, Italian authorities had gained critical information from an informant and were able to launch a successful rescue under the auspices of the Nucleo Operativo Centrale di Sicurezza (NOCS, or Central Security Operations Service). General Dozier, who had been held for 42 days, would later report that as police stormed the apartment, one of his captives was "leveling a gun at his head."

After this rescue, the BR experienced further defections of their members, who in turn acted as informants for the government. Back in the United States, Dozier received a hero's welcome and was celebrated by President Ronald Reagan at the annual National Prayer Breakfast, following which both men traveled in a motorcade to the White House, where they posed for pictures.

Dozier continued his army career and was promoted two years later to the rank of major general. In 2006, he addressed a conference on terrorism sponsored by the U.S. Air Force, and told the group that many of the lessons he learned from his experience with the BR were still applicable to contemporary terrorist groups.

Paul Smith

See also: Pearl, Daniel; Terrorism

Further Reading

Dozier Kidnap Defendant Says Bulgaria Sought Role." *Gazette News Service*, March 17, 1982. Available online at http://news.google.com/newspapers?nid=1946&dat=198220317.

"1982: US General Rescued from Red Brigades." *BBC*, January 28, 1982. *BBC on This Day*. http://news.bbc.co.uk/onthisday/hi/dates/stories/jawag/28/newsid-4202000/4202723.

Philipps, Thomas. "The Dozier Kidnapping: Confronting the Red Brigades." *Air and Space Power Journal*, February 7, 2002. http://www.airpower.maxwell.af.mil/airchronicles/cc/philipps.html.

Smith, Paul. *The Terrorism Ahead: Confronting Transnational Violence in the Twenty-First Century*. Armonk, NY: M. E. Sharpe, 2008.

Wilson, George. "Kidnapped Officer Seen as a 'Soldier's Soldier.'" *Washington Post*, December 18, 1981, A52.

Drones. *See* Unmanned Aerial Vehicles

E

Eagle Claw, Operation

(April 25, 1980)

A failed U.S. mission to rescue American hostages being held in Iran on April 25, 1980, was code-named Operation Eagle Claw. On November 4, 1979, during the Iranian Revolution, radical Iranian students seized the United States embassy in Tehran, taking 52 Americans captive. The ensuing hostage crisis created a division within the Jimmy Carter administration. National Security Advisor Zbigniew Brzezinski believed that the president had to take a hard stance and was an ardent proponent of a rescue operation. Secretary of State Cyrus Vance opposed military action and believed that persistent and carefully constructed negotiations could resolve the crisis. He maintained that a rescue attempt would place the captives in greater danger. Vance considered the Iranian threats against their lives to be purely rhetorical, as dead hostages would be of no value to the Iranians. He argued that if the captives were rescued, the terrorists would simply take more hostages. The secretary of state also asserted that military action against Iran could turn the entire Muslim world against the United States.

President Carter resisted Brzezinski's initial pressure for a rescue mission. Carter, like Vance, feared that any military action would result in the execution of the hostages. The president did allow for tentative mission planning and preparation to begin, however.

On April 11, 1980, after the Iranian students publicly threatened the hostages, Carter approved a rescue attempt. Carter dismissed Vance's warnings about reprisals from other Middle Eastern countries, believing that Islamic fundamentalist Iran enjoyed little support from its Arab neighbors. The president determined that not taking action would be more costly than taking action. Indeed, he was especially concerned that the United States not appear soft on terrorism and weak in the eyes of leaders of the Soviet Union, with which relations had already rapidly deteriorated. Vance then resigned, having protested the proposed rescue operation for nearly six months.

Carter and Brzezinski ordered the operation to proceed in accordance with four constraints: planning secrecy, protecting the lives of the hostages, keeping Iranian casualties to a minimum, and maintaining a small task force. The element of surprise was also encouraged. Carter met with the task force planners personally on April 16. The U.S. Army's Delta Force, commanded by Colonel Charles Beckwith, was charged with executing the raid, while Colonel James Kyle commanded the mission's air force elements. Meanwhile, White House Chief of Staff Hamilton Jordan met with representatives from Iran on April 18 in a final attempt to reach a diplomatic solution to the hostage crisis. He was informed that the Iranian government would not be able to address the issue until after parliamentary elections in mid-May. With his efforts to achieve an immediate diplomatic resolution frustrated, and under increasing pressure from the American public and media to take action, Carter authorized Operation Eagle Claw on April 23. He made a fateful pledge to the task force commanders that he would accept full responsibility for the mission.

The ill-fated rescue mission never reached Tehran. The plan failed because of weather conditions over the Iranian desert and an unfortunate set of circumstances that occurred at the mission's forward refueling point, code-named Desert One. On April 24, when the mission began, sandstorms caused the operation to fall an hour behind schedule. Mechanical failures reduced the eight navy RH-53D Sea Stallion helicopters in the mission to only five. Meanwhile, civilians in automobiles threatened operational secrecy by stumbling upon the forward refueling point. The decision to abort the mission because of the lack of serviceable helicopters had already been made when an accident occurred around 2:00 a.m. on April 25. A helicopter rotor struck an MC-130 transport aircraft on the ground, causing a massive explosion at Desert One. The task force, including five wounded, was evacuated immediately. Eight dead American servicemen and the four remaining Sea Stallions were abandoned in the desert.

The failed operation was a dark episode in Carter's presidency. In August 1980, an investigative body led by Admiral James L. Holloway analyzed Operation Eagle Claw. It concluded that the accident at the forward refueling point was the result of human error brought on by the dark, dusty, and cluttered conditions at Desert One. The government examined the state of U.S. special operations forces after the catastrophe at Desert One. The Senate Armed Services Committee consulted with Colonel Beckwith and drew several conclusions from the failed mission, including the importance of standardized training for all special operations forces and the need to create a permanent joint command. It also recommended the establishment of forward staging areas around the globe. These would allow special operations forces to be deployed faster and more efficiently. Based upon these findings and those of the Holloway Committee, the Joint Special Operations Command (JSOC) was formed on December 15, 1980. In 1987, Congress created the position of Assistant Secretary of Defense for Special Operations and Low Intensity Conflict and the U.S. Special Operations Command (USSOCOM). Passage of this legislation guaranteed regular funding, standardized training, and specialized weapons and equipment for special operations forces in all branches of the U.S. military.

The American hostages were not released until January 20, 1981. The failure to secure their freedom earlier undoubtedly helped Republican Ronald Reagan win the presidency in the November 1980 elections.

Jeffrey Lamonica

See also: Carter Doctrine; SEAL Teams, U.S. Navy

Further Reading

Beckwith, Charlie A., and Donald Knox. *Delta Force: The Army's Elite Counterterrorist Unit.* New York: Avon, 2000.

Carter, Jimmy. *Keeping Faith: Memoirs of a President*. Fayetteville: University of Arkansas Press, 1982.

Cogan, Charles. "Desert One and Its Disorders." *Journal of Military History* 67 (2003): 273–296.

Jordan, Hamilton. *Crisis: The Last Year of the Carter Presidency*. New York: Putnam, 1982.

Kyle, James, and John Eidson. *The Guts to Try: The Untold Story of the Iran Hostage Rescue Mission by the On-Scene Desert Commander*. New York: Orion Books, 1990.

Economic Impact of the September 11, 2001, Attacks

The financial impact of the September 11, 2001, terrorist attacks on the United States was particularly devastating to New York City and to the commercial airline industry. It was this economic damage as much as the physical damage that had appealed to Osama bin Laden when he helped plan the assaults. Indeed, he hoped to attack the United States at its source of strength and cause it considerable economic distress. Because New York City is the hub of the nation's financial industry, it was very high on Al-Qaeda's list of targets.

Bin Laden was successful in achieving his goals. Property losses, particularly in New York City, were high. Southern Manhattan, where the World Trade Center was located, was the center of New York City's government and international finance, and both were paralyzed for weeks. Nearby office buildings remained empty, and the subways stopped running. Also, tens of thousands of New Yorkers who lived below Canal Street were prevented from going there. All of the city's schools and bridges were also closed.

The economic impact was greatest and most long-lasting in the airline industry

because the attacks had been carried out using commercial airliners. The airlines were hit by massive insurance and litigation claims from the thousands of families of those killed or wounded in the attacks, and greatly enhanced postattack airport security also cost the airlines millions of dollars to implement and administer.

It took the American airline industry nearly five years to recover completely from 9/11. Both American and United airlines lost two aircraft each to the hijackers, but insurance covered most of those losses. What hurt the airlines the most was the loss of customers, many of whom were afraid to fly. Airports had been shut down around the country for several days, meaning millions of dollars in lost revenue. Ten days after the September 11 attack, New York City's three main airports were operating 80 percent of their flights but with only 35 percent of passenger seats filled. Lost revenue from the three New York airports alone was around $250 million a day.

Compounding the problem was the rocketing cost of oil and the higher aviation premiums from insurers. In the period from September 11, 2001, to September 2004, the airline industry lost $23 billion. In October 2001, airline passenger traffic had dropped 23.2 percent in comparison to October 2000. An infusion of $1.5 billion of federal aid helped the airline industry, but a series of bankruptcies and mergers occurred in the next few years. Only gradually were the airlines able to move back toward financial health.

New York City experienced massive job losses and saw many buildings damaged or destroyed. Job losses have been estimated at 143,000 a month, with lost wages of $2.8 billion. Nearly 70 percent of the jobs lost and 86 percent of the wages lost were to persons with well-paying positions in finance, insurance, and banking, the industries that were hit the hardest. Building and property-damage losses have been assessed at $34 billion, with only about half that insured at value. It has been estimated that the city lost $60 billion in revenue, with $82 million coming from lost parking ticket revenue alone.

Perhaps the least long-lasting economic impact was in the stock market. On September 11, 2001, the hijacked aircraft crashed into the World Trade Center complex before the opening of the stock market. Damage to communications, evacuation orders, and rescue efforts led to the closing of the market for the next four days. When the stock market reopened on Monday, September 17, there was an immediate sell-off. On September 10, the Standard & Poor's 500 Index had closed at 1,092.54; when trading closed on September 17, the index stood at 891.10. By September 24, however, the stock market was climbing again, and by October 11, the index closed at 1,097.43, having erased all of the earlier losses.

The American economy as a whole rebounded from the September 11 attacks within months. One reason that the attacks did not have a more lasting impact was that they had been concentrated by geography and industry. Whereas New York City, and to a much lesser extent Washington, D.C., suffered economic dislocation from unemployment and property damage, the rest of the country was left relatively untouched. The economy dipped into a mild recession from which it rebounded some 15–18 months later.

The most difficult area to assess is the economic cost of confronting Al-Qaeda in military actions in Afghanistan and Iraq and in new procedures and agencies created worldwide to confront terrorism. Al-Qaeda strategists have often pointed out the enormous sums of money now being expended by the United States and other Western countries on this effort as opposed to the relatively modest amounts for Al-Qaeda in waging jihad.

Stephen E. Atkins

See also: Impact of 9/11 on Presidential Power; Impact of 9/11 on U.S. Foreign Policy; Impact of 9/11 on U.S. Public Opinion; September 11 Attacks, International Reactions to; Terrorism

Further Reading

Griffiths, Katherine. "US Airline Industry in Tailspin to Disaster." *Independent* (London), September 10, 2004, 46.

Kawar, Mark. "9/11 Shock Didn't Bring Bears to Stock Market." *Omaha World Herald*, September 17, 2002, 1D.

Polgreen, Lydia. "Study Confirms 9/11 Impact on New York City Economy." *New York Times*, June 30, 2004, B6.

Zuckerman, Sam. "9/11 Before & After: It's the Rebound, Stupid." *San Francisco Chronicle*, December 30, 2001, D7.

Enduring Freedom, Operation

Enduring Freedom was the code name given to the U.S.-led invasion of Afghanistan that began on October 7, 2001. The purpose of the invasion was to topple the Taliban government and kill or capture members of the Al-Qaeda terrorist group, which had just carried out the terror attacks of September 11, 2001. The Taliban had sheltered Al-Qaeda and its leader, Osama bin Laden, on Afghan territory and provided the terrorists with bases, training facilities, and quite possibly financial support.

The United States faced major problems in planning a war against the Taliban

Soldiers from the U.S. Army 10th Mountain Division detain suspected Taliban fighters after an army base was attacked with rocket-propelled grenades and small arms fire on August 4, 2006, in the Paktika Province of Afghanistan. (U.S. Department of Defense)

and Al-Qaeda. Prime among these were logistical concerns, for Afghanistan is a landlocked country distant from U.S. basing facilities. American planners decided that an alliance would have to be forged with the Afghan United Front (also known as the Northern Alliance), an anti-Taliban opposition force within Afghanistan. The Northern Alliance would do the bulk of the fighting but would receive U.S. air support along with assistance, advice, and cash from U.S. special operations forces.

The war began with American air strikes from land-based B-52 and B-1 bombers, carrier-based F-14 Tomcat and F-18 Hornet aircraft, and Tomahawk cruise missiles. These attacks were intended to knock out the Taliban's antiaircraft defenses and communications infrastructure. However,

desperately poor Afghanistan had a very limited infrastructure to bomb, and the initial air attacks had only minimal impact. Al-Qaeda training camps were also targeted, although they were quickly abandoned once the bombing campaign began. U.S. special operations forces arrived in Afghanistan on October 15, at which time they made contact with the leaders of the Northern Alliance.

The first phase of the ground campaign was focused on the struggle for the northern city of Mazar-e Sharif, which fell to the Northern Alliance forces led by generals Abdul Dostum and Ustad Atta Mohammed on November 10, 2001. The fighting around Mazar-e Sharif was intense, but U.S. air strikes, directed by special operations forces on the ground, did much to break Taliban and Al-Qaeda resistance.

As the fighting progressed, the Taliban and Al-Qaeda improved both their tactics and combat effectiveness. Camouflage and concealment techniques were also enhanced, helping to counter American air power. However, the Taliban's limited appeal to the population meant that the regime could not withstand the impact of a sustained assault. The repressive rule of the Taliban ensured that it never widened its base of support beyond the Pashtun ethnic group from which it originated.

Northern Alliance forces captured the Afghan capital of Kabul without a fight on November 13. On November 26, a besieged garrison of 5,000 Taliban and Al-Qaeda soldiers surrendered at Kunduz after heavy bombardment by American B-52s. Meanwhile, an uprising by captured Taliban fighters held in the Qala-e-Gangi fortress near Mazar-e Sharif prison was suppressed with great brutality in late November.

The scene of the fighting then shifted to the city of Kandahar in southern Afghanistan. Because the Taliban had originated in Kandahar in the early 1990s, it was expected to put up a stiff fight for the city. Kandahar was attacked by Northern Alliance forces led by generals Hamid Karzai and Guyl Agha Shirzai, with U.S. special operations forces coordinating the offensive. The Taliban deserted Kandahar on December 6, and Taliban leader Mohammed Mullah Omar and the surviving Taliban elements went into hiding in the remote mountain regions of Afghanistan and Pakistan. The fall of Kandahar marked the end of Taliban rule in Afghanistan, only nine weeks after the beginning of the bombing campaign. On December 22, 2001, an interim administration chaired by Hamid Karzai took office.

Despite the rapid and efficient progress of Operation Enduring Freedom, Taliban and Al-Qaeda elements remained at large in Afghanistan, and the operation failed to capture or kill either Osama bin Laden or Omar. Bin Laden was believed to be hiding in mountain dugouts and bunkers located in the White Mountains near Tora Bora. A 16-day offensive in early December 2001 failed to find bin Laden. For this offensive, the United States once again relied on Northern Alliance ground troops supported by U.S. special operations forces and American air power. Later there would be charges that this offensive was mishandled, and an opportunity to take bin Laden was lost. Bin Laden escaped, probably into Pakistan through the porous border that separates Afghanistan from Pakistan.

Despite the failure to capture or kill bin Laden, the United States could point to notable success in the so-called war on terror by the end of 2001. The Taliban had been deposed and Al-Qaeda was on the run, with many of its members and leaders having been killed or captured. This occurred despite the fact that the United States had deployed only about 3,000 service personnel, most of them special operations forces, to Afghanistan by the end of the year. The U.S. death toll was remarkably light, with only two deaths attributed to enemy action. Estimates of Afghan fatalities are approximate at best. As many as 4,000 Taliban soldiers may have been killed during the campaign. Afghan civilian deaths have been estimated at between 1,000 and 1,300, with several thousand refugees dying from disease and/or exposure. Another 500,000 Afghans were made refugees or displaced persons during the fighting.

The United States attempted a different approach in March 2002, when Al-Qaeda positions were located in the Shahi-Kot Valley near Gardez. On this occasion, U.S. ground troops from the 10th Mountain Division and the 101st Airborne Division led the way, along with special operations forces from Australia, Canada, and Germany, and Afghan government troops, in an offensive code-named Operation Anaconda. Taliban reinforcements rushed to join the Al-Qaeda fighters, but both were routed from the valley with heavy losses.

Since 2002, the Taliban and Al-Qaeda remnants have maintained a steadily increasing insurgency in Afghanistan. Troops from the United States and allied countries, mainly from North Atlantic Treaty Organization (NATO) member states, remain in Afghanistan operating ostensibly under the banner of Operation Enduring Freedom. Efforts at achieving and maintaining lasting stability, however, have met with little success.

In late 2009, President Barack Obama announced that the United States would begin a troop surge in Afghanistan similar to that used in Iraq. This new strategy witnessed the insertion of some 33,000 additional troops into Afghanistan, which began in early 2010. By September 2012, per the timetable worked out by the White House and Pentagon, most of those troops had been withdrawn, although there were still over 60,000 foreign troops remaining in Afghanistan. The surge did little to end the growing Taliban–Al-Qaeda insurgency, however, and it is generally acknowledged that the effort was not nearly as successful as the earlier troop surge in Iraq. Today, Afghanistan stands on the precipice of chaos, a situation made worse by the corrupt and inept Hamid Karzai administration. The troop surge failed to achieve success partly because Karzai never fully supported the effort and did not fully cooperate with it. It was also unsuccessful because the Pakistanis never cracked down on insurgents and terrorists who were using the northern and western parts of that nation as staging areas for terror operations in Afghanistan.

Some commentators have also suggested that the troop surge did not work because it was too little, too late and was hampered at the onset by an inflexible timetable, which the Obama administration had insisted upon.

Paul W. Doerr

See also: Al-Qaeda; Bin Laden, Osama; Bush Administration; Bush Doctrine; Global War on Terror; Obama Administration; Pentagon Attack; Taliban; World Trade Center, September 11, 2001

Further Reading

Biddle, Stephen. *Afghanistan and the Future of Warfare: Implications for Army and Defense Policy*. Carlisle, PA: Strategic Studies Institute, 2002.

Hanson, Victor Davis. *Between War and Peace: Lessons from Afghanistan to Iraq*. New York: Random House, 2004.

Kagan, Frederick. *Finding the Target: The Transformation of American Military Policy*. New York: Encounter Books, 2006.

Maley, William. *The Afghanistan Wars*. New York: Palgrave Macmillan, 2002.

F

Fahrenheit 9/11

Fahrenheit 9/11 is an award-winning documentary by the filmmaker Michael Moore. It is highly controversial because of its pronounced bias against President George W. Bush and his policies. The documentary opened in movie theaters across the United States on June 25, 2004, and it received mixed reviews, which often reflected the political persuasion and beliefs of the reviewers. Moore had a reputation for making documentaries that evinced a liberal bias, and this documentary fit into that category as well.

The film highlights President George W. Bush's conduct before and after the events of September 11, 2001. Moore is particularly harsh toward President Bush's passivity and apparent lack of action against the threat of terrorism before September 11. In his documentary, Moore reported that Bush spent 42 percent of his time on vacation in the period leading up to September 11. Moore also spotlighted the close personal and business relationship between President Bush (and his family) and the Saudi regime. This relationship led to the evacuation of Osama bin Laden's family from the United States just after September 11 in such haste that there was no time for debriefing by law enforcement and intelligence officials. Moore was also highly critical of the rationale for the invasion of Iraq. Finally, Moore criticized the national media for cheering on the Bush administration's war against terror and the invasion of Iraq.

Specifically, *Fahrenheit 9/11* makes the following points about Bin Laden and about Afghanistan, and makes them in this order:[1]

1) The Bin Laden family (if not *exactly* Osama himself) had a close if convoluted business relationship with the Bush family, through the Carlyle Group.
2) Saudi capital in general is a very large element of foreign investment in the United States.
3) The Unocal company in Texas had been willing to discuss a gas pipeline across Afghanistan with the Taliban, as had other vested interests.
4) The Bush administration sent far too *few* ground troops to Afghanistan and thus allowed far too many Taliban and al-Qaida members to escape.
5) The Afghan government, in supporting the coalition in Iraq, was purely risible in that its non-army was purely American.

Even before its appearance in movie theaters, the documentary was so controversial that it had trouble finding a distributor. Harvey Weinstein, the CEO of Miramax Films, had provided most of the $6 million financial support for the documentary. Miramax is a subsidiary of Walt Disney Company, and Michael Eisner, then the CEO of Walt Disney Company, refused to allow Miramax to distribute the film. This decision was made by Eisner despite the fact that he had not yet seen the documentary. Moore claimed that Eisner had been concerned about retaliation from Florida governor Jeb Bush, the brother of George W. Bush, concerning Disney's major real estate holdings and other interests in Florida. In the trade journals it was already common knowledge that *Fahrenheit 9/11* was going to be a hot property and that it would draw interest from a number of distributors. Weinstein discussed the issue with Eisner, but he lost the argument and the documentary was ultimately not distributed by Miramax. Moore then turned to a second distributor, Lions Gate Entertainment Corporation, a Canadian distributor based in Vancouver, British Columbia. To handle such a large booking, Lions Gate had to conclude a secondary partnership with IFC Films and Fellowship Adventure Group.

The documentary was fabulously successful financially. During its opening weekend alone (July 25–27, 2004), it generated box office revenues of $23.9 million in the United States and Canada despite opening in only about 40 percent of the theaters normally available for top-flight movies. In less than a year, the documentary had grossed over $120 million in the United States and over $220 million worldwide. Because of its anti-Bush theme and opposition to the Iraq War, the documentary was also an international best seller. Moore decided to release the documentary in a DVD format, which was made available in stores on October 5, 2004. Around 2 million copies of the DVD were sold on the first day.

Besides producing controversy, the documentary has also received some critical acclaim. In April 2004, the documentary was entered to compete for the prestigious Palme d'Or (Golden Palm) Award at the 57th Cannes Film Festival. It was received with great fanfare at its first showing. The nine-person panel for the award had four Americans and only one Frenchman on it whom had already stated criticism of the war, according to critics of the movie. This majority of votes provided *Fahrenheit 9/11* as the winner of the 2004 Palme d'Or award.

Supporters of President Bush and the conservative movement tried in various ways to block the release of the documentary. They were worried that it might have a negative effect on Bush's 2004 reelection campaign. Organizations such as Patriotic Americans Boycotting Anti-American Hollywood (PABAAH) launched an anti-Moore campaign. Subsequently, some Bush supporters held an anti-Moore film festival, called the American Film Renaissance, in Texas, showing films that attacked Moore and his views regarding the Bush administration. The key feature was Michael Wilson's film *Michael Moore Hates America*. To counter the charges from conservatives that he distorted facts in his documentary, Moore hired a staff of researchers and two lawyers to check the facts and claims in *Fahrenheit 9/11*. The group found no false claims and there appeared to have been a backlash against this anti-Moore campaign and the documentary continued to be shown in theaters, attracting more viewers and making more money.

Stephen E. Atkins

See also: Bush Administration; Bush Doctrine; Cheney, Richard Bruce; Tenet, George

Note

1. Christopher Hitchens, "Unfairenheit 9/11," *Slate*, June 21, 2004, http://www.slate.com/articles/news_and_politics/fighting_words/2004/06/unfairenheit_911.html.

Further Reading

Booth, William. "Fahrenheit 9/11 Too Hot for Disney?" *Washington Post*, May 6, 2004, C1.

Denby, David. "Michael Moore's Viciously Funny Attack on the Bush Administration." *New Yorker*, June 28, 2004, 108.

Donegan, Lawrence, and Paul Harris. "American Right Vows to Settle Score as Bush's Nemesis Turns Up the Heat." *Observer* (London), June 27, 2004, 18.

Moore, Michael. *Will They Ever Trust Us Again?* New York: Simon and Schuster, 2004.

Smith, Gavin. "Michael Moore Gives Much More." *New Statesman*, July 19, 2004, 1.

Failed States and the Global War on Terror

A failed state is characterized as a nation whose governing institutions do not provide minimum services to its population, especially in terms of security. Although still not accepted by many political experts, the concept of failed states gained currency during the George W. Bush presidency as a way of rationalizing interventionism in the global war on terror or explaining how the terrorist attacks of September 11, 2001, could have arisen. The concept of failed states was discussed in a volume edited by Robert Rotberg and then became part of an index in the influential journal *Foreign Policy* to measure certain facts in a number of countries.

In the popularized concept of failed or collapsed states, these states may be paralyzed by corruption, unable to initiate or maintain economic or development programs, and have ineffective judicial systems and little democracy. Currently, the true test of failure is seen as the presence of large-scale endemic violence. The concept of failed states was specifically crafted to explain the rise of Osama bin Laden, so it was employed to identify ungoverned or poorly governed areas that harbor those who are violent.

A primary function of the state is to provide security for its citizens by means of what German sociologist Max Weber referred to as a monopoly on the legitimate use of violence. Failure to maintain this monopoly by permitting or being unable to prevent nonstate groups to exercise violence on a large scale within the borders of the state calls into question the existence of the state as a system of governance.

Those who employ the label of failed states may point to Afghanistan, Lebanon, and perhaps Pakistan. Failed states became an issue in the years following World War II as new nation-states were established in the European powers' former colonial empires and as former colonies rebelled and abruptly gained their independence. Some of these new states lacked strong central-governing bureaucratic institutions or well-trained government officials and civil servants. They were unable to govern their territories and populations in an efficient manner, leaving many of their citizens to search for other sources of basic services and security.

Many of the new states' borders were not aligned with ethnic or tribal boundaries that had been in place for decades and in some cases centuries, creating new territorial conflicts or making old ones worse. This resulted in groups within the states attempting to take on some of the powers normally held by the state, either as a means to provide security for themselves and their constituents or simply to attain autonomous power within the state's boundaries.

One supposed central characteristic of a failed state is the breakdown of law and order. This is often the result of the increased power of criminal organizations such as drug cartels, militias, insurgents, and terrorist organizations arrayed against the poor-quality military and security forces of the state. With the weakening and failure of the state, areas of these nations may come under the control of such organizations, especially as they become more capable of imposing their will on the security forces and leadership of the state. The concept of failed states has been particularly important in the U.S. approach to the global war on terror because most terrorist organizations seek areas of weak governmental control, which they take advantage of for the purposes of training, organization, and staging attacks.

Terrorist organizations may take advantage of state weakness in a number of ways. Terrorists often seek to operate from regions that are difficult to reach due to geographical distances from the country's center or because of difficult, typically mountainous, terrain, or both. In some cases, such as in Afghanistan under the Taliban, the central government may welcome a terrorist organization such as Al-Qaeda as an ideological ally. Sometimes the terrorists will come to an informal agreement of "live and let live" with the government, promising not to challenge government authority or get involved in domestic politics in return for a free hand to operate in their sanctuaries. Attacks in Pakistan by a rebuilt Taliban in 2008 led to attempts by the Pakistani government to arrange such an agreement with the terrorists, but that effort has had decidedly mixed results. Because failed states are still considered sovereign by their citizens and governments, military action by other states against terror-

ist organizations in their territory involve issues of international law and politics that relate to interstate conflict and war.

While the American-led invasion of Afghanistan in 2001 was aimed at Al-Qaeda, it was premised on the overthrow of the Taliban regime and reconstructing Afghanistan so that it would no longer serve as a haven for terrorist organizations. However, the Taliban remains active in Afghanistan, and the insurgency that followed the quick 2001 American victory over the Taliban and Al-Qaeda illustrates how difficult it can be to establish a strong state until adequate leadership and institutions can be established, positioned, and strengthened. Indeed, by early 2014, the situation in Afghanistan remained chaotic, some four years after the Obama administration had implemented a troop surge strategy that sent some 33,000 additional troops to that country. The surge was generally considered to be a failure. As of this writing, some 50,000 foreign troops remain in Afghanistan, but the future of that nation remains an open question.

Elliot Paul Chodoff

See also: Al-Qaeda; Democratization and the Global War on Terror; Enduring Freedom, Operation; Global War on Terror; Taliban; Terrorism

Further Reading

Fearon, James D., and David D. Laitin. "Ethnicity, Insurgency, and Civil War." *American Political Science Review* 97 (2003): 75–76.

Hironaka, Ann. *Neverending Wars: The International Community, Weak States, and the Perpetuation of Civil War.* Cambridge, MA: Harvard University Press, 2005.

Jones, Seth G. "The Rise of Afghanistan's Insurgency: State Failure and Jihad." *International Security* 32 (2008): 7–40.

Rotberg, Robert I., ed. *When States Fail: Causes and Consequences.* Princeton, NJ: Princeton University Press, 2003.

Federal Emergency Management Agency (FEMA)

The Federal Emergency Management Agency (FEMA) has had a mixed record in dealing with the aftermath of September 11, 2001. The legislative mandate for FEMA was to provide direct assistance to those who had been impacted by a natural or a human-made disaster. In September 2001 it was a large agency, with 2,600 employees and nearly 4,000 standby reservists. On September 11, 2001, Joe M. Allbaugh was the director of FEMA. Allbaugh was a Texan with close ties to President George W. Bush.

Where FEMA excelled was in its prompt response to the disaster. Emergency services personnel from 18 states responded almost immediately to the sites of the attacks. FEMA sent 28 urban search-and-rescue task forces to the sites of the disasters. Each task force had 62 members. The urban search-and-rescue task forces sent to the World Trade Center complex site to locate survivors worked 24-hour days, with the personnel working two 12-hour shifts. Conditions were horrible, and the dust from the debris made the task extremely difficult for the searchers. They employed portable cameras to spot survivors, sniffer dogs to smell for survivors, and sensitive life-detector sensors to look for signs of life. Despite these heroic efforts, few survivors were found because of the horrendous impact of the collapse of the Twin Towers. As it became apparent that there would be no more survivors, FEMA started pulling out its

search-and-rescue teams. The last to leave was an Oakland, California, unit, which left on October 6, 2001. A spokesperson for FEMA stated that the site had been turned over to the Fire Department City of New York (FDNY) and the Army Corps of Engineers.

FEMA also sent in critical incident stress management (CISM) teams to help the workers at the site of the attacks. These teams had psychologists, psychiatrists, social workers, and professional counselors whose mission was the prevention and mitigation of disabling stress among the personnel working at the World Trade Center site. There were nearly as many members of these CISM teams as there were workers at the site. This caused some difficulty because members of these teams were so eager to help that they became intrusive. They soon earned the nickname "therapy dogs" from workers at the site. Members of these teams undoubtedly helped some of those working at the site, but others resented their constant interference with the urgent job at hand.

FEMA's biggest failure was in its handling of the September 11 disaster relief funds. September 11 had caused the loss of 75,000 jobs and $4.5 billion in lost income. Despite promises of quick financial relief for those who had lost their jobs, FEMA's administrators changed the rules in the aftermath of September 11, making it more difficult for people to qualify for financial relief. Thousands of people were denied housing aid after FEMA decided to limit benefits to those who could prove that their lost income was a "direct result" of the attacks rather than merely the "result" of the attacks, which had been the previous standard. This seemingly minor change in language led to FEMA's rejection of the claims of 70 percent of the people applying for relief under the mortgage and rental program after losing their jobs. Between September 11, 2001, and April 2002, less than $65 million was paid out by FEMA to help families in the disaster area pay their bills, avoid eviction, and buy food.

Decisions on accepting or rejecting claims were made by FEMA agency evaluators (two-thirds of whom were temporary workers) at processing centers in Texas, Maryland, and Virginia. These evaluators had little or no knowledge of New York City or its culture, institutions, or geography. Moreover, the application form had not been changed to make it possible for evaluators to determine whether job losses were directly related to the disaster, and all the forms were printed exclusively in English. It was only on November 14, 2001, that the application form was revised and issued in six languages, but even the new forms did not explain how FEMA defined "direct result."

Furthermore, some odd decisions were made by the FEMA evaluators. One applicant provided the name of the restaurant where he had worked in the World Trade Center and his supervisor's telephone number, as required by the application. His application was denied because the evaluator was unable to make contact by telephone with the restaurant, which had of course been destroyed on September 11.

Criticisms of FEMA soon reached the halls of Congress. Under pressure from politicians, FEMA reevaluated its program in late June 2002 and eased its eligibility criteria. But the bad feelings were hard to overcome.

Stephen E. Atkins

See also: International Emergency Economic Powers Act; Pentagon Attack; World Trade Center, September 11, 2001

Further Reading

Chen, David W. "More Get 9/11 Aid, but Distrust of U.S. Effort Lingers." *New York Times*, August 27, 2002, B1.

Keegan, William, Jr., with Bart Davis. *Closure: The Untold Story of the Ground Zero Recovery Mission.* New York: Touchstone Books, 2006.

Mitchell, Kirsten B. "Government Trying to Decide FEMA's Fate." *Tampa Tribune*, August 7, 2002, 1.

Feith, Douglas

(July 16, 1953–)

Douglas Feith is an attorney, foreign and military policy expert, and noted neoconservative, and was undersecretary of defense for policy from 2001 to 2005. Born on July 16, 1953, in Philadelphia, he attended Harvard University, earning a BA degree in 1975. In 1978, he earned a law degree from Georgetown University. While in law school, Feith interned at the Arms Control and Disarmament Agency, where he met Fred Iklé, John Lehman, and Paul Wolfowitz. After graduation, Feith practiced law in Washington, D.C., and wrote articles on foreign policy. As he grew older, he developed positions on foreign policy that would eventually identify him as a neoconservative who believed in the use of force as a vital instrument of national policy.

Feith entered government service in 1981 during the Ronald Reagan administration, working on Middle East issues for the National Security Council. Feith then transferred to the Department of Defense as special counsel for Assistant Secretary of Defense Richard Perle, and later served as deputy assistant secretary of defense for negotiations from March 1984 to September 1986. After that Feith left government to

U.S. undersecretary of defense Douglas Feith at the U.S. embassy in Kabul, Afghanistan, in September 2002. Feith and his staff were subsequently accused of developing dubious intelligence linking Iraqi leader Saddam Hussein and Al-Qaeda as a justification for launching the Iraq War. (AP/World Wide Photos)

form a law firm, Feith & Zell, P.C., which he managed until 2001, although he continued to write and speak on international affairs.

In April 2001, President George W. Bush nominated Feith as undersecretary of defense for policy. Confirmed in July 2001, Feith held that position until August 2005. His tenure would prove to be highly controversial. At the Pentagon, Feith's position was advisory; he was not within the military chain of command, yet his office held approval authority over numerous procedures. He was the number three civilian in the Pentagon, next to Secretary of Defense Donald Rumsfeld and Deputy Secretary of Defense Paul Wolfowitz.

As undersecretary, Feith became associated with three projects that, although well

known, did not bear fruit. First, he hoped to engage America's opponents in the global war on terror in a battle of ideas. In the late autumn of 2001, Feith supported the development of the Office of Strategic Influence (OSI), a division of the Department of Defense that would seek to counter propaganda sympathetic to terrorist groups such as Al-Qaeda through psychological campaigns. The clandestine nature of the OSI and a lack of oversight forced Rumsfeld to close it down in February 2002.

Second, Feith advocated the arming of a force of Iraqi exiles to accompany the U.S. invasion of Iraq in 2003. According to Feith, the idea was not well received in the Pentagon, the State Department, or the Central Intelligence Agency (CIA). Third, before Operation Iraqi Freedom began, Feith and his staff developed a plan for the creation of an Iraqi Interim Authority (IIA), which would have allowed for joint American-Iraqi control of Iraq after the defeat of Saddam Hussein's regime, as a prelude to a new Iraqi government. This plan was nixed by the U.S. administrator in Iraq, L. Paul Bremer, in the autumn of 2003.

During his time at the Pentagon, Feith became a lightning rod for criticism of the Bush administration's conduct of the global war on terror and the Iraq War. He has been blamed for a myriad of policy miscues in Afghanistan and Iraq, and some have accused him of pursuing policies that led to the highly damaging Abu Ghraib Prison scandal in 2004. Former vice president Al Gore called for Feith's resignation in a speech at New York University on May 26, 2004.

In various press accounts, Feith has been accused of setting up a secret intelligence cell designed to manipulate the prewar intelligence on Iraq to build a case for war. Feith's account of events in his memoirs differs considerably, however.

He presented the Policy Counter Terrorism Evaluation Group, which evaluated prewar intelligence, as a small group of staffers tasked with summarizing the vast amounts of intelligence that had crossed his desk. Far from being a cadre of Republican political operatives, he argued, the small staff included Chris Carney, a naval officer and university professor who won a seat in Congress in 2006 as a Democrat.

In addition, Feith was accused of attempting to politicize intelligence and to find and publish evidence of links between Iraq and Al-Qaeda that did not exist. In his memoirs, Feith states that he tasked career intelligence analyst Christina Shelton with reviewing intelligence on Iraqi–Al-Qaeda connections and that she developed a view that was critical of the methods by which CIA analysts examined that intelligence. A subsequent Senate Intelligence Committee investigation concluded that staffers of the Office of the Undersecretary of Defense for Policy did not, in fact, pressure intelligence analysts into changing their product. However, intelligence and military analysts as well as other policy experts and media were either concerned by the scrutiny of or influenced by Rumsfeld and Feith's office, and this did in fact affect their products.

In August 2005, with both Rumsfeld and Wolfowitz gone and discredited and the Bush administration's war and national security policy under attack from both Democrats and Republicans, Feith tendered his resignation and left government service. In 2006, he took a position at Georgetown University as visiting professor and distinguished practitioner in national security policy. His contract at Georgetown was not renewed in 2008. Also in 2006, Feith published his memoirs, *War and Decision: Inside the Pentagon at the Dawn*

of the War on Terrorism, which offered a sustained defense of his reputation and an explanation of the decisions that he made while serving in government. The book hardly appeased his legion of critics and detractors, however, and Feith now operates on the margins of policy, though his ideas still retain influence. Feith was last affiliated with the Hudson Institute, a public policy think tank.

Mitchell McNaylor

See also: Abu Ghraib; Bush Administration; Global War on Terror

Further Reading

Feith, Douglas. *War and Decision: Inside the Pentagon at the Dawn of the War on Terrorism*. New York: Harper, 2008.

U.S. Senate. *Report of the Select Committee on Intelligence on the U.S. Intelligence Community's Prewar Assessments on Iraq*. Washington, DC: U.S. Government Printing Office, 2004.

Woodward, Bob. *State of Denial: Bush at War, Part III*. New York: Simon and Schuster, 2006.

Foreign Intelligence Surveillance Act of 1978

The Foreign Intelligence Surveillance Act (FISA) of 1978 was passed as a result of the abuses of the Federal Bureau of Investigation (FBI) in conducting warrantless surveillance of American citizens in the 1960s and early 1970s. Recommendations came out of the 1975 Church Committee on ways to prevent the warrantless surveillance of U.S. citizens by the FBI. Committee members also wanted to end decades of presidentially approved electronic surveillance for national security purposes without a judicial warrant, and thus prevent irregularities in surveillance activities. This committee also believed that the U.S. judiciary lacked the expertise to rule on matters concerning foreign intelligence surveillance. Provisions of the FISA allowed for a special court to be established that would issue warrants after receiving requests from law enforcement agencies. This court was given the name of Foreign Intelligence Surveillance Court (FISC). A search warrant or a wiretap could be issued by the FISC if the subject was an agent of a foreign power, which was defined as either a foreign country or an international terrorist group, or if the subject was engaged in international terrorism or activities in preparation for terrorism on behalf of a foreign power. FISC's orders are classified and kept secret. In the history of the FISC, only a few warrants have ever been turned down, because FISA permits search warrants to be issued based on a lower standard than the standard of probable cause used for criminal search warrants.

Despite the reputation of the FISC for almost never turning down a request from a law enforcement agency, the FBI had been reluctant to apply for warrants from the court before September 11, 2001. An elaborate and time-consuming procedure had to be followed to apply for a warrant from the FISC. Once the agents at a field office had determined that there was probable cause for a FISA warrant, an electronic communication (EC) with supporting documents would be sent to the FBI headquarters unit overseeing the investigation. That unit would add any supporting documents and send the package to the National Security Law Unit (NSLU). This unit comprises lawyers with expertise in national security law. Lawyers in the NSLU would review the case on its merits. If these lawyers agreed that the case met the threshold of probable

cause, then the dossier would be forwarded to the Department of Justice. If not, the case would end at the NSLU. At the Department of Justice, the case would be examined anew by its Office of Intelligence Policy Review (OIPR), where lawyers would once again examine the case for a FISA warrant. Only if the case could pass all of these roadblocks could it be forwarded to the FISA court in the form of a declaration and be signed off by a FISA court judge.

Part of the problem was that the FBI's lawyers interpreted the FISA law in a more restrictive manner than the legislation had intended. This strict interpretation of the law was the case with the FISA request from the Minneapolis field office for a warrant concerning Zacarias Moussaoui, the so-called 20th hijacker on September 11, 2001. FBI agents had requested authority for a warrant several times for Moussaoui, including one from the FISC, but each time their request was turned down by FBI headquarters. Moussaoui had been in Chechnya assisting the Chechen rebels fighting against Russia. The head of the Radical Fundamental Unit (RFU) at FBI headquarters refused to classify the Chechen rebels as part of a so-called recognized foreign power.

The final interpretation of FBI headquarters in the Moussaoui case was that Moussaoui was not associated with a foreign power, nor was the Chechen rebel group a recognized terrorist group. This decision was made despite the warning from French security agents that Moussaoui had been associating with Muslim extremists and even though it was well known in intelligence circles that the Chechen rebels had extensive contacts with Al-Qaeda.

Everything changed after the events of September 11, and the FBI had no trouble obtaining a criminal warrant against

Moussaoui in the aftermath of the attacks. An examination of his computer after September 11 revealed his contacts with the Hamburg Cell, which had carried out the 9/11 attacks, and Al-Qaeda. The FBI's strict adherence to its interpretation of the FISA has been blamed as part of the "Wall" that hindered the flow of information and thwarted the effectiveness of the FBI's efforts against terrorism.

Since September 11, 2001, the controversy over the FISC intensified. The George W. Bush administration made its view known that the onerous requirements of FISA stood in the way of intelligence gathering. In a secret court proceeding before the FISA Appeals Court on September 9, 2002, with only government lawyers present, the Bush administration presented its case that the FISC had hindered the flow of information and had obstructed the president's authority to conduct warrantless searches to obtain foreign intelligence information. The court accepted the government's position and the U.S. Supreme Court refused to hear any appeals. This judgment was the legal grounds for subsequent warrantless searches, which were conducted by the National Security Agency (NSA) in secret and under presidential authority. After news of the warrantless searches became public in December 2005, however, Bush instructed the various intelligence organizations that the FISC system be used for all intelligence-gathering activities. Since taking office in January 2009, Barack Obama and other members of his administration have reiterated Bush's view that it is the president's executive prerogative to circumvent FISA.

Several acts have amended FISA over the years. In 2004, a "lone wolf" provision was added, allowing FISA courts to grant warrants for the surveillance of a non-U.S. citizen believed to be engaging in international terrorism but not linked to a particular government or organization. The Protect America Act of 2007, signed into law on August 5, 2007, officially allowed for the warrantless surveillance of international communications by the U.S. government without FISA oversight. The act, however, expired on February 17, 2008. The Foreign Intelligence Surveillance Act of 1978 Amendments Act of 2008, enacted on July 10, 2008, prevents telecommunications companies from being prosecuted for their complicity in the government's warrantless wiretapping programs. It extends the period of time the government may conduct surveillance on an individual without a warrant from two days to seven days. It also permits the government to not keep records of its searches and surveillance and allows it to destroy existing records after 10 years.

Despite the efforts of the Bush and Obama administrations to bypass the FISC system, FISA courts still exist and the number of warrant requests coming before them has increased significantly in recent years. The use of FISA and its courts does, however, protect the government from accusations that it violates the Fourth Amendment rights of U.S. citizens. The debate over FISA and its courts is ongoing, with many critics believing that both the law and its implementation are hindering the war on terrorism. The issue of surveillance of U.S. citizens and data gathering by the NSA was revisited with a vengeance in 2013, when leaks by Edward Snowden, a U.S. defense contractor with a top security clearance, revealed that the U.S. government was collecting phone numbers, dates of phone calls, length of phone calls, and other information from electronic footprints left by Americans citizens and foreigners alike. In mid-January 2014, President Obama announced limitations on these types of activities, but many civil libertarians argue that they did not go far enough.

Stephen E. Atkins

See also: Bush Administration; Moussaoui, Zacarias; Obama Administration; USA PATRIOT Act

Further Reading

Graham, Bob. *Intelligence Matters: The CIA, the FBI, Saudi Arabia, and the Failure of America's War on Terror*. New York: Random House, 2004.

Meason, James E. "The Foreign Intelligence Surveillance Act: Time for Reappraisal." *International Lawyer* 24 (Winter 1990): 1043.

Schmitt, Gary. "Constitutional Spying: The Solution to the FISA Problem." *Weekly Standard* 11, no. 16 (January 2–9, 2006): 1–2.

Yoo, John. *War by Other Means: An Insider's Account of the War on Terror*. New York: Atlantic Monthly Press, 2006.

Fort Dix Plot

On May 7, 2007, agents from the Federal Bureau of Investigation (FBI) arrested six Muslim extremists originally from the Middle East after two tried to buy automatic weapons from an undercover officer in a plot to attack the Fort Dix military base in New Jersey. They were charged and convicted for trying to kill military personnel and, although not connected to Al-Qaeda, were alleged to have been inspired by Osama bin Laden and his concept of jihad in the defense of Islam.

The group included three brothers: Dritan Duka, 28; Shain Duka, 26; and Eljvir Duka, 23. The trio were ethnic Albanians from Debar in the Republic of Macedonia and had first entered the United States illegally in 1984. Between 1996 and 2006, police had charged Dritan and Shain with a number of traffic citations and minor offenses, including marijuana possession. Court records show they were fined amounts varying from $20 to $830.

The other three were Agron Abdullahu, 24, an Albanian from Kosovo who was living legally in New Jersey and who gave the group weapons training; Mohamad Ibrahim Shnewer, 22, Dritan's brother-in-law and a Palestinian cab driver from Jordan who became a naturalized U.S. citizen; and Serdar Tatar, 23, born in Turkey, who resided in Philadelphia legally and who had worked at a Super Mario Pizza owned by his family.

The six men trained on firing semiautomatic weapons at a Gouldsboro, Pennsylvania, shooting range and used cell phones to videorecord their sessions while shouting in Arabic, "God is great." On January 31, 2006, the group went to a Circuit City store in Mount Laurel, New Jersey, to convert the electronic images into a DVD. However, they failed to effectively screen the cell phone from outside purview, and after store employee Brian Morgenstern saw the content, he contacted authorities.

The FBI then began a 16-month investigation and infiltrated the group with two paid informants who recorded the members planning their attacks. Additional incriminating evidence was extracted from their cell phones, which clearly indicated they wanted to kill as many Americans as possible at the military base. According to U.S. attorney Christopher J. Christie, the members all seemed to feed off each other and obviously had aspirations to be jihadists.

The 26-page indictment showed that the group had no formal military training, no apparent connection to Al-Qaeda or other foreign terrorist organizations, no clear ringleader (although some reports cited Shnewer as the main commander), and very little chance of actually succeeding in pulling off that operation. Court records said the cell had first considered attacking Fort Monmouth in New Jersey, Delaware's Dover Air Force Base, and the U.S. Coast Guard Building in Philadelphia. However, the six settled on Fort Dix because Tatar had delivered pizzas there from his family's Super Mario Pizza and had a map of the installation.

A conversation involving members of the group, recorded by one of the informants, revealed that the cell planned to hit four, five, or six Humvees; rampage through the base, killing people as they went; and then completely retreat without suffering any losses. To do this they had attempted to purchase weapons from an undercover FBI agent, including AK-47s, M16s, M60s, and rocket-propelled grenades.

On May 11, 2007, all six were ordered held without bail at the federal detention facility in Philadelphia. Their trial opened the following October, and after a month the following convictions were handed down: the Duka brothers and Shnewer all received life sentences; Tatar was imprisoned for 23 years; and Abdullahu accepted a plea bargain deal for five years in jail.

Donna Bassett

See also: Al-Qaeda; Terrorism

Further Reading

Emerson, Steven. *Jihad Incorporated: A Guide to Militant Islam in the US.* Amherst, NY: Prometheus Books, 2006.

Lawrence, Bruce. *Messages to the World: The Statements of Osama bin Laden.* London: Verso, 2005.

Temple-Raston, Dina. *The Jihad Next Door: The Lackawanna Six and Rough Justice in the Age of Terror.* New York: Perseus Books, 2007.

G

Gates, Robert Michael

(September 25, 1943–)

U.S. Air Force officer, president of Texas A&M University, director of the Central Intelligence Agency (CIA), and secretary of defense from 2006 until 2011, Robert Michael Gates was born in Wichita, Kansas, on September 25, 1943. He graduated in 1965 from the College of William and Mary with a bachelor's degree in history, then earned a master's degree in history from Indiana University in 1966, and a PhD in Russian and Soviet history from Georgetown University in 1974.

Gates served as an officer in the U.S. Air Force's Strategic Air Command (1967–1969) before joining the CIA in 1969 as an intelligence analyst, a post he held until 1974. He was on the staff of the National Security Council (NSC) from 1974 to 1979, before returning to the CIA as director of the Strategic Evaluation Center in 1979.

Nominated to become director of the CIA in 1987, he withdrew his nomination when it appeared that his connection with the Iran-Contra Affair might hamper his Senate confirmation. He then served as deputy assistant to the president for National Security Affairs (March–August 1989) and as assistant to the president and deputy national security adviser from August 1989 to November 1991.

The Iran-Contra Affair erupted in 1987 when it was revealed that members of President Ronald Reagan's administration had sold weapons to Iran and illegally diverted the funds to the Nicaraguan Contras, the rightist anti-Sandinista rebels. Gates's political enemies assumed that he was guilty because of his senior status at the CIA, but an exhaustive investigation by an independent counsel determined that Gates had done nothing illegal, and on September 3, 1991, the investigating committee stated that Gates's involvement in the scandal did not warrant prosecution. The independent counsel's final 1993 report came to the same conclusion. In May 1991, President George H. W. Bush renominated Gates to head the CIA, and the Senate confirmed Gates on November 5, 1991.

Gates retired from the CIA in 1993. He remained active in public service, cochairing in January 2004 a Council on Foreign Relations task force on U.S.-Iran relations, which suggested that the United States engage Iran diplomatically concerning that nation's pursuit of nuclear weapons. Gates was a member of the Iraq Study Group, a bipartisan commission charged with studying the Iraq War also known as the Baker-Hamilton Commission, from March 15, 2006–December 6, 2006, when he was nominated to succeed the controversial and discredited Donald Rumsfeld as

Defense Secretary Robert Gates announces on March 2, 2007 that he has accepted the resignation of U.S. Army secretary Francis J. Harvey, who stepped down as a result of the fallout from a scandal over substandard conditions at Walter Reed Army Medical Center's outpatient facilities. Many of the patients served in the War on Terror. (U.S. Department of Defense)

defense secretary. Gates assumed the post on December 18, 2006.

In addition to the challenges of the Iraq War, in February 2007, Gates was faced with a scandal concerning inadequate and neglectful care of returning veterans by Walter Reed Army Medical Center. In March 2008, Gates accepted the resignation of Admiral William Joseph "Fox" Fallon, commander of the U.S. Central Command (CENTCOM), a departure due in part to the controversy surrounding an article by Thomas P. M. Barnett titled "The Man between War and Peace," published in *Esquire* magazine on March 11, 2008. The article asserted that there were policy disagreements between Fallon and the Bush administration on the prosecution of the war in Iraq and potential conflict with Iran over that nation's nuclear arms program. Gates rejected any sugges-

tion that Fallon's resignation indicated a U.S. willingness to attack Iran in order to stop its nuclear weapons development.

Unlike his abrasive predecessor, Gates brought an era of calm and focus to the Pentagon and appeared far more willing to engage in discussion and compromise over matters of defense and military policy. Indeed, he was so conciliatory that President Barack Obama, who took office in January 2009, decided to keep him on as defense secretary. In April 2009, Gates proposed a major reorientation in the U.S. defense budget that would entail deep cuts in more traditional programs that provide for conventional warfare with such major military powers as Russia and China, and shift assets to those programs that would aid in fighting the insurgencies in both Iraq and Afghanistan. Among his proposed cuts were missile defense, the army's future combat systems, navy shipbuilding, new presidential helicopters, and a new communications satellite system. Gates proposed delaying development of a new air force bomber and ordering only 4 additional F-22 fighters for a total of 197, while purchasing as many as 513 of the less expensive F-35 strike fighters over the next five years. Purchases of large navy ships would be delayed. At the same time, the new budget would provide for a sharp increase in funding for surveillance and intelligence-gathering equipment, to include the Predator-class unmanned aerial vehicles, and would increase manpower in the army to include Special Forces and the Marine Corps. These decisions triggered major debate in Congress over defense spending and priorities. In December 2009, Gates was the first senior U.S. official to visit Afghanistan after President Barack Obama announced his intention to deploy some 30,000 additional military personnel to that country.

In 2010, Gates lifted the ban against women crew members aboard U.S. Navy submarines and helped engineer the repeal of the controversial "Don't Ask Don't Tell" policy toward gays in the military. By the fall of 2011, gays were permitted to serve openly in the U.S. military without fear of being intimidated, ostracized, or expelled. Gates retired in July 2011, at which time he was awarded the Presidential Medal of Freedom. In 2012, Gates became chancellor of the College of William and Mary in Virginia. In January 2014, Gates's newly published autobiography, *Duty: Memoirs of a Secretary of War*, sparked controversy because in it he stated that Obama had seemed ambivalent toward the troop surge in Afghanistan, which began in 2010. He went on to say, however, that he never had any doubt that the president supported U.S. military forces. Gates reserved his most notable criticism for Vice President Joe Biden. Gates pointedly claimed that Biden had been consistently wrong on almost every major military or national security debate over the preceding 25 years.

Richard M. Edwards

See also: Bush Administration; Bush Doctrine; Central Intelligence Agency; Enduring Freedom, Operation; Iraqi Freedom, Operation; Obama Administration; Rumsfield, Donald Henry

Further Reading

Barnett, Thomas P. M. "The Man between War and Peace." *Esquire*, March 11, 2008, 1–4.

Gates, Robert M. *Understanding the New U.S. Defense Policy through the Speeches of Robert M. Gates, Secretary of Defense.* Rockville, MD: Arc Manor, 2008.

Gates, Robert M. *From the Shadows: The Ultimate Insider's Story of Five Presidents and How They Won the Cold War.* New York: Simon and Schuster, 1996.

Oliphant, Thomas. *Utter Incompetents: Ego and Ideology in the Age of Bush.* New York: Thomas Dunne Books, 2007.

Gemayel (Bashir) Assassination

On September 14, 1982, a 77-pound improvised explosive device (IED) killed Bashir Gemayel, a Lebanese senior politician, militia commander, and president-elect, at his Christian Phalangist Party headquarters in East Beirut. In addition to Gemayel, the bomb killed 25 others, including Phalangist Party head John Nazir. Fifty people were injured by the blast.

Habib Shartouni, a member of the Syrian Social Nationalist Party, confessed to planting the IED in his sister's apartment above the room Gemayel was in.

After calling and telling her to evacuate the building, he detonated the bomb from a few miles away. When Shartouni came back to check on his sister, he was immediately arrested. He later justified his actions on the grounds that Gemayel "had sold the country to Israel." He was imprisoned for eight years until Syrian troops took over Lebanon at the end of the war and freed him on October 13, 1990.

Prior to the assassination, Israeli defense minister Ariel Sharon had informed Gemayel that the Jewish state was going to invade Lebanon to root out the Palestine Liberation Organization (PLO). Gemayel, who had already angered many Lebanese Muslims and leftists by working with the Israeli political and military establishment, accepted the notification and duly warned the main Palestinian spokesman in the country that his organization should immediately leave or be wiped out. The representative refused, and in the summer of 1982, Israel invaded, successfully driving out the PLO. The casus belli was the attempted assassination of Israeli ambassador Shlomo Argove by Abu Nidal Organization (ANO) members in London on June 4, 1982.

Following the invasion and Gemayel's subsequent election, Israeli prime minister Menachem Begin demanded that the new Lebanese leader sign a peace treaty in return for Israel's earlier support of his Lebanese forces. If Gemayel did not comply, Begin warned that Israel would stay in South Lebanon indefinitely. Infuriated, Gemayel said that he had not fought for seven years to rid Lebanon of the Syrian Army and the PLO so that Israel could take their place. Begin relented and agreed that Israel's troops would cooperate with the Lebanese Army to force out the Syrian Army and then depart from the country.

Begin also accepted that Gemayel needed to mend Lebanon's internal conflicts before he could consider signing a peace accord. The 1982 assassination abruptly ended those plans.

Following Gemayel's death, his brother Amin was elected as president. Although Amin was a member of parliament and an experienced political operator, he lacked Gemayel's charisma; moreover, he did not inherit control of the armed forces, and he failed to win the support of the Maronite community. He was largely dependent on the support of the Israelis, who liked him less than his brother, and on the United States and a narrow domestic power base. This did not provide him with the necessary personal authority to either heal Lebanon's fractious internal conditions or consolidate a peace agreement with Israel.

Spencer C. Tucker

See also: Arab-Israeli Conflict, Overview; Democratization and the Global War on Terror

Further Reading

Fisk, Robert. *Pity the Nation: The Abduction of Lebanon.* New York: Touchstone, Simon & Schuster, 1990.

Oren, Michael B. *Power, Faith, and Fantasy: America in the Middle East 1776 to the Present.* New York: W. W. Norton, 2007.

Parker, Richard B. *The Politics of Miscalculation in the Middle East.* Bloomington: Indiana University Press, 1993.

Tyler, Patrick. *A World of Trouble: The White House and the Middle East—from the Cold War to the on War Terror.* New York: Farrar Straus Giroux, 2009.

Global War on Terror

This is a term used to describe the military, political, diplomatic, and economic measures employed by the United States and other allied governments against organizations, countries, or individuals that are committing terrorist acts, that might be inclined to engage in terrorism, or that support those who do commit such acts. The global war on terror is an amorphous concept and a somewhat indistinct term, yet its use emphasizes the difficulty in classifying the type of nontraditional warfare being waged against U.S. and Western interests by various terrorist groups that do not represent any nation. The term was coined by President George W. Bush in a September 20, 2001, televised address to a joint session of the U.S. Congress, and has been presented in official White House pronouncements, fact sheets, State of the Union messages, and such National Security Council (NSC) position papers as the National Security Strategy (March 2006) and the National Strategy for Combating Terrorism (February 2003 and September 2006 editions). Since 2001, the global war on terror has been directed primarily at Islamic terrorist groups, but has also been expanded to include actions against all types of terrorism. During the Bush administration, Secretary of Defense Robert Gates also called it the "long war."

As with the Cold War, the global war on terror is being waged on numerous fronts, against many individuals and nations, and involves both military and nonmilitary tactics. President George W. Bush's September 20, 2001, announcement of the global war on terror was in response to the September 11, 2001, terror attacks against the United States, which led to the deaths of some 3,000 civilians, mostly Americans but representing civilians of 90 different countries.

Although the war constitutes a global effort, stretching into Asia, Africa, Europe, and the Americas, the Middle East remains a focal point of the effort. The ongoing conflict and the manner in which it has been waged has been the source of much debate. There is no widely agreed-upon estimate regarding the number of casualties during the global war on terror because it includes the invasion of Afghanistan in 2001 and the war in Iraq, as well as many acts of terrorism around the world. Some estimates, which include the U.S.-led coalition invasion of Afghanistan in 2001 and the invasion of Iraq in March 2003, claim that well over 2 million people have died in the struggle.

Following the September 11, 2001, terror attacks, the United States responded quickly and with overwhelming force against the organizations and governments that supported the terrorists. Evidence gathered by the U.S. government pointed to the Al-Qaeda terrorist organization. Al-Qaeda at the time was being given aid and shelter by the Taliban regime in Afghanistan. On September 20, 2001, President George W. Bush announced to a joint session of Congress that the global war on terror would not end simply with the defeat of Al-Qaeda or the overthrow of the Taliban, but only when every terrorist group and terrorist-affiliated government with a global reach had been defeated. These broad aims implied attacks on countries known to support terrorism, such as Iran and Syria. Bush further assured the American people that every means of intelligence, tool of diplomacy, financial pressure, and weapon of war would be used to defeat terrorism. He told the American people to expect a lengthy campaign. Bush also issued an ultimatum to all other nations, stating that each had to choose whether they were with the United States or against it. There would be no middle ground. Clearly, Bush's pronouncements were far-reaching, yet the enemies were difficult to identify and find.

Less than 24 hours after the September 11 attacks, the North American Treaty Organization (NATO), declared the terrorist attacks of September 11 to be against all member nations, the first time the organization had made such a pronouncement since its inception in 1949.

On October 7, 2001, U.S. and coalition forces (chiefly British) invaded Afghanistan to capture Osama bin Laden, the head of Al-Qaeda, to destroy his organization, and to overthrow the Taliban government that supported him. Eventually Canada, Australia, France, and Germany, among other nations, joined that effort. However, when a U.S.-led coalition invaded Iraq in March 2003, there was considerable international opposition to this campaign being included under the rubric of the global war on terror. One problem for national leaders who supported President Bush's policies was that many of their citizens did not believe that the overthrow of Iraqi dictator Saddam Hussein was really part of the global war on terror and questioned other reasons stated by the Bush administration to justify the U.S.-led invasion. International opinion polls have shown that support for the war on terror has consistently declined since 2003, likely the result of opposition to the Bush administration's preemptive invasion of Iraq in March 2003 and later revelations that Iraq possessed neither ties to Al-Qaeda nor weapons of mass destruction. Although virtually all U.S. troops were withdrawn from Iraq by late 2011, that country has been plagued by an accelerating insurgency spawned by continued sectarian strife and groups like Al-Qaeda in Iraq, who by early 2014 had seized several sizable cities in Anbar Province. The

future of Iraq remains very much an open question.

The global war on terror has also been a sporadic and clandestine war since its inception in September 2001. U.S. forces were sent to Yemen and the Horn of Africa in order to disrupt terrorist activities, while Operation Active Endeavor is a naval operation intended to prevent terror attacks and limit the movement of terrorists in the Mediterranean. Terrorist attacks in Pakistan, Indonesia, and the Philippines led to the insertion of coalition forces into these countries as well and concerns about the situation in other Southeast Asian countries. In the United States, Congress has also passed legislation intended to help increase the effectiveness of law enforcement agencies in their search for terrorist activities. In the process, however, critics claim that Americans' civil liberties have been steadily eroded, and government admissions that the Federal Bureau of Investigation (FBI) and other agencies have engaged in wiretapping of international phone calls without requisite court orders and probable cause have caused a storm of controversy, as have the methods used to question foreign nationals. In 2013, leaks by U.S. defense contractor employee Edward Snowden further revealed that the National Security Agency (NSA) has been collecting phone logs of many American citizens in the name of the war on terror. This sparked outrage in America and compelled President Barack Obama to scale back such NSA programs in January 2014.

The Bush administration has also greatly increased the role of the federal government in the attempt to fight terrorism at home and abroad. Among the many new government bureaucracies formed is the Department of Homeland Security, a cabinet-level agency that counts at least 210,000 employees. The increase in the size of the government, combined with huge military expenditures—most of which went to the Iraq War—only added to the massive U.S. budget deficits.

Proponents of the global war on terror believe that proactive measures must be taken against terrorist organizations to effectively defeat global terrorism. They believe that in order to meet the diverse security challenges of the 21st century, a larger, global military presence is needed. Without such a force, they argue, terrorist organizations will continue to launch strikes against innocent civilians. Many of the people argue that the United States, Great Britain, Spain, and other countries, which have been the victims of large-scale attacks, must go on the offensive against such rogue groups and that not doing so will only embolden the attackers and invite more attacks. Allowing such organizations to gain more strength may allow them to achieve their goal of imposing militant Islamist rule.

Critics of the global war on terror claim that there is no tangible enemy to defeat, as there is no single group whose defeat will bring about an end to the conflict. Thus, it is virtually impossible to know if progress is being made. They also argue that "terrorism," a tactic whose goal is to instill fear into people through violent actions, can never be truly defeated. There are also those who argue against the justification for preemptive strikes, because such action invites counter responses and brings about the deaths of many innocent people. Many believe that the Iraqi military posed no imminent threat to the United States when coalition forces entered Iraq in 2003, but the resultant war has been disastrous for both the Iraqi and American people. Civil right activists contend that measures meant to crack down on terrorist activities have infringed on the rights of American citizens as well as the rights of foreign detainees. Furthermore, critics argue that the war and the amount of spending apportioned to military endeavors negatively affects the national and world economies. Others argue that the United States should be spending time and resources on resolving the Arab-Israeli problem and trying to eradicate the desperate conditions that feed terrorism.

As support for the global war on terror effort has diminished, the debate over its effectiveness has grown. From late 2007 to early 2014, terrorist attacks have continued, and the deliberation over the best way to ensure the safety of civilian populations around the world continues. In April 2013, two young men with alleged ties to Islamic extremists in Chechnya bombed the Boston Marathon, killing 3 and wounding more than 250 others. The attack demonstrated that despite all of the increased security after 2001, America is still vulnerable to terror plots on its soil.

As of March 2009, the Barack Obama administration decided not to use the terms "global war on terror" or "long war." It instructed U.S. government agencies to use the term "overseas contingency operations." White House officials explained that Obama is "using different words and phrases in order to denote a reaching out to many moderate parts of the world that we believe can be important in a battle against extremists." However, the term "global war on terror" is still deeply embedded in the collective psyche.

In a much-anticipated speech at the National Defense University on May 23, 2013, President Obama said that it was time to narrow the scope of the grinding battle against terrorists and begin the transition to a day when the country will no longer be on a war footing. Declaring that "America is at a crossroads," the president called for redefining what has been a global war into a more targeted assault on terrorist groups threatening the United States. As part of a realignment of counterterrorism policy, he said he would curtail the use of drones, recommit to closing the prison for terror suspects at Guantánamo Bay, Cuba, and seek new limits on his own war power. Instead, the president suggested that the United States return to the state of affairs that existed before Al-Qaeda toppled the World Trade Center, when terrorism was a persistent but not existential danger. With Al-Qaeda's core now "on the path to defeat," he argued, the nation must adapt.

Gregory Wayne Morgan

See also: Counterterrorism Strategy; Enduring Freedom, Operation; Iraqi Freedom, Operation; Terrorism

Further Reading

Bacevich, Andrew J. *The New American Militarism: How Americans Are Seduced by War.* New York: Oxford University Press, 2005.

Mahajan, Rahul. *The New Crusade: America's War on Terrorism.* New York: Monthly Review, 2002.

Woodward, Bob. *Bush at War.* New York: Simon and Schuster, 2002.

Ground Zero Mosque Controversy

Commonly referred to as the "Ground Zero Mosque," Park51 is an Islamic community center under development in New York City. Although often identified in the media as a mosque, the 13-story building would feature many facilities, including a 500-seat auditorium, performing arts center, swimming pool, fitness center, bookstore, culinary school, art studio, and September 11 memorial, in addition to a prayer space that could accommodate up to 2,000 people. Although the community center would not actually be located at Ground Zero, the project has sparked significant debate because of its proximity to the site of the September 11 attacks.

The community center would occupy 45–51 Park Place, about two blocks north of the World Trade Center site. In July 2009, Soho Properties bought half of the lot (45–47 Park Place), which was occupied at the time by a three-story building that had been heavily damaged during the September 11 attacks. The other half of the lot (49–51 Park Place) is owned by the utility Con Edison and leased to Soho Properties. Although Soho Properties CEO Sharif El-Gamal initially intended to turn the site into a condominium complex, he was convinced by Imam Feisal Abdul Rauf, a well-known Muslim religious leader in New York City, to construct a community center instead. The project's chief investors—the American Society for Muslim Advancement (ASMA) and the Cordoba Initiative—are both nonprofit organizations founded by Rauf.

Plans to build the community center were first made public in the *New York Times* on December 9, 2009, although they attracted little notice. On May 25, 2010, Lower Manhattan Community Board 1 backed the secular aspects of the project through a nonbinding vote of 29 to 1, although the religious component of the planned community center caused some anxiety among board members. By mid-2010, Pamela Geller and Robert Spencer, founders of the group Stop Islamization of America, had brought national attention to the project, which they vocally criticized and dubbed the Ground Zero Mosque.

Most Park51 opponents assert that this is not an issue of religious freedom or racism and that they object only to the location of the community center. They argue that building Park51 only a few blocks from Ground Zero is insensitive to the memory of 9/11 victims, who lost their lives at the hands of Islamic terrorists, and their families. More extreme opponents, however, have labeled the construction project a blatant Islamic threat. Others have speculated about Park51's funding sources, voicing concerns that the project's investors might take money from Hamas, Iran, or other entities hostile to the United States. Those opposed to Park51 include a number of families of 9/11 victims, the American Center for Law & Justice, the Zionist Organization of America, and the Center for Islamic Pluralism. Prominent politicians who have spoken out against the project include Republican senator John McCain, former Alaska governor Sarah Palin, former Speaker of the House New Gingrich, and former New York City mayor Rudy Giuliani.

Supporters counter that opponents are motivated by intolerance and baseless fear and hatred. They assert that it is important to distinguish between mainstream Islam and the radical brand of Islam practiced by those who committed the September 11 attacks. Concerns have also arisen that the controversy over Park51 will fuel anti-Americanism around the world and serve as a powerful recruiting tool for Islamic extremist groups. Supporters of the project include the September 11th Families for Peaceful Tomorrows, the Council on American-Islamic Relations (CAIR), the Muslim Public Affairs Council, and the American Civil Liberties

Union (ACLU). Many New York City officials have backed Park51, including former New York Mayor Michael Bloomberg and Manhattan Borough president Scott Stringer. Former president Bill Clinton, Texas representative Ron Paul, and other well-known politicians have also given their support.

Polls reveal that the majority of Americans, as well as the majority of residents living in New York State and the larger New York City metropolitan area, oppose the building of Park51 near the World Trade Center, although a majority of respondents also agree that the developers have a legal and constitutional right to build the community center at that site. A majority of Manhattan residents, however, support the building of Park51 at its planned location.

In addition to the issue of location, even the community center's name has proven controversial. The development's original name—Cordoba House—was inspired by Cordoba, Spain, where, according to Rauf, Muslims, Jews, and Christians lived harmoniously and cooperatively during the 8th through 11th centuries. Detractors contend that the name was a clear and hostile reference to the Muslim conquest of the Iberian Peninsula. To minimize objections, the community center's name was changed to Park51, referring to its address on Park Place. Supporters of the project argue that the popular nickname "Ground Zero Mosque" is inaccurate and misused by the media in order to increase public anxiety about the development. In late September 2011, the developer of Park51 opened a small, 4,000-square foot Islamic center at the site; however, the larger 13-story project remained in limbo as of late 2013. In late September 2011, a temporary 4,000-square-foot (370 m2) Islamic center opened in renovated space at the Park51 location.

Spencer C. Tucker

See also: Al-Quds Mosque; Global War on Terror; September 11 Terrorist Trial Controversy; World Trade Center, September 11, 2001

Further Reading

Barret, Devlin. "Mosque Debate Isn't Going Away." *Wall Street Journal*, August 3, 2010.

Ghosh, Bobby. "Mosque Controversy: Does America Have a Muslim Problem?" *Time*, August 19, 2010.

Hernandez, Javier C. "Vote Endorses Muslim Center Near Ground Zero." *New York Times*, May 25, 2010.

Rauf, Feisal Abdul. "Building on Faith." *New York Times*, September 7, 2010.

Guantánamo Bay Detainment Camp

The Guantánamo Bay Detainment Camp, operated by the U.S. government to hold enemy combatants taken prisoner during the global war on terror, which began in late 2001 after the September 11, 2001, terror attacks against the United States, is situated on the Guantánamo Bay Naval Base, operated by the United States in southeastern Cuba. The base is an area of 45 square miles that has been formally occupied by the United States since 1903, a result of the 1898 Spanish-American War. The original intent of the base was to serve as a coaling station for the U.S. Navy. A subsequent lease was signed on July 2, 1906, on the same terms. A new lease was negotiated between the Cuban and U.S. governments in 1934.

Shortly after the 1959 Cuban Revolution, the Castro government demanded that the Guantánamo Bay area be returned to Cuban sovereignty, but the U.S. government refused, citing that the lease required the agreement of both parties to the modification or abrogation of the agreement. Since then, the United States has continued to send a check to the Cuban government for the lease amount every year, but the Cuban government has steadfastly refused to cash them.

During its invasion of Afghanistan that began in October 2001, the U.S. military captured a large number of Al-Qaeda fighters and other insurgents. The George W. Bush administration determined that those captured were enemy combatants, not prisoners of war.

This decision came after lawyers from the White House, the Pentagon, and the Justice Department issued a series of secret memorandums maintaining that the prisoners had no rights under federal law or the Geneva Conventions. In this ruling, enemy combatants could be held indefinitely without charges. A number of conservative lawyers in the Justice Department's Office of Legal Counsel (OLC) provided the legal opinions for this decision. The Bush administration issued this decision on January 22, 2002.

Finally, after considering several sites to hold these prisoners, the U.S. military decided to build a prison at Guantánamo Bay, Cuba, the Guantánamo Bay Detainment Camp. Camp X-Ray was the first facility, and the first 110 prisoners arrived there on January 11, 2002. They were held in wire cages. Later, Camp Delta was constructed, but neither camp was up to standards for prison inmates in the United States. At their peak, the camps held 680 prisoners.

U.S. military police escort a detainee to his cell at the naval base at Guantánamo Bay, Cuba, on January 11, 2002. (U.S. Department of Defense)

The Bush administration selected Guantánamo Bay for a specific reason. If the prisoners were held on U.S. soil, they might claim access to legal representation and American courts. Guantánamo Bay fell under a unique legal situation because the land is leased from Cuba and thus is not technically American soil. Furthermore, because the United States has no diplomatic relationship with Cuba, the prisoners had no access to the Cuban legal system. There the prisoners reside in legal limbo with few, if any, legal rights.

The detainment camp is run by the U.S. military. At the beginning, command responsibility for the base was divided between Major General Michael Dunlavey, an army reservist, and Brigadier General Rick Baccus, of the Rhode Island National Guard. Dunlavey maintained a hard-line attitude toward the detainees, but Baccus was more concerned about their possible

mistreatment. They often quarreled over interrogation techniques and other issues. This situation changed when U.S. Army major general Geoffrey Miller replaced them and established a unitary command at Guantánamo in November 2003.

Miller had no experience running a prison camp, and he was soon criticized for allowing harsh interrogation techniques including the controversial waterboarding technique, which the Bush administration insisted was not torture. Later, Miller was transferred to Iraq, where he took over responsibility for military prisons there.

After Camp Delta was built, the detainees lived in better, but still restrictive, conditions. At Camp X-Ray, the original camp, the detainees lived behind razor wire in cells open to the elements and with buckets in place of toilets. At Camp Delta, the detainees were held in trailerlike structures made from old shipping containers that had been cut in half lengthwise, with the two pieces stuck together end to end. Cells were small, six feet eight inches by eight feet, with metal beds fixed to the steel mesh walls. Toilets were squatting-style flush on the floor, and sinks were low to the ground so that detainees could wash their feet before Muslim prayer. There was no air conditioning for the detainees, only a ventilation system that was supposed to be turned on at 85 degrees but rarely was. Later a medium-security facility opened up, and it gave much greater freedom and better living conditions to the detainees.

The Bush administration gave the Central Intelligence Agency (CIA) responsibility for interrogations. Because these enemy combatants had no legal standing in American courts, they were treated merely as sources of intelligence. President Bush had determined this stance after deciding that Al-Qaeda was a national security issue, not a law enforcement issue. Consequently, the Federal Bureau of Investigation (FBI) was completely left out of the loop. But this did not mean that the FBI gave up on questioning prisoners. For various reasons, FBI personnel did interrogate the detainees on occasion.

To encourage cooperation, levels of treatment for detainees are determined by the degree of a detainee's cooperation. Level one was for cooperating prisoners, and they received special privileges. Level two included more moderately cooperative detainees, and they received a few privileges, such as a drinking cup and access to the library. Level three was for the detainees who absolutely refused to cooperate. They were given only the basics: a blanket, a prayer mat and cap, a Koran, and a toothbrush.

The CIA ultimately determined that the most important Al-Qaeda prisoners should not be held at the Guantánamo Bay Detainment Camp. There were simply too many American officials from too many agencies trying to interrogate the prisoners. Moreover, it was too public. CIA leaders wanted a secret location where there would be no interference in the interrogations. Several secret interrogation sites were then set up in friendly countries where the CIA could do what it wanted without interference.

Soon after the prisoners had been transferred to the Guantánamo Bay Detainment Camp, reports began to surface about mistreatment of the detainees, which caused considerable consternation abroad. In the late spring of 2002, a CIA analyst visited the camp and was aghast at the treatment of the prisoners. Because he spoke Arabic, he was able to talk to the detainees. In his report the analyst claimed that half of the detainees did not belong there. This report traveled throughout the Bush administration, but no action was taken regarding it. The American public was still upset over the September 11 attacks, and public reports about mistreatment of those held at Guantánamo Bay garnered little sympathy.

The Bush administration decided in the summer of 2006 to transfer the top captured Al-Qaeda leaders to the Guantánamo Bay Detainment Camp. In September 2006, the transfer of these 14 detainees was complete. Then, beginning in March 2007, court proceedings were begun to determine their status. In the most important case, that of Khalid Sheikh Mohammed, the accused made a total confession of all his activities both in and outside Al-Qaeda. However, his confessions were elicited through torture and physical abuse. Among these were the planning for the September 11 attacks and the execution of U.S. journalist Daniel Pearl. Mohammed's justification was that he was at war against the United States. Proceedings against the other detainees continued in the spring of 2007.

Meanwhile, growing public criticism in the United States and elsewhere about the status of the detainees led to a series of court cases in the United States in 2007 and 2008 that tried to establish a legal basis for them. Finally, in June 2008, the U.S. Supreme Court ruled that Guantánamo detainees were indeed subject to protection under the U.S. Constitution. By that time the situation in Cuba had become a public relations fiasco for the Bush administration. In October 2008, a federal court judge ordered the release of five Algerians being held at Guantánamo because the government had shown insufficient evidence for their continued incarceration. More detainees were likely to be reevaluated, which would result in their potential release or a trial. Experts have recommended exactly such a process, which they termed R2T2: (1) review, (2) release or transfer, and (3) try. In January 2009, on his second full day in office, President Obama signed an executive order that was a declaration of American renewal and decency hailed around the globe. It called for the closure, in no more than a year, of the detention camp at the United States Naval Station at Guantánamo Bay, Cuba. As of 2014, however, the detention camp continued operations.

Stephen E. Atkins

See also: Bush Administration; Bush Doctrine; Coercive Interrogation Techniques; Global War on Terror; Mohammed, Khalid Sheikh; Obama Administration; Torture of Prisoners

Further Reading

Hersh, Seymour. *Chain of Command: The Road from 9/11 to Abu Ghraib.* New York: HarperCollins, 2004.

Mendelsohn, Sarah E. *Closing Guantanamo: From Bumper Sticker to Blueprint.* Washington, DC: Center for Security and International Studies, 2008.

Saar, Erik, and Viveca Novak. *Inside the Wire: A Military Intelligence Soldier's Eyewitness Account of Life at Guantanamo.* New York: Penguin, 2005.

Yee, John. *War by Other Means: An Insider's Account of the War on Terror.* New York: Atlantic Monthly, 2006.

H

Hamburg Cell

A group of radical Islamists formed a terrorist cell affiliated with Al-Qaeda in Hamburg, Germany. This cell began when Mohamed Atta, Ramzi bin al-Shibh, and Marwan al-Shehhi began rooming together on November 1, 1998, in an apartment at 54 Marienstrasse in Hamburg. They were members of a study group at the al-Quds Mosque run by Mohammad Belfas, a middle-aged postal employee in Hamburg originally from Indonesia. Both in the study group and at the apartment they began talking about ways to advance the Islamist cause. Soon the original three attracted others of a like mind. The nine members of this cell were Mohamed Atta, Said Bahaji, Mohammad Belfas, Ramzi bin al-Shibh, Zakariya Essabor, Marwan al-Shehhi, Ziad Jarrah, Mounir el Motassadez, and Abdelghani Mzoudi. Belfas was the initial leader of the group, but he was soon replaced by Atta and left the cell. Atta then became the formal leader of the Hamburg Cell, but bin al-Shibh was its most influential member because he was better liked in the Muslim community than the dour Atta.

At first, the members of the Hamburg Cell wanted to join the Chechen rebels in Chechnya in fighting against the Russians. Before this move could take place, the leaders of the cell met with Mohamedou Ould Slahi, an Al-Qaeda operative in Duisburg, Germany, who advised that they undertake military and terrorist training in Afghanistan first. Atta, bin al-Shibh, Jarrah, and al-Shehhi traveled to Kandahar, Afghanistan, where they underwent extensive training in terrorist methods. They also met with Osama bin Laden, at which time Atta, Jarrah, and al-Shehhi were recruited for a special martyrdom mission to the United States.

Bin al-Shibh was to have been a part of this mission, but he was never able to obtain a visa to travel to the United States. Instead, he stayed in Hamburg, serving as the contact person between the Hamburg Cell and Al-Qaeda. He also served as the banker for the September 11, 2001, plot.

The most dedicated members of the Hamburg Cell participated in the September 11 plot. Other members of the group, however, provided moral and technical support. Mamoun Darkanza was the money man for the Hamburg Cell. What made those in the Hamburg Cell so important was that they were fluent in English, well educated, and accustomed to the Western lifestyle, so they could fit in without arousing suspicion in any of the Western countries. They also had the capability to learn how to pilot a large aircraft with some training.

Bin al-Shibh shut down the Hamburg Cell as soon as he learned the date of the attacks. He made certain that anyone connected with the Hamburg Cell was forewarned so that they could protect themselves. Bin al-Shibh destroyed as much material as possible before leaving for Pakistan. Only later did German and American authorities learn of the full extent of the operations of the Hamburg Cell.

German authorities had been aware of the existence of the Hamburg Cell, but German law prevented action against the cell's members unless a German law was violated. This restriction did not prevent a veteran Central Intelligence Agency (CIA) officer attached to the American consulate in Hamburg, Thomas Volz, from attempting to persuade the German authorities to take action against the Islamist extremists in the Hamburg Cell. Volz had become suspicious of several members of the Hamburg Cell and their connections with other Muslim terrorists. He hounded the German authorities to do something until his actions alienated them to the point that they almost had him deported from Germany.

After the September 11 attacks, German authorities began a serious investigation of the Hamburg Cell and its surviving members. By this time there was little to examine or do except to arrest whoever had been affiliated with it. German authorities learned the extent to which Al-Qaeda had been able to establish contacts in Germany and elsewhere in Europe.

Stephen E. Atkins

See also: Al-Qaeda; Al-Quds Mosque; Atta, Mohamed el-Amir Awad el-Sayed; Pentagon Attack; World Trade Center, September 11, 2001

Further Reading

Bernstein, Richard. *Out of the Blue: The Story of September 11, 2001, from Jihad to Ground Zero*. New York: Times Books, 2002.

McDermott, Terry. *Perfect Soldiers: The 9/11 Hijackers; Who They Were, Why They Did It*. New York: HarperCollins, 2005.

Posner, Gerald. *Why America Slept: The Failure to Prevent 9/11*. New York: Ballantine, 2003.

Sageman, Marc. *Understanding Terror Networks*. Philadelphia: University of Pennsylvania Press, 2004.

Hanjour, Hani Saleh Husan

(1972–2011)

Hani Saleh Husan Hanjour was the leader and probable pilot of the terrorist group that seized American Airlines Flight 77 and crashed it into the Pentagon on September 11, 2001. He was a last-minute recruit because the September 11 conspirators needed one more pilot. Although Hanjour was a terrible pilot, he had enough skill to guide an airliner into a stationary target.

Hanjour had advantages in life, but he lacked the abilities to capitalize on them. He was born on August 30, 1972, in Ta'if, Saudi Arabia. His father was a successful food-supply businessman in Ta'if. Hanjour was a devout Muslim, and it colored all of his conduct. Because he was an indifferent student, Hanjour was only persuaded to stay in school by his older brother. This older brother, who was living in Tucson, Arizona, encouraged him to come to the United States. Hanjour arrived in the United States on October 3, 1991. He stayed in Tucson, where he studied English at the University of Arizona.

Frustrated in his job hunting, Hanjour traveled to Afghanistan. He arrived there just as Khalid Sheikh Mohammed's men were looking for another pilot for the September 11 plot. Hanjour was made to order. After being recruited by Al-Qaeda, he returned to the United States. In September 2000, when he moved to San Diego, California, Hanjour met up with Nawaf al-Hazmi. Hanjour returned to Phoenix to continue his pilot training at the Jet Tech Flight School. He was so inept as a flyer, and his English was so bad, that the instructors contacted the FAA to check whether his commercial license was valid. The FAA confirmed that his commercial license was indeed valid. Hanjour spent most of his time there on the Boeing 737 simulator. Next, he moved to Paterson, New Jersey, in the early spring of 2001. There, he met several times with other members of the September 11 conspiracy. On September 11, 2001, Hanjour was the hijackers' pilot on American Airlines Flight 77. Despite his lack of ability, he managed to fly that aircraft into the Pentagon. All 58 passengers aboard the jetliner perished, including all of the hijackers. Another 125 people died on the ground.

Stephen E. Atkins

See also: Mohammed, Khalid Sheikh; Pentagon Attack

Further Reading

Graham, Bob. *Intelligence Matters: The CIA, the FBI, Saudi Arabia, and the Failure of America's War on Terror.* New York: Random House, 2004.

McDermott, Terry. *Perfect Soldiers: The Hijackers: Who They Were, Why They Did It.* New York: HarperCollins, 2005.

Harakat ul-Jihad Al-Isalami (HuJI)

Harakat ul-Jihad al-Islami (HuJI, or Islamic Struggle Movement) is a Pakistan-based terrorist group that adheres to the Deobandi sect of Islam and espouses a virulent anti-Indian, anti–United States, and anti-Pakistani government agenda. Conflicting reports exist regarding the precise date of HuJI's founding and its creators; however, most sources agree that the organization was established during the Afghan jihad to fight against occupying Soviet forces, and that Qari Saifullah Akhtar and Maulana Irshad Ahmed were prominent early members. Following Moscow's withdrawal from Kabul in 1989, HuJI refocused its efforts toward fighting Indian rule in the predominantly Muslim state of Jammu and Kashmir with the prominent support and backing of Pakistan's InterServices Intelligence (ISI) Directorate.

HuJI developed strong ties with the Taliban government in Afghanistan during the late 1990s, and several sources suggest that by this time Akhtar was serving as a political advisor to Mullah Omar. HuJI relocated much of its training infrastructure to Afghanistan, establishing a major training camp in Rishkot, and assisted the Taliban in combat operations against the Northern Alliance—eliciting perhaps the first known use of the term *Punjabi Taliban.* HuJI's leadership was also reportedly close to Al-Qaeda, and is believed to have been a principal force in helping to solidify links between Osama bin Laden and Mullah Omar.

Following the fall of the Taliban in late 2001, much of the group's membership relocated to Pakistan, establishing a strong presence in the Federally Administered Tribal Areas (FATA) and the Northwest Frontier Province (NWFP), now known as Khyber-Pakhtunkwha. The group also set up various smaller branches in other parts of the country. Akhtar reportedly fled from

Afghanistan first to South Waziristan, then to Saudi Arabia, and finally to Dubai. He was deported to Pakistan in 2004 following suspicions of his involvement in two foiled plots to assassinate then president Pervez Musharraf, and was held in custody until 2007, when he was evidently released.

Following the storming of the Lal Masjid mosque, HuJI was suspected of involvement in a number of high-profile terrorist attacks in Pakistan. These included, notably, two assassination attempts against Benazir Bhutto in 2007—the second of which proved successful—and the bombing of a Marriott hotel in Islamabad in 2008. At this time Akhtar moved to Waziristan, where under his auspices HuJI continued to foster links to Al-Qaeda as well as the newly formed Tehrik-e-Taliban Pakistan (TTP, or Pakistani Taliban). Until his death in June 2011, HuJI's operational commander, Ilyas Kashmiri, emerged as a top commander for joint operations conducted by his group, Al-Qaeda, the TTP, and other Deobandi terrorist outfits. HuJI itself has been tied to an assault on the Pakistani Army's general headquarters in 2009, a plot to attack a Danish newspaper that had published offensive cartoons of the prophet Muhammad, and the assassination of Khalid Khwaja, an ex-ISI squadron leader, in 2010 (the latter being claimed under the name Asian Tigers).

Despite these operations, HuJI's overall level of activity has declined in recent years as the group has been eclipsed by other terrorist organizations based in Pakistan. HuJI's current infrastructure in India is unknown at the present time, although its affiliate in Bangladesh—Harakat-ul-Jihad-Islami Bangladesh (HuJI B)—is thought to retain a strong network in the country, particularly in the state of West Bengal.

Ben Brandt

See also: Al-Qaeda; Al-Qaeda in the Arabian Penisula; Bin Laden, Osama; Taliban

Further Reading

"Harakat_ul-Ansar (now known as Harakar-ul-Mujahideen): Evolution of the Outfit." South Asia Terrorism Portal (SATP). Accessed on June 15, 2014. http://www.satp.org/.
"HuJI Chief behind EX-ISI Man's Killing?" *Times of India*, May 2, 2010. http://www.satporg/satporgtp/countries/india/states/jandk/terrorist outfits/harakat_ul_ansar_or_harakat_ul_jehad_e_islami.htm.

Heathrow Liquid Bomb Plot

In August 2006, United Kingdom (UK) authorities arrested 24 individuals alleged to have been plotting to detonate a number of explosive devices aboard transatlantic commercial aircraft while in flight from Heathrow airport to a number of destinations in the United States and Canada. British and American authorities claimed that this plot had strong links to Al-Qaeda militants based in Pakistan. Those arrested were said to have intended to utilize a novel form of liquid explosives to attack passenger aircraft; as a result of this plot, a range of new airport security measures were introduced.

The leader of the cell, Ahmed Abdullah Ali, was identified as a person of interest by UK authorities as part of investigations into potential violent extremists following the July 2005 underground bombings in London. When Ali returned from a trip to Pakistan in June 2006, his luggage was covertly searched, and a bottle of powdered soft drink (Tang) and a large number of batteries were discovered. Concern over this discovery led the authorities to begin a large-scale surveillance operation targeting Ali and his associates; it has also been reported that a member of the British Security Service (MI5) penetrated the group. In June 2005, intelligence officials learned that members of the apparent homegrown terror cell had made a cash purchase of an apartment on Forest Road, London. The property was subsequently searched, and video and listening devices installed. During this and later covert searches, officers found what appeared to be bomb-making equipment, including batteries and chemicals. As the surveillance operation continued, the scale of the alleged plot became apparent, and it is thought up to 19 attackers may have been involved (mirroring the number of hijackers involved in the attacks on September 11, 2001).

Surveillance of the London cell may have continued for considerably longer than was the case if it had not been for the detention in Pakistan of Rashid Rauf, a British-born Pakistani thought to have been a key player in the plot. This arrest apparently took the UK authorities by surprise and compelled the security forces to move against the alleged plotters earlier than may have been planned. It was alleged at the time of the apprehensions that the U.S. and UK authorities had disagreed over when to act. Reportedly, the British wished to continue to observe the terrorists, while the Americans were pushing for an early intervention to bring the plot to a halt. Rauf subsequently escaped from Pakistani custody, although he was later killed in 2008 during a U.S. air strike.

Of the 25 individuals initially arrested, 8 were eventually charged with conspiring to cause explosions with intent to endanger life and conspiring to cause explosions on board passenger aircraft. Several other men were accused of lesser terrorism offenses. During their trials those involved claimed that their preparations were part of an elaborate publicity stunt rather than an attempt to destroy a number of aircraft in flight.

The key individuals in the case were:

- Ahmed Abdullah Ali, the alleged ringleader of the plot, who claimed that the intention had been to plant a number of small explosive devices at Heathrow to draw attention to UK foreign policy and that there was no intention to endanger life. Ali admitted to having researched over the Internet how to construct an explosive device using a drink bottle, batteries, and bleach.
- Assad Sarwar, described during the trial as the cell's quartermaster responsible for buying and concealing bomb-making materials. Reported to have met Ali while volunteering at a refugee camp in Pakistan, Sarwar admitted to having learned how to make explosives in Pakistan.
- Tanvir Hussain, who was already known to the UK authorities and who had been approached by MI5 prior to the emergence of this plot. Despite this, he persisted in his involvement and helped manufacture the devices to be used in the attacks. He also recorded a "living will" or martyr video that was recovered and formed a key element in the prosecution's case.
- Arafat Waheed Khan, who also recorded a martyr video and was alleged to have helped procure bomb-making materials for the attack. Khan had been at school with Ali and had failed a business course at Middlesex University. He was reportedly approached by the security service to act as an informant but refused to cooperate.
- Waheed Zaman, who claimed he only wanted to raise public awareness of the oppression of Muslims and denied he knew what Ali had been planning.

- Ibrahim Savant, a convert to Islam who also recorded a martyr video. He later claimed that he had done so at Ali's behest and did not adhere to the radical statements made in the video.
- Umar Islam, another convert to Islam and a close associate of Ali and Sarwar. He helped in refugee camps in Pakistan and recorded a video in which he stated, "I say to you disbelievers that as you bomb, you will be bombed. As you kill, you will be killed. And if you want to kill our women and children then the same thing will happen to you. This is not a joke."
- Adam Katib, who was described as being Ali's lieutenant and had conducted research into the chemicals to be used in the manufacture of detonators.
- Mohammed Gulzar, who was accused of being an international terrorist and of being the superintendent of the plot.

At the end of the original trial in September 2008, Ali, Sarwar, and Hussain were found guilty of conspiring to commit murder, but no verdict was reached on the charges that they intended to detonate an explosive device on an aircraft. Khan, Zaman, Savant, and Islam all pleaded guilty to conspiracy to commit a public nuisance—the jury was unable to reach a verdict on the charges of murder.

In September 2009, a second trial found Ali, Sarwar, and Hussain guilty of attempting to cause explosions in passenger aircraft and convicted Islam of conspiracy to commit murder. However, the jury was unable to reach a verdict on the remaining defendants. A third trial found Savant, Khan, and Zaman guilty of conspiracy to murder in July 2010. Gulzar was cleared on all charges. Those convicted were sentenced to serve between 20 and 36 years in prison.

Prior to deciding on their final targets, the cell appeared to have looked into the feasibility of attacking other venues. During searches following the arrest of the plotters, a diagram of the layout of the Bacton gas terminal in Norfolk was discovered, along with plans of the Coryton oil refinery in Essex. During the trial Sarwar, alleged to have been the chief target scout for the cell, admitted he had also conducted research on the Internet into possible targets, including the Houses of Parliament and the Heathrow, Gatwick, Stansted, and Birmingham airports. Further evidence of potential alternate targets emerged with the discovery of CD-ROMs containing photographs of the area around a pedestrian tunnel under the Thames, along with photographs of a nearby university campus and closed-circuit television camera locations.

A notable aspect of this plot was the plan to utilize a novel explosive device to circumvent the stringent security procedures instituted at airports in light of the September 11, 2001, attacks in the United States. The plotters' intent was to use a peroxide-based liquid explosive, which would be injected into sealed plastic soft drink bottles. A second element of the device was a disposable camera containing a small quantity of hexamethylene triperoxide, which would be triggered by the camera's flash unit. When held beside the bottle of liquid explosive, this would act as a detonator for the main explosive charge. As part of the evidence for the various trials, British government technical experts claimed to have replicated the devices and found that they would have been viable if properly constructed and executed. It was alleged that the cell was on the verge of conducting a dummy run, aimed at testing airport security to see if the liquid explosives could be successfully smuggled aboard the aircraft without detection.

Parallels have been drawn between this attempt and the mid-1990s Bojinka plot, which sought to use a series of small nitroglycerine-based devices to bring down commercial aircraft in flight.

The cell had apparently also given consideration to the possibility of using other measures to get their devices through security. Specifically, Ali had suggested that the alleged bombers should take pornographic magazines and condoms in their hand luggage to allay any suspicions security staff might have. It has also been claimed that the plotters discussed bringing their wives and children with them for the attacks.

The innovative use of liquid explosives in this plot led to the introduction of a range of new security measures at North American and European airports. These included a ban on any liquids or gels over three ounces (100 milliliters) in passengers' carry-on luggage and the institution of more stringent search and screening procedures. The new rules remained in place at the time of this writing.

Greg Hannah

See also: Al-Qaeda; Anglo-American Alliance; Bojinka, Operation; Madrid Airport Bombing

Further Reading

Bennett, Brian, and Douglas Waller. "Thwarting the Airline Plot: Inside the Investigation." *Time*, August 10, 2006.

"The Terrorists Who Changed Air Travel Forever." *The Independent* (UK), September 9, 2008.

Hezbollah (Party of God)

Hezbollah (the Party of God) is a Lebanese Shiite Islamic group with ideological and strategic ties to Iran. It officially came into being with the promulgation of its first manifesto, the 1985 "Open Letter." Today it acts simultaneously as a vast social services provider, a recognized political party with elected representation in the Lebanese National Assembly, an illegal armed militia, and a terrorist organization implicated in a variety of global criminal enterprises. The group's objectives upon its creation were to end the Israeli invasion of Lebanon, oppose any "imperial" occupation in that same country, and ultimately create a representative Lebanese government with a noted commitment to Shiite Islam. As a resistance movement conducting asymmetrical warfare against Israel, Hezbollah was one of the first Islamist organizations to employ tactical suicide attacks in the Middle East. The organization is listed, in whole or in part, as a terrorist organization by the United States, Israel, the United Kingdom, Australia, Canada, Bahrain, Egypt, and the Netherlands.

Hezbollah's foundations can be traced back to the early 1960s, when Lebanon and the entire Arab world were exposed to a revival of Islamism in the political and cultural scenes. The movement was largely a result of widespread disillusionment with the failure of Gamal Abdel Nasser's pan-Arabism both to create a unifying identity in the Middle East and to defeat Israel. Greatly inspired by the teachings of clerics such as Ayatollah Imam Musa al-Sadr and Ayatollah Sayyed Muhammad Hussein Fadlallah, as well as the 1979 Iranian Revolution, the group's founding members sought to create a united Islamic organization whose objectives would rest on three pillars: (1) Islam, to provide the structure and guiding principles for managing the intellectual, religious, ideologi-

Shiite Muslim members of Hezbollah beat their chests during a procession organized by the movement in the southern Lebanese town of Nabatiyeh. (AP/Wide World Photos)

cal, and practical aspects of personal and public life; (2) resistance against Israel's occupation of Lebanon through jihad; and (3) the jurisdiction and the unquestionable authority of the Jurist-Theologian (Wilayat al-Faqih)—the successor of the Prophet and the imams—to guide the faithful toward a nation of Islam. These pillars resonated with Lebanese Shiites, many of whom felt excluded from and underrepresented in the country's Sunni-Maronite-dominated political system, despite having become the largest confessional group by the early 1980s.

Hezbollah's organizational structure derives from the religious leaders, the ulema, who represent the supreme authority from which all decisions derive to the community. The leader of Iran is the ultimate clerical authority that provides the Hezbollah leadership with guidance and directives in

case of dissent. The decision-making bodies of Hezbollah are divided as such:

1. The Consultative Assembly, or Majlis Shura, composed of 12 clerical members who oversee Hezbollah's activity within Lebanon and all related tactical decisions. It also has responsibility for the functioning of seven subcommittees that tackle ideological, military, political, financial, judicial, and social matters within Hezbollah.
2. The Deciding Assembly, or Majlis al-Shura al-Karar, again composed of 12 clerical members (headed by Fadlallah) who take charge of all strategic decisions.

According to the Gulf Research Centre, Hezbollah's military force is estimated at approximately 1,000 full-time members and between 6,000 and 10,000 volunteers. Its military arsenal includes long-range and antitank guided missiles, as well as surface-to-air and antiship missiles.

As a political organization, by the latter half of 2011, Hezbollah held 12 of the 128 seats in the Lebanese parliament and 2 of the 30 seats in the cabinet. As a social services organization, it runs a number of construction companies, a minimum of four hospitals, 12 clinics, 12 schools, and three agricultural centers. Militarily, it has evolved from the use of terrorist tactics in the 1980s to highly professional guerrilla warfare tactics, as was demonstrated in its confrontation with the Israel Defense Forces (IDF) in 2006.

Hezbollah relies on a number of sources for financing, Iran being one of the more substantial. It is estimated that the group receives roughly $100 million every year from Tehran, although some sources have placed the figure as high as $200 million. In addition to financial assistance, Iran helped with the early development of Hezbollah by dispatching a contingent of the Iranian Revolutionary Guard (al Quds) to the Lebanese Bekaa Valley to set up and run training camps for the organization.

Hezbollah also receives significant financial support from expatriates living in the United States, Latin America, and African countries with large wealthy Lebanese Shiite communities. These funds are transferred directly to the group, sent via front charity organizations, or smuggled into the country by human couriers.

Hezbollah has also been known to link itself to various global criminal enterprises, including drug trafficking, "blood" diamond smuggling, and fraud networks. Although the group engages in these pursuits in the Americas, Africa, and the Middle East, it is the Tri-border Area of South America that has been the most important to Hezbollah, providing it with an annual income thought to be in the range of $10 million. The group has also profited financially and operationally from the growth of and trade in hashish (poppy crop) in the Lebanese Bekaa Valley itself.

Domestically, Hezbollah has undergone a series of metamorphoses in its identity, largely a function of the changing political and security conditions in Lebanon. In its development from its foundations within the Islamic movement of social and political protest (1978–1985) to a social movement (1985–1991) to a parliamentary political party (1992–present), the group has expanded its framework beyond a purely military wing dedicated to resisting the Israeli presence to a broader movement aimed at supporting the Lebanese Shiite community through the provision of health care, social services, educational services, and monetary and communal assistance. Stepping up in areas traditionally neglected by the Lebanese government, such as South Lebanon and the Bekaa Valley, Hezbollah has made use of its social leverage to transition into the political sphere as a representative of the Shiite community. In May 2008, for the first time Hezbollah managed to obtain sufficient votes to secure veto power in the Lebanese cabinet, thus greatly enhancing its political role.

Internationally, Hezbollah has so far successfully walked the fine line between preserving its Islamic identity and recognizing and working within the confines of the Lebanese state. The organization maintains its strategic ideological alliance with Iran and continues to enjoy a political partnership with Syria. With regards to the relationship with Tehran, Hezbollah initially served as a proxy organization, with the Majlis al-Shura deferring to the ayatollah as its supreme clerical authority on all matters of contention, and Hezbollah's military wing training directly under the Iranian Revolutionary Guard. The relationship seems to have taken a step down over the years toward more of a partnership, as Hezbollah has sought to further integrate itself into Lebanese politics and adapt its ideology within a more nationalistic sphere.

The United States has placed Hezbollah on its list of foreign terrorist organizations. A 2003 U.S. court decision ruled that the Islamic Jihad Organization (IJO) and Hezbollah were one and the same. The IJO is a terrorist organization that was responsible for a number of suicide attacks in Lebanon and Europe, including bombings in Beirut, Lebanon, that targeted the U.S. embassy and the American Marines (and French Paratrooper) military barracks in 1983. The latter attacks were especially destructive and have only been superseded by Al-Qaeda's strike on September 11, 2001, in terms of American casualties. However, given the organizational structure of Hezbollah at the time, it remains unclear just how much involvement and operational control the group's leadership had over the attacks. It has been argued that at the time, the group's external security organization operated independently of the party and reported directly to Iranian intelligence. The 2011 Hezbollah Anti-Terrorism Act was passed in the U.S. Congress, ensuring that no American aid to Lebanon reach Hezbollah. Hezbollah does not figure on the European Union's terrorist list.

In July 2006, a confrontation between Hezbollah members and an Israeli border patrol, and the subsequent abduction of two members of the IDF, prompted Israeli air strikes and artillery fire against Lebanese infrastructure. This incident triggered a 33-day war between Israel and Hezbollah that in many ways saw the latter emerge as the victor. The conflict was a testimony to Hezbollah's guerrilla warfare capabilities and considerable military arsenal.

In 2008, an attempt by the Lebanese government to shut down Hezbollah's telecommunications network and remove Beirut International Airport's chief of security, Wafic Shkeir, because of his alleged ties to Hezbollah spurred fighting in Beirut on May 7. Hezbollah fighters took over a number of neighborhoods in the west of the city of Beirut, which they then handed over to the Lebanese Army. The conflict ended with the signing of the May 21 agreement between rival government factions, ending what had become an 18-month political feud between government and opposition forces.

In 2009, the United Nations Special Tribunal for Lebanon, investigating the assassination of former Lebanese prime minister and multimillionaire Sunni tycoon Rafiq Hariri in 2005, reportedly uncovered evidence potentially linking Hezbollah to the murder. To date, Hezbollah vehemently denies any involvement in the incident, with Hassan Nasrallah maintaining that he and the former prime minister were in the process of overcoming ideological differences and were moving to draft a unifying vision for Lebanon in an unprecedented Sunni-Shiite exchange prior to Hariri's death. According to Hezbollah, the two leaders frequently met at Nasrallah's headquarters in the southern suburbs of Beirut for late-night chats, the last of which occurred a mere two days before the explosion. Despite Hezbollah's protestations, the special tribunal investigating Hariri's death issued a warrant for the arrest of four senior Hezbollah members on June 30, 2011. Those named were Mustafa Badr el-Din, Salim al-Ayyash, Assad

Sabra, and Hassan Unaisi. Nasrallah has stated that these individuals will not be arrested under any circumstances. Hezbollah continues to sponsor terror activities, particularly in the Middle East, and remains a staunch foe of Israel.

Yara Zogheib

See also: Arab-Israeli Conflict, Overview; Islamic Radicalism

Further Reading

Alagha, Joseph. *Hezbollah's Documents: From the 1985 Open Letter to the 2009 Manifesto*. Amsterdam: Pallas, 2001.

Blanford, Nicholas. *Killing Mr. Lebanon: The Assassination of Rafik Hariri and Its Impact on the Middle East*. New York: I. B. Tauris, 2006.

Jackson, Michael. *Hezbollah: Organizational Development, Ideological Evolution, and a Relevant Threat Model*. Washington, DC: Georgetown University Press, 2009.

Levitt, Matthew. "Hezbollah Finances: Funding the Party of God." In Jeanne Giraldo and Harold Trinkunas, eds., *Terrorism Financing and State Responses: A Comparative Perspective*, 227–51. Stanford, CA: Stanford University Press, 2007.

Norton, Augustus Richard. *Hezbollah: A Short History*. Princeton, NJ: Princeton University Press, 2007.

Human Shields

The term "human shield" can refer to civilians who are forced by military or paramilitary forces to precede them in an attack. More recently, the media and others began using the term to refer to a person or group of people who are voluntarily or involuntary positioned at or near a potential military target as a means to deter enemy fire or attack. States and military establishments have often claimed that their opponents have employed civilians as human shields in order to explain civilian casualties resulting from military action.

A potential enemy may choose not to use force against the employers of the shield for fear of harming the person or persons who form the shield. A potential attacker's inhibition regarding the use of force depends on various considerations, such as fear for his or her own security, societal norms, the inclination to abide by international law forbidding attacks on civilians during an armed conflict, fear of negative international or national public opinion, or a close affiliation with the person or group of people forming the shield.

Human shields are similar to hostages, but there are important differences. In contrast to hostages, who are invariably taken involuntarily, human shields might be civilian volunteers utilized by a government at a particular site to deter an enemy from attacking it. The term also refers, however, to the involuntary use of civilians to shield combatants during attacks. In such incidents, the civilians are forced to move in front of the soldiers in the hope that the enemy force will be reluctant to attack, or if it does so and the civilians are killed, this might have propaganda value.

When there is a case of deliberate seizure of civilians to act as human shields, in most cases once the threat is over the seized are released. Usually, no ransom is involved. Historical records indicate that human shields have been used by state authorities, nongovernmental organizations, and terrorists alike.

Despite attempts to prevent the use of human shields through the development of international law during the second half of the 20th century, the use of human shields was recorded and discussed in the context of several conflicts, mainly in the 1991 Persian Gulf War, the Bosnian conflict of 1992–1995, the Kosovo War (1999), the Iraq War of 2003, as well as the ongoing Israeli-Palestinian conflict.

Both in Bosnia in 1995 and in Kosovo in 1999, human shields were used extensively by the Serbs. In the war in Bosnia, Bosnian-Serb armed units chained captured United Nations (UN) soldiers to potential North Atlantic Treaty Organization (NATO) air-strike targets. This strategy was effective in paralyzing the UN military forces' operations in Bosnia in May 1995. The nations participating in the UN operation refused to support the use of force against Serbian military targets, as their soldiers' lives were in jeopardy. In 1999, Serbian forces compelled civilian Kosovars to remain near Serb military bases to deter NATO from bombing the bases.

Iraqi dictator Saddam Hussein's regime used human shields of both Westerners and Iraqi civilians on several occasions during the 1990s and right up to the Anglo-American–led invasion of Iraq in March 2003 to safeguard potential military targets. After Iraq's armed forces occupied Kuwait on August 2, 1990, the Iraqi government held dozens of foreign nationals as human shields in strategic locations. To emphasize that human shields were in place, the Hussein regime released videos showing the human shields, some of them interacting with Hussein himself. Only after coming under intense international pressure did the Iraqi government allow these individuals to leave the country. The last human shields left Iraq by December 1991, several weeks before the beginning of Operation Desert Storm.

In November 1997, a crisis developed between Iraq and the UN concerning weapons inspection in the country. There have been charges that the Iraqi government then encouraged hundreds of civilians to move into palaces and other strategic locations in order to deter attacks there.

Human shields were used again in Iraq in early 2003, this time by antiwar protesters. The human shield operation was termed the Human Shield Action to Iraq, and it deployed several hundred Western volunteers to potential civilian strategic targets like water and power plants and a communications center.

When Operation Iraqi Freedom began on March 20, 2003, many of the volunteers left the country, but approximately 100 remained. The Human Shield Action to Iraq claimed that none of the strategic facilities to which it deployed volunteers were bombed while human shields were present.

Beginning in 2002, records kept by the Israeli human rights group B'Tselem indicate that some IDF units used Palestinian civilians as human shields during their operations in order to prevent Palestinian terrorists from firing at them. In these instances, the IDF forced persons held as hostages to precede them into buildings and certain areas. This practice was outlawed by the Israeli Supreme Court in October 2005. Nevertheless, since then, and on several occasions, human rights groups have recorded the use of Palestinian civilians as human shields by IDF units. In some cases, the IDF took disciplinary measures against its officers who employed this practice.

Chen Kertcher

See also: Global War on Terror; Hezbollah (Party of God); Iraqi Freedom, Operation; Islamic Radicalism; Persian Gulf War

Further Reading

Ezzo, Matthew V., and Amos N. Guiora. "A Critical Decision Point on the Battlefield—Friend, Foe, or Innocent Bystander." *U of Utah Legal Studies Paper* 8, no. 3 (2008): 128–50.

Gross, Emmanuel. "Use of Civilians as Human Shields: What Legal and Moral Restrictions Pertain to a War Waged by a Democratic State against Terrorism?" *Emory International Law Review* 16 (2002): 445–524.

Skerker, Michael. "Just War Criteria and the New Face of War: Human Shields, Manufactured Martyrs, and Little Boys with Stones." *Journal of Military Ethics* 3, no. 1 (2004): 27–39.

Impact of 9/11 on Presidential Power

On September 11, 2001, a transnational terrorist organization rooted in Afghanistan struck targets in New York and Washington, D.C., killing more than 3,000 civilians. These events led to several vigorous government actions granting the executive branch additional powers. Critics suggested that during this time, Congress submitted to presidential urgings for expanded authority, allowing the president wide latitude regarding national security. Conversely, Supreme Court rulings generally constrained presidential policy initiatives intended to expand presidential power.

Soon after 9/11, President George W. Bush sought congressional authority to proceed with military action against Afghanistan. The administration asserted that the Taliban regime in Afghanistan provided a safe haven for those responsible for 9/11: Al-Qaeda and its leader Osama bin Laden. Encouraged by the president, Congress passed the Authorization for Use of Military Force (AUMF) Act within weeks of the 9/11 attacks. This legislation provided the president with the ability to deter and preempt future acts of terrorism using "all necessary and appropriate force against those nations, organizations, or persons he determines planned, authorized, committed, or aided the 9/11

attacks." Close to a year later, Congress passed the Iraqi Resolution of October 2002 that granted the president authority to decide on the necessary military actions to take against Iraq and its dictator, Saddam Hussein. Again, this legislation was moved through Congress with the urging of the president. The administration claimed that Hussein was connected to Al-Qaeda and possessed weapons of mass destruction (WMDs), thus posing a threat to U.S. national security. Both of these congressional actions granted the president wide authority in implementing policies to fight terrorism. While each example typifies executive power, this imbalance in power between branches during times of war is not without precedent. Abraham Lincoln, for example, began the Civil War without congressional authorization after several Southern states seceded. President Franklin D. Roosevelt signed Executive Order 9066 in 1942, establishing internment camps for more than 100,000 U.S. citizens of Japanese descent.

Congress gave the president wide-ranging and vaguely defined powers with the AUMF and Iraqi Resolution in order to combat terrorism. These pieces of legislation provided the president an opportunity to act more unilaterally when conducting the global war on terror.

Congress passed a law creating the Department of Homeland Security (DHS) soon after 9/11. The DHS brought under one department different entities involved in homeland security. The DHS is a cabinet-level agency operating under the direction of the executive branch. The president appoints the cabinet head, the Secretary of Homeland Security, as well as several undersecretaries in the new department, including the new director of national intelligence.

The DHS contains portions or all of 22 federal agencies, such as the U.S. Coast Guard, Federal Emergency Management Agency (FEMA), U.S. Customs and Border Protection, and the U.S. Secret Service. When the DHS was first created, it had 170,000 employees and was a $37 billion dollar organization, although it has grown substantially since that time. With the addition of the DHS the executive branch greatly expanded, and this expansion likely correlates with its power vis-à-vis other branches of government.

In the aftermath of 9/11, presidential power experienced both expansion and contraction. The Supreme Court rejected several presidential prerogatives, while Congress often acceded to presidential urgings in conducting the war on terror. It is difficult to say whether the presidency has experienced an overall increase in power since 9/11. However, presidential power expansion and contraction during this time will likely have implications for future presidents and the citizens they govern.

Paul Martin and Joseph K. Young

See also: Economic Impact of the September 11, 2001, Attacks; Impact of 9/11 on U.S. Foreign Policy; Impact of 9/11 on U.S. Public Opinion; Pentagon Attack; World Trade Center, September 11, 2001

Further Reading

Ball, Howard. *Bush, the Detainees, and the Constitution: The Battle over Presidential Power in the War on Terror*. Lawrence: University Press of Kansas, 2007.

Banks, William C., Renee de Nevers, and Mitchell B. Wallenstein. *Combatting Terrorism: Strategies and Approaches*. Washington, DC: CQ Press, 2008.

Fisher, Louis. *Presidential War Power*. Lawrence: University Press of Kansas, 2013.

Fisher, Louis. *Military Tribunals and Presidential Power: American Revolution to the War on Terrorism*. Lawrence: University Press of Kansas, 2005.

Noftsinger, John B., Jr., Kenneth F. Newbold, Jr., and Jack K. Wheeler. *Understanding Homeland Security: Policy, Perspectives, and Paradoxes*. New York: Palgrave Macmillan, 2007.

Pfiffner, James P. *Power Play: The Bush Presidency and the Constitution*. Washington, DC: Brookings Institution Press, 2008.

Impact of 9/11 on U.S. Foreign Policy

Terrorism's influence on American foreign policy can be traced back to the early years of the American Republic, when George Washington dealt with terroristic piracy and hostage-taking by the Barbary pirates. After failed rescue attempts, President Washington paid out almost $1 million, agreed to an annual $21,600 tribute for protection, and sold the pirates a heavily armored war cruiser, which amounted to a sale of arms for hostages. In the 20th century, American administrations have wavered between various policies for handling terrorism. The administration of President Richard M. Nixon sought to diminish terrorism through law enforcement, a policy of no concessions, and collective security agreements based on international law meant to expedite extradition and prosecution. President Jimmy Carter attempted to address the problem by focusing on the root causes of terrorism, including poverty, ethnic conflict, and government repression. President Ronald Reagan sought to answer terrorism with military instruments, treating counterterrorism as roughly equivalent to President John F. Kennedy's view of counterinsurgency.

U.S. foreign policy concerning terrorism has been a patchwork of various strands of political thought, ranging from attempts to ignore it to overstating the threat and Americans' abilities to prevent the violence and apprehend its perpetrators. Political expediency has often trumped the tedious but necessary institution of a definitive counterterrorism policy. In general, America has dealt with terrorists on an ad hoc basis and has experienced difficulties in achieving cooperation and understanding between military and civilian officials. Various administrations have emphasized counterterrorism over antiterrorism, or vice versa. Counterterrorism is "active, offensive actions intended to suppress terrorist activities by denying the terrorists the ability to engage in such acts, including physical acts of violence against terrorist organizations and individual terrorists." Counterterrorism focuses on the apprehension or punishment of terrorists, and it often includes the activities of law enforcement, targeted intelligence collection, and military operations aimed at preemption. Antiterrorism includes actions that change or prevent terrorist activity by passively deterring it or mitigating its effects. It generally refers to "defensive measures taken to decrease the vulnerability of society to terrorist attacks, such as increased security at airports or monitoring the whereabouts of known terrorist groups through international police cooperation." Antiterrorism also encompasses a vast array of techniques meant to shield facilities from danger or to diminish factors that may precipitate terrorist violence. The United States has displayed no internal consensus on how to prevent and respond to terrorism, no common philosophical basis for accepting counterterrorism and antiterrorism failures, and "no internationally recognized commitment for firm, retributive deterrence of such violence."

Historically, the United States has treated terrorism almost solely as an international concern. Abroad, America attempted to thwart terrorism through occasional military actions, as evidenced by the aborted rescue of the Iranian embassy hostages in 1980, the Libyan bombings of 1986, and the cruise missile attacks on Afghanistan and Sudan in retaliation for the East African embassy bombings in 1998. Prior to 9/11, conventional terrorism was not seen as presenting a grave danger to the United States, though the threat posed by weapons of mass destruction (WMDs) raised the stakes. The administration of President Bill Clinton expressed a strong desire to address the threat of unconventional terrorism. After the sarin attack in the Tokyo subway in 1995, President Clinton made preventing and managing the consequences of a terrorist attack with WMDs the highest priority for the United States through Presidential Decision Directive 39. He asked that the American government approach the new terrorist challenges of the 21st century "with the same rigor and determination we applied to the toughest security challenges of this century," and he stated a determination "to see that we have a serious, deliberate, disciplined, long-term response to a legitimate potential threat to the lives and safety of the American people." The U.S. budget for federal counterterrorism agencies grew from $5.7 billion for fiscal year

1996 to $10 billion for fiscal year 2000, with nearly half of those funds devoted to countering WMDs.

Despite these attempts to increase the focus on terrorism, the issue was not at the forefront of the security agenda during the transition to the George W. Bush administration. Al-Qaeda represented an unprecedented global threat, with organized groups and radicalized converts in many countries.

The 9/11 attacks made terrorism the predominant foreign policy concern of the first years of Bush's presidency, leading to the declaration of a war on terror and development of the Bush Doctrine, in which President Bush declared that nations that harbor terrorists were as guilty as the terrorists themselves and would be held to account. Security became the primary lens for viewing foreign policy, changing relations with various governments in Asia and the Middle East, increasing engagement with unsavory regimes, and redefining security alliances. The 9/11 attacks led to the first invocation of Article 5 of the North Atlantic Treaty Organization (NATO) charter, a collective security clause that later drew NATO into the war in Afghanistan. After initial success in Afghanistan, the Bush administration began to advance a policy of preventive war against terrorists and rogue states, suggesting that the United States had a right to defend itself against threats before they had fully materialized. Using the 9/11 attacks as a warning of things to come, President Bush and his advisers suggested that the danger posed by terrorists seeking large body counts, the proliferation of WMDs, and the support of rogue states had grown too grave to tolerate any further. Against this backdrop, the United States launched a largely unilateral war in Iraq, based in part on the ideological belief that spreading democracy in the Middle East would prevent further terrorism. The unilateral nature of the Iraq War and the heated pursuit of terrorists led to strained relations with many of America's traditional allies, especially in Europe. The United States used a variety of controversial techniques to fight terrorists—including covert operations, extraordinary renditions, secret prisons, and Predator drone strikes—that many allies believed undermined fundamental sovereignty and legal regimes. Similarly, the establishment of a prison at Guantánamo Bay, use of coercive interrogation techniques to include waterboarding, and special military commissions for Afghan enemy combatants and terrorists undermined America's international credibility for respecting the rule of law, adhering to the Geneva Conventions, and following basic rights to speedy trials and habeas corpus proceedings.

Although striking a different rhetorical tone, President Barack Obama has largely continued the major elements of the Bush administration's counterterrorism policies abroad. The Obama administration has yet to transfer detainees from Guantánamo Bay, despite election-year promises to do so, and has significantly increased the use of unmanned drone strikes in Pakistan and Afghanistan. Similar to the previous administration, President Obama's goal for the war in Afghanistan is to "disrupt, dismantle, and defeat Al-Qaeda in Pakistan and Afghanistan, and to prevent their return to either country in the future." President Obama also employed a controversial troop surge strategy in Afghanistan patterned on the one advocated by President Bush in Iraq. That effort was largely unsuccessful, and the Taliban/Al-Qaeda insurgency in Afghanistan began to accelerate significantly during 2013, after the additional troop deployment had been withdrawn.

Vacillation in American foreign policy concerning terrorism has hampered the country's ability to reduce terrorist threats over the long-term. Following the end of the Cold War, terrorism came to replace communism as the most feared American security threat. The 9/11 attacks dramatically elevated the importance of counterterrorism in U.S. foreign policy, reordered its security alliances, prompted the initiation of two major wars, and reasserted military and intelligence operations as primary tools for fighting terrorism abroad.

James O. Ellis III

See also: Economic Impact of the September 11, 2001, Attacks; Impact of 9/11 on Presidential Power; Impact of 9/11 on U.S. Public Opinion; Pentagon Attack; World Trade Center, September 11, 2001

Further Reading

Carter, Ashton B., and William J. Perry. *Preventive Defense: A New Security Strategy for America*. Washington, DC: Brookings Institution Press, 1999.

Roberts, Brad. "Conclusion." In *Hype or Reality? The 'New Terrorism' and Mass Casualty Attacks*, edited by Brad Roberts, 263–75. Alexandria, VA: Chemical and Biological Arms Control Institute, 2000.

Snow, Donald M. *Distant Thunder: Third World Conflict and the New International Order*. New York: St. Martin's, 1993.

Impact of 9/11 on U.S. Public Opinion

National tragedies, such as the September 11, 2001, attacks on the United States, have a direct and profound impact not only on the immediate victims and their families but also on the general public. An opinion poll conducted by Zogby International in September 2007 reported that a large majority (81%) of those surveyed either "strongly agreed" or "somewhat agreed" that the 9/11 attacks permanently altered how the American public "views the world." Moreover, this same poll reported that, six years after 9/11, more than 60 percent of those surveyed thought about the events of that day at least "once per week."

There have been several incidents in the history of the United States that have created a sense of unity and patriotism. The bombing of Pearl Harbor on December 7, 1941, and the assassination of President John F. Kennedy on November 22, 1963, are two such events. As the Zogby poll makes clear, the terrorist attacks on 9/11 were another such defining moment.

The initial reaction of most Americans to the attacks was shock, disbelief, and anger. Among many there was an imminent sense that the United States was about to go to war. One of the few uncertainties in this regard was the place and time. A large majority of the population rallied around President George W. Bush and other leaders in government and the military services. Those individuals would be responsible for determining a course of action in response to this blatant act of violence perpetrated against the United States. Following that day, many Americans' sense of security was gone, replaced by feelings of extreme vulnerability. The attacks also united the nation, and the diversity that was apparent prior to that day was largely replaced with a feeling of heightened nationalism, at least in the short term. Patriotism was at its highest level since the early days of World War II as a majority of Americans

Transportation Security Administration officials use wands to check over passengers as they pass through the security checkpoint in the terminal of Denver International Airport, on September 11, 2002. Full-body scanners later became a secondary security screening measure at the airport. (AP Photo/David Zalubowski)

(65%) openly displayed the flag, compared to 25 percent who flew the Stars and Stripes prior to 9/11.

Interestingly, some studies indicate that American attitudes regarding minorities, specifically Muslims, were not changed as a result of 9/11. Generally speaking, among minorities Muslims have been "rated lower" than other groups both prior to and following the events of 9/11. Nevertheless, physical and verbal attacks on Muslim Americans did escalate in the immediate aftermath of 9/11. Additionally, following the attacks, law enforcement agencies focused their attention more heavily on individuals of South Asian

and Middle Eastern origin. Thousands of Muslim men were detained without being formally charged with the commission of a crime—some for long periods of time—while others were arbitrarily deported for illegal behavior considered negligible. Furthermore, following the 9/11 attacks, a large percentage of Caucasians and African Americans supported the racial profiling of individuals whose facial features appeared Middle Eastern.

With respect to impingements on civil liberties, the attitude of many Americans was initially one of acceptance and tolerance. In their view, 9/11 demanded some curtailment of civil liberties and a more intrusive role by government in the lives and activities of the average citizen. For example, enhanced airport security screening and other measures that restricted certain items from entering an aircraft's passenger sections, although irritating and inconvenient to travelers, were, for the most part, viewed as necessary in a heightened security environment. Most people realized that the "new normal" spawned by 9/11 necessitated some impact on activities that were heretofore taken for granted.

An immediate response to the 9/11 attacks was the passage of the USA PATRIOT Act, legislation that, in part, increased the investigative powers of U.S. law enforcement agencies and provided additional tools and capabilities to those charged with combating terrorism. Among its provisions are measures to combat money laundering, further safeguard U.S. borders, and allow for interagency criminal information-sharing during the course of an investigation. Additionally, the act adopted specific measures regarding terrorism-related crimes. The USA PATRIOT Act was signed into law on October 26, 2001, after garnering overwhelming support across the political spectrum. However, although the American public generally supported the act, opinions diverged according to its specific stipulations. While many viewed the act as a safeguard on civil liberties and an instrument that strengthened national security, others were of the opinion that some of the law's provisions infringed and restricted rights guaranteed under the U.S. Constitution.

Another hotly debated subject in the weeks, months, and years following 9/11 was border and immigration control. It remains a very contentious issue and a consistent topic for discussion by the news media as well as the general public. Indeed, heightened post-9/11 security put this issue on the floor of the U.S. Congress, which passed the Border Protection Antiterrorism and Illegal Immigration Control Act in December 2005. In October of the following year, the Secure Fence Act was passed. This act authorized the construction of a 700-mile fence with state-of-the-art tracking and monitoring devices to restrict the flow of illegal aliens crossing the border areas between Mexico and the United States. A telephone survey conducted by Rasmussen Reports in August 2007 found that 56 percent of those questioned supported the building of the security fence. Moreover, in the same poll, 71 percent said they would support a measure requiring "foreign visitors" to carry an identification card and a greater number (74 percent) would support the establishment of a "central database" to monitor all foreign nationals visiting the United States. Government, law enforcement, and the average American have long known that the porous U.S. borders to the north and south have served as smuggling channels for terrorists, drug traffickers, and criminal gangs and, in the case of the

southern border, as a conduit for Mexicans seeking employment. The debate continues regarding the effectiveness of these established and proposed security measures.

Several polls conducted in the first few weeks following the attacks showed that the American public was generally supportive of and trusted the government's response to 9/11; regarding the use of military force, this remained true 18 months after 9/11. On October 7, 2001, the date the U.S.-led coalition invaded Afghanistan (Operation Enduring Freedom), an *ABC News/Washington Post* poll indicated that 94 percent of those surveyed supported the U.S. attack on that country. In July 2008, however, this same organization reported that only 51 percent of those surveyed believed that the war in Afghanistan was worth fighting. Moreover, various opinion polls revealed that between 69 percent and 80 percent of those surveyed initially supported military action against Iraq. This support remained high into and following the March 2003 invasion. A *CBS News* opinion poll taken in March 2003, one week after the United States launched a ground and air assault on Iraq, found that 69 percent of those surveyed viewed the invasion of that country as the right course of action. This number differs significantly from another *CBS News* poll that in August 2008 reported that only 38 percent of those surveyed viewed the U.S. invasion as the right course of action.

Clearly, U.S. public opinion varies as more time elapses since the 9/11 attacks; the "fear factor" lessens and the cost is internalized. Furthermore, other issues become more germane to the here and now. However, while this may be viewed as a reasonable assumption, there are various triggers and circumstances that have the potential to reignite the passions of 9/11.

For example, a fairly recent issue that garnered quite a bit of controversy was a proposal by a New York imam to build an Islamic community center and mosque near the site of the 9/11 attacks. In August 2010, a public opinion poll published by Rasmussen Reports indicated that over 60 percent of the respondents were against the building of a mosque near Ground Zero, while an equal number considered the proposal to be "insensitive" to the family members of victims of this tragedy.

Additionally, after the 9/11 attacks, Americans continue to be troubled over the two wars that have cost many lives and the expenditure of billions of taxpayer dollars. Regarding Afghanistan, many Americans question whether spending more than 15 years in the country, after the last troop leaves in 2016, if the resources (military and civilian lives, and financial) was worth a conflict. Furthermore, for Americans with family members or friends serving in the military, the sacrifices that these attacks demanded prompt reflection on that day in September 2001 and thoughts of those who are putting their lives on the line in an effort to prevent other attacks like the one that occurred on 9/11. For many Americans, the events of 9/11 will always spawn feelings of anger, frustration, and a sense of vulnerability.

The events of 9/11 have altered the views and perceptions of many Americans on a variety of security-related issues. For the families of those who perished in the 9/11 attacks and those who lost their lives or sustained permanent injuries in the war on terror, the tragedy of that day has profoundly illustrated that the rights and freedoms that some Americans take for granted come with a heavy price tag.

Finally, public opinion is a powerful catalyst for action. It has elected presidents, initiated wars, defined moral parameters and legislative agendas, and, to a large degree, determines how Americans live their daily lives. As a nation, the United States must utilize this powerful tool by collectively engaging in useful dialogue aimed at solving some of the world's most pressing issues.

Frank Shanty

See also: Economic Impact of the September 11, 2001, Attacks; Impact of 9/11 on Presidential Power; Impact of 9/11 on U.S. Foreign Policy; Pentagon Attack; World Trade Center, September 11, 2001

Further Reading

Bowman, Karlyn. "Public Opinion on the War with Iraq." Updated March 19, 2009. American Enterprise Institute, AEI Public Opinion Studies, http://www.aei.org/publicopinion2.

Kalkan, Kerem, and Yu-Sung Su. "A Change in Attitudes Toward Muslims? A Bayesian Investigation of Pre and Post 9/11 Public Opinion." Paper presented at the annual meeting of the MPSA Annual National Conference, Chicago, IL, April 3, 2008. http://citation.allacademic.com/meta/p266549_index.html.

Morin, Richard, and Claudia Deane. "Poll: Strong Backing for Bush, War: Few Americans See Easy End to Conflict." *Washington Post*, March 11, 2002, A1.

"Most Back Extending the PATRIOT Act, but Concerns about Intrusions Grow." *ABC News/Washington Post* poll, analysis by Gary Langer, June 9, 2005, http://abcnews.go.com/images/Politics/983a2PatriotAct.pdf.

Rasmussen Reports. "71% Favor Requiring Foreign Visitors to Carry Universal ID Card," August 18, 2007, http://www.rasmussenreports.com/public_content/politics/current_events/immigration/71_favor_requiring_foreign_visitors_to_carry_universal_id_card.

Rhine, Staci L., Stephen Bennett, and Richard Flickinger. "After 9/11: Television Viewers, Newspaper Readers and Public Opinion about Terrorism's Consequences." Paper presented at the annual meeting of the American Political Science Association, Boston Marriott Copley Place, Sheraton Boston & Hynes Convention Center, Boston, MA, August 28, 2002, http://fs.huntingdon.edu/jlewis/Terror/FlickingerAPSA02ppr.pdf.

Schafer, Chelsea E., and Grey M. Shaw. "The Polls Trends: Tolerance in the United States." *Public Opinion Quarterly* 73, no. 2 (Summer 2009): 404–431.

Improvised Explosive Devices

Improvised explosive devices (IEDs) have been employed in warfare almost since the introduction of gunpowder. They remain the weapon of choice for insurgent and resistance groups that lack the numerical strength and firepower to conduct conventional operations against an opponent. IEDs are the contemporary form of the booby traps employed in World War II and the Vietnam War. Traditionally, they are used primarily against enemy armor and thin-skinned vehicles.

A water cart filled with explosives was employed in a futile effort to assassinate Napoleon Bonaparte in Paris as he traveled to the opera on Christmas Eve 1800. The emperor escaped injury, but the blast killed the little girl the conspirators paid to hold the horse's bridle and killed or maimed a dozen other people. In more recent times, IEDs have been employed against civilian targets by Basque separatists and the Irish Republican Army. Molotov cocktails, or gasoline bombs, are one form of IED. The largest, most deadly IEDs in history were the U.S. jetliners hijacked by members of the terrorist organization Al-Qaeda on September 11, 2001, and used to attack the World Trade Center in New York City and the Pentagon in Washington, D.C.

IEDs became one of the chief weapons employed by insurgents during the Iraq War (2003) and its aftermath to attack U.S. forces and Iraqi police to carry out sectarian violence. IEDs have also been employed by insurgents in Afghanistan, but with less frequency and lethality compared to those used in Iraq. The simplest type of IED was a hand grenade, rigged artillery shell, or bomb triggered by a tripwire or simple movement. It might be as simple as a grenade with its pin pulled and handle held down by the weight of a corpse; once the corpse is raised, the grenade explodes. Bombs and artillery shells are also used as IEDs. Such weapons may be exploded remotely by wireless detonators in the form of garage door openers and two-way radios or infrared motion sensors. More powerful explosives and even shaped charges can be used to attack armored vehicles. Casualty totals are one way to judge the effectiveness of a military operation, and growing casualties from IEDs in the 1980s and 1990s induced the Israeli Army to withdraw from southern Lebanon.

The explosives that killed three people and injured more than 200 during the Boston Marathon on April 15, 2013, were rudimentary IEDs made from ordinary kitchen pressure cookers, except they were rigged to shoot sharp bits of shrapnel into anyone within reach of their blast and maim them severely. The pressure cookers were filled with nails, ball bearings, and black powder, and the devices were triggered by "kitchen-type" egg timers. The resulting explosions sent metal tearing through skin and muscle, destroying the lower limbs of some victims, who had only shreds of tissue holding parts of their legs.

Spencer C. Tucker

See also: Al-Qaeda; Boston Marathon Bombing; Predator; Terrorism; Unmanned Aerial Vehicles

Further Reading

Crippen, James B. *Improvised Explosive Devices (IED)*. New York: CRC Press, 2007.

DeForest, M. J. *Principles of Improvised Explosive Devices*. Boulder, CO: Paladin, 1984.

Tucker, Stephen. *Terrorist Explosive Sourcebook: Countering Terrorist Use of Improvised Explosive Devices*. Boulder, CO: Paladin, 2005.

Indian Embassy (Kabul) Bombing

On July 7, 2008, a suicide car bomb exploded at the entrance of the Indian embassy in Kabul, killing 58 people and injuring another 141. The attack took place at the height of the morning rush hour. Among the dead were an Indian defense attaché, a political information officer, two Indian security officials, and nine police officers.

The car used in the bombing, an explosives-packed Toyota Camry, was rammed into two Indian diplomatic vehicles entering the embassy and detonated at approximately 8:30 a.m. on a busy street outside the diplomatic mission where people usually line up to apply for visas. The *Times of India* later reported that the suicide operative was Hamza Shakoor, 22, of the Gujranwala district in Pakistan.

India had been raising the issue of security for its law enforcement and diplomatic staff in Afghanistan for months. The government's consulate in Jalalabad had already been attacked twice by hand grenades in 2007, while a Taliban ambush on the Indo-Tibetan Border Police (ITBP) a month prior to the embassy bombing left one officer dead and four others injured. In the aftermath of the second incident, Delhi's Home Ministry issued a warning to the ITBP (an elite force that had been deployed to Afghanistan to protect Indian nationals and projects) to take necessary precautionary measures and remain on guard against possible suicide attacks; it also noted that the security provided by the Afghan police was not up to the mark.

On August 1, 2008, just a month after the bombing, U.S. authorities leaked to the *New York Times* that Islamabad's InterServices Intelligence (ISI) Directorate planned and coordinated the attack. Their conclusions were based on intercepted communications between Pakistani intelligence officials and the perpetrators before the attack as well as statements from an ISI officer inside Afghanistan. That same day, the *Washington Post* reported that American security agencies had reason to believe the ISI had provided logistic assistance to the bombers, who were in turn linked to Jalaluddin Haqqani, a Pashtun and pro-Taliban insurgent leader.

The news stories were consistent with revelations that Central Intelligence Agency (CIA) deputy director Stephen R. Kappes had visited Islamabad just before the attack. The reason for his trip was to present senior Pakistani officials with information that members of the ISI were actively supporting militant Islamist groups and that this was both known and sanctioned by their superiors.

Following the bombing, questions were raised about Pakistan's reliability as an ally in the U.S.-led war on terror. President George W. Bush confronted Pakistani prime minister Yousuf Raza Gilani in Washington, D.C., with evidence that the ISI had at least known about, if not been directly involved in, the attack, and stated

An Indian Embassy guard stands at the embassy's entrance gate in central Kabul, Afghanistan, on July 7, 2008. A suicide car bomb exploded outside the embassy, killing over 40 people in the deadliest attack in Afghanistan's capital that year. (AP Photos/Rahmat Gul)

that serious action would be taken if another bombing occurred.

The embassy bombing occurred in the context of a rapidly strengthening Indo-Afghan partnership after 2001. During Operation Enduring Freedom (OEF), Delhi had offered intelligence and other logistic support to Allied forces to help overthrow the Taliban. In 2002, India established diplomatic relations with the newly elected government in Kabul and provided aid and workers to help with the country's reconstruction efforts. By 2007, India had pledged $850 million in development assistance and support, the largest amount from any country without a military presence in Afghanistan.

Donna Bassett

See also: Enduring Freedom, Operation; Suicide Bombings; Terrorism

Further Reading

"Bomb Rocks Indian Embassy in Kabul." *BBC News*, July 7, 2008. http://news.bbc.co.uk/2/hi/7492601.stm.

"Indian Embassy Bomb Kills 41 in Kabul." *The Telegraph* (UK), July 7, 2008. http://www.telegraph.co.uk/news/worldnews/asia/afghanistan/2261882/Indian-embassy-bomb-kills-41-in-Kabul.html.

Miller, Frederic. *2008 Indian Embassy Bombing in Kabul.* Beau-Bassin, MU: Vdm, 2010.

International Emergency Economic Powers Act

The International Emergency Economic Powers Act is a U.S. federal law that grants presidents the power to identify and respond to any unusual or extraordinary threat originating outside the United States by confiscating property and prohibiting fiscal transactions under Title 50, Chapter 35, Sections 1701–1707. These confiscations and controls can be applied to individuals, groups, organizations, and foreign nations.

Congress passed the International Emergency Economic Powers Act (IEEPA) on October 28, 1977. As Public Law 95-223, 91 Stat. 1626, this act falls under the provisions of the National Emergencies Act (NEA), passed in 1976, which means that an emergency declared under the act is subject to annual renewal and may be repealed at any time by a joint congressional resolution. The act is a further clarification of the Trading with the Enemy Act, which had provided a source of both presidential emergency authority and wartime authority.

The origins and evolution of IEEPA date back to the Great Depression. In 1933, when President Franklin D. Roosevelt assumed office, his New Deal legislation implied that the president had the power to declare emergencies without limiting their scope and length of time. The Roosevelt administration claimed that there was no need to cite pertinent statutes and that it did not have to report to Congress. Subsequent presidents followed this line of thinking, including President Harry S. Truman in his response to the nationwide steel strike during the Korean War, until the U.S. Supreme Court in *Youngstown Sheet & Tube Co. v. Sawyer* (1952) limited what a president could do in such an emergency. The court did not, however, limit the power of emergency declaration itself. Shortly after the Vietnam War, a 1973 Senate investigation revealed that four declared emergencies were still in existence: the 1933 gold issue; the 1950 Korean War emergency; the 1970 postal workers strike; and the 1971 response to rampant inflation. The NEA officially terminated these emergencies in 1976, and the IEEPA was passed the next year to restore executive emergency powers, albeit in a limited fashion and with oversight by Congress.

The first time the IEEPA was used was during the Jimmy Carter administration in reaction to the Iranian hostage crisis of 1979–1981. Since then, the IEEPA has been invoked by presidents against Iraq (1990–2004), for its invasion of Kuwait; Libya (1986–2004), for sponsoring terrorism; Liberia (2001–2004), for human rights violations; Panama (1988–1990), for the military coup by Manuel Noriega; South Africa (1985–1991), for its apartheid policy; Zimbabwe (since 2003), for undermining democratic institutions; North Korea (since 2008), for the risk of the proliferation of weapon-usable fission material; and other countries for supporting terrorism, including the former Taliban regime in Afghanistan.

Some of the terror organizations and terrorists targeted by the IEEPA are the Egyptian Islamic Jihad, Al-Qaeda, the Abu Sayyaf group, the Taliban, Ayman al-Zawahiri, Abu Abdullah, and Osama bin Laden. One of the more notable cases involving an American was in 1983, when financier Marc Rich was accused and convicted of violating the act by trading in Iranian oil during the Iranian hostage crisis. Rich was later pardoned by President Bill Clinton.

Over the years, new restrictions on certain powers have amended the IEEPA. Presidents no longer have the authority to regulate or prohibit personal communications that do not involve the transfer of items of value. Presidents cannot regulate or prohibit the transfer of articles for humanitarian aid unless it is deemed that such transfers would interfere with the ability to deal with the emergency or endanger U.S. military forces. Nor can a president regulate or prohibit the importation from any country or exportation to any country informational materials such as records, photographs, compact discs, CD-ROMs, artworks, and publications.

When the act was first passed, presidents used it to order sanctions directed at specific nations. Since then, presidents have used the IEEPA to shut down terrorist organizations and to cut off aid and support to individuals. One recent case occurred in 2006, when Javed Iqbal was arrested and charged with conspiracy for violating the act by airing material produced by Al-Manar Television in New York City during the Israel-Lebanon conflict that summer. The IEEPA has taken on greater importance as well as more scrutiny in light of the global war on terror.

Charles Francis Howlett

See also: Al-Qaeda; Bin Laden, Osama; Global War on Terror; Television, Middle Eastern; Taliban

Further Reading

Carter, Barry E. *International Economic Sanctions*. Cambridge: Cambridge University Press, 1988.

Malloy, Michael P. *United States Economic Sanctions: Theory and Practice*. Alphen aan den Rijn, NL: Kluwer Law International, 2001.

Patterson, Thomas G., et al. *A History of American Foreign Relations since 1895*. Boston: Houghton Mifflin, 2005.

International Red Cross Headquarters (Baghdad) Bombing

On October 27, 2003—the first day of Ramadan of that year—a series of bombs ripped through downtown Baghdad in a coordinated string of attacks unprecedented in both scale and scope. Among the targets of the bombings was the headquarters of the International Committee of the Red Cross (ICRC), located in central Baghdad. The attack on the ICRC came on the heels of a number of high-profile bombings targeting other civilian entities in Iraq, such as the Jordanian embassy and the offices of the United Nations (UN). Still, it sent shock waves through nongovernmental organizations operating in Iraq and prompted most of those that had not already left the country to further scale back their operations or withdraw altogether.

The months preceding the ICRC bombing saw substantial changes in the overall security environment in Iraq. In the immediate aftermath of the March 2003 U.S.-led invasion, looting posed a serious problem, and an Iraqi nationalist and ex-Baathist insurgency was percolating. While there were some portentous developments—the July 22, 2003, killing of a Sri Lankan ICRC employee and a handful of attacks on members of Iraqi civil society—the vast majority of attacks took the form of ambushes, roadside bombings, and improvised explosives primarily targeting U.S. forces. In effect, through the spring and midsummer of 2003, there was still reason for optimism about the future of Iraqi security.

By the late summer of 2003, however, the security environment in Iraq had changed drastically. On August 7, 2003, a car bomb detonated in central Baghdad outside the headquarters of the Jordanian embassy, killing 18 and wounding scores more. Less than two weeks later, on August 19, 2003, the headquarters of the UN Assistance Mission in Iraq were rocked by a suicide

Iraqi children pass by the destroyed headquarters of the International Red Cross in Baghdad on October 28, 2003. (AP Photo/Anja Niedringhaus)

car bombing that decimated the UN staff and killed the UN's special envoy, Sergio Vieira de Mello, a veteran with 33 years of experience working in some of the world's toughest conflict zones. The UN bombing was followed a mere 10 days later by a car bomb attack on a crowd outside the Imam Ali shrine in the southern city of Najaf on August 29, 2003. This incident marked the first major sectarian attack of the Iraq War and left 83 people dead, including the influential Shi'ite Ayatollah Muhammad Baqir al-Hakim. The attack also wounded 500 others. In sum, these three bombings loudly announced the presence of foreign jihadists within Iraq and obliterated any notion of an insurgency strictly characterized by Saddam Hussein loyalists and ex-Baathists.

Despite this violence, Iraq still had not seen anything near the scope, scale,

and coordination of the attacks that took place on October 27, 2003. Beginning at roughly 8:30 a.m. local time, a flurry of coordinated suicide attacks rocked Baghdad. First, a suicide bomber detonated his explosives-laden vehicle at Dora patrol station in Baghdad's Bayaa neighborhood. The attack killed at least 15 people, including one U.S. soldier. Just minutes after this explosion, a suicide bomber in a Peugeot ambulance marked with the emblem of the Red Crescent—the Muslim equivalent of the Red Cross and the type of vehicle ubiquitous in post-invasion Iraq—sped toward the ICRC headquarters. Approximately 30 meters (98 feet) from the organization's offices, the bomber slammed into the protective barrier surrounding the building, which was comprised of little more than loosely strung together oil barrels filled with sand. The collision detonated the explosives.

The blast was devastating. Its impact created a hole 21 feet deep by 53 feet wide, tore a 129-foot hole in the sandbag-reinforced front wall of the building, and caused extensive damage to the interior of the building. The explosion sent shrapnel flying hundreds of feet in all directions and ultimately killed 12 people and wounded 22. Among the dead were two ICRC staff members. Both were unarmed security guards, and both were Iraqis. Given that the blast occurred early in the morning, the death toll at the organization would have been substantially higher had the staff not been instructed to arrive one hour later because of Ramadan. It is believed that as few as 10 staff members were inside the ICRC's offices at the time of the attack.

In the immediate aftermath of the ICRC bombing, U.S. forces arrived on the scene to cordon off the area and assist those wounded in the explosion. Immediately after their arrival, however, a series of three other coordinated blasts occurred at police stations scattered throughout downtown Baghdad. A fifth attempted suicide bombing on a police station was foiled when Iraqi police forces shot and wounded the driver, who was caught in a Toyota Land Cruiser filled with approximately 400 pounds of TNT and three 120-millimeter mortar rounds. His capture was a boon for the Iraqi security services as it shed substantial light on the identity of those behind the October 27, 2003, bombings. Claiming at first to be a Syrian national and possessing a Syrian passport, the bomber later told authorities he hailed from Yemen.

Even without the knowledge of the exact nationality of the bomber, the tactics and the targeting of the bombings bore the mark of sophisticated foreign jihadists. First, the fact that the bombings were so closely coordinated revealed significant technical and operational expertise on behalf of the perpetrators. Routes to the police stations were carefully planned out in advance, and eyewitness reports suggested that the vehicles used were either stolen police cars or, in the case of one vehicle, a truck painted with the exact same color scheme as an Iraqi police vehicle. Moreover, all of the bombings were specifically timed to take place within a span of only 45 minutes. Second, the choice of weapon, a suicide vehicle–borne improvised explosive, was another tactical hallmark of Al-Qaeda. Finally, the fact that the attackers targeted an international organization such as the ICRC, which had operated in Iraq for 23 years and through three separate wars, suggested the work of foreign jihadist elements rather than Iraqi nationalists.

Overall, the ICRC bombing, like the UN bombing and the Jordanian embassy bombing, is remembered as a substantial turning point in the Iraqi insurgency. In concert, the three blasts violently proclaimed that no entity, no matter how well regarded by Iraqis or the international community, was safe in Iraq. With the attack, foreign jihadists announced that they would ruthlessly kill civilians in their efforts to oust any Western presence from Iraq and topple the Iraqi government.

Nate Shestak

See also: Iraqi Freedom, Operation; Jamaa al-Tawhid wa'a Jihad (JTJ); Joint Direct Attack Munitions and Small Diameter Bomb; London Bombings

Further Reading

Chandrasekaran, Rajiv. "Car Bombs Kill at Least 35 in Baghdad." *Washington Post*, October 28, 2003.

Filkins, Dexter, and Alex Berenson. "Suicide Bombers in Baghdad Kill at Least 34." *New York Times*, October 28, 2003.

Hanley, Charles J. "36 Killed in Bomb Attack upon Baghdad Red Cross Headquarters, Police Stations." Associated Press, October 27, 2003.

Labbe, Theola, and Keith B. Richburg. "Decades of Good Deeds Provide No Armor; Red Cross Reassesses Its Presence in Iraq." *Washington Post*, October 28, 2003.

International Security Assistance Force

The International Security Assistance Force is a multinational military security and assistance mission to Afghanistan, currently led by the North Atlantic Treaty Organization (NATO) and formed by the United Nations (UN) Security Council on December 20, 2001. The International Security Assistance Force (ISAF) is composed of a military headquarters, an air task force, regional commands, forward support bases, and Provincial Reconstruction Teams (PRTs). Its mission is to help the Afghan central government extend its authority throughout the provinces, mentor and train the Afghan National Army and Afghan National Police, conduct military operations in coordination with Afghan security forces to stabilize and secure the country, assist the Afghan government in disarming illegal militias, support Afghan counternarcotics programs, and provide humanitarian assistance when needed.

In December 2001, two months after the United States and coalition forces began Operation Enduring Freedom to destroy Al-Qaeda and topple the Taliban government in Afghanistan, the international community held a conference in Bonn, Germany, to assist Afghanistan in creating a stable government and reconstructing the country. This international effort, known as the Bonn Agreement, included a military component. On December 20, 2001, the United Nations Security Council authorized the deployment of an International Security Assistance Force to operate in the Afghan capital at Kabul. Its mission was to assist with stabilizing the country and to create conditions for the establishment of peace. The ISAF was not a United Nations force, but rather an organization created by volunteer countries acting under the authority of the United Nations Security Council.

The United Kingdom headed the first ISAF rotation, from December 2001 to July 2002. Eighteen additional countries contributed troops, equipment, and other assets, bringing the initial number of troops to 5,000. According to the United Nations Security Council mandate, this force could only operate in Kabul. Turkey commanded ISAF II from July 2002 to January 2003. Germany, Canada, France, Turkey, and Italy each led a subsequent ISAF rotation, with each rotation lasting six months. In addition, the United Kingdom led a 10-month rotation from May 2006 to February 2007. U.S. lieutenant general Dan K. McNeill served as ISAF commander from February 2007 to May 2008, followed by General David D. McKiernan, another American, who took over as ISAF commander in June 2008. U.S. general Stanley A. McChrystal succeeded McKiernan in June 2009. He was replaced by U.S. general David Petraeus (July 2010–July 2011). From July 2011 until February 2013, U.S. general John R. Allen commanded ISAF; he was succeeded by U.S. general Joseph F. Dunford, Jr. ISAF commanders coordinate their activities with the United Nations

Assistance Mission in Afghanistan and other top coalition leaders.

One problem of the ISAF command arrangement early on was that each rotation lasted only six months, which required a constant search for another coalition partner to volunteer to lead the organization. Even with briefings and coordinated handovers from one command to the next, the new, incoming staff usually lacked sufficient knowledge or understanding of conditions in Afghanistan. This inexperience led to uneven transitions in programs and operations.

NATO finally provided the solution to the rotating ISAF headquarters problem. In April 2003, the North Atlantic Council authorized a peacekeeping force in Afghanistan, which would be responsible for the command, coordination, planning, and headquarters for ISAF. A permanent NATO command also allowed smaller coalition nations to participate more fully in what would become a multinational headquarters, since it was too difficult for them to lead a 1,700-strong ISAF staff on their own. NATO formally assumed command of the ISAF on August 11, 2003. Its primary mission was to focus on stabilization, reconstruction, and maintaining security in relatively quiet areas of Afghanistan, while U.S. forces concentrated on combat operations against insurgent forces as well as training the Afghan National Army.

In 2003, ISAF headquarters and coalition troops consisted of 5,882 personnel from 32 nations and still operated exclusively in Kabul. In October 2003, however, the UN Security Council approved the expansion of ISAF into other areas of Afghanistan. The first extension was into the northern provinces. The joint civil-military Provincial Reconstruction Teams, which conducted reconstruction efforts and supported the expansion of the central Afghan government's authority into the provinces, provided the means to begin the expansion. The ISAF took control of the Kondoz PRT from Germany in December 2003. Soon after, the ISAF assumed control of four additional PRTs—in Mazar-e Sharif, Meymaneh, Fayzabad, and Baghlan. By October 2, the ISAF became responsible for operations in the nine northern provinces.

Stage two of the expansion occurred in the western provinces in May 2006. The ISAF took control of the Herat and Farah PRTs as well as a forward support base in Herat. The ISAF opened new PRTs in Chaghcharan and Qala-i Now in September 2006. The northern and western provinces constituted about half of Afghanistan's territory, and were the most stable and secure areas. The expansion of the ISAF into the violent southern and eastern provinces proved more difficult. Beginning in July 2006, the ISAF took responsibility for the volatile southern provinces, including the heart of the Taliban-led insurgency in the Helmand, Kandahar, and Uruzgan provinces. At this time, the number of ISAF forces increased from 10,000 to 20,000 troops. The ISAF completed the final phase of the expansion in October 2006. As of January 2014, the ISAF commanded some 57,000 troops in Afghanistan, including some 38,000 troops from the United States; operated 26 PRTs; and represented the contributions of 49 nations. An additional 19,000 U.S. troops operated independently from the ISAF along the Afghan-Pakistan border.

While the ISAF commander is headquartered in Kabul, his chain of command extends back through multiple headquarters in Europe. The ISAF commander reports to the Allied Joint Force

Command Headquarters Brunssum (JFC HQ Brunssum) in the Netherlands and the joint force commander, currently in Germany. The joint force commander reports to the Supreme Headquarters Allied Powers Europe (SHAPE), located in Mons, Belgium. The distance of the chain of command and the differing rules governing how each of the various nations can engage in combat has often limited the effectiveness of ISAF operations. Some nations limit the kinds of engagements their troops may engage in, and some do not allow their troops to engage in combat operations at all. These national caveats hamper the effective use of coalition troops and shift the burden of heavy fighting to those nations with more freedom to conduct military operations, such as Canada, the United Kingdom, and the United States, among others. The constraints have been a constant source of tension between the NATO-led ISAF and the United States.

In addition to supplying headquarters personnel and combat forces for operations in Afghanistan, ISAF member nations contribute funding and equipment for the Afghan security forces. Slovenia, Hungary, and Latvia have provided small arms, mortars, and ammunition, while others, including Poland, Germany, and Romania, have donated uniforms and spare parts for weapons systems. Other nations have donated such military equipment as howitzers, tanks, aircraft, and helicopters. The ISAF currently participates in Task Force Phoenix, the military organization whose mission is to train the Afghan National Army and Afghan National Police by providing personnel for the headquarters and for the embedded mentoring and training teams that deploy with Afghan army units.

Since the ISAF has taken control of most military operations in Afghanistan, the level of violence has risen considerably in the southern and eastern provinces, while areas in the north and west remain stable. The Taliban and other enemy forces have adopted such guerrilla and terrorist tactics as ambushes, roadside bombs, and suicide bombs in the south and east. For example, roadside bombs increased from 60 detonations in 2003 to 1,256 in 2007. Since 2006, the worst fighting has taken place in the southern province of Helmand, where British and Canadian troops serve. In December 2007, the Afghan National Army, supported by ISAF troops, engaged in several days of hard fighting to liberate Musa Qala from Taliban control.

In more stable areas, ISAF has contributed to reconstruction efforts, building infrastructure such as roads and bridges as well as supporting provincial and local governments. As of April 2008, over 5,600 civil-military reconstruction projects had been completed. While the economy is improving in Afghanistan, the population's reliance on growing poppy for the illegal narcotic drug trade in opium and for heroin production continues to be one of the more difficult problems to solve. There is ample evidence that illegal drug money is helping to fund the Taliban insurgency, but other evidence shows deep involvement in the drug trade by associates and relatives of the current Afghan government. The initial American strategy in Afghanistan of the Barack Obama administration was to target individuals higher up in the drug trade as well as to destroy crops. While some Afghans do support the Taliban, a December 2007 poll suggested that the population supported international involvement in Afghanistan, including the presence of international military forces and the reconstruction efforts of the coalition.

In late 2009, the Obama administration announced a troop surge strategy in Afghanistan to begin early the following year. That witnessed the insertion of some 33,000 additional U.S. troops, who were to remain in that nation for a maximum of 18 months. At the height of the deployment, the United States had a total of about 68,000 troops on the ground in Afghanistan, or about eight times as many troops as the United Kingdom, the ISAF's second-largest contributor. The troop surge had a rather negligible impact on the growing insurgency in Afghanistan, however, and by 2011 a number of nations contributing to the ISAF had begun to draw down their forces. Many blamed the limited success of the American troop surge on the Hamid Karzai administration's failure to fully embrace the mission, Pakistan's unwillingness or inability to crack down on insurgents using its border with Afghanistan as a base of operations, and the Obama administration's insistence on a specific time table for deployment and its unwillingness to increase the number of troops above the 33,000 figure. By late 2011, virtually all of the 33,000 troops had been withdrawn. The situation in Afghanistan remains tense, however, and insurgents have steadily increased their attacks against both Afghanis and ISAF interests. On May 27, 2014, President Obama announced that he aims to keep 9,800 U.S. troops in Afghanistan after the war formally ends that year, while pledging a near-total withdrawal by the end of 2016. The plan would shrink the U.S. troop presence from its current force of 32,000 to 9,800 by the start of 2015, and to roughly half that size by the end of that year. Nearly all those forces are to be out by the end of 2016.

Estimated International Security Assistance Force (ISAF) Troop Strength (as of January 2014)

Country Organization	Affiliation Troop Strength
Albania NATO	74
Armenian None	121
Australia None	348
Austria EAPC	3
Azerbaijan EAPC	94
Belgium NATO	140
Bosnia and Herzegovina None	53
Bulgaria NATO	417
Canada NATO	265
Croatia NATO	140
Czech Republic NATO	219
Denmark NATO	263
El Salvador None	12
Estonia NATO	156
Finland EAPC	110
France NATO	205
Georgia EAPC	1,560
Germany NATO	3,077
Greece NATO	7
Hungary NATO	131
Iceland NATO	2
Italy NATO	2,159
Latvia NATO	131
Lithuania NATO	99
Luxembourg NATO	10
Malyasia None	1
Mongolia None	40
Netherlands NATO	200
New Zealand None	2
Norway NATO	109
Poland NATO	967
Portugal NATO	78
Romania NATO	505
Slovakia NATO	274
Slovenia NATO	34
Spain NATO	259
Sweden EAPC	270
Tonga None	55
Turkey NATO	458
Ukraine EAPC	28

Country Organization	Affiliation	Troop Strength
United Arab Emirates		
None		35
United Kingdom	NATO	5,200
United States	NATO	38,000
Total		**56,849**

Lisa Marie Mundey

See also: Enduring Freedom, Operation; Taliban; Taliban, Destruction of Bamiyan and Pre-Islamic Artifacts; U.S. Central Command

Further Reading

Combat Studies Institute Contemporary Operations Study Group. *A Different Kind of War: The United States Army Operation Enduring Freedom (OEF)*, September 2001–September 2005. Fort Leavenworth, KS: Combat Studies Institute Press, 2009.

Jalali, Ali A. *Enduring the Freedom: A Rogue Historian in Afghanistan*. Washington, DC: Potomac Books, 2007.

Jalali, Ali A. "The Future of Afghanistan." *Parameters* (Spring 2006): 4–19.

Sundquist, Leah R. *NATO in Afghanistan: A Progress Report*. Carlisle Barracks, PA: U.S. Army War College, 2008.

Iraqi Freedom, Operation

(March 20, 2003–May 1, 2003)

Those who take the long view of history may be inclined to blame British prime minister David Lloyd George as much as U.S. president George W. Bush for the current situation in Iraq. British and French actions after World War I to fill the Middle Eastern void left by the collapse of the Ottoman Empire created modern Iraq and other Arab nations without regard for traditional ethnic and religious boundaries. Conditions in the European-created, artificial country of Iraq (especially the long-held animosity between the country's three major ethnic and religious populations of Kurds, Sunni, and Shia) made it a perfect breeding ground for such strong-arm dictators as Saddam Hussein to seize and hold power over a divided population, while incubating simmering ethnic and religious rivalries.

Iraq, compared with Afghanistan, the other major theater of combat operations for President Bush's global war on terror, played out with mixed success in two very different campaigns: a stunning conventional assault that rapidly destroyed the Iraqi army, captured Baghdad, ousted Saddam Hussein, and paved the way for a U.S.-led occupation of the country, and a smoldering insurgency conducted by Al-Qaeda fighters and both Sunni and Shia faction Iraqi militia groups that began shortly after Hussein's defeat.

Although the two Iraq campaigns bear a superficial similarity to what transpired in Afghanistan (large-scale conventional combat operations to defeat the enemy's main forces followed by an insurgency), the Iraq War and occupation have shown striking differences in scope, intensity, and even in the justification U.S. leaders gave for invading the country. While Operation Enduring Freedom was launched to strike directly at those presumed responsible for masterminding the September 11, 2001, terror attacks and the Afghan Taliban regime that harbored them, no such justification can be claimed for the Bush administration's decision to launch the March 2003 invasion of Iraq. Despite Iraqi president Saddam Hussein's track record of general support for terrorist organizations

CH-47 Chinook helicopter crew members of the 101st Airborne Division in Kuwait converse shortly before flying across the border into Iraq on March 23, 2003. US-led Coalition airborne forces first entered Iraq only three days previously as part of Operation Iraqi Liberation, later renamed Operation Iraqi Freedom. (U.S. Army)

hostile to the United States and the West, no direct link to Al-Qaeda has ever been proven. And while U.S. strategy regarding Afghanistan might be classified as *reactive*, the decision of America's leaders to invade Iraq can only be termed *proactive*, a surprising and controversial preemptive action.

In the wake of the 1990–1991 Persian Gulf War, Hussein used chemical weapons on Iraq's Kurdish minority. Subsequently, Hussein was often vilified for using chemical weapons on "his own people," but he did not consider the Kurds to be "his people"; his loyalty lay only with his Baathist Party cronies and his own tribe. What is perhaps surprising about his use of chemical weapons is that he did not use them more extensively. Iraqi officials were reluctant to inspections by the United Nations (UN) and failed, by late 2002, to produce

an adequate accounting of the disposition of the weapons of mass destruction the country was known to possess (and use) in 1991. Further, the Iraqis failed to provide a full and open disclosure of the status of its suspected nuclear weapons program. If Iraq had added nuclear weapons to its 1991 chemical arsenal, as was charged by Iraqi émigrés (such as Khidhir Hamza, self-proclaimed as "Saddam's Bombmaker," who toured U.S. college campuses in the autumn of 2002 trumpeting his "insider" knowledge of Iraq's alleged nuclear program), it would have been foolish to ignore the threat such weapons posed. By failing to cooperate promptly, fully, and openly with UN weapons inspectors, Hussein had almost literally signed his own death warrant.

Opting for a preemptive strategy instead of risking a potential repeat of the

September 11 terror attacks—with the added specter of chemical, biological, or nuclear weapons—Bush and his advisers (principally Vice President Dick Cheney and Deputy Secretary of Defense Paul Wolfowitz, described as "a major architect of Bush's Iraq policy . . . and its most passionate and compelling advocate") decided to act, unilaterally if necessary. Armed chiefly with what would later be exposed as an egregiously inaccurate Central Intelligence Agency (CIA) report about Iraq's possession of nuclear and other weapons of mass destruction, Bush obtained a legal justification for invading Iraq when the Senate approved the Joint Resolution "Authorization for Use of Military Force against Iraq Resolution of 2002" in October 2002. In February 2003, Secretary of State Colin Powell addressed the UN Security Council with information based largely on the same flawed CIA report, but action was blocked by France, Germany, and Russia. Although the three powers bolstered their opposition with claims that military action against Iraq would threaten "international security," their true motives were suspect to some who supported military action (France and Germany, for example, already had made billions of dollars by illegally circumventing the UN Oil-for-Food Programme with Iraq). Regardless of their motives, all three countries had a vested interest in maintaining the status quo in Iraq and little motivation to participate in an American-led preemptive strike. Although Britain joined Bush's "coalition of the willing" (from 2003, 75 countries contributed troops, matériel, or services to the U.S.-led effort), the absence of France and Germany left his administration open to strong criticism for stubbornly proceeding without broad-based European support.

Bush's proactive rather than reactive strategy was heavily criticized by administration opponents as a sea-change departure from that of past U.S. presidents and slammed for its unilateralism. Yet, as historian John Lewis Gaddis points out in *Surprise, Security and the American Experience*, it was not without historical precedent. He cites the preemptive, unilateral actions of presidents John Adams, James K. Polk, William McKinley, Woodrow Wilson, and even Franklin D. Roosevelt. Yet, with U.S. ground forces already stretched thin by Operation Enduring Freedom, mounting a major, preemptive invasion of Iraq was considered by many—particularly U.S. military leaders—as risky. Military drawdowns during Clinton's presidency, for example, had reduced U.S. Army active duty strength from 780,000 to about 480,000.

On March 20, 2003, U.S. and British forces (plus smaller contingents from Australia and Poland) invaded Iraq in Operation Iraqi Freedom. The 297,000-strong force faced Iraqi forces numbering approximately 375,000, plus an unknown number of poorly trained citizens' militias. U.S. combat strength was about half of that deployed during the 1990–1991 Persian Gulf War. With U.S. Central Command general Tommy Franks in overall command, the U.S. ground forces prosecuting the invasion were led by U.S. V Corps commander Lieutenant General William Scott Wallace.

Preceded by a shock-and-awe air campaign reminiscent of the one that blasted Hussein's forces and Iraqi infrastructure in the Persian Gulf War, ground forces (including U.S. Marines and British combat units) executed another "desert blitzkrieg" that quickly smashed the Iraqi Army. Despite the failure of the Turkish government at the last minute to allow the United States to mount a major invasion of northern Iraq from its soil, two ground prongs struck north from Kuwait, while Special Forces and airborne forces worked with the Kurds in the north in a limited second front. The ground advance north was rapid. Baghdad fell on April 10, and Hussein went into hiding. (He was captured in December 2003, brought to trial, found guilty, and executed on December 30, 2006.)

President Bush declared the "mission accomplished" and the end of major combat operations while aboard the U.S. aircraft carrier *Abraham Lincoln* on May 1, 2003. Subsequent events during the post-invasion occupation of Iraq would prove Bush's dramatic statement to be wildly premature: although only 139 U.S. personnel and 33 British soldiers died during the invasion, more than 4,000 Americans were to die thereafter in the insurgency that accompanied the occupation. Bush administration decisions to include the dismissal of Baathist Party officials (essentially, Iraq's only trained administrators), and the disbanding of the Iraqi Army (which at one stroke dumped nearly 400,000 trained soldiers and potential insurgent recruits into the Iraqi general population) contributed to the insurgency.

Jerry D. Morelock

See also: Bush Administration; Cheney, Richard Bruce; Iraq War; Persian Gulf War; Powell, Colin Luther; Rumsfeld, Donald Henry; U.S. Central Command

Further Reading

Gaddis, John L. *Strategies of Containment: A Critical Appraisal of Postwar American National Security Policy.* New York, NY: Oxford University Press. 1982; revised 2005.

Gordon, Michael R., and General Bernard E. Trainor. *Cobra II: The Inside Story of the Invasion and Occupation of Iraq.* New York: Pantheon Books, 2006.

Murray, Williamson, and Robert H. Scales, Jr. *The Iraq War: A Military History.* Cambridge, MA: Belknap, 2005.

Ricks, Thomas E. *Fiasco: The American Military Adventure in Iraq.* New York: Penguin, 2006.

Woodward, Bob. *State of Denial: Bush at War, Part III.* New York: Simon and Schuster, 2006.

Woodward, Bob. *Plan of Attack.* New York: Simon and Schuster, 2004.

Woodward, Bob. *Bush at War.* New York: Simon and Schuster, 2002.

Iraqi Insurgency

(2003–Present)

A violent resistance by segments of the Iraqi population against the foreign occupation powers deployed in Iraq and the new Iraqi government set up after the fall of the Baathist state. The term "insurgency" is employed in U.S. governmental circles and by coalition forces but is not used in the Arab media, except in discussions with U.S. spokespersons. The term was not initially employed by the U.S. government, but its appearance in 2004 onward led to a major emphasis on insurgency theory and new approaches to counterinsurgency.

The Iraqi insurgency commenced soon after the official end of hostilities that followed the overthrow of Iraqi president Saddam Hussein in the spring of 2003. Until the U.S. military gained control of Iraq and President George W. Bush declared "mission accomplished" on May 1, 2003, Operation Iraqi Freedom was essentially a war between the Iraqi government and military and the coalition powers that overthrew it. Afterward, Iraqi Freedom morphed into a battle between coalition and allied Iraqi forces and a wide array of insurgent groups, which was characterized as an insurgency war. Following the withdrawal of U.S. and coalition troops from Iraq in December 2011, the insurgency continued, but it essentially morphed into a Sunni-Shia sectarian conflict and an insurrection by various insurgent groups against the Shia-dominated government of Nuri al-Maliki.

A number of factors led to the insurgency, but the chief cause was the power vacuum created by the sudden collapse of the highly centralized Iraqi government and the failure of the U.S. armed forces to properly fill that void in a timely manner with a power structure acceptable to those governed. Many Iraqis did not welcome a change in government, or feared the opposition elements that assumed power. Coalition forces have sometimes argued that the lack of electricity, fuel, potable water, and basic social services created daily personal grievances among many Iraqis, but far more resentment was engendered by attacks, arrests, and detentions, and later, by Iraqi-on-Iraqi campaigns that led those who could afford or were able to flee Iraq to do so. The Iraqi people expected the occupying American forces to provide for their security, but the latter either had insufficient numbers to do so effectively or were not assigned to protect Iraqis, their property, or their state institutions.

The U.S.-led invasion of Iraq and subsequent fall of the country's dictator, Saddam Hussein, made conditions ripe for power struggles to emerge among various sectarian and political groups. Even though Iraqis had a history of intermarriage and mixed communities, many had been suppressed and mistreated by Hussein's government and had scores to settle. The U.S. government hoped that the period immediately following the overthrow of Hussein would see the installation of a broadly based Iraqi government led by those who had opposed Saddam. However, the Iraqi people viewed many of the new leaders as pursuing their own narrow interests or those of their parties.

Also, the initial U.S. governmental appointees in the Interim Authority were intent on wiping out all vestiges of the previous government and institutions through de-Baathification. This led many Sunni Iraqis to conclude that they had absolutely nothing to gain and could possibly force the occupying troops to leave Iraq if they took up arms and established control in those areas of the country where they were a majority. Initially, the coalition refused to accept both the severity of this fighting and its toll on Iraqis, but a virtual civil war began to engulf Iraq in 2006.

A telling feature of the Iraqi insurgency has been its decentralized nature. It is conducted by a large number of disparate groups, many of which are ideologically different, although temporary alliances are not uncommon. For example, there were at least 40 different Sunni Muslim insurgent factions, although the coalition primarily focused on the threat presented by Al-Qaeda in Iraq. Others were local nationalists, made up of former Iraqi security service members and soldiers of the old Iraqi armed forces, some of whom aligned with new Islamist groups. Their goal, broadly speaking, was to drive the United States and its allies from Iraq and regain the power that they once had enjoyed, or at least sufficient power to force the central Shia-dominated Iraqi government to grant them autonomy in certain areas. This segment of the resistance was motivated by a mixture of nationalism, opposition to occupation, loss of status and income, fear of future discrimination, and the lure of financial incentives provided by various groups. These predominantly Sunni groups had valid reasons to fear that the new security services dominated by Shia and Kurds would oppress them. Some of these insurgents were believed to be trained and equipped soldiers with previous combat experience and knowledge of the local terrain.

A second element within the Sunni Iraqi community consisted of jihadist salafiyya (or salafis) whose ultimate goal was the establishment of an Islamic state in Iraq while excluding the Shia and/or non-Islamists from power altogether. The U.S. government identified this group as consisting primarily of foreign volunteer fighters who had traveled to Iraq from Saudi Arabia, Jordan, Syria, Egypt, and Libya. Actually, there were far fewer of these foreign volunteers than was claimed, and a far larger number of salafist or jihadi salafists were Iraqis who adopted this role in desperation, or who had become salafist in the Saddam Hussein era. These groups targeted coalition forces as well as Iraqi military, police, government, and civilians in suicide attacks. Among these groups was Al-Qaeda in Iraq, which was originally the Tawhid wal-Jihad group headed by now-deceased Abu Musab al-Zarqawi.

Although Al-Qaeda leaders in Afghanistan warned the Iraqi group, which had sworn allegiance to them, that attacking Iraqi Shia was a dubious policy, they went on doing so. The leaders of Al-Qaeda in Iraq considered the Shia to be renegades (and apostates) and held them accountable for collaborating with the occupying forces.

In 2008, the coalition began to claim that many insurgents were not ideologically committed (perhaps because efforts to convince Iraqis that they were un-Islamic were failing). They asserted that many fighters were motivated by the need for a source of income because of the economic collapse of Iraq and the general state of lawlessness. This claim appears to have been true in some limited areas where kidnapping rings operated just after the initial defeat of Hussein's government. It is the type of claim that can be made in civil wars generally, but is demonstrably untrue, for most of the insurgent statements claim religious convictions.

The insurgents have employed a wide array of tactics against their targets. Some rely on sabotage of electric stations, oil pipelines and facilities, and coalition reconstruction projects. Others use small-arms gunfire against coalition forces and attempt assassinations of public officials and private citizens. Firing rockets and mortar shells at fixed coalition positions has also been an insurgent tactic. The use of improvised roadside bombs and improvised explosive devices (IEDs) proved especially lethal to coalition troops as well as Iraqi military and security personnel. Suicide bombers, car bombs, and truck bombs, many of which have killed scores of innocent civilians, have also been used to great effect by the insurgents.

Insurgents have deployed ambushes that involve the simultaneous use of mines, grenades, and rocket-propelled grenades. They also engage in the kidnapping of local citizens and foreigners to exchange them for ransom, or simply to execute them. Initially, insurgent violence was primarily directed at coalition forces. As the occupation has persisted, however, attacks by various insurgency groups began shifting toward the Iraqi police and security forces as well as opposing militias representing the various warring sects. Attacks on Iraqi civilians, especially those associated with the government or seeking employment with the police force, also escalated after 2004.

The United States has accused Syria and Iran of aiding various insurgency groups in the funding and planning of their activities. There was evidence that some former Baathists, including the acknowledged leader of the resistance, Ibrahim al-Duri, were in Syria. Both Syria and Iran oppose the establishment of a pro-American democracy in Iraq, and fear that their influence in the region would be jeopardized by the long-term stationing of U.S. troops in Iraq.

The United States employed several strategies to squelch the insurgency in Iraq. The initial phase of counterinsurgency efforts in late 2003 and early 2004 consisted mainly of occupation forces engaging in indiscriminate and sometimes culturally insensitive tactics that alienated many Iraqis, such as mass arrests, night searches, heavy-handed interrogations, and blanket incarcerations. Such actions enraged and embittered formerly friendly or neutral Iraqis. The United States then responded to insurgents by engaging in a variety of counterinsurgency measures, including Operation Desert Thrust, Operation Phantom Fury in Fallujah, Operation Together Forward, and Operation Phantom Thrust, just to name a few. These full-scale assaults on insurgency bases have had only a temporary and limited effect, however.

The most notable counterinsurgency effort was mounted during 2007. The so-called troop surge undertaken by the Bush administration accounted for an increase in U.S. troop size by about 30,000 additional soldiers. The move was hailed a success by U.S. officials for bringing down the levels of violence in Iraq. Critics, however, contend that the levels of violence went down only in some areas of the country, and only through methods that cordoned off and imposed barriers around neighborhoods that had been cleansed on a sectarian basis. In spring 2009, for example, there was an upsurge of bombings targeting both Shia and Sunni areas in Baghdad. While most insurgent activity involved only Sunnis, other groups have also been involved. Thus, there was also armed resistance by members of Muqtada al-Sadr's Mahdi Army when Iraqi government forces engaged them. They had not been a part of the insurgency but rather sought to enhance their power within the body politic.

Another reason for a drop in the violence was the fact that the U.S. military struck a bargain with various Sunni groups, some of them jihadist salafists. This permitted coalition forces to concentrate on fighting Al-Qaeda in Iraq in these areas. However, these so-called Awakening Councils were subject to numerous attacks and began clashing with the government. Since their support rested on financial incentives, their continued compliance was not assured.

When he ran for president in 2008, Democratic presidential candidate Barack Obama, who opposed the war in Iraq, pledged to withdraw all U.S. troops from Iraq within two years of taking office. When he took office in January 2009, high on his agenda was a gradual U.S. military disengagement from Iraq, with a goal of complete withdrawal before the end of 2011. With the Bush troop surge still showing some signs of having promoted more stability in Iraq, the United States and its coalition partners began a major drawdown of forces beginning in late 2009. Soon, however, there were signs that sectarian strife and Islamic extremism in Iraq, egged on and supported by the Syrians and Iraqis, were beginning to reemerge as major problems. Despite this, the Obama administration was committed to its timetable for the withdrawal of American troops, which was concluded in December 2011.

The situation in Iraq then deteriorated rapidly, especially during 2013. Al-Maliki's government has been largely unable to stem a new, growing insurgency, and has been attempting to further marginalize the Sunni opposition. During 2012–2013 and into early 2014, bombings, kidnappings, assassinations and other violence accelerated, and more and more civilians were being caught in the crossfire of a potential civil war in Iraq. Al-Qaeda had now become a major player in the insurgency, as had numerous Shiite militias. At the same time, the number of foreigners taking part in the insurgency increased, and Iran was playing a larger role in funding and supporting the rebels. By early January 2014, Al-Qaeda insurgents and their allies had seized control of a large portion of Anbar Province, including its two major cities—Ramadi and Fallujah. The future of Iraq remained very much in doubt by early 2014, and the Al-Maliki government was exhibiting little success in breaking the growing momentum of the Iraqi insurgency.

Kristian P. Alexander and Sherifa Zuhur

See also: Al-Qaeda; Al-Qaeda in Iraq; Iraqi Freedom, Operation; Iraq War

Further Reading

Chehab, Zaki. *Iraq Ablaze: Inside the Insurgency.* New York: I. B. Tauris, 2006.

Cordesman, Anthony. *Iraqi Security Forces: A Strategy for Success.* Westport, CT: Praeger Security International, 2005.

Hafez, Mohammed. *Suicide Bombers in Iraq: The Strategy and Ideology of Martyrdom.* Washington, DC: United States Institute of Peace Press, 2007.

Hashim, Ammed S. *Insurgency and Counterinsurgency in Iraq.* Ithaca, NY: Cornell University Press, 2006.

Pelletiere, Stephen. *Losing Iraq: Insurgency and Politics.* Westport, CT: Praeger Security International, 2007.

Iraq War

The Iraq War of 2003 pitted a coalition led by the United States and the United Kingdom against the government of Iraqi president Saddam Hussein and his Arab Baath Socialist Party. Hostilities commenced with U.S.-led attacks on March 20, 2003—without the approval of the United Nations (UN)—following months of U.S. and British assertions that Hussein was harboring weapons of mass destruction (WMDs).

The war had much longer-lasting effects in the Middle East and the international community than the Persian Gulf War of 1990–1991. Sparking a great deal of controversy, the war triggered arguments among UN member states regarding the appropriate action to take and spurred millions of people around the world to march in protest of the military action. In addition, a great deal of suspicion arose regarding the U.S.-led coalition forces' motives behind the war, with pundits suggesting that the coalition desired more to control Iraq's great oil reserves than to liberate a people long oppressed by Hussein.

Following the Persian Gulf War, the UN imposed sanctions on Iraq, calling for Hussein to destroy the country's arsenal of WMDs. Over the next decade, however, Hussein repeatedly evaded attempts by UN weapons inspectors to ensure that the sanctions were enforced. Upon assuming the U.S. presidency in January 2001, George W. Bush and his administration immediately began calling for renewed efforts toward ridding Iraq of WMDs—an endeavor that greatly intensified after the September 11, 2001, World Trade Center and Pentagon attacks.

In Bush's 2002 State of the Union message, he castigated Iraq for continuing to "flaunt its hostility toward America and to support terror" and called the Middle Eastern nation part of "an axis of evil, arming to threaten the peace of the world." In the months that followed, he increasingly spoke of taking military action in Iraq. Bush found an ally in British prime minister Tony Blair, but pressure from citizens of both countries pushed the two leaders to take the issue before the UN Security Council in the form of UN Resolution 1441, which called for UN weapons inspectors, led by Hans Blix, to return to Iraq and issue a report on their findings.

On November 8, 2002, the 15-member Security Council unanimously passed the resolution, and weapons inspectors began work on November 27. On December 7, Iraq delivered a 12,000-page declaration of its weapons program, an insufficient accounting according to Blix, and a month later, Bush stated: "If Saddam Hussein does not fully disarm, we will lead a coalition to disarm him." Bush and Blair actively sought the support of the international community, but their announcement that they would circumvent the UN if necessary ruffled many nations' feathers, most notably drawing the ire of France, Germany, and Russia, all of which pushed for further inspections. Spain joined with the United Kingdom and the United States to propose a second UN resolution declaring Iraq to be in "material breach" of Resolution 1441. Although a small number of other nations pledged their support for military action in Iraq, only Australia

committed troops to fight alongside British and U.S. forces.

Blair in particular incurred negative reaction from his country's citizens, and reports indicated he might lose his job. As a result, Blair pushed for a compromise that would give weapons inspectors a little more time to inspect Iraq. However, with two permanent members of the Security Council—France and Germany—threatening to veto the resolution, the proposal was withdrawn. Undeterred by that set of events, as well as the Turkish government's refusal to allow coalition troops to use Turkey as a platform for a northern invasion of Iraq and increasing protestations by antiwar groups around the world, on March 17, Bush issued an ultimatum to Hussein that he leave Iraq within 48 hours or face military action. Hours before the deadline was to expire, Bush received intelligence information that Hussein and several top officials in the Iraqi government were sleeping in an underground facility in Baghdad. Bush ordered a "decapitation strike" aimed at killing Hussein, and on March 20, around 2:30 a.m. local time, three dozen Tomahawk missiles with 1,000-pound warheads were launched from warships in the Persian Gulf and Red Sea. Three hours later, they hit their targets in Baghdad and were followed immediately by 2,000-pound bunker-busters. The war had started.

Although intelligence reports suggested that Hussein was carried from the facility on a stretcher, it became clear in the coming weeks that the decapitation strike had failed and Hussein was still alive. U.S.-led coalition troops crossed the border from Kuwait into Iraq on March 20. Armed with new technology that included stealth bombers and smart bombs—which constituted 80 percent of the coalition arsenal, as opposed to 10 percent during the Persian

Gulf War—the coalition commenced its "shock and awe" campaign, designed to stun and demoralize the Iraqi Army so it would quickly surrender.

Iraqi soldiers did not surrender with the same celerity as in the Persian Gulf War, but within a matter of days, the coalition had overtaken Iraq's second-largest city, Basra; the port city of Umm Qasr; and Nasiriya. The coalition also destroyed Hussein's government buildings and palaces on the Tigris River in Baghdad, symbolizing the end of the Iraqi regime. Nearly 10,000 Iraqi troops surrendered to coalition forces during those first days. Still, the coalition troops were caught unprepared by some of the Iraqis' guerrilla tactics, including faking surrenders and ambushing troops from the rear. Throughout the fighting, news reporters and camera crews "embedded" in military units brought live action to television viewers worldwide.

After securing southern Iraq and its oil fields, coalition soldiers began moving toward Baghdad; they secured an airfield in western Iraq and Hussein International Airport (immediately renamed Baghdad International Airport) with little difficulty. On April 5, coalition forces entered Baghdad, and six days later, the United States declared the end of Hussein's regime. One last hurdle remained, and by April 14, coalition forces accomplished it by capturing Hussein's hometown of Tikrit. Formal military action ceased, with fewer than 200 confirmed coalition deaths.

In the weeks after the Battle of Tikrit, coalition forces began searching for WMDs, as well as Hussein and other top Iraqi officials. Although there was a degree of success in the latter endeavor, the troops were unable to find WMDs or Hussein (though he was eventually captured by U.S. soldiers on December 13, 2003).

Those failures drew criticism from many who already questioned the coalition presence in Iraq, as did the looting of historic treasures from Iraqi museums, which the coalition failed to protect. In addition, though many Iraqi citizens and neighboring countries were very happy to see Hussein's regime toppled, many others protested the continued presence of coalition forces and the influence they, particularly the United States, would have in the new Iraqi government.

Bush appointed Paul Bremer to govern Iraq through the Coalition Provisional Authority, whose stated aim was to reconstruct Iraq as a liberal, pluralist democratic state. The occupation has been plagued by violent resistance, which has greatly hampered the economic and political reconstruction of the country, preventing international aid organizations from working in Iraq and discouraging badly needed capital investment. An interim constitution was signed in March 2004, and on June 28, 2004, sovereignty was transferred to the Iraqi people. On January 30, 2005, Iraq held its first open election in half a century, selecting a 275-member transitional National Assembly. Despite the withdrawal of several Sunni parties from the poll and threats of Election Day violence from insurgents, turnout was high. After two months of deadlock, on April 6, the new legislature elected Kurdish leader Jalal Talabani as president and Ibrahim al-Jaafari as prime minister. In April 2006, Talabani was reelected and Nouri al-Maliki was selected to succeed al-Jaafari as prime minister. The country continues to be racked by sectarian violence as the new government struggles to unite disparate parties and warring factions.

Although Bush declared major combat operations over on May 1, 2003, deadly guerrilla attacks against U.S. troops continued and increased. In addition, major violence broke out between Shiite and Sunni insurgents, causing many observers to begin calling the conflict a civil war. By late 2008, the U.S. public's support for the Iraq War had plummeted. A status of forces agreement was made by the U.S. and Iraqi governments that required U.S. combat troops to leave Iraqi urban areas by the end of June 2009 and to leave the country entirely by the end of 2011. Soon after taking office in early 2009, President Barack Obama announced that most U.S. troops would exit Iraq by the end of August 2010, with a smaller transitional force remaining until the end of 2011. The war was declared officially over by the U.S. military on December 15, 2011; by that time, more than 1 million members of the armed forces had served in Iraq, nearly 4,500 Americans had died in the conflict, and more than 32,000 were wounded in action.

Unfortunately, sectarian violence and radical Sunni Islamic extremism in Iraq have been on the increase since 2012. By January 2014, rebels associated with the Islamic State of Iraq and the Levant had seized control of virtually all of Anbar Province, including Fallujah, where U.S. forces had fought two bloody battles during the Iraq War. Within days, the Sunni rebels had also captured the city of Ramadi, also in Anbar Province. The situation underscores the inability of Iraqi president Nouri al-Maliki to govern his country effectively and demonstrates the pitfalls of al-Maliki's governing style, which has excluded Iraq's Sunni minority from political and governmental decision making. Whether Iraq will manage to avert another civil war or sectarian dismemberment remains an open question.

During 2013, more than 8,000 Iraqis died as a result of sectarian violence and other strife. January 2014 proved to be the deadliest month in Iraq in six years, with more than 1,000 Iraqis killed in car bombings, suicide bombings, and other violence. Among the dead were 795 civilians. The violence and instability in Iraq are deeply troubling to the West, particularly the United States, because numerous radical Islamist groups, including Al-Qaeda, have begun to put down roots in the country. Indeed, Al-Qaeda elements were largely responsible for the seizure of Fallujah and Ramadi. Although the United States has ruled out any new troop deployments to Iraq, the Obama administration has begun selling and shipping armaments to the al-Maliki government, including Hellfire missiles and Scan Eagle surveillance drones.

Lori Weathers

See also: Bush Administration; Iraqi Freedom, Operation; Iraqi Insurgency; Persian Gulf War

Further Reading

Atkinson, Rick. *In the Company of Soldiers: A Chronicle of Combat.* New York: Henry Holt, 2004.

Boyne, Walter J. *Operation Iraqi Freedom: What Went Right, What Went Wrong, and Why.* New York: Forge, 2003.

Fontenot, Gregory, E. J. Degen, and David Tohn. *On Point.* Washington, DC: U.S. Army, 2004.

Woodward, Bob. *Bush at War.* New York: Simon & Schuster, 2003.

Islamic Army of Aden (IAA)

The Islamic Army of Aden (IAA) operated as an Al-Qaeda regional affiliate in southern Yemen. The group's name is based on the alleged revelation of the prophet Muhammad that "twelve thousand will appear from Aden Abyan who will aid God and His Messenger." The IAA emerged in the mid-1990s as one of several loosely connected organizations established by Afghan-Soviet War veterans and various local and international Islamic jihadists. The battlefield experience of the former mujahideen, combined with the extraordinarily large number of weapons available in Yemen (estimated at three firearms to each resident), expedited the creation of a formidable movement.

The IAA emerged under the leadership of Zein al-Abidin al-Mihdar (aka Abu al-Hassan) against the backdrop of civil unrest following the shaky unification of North and South Yemen in 1990. The group called for the overthrow of the government in Sana'a and the removal of all U.S. and British ambassadors from the country. Despite this dual-track agenda, the IAA targeted only foreigners, never the Yemeni government itself.

The IAA gained notoriety through statements applauding the 1998 U.S. embassy attacks in Kenya and Tanzania and the group's subsequent kidnapping of 16 Western tourists, who were seized in the name of Osama bin Laden. Yemeni forces captured Abu al-Hassan in an operation to free the hostages, four of whom were killed. He was executed and succeeded by Hatem bi Fareed.

The IAA set up a training camp in the mountains of Abyan and adjusted its strategy to focus on high-visibility targets. In coordination with local Al-Qaeda members, the organization carried out a failed attack on USS *The Sullivans* and took credit for the bombings of the USS *Cole* and the M/V *Limburg* (although primary responsibility for these strikes has always lain with Al-Qaeda). The day after the *Cole* incident, another IAA member was charged with throwing a hand grenade into the British embassy.

The IAA issued most threats and statements through Abu Hamza al-Masri, a British-Egyptian dual-national cleric known for preaching a violent and politicized interpretation of Islam. The Bush administration froze his assets in 2002 on the grounds that he was a primary financier for the IAA, and the UK government revoked his citizenship a year later, after he was determined to be a threat to national security. Al-Masri was arrested in London on May 27, 2004, and has since been fighting deportation to both Yemen and the United States.

The IAA itself has suffered from a number of setbacks as a result of heightened counterterrorist efforts since September 11, 2001. In 2002, a missile from an unmanned U.S. Predator aircraft struck a car carrying four suspected IAA members along with an Al-Qaeda regional commander and a Yemeni-American recruiter. The next year, Yemeni forces stormed one of its main compounds, killing several senior members. Following the raid, Abd al-Nabi accepted President Ali Abdullah Saleh's offer of a full pardon for all insurgents who surrendered to the government. Deprived of its leader, the IAA effectively collapsed, and there is little evidence that the group has been active since 2003. That said, there have been periodic reports of ex-IAA militants joining jihadist extremists in Yemen, Iraq, and elsewhere.

Julie Manning

See also: Al-Qaeda; Al-Qaeda in the Arabian Peninsula; USS *Cole* Bombing

Further Reading

Cook, David. *Paradigmatic Jihadi Movements.* West Point, NY: Combating Terrorism

Center, 2006. http://www.ctc.usma.edu/posts/paradigmatic-jihadi-movements.

McGregor, Andrew. "Strike First." *The World Today* 58, no. 12 (2002).

Schanzer, Jonathan. "Behind the French Tanker Bombing: Yemen's Ongoing Problems with Islamist Terrorism." *Columbia International Affairs Online*, October 21, 2002. http://www.ciaonet.org/pbei/winep/policy_2002/2002_670.html.

"Yemen: Coping with Terrorism and Violence in a Fragile State." *ICG Middle East Report* 8 (2003).

Islamic Radicalism

This term is used to describe radical movements, organizations, and parties that, regardless of doctrinal and political differences, promote and legitimize their political objectives by invoking Islam. A radical is an individual who espouses extreme views and seeks major, if not revolutionary, change in government and society and often favors illegal means, including violence, to promote such change.

Islamic radicals, also known as Islamic fundamentalists, espouse a literal interpretation of Islam and sharia (Islamic law) and favor the establishment of an Islamic state based on that law. They share these goals with Islamists, who are sometimes incorrectly deemed radicals, since not all support revolutionary means for Islamization. Some claim that Islamic radicals eschew Western ideas and values, including secularism, democracy, and religious tolerance and pluralism. However, this is untrue of many who value Western ideas but not existing morals in Western society. To certain extreme Islamic radicals, governments and laws that are based on anything but their interpretation of Islam are considered heretical. These radicals feel bound to impose their values on others, and even, if possible, to overthrow heretical governments.

Al-Qaeda, the Taliban, the Armed Islamic Group of Algeria, the Salafist Group for Preaching and Combat of Algeria, Laskar Jihad, and Egyptian Islamic Jihad are some of the better-known radical Islamic groups. Others, such as the Muslim Brotherhood in Egypt, have largely forsworn violence and imposing change on others, and are thus less radical. Hezbollah and Hamas have employed violence against Israelis.

Some Islamic radical groups are Shia, and some are Sunni movements. Iran, one of the few countries with a majority Shia population, is an example of a radical Islamic state, but radical Shia movements also exist in Iraq, Yemen, and the Gulf States.

The origins of Islamic radicalism are threefold. First, although the Islamic world was once a great and powerful civilization, beginning in the 11th century with the Crusades, followed by Ottoman rule and then European colonial rule after World War I, it has been in decline, eclipsed, and in its own view, dominated and exploited by the West. This view is also shared by Bernard Lewis and other such Western thinkers as Samuel Huntington, but many Muslims argue that the reason for the domination and exploitation is their own fault—that Muslims abandoned jihad in its fighting form and must now return to it. Second, other movements, like nationalism and socialism, failed to bring about a better political solution, and Muslims sought out Islamist or radical Islamic groups as an alternative. Third, many Muslims have come to regard the West, and particularly the United States, with contempt for its alleged social, moral, and economic decadence. They also see that while preaching democracy, the Western powers have supported the very authoritarian governments that have oppressed them.

To Islamic radicals, the Islamic world has lost its way because it has forsaken Islamic values, amalgamated Western and Islamic law, and transposed foreign cultures onto its own peoples. Accordingly, the solution for the revival of Islamic civilization is a return to an allegedly authentic or purified Islamic way of life. Islamic radicalism is thus, in many ways, an explicit rejection of the current ills of Muslim society. Certain, but not all, Islamic radicals thus seek to overthrow the regimes and rulers they regard as un-Islamic, and some of these are—or have been—supported by the West and the United States, such as those in Saudi Arabia, Egypt, Jordan, and Kuwait. Islamic radicals were responsible for the overthrow in 1979 of the pro-American Mohammad Reza Shah Pahlavi in Iran and the assassination two years later of President Anwar Sadat of Egypt. They have also been responsible for myriad terror attacks against Western interests, including the September 11, 2001, attacks in the United States that killed some 3,000 people.

Stefan M. Brooks

See also: Al-Qaeda; Global War on Terror; Hezbollah; Shia Islam; Sunni Islam; Taliban; Terrorism

Further Reading

Choueri, Youssef. *Islamic Fundamentalism.* New York: Continuum Publishing Group, 2002.

Esposito, John. *Unholy War: Terror in the Name of Islam.* New York: Oxford University Press USA, 2003.

Esposito, John. *What Everyone Needs to Know about Islam.* New, York: Oxford University Press, 2002.

Lewis, Bernard. *The Crisis of Islam: Holy War and Unholy Terror.* New York: Random House, 2003.

Lewis, Bernard. *What Went Wrong? The Clash between Islam and Modernity in the Middle East.* New York: Oxford University Press, 2002.

Milton-Edwards, Beverly. *Islamic Fundamentalism since 1945.* New York: Routledge, 2002.

Sidahmed, Abdel Salam. *Islamic Fundamentalism.* Boulder, CO: Westview, 1996.

Tibi, Bassam. *The Challenge of Fundamentalism: Political Islam and the New World Disorder.* Berkeley: University of California Press, 1998.

J

Jamaa al-Tawhid wa'a Jihad (JTJ)

Jamaa al-Tawhid wa'a Jihad (JTJ), a name that translates to "Monotheism and Jihad," was a Sunni salafist-jihadist group operating in Iraq during the early stages of the Iraq War. One of the most violent and disruptive insurgent movements in postinvasion Iraq, the group was founded and led by Abu Musab al-Zarqawi. Al-Zarqawi would ultimately pledge allegiance to Osama bin Laden and formally rebrand the group as Tanzom Qa'idat al-Jihadi Bilad al-Rafidyan (QJBR), more commonly known as Al-Qaeda in Iraq (AQI). As the successor to JTJ, QJBR operates in Iraq as of this writing under the name of its umbrella organization, the Islamic State of Iraq.

While the exact date of JTJ's founding is unknown, one can trace its roots through the life of al-Zarqawi and his relationship to various militant groups, portions of whose cadres would ultimately form JTJ. Following a short stint in prison for sexual assault, al-Zarqawi left Jordan in 1989 to participate in jihad against the Soviets in Afghanistan. While he arrived too late to take part in the heavy fighting, this visit provided al-Zarqawi with his first chance to forge ties with veterans of the Afghan jihad. After he returned to Jordan, he fell in with the Jordanian militant group Bayat al-Imam, led by al-Zarqawi's mentor Abu Muhammad al-Maqdisi, many of whose members were Jordanian veterans of the Afghan jihad. Al-Zarqawi was thrown into prison a second time for plotting against the Jordanian state in 1994. This stint in jail merely served as a chance for al-Zarqawi to make connections and mature into a leader, for he was admired by fellow prisoners for his religious discipline and ultimately supplanted al-Maqdisi. Upon his release as part of King Abdullah's amnesty program in 1999, al-Zarqawi took part in the millennium bomb plot, which aimed to bomb a series of luxury hotels in Jordan. However, the plot was uncovered, and al-Zarqawi fled to Afghanistan via Pakistan.

It was in Herat, Afghanistan, that al-Zarqawi began to truly forge the core leadership of what would ultimately become JTJ. Drawing on his previous connections to various jihadist groups, he set up camp in Herat province in the northwestern part of the country. Before doing so, he first had to receive permission from bin Laden. Al-Zarqawi founded his organization as a wholly separate entity from bin Laden's Al-Qaeda organization, chiefly because al-Zarqawi believed in first targeting the "near enemy" (Arab regimes deemed to be apostates), while bin Laden believed jihadist efforts should be targeted at the "far enemy" (the United States and other Western regimes). In spite of these differences, al-Zarqawi was permitted to remain in the country and run his camp out of northwestern Afghanistan in 1999.

The U.S.-led invasion of Afghanistan in 2001 disrupted al-Zarqawi's network. While al-Zarqawi and his cadres briefly participated in the fighting, he and his network were ultimately forced to flee from his base in Herat to Iraq, via northern Iran. In Iraq, al-Zarqawi was able to link up with members of Ansar al-Islam (AaI), a Kurdistan-based Iraqi militant group, in early 2002. As a charismatic figure with extensive ties to Arab jihadist networks in the region, al-Zarqawi quickly broadened beyond AaI and eventually branched off to form his own independent organization, JTJ. Under al-Zarqawi's guidance JTJ engaged in international terrorism. The group assassinated Laurence Foley, an American employee of the U.S. Agency for International Development, outside of his home in Amman in 2002. It also was implicated in plots involving the use of ricin in France and Europe. However, perhaps owing to al-Zarqawi's emphasis on the near enemy, JTJ maintained a focus on Iraq, basing itself in the country's Sunni triangle, already home to a number of different Sunni insurgent movements.

Following the U.S. invasion of Iraq, JTJ blossomed. It executed a number of deadly attacks on Western targets. As a successful facilitator of foreign fighters, al-Zarqawi helped to send a steady stream of suicide bombers for a wave of attacks he unleashed on the country. Among the most devastating was the August 7, 2003, car bombing at the Jordanian embassy, which marked the first major attack of the war against a non–coalition forces target and set the tone for the rampant violence that would soon engulf the country. JTJ then followed this attack with the August 19, 2003, suicide car bombing at the headquarters of the United Nations (UN) Assistance Mission in Iraq, located in Baghdad's Canal Hotel. The attack proved especially devastating as it killed Sergio Vieira de Mello, the UN special representative for Iraq, and ultimately prompted the UN to withdraw from Iraq altogether. JTJ's descent into infamy reached its high-water mark a few months later when on May 7, 2004, it beheaded American businessman Nicholas Berg. The videotaped beheading, which allegedly included al-Zarqawi personally wielding the knife, made for gruesome international headlines. This act was but one of a number of beheadings JTJ carried out in postinvasion Iraq.

While JTJ might be best known for these high-profile attacks on international targets, the bulk of its operations targeted and killed Iraqis. The group is believed to have been behind numerous attacks on police recruiting centers, including a series of five coordinated blasts on October 27, 2003, which killed potential police recruits and civilian bystanders alike. JTJ also intentionally targeted the country's Shia, both because al-Zarqawi viewed them as apostates and because he saw strategic value in sowing the seeds of sectarian war between the country's Sunni and Shia. With this goal in mind, JTJ carried out a number of high-profile attacks against the Shia. Its first major attack took place on August 29, 2003, when it targeted the Imam Ali mosque in the Shiite holy city of Najaf in a bombing, killing a prominent Shiite cleric and 83 others. Though some sources allege that Iran had a hand in the attack, most attribute it to JTJ. The group then followed the Najaf bombing with a spate of other bombings in the Shiite-dominated cities of Karbala and Basra that left thousands of Iraqi Shia dead.

By mid-2004, these attacks catapulted the group to prominence as arguably the most important jihadist insurgents operating in the country. As one of the core elements of the Sunni insurgency, JTJ ultimately attracted U.S. attention. The United States conducted a number of air strikes in Fallujah aimed at JTJ targets in August 2004, and ultimately launched the second Battle of Fallujah partly in an effort to oust al-Zarqawi's network (alongside many Sunni nationalist groups) from what was perceived to be his main base of operations. U.S. efforts also included targeted raids on members of al-Zarqawi's network throughout central, western, and northern Iraq.

JTJ survived these onslaughts, which further fueled the reputation of al-Zarqawi and his network. At the same time, JTJ saw an opportunity to expand its role in Iraq by leveraging the broader Al-Qaeda network. Following eight months of lengthy negotiations, al-Zarqawi officially pledged allegiance to bin Laden in October 2004, renaming JTF as QJBR. This alliance was somewhat unexpected because al-Zarqawi had had the opportunity to join Al-Qaeda upon his arrival in Afghanistan in 1999 and chose not to do so, chiefly over the differences as to whether to prioritize attacking the near enemy or the far enemy.

Nonetheless, in 2004, al-Zarqawi believed he could overlook these differences since official Al-Qaeda affiliation offered JTJ a number of advantages. The move allowed al-Zarqawi greater access to Al-Qaeda's technical and operational expertise. Most important, Al-Qaeda offered al-Zarqawi both a brand name and a larger platform from which he could draw recruits. Already a successful facilitator of foreign fighter inflows, Zarqawi now had a much greater pool of personnel resources from which he could draw. Overall, these benefits outweighed the strategic differences between al-Zarqawi and bin Laden, and thus JTJ evolved to become QJBR. In its new form, the group would go on to become an even more brutal insurgent jihadist organization than its predecessor.

Nate Shestak

See also: Al-Qaeda; Bin Laden, Osama; International Red Cross Headquarters (Baghdad) Bombing

Further Reading

International Crisis Group. *Jordan's 9/11: Dealing with Jihadi Islamism.* Middle East Report no. 47, November 23, 2005.

Michael, George. "The Legend and Legacy of Abu Musab al-Zarqawi." *Defence Studies* 7, no. 3 (September 2007): 338–57.

Raphaeli, Nimrod. *'The Sheikh of the Slaughterers': Abu Mus'ab Al-Zarqawi and the Al-Qaeda Connection.* Washington, DC: The Middle East Media Research Institute. Inquiry and Analysis Series Report no. 23. July 1, 2005.

Joint Chiefs of Staff

The principal military advisory group to the president of the United States and the secretary of defense, composed of the chiefs of staff of the U.S. Army and the U.S. Air Force, the chief of U.S. Navy operations, the commandant of the U.S. Marine Corps, and the chair and vice chair of the Joint Chiefs of Staff (JCS). The National Security Act of 1947 changed the JCS from executive agents dealing with theater and area commanders to planners and advisers.

The JCS originally consisted of only the service chiefs of the U.S. Army, U.S. Navy, and U.S. Air Force and the chair. The commandant of the U.S. Marine

The United States Joint Chiefs of Staff on November 7, 1989. In the foreground is General Colin Powell, the 12th Chairman of the Joint Chiefs of Staff, the highest military position in the Department of Defense. The other members are, from left, Marine general Alfred M. Gray; Army general Carl Edward Vuono; Navy admiral Carlisle A. H. Trost; Air Force general Larry D. Welch; and Air Force general Robert T. Herres. (AP Photo/U.S. Department of Defense/Robert D. Ward)

Corps became a member later, and even later the position of vice chair was established by the Goldwater-Nichols Act. The chair and vice chair can be appointed from any of the four services.

Responsibilities as members of the JCS took precedence over duties as the chiefs of military services. The president nominated the chair for appointment, and the U.S. Senate confirmed the appointment. By statute, the chair was either a full (four-star) general or a full admiral and served a two-year tour of duty. The president had discretionary power to renominate the chair for additional two-year terms.

The 1986 Goldwater-Nichols Department of Defense Reorganization Act identified the chair of the JCS as the senior-ranking member of the armed forces.

As such, the chair of the JCS serves as the principal military adviser to the president, the secretary of defense, and the National Security Council (NSC). In carrying out the duties of the office, the chair of the JCS consults with and seeks the advice of the other members of the JCS and the combatant commanders, as the chair deems appropriate.

All JCS members are by law military advisers, and they can respond to a request or voluntarily submit, through the chair, advice or opinions to the president, the secretary of defense, or the NSC. The modern JCS has no executive authority to command combatant forces. In fact, the JCS members are bypassed in the chain of command so that responsibilities for conducting military operations flow from the president to the secretary of defense directly to the commanders of the Unified Combatant Commands. However, the JCS members have authority over personnel assignments, equipment, training, operational doctrine, and resource management of their respective services as well as oversight of resources and personnel allocated by their services to the combatant commands.

Collectively, the JCS serves as the second-highest deliberative body for military policy behind the NSC. The chair of the JCS is also a member of the NSC. As of 2008, there were eight directorates of the JCS: J1 Personnel and Manpower; J2 Intelligence; J3 Operations; J4 Logistics; J5 Strategic Plans and Policy; J6 Command, Control, Communications and Computer Systems; J7 Operational Plans and Joint Force Development; and J8 Force Structure, Resources, and Assessment.

The JCS participated in all the important decisions regarding Operations Desert Shield and Desert Storm. Once the ground invasion began in February 1991, the JCS proved particularly wary of what might go wrong and sensitive to avoiding needless American casualties. This attitude frequently put the JCS at odds with White House officials who were eager to teach Hussein a lesson by seriously degrading Iraq's military. Chairman Powell was a particular voice of caution and restraint, and he played a pivotal role in the controversial decision recommending a quick end to the war that did not include the toppling of Hussein's regime.

After the Persian Gulf War ended, U.S. Army general John M. D. Shalikashvili served as chairman of the JCS, replacing Powell in 1993. Shalikashvili stayed on until 1997. During his tenure, the JCS examined the lessons from the Persian Gulf War and focused on the long lead times required to move substantial forces and their logistical backing to the Gulf region. A result of this examination was the prepositioning of equipment and supplies in the Gulf. U.S. Army general Henry H. Shelton was JCS chairman during the September 11, 2001, terrorist attacks on the United States. He retired on October 1, 2001.

Having served as vice chairman of the JCS from March 2000 to September 2001, U.S. Air Force general Richard B. Myers became the chairman of the JCS on October 1, 2001. He served in that capacity during the earliest planning stages for the global war on terror, including Operations Enduring Freedom and Iraqi Freedom. As such, Myers served as the military's public face by conducting high-level media briefings. His air force experience as commander in chief of the U.S. Space Command clearly informed his keen understanding of the role that command, control, communications, and computers played in the battlefield. He also acknowledged the necessity for networked joint interagency computers and the need to link sensor and reconnaissance platforms with shooting platforms. Also, Myers promoted enhanced joint war-fighting capabilities.

Upon Meyer's retirement in 2005, U.S. Marine Corps general Peter Pace, who had become vice chairman of the JCS on September 30, 2001, became chairman. Pace was the first marine officer to hold either the vice chairman or the chairman positions. Pace's tenure coincided with a major escalation in the Iraqi insurgency. However, his comments in 2007 concerning homosexuals (he termed homosexual acts "immoral") and gays in the military caused an uproar that turned many against him. In 2005, Pace also publicly disagreed with Secretary of Defense Donald Rumsfeld concerning torture, and in 2007 Pace contradicted the White House's contention that Iran was supplying arms to Iraqi insurgents. In June 2008, Secretary of Defense Robert Gates recommended that Pace not be renominated for another term, fearing that he would be the object of protracted grilling by a Democratically controlled Congress upset with the progress of the war.

In turn, Admiral Mike Mullen became chairman on October 1, 2007. With considerable reluctance, the JCS endorsed the George W. Bush administration's troop surge strategy in Iraq, which began in the late winter of 2007. Likewise, the JCS acquiesced to President Barack Obama's intentions to drawn down forces in Iraq and send reinforcements to Afghanistan. On January 27, 2009, JCS chairman Admiral Mullen stated that America's most challenging security threat was centered in Afghanistan and Pakistan, which seemed to confirm the new president's military focus. Obama's Afghanistan troop surge, announced in late 2009, sent some 33,000 additional troops to Afghanistan; they were withdrawn by the end of 2012. Mullen was replaced by General Martin Dempsey on October 1, 2011. As of early 2014, he remained chairman of the JCS.

James Arnold

See also: Enduring Freedom, Operation; Iraqi Freedom, Operation; Powell, Colin Luther; Rumsfeld, Donald Henry; U.S. Central Command; U.S. European Command; U.S. Special Operations Command; War Powers Act

Further Reading

Burton, James G. *The Pentagon Wars.* Annapolis, MD: Naval Institute Press, 1993.

Gordon, Michael R., and General Bernard E. Trainor. *The Generals' War: The Inside Story of the Conflict in the Gulf.* New York: Little, Brown, 1995.

Scales, Robert H. *Certain Victory: The U.S. Army in the Gulf War.* Washington, DC: Brassey's, 1994.

Joint Direct Attack Munitions and Small Diameter Bomb

Two highly accurate, all-weather, autonomous air-delivered weapons developed by the U.S. Air Force that utilize the precise timing signal of the Navigation Signal Timing and Ranging (NAV-STAR) Global Positioning System (GPS) satellites for all-weather precision attacks of ground targets. The Joint Direct Attack Munitions (JDAM) is a tail kit that attaches to the rear of conventional 500-pound, 1,000-pound, or 2,000-pound gravity bombs. The carrying aircraft can launch the weapon up to 15 miles from the target and program each weapon it carries to strike separate targets. Once released, the bomb's Inertial Navigation System (INS)/GPS guides the bomb to its target regardless of weather conditions. The weapon can impact within 5 yards of the target in the GPS-aided INS mode or within 10 yards in INS-only mode.

The U.S. Air Force began developing the JDAM in the late 1980s but shelved it in 1989. During the Persian Gulf War, however, the air force discovered that clouds and smoke adversely affected the accuracy of its laser-guided bombs. Chief of staff of the air force General Merrill A. McPeak subsequently directed the development of an all-weather, low-cost, and highly accurate air-delivered weapon. In 1995, McDonnell Douglas (now Boeing) began producing the JDAM tail kits at a cost of $18,000 each. Today, every strike aircraft in the U.S. Air Force, the U.S. Navy, and the U.S. Marine Corps and many strike aircraft of U.S. allies can carry the JDAM.

During Operation Enduring Freedom, which began in October 2001, the JDAM quickly became the air-delivered weapon of choice to attack enemy forces in close proximity to friendly forces or civilian centers. Using laser range-finding binoculars and GPS receivers, special operations ground controllers with Northern Alliance forces identified targets and relayed the coordinates to the Air Operations Center in Kuwait or to aircraft over the battlefield.

After the Anglo-American–led invasion of Iraq in March 2003 and during the continuing combat in Afghanistan and in Iraq, U.S. and coalition aircraft continued to refine procedures to hit targets of opportunity with JDAMs in near real time. As combat operations continued, the war fighters in the Middle East identified the need for two additional capabilities: a JDAM capable of striking moving targets and a precise weapon with a smaller blast and fragmentation pattern than the 500-pound JDAM. By mid-2007, the Air Armament Center, Eglin Air Force Base, Florida, had developed the Laser JDAM with a laser seeker in the nose that tracks and hits a target moving up to 50 miles per hour, and awarded the production contract to Boeing.

The U.S. Air Force began development of the Small Diameter Bomb (SDB) in 2003. It is only six feet long and weighs 285 pounds. It comes in two variants, one with GPS/INS guidance only and one with GPS/INS guidance and a laser seeker to hit moving targets. Its special bomb carriage system can carry four SDBs on one weapons station. The weapon can be launched up to 60 miles from the target. Because of its smaller size, strike aircraft can carry more individual weapons, giving the fliers increased kills per mission. It also provides reduced collateral damage in urban areas (such as those in Iraq) in which the military struggles at times to find a weapon with the desired kill effect but without excessive blast or fragmentation effects.

The U.S. Air Force declared the SDB operational in September 2006 with initial integration with the F-15E Strike Eagle with follow-on integration on other air force strike aircraft. Because of its capabilities, the SDB system is an important air-delivered weapon in the ongoing global war on terror.

Robert B. Kane

See also: Enduring Freedom, Operation; Iraqi Freedom, Operation

Further Reading

History Office. *History of the Air Armament Center, 1 October 2006–30 September 2007.* Eglin Air Force Base, FL: Air Armament Center, 2008.

Lambeth, Benjamin S. *Air Power against Terror: America's Conduct of Operation Enduring Freedom.* Santa Monica, CA: RAND Corporation, 2005.

Lambeth, Benjamin S. *NATO's Air War for Kosovo: A Strategic and Operational Assessment.* Project Air Force Series on Operation Allied Force. Washington, DC: RAND Corporation, 2001.

Joint Terrorism Task Force

New York City's Joint Terrorism Task Force (JTTF) was a joint New York City Police Department (NYPD) and Federal Bureau of Investigation (FBI) effort to combat the domestic terrorism threat to New York City. It was formed in 1980 in the midst of a terrorist campaign by Puerto Rican nationalists, after it became apparent that better cooperation between the NYPD and the FBI was necessary. The original plan was for a unit of 10 FBI agents and 10 New York City police detectives, but over the years the size of the unit expanded. In 1990, Neil Herman, an FBI agent, assumed control of the JTTF.

The early focus of the JTTF was domestic terrorism. Besides Puerto Rican nationalists, the agents of the JTTF were involved in the investigation of the black nationalist group New Afrikan Freedom Fighters (NAFF). The acquittal of the eight defendants in a conspiracy trial angered members of the task force.

Another important case was the assassination of Israeli extremist Meir Kahane by Islamist El Sayyid Nosair. Members of the JTTF had monitored paramilitary training by militants before the assassination. Shortly after the assassination, the JTTF was shut out of the case and lost access to 16 boxes of intelligence information.

In the early 1990s, the JTTF recruited a Muslim agent. Emad Salem, a former Egyptian army officer, penetrated the al-Kifah Refugee Center militant circle. There he heard about a possible bomb plot against a dozen Jewish targets. The problem was that elements in the JTTF had reservations about Salem. He was simply too good to be true. Salem kept reporting about a bomb plot, but the details were vague. His handlers wanted Salem to wear a wire, but he refused to compromise himself. After his refusal, the JTTF let him go in July 1991. His parting remark was "Don't call me when the bombs go off." He had been their best access to Islamist militants in the New York City area, but the agents were more interested in winning a court case than in gathering intelligence.

The 1993 World Trade Center bombing made the unit begin to study international terrorism as well as domestic terrorism. Members of the JTTF were part of the 700 investigating agents assigned to the World Trade Center bombing. Within weeks, the JTTF team had arrested or identified all of the World Trade Center bombers. Now with more resources, the JTTF began to investigate other militants. Emad Salem was rehired, and the team sent him in to investigate the doings in the al-Kifah Mosque. There he learned that Sheikh Omar Abdel-Rahman was instigating a plot to assassinate Egyptian president Hosni Mubarak during a New York visit in April 1993. Because of questions about his safety, Mubarak canceled his New York City visit. The JTTF also became heavily involved in the investigation of the crash of United Airlines Flight 800 off the coast of the United States. Agents of the JFFT spent 17 months investigating the explosion and crash. It took a series of computer simulations to finally prove that the explosion had been an accident, not a terrorist attack. This investigation consumed most of the JTTF's attention at a time when it needed to be investigating potential terrorism conspiracies.

The members of the JTTF had no knowledge of the September 11 plot before it happened, although they had been suspicious of increased Al-Qaeda activity in the United States and were busy investigating leads. New York City was a prime target of any terrorist conspiracy. Then a Central Intelligence Agency (CIA) agent presented the JTTF staff with photos of possible terrorists on June 11, 2001, and he asked for information about them. After identifying the individuals in the photos, the CIA agent refused to give out any further information, infuriating the JTTF agents. The JTTF agents became even more suspicious when they received the news that two prominent Al-Qaeda operatives had been operating for more than a year in San Diego, California—Khalid al-Mihdhar and Nawaf al-Hazmi. The two had participated in a meeting of Al-Qaeda leaders in 2001. A formal request for more information was made to the FBI, but the staff of the JTTF did not receive the information until after September 11. Like the rest of the nation, the members of the JTTF watched the events of September 11 with horror.

Stephen E. Atkins

See also: Al-Qaeda; Bush Administration; Clinton Administration; World Trade Center Bombing; Terrorism

Further Reading

Miller, John, Michael Stone, and Chris Mitchell. *The Cell: Inside the 9/11 Plot and Why the FBI and CIA Failed to Stop It.* New York: Hyperion, 2002.

Naftali, Timothy. *Blind Spot: The Secret History of American Counterterrorism.* New York: Basic Books, 2005.

Justification for the September 11 Suicide Mission

The most difficult aspect of the September 11 attacks for Americans to understand was the use of suicide as a weapon. Nineteen young men bonded together to hijack four American commercial aircraft and crash them into preselected targets. They had no regard for their safety or for anybody else's. Each had received at least basic training at Al-Qaeda camps to prepare for such a mission. An important part of this training was religious instruction that prepared them for what they called a martyrdom mission.

What Is Jihad?

Jihad literally means "to struggle." In the military sense it is meant in the context, "to struggle against oppression." Jihad is therefore an act to liberate people from the oppression of tyrants. Jihad is not illegal acts against innocent people. When tabloid journalists mistakenly inform the masses that Jihad is "to commit illegal acts of terror," they are revealing their unprofessional approach by failing to educate themselves with the proper knowledge.

The religious justification for suicide missions is controversial among Muslim religious authorities. Both opponents and proponents refer to the religious teachings of the Prophet Mohammad as stated in the Koran or to the sayings of the Prophet in the hadiths. Personal suicide is not a part of Muslim religious practice, and this is reflected in the low personal suicide rate in the Muslim world. On the other hand, suicide undertaken as part of jihad, or holy war, is where it becomes controversial.

Jihad has two meanings in Muslim theology. Primarily, jihad means a personal struggle to adhere to the precepts of being a Muslim. The other meaning of jihad is war against the enemies of Islam. Again there are two meanings to this concept. There is jihad that aggressively wages war for the faith. This was the type of jihad that the Muslim successors to the Prophet Mohammad waged in the expansionary period of Islam's history. Then there is defensive jihad, which exists when the Islamic world is attacked by outsiders. According to this concept, it is the obligation of every able-bodied Muslim to participate in a war against an invader. Islamist groups consider the presence of Israel in the Middle East as part of an invasion of the Muslim world. Because the United States is an ally of Israel and has a presence in the Middle East, it is also considered a partner in this invasion. Al-Qaeda and other Islamist groups maintain that the war against Israel and the United States is a continuation of the war between the West and the Muslim world that dates back to the Crusades in the Middle Ages.

Suicide as a political weapon has a history in the Muslim world. The most famous historical cases of suicide used as a political weapon were those carried out by the assassins of the Ismaeli Shiite sect of Hassan ibn Sabbah, who established the Ismaeli Assassins in the Middle Ages (1034–1255); they carried out suicide missions against Muslim Sunnis and Christian Crusaders. After the collapse of this sect, there were sporadic suicide missions, mostly against European colonial targets. Only in the early 1980s did the use of suicide as a weapon reappear in the Middle East. It has appeared elsewhere mostly in association with the Tamil Tigers in Sri Lanka. The first incidence of a suicide mission in the Middle East in modern times was by the Shiite Amal organization, when a suicide bomber drove a car with explosives into the Iraqi embassy in Beirut on December 15, 1981, killing 61 people. Hezbollah (the Party of God) in Lebanon borrowed this tactic and has used it with lethal effect against American and Israeli targets. Later, both the Palestinian Islamic Jihad and Hamas began depending on suicide bombers for use against the Israelis. The military wing of Fatah, the al-Aqsa Martyrs Brigades, has also resorted to the use of suicide bombers.

Suicide terrorism is the most aggressive form of terrorism, pursuing coercion even at the expense of angering not only the target community but neutral audiences as well. What distinguishes a suicide terrorist is that the attacker does not expect to survive the mission and often employs a method of attack (such as a car bomb, suicide vest, or ramming an airplane into a building) that requires his or her death in order to succeed. In essence, suicide terrorists kill others at the same time that they kill themselves.

Noting the effectiveness of suicide bombers, Al-Qaeda's leadership adopted the practice. Suicide bombing is considered an effective weapon in a war in which one side is much stronger militarily than the other. Besides its lethal impact, a suicide bombing has the element of surprise. The suicide bomber is able to get close to the target before he or she detonates the bomb. Al-Qaeda leaders claim that it is the most successful tactic in inflicting damage and at the same time the least costly in terms of loss of its operatives. This belief is reinforced by the fact that suicide attacks claim 10 to 15 times the casualties of any other terrorist operation.

Stephen E. Atkins

See also: Al-Qaeda; Hamburg Cell; Islamic Radicalism; Terrorism

Further Reading

Atwan, Abdel Bari. The *Secret History of Al Qaeda*. Berkeley: University of California Press, 2006.

Pape, Robert A. *Dying to Win: The Strategic Logic of Suicide Terrorism*. New York: Random House, 2005.

Rubin, Barry, and Judith Colp Rubin, eds. *Anti-American Terrorism and the Middle East: A Documentary Reader*. New York: Oxford University Press, 2002.

K

Kill List

A regularly updated chart showing the world's most wanted terrorists used by President Barack Obama during kill or capture debates between the Central Intelligence Agency (CIA) and senior administration officials.

According to a front-page article that appeared in the *New York Times* on May 29, 2012, the administration—faced with a difficult reelection against Republican Mitt Romney—reportedly accelerated work in the weeks before the election in order to establish more specific rules for the killing of terrorists by unmanned CIA-controlled drones.

The U.S. drone program, which was initially launched by President George W. Bush, expanded under President Obama. Some media reports suggested that since Obama took office in January 2009, more than 300 drone strikes had been carried out by the U.S. military by 2012. It is believed that Obama personally approves every drone strike in Yemen and Somalia, and especially risky strikes in Pakistan. He is supposedly also responsible for deciding whether or not a strike against a suspected terrorist should occur when that person is accompanied by family or other noncombatants.

Media reports have suggested that some administration officials have expressed reservations about the justification for the "kill list," as well as the Obama administration's method of counting combatant and civilian casualties. The *New York Times* has said that this method in effect counts all men of military age in a strike zone as militants, unless there is intelligence proving otherwise.

Critics of the "kill list" launched a petition asking the White House to create a "Do Not Kill" list to protect U.S. citizens from drone strikes by their own government. The petition, however, failed to meet the 25,000-signature threshold required to elicit an official response from the White House.

Jan Goldman

See also: Martyrdom; Obama Administration; Predator; Suicide Bombings; Unmanned Aerial Vehicles

Further Reading

Finkelstein, Claire, and Jens David Ohlin. *Targeted Killings: Law and Morality in an Asymmetrical World*. New York: Oxford University Press, 2012.

Melzer, Nils. *Targeted Killing in International Law*. New York: Oxford University Press, 2009.

Scahill, Jeremy. *Dirty Wars: The World Is a Battlefield*. New York: Nation Books, 2013.

Kuala Lumpur Meeting

The Kuala Lumpur Meeting was a planning meeting of 18 terrorists that took place in Kuala Lumpur, Malaysia, on January 5, 2000. This meeting was one of convenience because it allowed midlevel Al-Qaeda operatives a chance to review their upcoming operations. They also wanted to explore possible operations in South Asia.

Even before the meeting, the National Security Agency (NSA) had intercepted communications indicating that such a gathering would take place. Late in 1999, the agency began intercepting communications between Nawaf and Salem al-Hazmi in Karachi, Pakistan, and Khalid al-Mihdhar in Yemen. These intercepts came from the telephone of a prominent Yemeni family—the Hada family—who had marriage ties to Al-Qaeda member Khalid al-Mihdhar. From these intercepts, the NSA learned there would be a major meeting of Al-Qaeda operatives in Kuala Lumpur. Yazid Sufaat, a former Malaysian Army captain and successful Malaysian businessman academically trained in biochemistry in Great Britain and the United States, provided his weekend retreat at the Bandar Sungai Long condominium complex outside Kuala Lumpur for the meeting. Exactly what was discussed at this gathering is unknown, but from informants it is known that planning occurred for the October 12, 2000, attack on USS *Cole*, and there was discussion of using aircraft as weaponry, possibly in South Asia. Khallad bin Atash and Muhammad Omar al-Harazi, operational chiefs of the attack on USS *Cole*, were in attendance. Representing the September 11, 2001, plot were Ramzi bin al-Shibh, al-Mihdhar, and Nawaf al-Hazmi.

Once American authorities learned of the meeting, they requested that Malaysian security officials photograph the attendees and bug the condo. Bugging was impossible because of the constant coming and going of the participants, but Malaysia's security service—the Special Branch—took photographs. Two photos came to have special importance—those of Khalid al-Mihdhar and Nawaf al-Hazmi. Both were Saudi citizens with combat experience in Bosnia and training at Al-Qaeda camps in Afghanistan. Although al-Mihdhar and al-Hazmi were known Al-Qaeda operatives, they left Kuala Lumpur and entered the United States without incident. They were eligible to be put on a watch list to prevent their entry, but the Central Intelligence Agency (CIA) neglected to do so. This inaction proved to be a monumental mistake, for al-Mihdhar and al-Hazmi were 2 of the 19 suicide hijackers on September 11, 2001.

Stephen E. Atkins

See also: Al-Qaeda; Bojinka, Operation; National Security Agency; USS *Cole* Bombing

Further Reading

Graham, Bob. *Intelligence Matters: The CIA, the FBI, Saudi Arabia, and the Failure of America's War on Terror*. New York: Random House, 2004.

Lance, Peter. *Triple Cross: How Bin Laden's Master Spy Penetrated the CIA, the Green Berets, and the FBI—and Why Patrick Fitzgerald Failed to Stop Him*. New York: ReganBooks, 2006.

McDermott, Terry. *Perfect Soldiers: The 9/11 Hijackers; Who They Were, Why They Did It*. New York: HarperCollins, 2005.

Strasser, Steven, ed. *The 9/11 Investigations; Staff Reports of the 9/11 Commission; Excerpts from the House-Senate Joint Inquiry Report on 9/11 Testimony from 14 Key Witnesses, Including Richard Clarke, George Tenet, and Condoleezza Rice*. New York: PublicAffairs, 2004.

L

La Belle Discotheque Bombing

On April 4, 1986, a bomb placed near the dance floor of the packed La Belle Discotheque in West Berlin exploded, killing 3 people and wounding 231 others, including 79 Americans. In response, the U.S. government launched a retaliatory strike on Libya (Operation El Dorado Canyon), which was widely suspected to have provided financial and logistical assistance for the attack.

The improvised explosive device blew a hole through the club's floor and ceiling, causing the walls to collapse inward. Two people died at the scene: Sergeant Kenneth Terrance Ford from the U.S. Army and Nermine Haney, a 28-year-old woman from Turkey. A third person, U.S. Army Staff Sergeant James E. Goin, succumbed to his wounds four days later.

A self-proclaimed spokesman for the Anti-American Liberation Front phoned a West German news agency in West Berlin and took credit for the attack. Another person told a London news agency that the Holger Meins Commando—an offshoot of the Rote Armee Fraktion (RAF, or Red Army Faction)—was behind the bombing. A third caller made contact with a West Berlin news agency and said the RAF was responsible.

During a press conference on April 9, U.S. president Ronald Reagan declared that the United States was prepared to retaliate militarily if there was definitive proof linking Libya to the discotheque bombing. Two days later, German chancellor Helmut Kohl phoned Reagan confirming the country's complicity.

On April 14, U.S. aircraft took off from Britain. After flying around France and Spain, they passed through the Strait of Gibraltar and launched a missile assault on Tripoli. The attack killed at least 15 civilians, including the 15-month-old adopted daughter of Libyan leader Colonel Muammar Qaddafi, and injured more than 2,000.

A week after the strike, West German police arrested Ahmed Nawaf Mansour Hasi, 35, as a prime suspect in the La Belle Discotheque attack. Although he denied playing a role in the incident, he did admit to bombing the Arab-German Friendship Society on March 29, 1986. His confession led to the arrests of two others, Farouk Salameh and Fayez Sahawneh, both of whom were later convicted as accomplices in the March 29 operation.

More than a month after the bombing, authorities unearthed evidence that a terrorist-for-hire group called the Jordanian Revolutionary Movement for National Salvation had been involved in the attack. The group had ties to Libya, Syria, and the Abu Nidal Organization (ANO). It was also connected to the Hindawi clan, which had risen to prominence on April 17, 1986, when its leader, Nezar Hindawi, had tried to use his pregnant Irish girlfriend to

German firefighters search through debris on April 5, 1986, after a bomb attack at a Berlin disco killed two American servicemen and a Turkish woman and injured 231 others. (AP/Wide World Photos)

unwittingly smuggle a bomb aboard an El Al flight to Tel Aviv. The 3.25-pound bomb was found by security. It was subsequently reported that Hindawi was already married and had apparently concluded that the best way to rid himself of his girlfriend and unwanted child was to use them to carry out a terrorist attack.

In 1996, three men and a woman were convicted of planning the La Belle Discotheque bombing. Two of the men, Musbah Eter and Ali Chanaa, worked for the Libyan embassy in East Berlin and doubled as spies for the Stasi. They were found guilty of aiding and abetting murder and sentenced to 12 years in prison. The third man, the alleged ringleader of the team, Yassar al-Shuraidi, received a 14-year jail term for multiple counts of homicide, as did Verena Chanaa, the German ex-wife of Ali Chanaa.

The judge said it was not clear whether Qaddafi or Libyan intelligence had actually ordered the attack, or not, although the speculation was that they had. Two weeks before the La Belle Discotheque blast, U.S. forces had sunk a Libyan patrol boat in the Mediterranean, killing 35 seamen. The presumed wisdom was that the operation in Germany was to avenge that incident. Whatever the truth of the matter, the U.S. raid on Tripoli served to galvanize anti-American sentiment in Libya and was almost certainly the trigger for the 1988 bombing of Pan Am Flight 103 over Lockerbie, Scotland, which killed all 259 passengers and crew on board as well as 11 people on the ground.

Donna Bassett

See also: Pan Am/Lockerbie Bombing; Terrorism

Further Reading

Davis, Brian. *Qaddafi, Terrorism, and the Origins of the U.S. Attack on Libya*. New York: Praeger, 1990.

Mickolus, Edward, Todd Sandler, and Jean M. Murdock. *International Terrorism in the 1980s: A Chronology of Events*. Vol. 2, *1984–1987*. Amcs: Iowa State University Press, 1989.

Stanik, Joseph T. *El Dorado Canyon: Reagan's Undeclared War with Qaddafi*. Annapolis, MD: Naval Institute Press, 2003.

Lashkar-e-Jhangvi (LeJ)

Lashkar-e-Jhangvi (LeJ) was founded in 1996 by a group of radical extremists—led by Muhammad Ajmal (also known as Akram Lahori)—who strongly endorsed the anti-Shia principles associated with Maulana Haq Nawaz Jhangvi (from whom the outfit derives its name), which stressed that the only way to effectively sanctify the Sunni faith in Pakistan was through violent means. LeJ has an estimated militant base of 300 cadres organized into semi-autonomous cells of five to eight members and retains most of its hard-core membership in the Punjab. The Pakistani government proscribed LeJ in August 2001.

LeJ has been at the forefront of sectarian violence in Pakistan—a conflict that left 1,518 dead and 2,817 injured between 2002 and 2008 alone. Attacks perpetrated by the group frequently involve suicide bombers and have targeted Shia religious sites, marches, funeral processions, and those at home or even in the hospital.

Although primarily focused on prosecuting its sectarian agenda in Pakistan, LeJ is widely suspected of having established links with Al-Qaeda. The group is known to have sent recruits to train at terrorist camps located near to the Sarobi Dam in Afghanistan, many of whom were subsequently retained for attacks against the Northern Alliance as well as Shiite enemies of the Taliban. LeJ is also thought to have benefited from the financial largesse of wealthy Gulf patrons with known sympathies for Osama bin Laden. The desert town of Rahimayar Khan in southern Punjab appears to have played a prominent role in this regard. Each year thousands of Arabs come to the region, spending several million dollars hunting local wildlife. Western officials suspect that a significant proportion of these monies have been transferred to the Sipah-ed Sahaba Pakistan (SSP) leadership, and through it to LeJ, to sustain and otherwise support anti-Shia activities in Pakistan.

There are also indications that LeJ has established ties to Al-Qaeda through the conduit of organized crime. The group is known to have established links with drug syndicates based in the port city of Karachi, facilitating the transfer of Afghan-sourced heroin across Pakistan's western borders for both internal consumption and distribution to Asia and Europe. Profits earned from these overseas markets are widely believed to form a substantial component of Al-Qaeda's war chest, which has, in return, paid LeJ with guns, explosives, and other matériel. Moreover, in common with Lashkar-e-Taiba, LeJ has been linked to Ibrahim Dawood's D-Company; Indian sources assert this international criminal enterprise retains at least residual links with bin Laden's wider jihadist network.

Finally, evidence (albeit nondefinitive) of an Al-Qaeda link has emerged in the testimony of Ajmal, the former leader of LeJ who was arrested in 2002. By his own admission, Ajmal has confirmed that members of his group (as well as cadres of HuM) swore an oath on the Koran to physically eliminate Pervez Musharraf at any cost. The basis for this commitment was apparently a conviction that the Pakistani president had both damaged and betrayed the true cause of jihad by siding with the United States in the post-9/11 global war on terror and was actively seeking to further a secular, Western-oriented agenda in Pakistan and throughout South Asia.

Violence perpetrated by LeJ continues to plague Pakistan and Afghanistan. LeJ claimed responsibility for an attack that left 26 Shia Muslim pilgrims dead during a September 20, 2011, attack in Balochistan. The Afghan government blamed the group for a December 2011 attack in Kabul that killed 59 civilians. LeJ was also thought to have been behind attacks in Pakistan in January, February, and June 2013 in which as many as 250 people died.

Peter Chalk

See also: Al-Qaeda; Bin Laden, Osama; Global War on Terror

Further Reading

Howard, Roger. "Probing the Ties That Bind Militant Islam." *Jane's Intelligence Review*, February 2000: 38–40.

Lawson, Alastair. "Pakistan's Evolving Sectarian Schism." *BBC News*, February 20, 2009. http://news.bbc.co.uk/2/hi/south/south_asia/7901094.stm.

Rabasa, Angel, Peter Chalk, Kim Cragin, Sara A. Daly, Heather S. Gregg, Theodore W. Karasik, Kevin A. O'Brien, and William Rosenau. *Beyond al-Qaeda Part 1: The Global Jihadist Movement*. Santa Monica, CA: RAND, 2006.

Lashkar-e-Taiba (LeT)

Lashkar-e-Taiba (LeT, literally, the Army of the Pure) dates back to 1993, when it was created as the military wing of the Markaz-ad-Da'awa Wal Irshad (MDI) madrassa. It is affiliated with the Ahl-e-Hadith sect of Wahhabism (which emphasizes statements attributed to the Prophet Muhammad) and was a creation of Pakistan's InterServices Intelligence (ISI) Directorate to act as a proxy force for prosecuting Islamabad's policy objectives in Jammu and Kashmir (J&K). The group is led by Hafiz Saeed (its spiritual emir) and Zaki ur-Rehman Lakhvi (its operational commander) and has a broader membership of around 150,000 cadres (including 750 insurgents on the ground in J&K). Under international pressure following the September 11, 2001, terror attacks in the United States, then president Pervez Musharraf banned the group in 2002. However, it has since operated more or less openly under the name Jama'at-ud-Da'awa (which Saeed leads purportedly as an Islamic charity), although this group was also banned in 2009.

LeT possesses a robust network in India and has made strenuous efforts to cultivate ties with various extremist groups in the country, including the Students Islamic Movement of India and the Indian Mujahideen. LeT also enjoys an established international network outside South Asia, with particular strength in the Middle East and a growing presence in the United Kingdom. Financially, most of the group's funds come from diaspora contributions, earnings from legitimate businesses (such as real estate and commodity trading), the Pakistani military, and the provincial government of the Punjab (in the form of donations). Its espousal of Ahl-e-Hadith, which is considered theologically similar to the Salafi Islam practiced in Saudi Arabia, has additionally helped it procure financial support from that country.

LeT has between 100,000 and 150,000 supporters and members and enjoys an extensive infrastructure in Pakistan that includes its sprawling compound in the town of Murdike outside Lahore, training camps in Pakistani Occupied Kashmir (POK, or Azzad Jammu o-Kashmir) offices, madrassas, schools, medical clinics, and mosques. The group publishes several periodicals in Urdu and English, has operated Web sites and promulgated news bulletins via outlets such as Yahoo Groups, recruits openly on Pakistani university campuses, and operates the MDI madrassa (which was heavily involved in relief efforts following the devastating 2005 earthquake in POK).

Although the group was established as a tanzeem to fight Indian rule in J&K, most of LeT's personnel are Punjabi and Pashtun, with relatively few Kashmiris in its ranks. In addition, the group has always defined its objectives in local and regional terms, articulating a twofold ideological and operational agenda that aims to exploit ethno-religious tension in Kashmir in order to trigger a wider religious revolution across the Indian state. To this end, the group has spearheaded terrorist attacks across J&K and has been directly tied to numerous assaults in India, including the attack on India's Red Fort in December 2000, the strike against the Indian National Parliament in December 2001, the Kaluchak massacre in May 2002, serial explosions in Delhi in October 2005, the Varanasi attack in March 2006, the Mumbai assaults in November 2008, and the bombing of a German bakery restaurant in Pune in February 2010. Of these, arguably the most serious and audacious were the November 2008 assaults, which were allegedly undertaken in collaboration with Ibrahim Dawood, the head of D Company (also known as the Bombay Mafia) and one of India's most wanted men.

LeT is known for its sophisticated intelligence and operational planning capabilities. The 2008 Mumbai attacks represent a case in point. David Headley, a Pakistani American, traveled to India on several occasions to reconnoiter targets for the assault, using a fake visa-processing business to establish his cover identity. The attacks were then executed by LeT cadres trained in marine operations and equipped with automatic weapons, grenades, and delayed explosive charges. Members of the strike team used Google Earth to familiarize themselves with Mumbai, hijacked a fishing trawler to make the trip to India, employed modern GPS receivers to navigate, and communicated with their Pakistani handlers via satellite phones routed through the Internet. The attackers operated in small, heavily armed units, exploiting news broadcasts to ascertain the position, size, and maneuvers of the security forces. These tactics allowed 10 men to not only strike multiple locations across the city but also decisively overwhelm Mumbai's massive but poorly trained and equipped police force.

LeT is set apart from other Pakistani terrorist groups by its relative obedience to the military and ISI as well as by its espousal of the Ahl-e-Hadith sect of Islam. These traits have frequently caused friction with the major Deobandi militant entities, although it has often cooperated on an operational and logistic level with groups in India and Bangladesh. Unlike many other Kashmiri tanzeems, LeT is additionally characterized by a relatively strong sense of internal cohesion, and at the time of this writing, there was little evidence to suggest that it was suffering from the type of internal hemorrhaging that has befallen groups such as Jaish-e-Mohammed and Harakat-ul-Mujahideen.

Despite LeT's growing connections to anti-Western violence, the Pakistani government has refused to act against the group, and both the military and the ISI are considered to enjoy somewhat cordial relations with it. Indeed, reports from the Indian media indicated that Saeed was the guest of honor at an iftar dinner (the evening meal that breaks the daily fast during the holy month of Ramadan) hosted by the Pakistani Army's 10th Corps in 2009, shortly before he was charged with preaching jihad and raising money for terrorist activities (all of these charges have since been dropped). The general reluctance to act against LeT is considered to be a product of the army's belief that the group continues to be a strategic asset vis-à-vis Pakistan's competition with India. A number of military and intelligence officers also share LeT's religious convictions, further strengthening bonds. A number of sources in Pakistan have additionally suggested that Islamabad is fearful of the consequences of attempting a wholesale crackdown on LeT, given its size and formidable capabilities.

Ben Brandt

See also: Global War on Terrorism; National Geospatial-Intelligence Agency

Further Reading

Fair, Christine C. "Antecedents and Implications of the November 2008 Lashkar-e-Taiba (LeT) Attack upon Several Targets in the Indian Mega-City of Mumbai." Testimony given before the House Homeland Security Committee, Subcommittee on Transportation and Infrastructure, March 11, 2009. Accessed June 15, 2014. http://home.comcast.net/~christine_fair/pubs/CT-320_Christine_Fair.pdf.

"Lashkar-e-Toiba: Army of the Pure." South Asia Terrorism Portal. Updated June 2014. http://www.satp.org/satporgtp/countries/india/states/jandk/terrorist_outfits/lashkar_e_toiba.htm

Tankel, Stephen. "Lashkar-e-Taiba: From 9/11 to Mumbai." International Center for the Study of Radicalisation and Political Violence, London, April/May 2009. Accessed January 1, 2011. http://www.iscr.info/news/attachments/12408469161SRTTankelReport.pdf.

Lindh, John Walker

John Walker Lindh, commonly referred to as the "American Taliban," was born in 1981 to a middle-class family in suburban Washington, D.C. His family moved to Marin County, an affluent area in northern California, when he was 10 years old. Lindh attended Tamiscal High School, an alternative institution for "self-directed" students, and was described as hard-working and musically inclined.

At a young age, Lindh was moved by the biography of Malcolm X, and by 16 had converted to Islam and changed his name to Sulayman. In July 1998, he went to Yemen, where he studied classical Arabic and Islam. Lindh returned to the United States a year later and began worshipping at a San Francisco mosque, although he found the experience dull and flew back to Yemen in February 2000. His e-mail correspondence began to take on an increasingly radical tone, and in one message sent to his parents he asserted that the Al-Qaeda attack on the USS *Cole* was justified because the ship's presence in the region constituted an act of war.

Around this time, Lindh informed his mother and father that he planned to enroll in a religious school in the Northwest Frontier Province (NWFP) of Pakistan. However, he never followed through, and in May 2001, he began training in a camp operated by Harakat-ul-Mujahideen (HuM), a militant Kashmiri group based north of

An undated photo of American Taliban fighter John Walker Lindh made available on February 6, 2002 by the Alexandria, Virginia Sheriff's Department. (AFP/Getty Images)

Islamabad. After 24 days, Lindh decided against joining HuM and instead agreed to fight with the Taliban in Afghanistan. In a subsequent interview with CNN, Lindh stated that he came to support the movement's religious doctrine after reading its literature and speaking with supporters in the NWFP.

In late May, Lindh crossed the border into Afghanistan with a letter of introduction from HuM. He was interviewed at a Taliban recruitment center in Kabul and then sent to Al-Qaeda's al-Farooq camp. He received seven weeks of training in weapons handling, topography, explosives, and battlefield operations, and swore an oath of allegiance to jihad. Following the completion of the course at al-Farooq, Lindh was presented with several options. These included fighting the Northern Alliance or leaving Afghanistan to carry out an attack against an American or Israeli target. Lindh decided to stay in Afghanistan and was deployed to Mazar-e Sharif. He fled to Kunduz on foot after U.S. air strikes began in October 2001; there, he was captured along with 3,000 other Taliban fighters.

In November 2001, Lindh was interviewed by an employee of the Central Intelligence Agency (CIA) at the Qala-i Janghi compound near Mazar-e Sharif. Shortly after the session ended, several hundred prisoners staged an uprising and killed the CIA officer. Lindh heard the commotion and tried to run; however, he was shot in the leg. His companions carried him to a basement, where, after hiding from the authorities for several days, he was eventually caught and apprehended. Having been identified as an American citizen, Lindh spent several weeks being interrogated on a U.S. Navy ship in the North Arabian Sea. He was flown back to the United States on January 23, 2002.

After reaching a deal with prosecutors in 2002, Lindh pled guilty to one count of supplying services to the Taliban and carrying weapons for use against the Northern Alliance. During the trial, Lindh apologized for his actions and stated, "Had I realized then what I know now . . . I would never would have joined [the Taliban.]" He is currently serving a 20-year term in prison at a supermax facility in Florence, Colorado. In 2009, Lindh's family requested a commutation of part of his sentence, but that request was turned down by the outgoing George W. Bush administration.

Horacio Trujillo

See also: Central Intelligence Agency; Combined Forces Command—Afghanistan; Enduring Freedom, Operation; Reid, Richard; Taliban

Further Reading

"The Case of the Taliban American." *CNN People in the News*, December 19, 2001. http://www.cnn.com/CNN/Programs/people/shows/walker/profile.html.

"Profile: John Walker Lindh." *BBC News*, January 24, 2002. http://news.bbc.co.uk/2/hi/americas/1779455.stm.

Serrano, Richard A. "Release of Lindh Again Urged." *Los Angeles Times*, April 5, 2007.

United States of America v. John Philip Walker Lindh. U.S. District Court for the Eastern District of Virginia, Alexandria Division, January 15, 2002. http://www.usdoj.gov/ag/criminalcomplaint1.htm.

London Bombings

(2005)

Four simultaneous suicide bombings of London's public transportation system

The aftermath of a series of coordinated terrorist bombings on July 7, 2005. At least four bombs exploded on London's subway trains and a double-decker bus, with a death toll of 56. A little-known group affiliated with Al-Qaeda claimed responsibility for the attacks. (AP Photo/Dylan Martinez)

on July 7, 2005, killed 56 people, including the bombers, and injured more than 700. The terrorist attacks targeted three key lines on the London Underground rail system and one commuter bus—all packed with passengers during the morning rush hour. They were Western Europe's first-ever suicide bombings, and the largest terrorist attack ever committed on British soil.

The three rail attackers detonated their bombs within 50 seconds of one another, at about 8:50 a.m., in trains just outside the Liverpool Street, Edgware Road, and King's Cross stations. The bus bomb, which hit a double-decker bus in Tavistock Square, exploded at 9:47 a.m. In the ensuing chaos, London police, medical staff, and communications systems struggled to cope. Mobile phone systems were overwhelmed, and a June 2006 report investigating the response to the bombings lamented a lack of medical supplies in

area hospitals. Hundreds of people were trapped underground without access to first aid supplies.

Two weeks later, on July 21, a virtually identical attack on three Underground stations and one bus failed when the bombers' detonating devices did not work. However, the incident again plunged London's transportation system into chaos, just as it had begun to function again after extensive investigations. It also raised questions about British security and antiterrorism efforts.

All but one of the suicide bombers responsible for the July 7 attacks were Muslims who had been raised in England; all but one, a Jamaican-born man who moved to England as a child, were born there. Their backgrounds and seemingly normal lives raised concerns about growing Islamic discontent within the United Kingdom. Many feared that British involvement in the Iraq War had motivated the bombers, but the writings and videos they left behind made no mention of Iraq. Instead, they noted Islamic ideals and anger toward Britain and other Western governments for their treatment of Muslims worldwide. One of the bombers, Mohammad Sidique Khan, said in a posthumous video: "Your democratically elected governments continuously perpetrate atrocities against my people all over the world. Until we feel security, you will be our targets."

Subsequent investigations into the bombings also revealed that two of the bombers, Khan and Shehzad Tanweer, had spent several months in Pakistan from November 2004 to February 2005. Both of their families had migrated to the United Kingdom from Pakistan, but investigators believe their 2004 visit included contact with, and training by, Al-Qaeda operatives. Khan, who was 30, is believed to have been the mastermind behind the attacks; Tanweer was 22, and the other two bombers were 18 and 19.

A May 2006 report issued after months of investigations into the July 7 attacks blamed a lack of security resources for intelligence agencies' failure to prevent the bombings. Security agents had information about two of the four bombers but had not fully investigated them because they were understaffed and had to address "more pressing priorities," including disrupting known plans to attack the United Kingdom. The nation's MI5 intelligence agency has estimated that at the time of the London bombings the agency was investigating about 800 people who were viewed as potential threats and had possible Al-Qaeda ties or sympathies. The figure rose to more than 1,000 over the next year. With several agents needed to monitor one person, intelligence officials said they were simply overwhelmed.

Terri Nichols

See also: Madrid Commuter Train Bombings; World Trade Center Bombing; World Trade Center, September 11, 2001

Further Reading
Benetto, Jason, and Ian Herbert. "London Bombings: The Truth Emerges." *Independent* (UK), August 13, 2005.

House of Commons. *Report of the Official Account of the Bombings in London on 7th July 2005*. London: Her Majesty's Stationery Office, May 11, 2006.

BBC News. "7 July Bombings." July 7, 2005. http://news.bbc.co.uk/2/shared/spl/hi/uk/05/london_blasts/what_happened/html/.

Intelligence and Security Committee. *Report into the London Terrorist Attacks on 7 July 2005*. London: Her Majesty's Stationery Office, May 11, 2006.

M

Madrid Airport Bombing

On December 30, 2006, a vehicular improvised explosive device (VIED) detonated at Spain's Madrid-Barajas International Airport. The blast killed 2 and injured 52; it damaged one terminal, and destroyed the entire parking structure where the van containing the VIED had been left. The Basque militant organization Euskadi Ta Askatasuna (ETA, or Basque Homeland and Freedom) claimed credit for the attack, effectively ending a nine-month cease-fire and prompting the government of José Luis Rodríguez Zapatero to call off all negotiations with the group.

Planning for the bombing commenced during the summer of 2006 after Miguel Garikoitz Aspiazu Rubina (also known as Txeroki)—the leader of ETA's "commando Elurra"—sanctioned the attack in clandestine meetings held at the Baztan Valley in Navarre province. Three members of the group were charged with carrying out the operation—Mattin Sarasola, Igor Portu, and Mikel Sebastián. The trio rehearsed the route to the airport twice the following October and identified an appropriate place to leave the VIED. On December 27, they stole a Renault Trafic van at gunpoint in the French town of Luz Ardiden—holding the owner for three days in a cabin located in the Pyrenees. During this period the bomb was assembled. Authorities later determined that the device contained between 500 and 800 kilograms (1,100–1,700 pounds) of explosives (a mixture of ammonium nitrate and hexogen), making it one of the largest VIEDs ever deployed by ETA.

On the morning of December 31, the attack team drove the Renault to the airport and left it in parking lot D of Terminal Four. They then phoned in three coded warnings that a powerful bomb had been deployed and had been primed to detonate. An hour later the VIED went off. The ensuing explosion demolished 90 percent of the car park, killing two Ecuadorians who were napping in their vehicle at the time of the blast. The terminal building was also damaged, sending shrapnel that injured at least 52 people.

On January 9, 2007, ETA took responsibility for the attack. The group insisted that the cease-fire was still in place and claimed that the bombing was not meant to cause any casualties—blaming the government for not properly evacuating the airport after receiving three warnings of an impending explosion. Prime Minister Zapatero dismissed these overtures and immediately announced that he had canceled the peace effort with ETA, arguing that the group had miscalculated and that violence was incompatible with negotiation.

All of those involved in the attack were arrested in 2008. Portu and Sarasola were detained on January 7 in Gipuzkoa. Just over a month later (on February 16) Sebastián was captured in the French town of Saint-Jean-de-Luz along with fellow ETA members Jose Antonio Martinez Mur and Asuncion Bengoechea. Finally, on November 17, Txeroki—at the time Spain's most wanted man—was apprehended in Cauterets, Hautes-Pyrénées.

After a 20-day trial, Sarasola, Portu, and Sebastián were found guilty of 2 murders and 48 attempted murders (Spanish authorities gave a figure of 48 injuries during the hearing) on May 21, 2010. They each received a sentence of 1,040 years in jail. On July 21, 2011, Txeroki was convicted on 20 counts of attempted terrorist assassinations and 1 count of causing property damage. He was sentenced to be imprisoned for 377 years. Three months later, ETA declared a unilateral end to its campaign of bombings and shootings, affirming that the organization wished to seize "an historical opportunity to reach a just and democratic resolution" of the Basque national conflict in northeastern Spain and southwestern France.

Edward F. Mickolus

See also: Heathrow Liquid Bomb Plot; Madrid Commuter Train Bombings; Millennium Plots; Terrorism

Further Reading

Burns, John. "Separatists Halt Violence to Advance Basque Goals." *New York Times*, October 21, 2011.

"Ex-Chief of ETA Gets 377-Year Sentence." *Tip News*, July 21, 2011. http://www.tipnews.info/international/NTk3NTE=/2011/07/22/exchief_eta_gets_377year_sentence.

Sciolino, Elaine. "Separatists Admit to Madrid Airport Attack but Stand by Cease-Fire." *New York Times*, January 10, 2007.

"Spain Confirms Arrest of 4 ETA Suspects in France." Reuters, February 16, 2008.

"Spanish PM Suspends ETA Dialogue." *BBC News*, December 30, 2006. http://news.bbc.co.uk/2/hi/europe/6219431.stm.

Madrid Bombings. *See* Madrid Commuter Train Bombings; Madrid Convention Center Bombing

Madrid Commuter Train Bombings

The Madrid bombings, also referred to as 3/11, occurred in Spain on March 11, 2004. The attacks were launched in the morning against the city's commuter train system and left 190 people dead and 1,755 injured. The victims included citizens of 17 countries.

The attacks took place during the morning rush hour on four commuter trains traveling between Alcala des Henares and the Atocha Station in Madrid in an obvious effort to inflict the greatest amount of casualties possible. Thirteen bombs, hidden in backpacks, had been placed on the trains, 10 of which exploded within a two-minute period beginning at 7:37 a.m. Police detonated two of the three additional devices as well as a suspicious package found near the Atocha Station. One unexploded bomb was taken intact and provided crucial forensic evidence for the investigation and subsequent trial of the terrorists.

Three days later, the ruling Partido Popular (PP, or Popular Party) was defeated in national elections and replaced by the left-leaning Partido Socialista Obrero Españo (PSOE, or Spanish Socialist Workers' Party). While Al-Qaeda later claimed that the bombings had directly led to the PP's electoral defeat, most experts agree that

Red Cross officials lift a body bag containing the victim of a bomb blast from a train outside the main train station in Madrid, on March 11, 2004. Ten simultaneous explosions killed 182 people on packed Madrid commuter trains in Europe's bloodiest attack for more than fifteen years. (Kai Pfaffenbach/Reuters/Corbis)

the former government's clumsy handling of the aftermath of the attacks was the primary factor in the PSOE victory. The PP had held only a narrow and shrinking lead in the polls prior to the attacks, and many saw the government's early blaming of ETA as influenced by electoral considerations; when the Basques were found to have had nothing to do with the attacks, the administration's credibility was badly damaged.

A few weeks after the attacks, on April 2, 2004, another bomb was found on the tracks of a high-speed rail line. Although the device was fully primed, it was not connected to any detonating device. Following the discovery, new investigations were launched, and Spanish police traced the likely perpetrators to a cell based in an area south of Madrid. During the subsequent raid to arrest them, an explosion (apparently detonated by one of the suspects) killed seven terrorists; between five and eight others managed to escape and have yet to be apprehended. Helped by the fact that seven of the alleged ringleaders blew themselves up, in a flat surrounded by police, three weeks after the attacks, conspiracy theories about who was responsible have appeared in Spain's right-wing press on numerous occasions.

In all, 29 people—20 Moroccans and 9 Spaniards—were eventually apprehended and charged for involvement in the Madrid bombings. Their trial began on February 15, 2007, and lasted four and a half months. The verdict, handed down on October 31, 2007, found 21 guilty of various crimes ranging from forgery to murder. Two of the convicted terrorists were sentenced to prison terms that added up to 42,924 years (although Spanish law limits actual imprisonment to 40 years).

The court sentences did not mention any direct links between the convicted terrorists and Al-Qaeda, however. While the latter may well have inspired the former, no irrefutable evidence has been found to connect Osama bin Laden's movement with the planning, financing, or execution of the Madrid operation. That said, the attacks have been interpreted as the first major success for an Al-Qaeda–type terrorist organization in Europe. Moreover, the incident arguably served as the stimulus for further incidents in the region, including the July 7, 2005, bombings in London.

Elliot Paul Chodoff

See also: Al-Qaeda; Bin Laden, Osama; Global War on Terror; Heathrow Liquid Bomb Plot; Madrid Airport Bombing

Further Reading

Puniyani, Ram. *Terrorism: Facts versus Myths.* New Delhi: Pharos Media, 2007.

Von Hippel, Karin. *Europe Confronts Terrorism.* New York: Palgrave Macmillan, 2005.

Madrid Convention Center Bombing

At 9:00 a.m. on the morning of February 9, 2009, a car bomb planted by the Basque separatist terrorist organization Euskadi Ta Askatasuna (ETA, or Basque Homeland and Freedom) exploded near the main Parque Ferial Juan Carlos I Conference Center in the Campo de las Naciones area of Madrid. Despite the size of the explo-

sion, an earlier telephoned warning ensured that there were no casualties, with all damage confined to local buildings. Nevertheless, the attack was significant, both because it was the first act of ETA terrorism since the December 2006 bombing of Terminal Four at the Madrid-Barajas International Airport (which killed two and shattered a nine-month truce with the government) and because it was strategically located in the heart of the capital.

The bombing occurred only hours after the Spanish Supreme Court had banned two separatist political parties linked to ETA from running in the forthcoming Basque regional elections. It was therefore initially assumed that the incident was staged in retaliation for this decision. However, another motivation for the attack soon became apparent. The Peugeot containing the bomb was parked outside the offices of Ferrovial. Authorities believe this company was the real target, as it was involved in the construction of a controversial high-speed train link that would pass through the Basque provinces of northern Spain to France. ETA had threatened numerous businesses associated with the project, labeling it as an illegal imposition by Madrid and Paris that was "anti-social, anti-ecological and wasteful of resources." It had also been prepared to actively demonstrate its opposition, as was made clear by the December 2008 assassination of Ignacio Uria as he was leaving a restaurant in Azpeitia, near San Sebastian. The justification for the murder was that the 70-year-old executive owned a firm that was directly involved in work on the high-speed rail link.

ETA had targeted the Parque Ferial building four years earlier when the group planted and detonated a car bomb that injured 42 people. The attack occurred on February 10, 2005, just before King Juan Carlos, Queen Sofia, and Mexican president Vicente Fox were scheduled to view an art exhibition being held at the convention facility. That attack effectively nullified Madrid's hopes of hosting the 2012 Olympic Games, as the center had been proposed as a site for a number of prominent sporting events during the competition.

Richard Warnes

See also: Heathrow Liquid Bomb Plot; Madrid Airport Bombing; Madrid Commuter Train Bombings; Millennium Plots; Terrorism

Further Reading

Keeley, Graham. "ETA Car Bomb Targets BAA Owner in Madrid." *The Times* (London), February 9, 2009.

"Madrid Bomb Blast Injures 42." *ABC News Online*, February 10, 2005. http://www.abc .net.au/news/newsitems/200502/s1299457 .htm.

Pinedo, Emma. "Suspected ETA Bomb Explodes in Madrid." Reuters, February 9, 2009. http://www.reuters.com/article/cdUS TRES1825120090209.

Marine Corps Barracks (Beirut) Bombing

On October 23, 1983, a five-ton suicide vehicle-borne improvised explosive device (VBIED) killed 241 U.S. servicemen and wounded 80 others at the U.S. Marine Barracks at Beirut Airport. Minutes later, another VBIED killed 58 French paratroopers and injured 15 others two miles north of the airport. The twin attacks raised serious questions about sending foreign troops to the Middle East to participate in so-called peacekeeping missions and the wisdom of

an American president flexing his military muscle around the world. They were also widely credited for the subsequent decision to withdraw the United Nations' Multi-National Force (MNF) from Lebanon, underscoring the asymmetric power of terrorism and its potential to "level the playing field" for substate actors confronting even the strongest, most advanced militaries.

The first terrorist drove a Mercedes truck loaded with the equivalent of 12,000 pounds of TNT enhanced with explosive gas cylinders. He slid through a gate that that had been left open, rammed through both barbed wire and a sandbagged sentry post, and detonated the vehicle in the lobby of a building housing the 1st Battalion, 8th Marines of the 2nd Marine Division. The bomb had been placed on top of marble covering a bottom layer of concrete in the back of the truck. This configuration was designed to direct the blast upward and collapse the four-story building. Even so, the explosive force drove the truck bed eight feet down into the earth and severed the supporting concrete columns, each of which was 15 feet in circumference and reinforced by steel rods. The entire structure then lifted and collapsed on itself. The death toll—220 marines, 18 navy personnel, and 3 army soldiers—was the highest for the marines since the World War II battle for Iwo Jima and the most serious for any American military unit since the first day of the 1968 Tet Offensive during the Vietnam War.

The VBIED was most likely composed of conventional explosives tightly packed around bottled gas canisters of either propane or butane. The ensuing blast left a crater 30 feet deep and 120 feet across. Marine sentries could not fire at the truck because under the terms of their deployment they were required to keep their

U.S. marines retrieve the body of a comrade from the Battalion Landing Team building in Beirut, Lebanon on October 23, 1983. A truck packed with explosives crashed into the building, killing 241 marines. President Ronald Reagan withdrew the rest of the troops. The marines had been stationed in Beirut to protect the fragile Lebanese government from the Israelis. (Bettmann/Corbis)

weapons unloaded while in the barracks building.

The second suicide bomber drove a car loaded with the equivalent of about 1,200 pounds of TNT into the eight-story apartment building housing the French 1st Parachute Chasseur Regiment in the central Beirut district of Ramel el-Baida. The resultant fatality count was the single worst French military loss since the Algerian War.

Islamic Jihad Organization (IJO, now thought to be the direct predecessor of Hezbollah) took responsibility for both bombings. In phone messages to Agence France-Press offices in Beirut and Paris, a caller claiming to be a spokesman for the group said, "We are the soldiers of God and we crave death. Violence will remain our only path if they [U.S. and French

troops] do not leave. We are ready to turn Lebanon into another Vietnam." Ten days later, IJO carried out a similar bombing against Israel's intelligence headquarters in the Lebanese town of Tyre. This attack killed 61 Palestinians as well as an unspecified number of Israelis.

The three bombings came on the heels of an earlier assault on the U.S. embassy in Beirut. That attack, which took place on April 18, 1983, and involved a VBIED composed of approximately 1,230 pounds of TNT, killed 64 people and wounded between 88 and 100. Among the fatalities was Robert Ames, the Central Intelligence Agency's (CIA) national intelligence officer for the Near East and Washington's key liaison to the Palestine Liberation Organization's (PLO) leadership. He had just walked into the building when the blast occurred.

A massive rescue operation commenced immediately after the Beirut explosions. Helicopters dispatched from the U.S. 6th Fleet quickly brought many of the wounded to the USS *Iwo Jima*, which had surgical operating facilities on board. Others were medevaced to various American and European hospitals in Egypt, Italy, Cyprus, and West Germany.

In Washington, a three-hour National Security Council meeting was held, after which President Reagan announced that Commandant General Paul X. Kelly would be dispatched to Beirut to investigate ways of better protecting marines deployed as peacekeepers in active conflict zones. In Israel, Prime Minister Yitzhak Shamir said those responsible for the bombing were motivated by a desire to halt the peace process in Lebanon. In Moscow, the Russian newspaper *Pravda* proclaimed, "It appears the Viet Nam story begins to repeat itself. The U.S. is getting drawn deeper into the fighting."

Naturally, the United States, France, and Israel wanted to strike back at the terrorists. However, because Western governments had very little information on IJO—up until that time almost all focus had been on the PLO—exactly how to do this was not immediately apparent. Moreover, there was the question of how to infiltrate a fiercely religious movement that obviously had good intelligence of its own and was well organized. Eventually, Paris carried out a retaliatory air strike against supposed Islamic Revolutionary Guards in Syria's Bekaa Valley. However, there was no serious response from Washington other than to relocate the marine peacekeepers offshore where they could not be targeted. That decision set in motion the subsequent withdrawal of the entire MNF, which was completed by April 1984—five months after the bombings.

The U.S. government eventually concluded that Hezbollah had carried out the attacks, operating under the banner of IJO with Iranian and Syrian backing. Washington also asserted that this same sponsor-proxy combination was behind the bombing of the U.S. embassy in Beirut on April 18, 1983. In 1985 an American grand jury secretly indicted Imad Mughniyah as the chief architect behind the operations. Although he was never caught, he was killed by a car bomb in Syria on February 12, 2008.

On October 3 and December 28, 2001, the families of those who died in the Marine Corps Barracks bombing, together with some survivors, filed civil lawsuits against the Iranian government and its Ministry of Information and Security (MIS). They sought a ruling that Tehran was responsible for the attack and was therefore obligated to pay both punitive and compensatory damages. Iran denied any link to the incident but, notably, did not file court papers to counter the claims.

Important new evidence surfaced during the trial. This included a National Security Agency electronic intercept that had originated with Iran's intelligence headquarters and that instructed Tehran's ambassador in Syria to organize a "spectacular" act against the marines. On December 18, 2002, the presiding judge in the case, Royce C. Lamberth, determined that the defendants were in default. Four months later he ruled that Iran had provided both financial and logistical support for the bombing, that Hezbollah had actually executed the operation, and that the group had operated with the direct aid of agents from the MIS. On September 7, 2007, Lamberth awarded $2,656,944,877 to the plaintiffs.

Following the bombing, the U.S. Department of Defense issued a report recommending that Washington look at other ways of reaching its goals in Lebanon. It suggested a broader range of "appropriate military, political, and diplomatic responses to terrorism" and said that the army was in urgent need of improving its doctrine, planning, organization, force structure, education, and training to better combat violent extremism.

The Investigations Subcommittee of the House Armed Services Committee was more explicit. It accused the marines of inadequate intelligence gathering and lax security, and asserted that the entire military chain of command was guilty of "very serious errors in judgment." The subcommittee went on to declare that the ground commander in Beirut was responsible for egregious security lapses and directly faulted the top military officials overseeing the peacekeeping operation for not thoroughly examining the "guts" of protective measures adopted at the barracks. The committee chairman's statement concluded, "If you want to speak of negligence, then it goes all the way up to the combined Joint Chiefs of Staff."

The findings of another commission appointed by President Reagan and led by Admiral Robert L. J. Long similarly lambasted officials for not exercising better judgment in force protection. It proclaimed that even basic measures could have reduced the casualty count, such as constructing concrete barriers around the barracks and allowing sentries to have loaded weapons. The report was held from release while the White House debated the thorny question of how the military could be blamed without conducting court-martials for negligent generals and, more pointedly, without holding the administration accountable for putting the marines in harm's way in the first place.

The 1983 bombings in Beirut vastly increased the dimensions of contemporary terrorism, heralding the dawn of a new type of militant extremism, which up until that time had been confined mostly to small-scale strikes designed to attract mass publicity rather than cause widespread physical damage per se. The startling success of the operations, pointedly demonstrated by the withdrawal of the MNF from Lebanon, also heralded the initiation of a new, deadly tactic—large-scale suicide bombings—that was to become a characteristic modus operandi in numerous conflict environments around the world. Indeed, the events of 1983 have since been portrayed as one of the most clear-cut cases demonstrating the coercive success of suicide terrorism inflicting unacceptable punishment. As President Reagan wrote later in his memoirs, "The price we had to pay in Beirut was so great, the tragedy at the barracks so enormous. . . . We had to pull out. . . . We couldn't stay there and run the risk of another suicide attack on the Marines."

Donna Bassett

See also: Hezbollah (Party of God); La Belle Discotheque Bombing; U.S. Embassy (Beirut) Bombing

Further Reading

Chalk, Peter, and Bruce Hoffman. *The Dynamics of Suicide Terrorism: Four Case Studies of Terrorist Movements*. Santa Monica, CA: RAND, 2005.

Davis, Mike. *Buda's Wagon: A Brief History of the Car Bomb*. New York: Verso Books, 2007.

Fisk, Robert. *Pity the Nation: The Abduction of Lebanon*. New York: Touchstone, Simon & Schuster, 1990.

Tyler, Patrick. *A World of Trouble: The White House and the Middle East—from the Cold

War to the War on Terror. New York: Farrar Straus Giroux, 2009.

Wright, Robin. *Sacred Rage: The Wrath of Militant Islam.* New York: Touchstone Books, Simon & Schuster, 2001.

Zisser, Eyal. "Hezbollah in Iran: At the Cross-Roads." *Terrorism and Political Violence* 8, no. 2 (Summer 1996): 90–100.

Martyrdom

The act of dying for principles or a particular cause, usually religious. The term is derived from the Greek martyrs, meaning "witness," and was first used in a religious context when referring to the apostles of Jesus Christ, who were "witnesses" of the life and deeds of Jesus, although the idea of death and suffering for religious beliefs appears earlier in Egyptian, Hindu, and Mesopotamian faiths.

Martyrdom acquired its current usage in the Western, Christian world in the early Christian period, when Christians were being persecuted by authorities of the Roman Empire. Those killed for upholding their beliefs were called martyrs, their acceptance of death being considered a testimony of their faith. Some Christian martyrs sought out and welcomed martyrdom as a means of emulating Jesus's willingness to be sacrificed on the cross. Judaism does not connect martyrdom to the idea of witnessing faith, but rather refers to it as sanctification of the name of God, or kiddush ha-Shem. In both Christianity and Judaism, martyrdom refers to a case in which the believer accepts death rather than denies or changes his or her religious beliefs.

In Islam, martyrdom (shuhada) or becoming a martyr for the faith (istishhad) is connected to the concept of declaring or witnessing Islam and to struggle for the sake of Islam (jihad). The most important verse of the Koran usually connected with martyrdom is 4:69: "Whosoever obeys Allah, and the Messenger—they are with those whom God has blessed, Prophets, just men, martyrs [shuhada], the righteous; the best of company are they!" According to Islam, martyrs are not questioned after death by the two angels Munkar and Nakir; they bypass purgatory, and do not require the intercession of the Prophet to proceed to paradise, as they are free of sin. Martyrs can serve as intercessors for others and are buried in the clothes they die in and not washed after death.

In the early period of Islam, martyrdom referred to those Muslims killed in battle against the armies of Mecca, for example at the Battle of Uhud, and to 11 of the Shia imams. Today, the term also refers to suicide attackers who believe they are defending the cause of Islam. A true martyr (shahid) is, according to doctrine, one who does not seek his or her own death deliberately but accepts it and is granted religious legitimacy and assured a place in heaven. However, suicide committed for personal reasons is prohibited by Islamic law and may be punished by an endless repetition of the same form of death in hell.

Present-day Islamic terrorist organizations alluded to the concept of martyrdom when they began using suicide attacks as a tactic. This was not a new phenomenon but both a revival of an ancient tradition dating back to the early wars of Islam and an adaptation of the discourse of radical Islamic leaders who believed that martyrdom was inevitable for those struggling in the Islamic cause.

Suicide attacks provide two significant advantages over standard attacks. First, if successful, they are tactically and logistically easier to execute, because no escape route or retreat is needed, and they are therefore more efficient. Second, they provide a shock to the enemy that goes beyond the actual casualty figure, as they suggest great vulnerability and further probable use of this tactic. Third, they provide a martyr symbol that makes recruiting new members for the organization an easier task by strengthening the ideology behind a group's agenda. The fact that the martyr is willing to commit suicide is used by the group as "testimony" and "evidence" of the worthiness of its cause.

Terrorist suicide attacks in contemporary times began outside the Middle East, in Sri Lanka, where they were carried out by Tamil separatists. Much used there, this strategy has no connection with Islamic ideology and demonstrated only the resolve of the attackers. Claims of martyrdom, however, were made for those killed in demonstrations against the Iranian government prior to the Islamic Revolution. Suicide attacks were not used in that revolution, however. Suicide attacks that involved claims of martyrdom did occur in Syria in the late 1970s and early 1980s in battles between Islamic groups and the Syrian government in Damascus, Hama, and Homs.

The term "martyr" was used in the Lebanese civil war by both Christians and Muslims. The connection between martyrdom and suicide attacks came with the Islamic resistance, which responded to the Israeli invasion and occupation of Lebanon in 1982. These actions were undertaken by only a few, but some of the large attacks launched in 1983, as by Islamic Jihad against the U.S. Marines and barracks and French forces, were truck bombings involving suicide.

Much of the present-day discussion of martyrdom comes out of the war on terror. This depends on one's point of view. Thus Americans refer to suicide bomber attacks in Iraq, while some Iraqis style such events as martyrdom operations and part of the resistance against the occupation.

A long-standing discussion of martyrdom in acts of resistance also arose among Palestinians opposing Israeli occupation of what they perceive to be their homeland. Those killed in all stages of the resistance to Israel—but particularly those active in political movements—have been referred to by most Palestinians as martyrs. Suicide attacks began to be employed in the Palestinian-Israeli struggle in 1994 and were at the time very controversial among Palestinians. Were these necessary acts of desperation or a bona fide tactic in a war of the weak? That question led to discussions among religious leaders that only expanded after the September 11, 2001, Al-Qaeda terrorist attacks on the United States. Although these later were largely condemned by Muslim leaders, Palestinian suicide attacks were not, because of the conditions of the Israeli occupation and collective punishment and other tactics employed by the Israeli government. Sheikh Qaradawi, a popular Egyptian preacher who now lives in Qatar, has pronounced those who engage in such attacks in Palestine to be reacting under defensive jihad, justified by the Koran.

Some prominent Muslim religious leaders have given their public support for various types of martyrdom. Iranian leader Ayatollah Ruhollah Khomeini approved self-sacrifice by Iranian troops and citizens during the war against Iraq (1980–1988), when these forces, which included civilian volunteers, were forced to advance in human wave assaults against Iraqi defensive fire, in what would have to be classified as suicidal attacks. Other organizations that adopted the suicide/martyr method for attacks include Al-Qaeda, Abu Sayyaf, and a Bedouin group called Tawhid wa-l Jihad by the Egyptian security services, as well as the non-Islamist al-Aqsa Martyrs Brigades. Even Al-Qaeda leaders such as Sayf al-Adl indicate that they have sought to rein in the desire for suicide attacks by younger and less self-controlled members for, if such fervor were uncontrolled, there would be few operatives to run the movement.

Controversial aspects of the present-day link between jihad and martyrdom include the deaths of innocent civilian victims who are not the primary targets of such attacks. Extremist groups employing suicide attacks excuse these victims away as simply additional martyrs. There is also the issue of motivation—whether the suicide bombers are impelled to act by the wrong intent (niyah)—because if so, then they are not true martyrs. According to the companion of the Prophet and early caliph Umar, those waging jihad should not set out deliberately to die and become martyrs in an egotistical aim to be known as a hero. There is also a financial aspect to this, as those who engage in jihad (including those who are martyred) are enjoined not to leave their families without support or in debt. In contemporary times, would-be suicide martyrs sometimes ignore or reinterpret these rules or organizations promise to provide for their widows and families.

All of this has led to a serious effort to deradicalize by uncoupling the concepts as jihad and martyrdom within Muslim communities and by Muslim governments. While not uniform in approach and content, these attempts generally stress moderation and peaceful efforts rather than violence to change society. This task is extremely difficult where foreign occupation and military campaigns are ongoing, as in Pakistan, Afghanistan, and Iraq, but also in Saudi Arabia, where alliances with the United States are blamed for violence against Muslims.

Elliot Paul Chodoff and Sherifa Zuhur

See also: Al-Qaeda; Hezbollah (Party of God); Islamic Radicalism; Justification for the September 11 Suicide Mission; Pentagon Attack; Suicide Bombings; Terrorism

Further Reading

Ayoub, Mahmoud M. *Redemptive Suffering in Islam: A Study of the Devotional Aspects of "Ashura" in Twelver Shi'ism.* The Hague. Brill, 1978.

Gambetta, Diego, ed. *Making Sense of Suicide Missions.* Oxford: Oxford University Press, 2005.

Janes, Dominic and Alex Houen, ed. *Martyrdom and Terrorism.* Oxford: Oxford University Press, 2014.

Oliver, Anne Marie, and Paul Steinberg. *The Road to Martyrs' Square: A Journey into the World of the Suicide Bomber.* Oxford: Oxford University Press, 2005.

Shay, Shaul. *The Shahids: Islam and Suicide Attacks.* New Brunswick, NJ: Transaction Publishers, 2004.

Smith, Jane I., and Yvonne Haddad. *The Islamic Understanding of Death and Resurrection.* Albany: State University of New York Press, 1981.

McChrystal, Stanley A.

(1954–)

U.S. Army general and commander of U.S. forces in Afghanistan (2009–2010), Stanley McChrystal was born on August 14, 1954, and graduated from the U.S. Military Academy, West Point, in 1976. Commissioned a second lieutenant in the U.S. Army, his first assignment was with the 82nd Airborne Division. In 1978, he underwent Special Forces training at Fort Bragg, North Carolina. He commanded a detachment of the 7th Special Forces Group (Airborne) until 1980, when he attended the Infantry Officer Advanced Course at Fort Benning, Georgia.

Promoted to brigadier general in January 2001, McChrystal was the assistant division commander for operations of the 82nd Airborne Division in 2000–2001. During 2001–2002, he was chief of staff of the XVIII Airborne Corps. This assignment included duty as chief of staff of Combined Joint Task Force 180, the headquarters formation charged with direction of Operation Enduring Freedom, the U.S.-led invasion of Afghanistan. From July 2002, McChrystal was director of operations on the Joint Staff in Washington, D.C., where he delivered public briefings on the military situation during the U.S.-led invasion of Iraq.

In September 2003, McChrystal took command of the Joint Special Operations Command (JSOC), first as commanding general of JSOC from September 2003 to February 2006 and then as commander, JSOC/Commander, JSOC Forward, from February 2006 to August 2008. Although the command was situated at Fort Bragg, McChrystal spent most of his time in Afghanistan, Qatar, and Iraq.

McChrystal's Task Force 6-26 was subsequently accused of abuses in prisoner interrogations at Camp Nama in Baghdad, and five army rangers were ultimately convicted of prisoner abuses at the facility. McChrystal also came under criticism for his handling of details surrounding the death by friendly fire of ranger and former professional football player Pat Tillman in Afghanistan in 2004. Although McChrystal was one of eight officers recommended for disciplinary action in the affair, the army declined to take action against him.

In February 2006, McChrystal was promoted to lieutenant general. His colleagues described him as a warrior-scholar. His JSOC was widely praised for its ability to find and kill Iraqi insurgents, and some observers have stated that it, rather than the so-called surge, was largely responsible for the decline in violence in Iraq during 2007–2008.

McChrystal was nominated to direct the Joint Staff in February 2008, but his confirmation was held up for a time in the Senate over charges of mistreatment of detainees by forces under his command in Afghanistan and in Iraq. He took up his new post in August 2008.

On May 11, 2009, Secretary of Defense Robert Gates announced that he was recalling General David McKiernan, the top U.S. commander in Afghanistan, and nominating McChrystal as his replacement. McKiernan had held the post for less than a year and been instrumental in securing additional U.S. forces for Afghanistan. Although Gates said that McKiernan had done nothing wrong, he also said that "new leadership and fresh eyes" were needed. The announcement came less than one week after President Barack Obama's meeting with the leaders of Afghanistan and Pakistan, during which he pledged a more coordinated effort to fight Taliban forces in both countries. It is believed that a planned shift in favor of counterinsurgency as opposed to conventional operations, and the fact that McKiernan did not get on well with Central Command commander General David Petraeus, was the principal reason for McKiernan's ouster and McChrystal's selection.

On June 24, 2010, following a brief meeting with McChrystal at the White House, President Obama removed him from command of U.S. and NATO forces in Afghanistan. McChrystal had been recalled to Washington following the release of the copy of an article to appear in *Rolling Stone* magazine with highly critical comments by McChrystal and his staff of Obama, Vice President Joseph Biden, and other key members of the administration. The last time a U.S. president stepped in to remove a commander in the middle of a war was in April 1951, when President Harry S. Truman removed United Nations Command (UNC) commander in Korea, General Douglas MacArthur, over the general's all-too-public criticisms of U.S. policy. McChrystal's replacement was Central Command commander General David H. Petraeus, whose appointment sent a clear signal that the current U.S. strategy in Afghanistan would continue. McChrystal announced his retirement from the army shortly after his dismissal. Since his retirement, the former general has sat on several corporate boards, and joined Yale University's Jackson Institute for Global Affairs as a fellow.

McChrystal's memoir, *My Share of the Task*, was released on January 7, 2013. The autobiography had been scheduled for release in November 2012, but it was delayed because it lacked appropriate security clearance approvals required by the Department of Defense. On January 8, 2013, McChrystal appeared on MSNBC's *Morning Joe* program, endorsing stronger U.S. gun control laws, saying that assault weapons were for the battlefield, not schools or streets.

Spencer C. Tucker

See also: Counterinsurgency; Enduring Freedom, Operation; Gates, Robert Michael; Iraqi Freedom, Operation; Petraeus, David Howell; Taliban

Further Reading

Bumiller, Elisabeth, and Mark Massetti. "General Steps from Shadow." *New York Times*, May 13, 2009.

Schmitt, Eric, and Carolyn Marshall. "In Secret Unit's 'Black Room,' a Grim Portrait of U.S. Abuse." *New York Times*, March 19, 2006.

Woodward, Bob. "Why Did Violence Plummet? It Wasn't Just the Surge." *Washington Post*, September 8, 2008.

Military Tribunals

Military tribunals are special courts administered by the U.S. military to try enemy combatants accused of crimes that violate the accepted rules of war. The tribunals operate outside the civilian legal system and are not to be confused with military courts-martial, which are designed exclusively to try soldiers, sailors, and military officers accused of committing crimes while members of the military establishment. In military tribunals, military officers act as the prosecutors, defense attorneys, jurors, and judges. Most military tribunals operate on an inquisitorial system, in which judges and jurors actively participate in proceedings, including the questioning of suspects, witnesses, and other members of the court. In the United States, criminal cases are based on an adversarial system of justice in which the court remains above the proceedings as an impartial referee, while the prosecutors and defense attorneys ask questions and probe defendants and witnesses. The use of military tribunals became a hot-button issue in the United States after the September 11, 2001, terror attacks, which resulted in the global war on terror. Since then, dozens of

Guantánamo detainee Omar Khadr, left, sits alongside his defense team. Left to right, Muneer Ahmad, Rick Wilson, Marine lt. col. Colby Vokey, and Army capt. John Merriam, as Vokey addresses the robed presiding officer Marine col. Robert Chester, during a hearing inside the Military Commission, at Guantánamo Bay U.S. Naval Base, Cuba, on April 5, 2006. Cameras are not allowed in the courtroom, thus, only drawings (such as this one) may record the proceedings. (AP Photo/Brennan Linsley)

suspected terrorists in U.S. custody have been awaiting trial in U.S. military tribunals.

Military tribunals are by no means a new invention. Indeed, U.S. history has recorded their use as far back as the Revolutionary War, during which General George Washington convened one during the Benedict Arnold treason scandal. The courts were also used during the War of 1812, the Mexican-American War, the Civil War, the Philippine-American War, and World War II. The famous Nuremberg Trials convened to try war criminals were essentially military tribunals, organized by the Allied occupation powers in Germany during 1945 and 1946.

Beginning in early 2002, after a number of terror suspects had been captured by U.S. forces in Afghanistan and elsewhere, the George W. Bush administration began incarcerating these enemy combatants in a special prison located at the U.S. naval station at Guantánamo Bay, Cuba. For a number of years, the prisoners at Guantánamo Bay were held without formal charges being brought against them, and without access to defense lawyers or any written evidence against them. When some critics questioned the legality of this, the Bush administration insisted that the prisoners were not subject to U.S. constitutional safeguards because they were enemy combatants being detained during a time of war. Practically speaking, this meant that they were being held under the sole authority of the executive branch.

The intention was to try these individuals using military tribunals convened at

Guantánamo Bay, but no trials occurred until 2007; meanwhile, several challenges to the legality of the detention and tribunal system wound their way through the U.S. civilian justice system. In 2004, the U.S. Supreme Court decided that the Guantánamo Bay detainees were indeed subject to certain constitutional safeguards, including *habeas corpus*, or the right of a suspect to be formally charged with a crime in a court of law or be released if no evidence or charges can be brought. Two years later, the high court went even further, ruling that prisoners at Guantánamo Bay could not be tried by military tribunals because such proceedings circumvented the U.S. Constitution as well as the Geneva Conventions.

Nevertheless, in 2006, the Republican-controlled Congress enacted the Military Commissions Act of 2006, which authorized the president to unilaterally declare certain suspects as "unlawful enemy combatants." This would deny them *habeas corpus* protections and paved the way for the convening of military tribunals.

In 2007, several trials and proceedings were conducted by military tribunals at Guantánamo Bay. As a result, a handful of detainees were tried. David Hicks was convicted in 2007, and Salim Hamdan and Ali Hamza Al-Bahul were convicted in 2008. Also in 2008, the Supreme Court declared the 2006 Military Commission Act unconstitutional because it abrogated suspects' *habeas corpus* rights.

As a result of this, further trials were suspended. Al-Bahul won an appeal of his conviction in 2013, and another suspect—Mohamed Jawad—won a *habeas corpus* petition in a U.S. civilian court. Charges against him were dropped in 2009. When Barack Obama became president in January 2009, he signed an executive order that suspended indefinitely all activity by military tribunals. About the same time, evidence that some of the Guantánamo Bay suspects had been subjected to "enhanced" or coercive interrogation further clouded the legality of the proceedings against terror suspects. For a time, the Obama administration sought to close the Guantánamo Bay detention facility (which Obama had promised to do when he ran for the presidency in 2008), but that process has stalled because no viable sites have been found to house the prisoners. As of March 2014, 154 prisoners remained in Cuba.

The Obama administration has also voiced its preference for trying terror suspects in U.S. civilian criminal courts, but this has become highly politicized. It has also showcased the considerable logistical obstacles that would go along with trying terror suspects in civilian courts. For these reasons, no new trials have been held since 2008, and the Obama administration now seems to favor the use of military tribunals that would safeguard certain constitutional rights.

When it comes to the use of military tribunals, both detractors and adherents of these courts have sound reasoning for their positions. Detractors claim that the tribunals subvert the U.S. Constitution and the American justice system, potentially threaten the civil liberties of all citizens, send the wrong message to the rest of the world, and embolden foreign radicals to launch punitive strikes against American interests. They rightly point out that other terror suspects, including those who perpetrated the 1993 bombing of the World Trade Center, were tried in civilian courts with no difficulty. Supporters of the courts, however, claim that civilian trials would invite retaliation and therefore imperil the civilian court system, would promote overzealous media reporting, and would lead to the revelation of secret government information and informants that might jeopardize national security. In the end, it remains unclear when—and how—the U.S. government will move forward with the treatment of enemy combatants.

Paul G. Pierpaoli, Jr.

See also: Bush Administration; Coercive Interrogation Techniques; Global War on Terror; Guantánamo Bay Detainment Camp; Kill List; Nineteen Martyrs; Obama Administration; Terrorism; World Trade Center Bombing

Further Reading

Ball, Howard. *Bush, the Detainees, and the Constitution: The Battle over Presidential Power in the War on Terror.* Lawrence: University Press of Kansas, 2007.

Fisher, Louis. *Military Tribunals and Presidential Power: American Revolution to the War on Terrorism.* Lawrence: University Press of Kansas, 2005.

Schlueter, David A. *Military Justice: Practice and Procedure.* 7th ed. Dayton, OH: Lexis-Nexis, 2008.

Millennium Plots

Leaders of Al-Qaeda planned for a series of terrorist operations to take place on or around January 1, 2000. At least three plots surfaced during investigations in the months and weeks before the millennium. Khalid Sheikh Mohammed has claimed credit for planning and financing these plots, whose targets were in three different places—Amman, Jordan; Los Angeles, California; and Aden, Yemen. Fortunately, none of the plots was carried out, but the news clearly indicated that Al-Qaeda's leadership was busy concocting plots to the detriment of the United States. Al-Qaeda operatives had planned to bomb the Radisson Hotel in Amman, along with Christian tourist sites in and around the city on January 1, 2000, hoping to kill as many Americans as possible. Jordanian authorities, however, learned of the plot and raided the terrorists' bomb factory, which was hidden in an upper-middle-class residence. The terrorists had planned to use poisons and other improvised devices to increase the casualties of their attacks, planning to disperse hydrogen cyanide in a downtown Amman movie theater. News of this plot reached American officials in mid-1999.

The terrorists also plotted to plant a large bomb at the Los Angeles International Airport, a plan that originated in Canada among Muslim militants there. Ahmed Ressam tried to smuggle the explosives from Canada to the United States through the British Columbia–Washington Ferry Entry Point. An alert U.S. customs officer, Diana Dean, suspicious of Ressam's nervousness, pulled him over and had begun to check the vehicle when Ressam attempted to escape. Dean and fellow customs officers soon captured him, and an examination of his vehicle revealed a large quantity of explosives and a map of the Los Angeles International Airport. American authorities believed that Ressam would have received assistance from Al-Qaeda members in the Los Angeles area, but no proof of this has surfaced.

Finally, the terrorists planned a marine bombing intended to sink the destroyer USS *The Sullivans* at its berth in the port of Aden, Yemen. Al-Qaeda operatives overloaded a small boat with explosives, to the point of sinking, and nothing remained but to cancel the operation. Because of the covert nature of this operation—and because of its failure—American authorities did not learn about this plot until much later, after the October 12, 2000 attack on the USS *Cole*.

Stephen E. Atkins

See also: Al-Qaeda; Ressam, Ahmed; USS *Cole* Bombing

Further Reading

Clark, Richard. *Against All Enemies: Inside America's War on Terror.* New York: Free Press, 2004.

Loeb, Vernon. "Planned Jan. 2000 Attacks Failed or Were Thwarted; Plot Targeted U.S., Jordan, American Warship, Official Says." *Washington Post*, December 24, 2000.

Mohammed, Fazul Abdullah

(1972–2011)

Fazul Abdullah Mohammed was an Al-Qaeda operative from Somalia. He was born in 1972 in Moroni, the capital of the Comoros Islands. In 1990, he studied briefly in Saudi Arabia and then Pakistan, but soon quit school to move to Afghanistan, where he began training with Al-Qaeda. He then traveled to Sudan and the Horn of Africa, where he joined fellow Al-Qaeda operative Mohammed Saddiq Odeh in recruiting Somali militants for combat against U.S. and UN forces. Both men reportedly participated in the 1993 Battle of Mogadishu, in which Odeh boasted that he provided the rocket launchers and rifles that brought down two American helicopters (the infamous Blackhawk Down incident). Fazul and his associates were credited with introducing two Al-Qaeda tactical hallmarks to the Somali insurgency: suicide bombings and roadside improvised explosive devices (IEDs).

By 1996, Fazul was living in Nairobi with Wadih el Hage, the former personal secretary of Osama bin Laden and the head of Al-Qaeda's East Africa cell. Together they planned and executed the 1998 U.S. embassy bombings in Kenya and Tanzania. The operation, which involved the detonation of trucks loaded with TNT, left 224 people dead and thousands more wounded. The day marked Al-Qaeda's first attack on an American target and was one of the most devastating since Hezbollah's 1983 suicide assault on the Marine barracks in Beirut, Lebanon. Following the bombings, the Federal Bureau of Investigation (FBI) included Fazul in a list of 22 most wanted terrorists, issuing a $5 million bounty for information leading to his capture.

In 2001, Fazul traveled to Liberia with Ahmed Khalfan Ghailani, another suspect in the 1998 embassy attacks. There the two reportedly established financing deals in illegally traded diamonds to fund further Al-Qaeda operations. Fazul returned to Nairobi in August 2002, when he began planning another mission. Carried out in November of that year, the attack involved synchronized assaults on Israeli targets in Mombasa: one against a charter jet as it took off from Moi International Airport, and one against the Israeli-owned Paradise Hotel. The first, which involved surface-to-air missiles, failed; however, the second, which took the form of a suicide attack, killed 16 and injured 80.

When the Ethiopian army ousted Somalia's Council of Islamic Courts (CIC) in 2007, Fazul was believed to be living in Mogadishu. The following year he ventured to the Kenyan resort town of Mandali to be treated for a kidney condition. When intelligence reports revealed he was in the country, Kenyan officials raided his residence. He narrowly escaped and made his way back to Somalia. He continued to lead the Islamist insurgency, becoming a military commander for al-Shabaab, the youth movement of the CIC. In November 2009, Fazul was inaugurated as Al-Qaeda's top commander in East Africa in the Somali town of Kismayo following the death of his predecessor, Saleh Ali Saleh Nabhan.

On June 8, 2011, Fazul and another operative lost their way in northwestern Mogadishu and accidentally drove into a checkpoint manned by troops of Somalia's Transitional Federal Government. When the two men refused to identify themselves, the soldiers opened fire and killed them both. After the shoot-out, the soldiers searched the vehicle and discovered $40,000 in cash, laptop computers, and other equipment. U.S. officials confirmed Fazul's identity after carrying out DNA tests on his corpse, and Secretary of State Hillary Clinton announced his death as "a significant blow to Al-Qaeda, its extremist allies, and its operations in East Africa."

Elinor Kasting

See also: Al-Qaeda; Benghazi Attacks; Somalia, International Intervention

Further Reading

"Attacks against al-Qaeda Continue in Somalia." *MSNBC News*, September 1, 2007. http://www.msnbc.msn.com/id/16531987/#.TzsPiphPaao.

"Elusive Al-Qaeda Operative Was 'Real Deal.'" *CBS News*, February 11, 2009. http://www.cbsnews.com/stories/2007/01/10/world/main2347258.shtml.

Gatsiounis, Ioannis. "Somali Terror Group Curtailed." *Washington Times*, July 10, 2011.

Mango, Caroline, Paul Gitau, and Cyrus Ombati. "Top al-Qaeda Man Now Back in Africa." *Africa Press International*, August 4, 2008. http://africanpress.me/2008/08/04/top-al-qaeda-man-now-back-in-kenya/.

Omar, Hamsa. "Somali Soldier Who Killed al-Qaeda Leader Is Injured in Retaliatory Attack." *Bloomberg News*, August 17, 2011. http://www.bloomberg.com/news/2011-08-17/somali-soldier-who-killed-al-qaeda-leader-is-shot-in-retaliation.html.

Prestholdt, Jeremy. "Phantom of the Forever War: Fazul Abdullah Mohammed and the Terrorist Imaginary." *Public Culture* 21, no. 3 (Fall 2009).

"Profile: Fazul Abdullah Mohammed." *New York Times*, June 13, 2011.

Rajan, Karim, and Fred Mukinda. "Two Arrested as Top Terror Suspect Flees." *Daily Nation* (Kenya), August 30, 2008. http://www.nation.co.ke/News/-/1056/446582/-/tj2yrs/-/index.html.

Mohammed, Khalid Sheikh

(March 1, 1964 or April 14, 1965–)

Khalid Sheikh Mohammed is an Al-Qaeda terrorist and operative who played a major role in the planning and execution of the September 11, 2001, terror attacks on the United States. He was born either on March 1, 1964, or April 14, 1965, to a religious family in Kuwait, although he traces his ethnic origins to the Baluchistan region of Pakistan. He studied mechanical engineering in the United States at North Carolina Agricultural and Technological State University, from which he graduated in 1986. The next year, Mohammed joined his brother Zahid in Peshawar, Pakistan, where he took an assignment performing administrative tasks for Abdullah Azzam, the leader of the Maktab al-Khidimat (Jihad Service Bureau). There he became acquainted with Ayman al-Zawahiri and Azzam's protégé, Osama bin Laden, who financed the bureau's operations in Afghanistan.

Following the final Soviet withdrawal from Afghanistan in 1989, Mohammed's terrorist activities were limited until he learned of his nephew Ramzi Ahmed Yousef's plans to attack the United States. In the early 1990s, Omar Abdel-Rahman, known as the "blind Sheikh," a spiritual guide to the Islamic Jihad movement, settled in Brooklyn, New York, and became imam of three mosques in the New York City area. A follower of Rahman, Yousef was involved in the bombing of the World Trade Center in February 1993. Mohammed wired Yousef $600 for his role in the attack.

Following the 1993 bombing, Mohammed and Yousef traveled to the Philippines to collaborate on the so-called Bojinka Plot, in which Mohammed proposed hijacking twelve U.S. airliners and destroying them over the Pacific Ocean during a two-day period. Both Mohammed and Yousef secured and prepared the explosives to destroy the aircraft, and succeeded in blowing up a Philippine Airlines aircraft flying between Manila and Tokyo. Yousef was arrested by Pakistani authorities in an Al-Qaeda safe house after Philippine military officials discovered his bomb-making facilities. Mohammed, however, eluded capture and fled to Afghanistan, while Yousef was extradited to the United States. In 1997, Yousef was convicted for his role in the 1993 World Trade Center bombing and the Bojinka Plot.

In Afghanistan, Mohammed met with bin Laden and outlined his plans for multiple terror attacks against the United States. According to Mohammed's testimony, bin Laden was initially unconvinced that such a plot would succeed. Following the 1998 attacks on the U.S. embassies in Nairobi, Kenya, and Dar es Salaam, Tanzania, Mohammed, bin Laden, and bin Laden's confidant Muhammad Atef began planning the September 11 attacks on New York City and Washington, D.C. Initially, Mohammed's plan called for attacks on both the Eastern and Western seaboards of the United States. He later stated, however, that he wanted to strike at the economic and political centers of the United States: New York and Washington. On September 11, 2001, 19 members of Al-Qaeda hijacked four U.S. airliners and crashed two of them into the twin towers of the World Trade Center in New York; a third crashed into the Pentagon in Arlington, Virginia, while the fourth aircraft, the target of which was presumably either the White House or the Capitol building in Washington, D.C., crashed into a field in western Pennsylvania. In response, the United States went to war in October 2001 against the Taliban regime in Afghanistan, which had harbored bin Laden and Al-Qaeda. Mohammed, like the other Al-Qaeda principals, initially eluded capture by the United States.

On March 1, 2003, Mohammed was arrested in Pakistan and placed in the custody of the Central Intelligence Agency (CIA) until his transfer to Camp Justice at Guantánamo Bay, Cuba, in September 2006. According to the U.S. Department of Defense, he confessed to masterminding the September 11 attacks in addition to other activities during his Combatant Status Review Tribunal in March 2007. During the proceedings, he also admitted to having beheaded *Wall Street Journal* reporter Daniel Pearl in Karachi, Pakistan, with "his own right hand." It seems that Mohammed admitted to many more actions than he could have committed, however. It is also unclear to what degree his admissions were compromised by torture. The March tribunal revealed that Mohammed had been subjected to enhanced interrogation techniques, including "waterboarding," a total of 183 times.

On June 5, 2008, Mohammed faced Colonel Ralph Kohlmann, the chief judge of the military tribunals at Guantánamo Bay during the initial tribunal proceedings and rejected his military- and civilian-appointed attorneys. He informed Kohlmann that he wished to represent himself during the war crimes trial. According to the Associated Press, the judge warned Mohammed that he faced execution if convicted, to which he responded that he wanted to "die as a martyr." The Military Commissions Act of 2006 requires that in order to be convicted and given a death sentence, a panel of at least 12 officers of the U.S. Armed Forces must unanimously concur on the death sentence and that the president of the United States must ultimately authorize it. Mohammed pleaded guilty to the charges against him in December 2008, but since then the case has been repeatedly stalled because of procedural concerns. In 2009, the Obama administration announced that Mohammed and his codefendants would be tried in a civil court, but that move created more procedural problems, so in 2011, Mohammed was remanded to a military tribunal to be convened at Guantánamo Bay, Cuba. That trial began in May 2012, but has been hamstrung by difficulties and continues as of this writing.

Ojan Aryanfard

See also: Al-Qaeda; Bin Laden, Osama; Coercive Interrogation Techniques; Martyrdom; Military Tribunals; Nairobi, Kenya, Bombing of U.S. Embassy; Pentagon Attack; Terrorism; World Trade Center Bombing; World Trade Center, September 11, 2001

Further Reading

Gunaratna, Rohan. *Inside Al Qaeda: Global Network of Terror*. New York: Berkley Publishing Group, 2003.

Kepel, Gilles, and Jean-Pierre Milelli, eds. *Al Qaeda in Its Own Words*. Cambridge: Harvard University Press, 2008.

9/11 Commission. *The 9/11 Commission Report: Final Report of the National Commission on Terrorist Attacks upon the United States*. Authorized edition. New York: Norton, 2004.

Moussaoui, Zacarias

(May 30, 1968–)

One of several individuals accused of being the "twentieth member" of the suicide hijacking mission of September 11, 2001, Zacarias Moussaoui (Zakariyya Musawwi) was born on May 30, 1968, in St. Jean-de-Luz, near Narbonne, France, to Moroccan parents. During Moussaoui's youth, his family moved around France before finally settling down in Narbonne. Moussaoui spent a year in an orphanage and had frequent and furious arguments with his mother, forcing him to leave home in 1986. A good student, he easily passed his vocational baccalaureate. After passing entrance exams, he opted to study mechanical and electrical engineering at a school in Perpignan. Moussaoui transferred to the University of Montpellier's Economic and Social Administration program, but he had begun to tire of school when the Persian Gulf War began in January 1991.

The plight of Iraqi civilians and Palestinians concerned Moussaoui, and he became increasingly politicized. He had experienced racism in France, and his sympathy for Muslim causes increased. While at the University of Montpellier, he came into contact with Muslim students advocating extremist Islamist views. He made a six-month visit to London in

Zacarias Moussaoui, a French citizen of Moroccan descent, was charged as the "20th hijacker" in the September 11, 2001 terrorist attacks, thus becoming the only person charged in the United States in connection with the 9/11 attacks. In April 2005, Moussaoui pleaded guilty to charges that he had conspired to commit acts of terrorism transcending national boundaries, commit aircraft piracy, and murder government employees. (AFP/Getty Images)

1992, but his stay in England proved disillusioning; he claimed that he found British society intolerant and class ridden. This experience did not prevent him from returning to England, where he stayed for the next three years. He attended the South Bank University in London, studying international business. Moussaoui earned his degree in 1995 and moved back to Montpellier.

Some time during his stay in England, he was attracted to the salafi jihadist cause, perhaps by the militant Islamic teacher Abu Qatada in London. His behavior during visits to France and Morocco alarmed his family fearing that Al-Qaeda recruiters convinced him to join the terrorist group. They were correct in their assumption.

Between 1995 and 2001, Moussaoui's association with Al-Qaeda became even closer. He received training in Afghanistan at Al-Qaeda's Khaldan camp in 1998, at the same time as Mohamed Atta. Moussaoui's trainers found him enthusiastic but questioned his stability. He was finally recruited for a suicide mission, but little evidence exists to show that it was the September 11, 2001, plot. In the hope of becoming a pilot, Moussaoui entered the United States, arriving at Chicago's O'Hare Airport on February 23, 2001, with a 90-day visa. Within days of his arrival, he began learning to fly small aircraft at the Airman Flight School in Norman, Oklahoma, but he became frustrated by his lack of progress after failing the written examination. After looking at other pilot schools, Moussaoui contacted the Pan Am International Flight Academy in Eagan, Minnesota, near Minneapolis, hoping to learn how to fly the huge Boeing 747-400. After only a few days of training in mid-August, the school's instructors became suspicious of Moussaoui, who showed more interest in flying than in either taking off or landing. He also inquired about the protocols used for communicating with flight towers and asked about cockpit doors. After a meeting of Moussaoui's instructors, one volunteered to contact a friend in the Minneapolis Federal Bureau of Investigation (FBI) field office. Instead, the call went to FBI Special Agent Harry Samit, a U.S. Navy aviation veteran and small-engine pilot who was immediately suspicious of Moussaoui.

The Minneapolis FBI field office was part of the Joint Terrorism Task Force (JTTF) system, and a brief investigation showed that Moussaoui's visa had expired on May 22, 2001. This led the Immigration and Naturalization Service (INS) agent in the JTTF to authorize the arrest of Moussaoui on August 16, 2001. Moussaoui refused to allow the FBI agents to search his belongings but agreed to allow them to be taken to the local INS building. Because of Moussaoui's French citizenship, the FBI requested information concerning him from French authorities, who deemed Moussaoui dangerous and conveyed this to the FBI office in Minneapolis.

The Minneapolis FBI agents sought a search warrant to examine Moussaoui's belongings—in particular, his laptop computer—but ran into difficulties at FBI headquarters in Washington, D.C. FBI headquarters found insufficient cause for a criminal warrant. The agents' request for a court-issued warrant was denied because Moussaoui was not affiliated with a recognized terrorist group, even though Moussaoui had contacts with Chechen rebels and close ties to Al-Qaeda.

After the September 11 attacks, the political climate changed, and Moussaoui became a key target for retribution. U.S. federal prosecutors charged Moussaoui with capital crimes, accusing him of six acts: preparing acts of terrorism, conspiracy to hijack an aircraft, destruction of an aircraft, use of weapons of mass destruction, murder of American officials, and destruction of property, even though Moussaoui had been in jail for 25 days when the events of September 11 occurred. Moreover, doubt still lingered about Moussaoui's role in the September 11 plot. The FBI had difficulty in proving that had Moussaoui cooperated with authorities, the September 11 attacks could have been prevented.

Nevertheless, U.S. Attorney General John Ashcroft insisted that the Justice Department seek the death penalty. Opposition to this position arose within the Justice Department because a death sentence would make plea-bargaining impossible. Although Moussaoui had information about Al-Qaeda, no attempt was made to extract it from him.

Moussaoui's 2006 trial was a national event, and his irrational behavior and sudden guilty plea created even more controversy. It became apparent that Moussaoui sought martyrdom. During the sentencing, prosecutors argued for the death sentence, but in May 2006, a dubious jury handed him a life sentence without chance of parole instead, reflecting Moussaoui's alleged role as an Al-Qaeda operative who intended to commit acts of terror rather than any action he might actually have taken. Moussaoui is now serving his sentence at a federal maximum-security prison.

Stephen E. Atkins

See also: Al-Qaeda; Bin Laden, Osama; Pentagon Attack; Rowley, Coleen; World Trade Center, September 11, 2001

Further Reading

Graham, Bob. *Intelligence Matters: The CIA, the FBI, Saudi Arabia, and the Failure of America's War on Terror.* New York: Random House, 2004.

Hersh, Seymour. *Chain of Command: The Road from 9/11 to Abu Ghraib.* New York: HarperCollins, 2004.

Joint Inquiry into Intelligence Community Activities before and after the Terrorist Attacks of September 11, 2001. *Hearings before the Select Committee on Intelligence U.S. Senate and the Permanent Select Committee on Intelligence House of Representatives.* Vol. 2. Washington, DC: U.S. Government Printing Office, 2004.

Moussaoui, Abd Samar, with Florence Bouquillat. *Zacarias, My Brother: The Making of a Terrorist.* New York: Seven Stories, 2003.

Multi-National Force—Iraq

The Multi-National Force—Iraq (MNF-I) was a U.S.-led military command of coalition forces in Iraq, established on May 15, 2004, and concluded on December 31, 2011. It was created ostensibly to combat the growing Iraqi insurgency, which began in earnest in late 2003 and early 2004; it replaced Combined Joint Task Force 7, which had been in operation from June 2003 to May 2004.

Commanders of the MNF-I have included lieutenant generals Ricardo Sanchez (May–June 2004), George W. Casey (June 2004–January 2007), David Petraeus (January 2007–September 2008), and Raymond Odierno (September 2008–January 1, 2010). The MNF-I was tasked with bringing the growing Iraqi insurgency to an end but was largely unsuccessful in that effort until the George W. Bush administration placed General Petraeus in command and implemented a troop surge in the winter of 2007 that placed as many as 30,000 additional U.S. troops on the ground in Iraq. The strategy seemed to have worked, for violence had fallen off markedly beginning by late 2007; Petraeus was given much of the credit for this development. At the same time, the so-called Anbar Awakening groups in Iraq also helped to curb sectarian and insurgent violence. MNF-I commander, General Odierno, acknowledged that the surge provided strengthened security forces and credited a change in counterinsurgency strategy more than the surge itself in reducing the level of violence. Referring to it as an "Anaconda strategy," Odierno has explained the strategy as a comprehensive approach that yielded success in, among other areas, cutting off insurgents from their support within the Iraqi population.

Since its inception, the MNF-I was overwhelmingly comprised of U.S. troops; the second-largest deployment was from Great Britain. The size of the MNF-I was fluid, but on average it contained around 150,000 combat-ready personnel, the vast majority of whom have been American. The troop surge brought the total closer to 180,000, but that number dwindled steadily as troop withdrawals began in 2008. Working with the MNF-I, but not falling under its direct command, was the United Nations (UN) Assistance Mission–Iraq, which provided humanitarian aid and observation, and the North Atlantic Treaty Organization (NATO) Training Mission–Iraq, whose goal was to train Iraqi security, police, and military personnel. The major component parts of the MNF-I were Multi-National Security Transition Command; Gulf Region Division, U.S. Corps of Engineers; Joint Base Balad; Multi-National Corps–Iraq; Multi-National Division–Baghdad; Multi-National Division–North; Multi-National Force–West; Multi-National Division Center; and Multi-National Division–Southeast.

In addition to battling the Iraqi insurgency and other indigenous violence, other goals of the MNF-I included support and aid to the Iraqi government, postwar reconstruction efforts, specialized training of Iraqi military personnel, intelligence-gathering, and border patrols. The December 2008 Status of Forces Agreement between the U.S. and Iraqi governments stipulated that all U.S. troops be withdrawn by December 31, 2011. Under the terms of this arrangement, U.S. troops vacated Iraqi cities by July 31, 2009. The Iraqis concluded similar agreements with other coalition forces that still maintained a presence in Iraq. By May 2011, all non-U.S. coalition forces had been removed from Iraq. As scheduled, the last of the U.S. troops were withdrawn by December 18, 2011.

The participating members, along with the peak size of their deployments as of December 2008, included the United States (145,000 troops), Great Britain (4,000), Romania (500), Australia (350), El Salvador (300), and Estonia (40).

Numerous other nations supplied troops to the MNF-I, many of which were withdrawn by the end of December 2008. Those nations that participated but withdrew by December 31, 2008, included (figures in parentheses represent peak deployments): South Korea (3,600), Italy (3,200), Poland (2,500), Georgia (2,000), Ukraine (1,650), Netherlands (1,345), Spain (1,300), Japan (600), Denmark (545), Bulgaria (458), Thailand (423), Honduras (368), Dominican Republic (302), Czech Republic (300), Hungary (300), Azerbaijan (250), Albania (240), Nicaragua (230), Mongolia (180), Singapore (175), Norway (150), Latvia (136), Portugal (128), Lithuania (120), Slovakia (110), Bosnia-Herzegovina (85), Macedonia (77), New Zealand (61), Tonga (55), Philippines (51), Armenia (46), Kazakhstan (29), Moldova (24), and Iceland (2).

To entice potential coalition partners to join the MNF-I effort, the U.S. government offered a plethora of financial aid and other incentives. Because the invasion of Iraq had not been sanctioned by the UN, the United States found it more difficult to convince other nations to become involved in the postwar stabilization effort in Iraq. Some nations, previously close allies, refused to take part in the mission, despite U.S. promises of financial and other rewards. The United States reportedly offered Turkey up to $8.5 billion in loans if the country sent peacekeeping troops to Iraq; Turkey, which had forbade the use of its bases during the March 2003 invasion of Iraq, demurred. France and Germany refused any participation in Iraq. Some countries, such as Great Britain and Australia, were offered lucrative private-contractor business that would help fuel their economies. The Bush administration, however, refused to acknowledge that there were any quid pro quo arrangements in the assembling of international forces in Iraq.

President Barack Obama, who took office in January 2009 and who had campaigned on a pledge to end American involvement in Iraq as quickly as possible, made certain that the December 2008 Status of Forces Agreement was adhered to scrupulously. Indeed, by December 18, 2011, almost two weeks ahead of schedule, all American troops had been withdrawn from the country. Unfortunately, a renewed sectarian-based insurgency has reignited in Iraq since the MNF-I completed its mission. Violence, including bombings, kidnappings, assassinations, and mass murder, accelerated rapidly during 2012–2013, and by early 2014, Iraq was poised on the precipice of a full-scale civil war. By January 2014, Al-Qaeda and allied forces had taken over large parts of Anbar Province. The government of Nuri al-Maliki, meanwhile, appeared unable to quash the building insurrection.

Paul G. Pierpaoli, Jr.

See also: Al-Qaeda; Counterinsurgency; Iraqi Freedom, Operation; Petraeus, David Howell

Further Reading

Cockburn, Patrick. *The Occupation: War and Resistance in Iraq.* New York: Verso, 2007.

Keegan, John. *The Iraq War: The Military Offensive, from Victory in 21 Days to the Insurgent Aftermath.* New York: Vintage, 2005.

N

Nairobi, Kenya, Bombing of U.S. Embassy

(August 7, 1998)

On August 7, 1998, the U.S. embassy compound in Nairobi, Kenya, was bombed by Al-Qaeda terrorists. The bombing occurred almost simultaneously with an Al-Qaeda bombing of the U.S. embassy in Dar es Salaam, Tanzania. The two bombings were among the largest terrorist attacks on U.S. interests to date, and precipitated a military response by the United States in the form of Operation Infinite Reach, which took place on August 20, 1998. The retaliatory action featured cruise missile strikes on terrorist camps in Afghanistan and an attack on the El Shifa pharmaceutical factory in Khartoum, Sudan.

In retrospect, the embassy bombings in Kenya and Tanzania were part of an escalating spiral of violence involving Al-Qaeda terrorists. After President Bill Clinton's administration struck Sudan and Afghanistan with Tomahawk cruise missiles, Al-Qaeda leader Osama bin Laden vowed revenge in the way of a spectacular attack on American interests. This came about on U.S. soil during the September 11, 2001, attacks that destroyed the World Trade Center in New York, damaged the Pentagon in Virginia, and forced the crash of another jetliner in rural Pennsylvania.

The destruction of the embassy in Nairobi was precipitated by a well-placed truck bomb and—it is believed—at least two determined suicide bombers. Timing their mission with the one occurring in Dar es Salaam, the suicide bombers struck at about 10:30 a.m. local time, or 3:30 a.m. Washington, D.C., time. The truck was apparently driven up to the rear entrance of the building. The detonation severely damaged the structure, which had to be torn down and rebuilt.

The death toll, which was staggering, included 200 Kenyans and 12 Americans. More than 4,000 people were injured, including 10 Americans and 12 foreign service nationals. The death toll was much higher in Nairobi than in Dar es Salaam for two principal reasons. First, the truck carrying the explosives to the Nairobi embassy was able to gain access to the inner embassy compound, which was not the case in Dar es Salaam. Second, the Nairobi embassy was in a densely populated area close to the center of the city, so when the bomb detonated, there were far more collateral casualties.

The resultant investigation of the bombings, which included the Federal Bureau of Investigation (FBI), concluded that bin Laden had approved the attacks. The U.S. government subsequently issued indictments against him and offered a $5 million reward for his capture. In addition, for the first time, he was placed on the FBI's

"Ten Most Wanted" list. In 2001, four men were convicted in a U.S. federal court in New York City, which heard impassioned testimony from the families of the victims. Two of the men, Khalfan Khamis Muhammad of Tanzania and Muhammad Rashid Daud al-Awhali of Saudi Arabia, had some direct role in the bombings and could have received the death penalty, but the jury could not reach a unanimous decision. The two others convicted were Muhammad Sadiq Awdeh, allegedly the adviser to the bombers, and Wadih al-Hage, an American who was convicted of being Al-Qaeda's leader in Nairobi. Their pleas for reduced sentences were rejected. All four were ordered to pay $7 million to the victims and $26 million to the U.S. government.

In October 2008, charges were brought against a Guantánamo Bay, Cuba, detainee, Tanzanian Ahmad Khaffan Gailani, to be tried in a special military tribunal for his role in the attack in Dar es Salaam. Rashid Swailah Hemed was acquitted in 2004 after a several years' trial in Tanzania.

In response to the bombings, President Clinton pledged to wage a war on terrorism. On August 20, 1998, the United States launched cruise missiles against terrorist camps in Afghanistan, where bin Laden was believed to reside, and the El Shifa pharmaceutical factory. The factory was a target because of allegations that bin Laden had some connection to it, which proved false, and because of allegations that the facility might have been producing nerve gas that was being shipped to Iraq. This latter claim was based on a soil sample; however pesticide decomposition can also produce the same trace chemical that was suspected.

The attacks in Afghanistan killed at least 20 people but failed to kill bin Laden. The attack on the plant in Sudan was severely criticized because it killed at least 20 people and because it had been producing pharmaceuticals necessary for Sudan to fight malaria and tuberculosis, among other diseases. These retaliatory U.S. strikes precipitated massive protests around the world, mostly in Muslim nations.

The U.S. State Department Bureau of Intelligence and Research had questioned the intelligence that linked El Shifa to bin Ladin in a report to Secretary of State Madeleine Albright prior to the attack, but it was disregarded. Some of Clinton's detractors charged that he ordered the strikes to take the public's attention off the Monica Lewinsky scandal. Just three days prior to the cruise missile strikes, Clinton had been forced to admit that he had had an affair with Lewinsky, a former White House intern.

On October 5, 2013, Nazih Abdul-Hamed al-Ruqai (also known as Abu Anas al-Libi) was captured by U.S. troops in Libya and subsequently indicted for planning the 1998 bombings of the U.S. embassies in Tanzania and Kenya. The operation, carried out by U.S. Special Forces, represented a rare foray by the U.S. military into the controversial practice of whisking terrorism suspects out of countries with which Washington does not have an extradition treaty. The Libyan government condemned what it called the "kidnapping" of one of its citizens, who was taken into custody outside his home in Tripoli.

Paul G. Pierpaoli, Jr.

See also: Al-Qaeda; Bin Laden, Osama; Clinton Administration; Dar es Salaam, U.S. Embassy Bombing; Islamic Radicalism; Terrorism; World Trade Center, September 11, 2001

Further Reading

Ferguson, Amanda. *The Attack against the U.S. Embassies in Kenya and Tanzania.* New York: Rosen, 2003.

Labévière, Richard. *Dollars for Terror: The United States and Islam*. New York: Algora, 2000.

Obwogo, Subiri. *The Bombs That Shook Nairobi & Dar es Salaam: A Story of Pain and Betrayal*. Nairobi: Obwogo and Family, 1999.

Nairobi, Kenya, Shopping Mall Attack

Beginning on September 21, 2013, the radical Islamist group known as al-Shabaab perpetrated a three-day terrorist attack against civilians in an upscale shopping mall in Nairobi, Kenya. The attack claimed the lives of at least 72 people, many of whom were foreign nationals or visitors. The death toll included 61 civilians, 5 attackers, and 6 Kenyan security officers. More than 200 other people were wounded. Al-Shabaab, which is operational in Somalia, is a cell of the radical Islamist terror organization known as Al-Qaeda. By the time of the attack, al-Shabaab controlled numerous areas in southern Somalia, where it had invoked sharia law. Al-Shabaab, which openly claimed responsibility for the attack, claimed that the killings were in retaliation for the Kenyan military's intervention in Somalia, which was part of a larger multinational effort to defeat al-Shabaab and restore some semblance of reasonable law and order to the war-torn nation.

Around noon on September 21, about 15 masked assailants began the attack on Westgate Mall. Some witnesses claimed that the shooting began even before the men had entered the mall, and at least one victim was later found dead near his car close to one of the mall's entrances. The men wore combat fatigues and carried automatic assault rifles. Some may also have carried hand grenades, as there were several reports of small explosions within the mall during the three-day standoff. The perpetrators hailed from several different countries. Kenyan police and military personnel responded quickly to the attack and had sealed off the mall by nightfall on September 21. By then the assailants were holding a number of shoppers hostage within the mall. In the end, more than 1,000 hostages would be rescued.

Intermittent arms fire continued until the evening of September 23, when it stopped, but it began again in the predawn hours of September 24. By then, all of the remaining hostages had been removed from the complex, and soldiers were conducting a careful sweep of the mall's interior. British and U.S. intelligence agents were reportedly involved in the stand-off as it neared an end. By early evening on September 24, the mall had been secured and Kenyan authorities had arrested 9 to 10 terrorists; the others are presumed dead.

A number of eyewitnesses reported that before the attack began, the terrorists instructed Muslims to leave the mall and asserted that only non-Muslims would be targeted. To determine if shoppers were indeed Muslim, some of the assailants asked people pointed questions that only Muslims were likely able to answer. The Associated Press (AP) termed the terrorists' effort as a "meticulous vetting process." The Nairobi mall attack was the worst terrorist incident in Kenya since the 1998 al-Qaeda bombing of the U.S. Embassy in Nairobi, when 224 people were killed. The Kenyan government received help from numerous countries and international organizations during its in-depth investigation of the attack. In November 2013, the Kenyan government charged four Somali nationals for having harbored the slain gunmen in their homes prior to the attack.

Paul G. Pierpaoli, Jr.

A security officer helps a wounded woman outside the Westgate Mall in Nairobi, Kenya, on September 21, 2013. Extremists had opened fire and threw grenades throughout the upscale shopping center. (AP Photo/Khalil Senosi)

See also: Al-Qaeda; Nairobi, Kenya, Bombing of U.S. Embassy; Terrorism

Further Reading

Bariyo, Nicholas, Heidi Vogt, and Cassell Bryan-Low. "Kenya Starts Probe in Wake of Mall Siege." *Wall Street Journal*, September 25, 2013. http://online.wsj.com/article/SB100014240527023045262045790967134971610 06.html.

Blair, Edmund. "Islamists Claim Gun Attack on Nairobi Mall, at Least 39 Dead." Reuters, September 21, 2013. http://www.reuters.com/article/2013/09/21/us-kenya-attack-idUSBRE98K03V20130921.

Narcoterrorism

Term used to describe terrorist-like tactics employed by narcotic traffickers to intimidate local populations and exert influence on governmental antidrug policies. The term "narcoterrorism" is credited to Fernando Belaúnde Terry, former president of Peru, who used it in a speech in 1983. He employed the descriptive when referring to the aggressive tactics used by his nation's drug traffickers and the rebel group Sendero Luminoso (Shining Path) against Peruvian antinarcotic police squads. In its original connotation, narcoterrorism referred to the tactics used by drug traffickers and dealers that often resembled terrorism.

Narcoterrorism was designed to keep local populations in fear, thus reducing the chances that they would cooperate with police, and to influence government policy that might be detrimental to the drug trade. Perhaps the most infamous of all narcoterrorists was the late Pablo Escobar, leader of the Medellin drug cartel in Colombia and considered one of the most ruthless outlaws of modern times. His narcoterrorism included the murder of at least 30 judges, more than 450 policemen, and as many as 500 other people. In more recent years, narcoterrorism has also been used to describe more traditional terror organizations that rely upon drug trafficking to fund their activities and recruit new members. Some of these include the Revolutionary Armed Forces of Colombia (FARC), the United Self-Defense Forces of Colombia (AUC), and the National Liberation Army of Colombia (ELN).

The U.S. government's war on drugs, which has been ongoing for several decades, was given a large boost in 1988 with the formation of the Office of National Drug Control Policy, the director of which is commonly referred to as the U.S. drug czar. Through this office, the U.S. government has centralized its antidrug efforts, including those in the United States and abroad. Although little is said about such programs, the United States routinely cooperates with other nations in drug interdiction efforts, and some even include the limited use of U.S. military troops and specially trained antidrug units.

In 1998, the United States became involved in major paramilitary efforts in Colombia (referred to as Plan Colombia) to destroy drug crops there and to detain and arrest drug traffickers who were aiding rebel and terrorist groups within Colombia. Since the September 11, 2001, terror attacks in the United States, the federal government has stepped up its antidrug efforts overseas, fearing that terrorist groups of all stripes might be using the lucrative drug trafficking business to fund their activities and recruit members.

The opium trade in Afghanistan helped fuel rebel groups there well before the September 11 attacks, and as Afghanistan has grown more unstable in the years after the overthrow of the Taliban, opium production is again on the rise. The opium crop is undoubtedly being exploited by elements in the Afghan government and also being employed by Afghan insurgents to secure funds with which to purchase arms and supplies, so the nation is becoming a part of narcoterrorism.

Drug trafficking certainly funds some Taliban activities. In addition, the radical organizations Hamas and Hezbollah have been identified with drug-smuggling activities. Programs aimed at curbing the international drug trade have become an integral part of the global war on terror.

Although Al-Qaeda is often said to finance its activities through drug trafficking, the *9/11 Commission Report* notes that "while the drug trade was a source of income for the Taliban, it did not serve the same purpose for al Qaeda, and there is no reliable evidence that bin Laden was involved in or made his money through drug trafficking."

Paul G. Pierpaoli, Jr.

See also: Al-Qaeda; Hezbollah (Party of God); Global War on Terror; Terrorism

Further Reading

Friman, H. Richard. *Narcodiplomacy: Exporting the U.S. War on Drugs*. Ithaca, NY: Cornell University Press, 1996.

Tarazona-Sevillano, Gabriela. *Sendero Luminoso and the Threat of Narcoterrorism*. New York: Praeger, 1990.

Valentine, Douglas. *The Strength of the Wolf: The Secret History of America's War on Drugs*. London: Verso, 2004.

Nashiri, Abd al-Rahim al-

Abd al-Rahim al-Nashiri (also known as Mullah Bilal Umar Mohammed al-Harazi, Abu Bilal al-Makki, Rahman Hussein al-Saafani, Abu al-Mohsin, Abu al-Hasan, Omar Mohammed al-Harazi, Khalid al-Safani, or Amm Ahmad) was born on January 1, 1965, in Mecca, Saudi Arabia. He is the alleged mastermind behind the 2000 attack on the USS *Cole* as well as the 2002 suicide strike on the M/V *Limburg*, and is also thought to have been the main strategic planner for Al-Qaeda's maritime operations.

Little is known about al-Nashiri's early life other than his participation in the Afghan mujahideen campaign against the Soviet Union during the 1980s. Some accounts state that he met Osama bin Laden during this time and stayed with him until after Moscow's withdrawal; others report that al-Nashiri did not meet bin Laden until the 1990s and, when asked to join Al-Qaeda, initially refused, considering the obligation to swear an oath of allegiance to be distasteful.

In 1997, al-Nashiri returned to Afghanistan and again refused to join bin Laden's organization. Instead, he fought with the Taliban against the Northern Alliance, although he did help with Al-Qaeda's weapons-smuggling efforts and is thought to have arranged for at least one Jordanian terrorist to obtain a passport. U.S. officials also allege that al-Nashiri was responsible for training the operatives that carried out the 1998 twin attacks on the U.S. embassies in Nairobi and Dar es Salaam. Although this has never been proven, one of the suicide bombers involved in the operation, Jihad Ali al-Makki (also known as Azzam), is believed to have been a relative of al-Nashiri, either a brother or a cousin.

Al-Nashiri apparently joined Al-Qaeda sometime around 1998–1999, reporting directly to bin Laden. It was at this time that he conceived of a plan to attack American ships in Yemen, which was both approved and funded. The first mission, launched against the USS *The Sullivans* in January 2000 as part of the millennium plots, failed, as the vessel carrying the suicide bombers and their explosives was overloaded and sank. The next attempt, against the USS *Cole* (October 2000), was successful, however, crippling the Arleigh Clarke–class destroyer warship and leaving 17 U.S. sailors dead and many more injured. The attack brought al-Nashiri greater prominence in Al-Qaeda, and he was made the organization's head of operations on the Arabian Peninsula.

In 2002, al-Nashiri masterminded another highly publicized suicide bombing, this time against the M/V *Limburg* (since renamed the *Maritime Jewel*)—a French-registered oil tanker transiting through the Gulf of Aden. Although the attack did not result in a large loss of life (only one crew member died), it triggered a temporary spike in worldwide petroleum prices, caused a short-term collapse of international shipping in the waters around Yemen, and underscored Al-Qaeda's stated intention of waging an economic war against the West.

The M/V *Limburg* incident was to be followed by further attacks on oil tankers passing through the Strait of Hormuz and on American and British warships in the Strait of Gibraltar. In addition, it is believed that al-Nashiri was looking into the feasibility of carrying out suicide bombings on cruise ships. However, before any of these operations could come to fruition, al-Nashiri was captured in the United Arab Emirates in November 2002. He was transferred to an undisclosed location, where he was interrogated and allegedly tortured. In 2004, a Yemeni court sentenced al-Nashiri to death in absentia for his role in the USS *Cole* bombing. Four years later, he was sent to the U.S. detention facility in Guantánamo Bay, Cuba, where he remains in prison while U.S. authorities decide whether to try him in a military or civilian court. Since then, procedural delays, motions filed by his defense counsel, and mental health evaluations have all conspired to delay the start of al-Nashiri's trial

Horacio Trujillo

See also: Al-Qaeda; USS *Cole* Bombing

Further Reading

"Suspected Al Qaeda Chief Cooperating." *CBS News*, November 22, 2002. http://www.cbsnews.com/stories/2002/11/17/attack/main529656.shtml.

United States Department of Defense. "Summary of Evidence for Combatant Status Review Tribunal—Al Nashiri, Abd Al Rahim Hussein Mohammad," March 14, 2007. http://www.defenselink.mil/news/ISN10015.pdf#1.

"U.S. Drops Guantanamo Charges per Obama's Order." Reuters, February 6, 2009.

National Commission on Terrorist Attacks upon the United States (9/11 Commission)

The creation of an independent commission to inquire into all aspects of the terror attacks of September 11, 2001, was prompted because of the stark limitations of earlier congressional inquiries. Congress's Joint Inquiry on Intelligence had outlined serious deficiencies in governmental intelligence-gathering and interagency cooperation, but the White House had refused to turn over documents to the investigators, citing constitutional separation of powers. Senator John McCain described the process as "slow-walked and stonewalled." A more in-depth inquiry into the policy miscalculations of the George W. Bush and Bill Clinton administrations engendered partisanship and found Republicans and Democrats attacking the other party's administration. The best way to mitigate such issues was to create an independent, bipartisan commission having unlimited access to all documents and officials.

However, conflicting interests caused delays in forming such a commission. The Bush administration was reluctant to support such a commission, fearing that it would concentrate chiefly on mistakes made during its tenure. Democrats feared a witch hunt for errors made during the Clinton administration. Intense pressure from the families of those killed during the attacks finally forced the creation of the commission. The survivors of the dead made it plain to all involved that they wanted an immediate investigation of the events surrounding September 11, but it was not until 14 months after the attacks that the 9/11 Commission was announced.

The National Commission on Terrorist Attacks upon the United States, or the 9/11 Commission, received a mandate from the president of the United States and the U.S. Congress to investigate the facts and circumstances of the attacks on the United States that occurred on September 11, 2001. Legislative authority for this commission was given by Public Law 107-306,

Thomas H. Kean, left, chairman of the National Commission on Terrorist Attacks upon the United States, and family members of victims of the attacks of September 11, 2001, at the start of the second day of hearings before the commission on April 1, 2003 in New York. The hearings were to assist the commission in their mandate to provide an authoritative account of the September 11 attacks and recommendations as to how to prevent such attacks in the future. (AP Photo/Tina Fineberg)

signed by President Bush on November 27, 2002. The five Republicans and five Democrats selected for this commission were a matter of some controversy. President Bush selected Henry Kissinger, once Richard Nixon's secretary of state, to chair the committee, and Senator Tom Daschle appointed George Mitchell, former Senate majority leader and chief negotiator of the Northern Ireland Peace Accords, as vice chair.

These appointees soon encountered political difficulties. The families of the victims confronted Kissinger about his consulting firm's clients, some of whom were suspected to be Saudis and even, possibly, the bin Laden family. Responding to pressure, the Senate Ethics Committee ruled that the members of the commis-

sion had to abide by congressional rules on the disclosure of possible conflicts of interest, which meant that Kissinger had to disclose his entire client list. He was unwilling to do so and resigned from the commission. Mitchell encountered the same problem with the client list of his law firm, so he, too, resigned from the commission. President Bush then turned to the well-respected former governor of New Jersey, Thomas H. Kean, and Senator Tom Daschle to former Indiana congressman Lee H. Hamilton. Neither Kean nor Hamilton had prior dealings with each other, but they soon began to work well together.

The final members of the commission were Thomas H. Kean (chair), Lee H. Hamilton (vice chair), Richard

Ben-Veniste, Fred F. Fielding, Slade Gorton, Max Cleland, John F. Lehman, Timothy J. Roemer, and James R. Thompson. Midway through the commission's deliberations, Cleland left the commission for a government job and was replaced by Bob Kerrey. In the interests of bipartisanship, Kean made Hamilton cochair.

The families of the victims maintained the momentum behind the creation of the 9/11 Commission, championing its subpoena powers by lobbying members of Congress and even the White House. These representatives formed the 12-member Family Steering Committee (FSC). Members of the FSC came mainly from four organizations: Families of September 11, Voices of September 11th, the Skyscraper Safety Campaign, and September 11th Advocates. Soon after the creation of the 9/11 Commission, representatives from the FSC met with Kean and Hamilton to express their desire for the commission to move swiftly and aggressively. They presented to Kean and Hamilton a document titled *September 11 Inquiry: Questions to Be Answered*, which consisted of 57 questions about 9/11 that reflected their greatest desire: accountability.

Almost immediately, the 9/11 Commission began to work with Philip Zelikow, who had a reputation as a presidential historian and who was the director of the Miller Center of Public Affairs at the University of Virginia. Zelikow's Republican connections included work on the National Security Council of President George H. W. Bush and on the transition team of the National Security Council of President George W. Bush. His coauthorship of a book with Condoleezza Rice on German unification, as well as his relationship with Stephen Hadley, the national security adviser, made Democratic commissioners leery of him. Members of the FSC were also unhappy with his selection and petitioned to have him removed. Both Kean and Hamilton, however, had confidence in his integrity, and he stayed. Zelikow became the mainstay of the 9/11 investigation, supervising the 80-person staff and playing a major decision-making role.

Much criticism was also directed at the composition of the 9/11 Commission staff, at least half of which was drawn from the agencies the commission was tasked to investigate. This raised worries that evidence would be looked at in a light that would exonerate the agencies and people implicated. Some critics feared that the 9/11 Commission was doomed—if not designed to fail: the commission would splinter down partisan lines; lose its credibility by leaking classified information; be denied the necessary access to do its job; or alienate the 9/11 families who had fought on behalf of its creation.

Although the 9/11 Commission had broad subpoena powers, it used these judiciously and only against those unwilling or unable to produce necessary documents. The most notorious offenders were the Federal Aviation Administration (FAA) and the North American Aerospace Defense Command (NORAD), both of which were so reluctant to produce documents regarding the events of September 11 that the commission was forced to subpoena documents from them. Both agencies complied with the subpoenas—which also acted as a warning to the White House to produce its own documents when required.

In its analysis of the failures to detect the September 11 conspiracy, the 9/11 Commission listed four contributing factors: (1) a "failure of imagination" to even conceive of the possibility of such an operation, (2) a "failure of capabilities" that allowed Al-Qaeda to operate in the United States despite agencies designed to prevent just such activity, (3) a "failure of management" by national security leaders whose agencies neither shared information nor collaborated in their activities, and (4) a "failure of policy" by both the Clinton and Bush administrations to prioritize counterterrorism.

The 9/11 Commission not only criticized the failures leading to September 11, but also made a series of recommendations. Among these recommendations were a National Counterterrorism Center, a national intelligence director, the reform of congressional oversight of national security, reform within the Federal Bureau of Investigation (FBI), more transparent levels of information sharing between government agencies, and smoother transitions between presidential administrations. It did recognize, however, that not all of its recommendations would find approval in both the White House and Congress.

In the course of the commission's investigations, members of the commission and its staff reviewed 2.5 million documents and interviewed more than 1,200 individuals in 10 countries. Nineteen days of public hearings and the testimony of 160 witnesses informed its investigation, but from the beginning, the commission was under pressure to achieve its objectives in a short time. Its request for an extension was greeted with little enthusiasm because the report would be produced too near to the 2004 presidential election. An extension of two months was granted, but still too little time remained to answer all the questions posed.

Stephen E. Atkins

See also: Able Danger; Atta, Mohamed el-Amir Awad el-Sayed; Bush Administration; Clinton Administration; Pentagon Attack; World Trade Center, September 11, 2001

Further Reading

Kean, Thomas H., Lee H. Hamilton, and Benjamin Rhodes. *Without Precedent: The Inside Story of the 9/11 Commission*. New York: Knopf, 2006.

May, Ernest R., ed. *The 9/11 Report with Related Documents*. Boston: Bedford, 2007.

Strasser, Steven ed. *The 9/11 Investigations: Staff Reports of the 9/11 Commission; Excerpts from the House-Senate Joint Inquiry Report on 9/11; Testimony from 14 Key Witnesses, including Richard Clarke, George Tenet, and Condoleezza Rice*. New York: PublicAffairs, 2004.

National Geospatial-Intelligence Agency

National Geospatial-Intelligence Agency (NGA) is the primary U.S. government agency responsible for mapmaking, imagery analysis, and geographic intelligence. Established in 2004, it is the product of more than two centuries of U.S. government involvement in geography and cartography that may be said to have begun with the U.S. Army's Lewis and Clark Expedition of 1803.

In the 1800s, the U.S. Army developed some of the country's first mapmaking capabilities, producing both large-scale and small-scale maps. The U.S. Navy developed a similar tradition for producing naval charts. Throughout the 1800s, maps and charts remained the principal focus of specialty units within these branches of the service, although some functions were gradually passed to civilian agencies, such as the U.S. Geological Survey (USGS), which was established in 1879.

During Operation Desert Storm, the organization produced more than 60 million maps. Although some were out of date and distribution problems arose, this marked a significant step forward. Likewise, imagery analysts processed unprecedented numbers of images, although delays in transmitting intelligence information to tactical units posed a problem. The development of smaller and lighter Global Positioning Systems (GPS) allowed troops to more accurately determine their locations. Cartographers developed sophisticated digital elevation models (DEMs), computer-generated 3-D terrain maps based on latitude, longitude, and elevation that are critically important to the guidance systems of smart weapons such as the Tomahawk cruise missile. These geospatial developments enabled the U.S. Navy to fire cruise missiles from the Persian Gulf and hit specific windows in targeted buildings in Baghdad. In the years following Desert Storm, the DMA systematically updated its regional maps for the Middle East and helped improve the distribution system, while other agencies refined the distribution process for imagery intelligence.

The September 11, 2001, terrorist attacks and subsequent combat in Afghanistan and Iraq provided the catalyst for further developments. The NGA continues to refine the technology that guided cruise missiles to Baghdad in 1991, making it increasingly available for frontline ground units. For instance, many units can now view DEMs of urban neighborhoods as they prepare and conduct combat operations. NGA personnel developed the Gridlock system to link intelligence, surveillance, and reconnaissance information to geospatial points, thus adding the capacity to provide tactical units with information that they can exploit on short notice. The NGA also assists in the development of precision-guided mini-munitions. A 500-pound bomb may be appropriate for bunkers and armored vehicles, but is not appropriate against a pickup truck driven by a terrorist, especially when civilians are in the vicinity. The development of mini-munitions allows troops to destroy hostile targets while reducing the likelihood of killing innocent civilians. This reduces the number of people likely to join the insurgents in pursuit of revenge.

The National Security Agency (NSA), which engages in signals intelligence (SIGINT), describes itself as the "ears of the nation." Likewise, the NGA sees itself as the "eyes of the nation." Geography is a holistic discipline, so it is not surprising that NGA personnel actively promote interagency cooperation, perhaps realizing that eyes and ears work better when they work together.

The NGA was credited by White House and military officials with providing critical information in support of Operation Neptune's Spear on May 2, 2011, in which the United States military raided a secret compound in Abbottabad, Pakistan, and killed Al-Qaeda leader Osama bin Laden.

Chuck Fahrer

See also: Al-Qaeda; Bin Laden, Osama; Central Intelligence Agency; Defense Intelligence Agency

Further Reading

Beck, Richard A. "Remote Sensing and GIS as Counterterrorism Tools in the Afghanistan War: A Case Study of the Zhawar Kili Region." *Professional Geographer* 55, no. 2 (May 2003): 170–79.

DeMers, Michael. *Fundamentals of GIS*. 3rd ed. Hoboken, NJ: Wiley, 2004.

Doty, John M. "Geospatial Intelligence: An Emerging Discipline in National Intelligence with an Important Security Assistance

Role." *DISAM Journal* 27, no. 3 (Spring 2005): 1–14.

National Security Agency

Headquartered at Fort Meade, Maryland, the National Security Agency (NSA) is a U.S. intelligence-gathering agency, specifically the component of the U.S. intelligence community that specializes in activities related to cryptography and signals intelligence (SIGINT). Established on November 4, 1952, by President Harry S. Truman in the wake of a series of intelligence failures regarding the Korean War, the NSA has served as the U.S. government's primary technical intelligence-collection organization since that time.

The United States was renowned for its success in the realm of SIGINT (the gathering and analysis of intercepted voice communications intelligence, or COMINT) and electromagnetic radiation (electronic intelligence, or ELINT) during World War II. Yet Americans entered the early years of the Cold War with a disorganized SIGINT apparatus loosely coordinated among the independent and oftentimes redundant cryptologic agencies of the U.S. Army, Navy, and Air Force. In line with the centralizing theme of the 1947 National Security Act, Secretary of Defense Louis A. Johnson established the Armed Forces Security Agency (AFSA) in 1949 to streamline SIGINT collection. Plagued by the weaknesses of limited jurisdiction and ill-defined authority, however, deficiencies in AFSA's relationship with the service agencies were made readily apparent prior to and during the outbreak of the Korean War in June 1950.

At the urging of President Truman, Secretary of State Dean Acheson appointed New York attorney George Abbott Brownell to head a probe investigating AFSA's failings. The resultant "Brownell Committee Report" advocated replacing AFSA with a centralized national agency capable of unifying all U.S. SIGINT efforts. Fully agreeing with this recommendation, within months, President Truman had dissolved AFSA and quietly signed into law the NSA.

Throughout the 1950s and early 1960s, the NSA established itself as a key intelligence player in virtually all major Cold War political and military conflicts. In 1953, the NSA began overflights of Soviet airspace using converted B-47 Stratojets equipped with various receivers capable of intercepting Soviet air defense radar signals. By intentionally triggering the activation of the Soviet air defense radar system, the B-47s could pinpoint and map the locations of Soviet systems on the ground, providing crucial information for U.S. pilots. By the late 1950s, the Stratojets had been replaced by the high-flying U-2 reconnaissance jet, and overflights to collect Soviet SIGINT data continued, focusing on radar emissions and telemetry information related to intercontinental ballistic missile (ICBM) launches.

The overflight program ended suddenly amid an international crisis. On May 1, 1960, U-2 pilot Francis Gary Powers was shot down over the central Soviet city of Sverdlovsk. Initially disavowing any knowledge of the overflight program, the Eisenhower administration, when faced with irrefutable evidence presented by Soviet premier Nikita Khrushchev, was forced to concede that it had ordered the flights.

Although direct flights over Soviet airspace were terminated in the wake of the

Powers controversy, the NSA maintained a robust collection effort utilizing ground-, air-, sea-, and space-based antennas and sensors to monitor the transmissions of the Eastern bloc as well as nonaligned and allied nations. In an often contentious relationship with the U.S. Navy, NSA listening posts were established on both adapted warships such as USS *Liberty* and on smaller dedicated collection platforms such as USS *Pueblo* to loiter in international waters collecting transmissions, while NSA-directed submarines tapped into undersea communication cables. Ground stations concentrating on intercepting shortwave and very high frequency (VHF) emissions were established in strategically important locations around the globe, including Ellesmere Island in the upper reaches of the Arctic Circle, Ayios Nikolaos in Cyprus, Field Station Berlin in West Berlin, and Misawa Air Force Base in Japan. After the undisclosed launch of the first SIGINT satellite in June 1960, the NSA also began to establish an array of ground-based relay centers in remote locations on the periphery of the Soviet Union.

By the late 1970s, the NSA was enjoying great success in decoding the encrypted Soviet messages that had previously eluded the U.S. intelligence community. As the NSA's mission grew, its budget increased exponentially. Exact budgetary figures from the Cold War period continue to be withheld as classified information, as is the current budget, but during that time, the NSA established itself as the largest U.S. intelligence agency in terms of both manpower and financial resources.

The proliferation of consumer-oriented electronic communication devices that began in the 1980s proved a boon to the NSA. With the advent of fax machines, cell phones, personal computers, and handheld computers, the NSA has greatly increased its ability to monitor transmissions of all kinds and from all around the world. Because of this, the NSA has been central in U.S. antiterrorism efforts. It is believed that the NSA has the capability of intercepting and monitoring transmissions of most of the planet's electronic devices. This ability has come in handy since the global war on terror began in 2001, but it has also caused much consternation among those who fear further encroachments on privacy and civil liberties. In December 2005, the NSA came under great scrutiny when the *New York Times* published a story about the George W. Bush administration's order to tap telephone conversations of select Americans placing calls out of the country. The operation was carried out largely by the NSA and without the requisite court warrants. There have also been concerns that the NSA, working with Internet service providers, may be monitoring customers' Internet communications even between Americans, a situation with serious implications regarding U.S. civil liberties.

In May 2013, Edward Snowden leaked to the media documents that he took while employed as an NSA contractor. It was a series of exposés revealing NSA programs such as the interception of U.S. and European telephone metadata and Internet surveillance programs that some observers have called the most significant leak of classified material in U.S. history.

A Quinnipiac University Polling Institute poll conducted June 28–July 8, 2013, found that in the wake of Snowden's disclosures, 45 percent of Americans thought the federal government went too far in restricting civil liberties, and 40 percent thought it did not do enough, in the context of the war on terror. A July 31–August

1, 2013 Quinnipiac poll found that 55 percent of respondents regarded Snowden as a whistleblower, while 34 percent viewed him as a traitor. In response to the leaks, changing public opinion, and fears that the NSA had overstepped its bounds, in mid-January 2014 President Barack Obama announced changes to the way in which the NSA handles and stores telephone and other electronic data gleaned from American citizens. The move did not, however, silence many critics of the NSA's activities.

Robert G. Berschinski

See also: Central Intelligence Agency; Defense Intelligence Agency; Global War on Terror; National Geospatial-Intelligence Agency

Further Reading

Bamford, James. *Body of Secrets: Anatomy of the Ultra Secret National Security Agency*. New York: Anchor, 2002.

Bamford, James. *The Puzzle Palace: A Report on America's Most Secret Agency*. New York: Penguin, 1983.

Johnson, Chalmers. *The Sorrows of Empire: Militarism, Secrecy, and the End of the Republic*. New York: Metropolitan Books, 2004.

Negroponte, John Dimitri

(July 21, 1939–)

A U.S. diplomat and the first director of national intelligence (2005–2007), John Dimitri Negroponte was born in London, England, on July 21, 1939. His father, Dimitri, was a Greek shipping tycoon. Negroponte attended elite schools in the United States, including Phillips Exeter Academy and Yale University, from which he earned an undergraduate degree in 1960. Attending Harvard University Law School for only a brief time, he joined the Foreign Service in 1960 and stayed with the State Department until 1997. During his long career, Negroponte served in eight overseas posts, including posts in Asia, Latin America, and Europe. He also held a series of increasingly important positions with the State Department in Washington, D.C. In 1981, he was appointed to his first ambassadorship, to Honduras, a post he held until 1985. He subsequently served as ambassador to Mexico (1989–1993) and the Philippines (1993–1996). From 1987 to 1989, Negroponte was deputy assistant to the director of national security affairs in the Ronald Reagan administration.

Negroponte retired from the Foreign Service in 1997 and joined the publishing firm of McGraw-Hill as a senior executive. In 2001, President George W. Bush tapped him to become the U.S. ambassador to the United Nations (UN), a post he held until 2004. Negroponte worked at the UN to secure support for U.S. policies in the aftermath of the September 11, 2001, terror attacks and vowed not to bend to international pressure in the ensuing global war on terror. This stance did not always make him popular among his UN colleagues. In the run-up to the 2003 Iraq invasion, Negroponte was the Bush administration's reliable point man in dealing with the UN.

In April 2004, Negroponte was named ambassador to Iraq. He assumed his duties on June 30, when Anglo-American occupation forces turned sovereignty of Iraq over to the provisional government. Negroponte, who replaced L. Paul Bremer, was immediately faced with a rapidly expanding insurgency and the problems of stabilizing and rebuilding a war-torn nation.

A year later, in February 2005, President Bush named Negroponte as the first

John Negroponte, National Intelligence Director during 2005–2007, shown testifying before the Senate Armed Services Committee on February 28, 2006. Negroponte introduced much needed reforms in the U.S. intelligence community. (AP Photo/Dennis Cook)

director of national intelligence, a new cabinet-level position. Negroponte was charged with coordinating the work of all of the nation's intelligence-gathering services. As such, he was largely responsible for establishing the budgetary requirements of the new intelligence apparatus, which approached $40 billion by 2006. Negroponte's appointment was lauded by many who saw in him the required steadiness of a diplomat combined with the ability to organize and lead. Having worked under both Democratic and Republican administrations, he was seen as a relatively bipartisan public servant who could be counted on to do the right thing in the face of considerable political pressures.

Negroponte wasted no time in instituting needed reforms in the intelligence community and reorganizing the intelligence-gathering apparatus to make it far more efficient and less vulnerable to leaks and political infighting. Indeed, his policies earned high praise from both executive-branch and congressional officials. In January 2007, Negroponte left to become deputy secretary of state, a position that he had long coveted, which he held until January 2009. After leaving public service, Negroponte accepted a teaching and fellowship position at the Jackson Institute of Global Affairs at Yale University.

Paul G. Pierpaoli, Jr.

See also: Bush Administration; Central Intelligence Agency; Iraqi Insurgency

Further Reading

Draper, Robert. *Dead Certain: The Presidency of George W. Bush.* New York: Free Press, 2008.

U.S. Senate, Committee on Foreign Relations. *The Nomination of Hon. John D. Negro-*

ponte to be U.S. Ambassador to Iraq, April 27, 2004. Washington, DC: U.S. Government Printing Office, 2004.

Network-Centric Warfare

Network-centric warfare is a technological theory of warfare developed by the U.S. Department of Defense in the late 1990s that has matured during the global war on terror, which commenced in 2001. It seeks to translate an information advantage, enabled in part by information technology, into a competitive war-fighting advantage through the robust networking of well-informed geographically dispersed forces. It is most widely embraced by the U.S. Air Force.

Most changes in the tactical level of warfare have occurred through advancing weapons technology. For example, the development of gunpowder weapons brought about revolutionary changes in the organization of military forces and battlefield tactics and eventually affected Western governments, economies, and social organizations. Since the late 1980s, technological changes in the acquisition of information about an adversary's infrastructure and military forces and the ways in which this information is processed, disseminated, and utilized by the combatants have been changing the way the U.S. Air Force conducts air warfare. Instead of changes in weapons technology, these current leaps in tactical warfare are being built upon a growing combination of sophisticated manned and unmanned aircraft, airborne sensors, data links, satellites, computers, and other elements through which information passes and is processed and forwarded to the fighters for their utilization.

By the late 1990s, the U.S. military began to realize a growing importance of command, control, communications, computers, intelligence, surveillance, and reconnaissance (C4ISR) through interoperability and systems integration. The North Atlantic Treaty Organization (NATO) Operation Allied Force against Serbia in 1999 provided the first signs of selective tactical uses of data links and collaborative analysis that provided a rough network between the Combined Air Operations Center (CAOC) in Italy and airborne command and control (C2) and strike aircraft over the Balkans. In late 2001, Operation Enduring Freedom brought together many new systems in joint operations and more extensive use of airborne networks to distribute sensor information, share tactical messages, and exert increased C2 over combat forces. For example, after the first three weeks of Enduring Freedom, coalition strike aircraft over Afghanistan ran out of preplanned targets, and ground controllers soon began talking directly to pilots above, a process dubbed immediate airborne close air support (XCAS), to request air strikes with precision-guided munitions against enemy targets in close proximity to coalition ground forces. Long-range bombers and carrier-based aircraft, tasked to strike preplanned targets in Afghanistan, began receiving updated targeting information through data links after they were en route and then reprogrammed their NAVSTAR Global Positioning System–guided weapons to strike new targets.

Additionally, digital networks, designed, developed, and tested in the years before Enduring Freedom began, linked aircraft and ground forces with operations centers thousands of miles away. For example, U.S. Central Command's

(CENTCOM) headquarters at MacDill Air Force Base, Florida, was successfully networked with the forward headquarters in Kuwait and a headquarters in Uzbekistan through satellites and related technologies to a degree not previously achieved. The growing use of surveillance unmanned aerial vehicles (UAVs) increased the quantity of battlefield surveillance and intelligence that was then passed to both ground forces and theater commanders, providing them with near–real-time and real-time battlefield situational awareness. For example, ground controllers and pilots above them could simultaneously view video streamed from a Predator UAV at a higher altitude through a satellite to the controller's computer and the pilot's cockpit and then talk to each other, using satellite communications, to identify in several minutes a prospective target from the video. Through networked communications, the CENTCOM commander directed the battle from his Mac-Dill Air Force Base headquarters at an unprecedented level, especially compared to Operation Desert Storm in 1991.

Network-centric warfare is still very much theory in progress and far from the magic bullet that its proponents claim for it. Exercise Millennium Challenge 2002 was a $250 million Department of Defense exercise that was supposed to showcase the new way of war fighting. But retired U.S. Marine Corps lieutenant general Paul Van Riper, acting as the commander of the Red Force, completely crippled the high-tech Blue Force by employing low-tech methods, such as motorcycle couriers and small reconnaissance boats that neutralized almost all of the technological overmatch of the Blue Force. The exercise was such a complete disaster that Secretary of Defense Donald Rumsfeld peremptorily

ordered it suspended. With the rules rewritten, the exercise was restarted, and the Red Force was ordered to stick to the script. Refusing to participate in the sham, Van Riper resigned in protest, but he had very dramatically managed to demonstrate the sort of threats that U.S. forces would face in both Iraq and Afghanistan in the coming years.

Network-centric warfare has largely failed to live up to the promises of its advocates in the insurgency warfare environments of both Iraq and Afghanistan. The entire concept has lost much of its former luster in recent years. There is no doubt that there is an upward and continuous technological trend in warfare, but the history of warfare is littered with high-tech innovations that have been neutralized or defeated by low-tech countermeasures. Improvised explosive devices (IEDs) are only the latest case in point. All the computers and communications connectivity in the world are not going to help a soldier caught in a kill zone when an IED goes off, nor will PowerPoint superiority or complete dominance of the air defeat determined insurgents.

Robert B. Kane

See also: "Axis of Evil"; Enduring Freedom, Operation; Global War on Terror; Iraqi Freedom, Operation; Iraqi Insurgency; Rumsfeld, Donald Henry; Satellites, Use of by Coalition Forces; Television, Middle Eastern

Further Reading

"Air Force Developing Handheld Video Receiver." *Aviation Week* (May 7, 2007): 46–47.

Grant, Rebecca. "Air Warfare in Transition." *Air Force Magazine* 87, no. 12 (December 2004): 120–32.

Lambeth, Benjamin S. *Air Power against Terror: America's Conduct of Operation*

Enduring Freedom. Santa Monica, CA: RAND Corporation, 2005.

Tiboni, Frank. "Information Becomes Weapon." *Federal Computer Week*, February 13, 2006, 10–13.

Zabecki, David T. "Landpower in History: Strategists Must Regain an Understanding of the Role of Ground Forces." *Armed Forces Journal* (August 2002): 40–42.

New York City Landmarks Bombing Conspiracy

The New York City Landmarks Bombing Conspiracy was another attempt to attack the United States following the 1993 World Trade Center bombing. Sheikh Omar Abdel-Rahman was the spiritual leader of this plot, but the actual work was done by his followers at the al-Kifah Refugee Center. The leaders were Ibrahim Siddig Ali, Mohammed Salah, Fares Kallafal, and Emad Salem. Almost immediately after the bombing of the World Trade Center on February 26, 1993, the conspirators began planning a series of bombings of New York City landmarks. By May 1993, they had selected four targets—the Federal Bureau of Investigation (FBI) building, the United Nations (UN), and the Lincoln and Holland tunnels. The plotters considered the George Washington Bridge, but they lacked the know-how to bring it down.

The conspirators then began building bombs, renting a workspace at 139-01 90th Avenue, Jamaica, Queens. Although they had selected four targets, they intended to build three large bombs. Because they lacked the bomb-making expertise of World Trade Center bomber Ramzi Yousef, they tested their bomb components constantly. However, an undercover agent had disclosed the nature of their plot to the Joint Terrorism Task Force (JTTF) from its beginning. Emad Salem, a former Egyptian military officer, carried a wire for the JTTF that recorded the conversations of the plotters. Salem acted as the chief bomb maker for the conspiracy. Some of the taped recordings implicated Abdel-Rahman. These taps allowed the JTTF to keep abreast of the progress of the terrorists in building the bombs. The terrorists were busy doing just that when JTTF agents raided the bomb-making facility and arrested eight men. Most of the conspirators were caught red-handed. Clement R. Hampton-El and Victor Alvarez were arrested later. A few days later the JTTF agents arrested Abdel-Rahman.

The trial of the 12 members of the conspiracy began in June 1995. In addition to those arrested earlier, El Sayyid Nosair, the assassin of Rabbi Meir Kahane, was the 12th defendant. Siddig Ali turned state's evidence and implicated the other conspirators. The defendants were convicted of 48 of the 50 counts on October 1, 1995. Abdel-Rahman and Nosair received life sentences in solitary confinement without chance of parole, and the other defendants garnered sentences ranging from 25 to 57 years. This trial ended the second attempt to launch a bombing campaign in the United States by Islamist terrorists.

Stephen E. Atkins

See also: Abdel-Rahman, Sheikh Omar; Joint Terrorism Task Force; Nosair, El Sayyid; World Trade Center Bombing; Yousef, Ramzi Ahmed

Further Reading
Bell, J. Bowyer. *Murders on the Nile: The World Trade Center and Global Terror.* San Francisco: Encounter Books, 2003.

Benjamin, Daniel, and Steven Simon. *The Age of Sacred Terror*. New York: Random House, 2002.

Posner, Gerald. *Why America Slept: The Failure to Prevent 9/11*. New York: Ballantine, 2003.

New York City Synagogue Bomb Plots

On May 20, 2009, four New Yorkers attempted to bomb two synagogues in the Riverdale neighborhood of the Bronx. The plots underscored the continuing threat posed by homegrown extremists seeking to attack the U.S. homeland.

Shortly before 9:00 p.m. on May 20, American citizens James Cromitie, David Williams, and Onta Williams and Haitian native Laguerre Payen planted an inactive improvised explosive device (IED) in the trunk of a car outside the Riverdale Temple and two mock bombs in the back seat of another vehicle parked at the nearby Riverdale Jewish Center. The men did not know that the IEDs, which they had obtained from an informant working for the Federal Bureau of Investigation (FBI) who had claimed to be a member of the Pakistani-based terrorist group Jaish-e-Mohammed, were fake.

The would-be terrorists had planned to remotely detonate the explosive-laden cars while simultaneously shooting down military aircraft with Stinger surface-to-air missiles (SAMs) at the New York Air National Guard Base located at Stewart International Airport in Newburgh. Located approximately 60 miles north of New York City, the facility stores aircraft used to transport military supplies and personnel to the U.S. military in Iraq and Afghanistan.

The investigation began a year before the attempted operation when Cromitie met a confidential informant at a Newburgh mosque. Subsequent conversations captured by the FBI plant—subsequently identified as Shahed Hussain—provide insight into the conspirators' motivations and intentions. Cromitie was recorded expressing a slew of highly virulent anti-Semitic invectives and anger over American military actions in Afghanistan and Pakistan. Similar sentiments were also expressed by Onta Williams, who is taped saying, "They [the United States military] are killing Muslim brothers and sisters in Muslim countries, so if we kill them here with IEDs and Stingers, it is equal."

Two weeks before the attempted attack, the men went to a warehouse in Stamford, Connecticut, to obtain what Hussain claimed was a SAM guided-missile system and three IEDs. However, all the bombs contained inert plastic explosives, while government officials had rendered the antiaircraft missiles safe prior to the arranged meeting at the warehouse.

The men were immediately taken into custody after planting the explosives. A federal indictment filed on June 2, 2009, charged all four with conspiracy, attempts to acquire weapons of mass destruction and SAMs, and intent to kill officers and employees of the United States. On October 18, 2010, Cromitie and David Williams were found guilty of all counts; Onta Williams and Payen were convicted for seeking to procure munitions but not for attempted murder. All received 25-year prison terms in 2011.

Some civil rights and legal experts have branded the case a product of government entrapment. Their criticism is based on the notion that four impoverished

Muslim converts were offered financial inducements upwards of $250,000 to carry out the plot. They also note that Hussain failed to record the first four months of meetings with Cromitie and have questioned seemingly unexplained gaps in the tapes.

It seems that the FBI has since softened some of its tactics in the wake of these allegations. In November 2011, for instance, the bureau did not move to investigate Jose Pimentel, who had been arrested by the New York City Police Department for allegedly planning to attack American military personnel and other targets. The case was not pursued due to the apparent facilitation by a confidential informant. In the end, Pimentel was merely charged in a New York State court for criminal possession of a weapon.

Taryn Wolf

See also: New York City Landmarks Bombing Conspiracy; Times Square Bomb Plot; Terrorism

Further Reading

"Four Convicted in New York for Terrorist Plot against Synagogues." Anti-Defamation League, New York, May 21, 2009. Accessed February 1, 2012. http://www.adl.org/main_terrorism/ny_synagogue_plot_arrests.htm.

Harris, Paul. "Newburgh Four: Poor, Black, and Jailed under FBI 'Entrapment' Tactics." *The Guardian* (UK), December 12, 2011. http://www.guardian.co.uk/world/2011/dec/12/newburgh-four-fbi-entrapment-terror.

"*USA v. Cromitie, James, et al.*" The Investigative Project on Terrorism. Accessed February 6, 2012. http://www.investigativeproject.org/case/324.

"*USA v. Pimentel, Jose.*" The Investigative Project on Terrorism. Accessed February 6, 2012. http://www.investigativeproject.org/case/602.

New York Stock Exchange Bomb Plot

On August 3, 2004, Dhirn Barot and 12 other suspects were arrested outside London on suspicion of conspiracy to carry out terrorist attacks in the United States and United Kingdom. Barot was found to have conducted detailed surveillance on the New York Stock Exchange (NYSE) and Citigroup buildings in New York, the Prudential building in New Jersey, and the World Bank and International Monetary Fund in Washington, D.C., in preparation for terrorist attacks.

Barot arrived in New York from the United Kingdom in August 2000, on the first of two trips to survey and assess potential targets for a large-scale attack. According to the 9/11 Commission, Khalid Sheikh Mohammed had sent Barot and another colleague, Nadeem Tarmohamed, to the city at the behest of Osama bin Laden. Barot and Tarmohamed's casing documents of the NYSE included details of the building's fire security system, ventilation ducts, security cameras, X-ray screening equipment, and construction materials as well as the location of nearby fire departments, hospitals, and police stations. Barot concluded his report with a recommendation that arson would be the most effective method of attacking the NYSE.

Similarly detailed surveillance documents on Barot's computer, complete with potential escape routes, also revealed proposals to attack Citigroup buildings in Manhattan and Queens. Barot laid out five possible attack methods: parking a vehicle-borne improvised explosive device (VBIED) next to one of the building's columns or near the front entrance on Lexington Avenue, planting a bomb in a rented space inside the Citigroup building itself, setting it on fire, or flying a plane directly into the structure. Barot and Tarmohamed also carried out reconnaissance of the Prudential headquarters in Newark, New Jersey, and recommended attacking this building with a VBIED left in the underground parking garage. During the same trip, Barot and Tarmohamed traveled to Washington, D.C., where they cased the headquarters of the International Monetary Fund and World Bank. Barot's computer revealed similarly detailed information to that collected about the NYSE.

After returning to Britain, Barot again traveled to New York in April 2001. He conducted video surveillance of the NYSE, the Citigroup Center, and other buildings in Manhattan's financial district. Barot flew back to London on April 8, 2001, and would not reenter the United States.

Back in the United Kingdom, Barot wrote several documents on the possibility of using radiological devices in a terrorist attack and worked on his "Gas Limos Project," which considered bombing London hotels with limousines packed with explosives. Like his surveillance of targets in the United States, Barot's plans were largely abstract and did not consider the difficulties of procuring explosives or other materials.

In 2004, a number of computers were seized in Pakistan that contained detailed surveillance files on buildings in the United States. A large-scale investigation was subsequently initiated, which eventually traced the electronic files back to Barot, who was immediately arrested in London. He pled guilty to conspiracy to murder in October 2006 and is serving a life prison term in the United Kingdom.

Peter Carey

See also: Al-Qaeda; Mohammed, Khalid Sheikh; New York City Landmarks Bombing Conspiracy; New York Times Square Bomb Plot

Further Reading

Carlisle, David. "Dhiren Barot: Was He an Al Qaeda Mastermind or Merely a Hapless Plotter?" *Studies in Conflict and Terrorism* 30, no. 12 (2007): 1057–71.

"The East Coast Buildings." Target: America, Report 4. NEFA Foundation, New York, October 2007. Accessed January 30, 2012. http://www.nefafoundation.org/miscellane ous/East_Coast_Buildings_Plot.pdf.

Mueller, John, ed. "Case 5: Barot and the Financial Buildings." *Terrorism since 9/11: The American Cases.* Columbus: Ohio State University Press, 2012. http://pswbe.sbs .ohio-state.edu/faculty/jmueller/since.pdf.

Tyler, Patrick. "British Charge 8 with Conspiracy in a Terror Plot." *New York Times*, August 18, 2004.

Nidal, Abu

(1937–2002)

Abu Nidal, which translates as "the father of struggle," was the nom de guerre of Sabri Khalil al-Banna, who was born in May 1937 in Jaffa, Palestine (now Tel Aviv-Jaffa), which at the time was under the British Mandate. In 1948, the Arab nations in the region rejected the United Nations partition plan, which ultimately led to war between the Jews and the Arabs. Jaffa soon became a battle zone. During the conflict, the new Israeli government confiscated Abu Nidal's father's expansive orange groves, and Abu Nidal and his family fled to refugee camps in Gaza. He later moved on to Nablus, which was under Jordanian governance.

While in Jordan, Abu Nidal joined the Arab nationalist Baath Party. He soon landed in a Jordanian prison for his political views. When the Baathists were suppressed by Jordan's King Hussein in 1957, Abu Nidal fled to Saudi Arabia. There he founded the Palestine Secret Organization (PSO) in 1967. After the Israelis won the Six-Day War in 1967, Abu Nidal was jailed again for his radical views, this time by the Saudis.

In Saudi Arabia, Abu Nidal joined al-Fatah, Yasser Arafat's faction within the Palestine Liberation Organization (PLO), whose stated objective was to free Palestine from Israeli control. Apparently dissatisfied with certain members of al-Fatah who sought diplomatic solutions, including a two-state solution to the Jewish problem, Abu Nidal left the group in 1973. He became enamored with the rejectionist position held by the Iraqi government, which opposed any solution to the Palestinian problem that allowed for the existence of a Jewish state. Abu Nidal soon accused the PLO of treason, formed the Abu Nidal Organization (ANO), and became Arafat's bitter rival. Meanwhile, al-Fatah sentenced Abu Nidal to death in absentia.

The ANO, operating out of Iraq, burst onto the international scene on September 5, 1973, when ANO gunmen took control of the Saudi embassy in Paris. This was followed by a number of spectacular acts of violence that were remarkable primarily because they seemed to show no concern for their effect on innocent civilians. The ANO has also assassinated a number of key PLO diplomats.

In 1981, Abu Nidal switched bases from Iraq to Syria because Damascus was interested in utilizing his brand of terrorism. Just one year later, the ANO critically wounded Schlomo Argov, Israel's ambassador to the United Kingdom. The Israelis wasted no time in retaliating and, only three days later, used the failed assassination attempt as a justification to invade Lebanon and attempt to destroy the PLO there.

By the mid-1980s, Abu Nidal was considered the world's most lethal terrorist and was the top target of the U.S. Central Intelligence Agency (CIA) and other counterterrorist organizations. At the same time, he became increasingly paranoid, subjecting his followers to endless security checks and bloody purges.

In 1985, Abu Nidal moved his base to Tripoli, Libya, where he became close friends with Libyan strongman Muammar Qaddafi. As the Syrians had, Qaddafi also found many ways to employ Abu Nidal's services. After American warplanes struck Tripoli in April 1986 as punishment for a West Berlin nightclub bombing, Qaddafi convinced Abu Nidal to strike the United States and Britain. The result was staggering. After a kidnapping that left three hostages dead, an ANO team hijacked Pan Am Flight 73 in Karachi, Pakistan, in September 1986, killing 22 people. The organization also provided the explosives that brought down Pan Am Flight 103 en route to New York City over Lockerbie, Scotland, on December 21, 1988, killing 270 people.

The ANO was also responsible for the 1988 attack on the Greek cruise ship *City of Poros* that killed 9 people and left 80 others injured. The attack was roundly criticized in Arab circles because its savagery did not serve either the Palestinian or the Arab political cause. As a result, some theorists accused Abu Nidal of being a Mossad agent or at least being on the Israeli payroll. Some have even argued that the ANO was Arafat's supreme deception in that it allowed Arafat to pose as a moderate while Abu Nidal carried out all of the PLO's truly violent acts.

He was living in a Baghdad home owned by the Iraqi Mukhabarat (Secret Service) when he allegedly committed suicide on August 19, 2002, suffering multiple gunshot wounds, after being detained by Iraq's internal security force.

From a Western perspective, Abu Nidal's violence may have seemed to be targeted at just Israeli interests. However, the bulk of his victims were Arabs. In fact, most of his killings were not even ideologically driven per se in that he served as a mercenary for such states as Iraq, Syria, and Libya, killing these nations' political enemies for financial gain. Abu Nidal's activities tended to put Palestinian demands in the worst possible light and diminish any hope of gaining broader international support. As a result, it should come as no surprise that the ANO was never popular among most Palestinians. Abu Nidal and the ANO were believed to have carried out some 90 terrorist attacks in 20 nations that may have killed as many as 1,000 people.

Peter Chalk

See also: Central Intelligence Agency; Hamburg Cell; Terrorism

Further Reading

Melman, Yossi. *The Master Terrorist: The True Story of Abu-Nidal*. New York: Adama, 1986.

Seale, Patrick. *Abu Nidal, a Gun for Hire: The Secret Life of the World's Most Notorious Arab Terrorist*. New York: Random House, 1992.

Tibi, Bassam. *Arab Nationalism: Between Islam and the Nation-State*. New York: St. Martin's, 2007.

Nineteen Martyrs

In parts of the Muslim world, the participants in the attacks on September 11, 2001, have been characterized as the Nineteen Martyrs. These 19 young men are revered in some areas of the Middle East, where it is believed that by giving up their lives they weakened the power of the hated United States. Yet several of the participants' families have denied that their sons were capable of such an act, and some of the families accuse the Central Intelligence Agency (CIA) of having them killed. Moreover, the identities of all but the leaders of the operation are in doubt. Reports have surfaced that some of them had entered the United States on false passports, and their names may never be known. Regardless, the 19 hijackers sought and found martyrdom, their apparent motivation the threat they believed the United States posed to Islam. They differed in the intensity of their religious beliefs, but they were united in their worldview, believing that the West had been corrupted by greed, sin, and selfishness. In contrast, they believed the Islamic world to be an oasis of faith threatened by the West—in particular, by the United States. Fifteen of the 19 hailed from Saudi Arabia. They were sons of well-to-do families, and most were well educated. Their fathers' occupations ranged from supermarket owners to tribal princes.

The members of the September 11 plot arrived in the United States at different times. Mohamed Atta and the other designated pilots arrived earliest for their pilot training and served as mentors of the later arrivals. Those later arrivals entered the United States from Dubai between March and June 2001, traveling in small groups and landing at four different airports to allay suspicion. Although they arrived in the United States knowing they were part of a martyrdom mission, for reasons of operational security they were not given the details of their mission. The plan called for more than 20 hijackers, but at least six of the men selected for the mission were unable to obtain visas to enter the United States. In all, the 19 terrorists entered and reentered the United States 33 times—most of that activity on the part of the four pilots. They flew back to Europe to consult with Al-Qaeda leaders on the progress of the mission, as well as on personal business.

The leader of the 19 was Atta, who was assisted by Marwan al-Shehhi, Hani Hanjour, and Ziad Jarrah. These individuals were also the pilots of the four hijacked aircraft: Atta of American Airlines Flight 11, al-Shehhi of United Airlines Flight 175, Hanjour of American Airlines Flight 77, and Jarrah of United Airlines Flight 93. The pilots bought tickets for flights on Boeing 757s and 767s because learning to fly these more modern models was much easier than learning to fly older aircraft. The secondary leaders of the plot were Nawaf al-Hazmi and Khalid al-Mihdhar. They had originally been selected to be pilots, but their lack of English and limited education made them poor choices. Their responsibilities then became providing logistical support. The remainder of the hijackers were muscle men sent over to the United States later, most of them from Saudi Arabia.

The 13 muscle men had been trained to hijack aircraft and provide physical support for the pilots. At Al-Qaeda camps in Afghanistan, they were trained in hand-to-hand combat and taught how to assault a commercial airliner's cockpit area.

Because the 19 men knew their mission to be one of martyrdom, each selected a name that honored an important person or event from the Golden Age of Islam, the decades that followed the death of the Prophet Muhammad. Each name was recognizable in the Muslim world and chosen for maximum mass appeal. On the morning of September 11, each team proceeded to its assigned airport, passing through security with only minimal interference. Each team member carried box cutters, utility knives, and chemical sprays. Both box cutters and chemical sprays were prohibited items. Teams had been divided into two groups: cockpit assault and passenger security. Two members of each team, including the designated pilot, were assigned to the cockpit assault unit and had seats near the cockpit door in the first-class section. The others were seated at the rear of the first-class section to provide security from the crew and the passengers, keeping them from interfering in the hijacking. Anyone who stood in their way was to be either killed or incapacitated.

The goal of the hijackers was to seize control of the aircraft within 15 minutes after takeoff. This goal was accomplished on American Airlines Flight 11, American Airlines Flight 77, and United Airlines Flight 175, but not on United Airlines Flight 93. Delay in seizing the aircraft, exacerbated by the time it took to reverse the aircraft's course, allowed the passengers and crew to organize resistance against the terrorists. This aircraft crashed rather than completing its mission. In the eyes of Osama bin Laden and Al-Qaeda's leadership, the mission was still a success. Some in the Muslim world perceived the events of September 11 as a just response to what they considered the many transgressions of the United States against the Muslim world. Many others, however, denounced the hijackings.

Stephen E. Atkins

See also: Atta, Mohamed el-Amir Awad el-Sayed; Islamic Radicalism; Pentagon Attack; World Trade Center, September 11, 2001

Further Reading

McDermott, Terry. *Perfect Soldiers: The 9/11 Hijackers; Who They Were, Why They Did It*. New York: HarperCollins, 2005.

Strasser, Steven. *The 9/11 Investigations: Staff Reports of the 9/11 Commission; Excerpts from the House-Senate Joint Inquiry Report on 9/11; Testimony from 14 Key Witnesses, Including Richard Clarke, George Tenet, and Condoleezza Rice*. New York: Public-Affairs, 2004.

North American Aerospace Defense Command

The North American Aerospace Defense Command (NORAD) has the military responsibility to defend the continental United States from enemy attacks, but on September 11, 2001, it failed. NORAD's mission includes defending the United States from foreign bombers or ballistic missiles; defending against civilian aircraft was not a part of this mission. On September 11, NORAD's radars were mostly directed outward to detect attacks from abroad. Because the Federal Aviation Administration (FAA) was responsible for domestic aviation, NORAD depended on information from the FAA, but the FAA was not a part of the infrastructure of defense against foreign attack. This gap in responsibility meant that both NORAD and the FAA lacked protocols for dealing with a scenario such as that surrounding the events of September 11.

The lack of protocols did not mean that no standard operating procedures (SOP) existed between the FAA and NORAD. In the event of a hijacking, the FAA was responsible for informing the Pentagon's National Military Command Center (NMCC), which would then seek approval from the secretary of defense for military assistance in the hijacking. Upon the secretary's approval, NORAD would receive orders from NMCC to scramble a flight of jets to find the aircraft and monitor it from a distance of five miles, at no time interfering with the hijacking. No guidelines were in place for dealing with a hijacking meant to end in a suicidal crash. Only a presidential order could be given to shoot down an American commercial aircraft—an order that had to be relayed through the chain of command.

Because of a lack of coordination and information between NORAD and the FAA, the actions of NORAD turned into a morass of errors on September 11. On that date, NORAD had 14 National Guard jets on standby throughout the country. Complicating the situation, NORAD was conducting three war games on September 11. One of the war games was with the Northeast Air Defense Sector (NEADS), which reduced the number of fighter jet flights available. FAA officials disregarded SOP and contacted NORAD directly. NEADS scrambled two F-15s from Otis Air National Guard Base in Massachusetts at 8:46 a.m., but the pilots had only a vague notion of their mission. They were vectored toward military-controlled airspace off Long Island. Within seconds of their take-off, American Airlines Flight 11 crashed into the North Tower of the World Trade Center complex. Eight minutes before the F-15s arrived in New York City at 9:10 a.m., United Airlines Flight 175 crashed into the South Tower of the World Trade complex. The jets' slowness in arriving indicates that they had not traveled at their maximum speed. Even if they had arrived sooner, they had no orders to intercept the hijacked aircraft, so it is uncertain just what they could have done to prevent the second crash. Much the same can be said about the two jets of the 177th Flight Wing of the New Jersey Air National Guard in Atlantic City, New Jersey, which, though available, were never called to assist.

By 9:00 a.m. it had become apparent that the hijacking plot involved more commercial airliners. At 9:24 a.m. a flight of F-16s of the National Guard's 119th Fighter Wing was ordered to immediately fly from Langley Air Force Base in Virginia, tasked with protecting the Washington, D.C., area after a report that American Airlines Flight 11 was heading in that direction. Flight 11, however, had crashed into the North Tower 40 minutes before. Lacking accurate information, the pilots of the F-15s and F-16s tried to keep visual contact with possible hijacked aircraft. Again, exactly what these pilots would have done if ordered to intercept a hijacked aircraft is unknown. Their orders were to "identify type and tail numbers of the hijacked aircraft"—nothing more.

Orders to intercept and possibly shoot down a hijacked aircraft had to be authorized by President George W. Bush. President Bush was in Sarasota, Florida, and Vice President Dick Cheney was in Washington, D.C. Cheney contacted President Bush and received authorization from him to shoot down hijacked aircraft shortly after 10:00 a.m. This order did not reach NORAD until 10:31—much too late to do anything, as American Airlines Flight 77 had already crashed into the Pentagon at 9:37. It was known by the FAA at this time,

however, that hijackers had seized United Airlines Flight 93, and that this airliner might be headed toward the Washington, D.C., area. For some reason, this information was not transmitted by the FAA to the NMCC, which did not learn that United Airlines Flight 93 had been hijacked until after it had crashed, when at last it was informed by the Secret Service.

The shoot-down order authorization was sent to NORAD at 10:31 a.m., but the 9/11 Commission reported that this order never reached the F-15 or F-16 pilots. It was a moot point because by the time this order would have reached the pilots, it was already too late. United Airlines Flight 93 had crashed near Shanksville, Pennsylvania, at 10:03 a.m. Shooting down an American commercial airliner would have been a traumatic experience for the pilots, even with a presidential order authorizing it. It is doubtful whether the pilots would have done so, especially if they were flying over heavily populated areas.

The confusion on September 11 extended into NORAD's record-keeping about the events of that day. So many contradictory accounts came out of NORAD that the 9/11 Commission staff had difficulty determining just what had happened. NORAD's leadership has been particularly defensive about its conduct on September 11, and so many discrepancies have appeared in its records that conspiracy theorists have used NORAD as an example of government complicity in the attacks. In fact, NORAD depended on the FAA for information, some of which proved to be both inaccurate and belated. As the 9/11 Commission pointed out, the military had "nine minutes' notice that American Airlines Flight 11 had been hijacked; two minutes' notice that an unidentified aircraft, American 77, was headed toward Washington, and no notice at all about United Airlines 175 or 93." The military, which depends heavily on contingency plans, had no contingency plan available to help NORAD handle hijackers determined to use commercial aircraft on suicide missions. Because NORAD was operating in the dark, it failed as much as any other agency in the government on that fateful day.

Stephen E. Atkins

See also: Pentagon Attack; National Commission on Terrorist Attacks upon the United States (9/11 Commission); World Trade Center, September 11, 2001

Further Reading

Kashurba, Glenn J. *Quiet Courage: The Definitive Account of Flight 93 and Its Aftermath.* Somerset, PA: SAJ Publishing, 2006.

Kean, Thomas H., Lee H. Hamilton, and Benjamin Rhodes. *Without Precedent: The Inside Story of the 9/11 Commission.* New York: Knopf, 2006.

Lance, Peter. *Triple Cross: How Bin Laden's Master Spy Penetrated the CIA, the Green Berets, and the FBI—and Why Patrick Fitzgerald Failed to Stop Him.* New York: ReganBooks, 2006.

Nosair, El Sayyid

(1955–)

The first major case of Islamist extremism in the United States was the assassination of the Israeli extremist politician Meir Kahane on November 5, 1990, by El Sayyid Nosair. Nosair stalked Kahane for several days before shooting him twice on a New York City street. He then escaped in a taxi. After a policeman accosted him, the two exchanged shots, and Nosair received a severe wound to the neck.

Nosair had a relatively normal upbringing. Born in 1955 in Port Said, Egypt, he was displaced along with his family during the Six-Day War with Israel in 1967. Nosair spent his adolescent years in Cairo, Egypt, where his academic achievements led to his graduation with a degree in industrial design and engineering from the Helwan University Faculty of Applied Arts. In July 1981, Nosair decided to immigrate to the United States. His first residence was in Pittsburgh, Pennsylvania, where he found work as a diamond cutter. Despite his distaste for the United States, he married an American woman who had recently converted to Islam. After Nosair lost his job as a diamond cutter because of a dispute with his employer, he held a variety of jobs, but none so prestigious or lucrative. Nosair decided to move his family to New York City.

Nosair had previously held moderate Islamic views, but after his move to New York City he became more militant. His religious home was al-Farooq Mosque in Brooklyn, which was affiliated with al-Kifah Refugee Center. At al-Kifah, Nosair became enamored with the jihadist philosophy of Abdullah Azzam. Nosair wanted to go to Afghanistan in 1987 to fight against the Soviets, but he lacked the funds to do so. Instead, he joined others in paramilitary training. Many of his compatriots were later to participate in the 1993 World Trade Center Bombing. Nosair also became an admirer of Sheikh Omar Abdel-Rahman, the blind Egyptian religious leader and militant terrorist. With Abdel-Rahman's blessings from Egypt, Nosair formed a terrorist cell. Now working as a janitor, Nosair began to consider schemes that ranged from assassinations to bombings. He threw a grenade at Mikhail Gorbachev when the Soviet premier visited

New York City on December 8, 1989, but it failed to explode. In April 1990, he exploded a crude bomb in a gay bar, causing minor injuries. After Abdel-Rahman arrived in the United States in May 1990, Nosair received more direction, as well as instructions on weapon use given by Ali Abdel Saoud Mohamed, who drew from his service in the Egyptian and American armed forces.

Nosair now decided to assassinate Meir Kahane. Kahane was an Israeli extremist, but Nosair believed that one day Kahane would be the leader of the Jewish state—and thus that his death would advance the Palestinian cause. He began stalking Kahane, looking for an opportunity to shoot him. When the opportunity arose, Nosair shot Kahane three times. After the assassination, the New York District Attorney's Office assumed jurisdiction of the case. The Federal Bureau of Investigation (FBI) turned over 16 boxes of information gathered in a search of Nosair's apartment to the Manhattan District Attorney's office, but the boxes promptly disappeared. The New York City Joint Terrorism Task Force (JTTF) became interested in the case because of its domestic terrorism aspects, but the FBI agents and New York City police detectives of the JTTF were removed from the case. The Nosair case was botched from its beginning. Nosair was charged with simple murder rather than participation in a conspiracy. The New York Police Department's chief of detectives, Joseph Borelli, refused to classify Kahane's assassination as a political assassination, instead calling Nosair a "lone deranged gunman," despite evidence to the contrary.

Kahane, though a victim, did not inspire sympathy. The case then took a strange turn. William Kunstler, the well-known defense lawyer, handled Nosair's defense, and Nosair was convicted of shooting two people after the assassination—but not of causing Kahane's death. He was sentenced to 7.5 to 22.5 years in prison. The lightness of his sentence caused great celebration in the Muslim community and convinced Islamist militants that the United States was merely a paper tiger.

From his prison cell, Nosair continued to advocate violence against the United States. Several of the 1993 World Trade Center Bombing conspirators visited Nosair in prison to confirm their plans. He constantly advocated terrorist projects, many of which were designed for his compatriots to break him out of prison. After government officials became aware of his activities and his participation in the 1993 World Trade Center Bombing, a subsequent trial sentenced him to life in prison.

Stephen E. Atkins

See also: Abdel-Rahman, Omar (aka the Blind Sheikh); World Trade Center Bombing

Further Reading

Benjamin, Daniel, and Steven Simon. *The Age of Sacred Terror*. New York: Random House, 2002.

Lance, Peter. *1000 Years for Revenge: International Terrorism and the FBI: The Untold Story*. New York: ReganBooks, 2003.

Miller, John, Michael Stone, and Chris Mitchell. *The Cell: Inside the 9/11 Plot and Why the FBI and CIA Failed to Stop It*. New York: Hyperion, 2002.

O

Obama Administration

In many respects, at least in terms of the war on terror, the Obama administration continued policies that were initiated by the George W. Bush administration, with some exceptions. The Obama administration waged a secret campaign against Al Qaeda in certain regions—the Arab peninsula and on Africa's east coast. In numerous press conferences, the White House acknowledged that it conducted lethal unmanned aerial attacks in Yemen and Somalia. Additionally, President Obama is credited with the attack and killing of Al-Qaeda leader Osama bin Laden on May 2, 2011. In public opinion polls, the Obama administration has routinely received high marks for handling the nation's security. Typically, most polls found that at least two-thirds of Americans approved of Obama's handling of the war on terror.

On May 23, 2012, President Obama announced at the National Defense University that "the global war on terror" is over. Obama went on to say that the military and intelligence agencies will not wage war globally, but rather focus on a specific group of networks determined to damage or destroy the United States. The Obama administration has generally sought to focus on efforts to defeat Al-Qaeda and its affiliates in the Arabian Peninsula, rather than pursuing a global approach to quashing terrorism. Nevertheless, mid-2014

several items remained on the agenda for the Obama administration before the war on terrorism could truly come to a close. These issues include the closing of the prison at Guantánamo Bay, Cuba; ending the use of enhanced interrogation techniques; ceasing the use of rendition; and employing military tribunals to try terror suspects.

During the 2008 presidential campaign, Obama was openly critical of the use of Guantánamo (Gitmo) for detaining enemy combatants for extended periods of time. On his second day as president, Obama issued an order to close the facility within a year. However, the Senate overturned this order by a vote of 90–6, thus denying his request for $80 million to close the prison. The problem, at least from the perspective of Congress (including both Democrats and Republicans), is the potentially high political cost of relocating these detainees to mainland prisons. No state or locality wants to accept suspected Al-Qaeda and Taliban terrorists within their borders.

Obama was also keen on ending the use of specific enhanced interrogation techniques, notably waterboarding, which many critics alleged constitute a form of torture. Obama also issued an executive order that required that the army field manual be used as the guide for interrogations as a way to end this practice. Some observers, however, believe that the Central Intelligence Agency (CIA) and other agencies involved in the war on terror have ways to skirt that order, sometimes by employing third parties to engage in such questionable interrogation activities.

Critics of the Obama administration point out that it has continued to permit extraordinary rendition, a policy that allows the CIA to capture suspected terrorists in foreign battlefields and detain them. They state that while the Obama administration order stated that these facilities be closed, it failed to specify whether third parties involved were allowed to conduct this practice. They point out that this has allowed the CIA to continue to use enhanced interrogation techniques by U.S. allies abroad, before transferring the enemy combatants to U.S. facilities.

The Obama administration still uses military tribunals and commissions that were established by the George W. Bush administration. Despite initial criticism of these and proposals recommending the use of civil courts, administration officials later stated that it was necessary to try enemy combatants by military tribunals, much as the prior administration had held.

In regards to the wars in Iraq and Afghanistan, Obama made good on his 2008 election promise to withdraw all American forces from Iraq. The last troops left that nation in December 2011. In Afghanistan, Obama rather reluctantly approved a troop surge to quash the growing Al-Qaeda/Taliban insurgency there. The surge began in 2010, and had ended by late 2012. The surge in Afghanistan did not make much of a dent in the growing insurgency, however, and that nation remains plagued by political corruption and chaos, not to mention growing violence. Iraq, meanwhile, has slid back into near civil war conditions, and by early 2014, the Iraqi government seemed powerless to staunch the violence being perpetrated by Al-Qaeda as well as Shiite and Sunni militias. In January 2014, a large portion of Iraq's Anbar Province had been overrun by Al-Qaeda and its allies. That summer, radical Islamist militants belonging to the Islamic State in Iraq and Syria, with the goal of establishing an Islamic state in the region, captured Mosul, Iraq's second-largest city. President Obama conceded that it is going to need more help from the U.S and the international community. He was not ruling out and future military and diplomatic actions.

Jan Goldman

See also: Al-Qaeda; Bush Administration; Enduring Freedom, Operation; Global War on Terror; Guantánamo Bay Detainment Camp; Iraqi Insurgency; Rendition; Torture of Prisoners

Further Reading

Bentley, Michelle and Jack Holland. *Obama Foreign Policy: Ending the War on Terror.* London: Routledge, 2013.

Katz, Mark. *Leaving without Losing: The War on Terror After Iraq and Afghanistan.* Baltimore: Johns Hopkins University Press, 2012.

Woodward, Bob. *Obama's Wars.* New York: Simon & Schuster, 2011.

P

Padilla, José

José Padilla was arrested in October 2002 on charges that he was planning to detonate a radiological dispersal device (or "dirty bomb") on U.S. soil. An American Muslim citizen, he was one of the first people to be officially declared an "enemy combatant" in the post 9/11 era and was held for several years in a military brig without trial or access to lawyers.

Padilla was born in Brooklyn, New York, on October 18, 1970. At the age of four, he moved with his mother to the northwest side of Chicago, Illinois. As a child he attended Charles Darwin Elementary School across the street from his home. He spent his teenage years in and out of detention centers and between short-term jobs as a busboy or dishwasher; he drifted into an affiliation with the Latin Disciples, one of the most notorious of Chicago's many street gangs, and acquired the nickname "Pucho."

During his gang days Padilla maintained several aliases, including José Rivera, José Alicea, José Hernandez, and José Ortiz. He was arrested on several occasions, and it was while he was in prison that he converted from Roman Catholicism to Islam. Upon his release, Padilla sought out the Masjid Al-Iman mosque in Fort Lauderdale, Florida, where he was befriended by Adham Amin Hassoun—a registered agent for the Benevolence International Foundation, a charitable organization that U.S. investigators have accused of funding terrorist activities. The U.S. Justice Department later determined that Hassoun was communicating with radical Islamic fundamentalists, including possibly Al-Qaeda, and in 2002 arrested him for overstaying his visa.

Padilla later traveled to Egypt, Saudi Arabia, Afghanistan, and Pakistan. He returned to the United States on May 8, 2002, and was arrested by federal agents at Chicago's O'Hare International Airport. He was subsequently declared an enemy combatant and accused of participating in the construction of a radioactive dirty bomb. No evidence for the charges was ever presented and no legal proceedings were authorized; moreover, he was kept from talking to his lawyer. He was then detained by the U.S. military and held at a naval brig in Hanahan, South Carolina.

On December 18, 2003, the U.S. Second Circuit Court of Appeals declared that the Bush administration had acted without proper authority in designating a U.S. citizen arrested on American soil an enemy combatant without first gaining clear congressional authorization. Although the court ordered Padilla to be released from military custody within 30 days, it agreed to stay this judgment pending a government appeal, which was presented on February 20, 2004. The case was resubmitted to the

Supreme Court in April 2004, but thrown out three months later due to a technicality.

On November 22, 2005, a federal grand jury in Miami indicted Padilla and four others on three counts of conspiracy to "murder, maim and kidnap" people overseas. Although these new charges suggested that Padilla was part of an American-based terrorism cell, they did not specifically state that he planned on carrying out attacks within the United States. Following the indictment, Padilla was transferred from military custody to the Justice Department.

In April 2007, the federal trial against Padilla and two codefendants, Hassoun and Kifah Wael Jayyousi, began. All three were charged with plotting to murder, maim, and kidnap people overseas; conspiring to materially support terrorism; and physically providing support to terrorists. On August 16, the three defendants were found guilty on all counts, which combined carried a maximum penalty of life imprisonment. On January 22, 2008, Judge Marcia Cooke sentenced Padilla to 17 years of jail time, Hassoun to 15 years, and Jayyousi to 12 years.

Eric Harris and Karl R. DeRouen

See also: Al-Qaeda; Global War on Terror; Terrorism

Further Reading

Benjamin, Daniel, and Steven Simon. *The Next Attack: The Failure of the War on Terror and a Strategy for Getting It Right*. New York: Times Books, 2005.

Clarke, Richard A. *Against All Enemies: Inside America's War on Terror*. New York: Free Press, 2004.

Levy, Robert. "Jose Padilla: No Charges and No Trial, Just Trial." CATO Institute, Washington DC, August 11, 2003. Accessed September 16, 2011. http://www.cato.org/pub_display.php?pub_id=3208.

"Profile: Jose Padilla." *BBC News*, August 16, 2007. http://news.bbc.co.uk/2/hi/203744.stm.

Pan Am/Lockerbie Bombing

On Wednesday, December 21, 1988, Pan Am Flight 103, en route from London to New York, exploded less than 40 minutes into the flight at approximately 31,000 feet over Lockerbie, Scotland. All 259 passengers and crew aboard the Boeing 747 aircraft (dubbed "Clipper Maid of the Seas") were killed, as were 11 people on the ground. Of those who died, 189 were U.S. citizens. Resultant debris rained down over an expansive section of rural Scotland, and preliminary investigations quickly suggested that an explosive device had caused the disaster.

An unprecedented multinational investigation ensued, involving both intelligence and law enforcement resources. After a painstaking inquiry and a detailed reconstruction of the incident, authorities concluded that a high-performance explosive device had been hidden inside a radio/cassette player that was packed in a suitcase left in the forward cargo hold of the aircraft. The unaccompanied luggage had originated in Malta and had been flown to London on board an affiliated air carrier.

Amazingly, investigators were able to identify other contents from within the suitcase, specifically, a number of pieces of clothing specific to a vendor in Malta and the remains of an umbrella. A fragment of a timer was also discovered, traced to the Swiss firm MEBO, which designed and manufactured various electronic items.

A Central Intelligence Agency (CIA) source working at Libya's Jamahariya Security Organization (later named the

The nose section of Pan Am Flight 103 lies in a field outside the village of Lockerbie, Scotland. The airliner was bombed on December 21, 1988. In January 2001, Libyan Abdelbaset Ali Mohmed al-Megrahi was convicted of the bombing, and the co-accused, Al Amin Khalifa Fhimah, was found not guilty and returned to Libya. (AP Photo/Martin Cleaver)

External Security Organization) subsequently provided an alert about two men: Abdelbaset Ali Mohmed al-Megrahi and Al Amin Khalifa Fhimah. Though the veracity of his information was questionable, he suggested that the pair were both intelligence officers tasked with performing "cover duties" that would afford them the necessary know-how and access to introduce an explosive device into the aviation system via the Luqa Airport in Malta. According to the source, al-Megrahi had acted as the head of security for Libyan Arab Airlines (LAA) until January 1987 (after which he took up the post of director of the Centre for Strategic Studies), while Fhimah had served as the local station manager for LAA at Luqa Airport. The CIA contact also indicated that the two had access to explosives and separately recounted seeing them with a suitcase (similar to that containing the explosive device aboard the doomed airliner) in Malta close to the time of the bombing.

Separately, investigators approached the Maltese vendor, who was able to recollect that a Libyan male had purchased the clothing items and umbrella found in the suitcase. He later identified the man as al-Megrahi after being shown pictures and upon seeing him in a lineup. At the same time, representatives of MEBO confirmed that the company's principal customer for MST-13 timers was the Libyan government, and that the firm had had previous business dealings with al-Megrahi. Additional evidence suggested that the Libyan had been in Malta at the same time the explosive was introduced into the aviation system, albeit under a passport with a different name (Ahmed Khalifa Abdusamad).

A journal belonging to Fhimah was later found to contain the inscriptions "Take/collect tags from the airport (Abdelbaset/Abdusamad)" and "Take taggs [sic] from Air Malta." It was presumed that these were instructions on how to load an unaccompanied bag onto a plane at Luqa. In addition, call records surfaced showing that al-Megrahi and Fhimah had met in Malta prior to the bombing.

Together, these and other related investigative leads led authorities to conclude that al-Megrahi and Fhimah had placed the explosive device on board Pan Am Flight 103 and that the "conception, planning, and execution of (the act) . . . was of Libyan origin." On November 14, 1991, a U.S. grand jury and Scotland's Lord Advocate indicted the pair for the downing of the aircraft. Libya denied any knowledge of, or association with, the incident, and was reluctant to turn over the accused men, offering instead to send them to the Arab League or another neutral site for trial.

Meanwhile, the United Nations (UN) Security Council passed a series of resolutions that collectively called on Tripoli to extradite al-Megrahi and Fhimah, imposed select sanctions against Libya, and placed a limited freeze on the country's foreign assets. The Qaddafi regime ultimately agreed to the trial of the two men at The Hague after receiving the following assurances from UN secretary-general Kofi Annan: the court would be overseen by Scottish judges and would follow Scottish legal procedures; the hearing would be limited to the two suspects (who would not be interrogated by either British or American authorities) and would not address the issue of Libyan government involvement; and the men, if convicted, would serve their terms in Scottish jails under UN

monitoring. On April 5, 1999, al-Megrahi and Fhimah were transferred to the Netherlands for the trial. That same day, the UN suspended, but did not drop, the sanctions against Libya.

The court commenced its work on May 3, 2000. Al-Megrahi was convicted of murder and sentenced to life in a Scottish prison on January 31, 2001. Fhimah was acquitted and returned to Libya. Al-Megrahi unsuccessfully appealed the ruling in 2001 and 2003. Though there was some suspicion that the Popular Front for the Liberation of Palestine–General Command (PLFLP-GC) had played a role in the incident, the trial found no evidence to support it.

In August 2003, Libya accepted responsibility for the bombing of Pan Am Flight 103 and agreed to financially compensate the families of the victims in return for the lifting of sanctions against the country and the United States rescinding its designation as a state sponsor of terrorism. The Qaddafi regime subsequently paid $4 million per victim after sanctions were terminated in September 2003, another $4 million after Washington suspended bilateral sanctions in September 2004, and a final $2 million once it was removed from the State Department's list of state sponsors of terrorism.

On August 20, 2009, Scottish government officials released al-Megrahi on compassionate grounds after doctors diagnosed he had prostate cancer and only a few months to live. The decision was highly controversial, particularly as al-Megrahi's prognosis ultimately proved to be less grim (he eventually died in May 2012).

The bombing of Pan Am Flight 103 was one of the most lethal acts of terrorism involving a commercial aircraft prior to the attacks of September 11, 2001. The resultant investigation was also unprecedented and led to sweeping changes in airline security procedures.

Paul Kemppainen

See also: Global War on Terror; Justification for the September 11 Suicide Mission; Madrid Airport Bombing; North American Aerospace Defense Command

Further Reading

Blanchard, Christopher. *Libya: Background and U.S. Relations*. Washington, DC: Congressional Research Service, 2007. http://www.opencrs.com.

Department of Transport Air Accidents Investigation Branch. *Aircraft Accident Report 2/90*. London: Royal Aerospace Establishment, 1990. http://www.aaib.gov.uk/home/index.cfm.

Gillibrand, Senator Kristen, Senator Frank Lautenberg, Senator Robert Menendez, and Senator Charles Schumer. *Justice Undone: The Release of the Lockerbie Bomber*. Washington, DC: U.S. Senate, 2010. Accessed February 16, 2012. http://www.hsdl.org.

Pearl, Daniel

Daniel Pearl, a reporter for the *Wall Street Journal*, was captured and brutally executed on February 1, 2002, by Pakistani militants. His beheading was filmed and broadcast on cable and Internet outlets, raising complicated and painful questions for news organizations regarding the use of such material.

Pearl was born on October 10, 1963, in Princeton, New Jersey, but was raised and educated in Los Angeles. He attended Stanford University, and began working for the *Wall Street Journal*'s Atlanta bureau in 1990. He moved to the Washington, D.C., bureau in 1993, then to London in 1996.

Pearl was working as the South Asia bureau chief for the *Wall Street Journal* based in Mumbai, India, when, on January 23, 2002, as part of his investigation of shoe-bomber Richard Reid, he traveled to an interview in Karachi, Pakistan. The interview was a trap, and Pearl was kidnapped by a militant group calling itself "The National Movement for the Restoration of Pakistani Sovereignty." Claiming that Pearl was actually a CIA agent, the group issued a series of demands, including the release of Pakistani prisoners and resumption of U.S. sales of fighter aircraft to Pakistan. Pearl was executed on February 2, and on February 21, a video of his beheading was released. His dismembered body was found in a shallow grave on May 16.

Four suspects were arrested in connection with Pearl's murder, and one, Ahmed Omar Saeed Sheikh, was convicted and sentenced to death. However, Al-Qaeda leader Khalid Sheikh Mohammed claimed to have been the person who actually beheaded Pearl.

Pearl's widow Mariane wrote a memoir entitled *A Mighty Heart*, which was made into a motion picture starring Angelina Jolie.

Clarence R. Wyatt

See also: Guantánamo Bay Detainment Camp; Mohammed, Khalid Sheikh; Terrorism

Further Reading

Lévy, Bernard-Henri. *Who Killed Daniel Pearl?* Brooklyn, NY: Melville House Publishing, 2003.

Pearl, Daniel. *At Home in the World: Collected Writings from the Wall Street Journal*. New York: Free Press, June 2002.

Pearl, Mariane, and Sarah Crichton. *A Mighty Heart: The Brave Life and Death of My Husband, Danny Pearl*. New York: Scribner, 2003.

Pearl, Ruth, and Judea Pearl, eds. *I Am Jewish: Personal Reflections Inspired by the Last Words of Daniel Pearl*. Woodstock, VT: Jewish Lights Publishing, 2004.

Penn Station Bomb Plot

On August 27, 2004, federal authorities arrested two New Yorkers for plotting to attack one of New York City's busiest subway stations with explosive-laden backpacks. The incident underscores the inclinations of lone wolf extremists who, though unaffiliated with international terrorist organizations, share their radical ideologies and violent propensities.

Three days before the Republican National Convention was held at Madison Square Garden, authorities detained Shahawar Matin Siraj and James Elshafay for planning to detonate explosives at the subway station in Herald Square, a dense shopping area one block from the Garden. Prosecutors said the men sought to avenge the perceived abuse of prisoners at Abu Ghraib and to show solidarity with the Palestinians.

Siraj, a 22-year-old Pakistani national who immigrated to the United States illegally five years before his arrest, first came to the attention of law enforcement for virulent anti-American rants. An undercover police informant, since identified as Osama Eldawoody, met Siraj at the Islamic bookstore where he worked and subsequently recorded their conversations.

Siraj later introduced the informant to Elshafay, the 19-year-old American-born son of an Irish American mother and an Egyptian father. Elshafay, who had previously drawn crude maps of several New York landmarks and police precincts, was taped telling Siraj of his idea to plant bombs on four bridges connecting Staten Island with Brooklyn and New Jersey. The objective was to incur economic damage and business disruption in the hope that this would force the United States to withdraw its troops from Iraq. However, the men abandoned the scheme because of the difficulty of rigging the bridge with explosives while avoiding detection.

Recorded conversations also featured discussions about attacking the U.S. Army with nuclear weapons and bombing various other subway stations. Siraj and Elshafay also apparently thought about assassinating the iconic founder of Microsoft, Bill Gates, before deciding to target Herald Square.

Six days before their arrests, Siraj, Elshafay, and the undercover informant conducted surveillance of the subway station to determine the best location to place the explosives. The men also left their backpacks on the platforms to test law enforcement responses. Elshafay, who has since described himself as a schizophrenic, proposed that he would avoid suspicion when actually planting the bombs by dressing like an Orthodox Jew in a long black coat and side curls.

While the men did not possess a bomb at the time of their arrests, Siraj did have a computer disk containing instructions for making improvised explosive devices (IEDs). Furthermore, the undercover informant had claimed he could obtain the necessary components for making an IED from a fictitious terrorist organization called "The Brotherhood."

Elshafay immediately agreed to cooperate with the government and, two months later, pleaded guilty to conspiring to blow up the subway station. He was sentenced to five years in prison on March 2, 2007. Elshafay also testified as a witness against Siraj, who was convicted on all counts after a five-week trial. He is currently serving a 30-year jail term.

Taryn Wolf

Further Reading

Horowitz, Craig. "Anatomy of a Foiled Terrorist Plot: Two Would-Be Bombers of the Herald Square Subway Station Find That Three Is a Crowd." *New York Magazine*, May 21, 2005. http://nymag.com/nymetro/news/features/10559/.

Rashbaum, William. "In Tapes of Subway Plot Suspect, a Disjointed Torrent of Hatred." *New York Times*, April 26, 2006.

Silber, Mitchell D., and Arvin Bhatt. "Radicalization in the West: The Homegrown Threat." New York: New York Police Department Intelligence Division, 2007.

"*United States v. Shahawar Matin Siraj.*" Investigative Project on Terrorism. Accessed February 8, 2012. http://www.investigativeproject.org/case/164.

Pentagon Attack

The terror attack on September 11, 2001, badly damaged the west side of the Pentagon and caused heavy loss of life. The building was built between 1941 and 1943, during World War II. As the headquarters of the United States Department of Defense, the Pentagon was an obvious target in any type of hostilities, including terrorist acts. It is considered the world's largest office building. The building is huge, covering 29 acres. Ten numbered corridors provide 17.5 miles of hallways. Although the building was constructed to house as many as 50,000 military and civilian personnel, on September 11, 2001, approximately 18,000 employees as well as about 2,000 nondefense support personnel were working there. Its unique construction incorporates five concentric rings named A, B, C, D, and E, from the inner ring facing the courtyard (A) to the outermost ring (E).

On the morning of September 11, five terrorists seized American Airlines Flight 77 as it traveled from Dulles International Airport outside Washington, D.C., to Los Angeles, California, and crashed it into the Pentagon. The five hijackers—Hani Hanjour, Nawaf al-Hazmi, Salem al-Hazmi, Khalid al-Mihdhar, and Majed Moqued—had little trouble passing through the Dulles checkpoint with weapons that they subsequently used to take over the aircraft. Seated in the first-class section, they seized control of the aircraft shortly after takeoff. As air traffic controllers at Dulles tried to regain contact with the airliner, the hijackers redirected the aircraft toward the Washington, D.C., area. A request was made to a U.S. Air Force transport for a visual sighting, and the pilot replied that he had the airliner in sight. An air traffic controller asked the C-130 pilot, Lieutenant Colonel Steve O'Brien, to monitor the airliner. He reported that the airliner was moving low and fast, and then he watched it crash into the west side of the Pentagon. The flight hit at first-floor level and penetrated three of the five rings of that section of the Pentagon.

The personnel at the Pentagon had no warning of the approaching aircraft. Many of the Pentagon workers were watching news footage on TV of the attacks on the World Trade Center complex. Several of the survivors remarked later that they talked about how vulnerable the Pentagon was to a similar type of attack. Suddenly there was a tremendous explosion. Those not killed or injured in the original explosion had to face fire and reduced visibility from the smoke. Most of those working in the Pentagon were evacuated, but those trapped in the west side of the building were unable to escape.

On September 11, 2001, United Flight 77 slammed into the Pentagon in Arlington, Virginia, killing everyone on the plane and 125 in the building, including 74 military personnel. (U.S. Army)

It took 10 days after the attack for all human remains to be removed from the Pentagon. A body-recovery team of one or more Federal Bureau of Investigation (FBI) agents, one or two Federal Emergency Management Agency (FEMA) representatives, a photographer, and a four-body carrier unit from the 3rd Infantry Regiment (Old Guard) looked for remains. Each body or body part was photographed at the site. Later, cadaver-sniffing dogs were brought in to help the body-recovery teams. One hundred and twenty-five people died in the Pentagon attack, and hundreds more were injured.

Stephen E. Atkins

See also: Global War on Terror; Islamic Radicalism; Justification for the September 11 Suicide Mission; Martyrdom; Suicide Bombings; Terrorism; World Trade Center, September 11, 2001

Further Reading

Bernstein, Richard. *Out of the Blue: The Story of September 11, 2001, from Jihad to Ground Zero*. New York: Times Books, 2002.

Goldberg, Alfred, et al. *Pentagon 9/11*. Washington, DC: Historical Office, Office of the Secretary of Defense, 2007.

Hedges, Michael. "Workers at Pentagon Recount Horrific Scene." *Houston Chronicle*, September 12, 2001, A22.

Perle, Richard

(September 16, 1941–)

Highly influential lobbyist, political adviser and pundit, and vocal leader of the neoconservative movement. Richard Perle was born in New York City on September 16, 1941, but moved to southern California with his family as a youth. He graduated from the University of Southern California in 1964, studied in Copenhagen and at the London School of Economics, and earned a master's degree in political science from Princeton University in 1967. Perle entered the public arena in 1969, when he took a job on Senator Henry M. "Scoop" Jackson's staff. As a Senate staffer from 1969 to 1980, Perle gained considerable political insight and expertise and soon became known as an expert on arms control and national security issues.

Despite his considerable reputation, Perle preferred to work behind the scenes and was not a well-known figure outside the halls of Congress. By the late 1970s, he had become an anti-Soviet hard-liner and derided the Jimmy Carter administration's attempts to engage in arms control agreements with the Kremlin, which Perle believed were detrimental to U.S. defense and global security. During this time, he also forged lucrative contacts with the private sector, which caused some to question his motives.

In 1981, the incoming Ronald Reagan administration named Perle assistant secretary of defense for international security policy, a post he held until 1987. Perle was, predictably, a champion of Reagan's get-tough approach with the Soviets and endorsed efforts to fight communism in Central America as well as the arming of the mujahideen in Afghanistan, who were waging an anti-Soviet insurgency.

His tenure in office was not without controversy. In 1983, he was accused of conflict of interest after recommending that the Pentagon purchase an Israeli-made weapons system. The company that made the system had recently paid Perle a $50,000 consulting fee. Perle pointed out that the payment was for work done prior to his joining the Reagan administration, but his detractors used the incident to tarnish his image.

When not employed in the public sector, Perle busied himself with lucrative consulting jobs, served as an informal political adviser, wrote several books, composed myriad essays and op-ed pieces for foreign and domestic newspapers and magazines, and often appeared on television as a political commentator. He has subscribed to numerous conservative and neoconservative causes and think tanks, including the Jewish Institute for National Jewish Affairs, the Center for Security Policy, the Hudson Institute, and the American Enterprise Institute for Near East Policy, among others. He was one of the signatories to the Project for the New American Century's open letter to President Bill Clinton in 1998 that advocated the overthrow of Iraqi dictator Saddam Hussein. Perle cultivated close ties to fellow neoconservative Paul Wolfowitz, deputy secretary of defense from 2001 to 2005 and a key architect of the Iraq War, as well as Secretary of State Donald Rumsfeld.

During 2001–2003, Perle was well placed to advocate for his neoconservative outlook as chairman of the Defense Policy Board Advisory Committee, which was charged with advising the Pentagon on matters of defense and national security issues. As such, he was an early and vocal proponent of war with Iraq, and within days of the September 11, 2001, terror attacks, he was on record as having linked Hussein to Al-Qaeda, a claim that has never been substantiated. Perle is also on record as having proposed to invade Iraq with as few as 40,000 ground troops, and he was dismissive of U.S. Army chief of staff General Eric Shinseki's call for more than 600,000 troops to attack Iraq. Perle envisioned a scenario in Iraq similar to that which had unfolded in Afghanistan during Operation Enduring Freedom, which had left most of the ground fighting to indigenous forces.

After the Iraqi insurgency began in earnest in 2004, Perle made a concerted attempt to distance himself from some of the

George W. Bush administration's policies in Iraq. While Perle has yet to call his Iraq War advocacy a mistake, he has expressed regret about the way in which the war was waged, and blamed "dysfunction" in the Bush administration for the failings of U.S. occupation and pacification policies. David Brooks, a conservative columnist, wrote in the *New York Times* in 2004 that Perle had "no noteworthy meetings with either Bush or [Vice President Dick] Cheney" after 2001 and intimated that Perle's influence over official policy was entirely overblown.

In 2004, Perle and other Hollinger executives were accused of fiduciary manipulation after they allegedly funneled company funds from stockholders' accounts into compensation packages for top company executives. Perle's compensation, at some $5.4 million, was questioned. In 2005, Perle publicly acknowledged he had been served a formal warning that the S.E.C.'s enforcement staff had found sufficient evidence of wrongdoing to bring a civil lawsuit. Perle was an advisor to Libyan dictator Muammar al-Gaddafi in 2006. Perle traveled to Libya with several other advisers to hold lectures and workshops, and promote the image of Libya and its ruler. In July 2008, he reportedly had made plans to invest in oil interests in Iraq, in collaboration with Iraqi Kurdish leaders in northern Iraq.

Paul G. Pierpaoli, Jr.

See also: Bush Administration; Bush Doctrine; Cheney, Richard Bruce; Feith, Douglas

Further Reading

Frum, David, and Richard Perle. *An End to Evil: How to Win the War on Terror.* New York: Random House, 2003.

Ricks, Thomas E. *Fiasco: The American Military Adventure in Iraq.* New York: Penguin, 2006.

Persian Gulf War

The Persian Gulf War resulted from the August 2, 1990, Iraqi invasion of neighboring Kuwait. In July 1990, U.S. intelligence detected an Iraqi military buildup along the Kuwaiti border. On July 17, Iraqi dictator Saddam Hussein threatened military action against Kuwait for its violation of Organization of Petroleum Exporting Countries (OPEC) oil caps. Overproduction had driven down the price of oil. Iraq's recently completed eight-year war with Iran (1980–1988) had generated a war debt of some $80 billion, and Baghdad was anxious to keep oil prices high. There was also an ongoing Iraqi border dispute with Kuwait over charges of Kuwaiti slant-drilling into Iraqi-controlled oil fields. Finally, Iraq had long claimed Kuwait as a "lost" province.

Washington had been increasingly concerned over Iraq's expanding nuclear industry and its chemical and biological weapons, some of which Hussein had used in the war against Iran and even against a group of Iraqi people, the Kurds. But U.S. policy was ambiguous, and Iraqis knew that Washington had tacitly supported them in the war with Iran, providing satellite intelligence information on Iran. U.S. Ambassador to Baghdad April Glaspie delivered mixed messages on behalf of the George H. W. Bush administration that seemed to allow Hussein free rein in the Persian Gulf. Hussein thus believed that Washington would probably not challenge a move against Kuwait. For its part, the State Department did not believe that Hussein would actually mount a full-scale invasion. If military action occurred, Washington expected only a limited offensive to force the Kuwaitis to accede to Iraqi oil production demands. Clearly, Washington underestimated Hussein's ambitions.

On August 2, 1990, Iraqi forces invaded Kuwait and speedily overran the country. The United States demanded that Hussein recall his troops from Kuwait. When he refused, the Bush administration took action. Washington feared that an unchecked Iraq would threaten Saudi Arabia, which possessed the world's largest oil reserves, and thus would be able to control both the price and flow of oil to the West. Bush also saw Hussein as a new Adolf Hitler and was determined that there would be no Munich-like appeasement of aggression. On paper, Iraq appeared formidable. Its army numbered more than 950,000 men, and it had some 5,500 main battle tanks (MBTs), of which 1,000 were modern T-72s; 6,000 armored personnel carriers (APCs); and about 3,500 artillery weapons. Hussein ultimately deployed 43 divisions to Kuwait, positioning most of them along the border with Saudi Arabia. In Operation Desert Shield, designed to protect Saudi Arabia and prepare for the liberation of Kuwait, the United States put together an impressive "coalition" that included Syria, Egypt, and Saudi Arabia as well as Britain, France, and many other states. Altogether, coalition assets grew to 665,000 men, 3,600 tanks, and substantial air and naval assets.

Hussein remained intransigent but also quiescent, allowing the buildup of coalition forces in Saudi Arabia to proceed unimpeded. When the deadline for Hussein to withdraw from Kuwait passed on January 15, 1991, coalition commander U.S. Army General H. Norman Schwarzkopf unleashed Operation Desert Storm on January 16. It began with a massive air offensive, striking targets in Kuwait and throughout Iraq, including Baghdad. In only a few days, the coalition had established absolute air supremacy over the battlefield. Iraq possessed nearly 800 combat aircraft and an integrated air defense system controlling 3,000 antiaircraft missiles, but it was unable to win a single air-to-air engagement, and coalition aircraft soon destroyed the bulk of the Iraqi Air Force. Air superiority assured success on the ground.

The air campaign destroyed important Iraqi targets along the Saudi border. Night after night, B-52s dropped massive bomb loads in classic attrition warfare, and many Iraqi defenders were simply buried alive. Schwarzkopf also mounted an elaborate deception to convince the Iraqis that the coalition was planning an amphibious assault against Kuwait. This feint pinned down a number of Iraqi divisions. In reality, Schwarzkopf had planned a return to large-scale maneuver warfare, which tested the U.S. Army's new AirLand Battle concept.

Schwarzkopf's campaign involved three thrusts. On the far left, 200 miles from the coast, XVIII Airborne Corps of the 82rd Airborne Division and the 101st Airborne Division (Airmobile), supplemented by the French 6th Light Armored Division and the U.S. 24th Infantry Division (Mechanized) and 3rd Armored Cavalry Regiment, were to swing wide and cut off the Iraqis on the Euphrates River, preventing resupply or retreat. The center assault, the mailed fist of VII Corps, was to be mounted some 100 miles inland from the coast. It consisted of the heavily armored coalition divisions: the U.S. 1st and 3rd Armored Divisions, the 1st Cavalry Division, the 1st Infantry (Mechanized) Division, and the British 1st Armored Division. VII Corps's mission was to thrust deep, engage, and then destroy the elite Iraqi Republican Guard divisions. The third and final thrust was to occur on the coast. It consisted of the U.S. 1st Marine Expeditionary force of two divisions, a brigade from the U.S. 2nd Armored Division, and allied Arab units, and was to drive on Kuwait City.

On February 24, Allied forces executed simultaneous drives along the coast, while the 101st Airborne Division established a position 50 miles behind the border. As the marines moved up the coast toward Kuwait City, they were hit in the flank by Iraqi armor. In the largest tank battle in the history of the U.S. Marine Corps, the marines, supported by coalition airpower, easily defeated the Iraqis. The battle was fought in a surrealist day-into-night atmosphere caused by the smoke of oil wells set afire by the retreating Iraqis.

As the marines, preceded by a light Arab force, prepared to enter Kuwait City, Iraqi forces fled north with whatever they could steal. Thousands of vehicles and personnel were caught in the open on the highway from Kuwait City and were pummeled by air and artillery along what became known as the "highway of death." The Allies now came up against an Iraqi rear guard of 300 tanks covering the withdrawal north toward Basra of four Republican Guard divisions. In perhaps the most lopsided tank battle in history, the Iraqi force was defeated at a cost of only one American death.

Lieutenant General Frederick Franks, commander of VII Corps to the west, angered Schwarzkopf by insisting on halting on the night of February 24 and concentrating his forces rather than risk an advance through a battlefield littered with debris and unexploded ordnance and subject to the possibility of casualties from friendly fire. When VII Corps resumed the advance early on February 25, its problem was not the Iraqis but the supply of fuel; because of the speed of the advance, the M1s needed to be refueled every eight to nine hours.

The afternoon of February 27 saw VII Corps engaged in some of its most intense combat. Hoping to delay the coalition, an armored brigade of the Medina Republican Guard Division established a six-mile-long skirmish line on the reverse slope of a low hill, digging in their T-55 and T-72 tanks. The advancing 2nd Brigade of the 1st Armored Division came over a ridge, spotted the Iraqis, and took them under fire from 2,500 yards. The American tankers used sabot rounds to blow the turrets off the dug-in Iraqi tanks. The battle was the largest single armor engagement of the war. In only 45 minutes, U.S. tanks and aircraft destroyed 60 T-72, nine T-55 tanks, and 38 Iraqi armored personnel carriers.

Allied tanks, especially the M1A1 Abrams and the British Challenger, had proved their great superiority over their Soviet counterparts, especially in night fighting. Of 600 M1A1 Abrams that saw combat, not one was penetrated by an enemy round. Conversely, the M1A1's 120-mm gun proved lethal to Iraqi MBTs. It could engage the Iraqi armor at 3,000 meters (1.86 miles), twice the Iraqis' effective range, and its superior fire control system could deliver a first-round hit while on the move. Overall, the coalition maneuver strategy bound up in the Air-Land Battle worked to perfection. As VII Corps closed to the sea, XVIII Corps to its left, with a much larger distance to travel, raced to reach the fleeing Republican Guards' divisions before they could escape to Baghdad.

In only 100 hours of ground combat, Allied forces had liberated Kuwait. On February 28, President Bush stopped the war. He feared the cost of an assault on Baghdad and was also concerned that Iraq might then break up into a Kurdish north, a Sunni Muslim center, and a Shiite Muslim south. Bush wanted to keep Iraq intact to counter a resurgent Iran.

The war was among the most lopsided in history. Iraq lost 3,700 tanks, more than 1,000 other armored vehicles, and 3,000 artillery pieces. In contrast, the coalition lost four tanks, nine other combat vehicles, and one artillery piece. In human terms, the coalition sustained 500 casualties (150 dead), many of these from accidents and friendly fire. Iraqi casualties totaled between 25,000 and 100,000 dead, with the best estimates being around 60,000. The coalition also took 80,000 Iraqis prisoner. Perhaps an equal number simply deserted.

Following the cease-fire, Hussein reestablished his authority. He put down, at great cost to the civilian population, revolts by the Shiites and Kurds. He also defied United Nations (UN) inspection teams by failing to account for all of his biological and chemical weapons, the so-called weapons of mass destruction (WMDs). Ultimately, President George W. Bush would use the alleged presence of WMDs as an excuse to send U.S. and allied forces to invade and occupy Iraq in another war in 2003, code-named Operation Iraqi Freedom.

Spencer C. Tucker

See also: Iraqi Freedom, Operation; McChrystal, Stanley A.; Multi-National Force—Iraq; U.S. Central Command

Further Reading

Dunnigan, James F., and Austin Bay. *From Shield to Storm.* New York: William Morrow, 1992.

Romjue, John L. *American Army Doctrine for the Post-Cold War.* Washington, DC: Military History Office and U.S. Army Training and Doctrine Command, 1997.

Scales, Robert H., Jr. *Certain Victory: The U.S. Army in the Gulf War.* Washington, DC: Brassey's, 1997.

Schubert, Frank N., and Theresa L. Kraus, eds. *Whirlwind War: The United States Army in Operations Desert Shield and Desert Storm.* Washington, DC: U.S. Army Center for Military History, 1994.

Schwarzkopf, H. Norman. *It Doesn't Take a Hero.* New York: Bantam, 1992.

Petraeus, David Howell

(1952–)

Davis Petraeus was born on November 7, 1952. He grew up and graduated from high school in Cornwall, New York. He graduated 10th in his class from the United States Military Academy, West Point, in 1974. Commissioned a second lieutenant of infantry, he graduated from Ranger School and served as a platoon leader in the 1st Battalion, 509th Airborne Infantry, in Italy. As a first lieutenant he served as assistant battalion operations officer, and as captain he served as company commander, battalion operations officer, and then commanding general's aide-de-camp, all in the 24th Infantry Division (Mechanized).

From 1982 to 1995, Petraeus served in a progression of command and staff assignments, with alternating assignments for both professional military and civilian academic education. He graduated from the Army Command and General Staff College in 1983, after which he attended Princeton University's Woodrow Wilson School of Public Affairs, where he earned a master's degree in public administration

U.S. Army general David Petraeus, commander of the U.S. Central Command (CENTCOM), confers with members of Combined Joint Task Force 101 at Combat Outpost Marghah in Afghanistan, on November 6, 2008. (U.S. Department of Defense)

in 1985 and a doctorate in international relations in 1987. His doctoral dissertation dealt with the U.S. Army in Vietnam and the lessons learned there.

Petraeus returned to West Point as an assistant professor of international relations and then was a military fellow at Georgetown University's School of Foreign Service. In 1995, he was assigned as the chief operations officer of the United Nations (UN) mission during Operation Uphold Democracy in Haiti.

Petraeus's commanded assignments included the 3rd Battalion, 187th Infantry Regiment, 101st Airborne Division, during 1991–1993, and the 1st Brigade, 82nd Airborne Division, from 1995 to 1997. He was promoted to brigadier general in 1999.

Petraeus's first combat assignment, at the rank of major general, came as commander of the 101st Airborne Division (Air Assault) in Operation Iraqi Freedom in March 2003. The division engaged in the Battle of Karbala and the Battle of Najar as well as the feint at Hilla. Petraeus later oversaw the administration and rebuilding of Mosul and Nineveh provinces. Subsequently, Petraeus commanded the Multinational Security Transition Command–Iraq and North Atlantic Treaty Organization (NATO) Training Mission–Iraq between June 2004 and September 2005. Petraeus's next assignment was as commanding general of Fort Leavenworth, Kansas, and the U.S. Army Combined Arms Center, where he exercised direct responsibility for the doctrinal changes to prepare the army for its continued efforts in Afghanistan and Iraq. He also coauthored *Field Manual 3-24, Counterinsurgency.*

On January 5, 2007, Petraeus, now a lieutenant general, was selected by

President George W. Bush and later unanimously confirmed by the U.S. Senate to command the Multi-National Force–Iraq. Petraeus took formal command on February 10, 2007, replacing Lieutenant General George Casey. The Petraeus appointment was the keystone in Bush's troop surge strategy in Iraq, designed to end the mounting violence there and bring about peace in Iraq. Many welcomed the change in command, but remained skeptical that Petraeus could reverse the violence in Iraq.

In April 2007, Petraeus was tasked with reporting to Congress on the progress of the Bush administration's troop surge strategy, begun that January, and met stiff and sometimes combative resistance. To his credit, however, Petraeus deftly handled the pressure and stated confidently that the strategy, given time, would show positive results. At the same time, he firmly argued against setting a timetable for the withdrawal of ground troops from Iraq. In July, he submitted to Congress his first progress report, which was positive and upbeat. It met with derision, however, because it did not appear that Iraq was any more secure than it had been in January. His September 2007 report cited progress on the military and security fronts but admitted that the political climate in Iraq remained troubled. The September report drew sharp criticism from some Democrats and the antiwar lobby, compelling a bipartisan group of congressional representatives and senators to sponsor resolutions—which eventually passed—that condemned the recent attacks on Petraeus. Petraeus was promoted to four-star rank in December 2007.

By early 2008, defying high odds and most critics of the war, the surge strategy appeared to be paying off, as violence had fallen off markedly in the last quarter of 2007. Talk of troop drawdowns, however, were still subject to interpretation, as the possible numbers being cited would account mainly for the surge, meaning that troop strength in Iraq would remain unchanged from January 2007, even after troop reductions.

By the spring of 2008, however, Petraeus could point to a significant reduction in sectarian and insurgency-based violence in Iraq. In addition, the Iraqis themselves seemed increasingly willing and able to take over security and police tasks. As a result, U.S. and coalition troop withdrawals accelerated throughout 2008, and violence in Iraq hit four-year lows. Petraeus was largely hailed in the United States for his efforts at undermining the Iraqi insurgency, and because of this President Bush tapped him to command CENTCOM. Petraeus took command on October 1, 2008; General Raymond Odierno succeeded him as commander of the Multi-National Force–Iraq.

During congressional hearings, Petraeus was careful to point out that talk of victory in Iraq was premature; instead, he viewed the situation with a great deal of realism, suggesting that an Iraq that is "at peace with itself, at peace with its neighbors, and has a government that is representative of—and responsive to—its citizens" might be considered a victory. As the head of CENTCOM, Petraeus became responsible for U.S. military operations in 20 nations from Egypt to Pakistan, as well as the ongoing conflicts in Afghanistan and Iraq.

On June 24, 2010, the same day that he removed General Stanley A. McChrystal as commander of U.S. and NATO forces in Afghanistan, President Barack Obama tapped Petraeus as McChrystal's successor, thereby sending a signal that there would no change in U.S. Afghanistan policy. Petraeus presided over the Obama administration's troop surge in Afghanistan, but that effort was not as successful as the one carried out in Iraq several years earlier. Less than a year later, the general found himself for the first time contemplating civilian life, but in 2011, Obama appointed Petraeus director of the Central Intelligence Agency; he took office on September 6, 2011. On November 9, 2012, however, Petraeus suddenly resigned from his post. The announcement came soon after Petraeus's extramarital affair with biographer Paula Broadwell was exposed.

Marcel A. Derosier

See also: Enduring Freedom, Operation; Iraqi Freedom, Operation; McChrystal, Stanley A.; U.S. Central Command

Further Reading

Atkinson, Rick. *In the Company of Soldiers: A Chronicle of Combat.* New York: Henry Holt, 2005.

Day, Thomas L. *Along the Tigris: The 101st Airborne Division in Operation Iraqi Freedom: February 2003–March 2004.* Atglen, PA: Schiffer, 2007.

Fontenot, Gregory, et al. *On Point: The United States Army in Iraqi Freedom.* Annapolis, MD: Naval Institute Press, 2005.

Phoenix Memo

The Phoenix Memo was an attempt by Federal Bureau of Investigation (FBI) field agent Kenneth Williams of the Phoenix FBI field office to warn FBI headquarters of a suspiciously large number of Middle Eastern males studying to become commercial pilots. His memo noted an "inordinate number of individuals of investigative interest" attending aviation training in Arizona. He believed that this might be part of "an effort to establish a cadre of individuals in civil aviation, who would be in position to conduct terrorist activity in the future" Williams also suspected that some of these pilot trainees had connections with Al-Qaeda.

Williams was right. One of the 10 trainees of whom he was most suspicious had contacts with Hani Hanjour. Williams sent the memo to individuals in the Usama Bin Laden Unit (UBLU) and the Radical Fundamentalist Unit (RFU) within the Counterterrorism Division at FBI headquarters and to several FBI special agents in the New York City field office.

Williams was a rookie FBI agent most of whose previous experience was with the San Diego Police Department and its SWAT team. He had become the counterterrorism expert in the Phoenix field office, but most of the attention was directed toward fighting the drug trade. In the middle of his investigation of Middle Eastern flight students, he received a six-month assignment to a high-profile arson case. This delayed his sending of the memo until after the end of the arson case.

Williams recommended in his memo that the FBI investigate the 3,000 or so commercial pilot schools for possible Al-Qaeda operations. This undertaking would have overloaded the FBI field offices, with little chance of FBI offices receiving any credit for their labor. Despite this failing, such an investigation might have identified some of the September 11 plotters and prevented the events of September 11. The problem was that this memo fell into a bureaucratic black hole, and no agent assumed responsibility for it.

The memo appeared at FBI headquarters on July 10, 2001, and elicited little interest. Nor was there any interest in it at the New York City field office's Joint Terrorism Task Force (JTTF). Agents in the New York City field office knew that Middle Eastern flight students were common, and they also knew that many of the students were affiliated with Al-Qaeda. These agents reasoned that bin Laden needed pilots to transport goods and personnel in Afghanistan. Personnel at FBI headquarters let the memo sit a week before deciding what to do with it. The FBI had a system where communications and memoranda were classified as a "lead," meaning that the office sending a communication can request that the receiving office or officers take some follow-up action or conduct additional investigation.

The lead was filed by the receiving office without notifying the officers' superiors of its existence. Finally, on July 30, 2001, the memo was assigned to an Intelligence Assistant (IA) in the RFU. This agent decided that the memo belonged to the UBLU. She was able to persuade a UBLU agent to take charge of the memo. This agent discussed the issue with colleagues over the legality of the proposal and whether it raised profiling issues. On August 7, 2001, the agents in the RFU and UBLU closed the file. They briefly considered assigning the Phoenix Memo to a headquarters analysis unit but decided against it.

This inaction remained hidden within FBI headquarters until the Joint Committee on Intelligence's investigators learned of its existence in 2003. Several of the participants then disclosed what had happened. This failure to respond to a warning was a black mark on FBI headquarters. Some of the FBI's field investigators were unhappy because no one in FBI headquarters was held responsible for this lapse of judgment.

Stephen E. Atkins

See also: Joint Terrorism Task Force; Pilot Training for September 11 Attacks; Rowley, Coleen; Terrorism

Further Reading

Graham, Bob. *Intelligence Matters: The CIA, the FBI, Saudi Arabia, and the Failure of America's War on Terror.* New York: Random House, 2004.

Joint Inquiry into Intelligence Community Activities before and after the Terrorist Attacks of September 11, 2001. *Hearings before the Select Committee on Intelligence U.S. Senate and the Permanent Select Committee on Intelligence House of Representatives.* Vol. 2. Washington, DC: U.S. Government Printing Office, 2004.

Pilot Training for September 11 Attacks

The key to the terrorist conspiracy of September 11, 2001, was pilot training. Khalid Sheikh Mohammed's original plan, as presented to Osama bin Laden and the other leaders of Al-Qaeda in mid-1996, envisaged the use of aircraft as flying bombs. Mohammed's nephew, Ramzi Yousef, had proved in the 1993 World Trade Center bombing in New York City that no bomb delivered by conventional means could cause enough damage to destroy a complex as large as the World Trade Center. The use of an aircraft as a flying bomb meant that the aircraft had to be large enough to carry a huge load of aviation fuel. The only candidates for such a mission were the aircraft flown by commercial airlines. Mohammed and his planners knew that seizing a commercial aircraft was possible, but the big problem was flying the aircraft to the target. Al-Qaeda knew that it could recruit intelligent, educated, and highly motivated suicide bombers, but training a handful of them to fly commercial aircraft was beyond them. Al-Qaeda was forced to send a select group of operatives to the United States and enroll them in commercial pilot training schools. Such training was expensive—about $30,000 per person—but Al-Qaeda had the necessary funds available. An additional risk that nevertheless had to be taken was the exposure of operatives to the attention of American authorities both on entry into the United States and during their stay in the country.

The United States has a thriving commercial pilot training industry. In 2000, around 3,000 commercial flight schools operated under the auspices of the National Air Transportation Association (NATS). These schools were located around the country, often in remote areas, operating from local airstrips and often training their students in airplane hangars—about 70,000 students annually, before September 11, 2001. Local interest in pilot training is steady, but some of the more ambitious schools actively recruited students from foreign countries. These schools had an agreement with the Immigration and Naturalization Services (INS) that allowed foreign students to enter the United States on the highly coveted I-20M immigration forms designed to help foreign students acquire visas to enter the United States as vocational students. Foreign students have flocked to the United States because a commercial pilot license in Europe or the Middle East would cost as much as $100,000 to earn, in contrast to $30,000 in the United States. In Florida's 220 commercial pilot training schools in 2000, 27 percent of the students were international students.

It was easy for Al-Qaeda to send a handful of its operatives to receive commercial pilot training. These operatives trained in at least 10 schools, from the Sorbi Flying Club in San Diego, California, to the Freeway Airport in Bowie, Maryland. After investigating the Airmen Flight School in Norman, Oklahoma, in July 2000 and finding it unsatisfactory, Mohamed Atta and Marwan al-Shehhi trained together at two Florida schools—Huffman Aviation in Venice, Florida, and Jones Aviation Flying Service at the Sarasota-Bradenton International Airport. After rejection by a flight instructor at the Jones Aviation Flying Service, they received most of their pilot training from Huffman Aviation.

After Atta and al-Shehhi received their commercial pilot licenses in December 2000, they began renting small aircraft to fly up and down the East Coast. It was on one such trip, on December 26, 2000, that Atta abandoned his rented aircraft on the taxiway at a Miami Airport after its engine sputtered before takeoff. The Federal Aviation Administration (FAA) complained about this but did nothing about it. In January 2001, Atta and al-Shehhi took even more flying lessons at the flight school at Gwinnett County Airport, near Atlanta, Georgia.

The other pilots trained at different schools. Several of them raised the suspicions of their flight instructors because of their apparent indifference to takeoffs and landings. All they seemed to be interested in was flying aircraft. This apparent disinterest made these pilots in training poor candidates for commercial pilots. Only one of the hijackers, Hani Hanjour, had ambitions to be a commercial pilot, but he was so poor a pilot that no commercial aviation company would hire him. Frustrated in his ambition, he joined the ranks of the hijackers.

The pilot flight schools have fallen on hard times after September 11, hurt by a combination of security-related red tape, diminished enrollment, and the stigma of association with the 9/11 hijackers. Florida and its pilot schools have suffered the most, but the hard times have affected the entire industry.

Stephen E. Atkins

See also: Atta, Mohamed el-Amir Awad el-Sayed; Hanjour, Hani Saleh Husan; Pentagon Attack; World Trade Center, September 11, 2001

Further Reading

Fainaru, Steve, and Peter Whoriskey. "Hijack Suspects Tried Many Flight Schools." *Washington Post*, September 19, 2001.

Hirschman, David. "I Didn't See Evil." *Atlanta Journal-Constitution*, January 27, 2002.

Klein, Barry, Thomas C. Tobin, and Kathryn Wexler. "Florida Flight Schools Decry Rush to Regulate after Attacks." *St. Petersburg Times*, September 24, 2001.

Sharockman, Aaron. "9/11 Hijackers Practiced Here." *St. Petersburg Times*, March 31, 2006.

Powell, Colin Luther

(April 5, 1937–)

Colin Luther Powell is a former U.S. Army officer, national security adviser during 1987–1989, chairman of the Joint Chiefs of Staff (JCS) during 1989–1993, and secretary of state during 2001–2005. He was born in New York City on April 5, 1937, the child of Jamaican immigrants. While pursuing a geology degree at the City College of New York, he joined the Reserve Officers' Training Corps (ROTC) and earned his commission as a second lieutenant in 1958. After paratrooper and ranger training, Powell was deployed as a military adviser to Vietnam. Even though

he was wounded and received a Purple Heart during his first tour, he chose to volunteer for a second tour before earning a master's degree in business administration at George Washington University in 1971. He was a White House fellow in 1972, followed by command assignments at the battalion, brigade, and division levels.

Powell served in executive assistant positions in the Energy Department and the Defense Department during the administration of President Jimmy Carter. Under President Ronald Reagan, Powell quickly moved up the ranks from senior military assistant to Secretary of Defense Casper Weinberger, whom Powell assisted during both the 1983 invasion of Grenada and the 1986 air strike on Libya. In 1986, Powell, now a lieutenant general, assumed command of the U.S. Army's V Corps in Germany. The following year, he became Reagan's national security adviser. In 1989, Powell was promoted to full general (four stars) and assumed command of Forces Command. Later that year, he became the youngest officer and the first African American to serve as chairman of the JCS.

As JCS chairman, Powell was responsible for developing the strategy that would allow a coalition of nations to push Iraqi president Saddam Hussein's invasion force out of Kuwait. Powell's strategy for dealing with the Iraqi Army was a simple one: "First we're going to cut it off, then we're going to kill it." Decisive force was the central tenet for the coalition strategy: overwhelming force should be brought to bear against the enemy. This approach led to a rapid and decisive victory over Iraqi forces in Operation Desert Storm. The victory came so quickly that some argued that it left the job unfinished, as Hussein remained in power. However, neither President George H. W. Bush nor Powell was

U.S. secretary of state Colin Powell tells reporters at the State Department on March 17, 2003, that President Bush will insist that Iraqi leader Saddam Hussein leave Iraq or face imminent war. (AP Photo/ Ron Edmonds)

eager to prosecute the war beyond the coalition's mandate or to make it appear as if the West was intent on punishing the Iraqi people.

The use of overwhelming force was one of the three tenets of the Powell Doctrine, which guided U.S. military strategy in the immediate aftermath of the Cold War. The doctrine also held that the United States should use its military only when the country's vital interests were at stake, only when there was a clear goal, and only when there was a clearly defined exit strategy. Unfortunately, as soon as Powell left the JCS in 1993, the Powell Doctrine began to be diluted.

Powell served as secretary of state under President George W. Bush beginning in 2001. It was clear from the start, however, that Powell would play a rather subordinate role to Vice President Richard Cheney, Secretary of Defense Donald Rumsfeld, Deputy Secretary of Defense Paul Wolfowitz, and National Security Advisor Condoleezza Rice. Except perhaps for Rice, all were considered neoconservatives, particularly in matters of national security and warfare. Powell, who did not subscribe to the rigid ideology of neoconservatism and was also the only senior civilian member of the administration with any practical experience in fighting wars, found himself in the difficult position of having to rally the international community around the global war on terror after the September 11, 2001, terrorist attacks. He walked a diplomatic tightrope between the Bush administration neoconservatives and the exigencies of the post-9/11 environment. Powell traveled less than any secretary of state in 30 years, demonstrating the demands that the global war on terror and the Iraq War exacted on his time.

Soon after 9/11, Powell was given the responsibility for building the case for a second invasion of Iraq to topple the Hussein regime and ensure that the nation did not harbor or use weapons of mass destruction (WMDs). Powell was generally opposed to the forcible overthrow of Hussein, arguing that it was better to contain him, which the international community had effectively done since 1991. Nevertheless, Powell agreed to work with the administration if it sought an international coalition to effect regime change in Iraq. Powell did convince Bush to take the case for war before the United Nations (UN); however, Powell had to serve as the point man for these actions.

As the United States moved toward war with Iraq, Powell addressed a plenary session of the UN on February 5, 2003, carefully building a case for international military action. Powell emphatically stated that the Iraqis had biological weapons in hand and that Hussein had many of the key components for the construction of a nuclear weapon. Powell's speech was immediately controversial, as many claimed even then that Powell's statements concerning Iraqi WMDs were unsubstantiated. Powell was himself skeptical about some of the intelligence presented to him, but nevertheless presented it as irrefutable. He would later refer to his UN speech as a blot on his record.

Powell must have been disappointed when the Iraq War was waged with insufficient numbers of troops to secure the peace in Iraq (a cardinal violation of the Powell Doctrine). The coalition that did invade Iraq in 2003 was not nearly as large, diverse, or unified as the 1991 coalition, another disappointment for Powell. Once Hussein had been toppled, Powell had the unenviable task of building international support for the rebuilding of Iraq, which was made far more difficult when a nearly two-year search found none of the WMDs that Powell and others had claimed were in Iraq.

As the war in Iraq began to deteriorate, Powell became even more marginalized with the administration. Realizing that his voice had been muted, he announced his intention to resign only days after Bush's November 2004 reelection. Powell left office in January 2005. He has since joined the venture capital firm of Kleiner, Perkins, Caulfield & Byers; embarked on an extended speaking tour; and has stayed active in moderate Republican political circles. In the summer of 2007, Powell revealed that he had spent much time attempting to persuade George W. Bush not to invade Iraq. Powell also stated that he believed that Iraq had descended into a civil war, the outcome of which could not be determined by the United States.

In 2007, Powell made a significant monetary contribution to Republican senator John McCain's 2008 presidential bid and reportedly advised McCain on both military and foreign policy matters. However, in the run-up to the 2008 election, Powell publicly endorsed the candidacy of McCain's Democratic Party opponent, Barack Obama. In October 2012, Powell endorsed Obama's 2012 reelection bid and expressed chagrin that some leaders in the Republican Party were unfairly demonizing Obama, which he believed was hurting the Republican Party.

Keith Murphy and
Paul G. Pierpaoli, Jr.

See also: Bush Administration; Cheney, Richard Bruce; Enduring Freedom, Operation; Global War on Terror; Iraqi Freedom, Operation; Rumsfeld, Donald Henry; Weapons of Mass Destruction

Further Reading

DeYoung, Karen. *Soldier: The Life of Colin Powell.* New York: Knopf, 2006.

Powell, Colin, and Joseph E. Persico. *My American Journey.* New York: Ballantine, 2003.

Roth, David. *Sacred Honor: Colin Powell; The Inside Account of His Life and Triumphs.* New York: HarperCollins, 1995.

Predator

The Predator is a medium-altitude, long-range, unmanned aerial vehicle (drone) used by the Central Intelligence Agency (CIA) and the U.S. Air Force (USAF) as an antiterrorist weapon. Developed by the USAF in the 1990s for long-range reconnaissance missions, it is about the size of a small SUV and is powered by a 101-horsepower propeller-driven engine that gives it a top speed of 135 miles per hour. It holds enough fuel to travel more than 750 miles. Its ability to hover in an area gives it an advantage over other, faster reconnaissance aircraft. When equipped with a pair of Hellfire antitank missiles, it also becomes an effective, lethal weapon. The Hellfire missile is an air-to-ground missile about five and a half feet long that weighs just over 100 pounds and can be fired from attack helicopters and the Predator.

The Predator is remotely controlled. A team of three—a pilot and two sensor operators—operate the Predator from a ground-control station that can be thousands of miles away. Controls for the system resemble those used in ultra-sophisticated model aircraft and advanced video games. It has a TV camera, an infrared camera, and a system that enables it to penetrate smoke and clouds.

The Predator has great potential for use against terrorists—particularly in remote areas—but its development was slowed by interagency gridlock. Both the CIA and the USAF wanted to gain control of the Predator program. Leaders of the CIA envisaged it as a counterterrorism weapon, but the USAF saw it as a reconnaissance asset. This infighting hindered the development of the program. Early versions of the Predator were used in Bosnia, and it was finally sent to Afghanistan in September 2000. President Bill Clinton authorized its use in Afghanistan to hunt down Osama bin Laden. Unfortunately, soon after it arrived in Afghanistan, one of the Predators crashed. It was suspected that news of its capabilities, or the possible capture of one of the aircraft, caused the Predator program to be shelved for improvements. Despite its obvious capabilities for neutralizing leaders of Al-Qaeda, the Predator program remained shut down until after September 11.

Revival of political fighting between the CIA and the U.S. Air Force caused most of the delay. The CIA still wanted to use the Predator as a weapon, and the USAF insisted that it be chiefly restricted to reconnaissance missions. The addition of the Hellfire antitank missile system sacrificed the Predator's ability to see through smoke and clouds. There was also argument about who would pay the $1 million price for each Predator. The George W. Bush administration finally ruled that the Department of Defense would pay for them, ending this part of the controversy.

A Predator-fired missile killed senior Al-Qaeda officials, including Mohammad Atef, in the early stages of the overthrow of the Taliban regime during Operation Enduring Freedom. Slow communications when seeking approval for a strike saved Mohammed Mullah Omar and most of the Taliban from a Predator attack on October 7, 2001. Then, in October 2002, a Predator launched its Hellfire missiles at a car carrying Abu Ali al-Harithi and Ahmed Hijazi, as well as four other Al-Qaeda operatives, on a road in Marib Province, Yemen. Al-Harithi had been part of the plot to attack USS *Cole* in October 2000. A National Security Agency (NSA) communications satellite intercepted a phone call from al-Harithi, and the Predator tracked the car before launching its missile. The car was destroyed with all its passengers, except one who escaped. This was exactly the type of mission the CIA had envisaged for the Predator system.

Despite this success, the Predator program has come under the operational control of the USAF after a decision made by the Bush administration. The CIA selects the target, but after the Predator is in flight, operational control is turned over to U.S. Air Force personnel in the United States. The job of completing a Predator's mission requires a task force of about 55 people to pilot the aircraft, check sensors, monitor communications, and manage the mission. Besides these personnel requirements, the Predator needs enough equipment for its ground control station that the equipment has to be hauled around by a C-130 transport aircraft. Despite this heavy logistical load, Predators have been frequently used in fighting the insurgencies in Iraq and Afghanistan. They have also been used against militants in Pakistan's Federally Administered Tribal Areas. Unfortunately, Predator missile strikes have also killed a number of civilians, leading to rising anti-American sentiment among local populations.

In 2002, a new version of the Predator, Predator B, appeared in the inventory of the U.S. military. Predator B is a larger model than its predecessor and has a more powerful jet engine. It lacks some of the loitering capability of the Predator, but it can fly twice as high and is much faster. Because it can carry a heavier armament package, the Predator B is more a hunter-killer than its earlier model. A third UAV, the MQ-1C Grey Eagle, became operational in 2009, with weaponized versions deployed to Afghanistan in late 2010. Predator drone strikes increased markedly during the Obama administration, which has deployed them with considerable success in Afghanistan and the border regions of Pakistan, as well as in Africa.

Stephen E. Atkins

See also: Bin Laden, Osama; Bush Administration; Central Intelligence Agency; Obama Administration; Unmanned Aerial Vehicles

Further Reading

Bigelow, Bruce V. "Predator, Part II: Spy Plane's New Version Is Bigger, Better, More Capable." *San Diego Union-Tribune*, August 27, 2002, C1.

Clarke, Richard A. *Against All Enemies: Inside America's War on Terror*. New York: Free Press, 2004.

Farren, Mick. *CIA: Secrets of "The Company."* New York: Barnes and Noble, 2003.

Huband, Mark, and Mark Odell. "Unmanned Weapon Makes Its Mark in Yemeni Sea of Sand." *Financial Times* (London), November 6, 2002, 24.

Miller, Judith, and Eric Schmitt. "Ugly Duckling Turns Out to Be Formidable in the Air." *New York Times*, November 23, 2001, B1.

Q

Qutb, Sayyid

Sayyid Qutb (alternative spellings are Said Qutub and Seyyid Kutb) was an Egyptian author, Islamic theoretician, and leader in the Muslim Brotherhood in the 1950s and 1960s. His writings have given rise to Qutbism, a strain of Islamic ideology that advocates the use of militant jihad to overcome Western power and culture. Due to the widespread popularity and influence of his works, he is commonly referred to as the father of modern fundamentalism. His two seminal pieces, *Milestones* and *Social Justice*, went on to form the ideological foundation of many radical Islamist groups, including Al-Qaeda. Qutb mainly focused on the social and political implications of Islam, but he also wrote extensively on his disapproval of the American way of life, which he believed to be fraught with moral pitfalls.

Qutb was born in 1906 in the Egyptian village of Musha. He was introduced to Islam largely through his father, who was well known for his political activism and devotion to the Koran. Qutb moved to Cairo in his twenties to start a career as a teacher in the Ministry of Public Instruction. During this early stage of his career, he devoted himself to literary critique and creative writing.

Qutb spent two years living in the United States as a student at the University of Northern Colorado, where he studied teaching. Many believe that it was during this trip that Qutb solidified his belief in America's moral bankruptcy. He wrote an influential piece titled "The America That I Have Seen" that summarized his disdain of the culture, drawing on aspects such as sexual promiscuity, materialism, racism, individual freedoms, and violence.

Upon his return from the United States, Qutb joined the Egyptian Muslim Brotherhood, where he started working as the editor of the group's newspaper and was later promoted to head of propaganda. The Muslim Brotherhood, founded in 1928 by Hasan al-Banna, shared many beliefs with Qutb, including a rejection of Western culture and influence in the Middle East. The Muslim Brotherhood opposed the Egyptian secular monarchy, and as a result, was banned for many of its early years. When Gamal Abdel Nasser and the Free Officers Movement overthrew the pro-Western monarchy, Qutb and the Brotherhood hoped that it would pave the way for a partnership toward an Islamic government. In fact, Qutb and Nasser had frequent secret meetings to discuss the Future of Egypt. Not until Qutb discovered that Nasser was exploiting their relationship and had created an organization to oppose the Muslim Brotherhood (the Tahreer) did he realize that the secular nationalist ideology of Nasserism would forever be incompatible with his own beliefs.

In 1954, Qutb was arrested for plotting against Nasser and was incarcerated for 10 years. He experienced many horrors during his time in jail, including being physically tortured and witnessing the deaths of fellow members of the Muslim Brotherhood. It was also during this time that he completed one of the most influential commentaries on the Koran ever written, entitled *In the Shade of the Qur'an*. Components of this 30-volume piece, along with letters he sent from prison, came to form the basis of his famous book *Milestones*. As the popularity of his works spread, the Nasser regime realized that his theories posed an existential threat to its ideology. Qutb was rearrested in 1965, sentenced to death, and killed a year later. Many considered him a martyr because he died at the hands of a government that he vehemently opposed.

The central tenets of Qutb's writings focus on the necessity of sharia law, arguing that following this code in its entirety is the only way to attain personal and societal peace. He believed that true implementation of sharia would not require a form of government, but rather would eventuate from and be organized in an anarcho-Islamic structure. Qutb believed that any system where men are subservient to other men instead of God could never truly be in accordance with the Koran. To combat this injustice, he advocated both proselytization and the abolishment of such institutions by physical power and jihad.

Stephanie Caravias

See also: Al-Qaeda; Bin Laden, Osama; Islamic Radicalism; Zawahiri, Ayman al-

Further Reading

Bergesen, Albert. *The Sayyid Qutb Reader: Selected Writings on Politics, Religion and Society*. New York: Routledge, 2007.

Calvert, John. *Sayyid Qutb and the Origins of Radical Islamism*. Chichester, NY: Columbia University Press, 2010.

Ibrahim, Raymond. *The Al Qaeda Reader: The Essential Texts of Osama bin Laden's Terrorist Organization*. New York: Broadway Books, 2007.

Musallam, Adnan. *From Secularism to Jihad: Sayyid Qutb and the Foundations of Radical Islam*. Westport, CT: Praeger, 2005.

Qutb, Sayyid. *In the Shade of the Quran*. Falls Church, VA: WAMY International, 1995.

R

Reid, Richard

(August 12, 1973–)

On December 22, 2001, Richard Colvin Reid, a citizen of the United Kingdom and convert to Islam, boarded American Airlines Flight 63 traveling from Paris to Miami. Approximately three hours after takeoff, Reid removed his shoes, each of which contained an improvised explosive device (IED) that he then tried to detonate by igniting a fuse with matches. Crew members and fellow passengers noted his actions and were able to tackle and subdue Reid before he was able to successfully carry out the attack. Reid was subsequently detained, and after pleading guilty to terrorism charges in 2003, he was sentenced to life in prison. In April 2005, Sajiid Badat, also a British national, was jailed for 13 years. He was accused of previously planning to attack another U.S.-bound commercial aircraft, but he had withdrawn from that plot.

Reid was born in South London on August 12, 1973. At the time of his birth, his father Robin was in prison for theft. Reid struggled at school and spent his free time experimenting with graffiti, but later graduated to more serious criminal activity. In 1992, he was arrested and convicted of four street robberies and sentenced to five years at the Feltham juvenile detention institution. It was during this incarceration that Reid's interest in Islam first began. Following his release, Reid attended the Brixton mosque in South London, where he adopted Salafi Islam. Here he also began to adopt a more militant stance, such as violent interpretations of jihad. After being challenged by the mosque's imam on these beliefs, Reid left and was drawn to the Finsbury Park mosque in North London, where the radical preacher Abu Hamza held sermons. Authorities believe that Djamel Beghal recruited him as an Al-Qaeda operative at this time. Reid appears to have spent part of 1999 and 2000 in Pakistan, where he attended a terrorist training camp. On his return to the United Kingdom, Reid came into contact with a number of other notable violent jihadists, including Nizar Trabelsi (later imprisoned for plotting to attack a North Atlantic Treaty Organization [NATO] base in Brussels).

Prior to Reid's abortive suicide attack, his Al-Qaeda handlers sent him on a series of intelligence-gathering tasks. On July 6, 2001, Reid flew from Karachi to Amsterdam, where he obtained a new passport from the British consulate. On July 12, Reid then took an El Al flight from Amsterdam to Tel Aviv, traveling in Israel for 10 days. On July 22, he boarded a bus to Cairo, leaving Egypt for Istanbul on July 29. He finally returned to Karachi on August 7. It is alleged that the purpose of this extended trip was to evaluate El Al security procedures at airports and in flight. Reid later claimed that the idea of placing explosives in his shoes resulted from these observations.

Authorities have also claimed that while in Israel, Reid identified a number of potential targets to attack, including the Tel Aviv train station. A journalist who bought a used laptop in Afghanistan after the fall of the Taliban subsequently found a copy of the report Reid (using the alias Abdul Ra'uff) is believed to have completed. The document reportedly showed that he had visited the Netherlands, Israel, Egypt, Turkey, and Pakistan, traveling on a British passport. Again the purpose appears to have been to scout venues for bombings.

In August 2001, Reid returned to Europe, spending time in Belgium and the Netherlands. On November 20, he again traveled to Pakistan, this time with Sajiid Badat, although the two men flew by different routes. From Pakistan, the pair crossed into Afghanistan, where they are thought to have received their "shoe bombs," which contained quantities of plastic explosive molded to fit into casual footwear. Tests would later show that the detonation cords for both devices had been cut from the same source. Reid and Badat then returned to the United Kingdom in early December 2001.

On December 5, 2001, Reid flew from Karachi to Brussels, where he obtained another new passport. On December 17, while in Paris, he booked a seat on Flight 63 to Miami; the following day he returned to the travel agency and paid for the ticket in cash. Meanwhile, Badat had booked a plane seat from Manchester to Amsterdam with the intent to take a U.S.-bound flight on December 21, the same day as Reid. However, at the last moment Badat had a change of heart and e-mailed his handlers

to say that he was unable to go through with the plan. He concealed the explosives in his parents' home and tried to return to normal life.

On December 21, Reid attempted to board the flight to Miami. However, airline and airport security personnel became suspicious, noting he had bought his ticket with cash and had no baggage to check in. Reid was subjected to additional questioning and screening, which caused him to miss his flight. Reid was rebooked for the following day and stayed in a local hotel. Despite the concerns raised on the previous day, he was allowed to board Flight 63, where he attempted to carry out the midair bombing.

Following the failure of the attack, the Federal Bureau of Investigation (FBI) took Reid into custody after the plane landed in Miami, and two days later he was charged with interfering with the operation of an aircraft. On January 16, 2002, Reid was indicted on eight additional charges, including the attempted use of a weapon of mass destruction, attempted murder, and attempted destruction of an aircraft. On October 4, 2002, Reid pleaded guilty to all counts and in January 2003, he was sentenced to three consecutive life sentences with no possibility of parole. Reid is currently serving his sentence in a super-maximum security prison in Colorado.

Greg Hannah

See also: Al-Qaeda; Global War on Terror; Terrorism

Further Reading

Belluck, Pam. "Unrepentant Shoe Bomber Is Given a Life Sentence for Trying to Blow Up Jet." *New York Times*, January 21, 2003.

Cullison, Alan, and Andrew Higgins. "Account of Spy Trip on Kabul PC Matches Travels of Richard Reid." *Wall Street Journal*, January 16, 2002.

Elliott, Michael. "The Shoe Bomber's World." *Time*, February 16, 2002.

O'Neill, Sean, and Daniel McGrory. *The Suicide Factory*. London: Harper Collins, 2006.

Rendition

Rendition is a legal term meaning "handing over." As applied by the U.S. government, rendition has been a controversial method of fighting terrorism. Overseen by the Central Intelligence Agency (CIA), its use was approved by presidents Bill Clinton, George W. Bush, and Barack Obama.

There are two forms of rendition: ordinary rendition and extraordinary rendition. Ordinary rendition occurs when a terrorist suspect is captured in a foreign country and then turned over to the United States. The individual is then transported to the United States or held at a foreign site for interrogation. Extraordinary rendition is the turning over of a suspected terrorist to a third-party country for detainment and questioning. Often, the suspect is wanted by the third-party country as well, for past offenses or crimes.

The first use of ordinary rendition occurred in 1986, during the Ronald Reagan administration, in regard to a suicide bombing in Beirut, Lebanon, the previous year. Fawaz Yunis had participated in the 1985 hijacking of a Jordanian aircraft, during which three Americans were killed. Federal Bureau of Investigation (FBI) agents and U.S. Navy SEALs seized him in a boat off the Lebanese coast.

Rendition as a policy lay largely dormant until the rise of more terrorism in the early 1990s. One such rendition involved the capture of Ramzi Yousef and his transportation to the United States. Yousef had been implicated in the 1993 World Trade Center bombing.

By the mid-1990s, there was a need for rules to standardize rendition. Michael Scheuer, then the head of the Bin Ladin Issue Station (code-named Alex, or Alec Station) in the Central Intelligence Agency (CIA), drew up the guidelines for a new rendition program in 1996. He ultimately ran the rendition program for 40 months.

The intent of the rendition program was to dismantle and disrupt the Al-Qaeda terrorist network and detain Islamic terrorists. Because the Clinton administration and the FBI did not want the captives brought to the United States, where the legal process gave them significant protection, the CIA focused on Al-Qaeda suspects who were wanted in a third country. In the early years, most of the extraordinary renditions were to Egypt, where torture and other methods of interrogation that are illegal in the United States were, and remain, in use.

The CIA has always been ambivalent about rendition. It has justified the practice with the contention that when allied governments had intelligence on terrorists that could not be used in a court of law, rendition was sometimes the only way to neutralize the terrorists. For renditions, the CIA has frequently used paramilitaries organized into teams and operating under the supervision of a CIA officer.

The rendition program has been effective, but it includes the danger that the information gathered is tainted by torture. Moreover, international law prohibits the forced return of any person, regardless of the crime, to a foreign location where that person would be subject to torture or mistreatment. Michael Scheuer has maintained that he warned the lawyers and policymakers about the dangers of turning over Al-Qaeda suspects to foreign countries.

In the George W. Bush and Barack Obama administrations, the CIA continued to handle rendition cases. Whereas rendition cases were infrequent in the Clinton administration, they became numerous during the Bush administration, especially after the September 11, 2001, terror attacks. Approximately 100 suspected Al-Qaeda operatives were captured and turned over to foreign governments for interrogation from 1996 to 2008. In recent years, a white Gulfstream V jet has been used to move prisoners around to various countries. Egypt, Afghanistan, and Syria have been principal destinations, but at least 14 European states have knowingly cooperated with the United States. Several Eastern European states are thought to have housed CIA detention centers.

In one case, two Egyptians were seized in Sweden and sent to Egypt. Ahmed Agiza and Muhammed al-Zery were radical Islamists, and they had sought political asylum in Sweden. On December 18, 2001, American agents seized both of them and placed them on a Gulfstream jet bound for Cairo, Egypt. The Swedish government cooperated after its representatives were assured that Agiza and Zery would not be tortured.

Once it was learned that both Agiza and Zery had indeed been tortured, there was a major political outcry in Sweden against the Swedish government and the United States. Egyptian authorities determined that Zery had no contacts with terrorists, and he was released from prison in October 2003. Agiza was less fortunate because he had been a member of Egyptian Islamic Jihad and close to its leader, Ayman al-Zawahiri. An Egyptian court subsequently sentenced Agiza to 25 years in prison.

Rendition has become more controversial after public revelations regarding several cases. The first such case was that of the radical Islamist cleric Abu Omar (full name Hassan Osama Nasr), who lived in Milan, Italy, under political refugee status. Omar had been under investigation for terrorist-related activities and support of Al-Qaeda when the CIA, with the assistance of Italian security personnel, seized him on the streets of Milan on February 17, 2002. He was taken to a North Atlantic Treaty Organization (NATO) base near Aviano, Italy, and then flown to Egypt on February 18. There, Omar was offered a deal to be an informant. After he refused, he was sent to a prison where he was tortured. Italian authorities became incensed over this rendition, and a judge charged 25 American CIA operatives and two Italian security officers with abduction. The Italian government requested extradition of the CIA operatives, and initiated court proceedings in 2008. The trial coincided with continuing popular Italian opposition to the Iraq War.

Two other cases of rendition also caused unease among U.S. allies. One was that of Maher Arar, a Canadian citizen from Ottawa and a software engineer. Arar arrived at JFK Airport in New York on an American Airlines flight from Zurich, Switzerland, on September 26, 2002, when U.S. authorities detained him. They were acting on inaccurate information given to them by the Royal Mounted Canadian Police (RMCP) that Arar was a member of Al-Qaeda. After interrogation and a stay at the Metropolitan Detention Center, he was flown to Jordan on October 8, 2002. CIA operatives then transferred him to Syria. In Syria, he was imprisoned and intensively interrogated for nearly a year. It took intervention by the Canadian government to win Arar's release in October 2003, after more than 10 months in captivity. Reportedly in 2012, Arar and his family remained on the U.S. No Fly List. His lawyers filed a lawsuit, *Arar v. Ashcroft*, which sought compensatory damages on Arar's behalf and also a declaration that the actions of the U.S. government were illegal and violated his constitutional, civil, and international human rights. After the lawsuit was dismissed by the Federal District Court, the Second Circuit Court of Appeals upheld the dismissal on November 2, 2009. The Supreme Court of the United States declined to review the case on June 14, 2010.

Meanwhile, a Canadian commission publicly cleared Arar of any links to terrorism, and the government of Canada later settled out of court with Arar. He received $10.5 million and Prime Minister Stephen Harper formally apologized to Arar for Canada's role in his "terrible ordeal."

Another noteworthy case was the December 2003 rendition of Khalid El-Masri, a German citizen. El-Masri was born in Kuwait but raised in Lebanon. In 1985 he immigrated to Germany, where he became a German citizen in 1994. He took a vacation in Skopje, Macedonia, but was arrested at the Macedonian border on December 31, 2003, because his name resembled that of Khalid al-Masri, the mentor of the Al-Qaeda Hamburg cell. CIA agents took him into custody on January 23, 2004, shortly after Macedonian officials had released him. He was sent to Afghanistan, where he was tortured during lengthy interrogations. El-Masri went on a hunger strike for 27 days in the confinement camp. American officials determined that he had been wrongfully detained, and he was released on May 28, 2004. He was dumped on a desolate road in Albania without an apology or funds to return home.

In early February 2013, an Italian court sentenced several former Italian intelligence agents to terms of up to 10 years for supporting the CIA in its 2003 kidnapping of Egyptian Muslim cleric Abu Omar. The CIA kidnapped Abu Omar in Italy and flew him first to the Ramstein air base in Germany and then to Egypt, where he says he was tortured. Milan appeals court judges sentenced Niccolo Pollari, former head of the Sismi military intelligence agency, to 10 years and jailed his former deputy Marco Mancini for nine years. The former head of the Rome CIA station and two other American officials were convicted in absentia and are unlikely to serve their sentences.

No charges were filed in Germany against CIA agents involved on German territory. The investigations conducted by prosecutor Eberhard Bayer, 62, were terminated because he was unable to determine which CIA operatives had been involved.

Numerous cases of torture have been verified, and they have made rendition a difficult policy to justify. Most of the rendition cases came during the first two years following September 11; there have been fewer of them after that time. Political fallout regarding rendition cases, however, continues both in the United States and among its allies.

Stephen E. Atkins

See also: Alec Station; Bush Administration; Central Intelligence Agency; Clinton Administration; Global War on Terror; Obama Administration

Further Reading

Drumheller, Tyler, and Elaine Monaghan. *On the Brink: An Insider's Account of How the White House Compromised American Intelligence*. New York: Carroll and Graf, 2006.

Grey, Stephen, and Ian Cobain. "From Secret Prisons to Turning a Blind Eye: Europe's Role in Rendition." *Guardian* (London), June 7, 2006, 1.

Scheuer, Michael. "A Fine Rendition." *New York Times*, March 11, 2005.

Whitlock, Craig. "In Letter, Radical Cleric Details CIA Abduction, Egyptian Torture." *Washington Post*, November 10, 2006.

Wilkinson, Tracy. "Details Emerge in Cleric's Abduction." *Los Angeles Times*, January 10, 2007.

Ressam, Ahmed

(May 17, 1967–)

Ahmed Ressam became infamous as the Al-Qaeda operative who was part of a plot to bomb the Los Angeles International Airport on January 1, 2000, earning him the nickname "the millennium bomber." Although this attempt failed, it was an indicator that Al-Qaeda was actively plotting against the United States.

Ressam had had a difficult childhood. He was born on May 19, 1967, in the town of Bou Ismail, Algeria. His father was a veteran of the Algerian War of Independence from France, and he worked as a government chauffeur. Ressam was the eldest of seven children. He was an active child and a good student. At age 16, however, a long-festering ulcer led him to have medical treatment and an operation in Paris. During this time, Ressam fell behind on his schoolwork, and even after repeating a year of school, he failed his final exam. This failure meant he was ineligible to attend a university. Ressam applied for jobs with the Algerian police and security forces, but was turned down. Unable to find meaningful employment, Ressam began working in a small café his father had opened.

In the meantime, he lived a secular life, drinking wine, smoking hashish, and dating girls. Political conditions in Algeria deteriorated in the early 1990s, with open warfare between the military-controlled government and the radical Front Islamique du Salut (FIS, or Islamic Salvation Front). Ressam decided that there was no future in Algeria, so he left for France.

Ressam arrived in Marseilles, France, on September 5, 1992. When his 30-day visa expired, and after obtaining a false French passport under the name Nasser Ressam, he traveled to Corsica, where he worked at odd jobs, mostly picking grapes and oranges. On November 8, 1993, French authorities arrested him in Ajaccio, Corsica, and charged him with immigration violations. Facing a March 1994 hearing and probable deportation to Algeria, Ressam fled to Canada.

Ressam arrived in Montreal on February 20, 1994. An immigration agent spotted the false passport and detained him. Ressam claimed political asylum to avoid deportation to Algeria. He insisted that the Algerian police had arrested him for selling firearms to a terrorist and had tortured him. Ressam was released on bond and told to have a lawyer represent him at a March 28, 1994, hearing. In the meantime, Ressam lived off welfare from the Canadian government.

Even after missing the March court date, Ressam was able to remain in Canada. Ressam began attending the Assuna Annabawiyah Mosque, where he ran into young men engaged in small-time criminal activity. To supplement his income, Ressam turned to small-scale crime. He was arrested once for shoplifting and then for pickpocketing, but in both instances he received only fines and probation. His theft of identifications and passports led him to an Al-Qaeda operative, Fateh Kemal, who bought the documents from Ressam. Kemal used the proceeds from these crimes to support Al-Qaeda's operations both in Canada and in the Middle East.

In 1996, an Al-Qaeda leader in Canada recruited Ressam for training as an operative. Ressam had made many contacts among Algerians in Canada. Hal Bernton, a reporter for the *Seattle Times*, noted that these were disaffected young men who spent their time "playing soccer, smoking cigarettes, and decrying the corrupt culture of their new country while simultaneously exploiting its generous immigration and welfare laws." Ressam developed a working relationship with members of the Algerian terrorist group Groupe Islamique Armeé (GIA, or Armed Islamic Group); this group also had ties with Al-Qaeda. Raouf Hannachi recruited Ressam to train at an Al-Qaeda camp in Afghanistan. On March 17, 1998, Ressam traveled to Peshawar, Pakistan, where he met Abu Zubaydah, the head of Al-Qaeda's training program.

Ressam's return to Canada had been easy, but the other members of his cell were detained elsewhere. These other members were to be the leaders of the cell, and their absence meant Ressam had to take a leadership role. He began to recruit others into his cell, including Abdelmajid Dahoumane, Mohktar Haouari, and Abdel Meskini, but none of them had received any Al-Qaeda training. Using a stolen Royal Bank visa card, Ressam and his cell began planning to build a bomb. His target was the Los Angeles International Airport; the plan was to place the bomb near a crowded security checkpoint for maximum casualties. In November 1999, the cell began the actual construction of the bomb in Vancouver, British Columbia.

After the bomb was built, the decision was made that only Ressam would transport it because it was thought that customs officers would be less likely to pull over a lone driver. Ressam started transporting the bomb on December 14, 1999. He took the M. V. Coho Ferry from Victoria, British Columbia, to Port Angeles, Washington. Customs inspector Diana Dean became suspicious about how Ressam was behaving. A close inspection found ingredients for a bomb in the spare-tire compartment. Ressam made a break for it but was soon captured. For a while, the custom agents had no idea that the materials they had found were intended for a highly sensitive bomb.

Ressam was unaware that he and his cell had been under investigation by the Canadian Security and Intelligence Service (CSIS) since 1996, and that agents knew of his connections to the GIA and later Al-Qaeda. Their surveillance of Ressam and his cell led these agents to conclude that they were relatively harmless. Even when a French terrorist expert, Jean-Louis Bruguiere, insisted that Canadian authorities arrest Ressam and his compatriots, CSIS was slow to respond. What CSIS did not know was that Ressam had been building a bomb to use in the United States.

After a four-week trial in the U.S. district court in Los Angeles, on April 6, 2001, Ressam was convicted of conspiracy to commit an international terrorist act, explosives smuggling, and lying to customs officials, among the nine counts with which he was charged. With the prospects of a prison sentence of 130 years, Ressam decided to cooperate for a reduced sentence. His information was used in the briefing paper titled "Bin Laden Determined to Strike in the U.S.," which President George W. Bush received on August 6, 2001. He also gave valuable information about Al-Qaeda and some of its operatives.

Ressam began to have second thoughts about cooperating in 2004 and stopped communicating with authorities. On July 27, 2005, U.S. district judge John Coughenour sentenced Ressam to 22 years in prison. The U.S. prosecutor appealed the sentence as too lenient, and the U.S. Ninth Circuit Court of Appeals panel ruled in January 2007 against one of the nine felony convictions. This was the count involving the use of false documents while transporting explosives. The U.S. Supreme Court, however, overturned this ruling on May 19, 2008, thereby reinstating the original convictions and sentence.

In a subsequent appeal, the U.S. Ninth Circuit Court of Appeals ruled on February 2, 2010, that the 22-year sentence was too lenient and did not meet the mandatory sentencing guidelines—65 years in prison—that had been in place at the time of the original trial. In October 2012, Ressam was resentenced to 37 years imprisonment. He is serving time at a supermaximum security prison in Colorado.

Stephen E. Atkins

See also: Al-Qaeda; Millennium Plots; Moussaoui, Zacarias; Zubaydah, Abu

Further Reading

Berton, Hal, Mike Carter, David Heath, and James Neff. "The Terrorist Within." *Seattle Times*, July 2, 2002.

Mulgrew, Ian. "Ressam Gets 22 Years in Prison." *The Gazette* (Canada), July 28, 2011.

Sageman, Marc. *Understanding Terror Networks*. Philadelphia: University of Pennsylvania Press, 2004.

Schwartz, John. "Appeals Court Throws Out Sentence in Bombing Plot, Calling It Too Light." *New York Times*, February 2, 2010.

Shepherd, Michelle. "Dossier Reveals Secrets of Forming al-Qaeda Cell." *Toronto Star* (Canada), April 25, 2011.

Shukovsky, Paul. "Terrorist Ahmed Ressam Is Sentenced but U.S. Judge Lashes Out." *Seattle Post-Intelligencer*, July 28, 2005.

Rowley, Coleen

(December 19, 1954–)

Coleen Rowley is the Federal Bureau of Investigation (FBI) agent from the Minneapolis field office who clashed with FBI headquarters over the handling of Zacarias Moussaoui's case. She was the principal legal adviser to the Minneapolis field office. She has been outspoken in her belief that the mishandling of the Moussaoui case by FBI headquarters contributed to the success of the terrorists on September 11, 2001.

Rowley was born on December 20, 1954, and raised in a small town in northeastern Iowa. After high school, she attended Wartburg College in Waverly, Iowa. She graduated summa cum laude in 1977 with a degree in French. Her next decision was to enter the College of Law at the University of Iowa, from which she received a JD in 1980, shortly thereafter passing the Iowa bar exam. Her career choice was to become an FBI agent. After passing the training at Quantico, Rowley was appointed a special agent with the FBI in January 1981. Her first assignment was in the Omaha, Nebraska, field office, but she soon was sent to the Jackson, Mississippi, field office. In 1984, Rowley was assigned to the New York field office, where she spent six years and specialized in organized crime. Because of her expertise in French, she received an assignment with the U.S. embassy in Paris, France, and later at the consulate in Montreal, Canada. Rowley received a promotion and an assignment to the Minneapolis field office as the chief legal adviser in 1990.

Rowley's chief claim to fame was her criticism of FBI headquarters for the mishandling of the Moussaoui case. Special agent Harry Samit received a communication from personnel at the Eagan flight school stating that Moussaoui might be attending their school to train for a terrorist attack. Moussaoui was arrested on a visa violation, but the agents at the Minneapolis office wanted a warrant to gain access to more information. Counterterrorism supervisors David Frasca and Michael Maltbie rejected the warrant requests. Bureau lawyers then turned down a Foreign Intelligence Surveillance Act (FISA) warrant request. Nothing was done, despite the growing frustration of the special agents at the Minneapolis field office, until after September 11. Rowley's frustration came to a head, and she reacted negatively to the statement by Robert Mueller, the director of the FBI, that an investigation of Moussaoui would not have prevented September 11. Her response was to send a 13-page letter to Mueller on May 21, 2002. In the letter, Rowley outlined the failures of FBI leadership on the Moussaoui case. Rowley accused these FBI leaders of effectively "deliberately sabotaging" the Moussaoui investigation. She indicated that certain facts had been "omitted, downplayed, glossed over, and/ or mischaracterized in an effort to avoid or minimize personal and/or institutional embarrassment on the part of the FBI and/ or even perhaps for improper political reasons." Rowley accused FBI headquarters of careerism, and she was indignant that those blocking the Moussaoui case and other terrorist cases were being promoted. Because Rowley knew that this letter was dynamite, she asked for whistle-blower protection against retaliation. At first Mueller kept the letter secret, but word got out and Rowley became an overnight sensation.

Rowley received an invitation to testify before the Senate Judiciary Committee in June 2002. The Moussaoui case was off limits, but she talked about the general weaknesses of the FBI organization. She was especially critical of the eight layers of bureaucracy encountered before reaching the director. Another aspect of the FBI found lacking was its inadequate computer system. Despite assurances that there would be no retaliation from Mueller, Rowley knew that her FBI career was at an end. She retired from the FBI in 2004 after 24 years of service. Rowley decided to run for political office in Minnesota. Her residence was in Apple Valley, Minnesota. She opted to run against incumbent representative John Kline for the Second Congressional District of Minnesota seat in the U.S. House of Representative in the November 2006 election. Rowley ran on an anti–Iraq War platform. Despite her popularity, she lost to Kline in the election. She is currently a blogger for the *Huffington Post*.

Stephen E. Atkins

See also: Counterterrorism Center; Counterterrorism Strategy; Moussaoui, Zacarias; Pentagon Attack; World Trade Center, September 11, 2001

Further Reading

Eggen, Dan. "Agent Claims FBI Supervisor Thwarted Probe." *Washington Post*, May 27, 2002.

Gordon, Greg. "Rowley Explains Criticisms." *Star Tribune* (Minneapolis), June 7, 2002.

Milligan, Susan. "FBI Whistle-Blower." *Boston Globe*, June 7, 2002, A33.

Powers, Richard Gid. *Broken: The Troubled Past and Uncertain Future of the FBI.* New York: Free Press, 2004.

Russo, Robert. "FBI Likened to Little Shop of Horrors." *Gazette* (Montreal), June 7, 2002, B1.

Rudolph, Eric

On July 27, 1996, Eric Rudolph bombed the Olympic Centennial Park in Atlanta, Georgia, during the 1996 Olympic Games being held there. The attack killed one spectator, Alice Hawthorne; a Turkish cameraman named Melih Uzunyol died of heart failure while running to the scene. Authorities said that 11 others were wounded. Forensic experts said that although the bomb was crude, it was designed to cause maximum casualties. The device was filled with masonry nails that served as shrapnel and hidden in a backpack specially designed with a steel plate to direct the blast outward. Apparently, it would have caused more damage if it had not tipped over at some point before detonating. Weighing in excess of 40 pounds, it was the largest pipe bomb in U.S. history.

Initially, suspicion for the bombing fell on the security guard Richard Jewell, who first spotted the backpack and started to clear the area. The working theory was that he had deliberately planted the bomb in order to defuse it so he could project himself as a public hero. However, no evidence was given to back up this line of inquiry, and authorities instead focused on other potential culprits. After Jewell was cleared, the FBI admitted it had no other suspects, and the investigation made little progress until early 1997, when two more bombings took place at an abortion clinic and a lesbian nightclub, both in the Atlanta area. The bombing of an abortion clinic gave the FBI crucial clues including a partial license plate. Other clues led the FBI to identify Eric Robert Rudolph as a suspect. Rudolph eluded capture and became a fugitive. Over a year later, on May 5, 1998, the FBI named him as one of its ten most wanted fugitives. A $1 million reward was offered for information leading to his arrest, but with the help of friends and accomplices, he managed to evade capture for another five years.

During the time Rudolph was on the run, both federal and amateur search teams carried out intensive searches for him. Quite naturally, his family supported him and maintained his innocence, while other hate groups called for more of his type of violence. Two country music songs were also written about his exploits, both of which made the national charts.

Federal authorities eventually captured Rudolph on May 31, 2003. In a subsequent statement, he declared that he was opposed to the U.S. government on account of its sanctioning of abortion on demand and had wanted to force the cancellation of the Atlanta Olympics to both embarrass Washington and negate the investment in the games. The statement also finally removed any lingering suspicion of Jewell and, indeed, vindicated him as a hero. In a deal to avoid the death sentence, Rudolph confessed to three other bombings: one on January 16, 1997, in Sandy Springs, Georgia; one on February 21, 1997, outside the Otherside Lounge, a lesbian bar in Atlanta; and one on January 29, 1998, at an abortion clinic in Birmingham, Louisiana. Together with the Centennial Games incident, these attacks left 3 people dead and more than 112 injured.

On August 21, 2005, a federal judge sentenced Rudolph, then 39, to four consecutive life sentences plus 120 years without parole. He was also fined $2.3 million in damages. He was sent to the super-maximum security prison in Colorado, where he spends more than 22 hours a day alone in his 80-square-foot cell.

Donna Bassett

See also: Centennial Olympic Park Bombing; Counterterrorism Center; Terrorism

Further Reading

Baird-Windle, Patricia, and Eleanor J. Bader. *Targets of Hatred: Anti-Abortion Terrorism.* New York: St. Martin's, 2001.

Hillard, Robert L., and Michael C. Keith. *Waves of Rancor: Tuning In the Radical Right.* New York: M. E. Sharpe, 1999.

Schuster, Henry. *Hunting Eric Rudolph.* New York: Penguin, 2005.

Rumsfeld, Donald Henry

(July 9, 1932–)

Congressman, government official, ambassador, and U.S. secretary of defense (1975–1977, 2001–2006), Donald Henry Rumsfeld was born in Chicago, Illinois, on July 9, 1932, and graduated from Princeton University in 1954. He was commissioned in the navy through the Naval Reserve Officers' Training Corps (NROTC), and served as a pilot and flight instructor from 1954 to 1957. Rumsfeld

remained in the reserves, retiring as a navy captain in 1989.

Rumsfeld began his long association with Washington as an administrative assistant to Representative David S. Dennison, Jr., of Ohio during 1957–1959, then joined the staff of Representative Robert Griffen of Michigan. During 1960–1962, he worked for an investment-banking firm. In 1962, Rumsfeld was elected to the U.S. House of Representatives as a Republican from Illinois and served until 1969, when he resigned to accept an appointment as director of the Office of Economic Opportunity and assistant to President Richard M. Nixon (1969–1970). He was then counselor to the president and director of the Economic Stabilization Program (1971–1973). During 1973–1974, he was U.S. ambassador to the North Atlantic Treaty Organization (NATO), and thus avoided any involvement with the Watergate scandal.

Nixon resigned and was succeeded by Gerald Ford, and in August 1974, Rumsfeld returned to Washington to serve as chair of the new president's transition team. He was then Ford's chief of staff. During 1975–1977, Rumsfeld served as secretary of defense. At age 43, he was the youngest person to hold that position. During Rumsfeld's 14 months in office, he oversaw the transformation of the military to an all-volunteer force, as well as post–Vietnam War reforms. He also actively campaigned for additional defense appropriations and to develop weapons systems, such as the B-1 bomber, the Trident missile system, and the MX missile. Ford honored Rumsfeld for his government service in 1977 with the Presidential Medal of Freedom, the nation's highest civilian award.

Rumsfeld left government service when President James (Jimmy) E. Carter took

Secretary of Defense Donald Rumsfeld defended U.S. treatment of terrorist suspects held at the detention facility in Guantánamo Bay, Cuba during press briefing on June 1, 2005. Rumsfeld said it was absurd to compare the Guantánamo facility with a Soviet-era "gulag." (U.S. Department of Defense)

office in January 1977. Following a brief period as a university lecturer, Rumsfeld entered private business. He was chief executive officer, then chairman, of G. D. Searle, the pharmaceutical company, from 1977 to 1985. From 1990 until 1993, Rumsfeld served as chairman and chief executive officer of General Instrument Corporation. During 1997–2001, Rumsfeld was chairman of Gilead Sciences, Inc. Concurrent with his work in the private sector, Rumsfeld served on numerous federal boards. He also served in the Ronald Reagan administration as special presidential envoy to the Middle East during 1983–1984.

In January 2001, newly elected President George W. Bush appointed Rumsfeld to be secretary of defense for a second time. Rumsfeld then became the oldest individual to hold the post. Bush charged him with transforming the military from its Cold War emphasis on major conventional warfare into a lighter, more efficient force capable of rapid deployment around the world. Rumsfeld worked to develop network-centric warfare, an approach to military operations that relies on technological innovation and integration of weapons and information systems to produce more firepower with fewer personnel.

In addition, Rumsfeld initiated the restructuring of the U.S. military presence throughout the world and the closure and consolidation of bases. Rumsfeld also refocused the strategic forces of the United States by emphasizing missile defense and space systems following the 2002 U.S. withdrawal from the Anti-ballistic Missile Treaty. He made certain of the loyalty of top officers by personally reviewing all higher promotion decisions at the three-star level and above. He angered a number of members of Congress when he canceled such weapons programs as the Comanche helicopter and Crusader self-propelled artillery system.

Rumsfeld's reform efforts and his restructuring of the military were overshadowed by his role in the post–September 11, 2001, global war on terror. As secretary of defense and a proponent of neoconservatism, Rumsfeld oversaw the military operation that overthrew the Taliban regime in Afghanistan (Operation Enduring Freedom), although the failure to capture Osama bin Laden tarnished the otherwise successful military campaign.

Rumsfeld was one of the foremost proponents of military action against Iraq, teaming up with President Bush and Vice President Richard Cheney to overcome opposition from within the cabinet by Secretary of State Colin Powell. Indeed, Rumsfeld was a major architect of the Bush Doctrine, which called for preemptive military action against potential adversaries. Rumsfeld then directed the 2003 invasion of Iraq (Operation Iraqi Freedom). In the campaign, Rumsfeld employed a strategy that relied on firepower and smaller numbers of "boots on the ground."

While the overthrow of the Iraqi regime of Saddam Hussein was highly successful, the subsequent occupation of Iraq did not go well. Within the Pentagon, there were complaints of Rumsfeld running roughshod over those who disagreed with him. Certainly he was much criticized for his outspoken, combative management style, as when he pointedly referred to the French and German governments, which had opposed the war, as "Old Europe." But there was good reason to criticize his military decisions and specifically his overly optimistic assessment of the situation that would follow the overthrow of Hussein. Disbanding the Iraqi Army to rebuild it from scratch came to be seen in retrospect as a major blunder. Rumsfeld had also ignored previous recommendations that 400,000 U.S. troops would be required for any occupation of Iraq. The actual number of troops involved was only about one-third that number. As a consequence, Iraqi arms depots, oil-production facilities, and even the national museum were looted in the immediate aftermath of the invasion.

Occupation troops were unable to halt a growing insurgency. As U.S. casualties escalated and Iraq descended into sectarian violence, calls for Rumsfeld's ouster came from Republicans as well as Democrats, and even a number of prominent retired generals. Just prior to the 2006 midterm elections, an editorial in all the *Military Times* newspapers demanded his removal.

Rumsfeld resigned on November 8, 2006. This came a week after President Bush had expressed confidence in his defense secretary and said that he would remain until the end of his term, but it was also one day after the midterm elections, in which the Republican Party lost its majorities in both the House of Representatives and the Senate. The election was widely seen as a referendum on the Iraq War, and by extension, Rumsfeld's leadership of it. President Bush named former Central Intelligence Agency (CIA) director Robert Gates to succeed Rumsfeld. In early 2011, Rumsfeld published his autobiography, *Known and Unknown: A Memoir*, a spirited defense of his policies in the George W. Bush administration.

Tom Lansford and Spencer C. Tucker

See also: Bush Administration; Bush Doctrine; Cheney, Richard Bruce; Enduring Freedom, Operation; Gates, Robert Michael; Iraqi Freedom, Operation; Powell, Colin Luther

Further Reading

Graham, Bradley. *By His Own Rules: The Ambitions, Successes, and Ultimate Failures of Donald Rumsfeld.* New York: PublicAffairs, 2009.

Scarborough, Rowan. *Rumsfeld's War: The Untold Story of America's Anti-Terrorist Commander.* Washington, DC: Regnery, 2004.

Woodward, Bob. *State of Denial: Bush at War, Part III.* New York: Simon and Schuster, 2006.

Woodward, Bob. *Plan of Attack.* New York: Simon and Schuster, 2004.

Woodward, Bob. *Bush at War.* New York: Simon and Schuster, 2002.

Rwanda

The death in a plane crash in 1994 of Rwanda president Juvénal Habyarimana, a moderate Hutu, marked the beginning of systematic attacks against Tutsis in Rwana. Although it is virtually impossible to get an accurate count of the resulting deaths, it is estimated that some 800,000–1,000,000 Tutsis and moderate Hutus were killed during the genocide, while many others fled Rwanda into neighboring countries. Except to rescue their own citizens, the Western powers, including the United States, were unwilling to intervene in Rwanda to stop the horrific bloodshed. Furthermore, the UN was powerless to act in the face of Western indifference.

In the aftermath of the genocide, the Rwandan Patriotic Front (RPF) continued fighting against the Hutu government, eventually taking over the country. Paul Kagame became president in 2000, and led Rwanda into an unsuccessful and bloody conflict with the Democratic Republic of Congo, which ended in 2002. During Kagame's administration, however, Rwanda slowly became safer and more stable.

The failure of the United States to intervene in Rwanda, its quick exit from Somalia (Operation Restore Hope) in 1995, and its limited responses to terrorist attacks against American interests in Yemen and Africa in the late 1990s seemed to demonstrate Americans' unwillingness to risk U.S. lives for a greater cause. Some have speculated that this may have played a part in the decision of the Al-Qaeda terrorist organization to attack the United States on September 11, 2001, believing it could do so with relative impunity. However, these attacks initiated the U.S. global war on terror, which then focused on the Middle East.

Since the early 2000s, Rwanda has slowly and steadily rebuilt its economy and infrastructure, and has voiced a keen interest in transforming its economy from one based largely on subsistence agriculture to one that is knowledge based. Such a transformation, however, will be slow going. Nevertheless, Kagame made a concerted effort to attract outside investment and boost economic activity. By 2007, the nation was deemed safe for tourists, and only one mortar attack, in a rural area, was launched during that entire year.

Wyndham E. Whynot

See also: Al-Qaeda; Global War on Terror; Somalia, International Intervention; Terrorism

Further Reading

Nugent, Paul. *Africa since Independence: A Comparative History*. New York: Palgrave Macmillan, 2004.

Schwab, Peter. *Africa: A Continent Self-Destructs*. New York: Palgrave Macmillan, 2001.

S

Satellites, Use of by Coalition Forces

Some military leaders and analysts have dubbed the 1991 Persian Gulf War the "first space war" because of the extensive use of satellite systems during that conflict. Although the U.S. military had used satellite systems to some degree in prior conflicts, it utilized every type of satellite system during Operations Desert Shield and Desert Storm. The use of satellite systems became even more prominent in the years since the end of that war.

When Iraqi troops invaded Kuwait in August 1990, the U.S. Central Command (CENTCOM) had begun updating its war plans, an indication of CENTCOM's intent to fully use space systems in a future Middle Eastern conflict. When hostilities by a U.S.-led coalition to drive Iraq from Kuwait began in January 1991, most of the satellites eventually used in the conflict were already in orbit and available. The Department of Defense eventually launched additional satellites to provide increased theater coverage and deployed more than 7,000 terminals and receivers so that the military could readily access and use the satellite data and imagery.

With the initial deployment to Saudi Arabia, CENTCOM contacted numerous space organizations, such as the Defense Communications Agency, Joint Chiefs of Staff (JCS), the Defense Mapping Agency (DMA), the U.S. Space Command, the Space and Missile Systems Center, the Strategic Air Command, the U.S. Navy's Space Command, and the U.S. Army's Space Command, to secure access to satellites, resolve technical issues, and arrange for data and imagery dissemination. The time it took to mobilize these capabilities depended upon ground equipment and satellite availability, launch windows, processing actions required to launch a spacecraft into orbit, time required to check out newly launched satellites or to reposition a satellite for better coverage, and the placement of trained personnel where needed. CENTCOM had received the use of 51 military and 12 commercial satellites by February 1991.

Perhaps the most important system of the Persian Gulf War was the Navigation Satellite Timing and Ranging (NAVS-TAR) Global Positioning System (GPS) satellite constellation. Coalition forces used GPS signals for numerous logistical, planning, and fighting applications. With GPS receivers, ground troops could readily navigate the nearly featureless desert, especially in the frequent sandstorms, and supply trucks were able to locate dispersed frontline units. Units conducted large-scale night maneuvers that in the past would have required numerous scouts and guides along the routes of advance. GPS allowed coalition forces to shift their attack plans back and forth virtually up to the moment of attack since they did not need fixed ground markers.

The Defense Meteorological Satellite Program (DMSP) satellites provided weather and climatic data and imagery directly to theater commanders in near real time. Commanders could now select targets and munitions for accurate targeting, plan and redirect aerial and ground missions, optimize night-vision equipment and night-capable targeting systems, and plan movement routes into Kuwait. DMSP satellites also provided information to alert troops to sandstorms, predict the possible spread of chemical agents, and monitor the extensive smoke plumes from the oil fires ignited by the Iraqi Army as it fled Kuwait in February 1991.

Satellite communications (SATCOM) provided essential command and control (C2) of deployed coalition forces. Within the first 90 days of deployment, U.S. military forces established more military communications connectivity to the Persian Gulf than had existed in Europe over the previous 40 years. Theater commanders communicated through a U.S. Navy Fleet Satellite Communications (FLTSATCOM) satellite, a Leased Satellite (LEASAT) program satellite, and two Defense Satellite Communications System (DSCS) satellites over the Indian Ocean. In addition, the Defense Department used FLTSATCOM satellites over the Atlantic and DSCS satellites over the Eastern Atlantic to communicate between CENTCOM headquarters in Saudi Arabia and various headquarters in the United States.

CENTCOM also used three early warning satellites of the Defense Support Program (DSP), normally used to provide ballistic missile early launch warning and other surveillance information. The DSP satellites detected Iraqi Scud missile launches, especially against targets in Israel, to provide timely warning to military forces and civilians.

During the course of the 1990s, the use of satellites by U.S. military forces grew as individual satellite systems, the integration of air and space elements to support joint war fighting, the development of digital data links, and increasing electronic airborne sensors to process information and deliver that information to field forces developed into network-centric warfare. More than 50 American and European satellites supported Operation Allied Force in March–June 1999 to force Yugoslavian president Slobodan Milosevic to end atrocities in Kosovo. Satellites connected the Combined Air Operations Center (CAOC) in Italy and other C2 centers to each other and to improved satellite sensors and other intelligence, surveillance, and reconnaissance (ISR) assets, such as the Predator unmanned aerial vehicles (UAV) and high-altitude U-2 reconnaissance aircraft. The Predators picked up ground imagery and relayed it through satellites to various C2 centers in real time, allowing commanders to calculate precise coordinates for the newly operational Joint Direct Attack Munition (JDAM), which used the NAVSTAR GPS signal to provide precise guidance to within 10 feet of its intended target and to improve timely battle damage assessment.

This short conflict made huge demands on SATCOM systems, especially the DSCS III satellites. After Desert Storm, the U.S. Air Force had contracted with Lockheed Martin to upgrade the last four DSCS satellites to provide greater tactical capability. DSCS satellites, the U.S. Navy's Ultra-High Frequency Follow-On satellites, and the newly operational Military Strategic and Tactical Relay (MILSTAR) satellite constellation provided bandwidth not only for voice and message communications but also for video-conferencing among the leaders of the coalition nations and coalition military leaders. Additionally, these satellites relayed video imagery from Predator and other airborne ISR platforms to dispersed C2 centers and linked command authorities, ground stations, and aircraft and ships during the conflict. Although SATCOM capability had risen by more than 100 percent since Desert Storm, the unprecedented demand during Operation Allied Force compelled the Defense Department and North Atlantic Treaty Organization (NATO) to lease commercial satellites to supply almost 75 percent of SATCOM's needs.

After the September 11, 2001, terrorist attacks on the United States, the Defense Department launched Operation Noble Eagle to deter a future air attack on the United States. Military, civil, and commercial space capabilities played an important part during this operation. SATCOM provided immediate communications to New York City and Washington, D.C., when they lost cell service from very high postattack use. Weather satellites provided weather data for decision makers involved in protection, response, and recovery actions. GPS provided precise data for search and rescue work and vehicle surveillance and tracking. Intelligence-gathering satellites helped monitor, locate, and intercept terror communications and networks.

In October 2001, U.S. military forces, assisting indigenous anti-Taliban forces in Afghanistan, launched Operation Enduring Freedom to destroy the Al-Qaeda terrorist infrastructure and overthrow the Taliban government. CENTCOM conducted an air campaign, relying on precision-guided weapons and U.S. Special Operations Forces (SOF) operating with the anti-Taliban forces. CENTCOM's newly operational CAOC at Prince Sultan Air Base, Saudi Arabia, served as the linchpin for the campaign's network-centric operations. Decision makers and planners could track every aircraft over Afghanistan, receive real-time video and data links from UAVs and other ISR platforms, and develop a common operating picture through global communications connectivity.

Coalition forces for this conflict utilized nearly 100 satellites of all types. Through a daily Space Tasking Order that paralleled the CAOC's Air Tasking Order, the Air and Space Operations Center of Fourteenth Air Force, the key provider of space support, could optimize coalition space capabilities by directing the appropriate space system to support a particular operational requirement and apportion space assets to meet both theater and global requirements. Because of greatly increased communications requirements, the military planners maximized the use of DSCS and MILSTAR satellites. Expanding use of UAV streaming-video imagery in real time to some strike aircraft and numerous worldwide C2 centers drove the need to obtain additional bandwidth and channels from civil and commercial communications satellites as the UAVs could not link through the military communications satellites. The widely dispersed and remote locations of coalition ground forces in Afghanistan increased the use of SATCOM between fielded forces and higher headquarters on the one hand and various control centers on the other hand.

Military and commercial weather and environmental satellites also made significant contributions to Enduring Freedom operations. This variety of satellites provided imagery and data on surface wind speed and direction, fog and cloud conditions, and dust storms. The GPS satellites have been the great enabler of network-centric and precision warfare in Operation Enduring Freedom. SOF controllers with the ground forces used laser-designator binoculars to determine the exact range of enemy ground forces, fed this data into a GPS receiver to produce accurate target coordinates, and then relayed these coordinates to airborne warning and control (AWAC) aircraft, the CAOC, or strike aircraft that released laser-guided bombs (LGBs) or GPS-guided munitions against the designated targets. Additionally, some strike aircraft obtained the capability to directly receive Predator video imagery through SATCOM links to actually see the targets on the ground and resolve any questions about target identification directly with the ground controllers.

Additionally, the use of the JDAM in Operation Enduring Freedom rose by almost 45 percent, while the use of LGBs dropped by nearly 32 percent. The U.S. Air Force increased its use of Boeing B-52 Stratofortress and North American/ Rockwell/Boeing B-1B Lancer strategic bombers, which released 46 percent of the total number of JDAMs in precision attacks on hostile ground forces. Increasingly, land- and carrier-based fighter aircraft handled most of the LGB missions. The larger bombers could carry up to 80 of the smaller, more accurate JDAMs and, more recently, the Small Diameter Bombs (SDB) that enabled them to strike more targets in a single mission with greater accuracy and less collateral damage. Data links allowed pilots to change preprogrammed target coordinates in flight to meet current needs of the ground forces.

Because the larger percentage of coalition forces in Afghanistan consisted of small parties of tactical air controllers with the anti-Taliban forces, the CAOC and other headquarters and control centers needed a means to track and locate these widely dispersed units in remote locations of Afghanistan. The U.S. Army had initiated a digital battle command system, called Force XXI Battle Command Brigade and Below (FBCB2). In this system, ground vehicles equipped with GPS transponders reported their location to a host vehicle, which in turn retransmitted its position to all networked units. Computer screens in these vehicles then displayed the locations of all networked vehicles as blue icons. Operational and intelligence personnel could then input data on enemy forces, which showed up as red icons.

Because of the limited range of line-of-sight radios, the Army attached SATCOM receivers onto the roofs of the vehicles of two 4th Infantry Division brigades. These receivers allowed the operators to receive an aggregated picture of the blue (friendly) force from a satellite ground station. This system, known as FBCB2-Blue Force Tracking (FBCB2-BFT), provided commanders with a tactical Internet that allowed them to control more decisive operations over vast distances more rapidly with greater force protection capability and allowed them to conduct operations in bad weather or at night in difficult terrain.

Space support for Operation Iraqi Freedom, which began in March 2003, was prominent, pervasive, and effectively more integrated than in previous operations. It produced a far greater level of coordination among air and space elements to support the fielded forces. As in Operation Enduring Freedom, the Space Cell in the CAOC worked even closer with the mission planners to integrate space assets into the operational plan and then work with space operations organizations in the United States to provide tailored space systems for particular combat requirements. DSP satellites detected and tracked Iraqi tactical ballistic missiles that resulted in the issuance of warning notices to targeted forces. Military, civil, and commercial satellites provided weather and environmental data and imagery to headquarters, C2 centers, mission planners, and fielded forces in virtually real time.

The use of GPS timing and ranging proved vital to Iraqi Freedom operations. With a full constellation, the GPS satellites provided unprecedented precise tracking, location, and targeting coordinates. The Enduring Freedom experience with FBCB2-BFT resulted in the expansion of the program as U.S. Army, U.S. Marine Corps, and British forces in Iraq received more than 1,200 BFT systems. The use of GPS-guided air-delivered munitions increased to about 68 percent of all munitions expended, almost 8 percent above the Enduring Freedom figure of 60 percent by late 2006.

SATCOM was another indispensable element in network-centric expeditionary warfare. The Defense Department increased available bandwidth capacity, especially from commercial satellites, by a factor of three to accommodate the growing requirements. Operation Enduring Freedom saw an increase in the use and quantity of satellite phones for communications and blue force situational awareness. The CAOC increased its use of MILSTAR satellites for secure communications, UAV surveillance video feeds, reach-back intelligence data, and facsimile and data message transmission among multiple users, such as the CAOC, headquarters, C2 centers, and deployed air, ground, and naval forces. Satellites will continue to take on even greater importance as technology continues to advance at a rapid pace.

Robert B. Kane

See also: Enduring Freedom, Operation; Iraqi Freedom, Operation; National Geospatial-Intelligence Agency; U.S. Central Command

Further Reading

Levis, Alexander H., John C. Bedford, and Sandra Davis, eds. *The Limitless Sky: Air Force Science and Technology Contributions to the Nation*. Washington, DC: Air Force History and Museums Program, 2004.

Spires, David N. *Beyond Horizons: A Half Century of Air Force Space Leadership*. 2nd ed. Maxwell Air Force Base, AL: Air Force Space Command and Air University Press, 2007.

Saudi Arabian Embassy (Khartoum) Attack

On March 1, 1973, ambassador Sheik Abdulla el-Malhouk was hosting a reception at the embassy of Saudi Arabia in Sudan for the departing American chargé d'affaires, George C. Moore. The party had just begun to break up at 7:00 p.m. when a Land Rover bearing diplomatic plates drove up to the largely unguarded gates of the compound. Eight Black September Organization (BSO) terrorists exited the vehicle and, armed with machine guns and revolvers, forced their way inside the building. They shot the Belgian chargé d'affaires, Guy Eid, in the leg and wounded the newly arrived U.S. ambassador, Cleo A. Noel, Jr., in the ankle. They then began to round up other guests as hostages.

The militants were well prepared. They had a guest list, security details, a diagram of the building, and a list of high-priority targets, including the ambassadors of West Germany, Great Britain, and the United States, as well as Moore.

The West German ambassador was kept away from the party by a diplomatic delegation from Bonn. British ambassador Raymond Etherington-Smith had been forced to leave the party early in order to pick up Anthony Kershaw, Britain's undersecretary of state, at the airport. These last-minute chores in all probability saved their lives.

The gunmen set a 24-hour deadline and demanded that Jordan free BSO leader Abu Daoud, and 16 others with ties to the group. In addition, they said they wanted the release of the two surviving hijackers who had carried out the May 8, 1972, attack on Sabena Airlines; Sirhan Sirhan, the Palestinian who had assassinated U.S. Senator Robert F. Kennedy in 1968; imprisoned members of the Baader-Meinhof Gang; and all women held in Israeli jails who had had been arrested for their activities on behalf of the Palestinian cause.

On March 2, Jordan and the United States rejected the BSO ultimatum. The terrorists responded by dropping their demands for prisoners to be released in Israel and West Germany. However, they strongly reaffirmed their commitment that those held in Jordan and Sirhan Sirhan should be set free.

Sixty minutes after the 24-hour deadline expired, the militants received an encrypted message from Lebanon that read, "Remember Nahr al-Bard. The people's blood in the Nahr-al Bard cries out for vengeance. These are our final orders. We and the rest of the world are watching you." This was a code ordering them to execute Noel, Moore, and Eid. At 9:30 p.m., the three men were taken to the basement

and shot to death. The militants released their remaining hostages on March 4 and surrendered to Sudanese authorities. Of the eight men who carried out the attack, two were set free for lack of evidence, and six were convicted of murder on June 24, 1974. They were handed over to Egypt and released to the Palestine Liberation Organization in November 1974.

Donna Bassett

See also: Benghazi Attacks; Bush Doctrine; Carter Doctrine; Dozier (James) Kidnapping; Hamburg Cell; Indian Embassy (Kabul) Bombing

Further Reading

Dobson, Christopher. *Black September: Its Short, Violent History*. London: Robert Hale, 1975.

Korn, David A. *Assassination in Khartoum*. Bloomington: Indiana University Press, 1993.

Mickolus, Edward F. *Transnational Terrorism: A Chronology of Events, 1968–1979*. Westport, CT: Greenwood, 1980.

Tyler, Patrick. *A World of Trouble: The White House and the Middle East—from the Cold War to the War on Terror*. New York: Farrar Straus Giroux, 2009.

Scheuer, Michael

(1952?–)

Michael Scheuer was head of the Central Intelligence Agency (CIA) Counterterrorism Center's Alec Station; he suspected Osama bin Laden's Al-Qaeda network of plotting violence against the Unites States well before the September 11, 2001, terror attacks. He believed from the first that bin Laden constituted a clear and present danger to the United States, but he had difficulty persuading the leadership of the CIA and the Bill Clinton administration about the threat. Scheuer's strident attacks on those in the CIA and the Clinton administration who prevented the Alec Station from assassinating bin Laden led to his removal as head of Alec Station in 1999, but he remained vocal on the issue. Since his resignation from the CIA in 2004, he has maintained a high profile by writing two books that castigate those who did not understand the threat of bin Laden and Al-Qaeda.

Little is known about Scheuer's personal background. He was born sometime around 1952, but there is little information about where or about the details of his upbringing. As with most CIA agents, personal data are hard to come by. What is known is that Scheuer attended Canisius College in Buffalo, New York, graduating in 1974. He then obtained a master's degree from Niagara University in 1976. His final educational degree was a PhD from the University of Manitoba in 1986. Based on the fact that he served 22 years in the CIA and retired in 2004, Scheuer must have joined the CIA in 1982. Scheuer was never a field officer; he worked as an analyst. Evidently he was good at analysis because in 1996, he was assigned to head the Usama bin Laden Unit (UBLU) in the Counterterrorism Center. This unit soon earned the name Alec Station, after Scheuer's adopted son Alec.

Scheuer directed all of the assets of the Alec Station to find ways to neutralize bin Laden. In his three years as head of this unit, he became extremely frustrated with the failure of the Clinton administration to carry out operations to eliminate bin Laden as a threat. Scheuer made plain that collateral damage was acceptable to him if the operation captured or killed bin Laden. The Clinton administration, however, was leery of collateral damage. Another of Scheuer's assignments was drafting the provisions of the rendition process that was later authorized by President Clinton.

Scheuer has a pugnacious personality, and this led to conflicts with key people in government circles. He also had difficulty sharing information with the Federal Bureau of Investigation (FBI). A personality conflict developed between him and John O'Neill, the counterterrorism expert with the FBI. O'Neill was just as aggressive as Scheuer, and they clashed. Both Scheuer and O'Neill kept material secret from the other agency. Scheuer's behavior became so aggressive that he was relieved as head of Alec Station in 1999. He stayed on in the CIA, and in September 2001, the CIA appointed him special adviser to the chief of Alec Station. He retained his position until he resigned from the CIA on November 12, 2004.

Since his retirement from the CIA, Scheuer has maintained a high profile as a critic of both the Clinton and George W. Bush administrations' counterterrorism efforts. While still with the CIA, he wrote a book that gave the view of the United States from bin Laden's perspective titled *Through Our Enemies' Eyes: Osama bin Laden, Radical Islam, and the Future of the United States* (2003). The outline of this book had originally been written as an unclassified manual for counterterrorism officers, but Scheuer expanded it and received approval from the CIA to publish it. This book created so much controversy that the CIA has amended its policy, now prohibiting CIA agents from writing books while still employed. After his resignation from the CIA, Scheuer wrote another book, *Imperial Hubris: Why the West Is Losing the War on Terror* (2004).

A lifelong Republican, Scheuer has been especially critical of President Clinton for not authorizing operations to neutralize bin Laden. He also attacked the American intelligence community for its failures of leadership. Finally, he was critical of the 9/11 Commission because of its failure to implicate and directly punish officials in the intelligence community who were negligent.

In February 2009, Scheuer was terminated from his position as a senior fellow of the Jamestown Foundation. Scheuer has written that he was fired by the organization for stating that the current state of the U.S.-Israel relationship undermined U.S. national security. More recently, Scheuer had been sharply critical of the Obama administration's foreign and national security policy, and in late 2012, he condemned the administration for having misled the American public concerning the true threat posed by Islamic radicalism. He also was adamantly opposed to any intervention in Libya after the so-called Arab Spring movement had begun.

Stephen E. Atkins

See also: Alec Station; Al-Qaeda; Bin Laden, Osama; Bush Administration; Central Intelligence Agency; Clinton Administration; Counterterrorism Center; Obama Administration

Further Reading

Goldenberg, Suzanne. "Agent Who Led Bin Laden Hunt Criticises CIA." *Guardian* (London), July 8, 2006, 14.

Gordon, Greg. "Ex-CIA Official: Bush Plays into Al Qaeda's Hands." *Sacramento Bee*, November 20, 2004, A12.

Lichtblau, Eric. "Officer Denounces Agency and Sept. 11 Report." *New York Times*, August 17, 2004, A14.

Priest, Dana. "Former Chief of CIA's Bin Laden Unit Leaves." *Washington Post*, November 12, 2004, A4.

Scheuer, Michael. "A Fine Rendition." *New York Times*, March 11, 2005, A23.

Wright, Lawrence. *The Looming Tower: Al Qaeda and the Road to 9/11.* New York: Knopf, 2006.

SEAL Teams, U.S. Navy

The U.S. Navy SEALs (Sea, Air, and Land) are part of the U.S. Navy Special Warfare Command, which in turn is a unit of the U.S. Special Operations Command (SOCOM). SOCOM was formed in 1987 to better coordinate military special operations, including the U.S. Army Delta Force, the U.S. Army Special Forces, and U.S. Air Force and U.S. Marine Corps special operations elements. U.S. Navy SEALs have played important roles in Operations Desert Storm, Enduring Freedom, and Iraqi Freedom as well as the global war on terror.

With nearly 2,500 members, SEALs have a distinguished tradition to draw upon. Tracing their heritage to the World War II navy frogmen who cleared underwater obstacles on Japanese-held islands in the Pacific prior to amphibious landings, SEAL teams were officially formed by order of President John F. Kennedy on January 1, 1962. From the Vietnam War in the 1960s to the invasion of Grenada in 1983 and the 1989 invasion of Panama, SEALs played an important role in American covert and special operations missions.

While SEALs operate in small units from two to eight members, the organizational structure of the SEAL teams is larger. There are eight SEAL teams (four on the West Coast and four on the East Coast). Each team is subdivided into six platoons, with supporting units that make up a naval special warfare squadron.

Members of Sea-Air-Land (SEAL) Team 8 prepare to enter the bridge of the fleet oiler USNS *Joshua Humphreys* during a boarding exercise. SEAL Team 8 provided boarding teams to assist ships of the Maritime Interdiction Force in their enforcement of U.N. sanctions against Iraq during Operation Desert Storm. (U.S. Department of Defense)

SEALs have become a lead element in executing the global war on terror. From 2002 to the end of 2008, SEALs were under-manned by about 12 percent, but a mandate to remedy the shortfall has resulted in a slow expansion in their numbers. Since augmentation efforts began in 2005, the rate of completion for the Basic Underwater Demolition/SEAL Course has risen from 26 percent to about 32 percent. Training, at a cost of around $350,000 per individual, takes on average about 30 months before a SEAL candidate is ready to deploy to a team.

The international response to the Iraqi invasion of Kuwait in August 1990 led to Operation Desert Shield and then to Operation Desert Storm. Beginning in August 1990, SEAL Teams 1, 3, and 5 were in country and served in various mis-

sions. Prior to combat they operated on the Kuwait-Iraq border, gathering intelligence on Iraqi dispositions and helping to train Kuwaiti and Saudi sailors. SEAL teams were the first U.S. combat forces to face Iraqi forces. When the war began in January 1991, SEALs performed maritime missions such as inspecting ships and capturing oil platforms. This included the first nonaerial combat of the war when SEALs assaulted Iraqis firing from a platform on U.S. helicopters. This SEAL operation killed 5 Iraqis and captured 23 others with no American casualties. Other tasks performed included combat search-and-rescue missions (including securing an American pilot who had ejected into the sea off Kuwait) and conducting beach reconnaissance to determine potential landing areas in

Kuwait. Additionally, SEALs performed mine-clearing operations. During a 16-day period in January 1991, SEALs destroyed or rendered harmless 25 maritime mines. This activity went undetected by the Iraqis.

The wars in Afghanistan and Iraq found the SEALs operating inland. During these conflicts, they have performed various missions including covert combat action, escorting VIPs in Iraq and Afghanistan, the rescue of American and allied prisoners of war (including the April 2003 rescue of U.S. Army private Jessica Lynch in Nasiriyah, Iraq), search and rescue of downed pilots, and the capture or apprehension of high-value targets. Some examples in Afghanistan include the search for Al-Qaeda organization leader Osama bin Laden and Taliban Mullah Khairulla Kahirkhawa in February 2002 and stability operations performed with indigenous forces. In January 2002, Seal Team 3 searched for weapons being smuggled into Afghanistan. In the Iraq War, SEAL operations have included safeguarding offshore oil platforms and dams (the latter included the April 2003 capture of Dam 57 in conjunction with Polish Special Operations forces before Saddam Hussein loyalists could destroy it) and reconnaissance and intelligence gathering.

Operations in conjunction with both conventional forces and special operations units of the other armed services have expanded the SEAL missions as well. A major strength of the SEAL teams continues to be their great flexibility, which gives them tremendous force-multiplying capability. They tie up more enemy troops defending against their real or perceived threats than their actual numbers would seem to dictate.

On May 2, 2011, a SEAL team infiltrated bin Laden's hideout and shot and killed him during a raid on his residential compound in Abbottabad, Pakistan. On May 28, 2012, SEALs, along with British special operations, rescued four British aid workers held captive by the Taliban in Badakhshan, Eastern Afghanistan. The SEALs assaulted the location, rescuing all hostages successfully. On December 8, 2012, SEALs rescued an American held captive by the Taliban. Navy SEAL Nicolas Checque died in the attack.

Scott R. DiMarco

See also: Al-Qaeda; Bin Laden, Osama; Enduring Freedom, Operation; Iraqi Freedom, Operation; Pentagon Attack; Taliban; World Trade Center, September 11, 2001

Further Reading

Couch, Dick. *Down Range: Navy SEALs in the War on Terrorism.* New York: Three Rivers, 2006.

Dockery, Kevin. *Navy SEALs: A Complete History from World War II to the Present.* New York: Berkley Books, 2004.

Fuentes, Gidget. "The Search for SEALs—Changes to Special-Warfare Recruiting, Training, Practices Shows Promise to Growing Unit." *Navy Times* (April 26, 2007): 18.

Luttrell, Marcus, with Patrick Robinson. *Lone Survivor: The Eyewitness Account of Operation Redwing and the Lost Heroes of SEAL-10.* Boston: Little, Brown, 2007.

Roth, Margaret. "Recent Conflicts Mark Turning Point for SEALs, Other Special Ops Forces." *Seapower* (February 2005): 14–16.

Sears Tower Bomb Plot

On June 22, 2006, American citizens Burson Augustin, Rothschild Augustine,

Narseal Batiste, Naudimar Herrera, and Stanley Grant Phanor, as well as the legal Haitian immigrant Lyglenson Lemorin and the illegal Haitian immigrant Patrick Abraham, were all indicted by a grand jury of the U.S. District Court for the Southern District of Florida on the following counts: (1) conspiracy to provide material support to a terrorist organization, (2) conspiracy to provide material support and resources to terrorists, (3) conspiracy to damage and destroy buildings by means of an explosive device, and (4) conspiracy to levy war against the government of the United States.

The seven were arrested shortly thereafter: Lemorin in Atlanta, where he had moved two months before the indictment, and Abraham, Augustin, Augustine, Batiste, and Herrera in Miami. Phanor was already in jail for a probation violation. The indictment alleged that the seven men, all of whom were from the Liberty City neighborhood of Miami, had met with a Federal Bureau of Investigation (FBI) informant posing as an Al-Qaeda operative on several occasions, beginning in November 2005. It further charged that they had sworn an oath of allegiance to Osama bin Laden and had plotted to bomb the FBI headquarters in North Miami Beach, the Willis Tower in Chicago, Illinois (formerly named and still commonly referred to as the Sears Tower), and various other government buildings. In preparation for the attacks—which were supposedly going to be levered for the purposes of waging war against the United States—the group had requested (on multiple occasions) and received (limited) material support from the informant and carried out surveillance on the potential targets. On December 13, 2007, the initial jury acquitted Lemorin, but it could not reach a verdict on the other six defendants,

resulting in a mistrial. The following day, the government transferred Lemorin to an immigration detention center and initiated deportation proceedings on the grounds that he posed a threat to national security. After several years in legal limbo—complicated by the massive earthquake that struck Haiti on January 12, 2010—he was eventually expelled on January 20, 2011.

A second trial of the remaining six suspects commenced on April 16, 2008, but again deadlocked. Finally, on May 12, 2009, a third jury acquitted Herrera and convicted Abraham, Augustin, Augustine, Batiste, and Phanor on all or a combination of the four counts against them.

Paul Kemppainen

See also: Al-Qaeda; World Trade Center, September 11, 2001

Further Reading

Bjelopera, Jerome, and Mark Randol. *American Jihadist Terrorism: Combating a Complex Threat.* Congressional Research Service (CRS) Report for Congress R41416. Washington, DC: Congressional Research Service, November 15, 2011. http://www.fas .org/sgp/crs/terror/R41416.pdf.

"FACTBOX: Miami Terrorism Trial of Liberty City Seven." *Reuters*, December 13, 2007. http://www.reuters.com/article/ 2007/12/13/us-usa-plot-profile-idUSN0 733513120071213.

Goodman, Amy, and Juan Gonzalez. "'Aspirational Rather than Operational'—7 Arrested in Miami Terrorism Plot." *Democracy Now*, June 26, 2006. Accessed February 18, 2012. http://www.democracynow.org/2006/6/26/ aspirational_rather_than_operational_7_ar rested.

Harnden, Toby. "Sect Inspired 'Leader of Sears Tower Plot.'" *Daily Telegraph* (London), June 25, 2006. http://www.telegraph .co.uk/news/worldnews/northamerica/ usa/1522288/Sect-inspired-leader-of-Sears -Tower-plot.html.

Reagan, Timothy. *National Security Case Studies Special Case-Management Challenges.* Washington, DC: Federal Judicial Center, 2010. http://www.fjc.gov/public/pdf.nsf/lookup/ts100222.pdf/$file/ts100222.pdf.

September 11 Attacks, International Reactions to

Although the terrorist attacks on September 11, 2001, targeted the United States, many other countries throughout the world were also affected. In addition to the 2,657 Americans killed, 316 foreign nationals from 84 different countries also died in the attacks, including 67 Britons, 28 South Koreans, 26 Japanese, and 25 Canadians. The shock and horror engendered by the attacks were truly international in scope.

Most public reaction and media coverage outside the United States was extremely sympathetic. The French national newspaper, *Le Monde*, declared *"Nous sommes tous Américains"* ("We are all Americans"). The British *Mirror* labeled the attacks a "War on the World." The Spanish paper *El Correo* ran a single-word headline: "Muerte" ("Murder"). Most world leaders were also quick to condemn the terrorists. Russian president Vladimir Putin urged that "the entire international community should unite in the struggle against terrorism," adding that the attacks were "a blatant challenge to humanity." Japanese prime minister Junichiro Koizumi said that "this outrageous and vicious act of violence against the United States is unforgivable." German chancellor Gerhard Schröder told reporters that "they were not only attacks on the people in the United States, our friends in America, but also against the entire civilized world, against our own freedom, against our own values, which we share with the American people."

Perhaps even more moving was the spontaneous outpouring of sympathy from average people around the globe. Tens of thousands of people left flowers, cards, and other personal mementos at U.S. consulates and embassies in many countries. Vigils and prayers were held throughout the world in a wide range of faiths. Thousands turned out in the streets of major capitals to protest the attacks, nearly 200,000 in Berlin alone. Ireland proclaimed a day of national mourning, while in Britain the American national anthem played at the changing of the guard in front of Buckingham Palace. With many international flights grounded for days after September 11, volunteers in 15 Canadian cities took care of 33,000 stranded passengers— mostly Americans—who had been aboard 255 planes diverted from U.S. airports.

Sympathy came from unlikely places. Libyan leader Muammar Qaddafi, himself linked to terrorism, called the attacks "horrifying" and counseled Muslims that "irrespective of the conflict with America it is a human duty to show sympathy with the American people." Iranian president Mohammed Khatami expressed his "deep regret and sympathy with the victims," while a visibly shocked Palestinian president Yasser Arafat denounced the attacks, repeating how "unbelievable" they were. Even the Democratic People's Republic of Korea (DPRK, North Korea), a rogue nation considered by many a sponsor of international terrorism, offered Americans sympathy following such a great "tragedy." In fact, few people demonstrated anything but sympathy for those who suffered in the attacks.

Sympathy for the United States and the victims of September 11 continued when in October 2001 the United States led an invasion of Afghanistan to destroy Al-Qaeda training camps, hunt its elusive leader Osama bin Laden, and overthrow the oppressive Taliban regime that had given refuge to the organization responsible for the carnage. On September 12 the North Atlantic Treaty Organization (NATO) had invoked Article 5 of its charter, which pledged mutual assistance in the war against Al-Qaeda. This was the first time in NATO's 52-year history that Article 5 was invoked.

Pakistan offered bases from which to plan operations in Afghanistan and support in tracking down Al-Qaeda and Taliban fighters. Simultaneously, British prime minister Tony Blair pursued multilateral antiterrorist planning within the European Union (EU). French president Jacques Chirac promised to stand with the United States, "fighting shoulder to shoulder" against terrorism. Many governments quickly arrested suspected terrorists operating in their countries. They also developed and implemented legislation aimed at combating terrorist organizations. While such measures were not without their critics, much of the world adopted more stringent security measures in the first few months after September 11.

This general outpouring of sympathy did not, however, translate into open-ended support for American foreign policy of its global war on terror. Many criticized U.S. president George W. Bush's worldview when he said a few days after September 11 that "you're either with us or with the terrorists." Some saw the global war on terror as a cover for extending U.S. power abroad, particularly when the Bush administration erroneously began to link September 11 terrorists with Iraq. Bush's controversial "axis of evil" perception of

the future, in which he grouped Iraq, Iran, and North Korea in his State of the Union address on January 29, 2002, struck many listeners as inflammatory and off the mark.

Reports by organizations such as Amnesty International would condemn the United States for the treatment of suspected terrorist prisoners in camps at Guantánamo Bay, Cuba, where detainees from the conflict in Afghanistan were held. More than anything, international sympathy for the United States was largely undermined by Bush's decision to invade Iraq in March 2003 despite the fact that its major allies and the United Nations (UN) refused to support such action. Thus, the legacy of September 11 turned from one of sympathy and commonality to one of suspicion and condemnation.

Arne Kislenko

See also: Al-Qaeda; Bin Laden, Osama; Bush Administration; Enduring Freedom, Operation; Global War on Terror; Iraqi Freedom, Operation; Pentagon Attack; Taliban; Terrorism; World Trade Center, September 11, 2001

Further Reading

Goh, Evelyn. "Hegemonic Constraints: The Implications of 11 September for American Power." *Australian Journal of International Affairs* 57, no. 1 (April 2003): 77–97.

Hirsh, Michael. "Bush and the World." *Foreign Affairs* 82, no. 5 (September–October 2002): 18–43.

Scheuer, Michael. *Imperial Hubris: Why the West Is Losing the War on Terror.* Washington, DC: Potomac Books, 2004.

September 11 Terrorist Trial Controversy

For several years, the U.S. government has been planning the trials of Khalid Sheikh

Mohammed and several other men accused of being involved in the September 11 terrorist attacks. Mohammed, a member of the terrorist organization Al-Qaeda, was captured in 2003 and confessed to playing a key role in the planning of the September 11 operation. After being held for more than two years in a remote prison in Pakistan, he was transferred to the Guantánamo Bay Detainment Camp in Cuba in September 2006.

On February 11, 2008, military prosecutors from the U.S. Department of Defense charged Mohammed and five other Guantánamo prisoners with war crimes and murder for their roles in the September 11 attacks and said they would seek the death penalty for the six men. During his arraignment hearing before a military tribunal in Guantánamo Bay in June 2008, Mohammed declared he wanted to be put to death and viewed as a martyr.

When U.S. attorney general Eric Holder announced in November 2009 that Mohammed and four coconspirators—Walid Muhammad Salih bin Attash, Ramzi Bin al-Shibh, Ali Abd al-Aziz Ali, and Mustafa Ahmed al-Hawsawi—would face a civilian trial in New York City, the news set off a firestorm of controversy. Most of the initial objections centered around the decision to try the five men in a civilian court rather than before a military commission. Several members of Congress asserted that the Al-Qaeda terrorists did not warrant the protections they would receive under the U.S. criminal justice system. They also expressed their concern that the trials would trigger more terrorist attacks in the United States and would also lead to the disclosure of classified material.

Initially, many Congressional Democrats and New York City officials supported the Barack Obama administration's plans for holding the trial in downtown Manhattan. When some relatives of September 11 victims voiced their opinion that holding the trial only blocks away from the site of the World Trade Center was insensitive, New York mayor Michael Bloomberg pointed out that the location of the trials was appropriate and a powerful symbol. Addressing concerns about the security challenges the trial presented, Bloomberg expressed his confidence that the New York Police Department was up to the task.

However, during the next few months, objections to the plan to hold the trial in New York City increased, with the New York Real Estate Board and Wall Street firms complaining that the security measures needed for the trial would be too disruptive to the business community. After security costs for the trial were estimated to be in the hundreds of millions of dollars annually, Bloomberg withdrew his support for holding the trials in Manhattan, explaining that the costs and disruptions would be too high. As a result, on January 29, 2010, the Obama administration dropped its plan to hold the trials in New York. Little progress has been made in choosing an alternate site for the trials of the five September 11 suspects. Until a location is agreed upon, Mohammed and the others will continue to be held indefinitely.

Spencer C. Tucker

See also: Al-Qaeda; Guantánamo Bay Detainment Camp; Mohammed, Khalid Sheikh

Further Reading

Calabresi, Massimo. "Prosecuting KSM: Harder Than You Think." *Time*, November 13, 2009.

Finn, Peter, and Anne E. Kornblut. "Opposition to U.S. Trial Likely to Keep Mastermind of 9/11 Attacks in Detention." *Washington Post*, November 13, 2010.

Savage, Charlie. "Accused 9/11 Mastermind to Face Civilian Trial in N.Y." *New York Times*, November 13, 2009.

Shane, Scott, and Benjamin Weiser. "U.S. Drops Plan for a 9/11 Trial in New York City." *New York Times*, January 30, 2010.

Shia Islam

The smaller of the two predominant branches of Islam, the larger being Sunni Islam. The name "Shia" derives from the Arabic term "Shiat Ali" (Party of Ali), whereas the name "Sunni" derives from the term "Ahl al-Sunnah wa al-Jama'ah" (People of the Prophet's Practice and Unified Community). Adherents to Shia Islam account for 12–15 percent of all Muslims worldwide. The Sunni sects or schools of Islam account for approximately 85 percent.

Shia Islam grew out of political struggles against the Umayyad caliphs. As a result of its political and theological evolution, it came to incorporate the descendants of several different trends: activists, moderates, and extremists. In addition, Shiite leadership is divided into different positions and differs in the degree of approved activism by clerics. The Ithna Ashariyya, called Twelvers by Westerners and Jafariyya by adherents for their school of Islamic law, were historically moderates; the Ismailiyya (Seveners) were labeled extremists, or *ghulat*, by their enemies; and the Zaydiyya (Fivers) were activists (in their support of Zayd in his jihad against the caliph). The three groups are named according to the prominent figures in the chain of religious leaders (*a'imah*, or imams) whom each recognizes as constituting the proper line of religious authority passed down to them from the Prophet Muhammad.

Shiism is the dominant branch of Islam in Iran (90% of the population), Iraq, Lebanon, Bahrain, and Azerbaijan. Shiism also has adherents in Syria, Yemen, East Africa, India, Pakistan, Afghanistan, Tajikistan, Turkey, Qatar, Kuwait, the United Arab Emirates, the Eastern Province of Saudi Arabia, and many areas outside the Middle East, such as the United States, Canada, South Asia, the United Kingdom, Europe, Australia, and East Africa. In the United States, Dearborn, Michigan, has a very large Shiite population.

The Shiat Ali (Party of Ali) preferred the succession of Ali ibn Abu Talib as *khalifa* (caliph) when the Prophet Muhammad died. Ali ibn Abu Talib was the son-in-law of Muhammad by marriage to Muhammad's only surviving daughter, Fatima. Some suggest that in the mixture of southern and northern Arab Muslim tribes, it was the southerners, Aws and Khazraj of Medina, who most strongly supported hereditary rights in leadership rather than a leader chosen on a different basis.

Ali accepted Abu Bakr as caliph, or political leader of the Muslims, even though Ali's supporters preferred Ali, and he also accepted the caliph Umar. The caliphate was then offered to him, but he was told he would have to follow the precedents of Abu Bakr and Umar, and Ali refused to do this. His supporters agitated again when Uthman became the third caliph. Uthman was so disliked for nepotism and the enrichment of his Umayyad relatives that a revolt occurred in which he was killed. Ali's followers recognized him as the fourth caliph in 656 CE. However, the Umayyads claimed the caliphate for Muawiya, and this led to two civil wars in Islam and Ali's assassination in 661. Following Ali's death, his son Hasan was forced to abdicate, and his other son Husayn fought the Umayyads and was killed at Karbala. These events are commemorated in Shiism and given a deeply symbolic meaning.

While all Muslims revere the Prophet and his family (known as Ahl al-Bayt, or People of the House), Sunni Muslims recognize a large number of the Prophet's early companions at Medina as transmitters of hadith, the short texts relating Muhammad's words, actions, or preferences. In contrast, the Shia do not recognize the authority of certain companions and teach the traditions (hadith) transmitted by others or the Ahl al-Bayt from the Prophet, his daughter Fatima, and Ali on to Ali's sons Hasan and Husayn and also the succession of imams who followed them. More importantly, because Ali had rejected the injunction to follow the precedents of the first two caliphs rather than the *sunnah* (traditions or practices) of the Prophet, the foundational logic for Shiism to develop its own *fiqh*, or legal school, was set.

In the Umayyad period, the followers of Ali began to develop their own attitudes and worldview in contrast to other Muslims. The Battle of Karbala in October 680 between the supporters and relatives of Muhammad's grandson Husayn ibn Ali and forces of Yazid I, the Umayyad caliph, reinforced the Shia belief in *walaya*, or devotion to the Prophet's family, and also provided a reason for rebellion. A movement called the *tawabbun* (penitents) rose up to fight the Umayyads a year after the Battle of Karbala because they had not defended Husayn then, and 3,000 of them were killed.

Shiites believe that Ali was the first imam, thereby inheriting the *nass*, or spiritual legitimacy, of the Prophet. The imam is the sole legitimate religious successor of the Prophet, and each imam designates his own successor. In Shia Islam, each imam is held to have special knowledge of the inner truth of the Koran, Muhammad's *sunnah*, and Islam. This institution is called the imamate in English (*a'imah*). The *a'imah*, or chain of imams, are believed to be infallible, sinless, and personally guided by Allah (God) and are also believed to possess the divine authority over Islam and humanity granted to Ali by the Prophet Muhammad. Shiites and Sunnis have the same beliefs about Allah, who has omnipotence over all beings and is also perceived as merciful and beneficent, closer to man than his own jugular vein and one who cares deeply about his creation. In both branches of Islam, there is also a dynamic between faith and the acceptance of divine will along with the responsibility of the human believer. Indeed, apart from the differences in the Shia view of leadership, the two sects are very similar in many aspects. They diverge, however, in their legal systems.

The Shia recognize all the same religious duties as the Sunnis, which are described in the study of Islam in the West as the Five Pillars with two additional duties. However, the Ismailiyya sect and its subsects also stress the inner truths, or esoteric knowledge of Islamic principles. Therefore, to their spiritual elite simply reading the Koran is inadequate; one must understand its hidden meaning.

The Shia stress the unicity or oneness (*tawhid*) of Allah, a strict monotheism, and the avoidance of any trace of polytheism. They support social justice (*'adalah*), which means equity within society, and aid to the oppressed and the needy. As with Sunni Muslims, the Shia adhere to the principle of the *hisba*, or commanding the good and forbidding the reprehensible. This refers to all that is licit or recommended in Islamic law as opposed to sins that are forbidden. Entrance into paradise is based on doing more good than evil or upon martyrdom. All Muslims, Shia as well as Sunni, respect the prophets, including Abraham, Moses, Jesus, and Muhammad, whom they believe revealed to humans the true religion of Allah.

The concept of the *a'imah* (imamate)—that specific leaders are appointed by Allah and then designated by other imams (*nass*)—grew in strength thanks to the sixth imam, Jafar al-Sadiq. His followers developed the Twelver legal and theological tradition. The last of these 12 imams, Muhammad al-Mahdi, did not make himself known at the death of the 11th imam, al-Hasan al-Askari; however, texts revealed his presence. Mahdi is believed to be hiding on Earth, neither alive nor dead but in a state of occultation, and will return at the Day of Judgment and the Resurrection (*qiyamah*) when Allah will decide the fate of all humanity, Muslim and non-Muslim alike.

The Twelvers believe that Mahdi, born in 689, was the son of Hasan. The Shia believe that Mahdi was in hiding from the caliph and that between the years 874 and 941 he communicated by letters with his people. During this period, called the Lesser Occultation, the community recognized four regents for Mahdi. In his last letter, he wrote that he would no longer communicate with humanity. Thus, the period from 941 to the present is known as the Greater Occultation.

In Islam, every human is held accountable for his or her deeds. The deeds of each individual are judged by Allah and weighed on a scale. If the good outweighs the evil, then the individual gains entrance into paradise. If the evil outweighs the good, the individual spends eternity in hell. The Shia, like the Sunni, also believe that the prophets, imams, and martyrs can intercede with Allah for a soul on the Day of Judgment and may seek this intercession (*shafa'a*) if possible through prayer, religious rituals, or appeals to the Fourteen Infallibles: the Prophet Muhammad, his daughter Fatima, the Twelve Imams, or martyrs. They also seek redemption through the ritual of repentance performed on the Day of Ashura, the commemoration of Imam Husayn's death.

Shiism's Twelvers, the largest Shia group, proclaim the necessity of obligatory religious duties or acts of outward worship. The first is the *shahada*, or testimony that there is no God but God and that Muhammad is his prophet and Ali his imam. The next is prayer (*salat*), recited five or more times a day. The third is fasting (*sawm*) during the daylight hours for all of the month of Ramadan, the ninth month of the Islamic calendar. The fourth religious practice is the pilgrimage (*hajj*), a journey to the holy city of Mecca that should be made at least once during a person's life if he or she is physically and financially able to undertake it. The fifth religious practice is the paying of *zakat*, a voluntary tax that is used to support the poor, to spread Islam, or sometimes for other purposes such as aid to travelers and the funding of jihad. The assessment of *zakat* should be 2.5 percent of one's income and assets in any given year. (All Muslims also give gifts of money during and at the end of Ramadan and the Id al-Adha, but these are in addition to *zakat*.) Another form of tithing, the *khums*, is a 20 percent tax on all annual profits from any source levied on all adult males and is used to support the mosque and the clerics. Jihad is also a commanded duty in Shiism and refers to the struggle of the faithful to please Allah as well as to defend Islam by waging war against those who attack Muslims. The idea of the *walaya* is important in Shiism (but also in Sufi Islam), as is the *tabarra*. These mean a special reverence for all members, past and descended, of the Ahl al-Bayt; the guardianship of the imamate; and the disassociation from all enemies of the Ahl al-Bayt.

In addition to the Shia groups mentioned above, there are others. The Shaykhiyya of Basra and Bahrain are a subsect of the Twelver Shia, influenced by Akhbari thought. The Druze (who call themselves *muwahiddun*, or unitarians) are an offshoot of the Ismailiyya sect, and the Alawites found in Syria and Turkey are a distinct subsect of Shiism. Sunni Muslims and some Shia, however, consider the Alawi sect extreme because of some of its syncretic practices. Nonetheless, it was declared a licit school of Islam in a fatwa issued by Imam Musa al-Sadr in order to legitimate the rule of President Hafiz al-Asad, an Alawi, in Syria. Although all branches of Islam believe in a divine savior, the Mahdi (the Guided One) who will come at the Day of Judgment, the Twelver branch of Shiism holds that the Twelfth Imam, or Hidden Imam since he is in occultation, is the Mahdi and call him the Imam Mahdi.

Mahmoud Ahmadinejad, former president of Iran, and his cabinet pledged to work to make the conditions right for the return of the Imam Mahdi, a return that Shia Muslims believe will lead Islam to world domination. In Iran, many believe that the Imam Mahdi will reappear from a well at the mosque in Jamkaran just outside of the holy city of Qum, Iran. The site is frequently visited by Shiite pilgrims who drop messages into the well hoping that the Hidden Imam will hear them and grant their requests. Along with the Imam

Mahdi's return at the Day of Judgment, there are various beliefs about other millenarian events and wars that will occur before this period.

Since the disappearance of the Twelfth Imam, the Shia *ulama* (clerics) have served as his deputies, interpreting the law and leading the Shiite faithful under the authority of the Hidden Imam. In Twelver Shiism, it is believed that four persons acted as the deputies or special vice-regents (*wakala al-khassa*) of the Hidden Imam during the Lesser Occultation. These persons were called the *bab* (gate) or *na'ib* (deputy) for the imam. From 941, there have been no overt claims of a *bab* except for Sayyid Ali Muhammad (known as "The Bab"), who established Babism in the 19th century, and the Shaykhi Shia, who put forth the idea of the perfect Shia who lives in each age. Generally in this period, the idea is that there is a *wakala al-'amma*, or a general vice-regency, that has been delegated to the Shia clerics. When Iran's Ayatollah Ruhollah Khomeini and his government established the system of rule of the cleric (*vilayat-e faqih*) in Iran, there were disputes about whether he was to be considered the *na'ib* al-Imam, or deputy of the Hidden Imam. The idea of rule of the cleric, developed from the increasingly activist opinions of one branch of Shiism—the Usulis (*usuliyya*)—opposed the Akhbaris, a different intellectual tradition. This notion that clerics should rule, therefore becoming a part of the political system, is still controversial even among many Usulis.

Khomeini's official title became "Supreme Faqih" (Jurist), and he governed the Council of Guardians as its supreme religio-political authority. There had been several clerics more senior to Khomeini who were, however, marginalized or even assassinated after the Islamic Revolution. Khomeini's successor, Ali Husayni Khamenei, was not the most senior of the clerics who might potentially have followed Khomeini in power. Khamenei was granted the title of ayatollah to ensure his authority. Some described him as a political appointee.

Ismaili Shiites, also known as Ismailiyya, or the Seveners, are followers of the living Agha Khan and constitute the second-largest branch of Shia Islam. Ismailis believe that the imamate is a position that continues unbroken since the caliphate of Ali, although the living imams since the Seventh Imam serve as regents awaiting the return of the Hidden Imam. Ismailis acknowledge only six of the Twelve Imams and assert that the real Seventh Imam was Ismail Ibn Jafar. Other Muslims assert that Ismail's son Muhammad was the Seventh Imam and that he is presently occulted awaiting the end of time to reveal himself as the last imam. The Ismaili movement spread through missionary activity as a secret organization beginning in the later ninth century. It split in a factional dispute about leadership in 899. Ismaili Shia are found primarily in South Asia, Syria, Saudi Arabia, Yemen, China, Tajikistan, Afghanistan, and East Africa but have also, in recent years, immigrated to Europe and North America.

Ismailis mandate the same religious practices as the Twelvers, but their emphasis is on esoteric teachings and thus on an inner or deeper interpretation of each that can make them distinct. As with the Twelvers, the Ismailis evince love and devotion (walayah) for Allah, the prophets, the Ahl al-Bayt, the imam, and the Ismaili da'i (preacher) and also believe in personal purity and cleanliness (taharah). As with

all other Muslims, they must also practice prayer and zakat, or almsgiving. In addition, they fast during Ramadan, carry out the hajj, and believe in jihad.

Zaydis, also known as Zaydiyya or the Fivers, are theologically and in the view of Islamic law closer to a Sunni school of the law. There are Zaydi communities in India, Pakistan, and Yemen. Zaydis derive their name from Zayd ibn Ali ibn Abi Talib, the son of Husayn ibn Ali ibn Abi Talib (626–ca. 680), the grandson of the Prophet Muhammad. Most Zaydis regard Husayn as the third rightful imam. After Ali, Hasan, and Husayn, the followers of Zayd had asserted that the succession of the imamate would be determined after engaging in armed rebellion against the Umayyad caliphs. Zayd's followers did not want a hidden imam, but a living one who would rule instead of the Umayyads, and so the Zaydiyya are considered activists. Although Zayd's rebellion against the corrupt Umayyad caliph Hisham ibn Abd al-Malik (691–743) in 740 was unsuccessful, his followers thereafter recognized Zayd as the fourth Zaydi imam.

Zaydism does not support the infallibility of the imams and asserts that no imam after Husayn received any divine guidance. Zaydis reject the Hidden Imam and the idea that the imamate must be passed from father to son, although they do believe that the living imam must be a descendant of Ali, and some of their own leaders passed on their leadership to their sons. Zaydi Islamic law (fiqh) is most like the Sunni Hanafi school.

While there was never a concept of Sunni Islam as a sect as it is described today, the non-Alid Muslims (those who did not insist on Ali gaining political leadership) accepted the institution of the caliphate even though the caliph was not a spiritual descendant of the Prophet. Still, the caliph received an oath of allegiance from his people and had to be pious and promote and protect Islam. Alids (supporters of Ali), later called the Shia, accepted their temporal rulers but did not regard them as being spiritually legitimate in the manner of the imams. For purposes of survival, they could deny their Shia beliefs if need be in the practice known as *taqqiya* (dis-simulation). There are major legal and philosophical differences in Shia Islam, such as the theme of the oppressed Muslims who act out their penitence for their inability to defend Husayn at Karbala, the imamate, the concept of the Occultation and the Return, and the concept of *marjaiyya*, the idea that a believer should follow a particular cleric as a guide. Minor differences pertain to aspects of daily prayer and the commencement of holidays, which often begin on one day in Iran and, typically, a day earlier in Saudi Arabia and other Sunni centers.

Shiite Islamic education is centered in Najaf and Karbala in Iraq, and in Qum and Mashhad in Iran, with other religious authorities in Tehran and additional centers of learning elsewhere. Shia clerics from Lebanon typically studied in Iraq or in Iran. One of the most influential Shia theorists in Iran following the Islamic Revolution was probably Abd al-Karim Sorush, who is famous for his idea of the expansion and contraction of Islamic law (*qabz va baste shari'at*). The most senior cleric in Iraq today is the Shia Grand Ayatollah Sistani. The clerical establishment in Iraq is referred to as the *hawzah*, and its duty is to train the future clerics of Shiism, provide judgments, and officiate over pilgrimages and those who wish to be buried at the holy sites. Other important cities of Shia learning are Qum, Mashhad, and Tehran, all in Iran. In Iran the great lead-

ers of Tehran, Ayatollah Sayyid Muhammad Tabatabai (1841–1920) and Sayyid Abd Allah Bahbahani (d. 1871), were part of the revolutionary organization of the constitutional movement early in the 20th century, but other clerics opposed that movement. Shiite authorities also resisted British colonialism and encroachments on their power by Reza Shah Pahlavi in Iran.

The last great single *marja' al-mutlaq* (the absolute source of emulation), Ayatollah Burujerdi, died in 1961. Debate then began between different reformist leaders and the degree of activism in which clerics should engage. In the 1960s, a more radical, or activist, Shiism began to develop. Informal gatherings and new publications began to spread new radical Shiite thought. Ayatollah Khomeini's resistance to Mohammad Reza Shah Pahlavi was significant, but so too was the work of Dr. Ali Shariati (1933–1977).

Educated in Mashhad and Paris, Shariati challenged the quietism of many religious scholars, writing essays and giving lectures to galvanize a new activism in Shiism that combined with existentialism and Third World views. Another major influence on radical Shiism in this period was Murtaza Mutahari (1920–1979).

Sunnis and Shiites have different approaches to jurisprudence, or the making of Islamic law, and therefore also in the issuance of fatawa to broader religious questions of Muslims. The different Sunni schools of law use as sources (*usul al-fiqh*) the Koran, the hadith, analogy (*qiyas*), and *ijma*, or the consensus of the community at Medina or of the jurists. In earlier periods, these legal schools also used *ray* (opinion of the jurist) or *ijtihad*, a particular technique of intellectual problem solving. In the 10th century, the Sunni jurists decided to stop using *ijtihad* so as to avoid the introduction of too many innovations into sharia (Islamic law). However, the Shia legal school of the Twelvers retained this principle. Consequently, Shia cleric-jurists who train in this technique and qualify receive the title of *mujtahid*, or one who can enact *ijtihad*. *Ijtihad* has come to mean more than a principle of Islamic jurisprudence. As contemporary activist Shiism was developing, Ali Shariati began to apply *ijtihad* to Muslim life, including a vibrant definition of monotheism and the application of Muslim principles.

There are various ranks of clerics in Shia Islam in addition to the *mujtahid*, such as the elevated designations of ayatollah and grand ayatollah that other clerics should agree on. In addition, the Shia may follow his or her own preferred *marja' al-taqlid* (source of emulation). Above all of these clerics, there may be one agreed-upon *marja' al-mutlaq*, or source of emulation of the age.

These are not the only differences between Sunni and Shia Islam. Shia constituted minorities in such countries as Lebanon and Saudi Arabia, where they were an underclass socially and economically. In the modern period, leaders such as Ali Shariati and Imam Musa Sadr in Lebanon supported populism and addressed the discrimination against and suffering of the Shiite masses.

While at times some Sunni groups have expressed both discrimination and hatred toward Shia Muslims, there have also been efforts at ecumenism and more cooperation between the sects. Al-Azhar University in Egypt teaches about the Jafariyya (Twelver) *madhhab*, or legal school of Islam, in spite of the government of Egypt having outlawed Shiism. It should also be noted that Shia and Sunni Muslims had coexisted peacefully and have frequently intermarried in Iraq. Shia Muslims were often members of the Communist Party or the Baath Party, and just like the Iranian clerics responding to the inroads made by secular ideologies in that country, the clerics in Iraq began an Islamic movement in part to encourage youths to reengage with Islamic education. When this movement developed from a clerical organization into an activist one, Iraqi president Saddam Hussein ruthlessly suppressed it. Sadly, the end of Hussein's rule brought Shia-Sunni sectarian conflict to Iraq, fueled in part by Sunni Islamists and nationalists who viewed the new Shia-dominated majority as conspirators with the Americans and who call the Shia apostates or renegades.

Richard M. Edwards and Sherifa Zuhur

See also: Martyrdom; Sunni Islam

Further Reading

Fuller, Graham E., and Rend Rahim Francke. *The Arab Shi'a: The Forgotten Muslims*. Hampshire, UK: Palgrave Macmillan, 2001.

Gregorian, Vartan. *Islam: A Mosaic, Not a Monolith*. Baltimore: Brookings Institute Press, 2004.

Halm, Heinz. *Shi'a Islam: From Religion to Revolution*. Princeton, NJ: Markus Wiener, 1997.

Sobhani, Ayatollah Jafar, and Reza Shah Kazemi. *Doctrines of Shi'i Islam: A Compendium of Imami Beliefs and Practices*. London: I. B. Tauris, 2001.

Somalia, International Intervention

(April 1992–March 1995)

Intervention in Somalia that lasted from April 1992 to March 1995 and was an

Somali children closely watch a U.S. marine on patrol in the city of Baidoa on December 1, 1992. The ill-fated peacekeeping mission ended with several U.S. soldiers being killed. (David Turnley/ Corbis)

international response to deteriorating humanitarian conditions in the war-torn nation. By 1992, continuing civil unrest in Somalia had rendered the government unable to react to a rising humanitarian crisis among its people, which threatened to bring wholesale starvation to millions of people. The intervention was made possible due largely to a consensus among the United Nations (UN) Security Council members to take action in a country where the central government had essentially ceased to exist. A major relief and humanitarian effort on the part of the United States, code-named Operation Restore Hope, became the backbone of the intervention. It began on December 9, 1993.

Modern Somali history has been repeatedly punctuated by international involvement and interventions. Somalia was forced into the European colonial system

at the end of the 19th century. Italy ruled its southern, central, and northeastern regions, while Great Britain ruled the northwestern region. During World War II, Great Britain conquered the entire country; after the war ended, Somalia was incorporated into the international mandate system. On July 1, 1960, all regions of Somalia were united to form one independent state.

Because Somalia had long been dominated by clan politics, forming a stable regime there proved to be impossible. In 1969, General Mohamed Siad Barre formed a dictatorship. In May 1988, the Somali National Movement (SNM), which represented the northwestern clan, the Isaaq, openly challenged Siad's rule. In the years that followed, a full-scale civil war unfolded in Somalia. Other clans joined the SNM's struggle against Siad, such as the Majerteen/Darod from the northeast and the Hawiye from the central region. Each clan formed its own political faction. When the clans' coalition finally defeated Siad's forces in early 1991, they turned against each other.

By 1992, the state was divided among the various warring factions. In the northwest, the Isaaq clan declared independence from Somalia and formed Somaliland. The Majerteen declared autonomy in the northeast of Somalia. The south-central region, which was the most populous, was dominated by the Hawiye, who formed the United Somali Congress (USC). The Haber-Gedir, a subclan of the Hawiye, split from the USC and formed the most powerful faction, the USC/SNA (United Somali Congress/Somali National Alliance). This faction was headed by General Mohammed Farrah Aidid (Aideed). The continuous fighting among the factions crushed whatever remained of Somalia's state authorities and infrastructure, threatening the well-being of millions of Somalis who were suffering from starvation, disease, and daily violence.

The first phase of the international intervention in Somalia lasted from April 1992 to December 1992. During this period, UN representatives tried to broker a peace deal among warring factions in Somalia while deploying a small peacekeeping force, called the United Nations Operation in Somalia I (UNOSOM I). The UN military contingent numbered approximately 500 soldiers from Pakistan stationed in the country's capital, Mogadishu. Another objective of the intervention was to deliver humanitarian aid to the country. But UN efforts failed to bring about change on the political, security, or humanitarian levels. The situation remained unchanged until the George H. W. Bush administration in the United States took the decision to lead

a United Task Force (UNITAF) comprised of multinational forces to help deliver humanitarian aid to approximately 2 million Somalis.

UNITAF numbered more than 30,000 men at its peak, with the United States contributing approximately two-thirds of this manpower. UNITAF troops were deployed solely in the south-central region of the country, encompassing some 40 percent of the country's territory, in the areas that had experienced the worst warfare and famine in the early 1990s. The international force took control of all ports, airfields, and main roads within its deployment areas.

Massive aid operations soon began reaching the needy, and within a few months UNITAF had succeeded in ameliorating the humanitarian conditions. All local Somali factions cooperated with the multinational forces, and in January and March 1993, signed the Addis Ababa Peace Agreements, calling for the establishment of a Transitional National Council, a political body that was to include all Somali factions and work as an interim government for the country.

During the intervention, a controversy developed between the U.S. government and the UN Secretariat concerning the disarming of the Somali factions. The UN Secretariat wanted UNITAF to disarm all Somalis, whereas the United States refused to do so, claiming that it had led UNITAF for strictly humanitarian reasons, not to impose peace. The Americans claimed that once the humanitarian crisis was over, it would be time for the UN to lead the international force.

As a compromise, instead of disarming the population, the international force concentrated its efforts on supervising the storage of the factions' heavy weapons under international supervision. Security Council Resolution 814 of March 26, 1993, established the United Nations Operation in Somalia II (UNOSOM II), which replaced the American-led UNITAF. For the first time in history, UN forces were authorized under Chapter VII of the UN Charter to use force. This authorization marked the third phase of the intervention in Somalia.

During the third phase, which lasted from March 1993 to February 1994, UNOSOM II numbered approximately 28,000 soldiers, civil police, and civilian personnel. These forces were supposed to assist the local Somali factions in implementing the Addis Ababa Peace Agreements. The UN forces had many objectives resulting from the agreements, such as establishing civilian institutions in Somalia, continuing the humanitarian aid, and instituting various development projects.

Instead of conciliation, however, UN actions strained the multinational force's relations with the most powerful Somali faction in the south-central region of the country, the USC/SNA. Aidid, the faction's leader, perceived the UN actions as efforts to undermine his faction's achievements from the civil war. He then encouraged his supporters to attack the UN forces. Tension between the UN and the USC/SNA reached a climax on June 5, 1993. Fighting erupted that day between Pakistani peacekeeping contingents and armed locals who were probably connected to the USC/SNA. The Pakistani soldiers were supposed to inspect a USC/SNA arms depot and to assist in the delivering of humanitarian aid. When the fighting ended, 24 Pakistani soldiers and approximately 50 Somalis were dead.

This fighting marked the beginning of a four-month war between the UN forces and Aidid and his allies. Between June and October 1993, the UN launched numerous operations to capture Aidid and his faction's co-leaders. Most of the operations were led by U.S. Special Forces units in the streets of southern Mogadishu, but these operations yielded bad results. Thousands of Somalis died, and Aidid was not caught. As a result of the high number of Somali casualties, many Somalis began to support Aidid against the international intervention.

The deadliest engagement occurred during October 3–4, 1993. A raid by U.S. Rangers and Delta Force troops on a USC/SNA house on Mogadishu was upset when, because of street fighting, the American force became disoriented and two U.S. Sikorsky MH-60 Black Hawk helicopters were shot down. Pakistani armor failed to arrive as intense fighting took place in southern Mogadishu between the American forces and hundreds of Somalis. At the end of battle there were many casualties, including 18 American soldiers. After the battle, Aidid declared a unilateral cease-fire.

Outraged and embarrassed by the turn of events, on October 7, President Bill Clinton declared his intention to withdraw all American forces from Somalia by March 31, 1994. After the Battle of Mogadishu, relative political and military stability prevailed in south-central Somalia until February 1994, but with no progress made regarding the core problems that had led to the intervention in the first place. The Somali factions retained their armaments, and the UN continued the rebuilding of civilian institutions under its auspices.

During 2006, a union of fundamentalist Islamic courts took hold of most of south-central Somalia. Their base of power was in Mogadishu, and they succeeded in defeating the clans' militias. The Islamists were able to restore law and order to the areas under their control by invoking

Islamic laws. However, their hard-line calls for religious war (jihad) put them at odds with Ethiopia. On December 24, 2006, Ethiopian military forces, aided by the TFG's forces, invaded the Islamist-held territories, defeating the Islamists in a series of battles. The Ethiopian victories paved the way for the TFG to finally take root in Mogadishu. However, the TFG faces continued insurgencies by Islamists and supporters of the various clans. In contrast to the turbulent history of south-central Somalia, relative political stability has prevailed in the northwestern self-declared state of Somaliland since 1991 and in the northeastern self-declared autonomy of Puntland since 1998.

Chen Kertcher

See also: Rwanda; Terrorism; U.S. Special Operations Command

Further Reading

Clarke, Walter S., and Herbst Jeffrey Ira. *Learning from Somalia: The Lessons of Armed Humanitarian Intervention.* Boulder, CO: Westview, 1997.

Kertcher, Chen. *The Search for Peace—or for a State: UN Intervention in Somalia, 1992–95.* Jerusalem: Harry S. Truman Research Institute for the Advancement of Peace, 2003.

Menkhaus, Kenneth. *Somalia: State Collapse and the Threat of Terrorism.* Oxford: Oxford University Press, 2004.

Oakley, Robert B., and John I. Hirsch. *Somalia and Operation Restore Hope: Reflections on Peacemaking and Peacekeeping.* Washington, DC: United States Institute of Peace Press, 1995.

Suicide Bombings

In suicide bombings, an explosive is delivered and detonated by a person or persons who expect to die in the explosion along with the intended target or targets. In recent years, the number of suicide bombings or attacks has risen exponentially, and not just in the Middle East. The United States was struck by four hijacked aircraft piloted by Islamic fanatics associated with the Al-Qaeda terrorist organization on September 11, 2001, resulting in the deaths of almost 3,000 people. Certainly, this was the most lethal—and most dramatic—example of a suicide operation to date.

Suicide bombers employ several different techniques. Japanese pilots in World War II were known for crashing their airplanes straight into targets, causing tremendous devastation. These were known as kamikaze ("divine wind"), the name given to a typhoon that destroyed a Mongol invasion fleet off Japan in the 13th century. Kamikazes exacted a heavy toll on Allied warships at the end of World War II, especially off Okinawa. The Tamil Tigers of Sri Lanka utilized suicide bombings during their long struggle against the central government in 1983–2009. Other attackers have employed bombs secured in cars or trucks.

Individual suicide bombers often strap explosives and shrapnel to their bodies and wear vests or belts specially designed for the purpose. They then drive or walk to their targets. Because military targets are heavily defended, typical targets include crowded shopping areas, restaurants, or buses. Suicide bombers may also approach softer targets directly linked to the military or police, such as a line of recruits in the street, as has occurred during the Iraq War. Detonating the explosives kills and injures people in the vicinity and can also destroy notable property, such as religious shrines. One technique is to send two or more suicide bombers against a single target; after

Masked members from al-Aqsa Martyrs Brigades, an armed group linked to Palestinian President Yasser Arafat's Fatah movement, are dressed as suicide bombers in the West Bank city, on October 23, 2003. (Abed Omar Qusini/Reuters/Corbis)

the first blast, the second bomber works his way into the crowd of responders and then detonates his explosives.

An explosion in an enclosed area is more destructive than one in the open, and suicide bombers pick their targets accordingly. Forensic investigators at the site of a suicide bombing can usually identify the bomber and the general type of device he or she used. A suicide vest decapitates the bomber; a belt cuts the bomber in two.

The explosive devices themselves are easily constructed. They might include an explosive charge, a battery, a cable, a light switch detonator, and a custom-made belt or vest to hold the explosives. Scrap metal might be employed to act as shrapnel, which in the blast would kill or maim those nearby. Explosives may also be carried in

a briefcase or other bag. The bomber sets off the explosive by flipping a switch or pressing a button, sometimes remotely as in the case of a car or truck bombing.

Muslim extremists in the latest wave of violence might leave a written or video *shahada*, which is partially a statement of their intent and partially a will and settlement of any debts. Suicide bombings have been used in the Middle East since the late 1970s. The Islamic resistance employed them in Syria against the Baathist government, although many more conventional attacks also occurred. During the Lebanese civil war, car bombings evolved in some cases into suicide attacks; and in 1981, the Islamic Dawa Party bombed the Iraqi embassy in Beirut. In response to the Israeli invasion of Lebanon in 1982, the Islamic

Resistance, a loosely organized group, formed, and some of its elements planned bombing attacks. In November 1982, an Islamic Resistance suicide bomber destroyed a building in Tyre, Lebanon, and killed 76 Israelis. The Organization of Islamic Jihad and other militant Islamist groups including Hezbollah, as well as numerous Christians, carried out another 50 suicide attacks between 1982 and 1999, when the Israelis withdrew from Lebanon. A massive suicide bombing of their barracks in October 1983 forced American and French troops from Lebanon.

The belief that such attacks bring martyrdom has encouraged suicide bombings in countries all over the world, including Afghanistan, Chechnya, Croatia, Tajikistan, Pakistan, Yemen, Panama, Argentina, and Algeria. In 1995, a suicide bomber dressed as a priest attempted to assassinate Pope John Paul II in Manila.

Suicide attacks by Palestinians began after the First Intifada, but were not regular events; however, many more took place during the Second (al-Aqsa) Intifada. The first Palestinian suicide bombing occurred in April 1994 in the West Bank. It killed eight Israelis and was carried out to avenge the deaths of 25 Muslims who had been praying in the Ibrahimi Mosque when they were killed by Israeli settler Baruch Goldstein. Hamas explained that its basic policy was only to attack Israeli soldiers, but if Palestinian civilians were slaughtered in deliberate attacks, then it would break that policy. There were 198 known suicide-bombing attacks in Israel and Palestine between 1994 and July 2002, which killed 120 people. The bombers died in 136 of those attacks.

Because many of the bombers were intercepted and/or the attacks otherwise failed, the numbers of casualties were far lower than in the numerous suicide attacks carried out in Iraq since 2003. Attacks increased after the beginning of the Second Intifada in September 2000. Although suicide bombings comprised only a small percentage of actual attacks launched by Palestinians against Israelis, they accounted for perhaps half the Israelis killed between 2000 and 2002. In 2003, there were 26 attacks killing 144, but in 2004, 15 attacks and 55 dead. In 2005, Hamas ordered a cease-fire, which was, however, not binding on the other groups that had engaged in attacks: the Abu Ali Mustafa Brigades of the Popular Front for the Liberation of Palestine, Islamic Jihad, and the al-Aqsa Martyrs Brigades. During 2005, there were seven attacks, killing 23, and then in 2006, only two attacks.

Suicide bombings have also been employed by insurgents in Afghanistan, although there were not as many casualties, most probably because the Taliban have chosen to target military personnel or politicians, rather than civilians, and because the planning for them is often poor. Large numbers of civilian casualties have resulted from certain attacks, as in the Baghlan in 2007, where the target was a politician and 70 people died, or when a local militia leader was targeted at a dogfight in Kandahar in February 2008, and 80 people died. After 2010, however, the number of suicide bombings in Afghanistan increased, with more civilians becoming victims compared to earlier bombings.

There are differing attitudes in the various states where suicide attacks have occurred. While most all people fear such attacks, many citizens support the notion of armed resistance. Since Al-Qaeda and groups similar to it have been active, counterterrorist agencies, police, and gendarmeries around the world have been focusing on ways to prevent suicide bombings. Suicide bombings are part of asymmetric warfare. Advantages for any violent radical group employing this tactic are that no escape need be arranged for the bombers and that they are not expected to live to reveal information. Also, the materials for the explosive devices are inexpensive.

Al-Qaeda tactics have created a new *fiqh al-jihad*, or rules of jihad, that are somewhat different from the past. For example, in a collective jihad, women, children, and parents of dependent children, or the children of the elderly, were not to volunteer for jihad, but in the five-year period when such attacks were most prevalent in Israel and in the last several years in Iraq, bombers have come from both genders, although most were men. It is a common assumption that suicide bombers are drawn from the poor and desperate, but a careful study of most suicide terrorist acts shows this is untrue; the bombers were, rather, the ideologically committed of different backgrounds.

On occasion, Afghani and Iraqi authorities have claimed that mentally impaired people have been induced to be bombers, but this must be only a small number. Sometimes those who were recruited to such actions were chosen for their psychological predispositions not to suicide but to suggestibility, and were prevented, if possible, from contacting their families once their mission was set, so as not to give any hint of their intent. In the case of Palestinian suicide bombers, those attackers who authorities said were traceable to Hamas and Islamic Jihad were persons with no major family responsibilities and who were over the age of 18. In some cases, recruiters sought individuals who could speak Hebrew well.

Understandably, suicide bombings are enormously upsetting to potential civilian victims. Suicide bombers turn up when they are least expected as their victims go about their daily business, and victims and bystanders are taken completely by surprise. The victims are often civilians, and children make up a sizable percentage of those killed. Because the bomber has no concern for his or her own life, it is difficult to prevent such attacks. In Israel and in Iraq, many individuals and businesses have hired security guards who are specially trained to spot potential bombers. Airport and general transport security has now been increased worldwide.

Amy Hackney Blackwell and
Sherifa Zuhur

See also: Al-Qaeda; Hezbollah (Party of God); Human Shields; Islamic Radicalism; Martyrdom; Taliban

Further Reading

Aboul-Enein, Youssef H., and Sherifa Zuhur. *Islamic Rulings on Warfare.* Carlisle Barracks, PA: Strategic Studies Institute, 2004.

Friedman, Lauri S. *What Motivates Suicide Bombers?* Farmington Hills, MI: Greenhaven, 2004.

Khosrokhavar, Farhad. *Suicide Bombers: Allah's New Martyrs.* Translated by David Macey. London: Pluto, 2005.

Rosenthal, Franz. "On Suicide in Islam." *Journal of the American Oriental Society* 66 (1946): 239–59.

Skaine, Rosemarie. *Female Suicide Bombers.* Jefferson, NC: McFarland, 2006.

Sunni Islam

Largest of the two predominant branches of Islam. Approximately 85 percent of Muslims worldwide are adherents of

Sunni Islam, although the exact proportions of the two branches are disputed. Muslims themselves seldom used the word "Sunni" prior to the 2003 invasion of Iraq and subsequent occupation or the Islamic Revolution in Iran. It derives from a medieval Arabic phrase, *ahl al-sunnah wa al-jama'a*, meaning those who live according to the Prophet's model, unified in a community. In the early period, this term did not refer to all Muslims but rather to those who were engaged in Islamic scholarship and learning. The *sunnah*, or way, of the Prophet Muhammad refers to his tradition, or practice, of Islam during his 23 years of life following the initial revelation of Allah's words to him. However, "sunnah" generally referred to any tradition of the ancient Arabs.

It is mostly in the West that Muslims are differentiated as Sunnis or Shia. If asked, a Muslim may instead identify himself by a school of Islamic law or jurisprudence, such as the Hanafi school, which was the official legal doctrine of the Ottoman Empire, or of a particular movement. Since the most recent Islamic revival (*sahwa islamiyya*) began in the 1970s, the term *sunniyyun* (plural of *sunni* used interchangeably with *Islamiyyun*) has acquired the meaning of a very devout Muslim, or a *salafi*.

In contrast with the more institutionalized clerics, courts, and systems of Sunni Muslim learning, Sufi Islam is a mystical movement within Islam, the goal of which is the spiritual development of the individual. Sufis seek out personal guides (*shaykh* or *pir*) and are organized into brotherhoods (*tariqat*). There are Shia as well as Sunni Sufi orders. Sufism can be highly ascetic, while mainstream Islam is not. In contemporary times, sometimes even official clerics are also Sufis; however, the *salafists* oppose Sufism.

Sunni Muslims do not adhere to the doctrine of the imams, as do several sects of Shia Muslims (excluding the Zaydiyya). In the past, they generally judged the validity of the caliph (the temporal political and military leader) or the caliphate (Islamic government) itself by his or its adherence to the faith and the order and harmony that he or it maintained. In contrast with the Shia, Sunni Muslims believe that Abu Bakr, Umar, and Uthman—the first three Rashidun caliphs following Muhammad—were legitimate successors of Muhammad and that they are of equal standing with the fourth caliph, Ali, Muhammad's son-in-law. Ali became the fourth caliph in 656 CE after the murder of Caliph Uthman and was himself assassinated in 661. However there were other Muslims, not Ali's supporters, who also opposed the Umayyads, so the political divisions over leadership were complex.

It was not a requirement that the political and religious leadership in Sunni Islam trace its lineage through Ali, although the requirements of a caliph as defined by the scholar Abu al-Hasan Ali Ibn Muhammad Ibn Habib al-Mawardi (972–1058) indicated that he must be of the Prophet Muhammad's Quraysh tribe, male, not physically impaired, and pious. Any link to the Ahl al-Bayt, the immediate family members of the Prophet was, however, highly regarded. The caliphs lost their real authority in 1055. They retained an element of religious authority only in name, as the caliph was mentioned in the Friday prayers. With the Mongol sack of Baghdad in 1258, the caliphs lost all power. For Sunni Muslims, other political leaders were acceptable, though they were supposed to uphold Islamic law. When the Ottoman sultans years later declared themselves to be caliphs in order to wage jihad, other Muslims questioned their religious claim. By the 20th century, some Muslims understood the caliphate as an ideal structure but one that could be replaced by other forms of authority. Others supported attempts to restore the caliphate.

In the absence of the caliphate, Muslim politics continued under the precept that other rulers, sultans, or emirs would rule to the best of their ability in accordance with sharia (Islamic law) and uphold the *hisba*, the principle of "commanding the good and forbidding the evil," a key principle in Islam. Clerics, or *ulama* (those who possess *'ilm*, religious knowledge), were to be consulted by the ruler, issue fatawa, and help to guide the believers.

To justify Islamic rule the Ottomans, who were Sunni Muslims, later governed under a particular theory called the circle of equity, in which mutual responsibilities were to provide equity, security, and justice. In the 20th century, both Sunni and Shia politicized Islamic movements have argued for a more intensely Islamic government. The Muslim Brotherhood, Hamas, Hezbollah, the Gamaat Islamiya, and Al-Qaeda have all taken this position. These groups draw on very important arguments about governance and the state that have developed in Islamic history. The Muslim Brotherhood relinquished jihad as armed struggle and sought to change society through *dawa*, a program involving recruitment, education, and social support. Hezbollah and Hamas argue for both armed struggle and *dawa*. Islamic Jihad (in Egypt), Gamaat Islamiya, and Al-Qaeda all argue that the groups who only conducted *dawa* are not supporting Muslims, that jihad as armed struggle is necessary. However, the Gamaat Islamiya and Egyptian Islamic Jihad (in Egypt, excluding those members who joined Al-Qaeda) recanted their use of jihad beginning in 1997 and reached a truce with the Egyptian government in 1999.

In general, individual interpretations of Islamic law by scholars may vary. There is no pope or central authority in Sunni Islam. In Sunni Islam, unlike Shia Islam, there is no *marjaiyya*, or formal policy of choosing a cleric as a "source of emulation." However there are today many very popular Sunni clerics and preachers whose followers are loyal to their various positions.

The Sunni legal schools employ a principle of lawmaking known as *ijma*, or consensus, that is not employed by the Shia legal schools. However, there are differences in the legal definitions of that consensus. Additionally, a Sunni Muslim could resort to a cleric of one school to obtain a ruling, or fatwa, and is generally expected to adhere to the commonly acknowledged features of his own school. But Muslims may also seek advice from other clerics or authorities, and advice columns in newspapers and on the Internet provide differing opinions, sometimes based on the positions of other legal schools.

Muslims believe that the Koran is the literal word of God delivered in Arabic by the angel Gabriel to Muhammad over a period of 23 years. Any desecration of the Koran is therefore a desecration of the very words of Allah. Although the Koran is the final statement of Allah to humanity, when it does not offer explicit advice on a particular matter, a Muslim may appeal to a jurist to look to the Prophet's *sunnah*, as recorded in the *ahadith*, or collected materials concerning the tradition, behavior, practices, and sayings of the Prophet. They may also use *qiyas*, or a type of analogy, in determining the licitness of any action, or behavior, or the principle of *ijma*.

The *hadith* are always introduced by listing the chain of their transmitters. Ideally, the first transmitter of the text was a companion (*sahabah*) of Muhammad. An important companion was Abu Bakr, also known as "The Most Truthful" (*al-Siddiq*), the first caliph. The next companions in level of importance are the next two caliphs, Umar and Uthman. The Shia reject the *hadith* transmitted by those they call Unjust Companions, who repudiated the leadership of Ali abi Talib. Although these three are important companions, there are ten who are thought to warrant paradise. A much longer list of *sahabah* exist because Sunnis consider anyone who knew or even saw Muhammad, accepted his teachings, and died as a Muslim to be a companion. Early Sunni scholars identified these companions, wrote their biographies, and listed them in various reference texts. This identification was essential because their testimonies and their reputation for veracity affirm and determine the content of the *hadith* and, therefore, the *sunnah*. There are many collections of these original oral traditions, but they are graded according to their soundness with six respected collections, two of which—that of Muslim and Bukhari—are considered most reliable. However, many Muslims repeat and believe in *hadith* that are not necessarily the most sound, and since the reform movement of the 19th century, some Muslims believe that the *hadith* brought many unwanted innovations or, conversely, too much imitation of tradition (*taqlid*) into Islam. Shia Islamic law generally uses *hadith* that pertain to Muhammad as told to members of Ali's family. These variations lead to some differences in Sunni Islamic law and Shia Islamic law.

Muslims must practice their faith through demonstrated religious rituals and obligations. Many sources speak of five religious practices or duties, often referred to as the Five Pillars. The first pillar is called bearing witness (*shahadah*) and is the recitation of the creed or confession of faith, called the Testimony of Faith: "There is no God, but Allah; and Muhammad is His prophet." The *shahadah* is also uttered as part of the Muslim call (*adhan*) to prayer and is part of the Tashahud, which follows each set of two prayer sequences, when they are recited at least five times daily (at different times two, three, or four sequences are the minimum required). The second pillar is prayer (*salat*), performed at least five times a day (dawn, noon, midafternoon, sunset, and evening). Muslims purify themselves before prayer by washing their hands, face, mouth, nose, ears, and feet. During prayer, all Muslims face Mecca. The third pillar is fasting (*sawm*) during the daylight hours for all of the month of Ramadan, the ninth month of the Islamic lunar calendar. This fasting means that no food or beverages are consumed and that there is no smoking or sexual intercourse. Those who are sick are excused from fasting and make up their fast. Other days of fasting may be observed, but it is obligatory during Ramadan.

The fourth pillar is almsgiving, effectively a tax (*zakat*) of 2.5 percent calculated on one's income and assets. But unlike a tax, it is supposed to be voluntary. It is used for the community's poor, the promotion of Islam, and the maintenance of the mosque and other religious institutions. The fifth pillar is the required pilgrimage (*hajj*) once in a lifetime to the holy city of Mecca, as commanded in the Koran (in surah XXII, al-Hajj, 22–33).

The responsibility for performing these duties falls on the individual, but stricter Muslims and Muslim governments hold that it is the duty of the state to command the good and thus to enforce their performance. There are other strictures as well. For example, Muslims must not drink alcohol, not simply as a forbidden substance but because it clouds alertness and judgment and makes it impossible to pray. Pork is forbidden, as are games of chance. Many Muslim women believe that covering their heads is a required individual duty, but others do not. Modest behavior is, however, required of both men and women.

Many Westerners know little about Islam, with the exception of the Five Pillars. Yet ethical behavior is very important to Islamic belief, including the commitment to social justice, as in protection of the weak and aid to the poor and socially disadvantaged. Islam seeks to promote an ethical life lived within a community. It is more difficult in many ways to be a good Muslim while fulfilling one's obligations to family and community than to live as a hermit, and the Prophet Muhammad is said to have promoted marriage and discouraged celibacy or an extreme ascetic lifestyle. Many of the rules regarding relations between men and women, which non-Muslims find very strict and hard to understand, are indeed intended to provide a moral and ethical grounding for the community.

Muslims are concerned with *iman*, or faith, as well as acts of submission (*islam*) and rightful intentions (*ihsan*), and many religio-philosophical principles guide them. The most basic aspect of Islam is belief in Allah and the Oneness (*tawhid*) of Allah. This monotheism is expressed in many ways. Muslims believe in the prophets and believe that they brought important messages to mankind, but Muhammad is considered the Seal of Prophecy, or the last prophet. Nonetheless, Jesus, Moses, Abraham, and others are revered. However, Muslims believe that some Jews did not heed the word of God in his divine message to them. Muslims, who believe that Jesus was only a prophet, also argue that Christians wrongly recognize Christ as Father and Divine Spirit. The doctrine of the Trinity violates the idea of the Oneness of Allah. Muslims recognize the scriptures as revelations of Allah. Allah was the creator, but he did not simply create the world and humankind and leave humanity to fend for itself. Rather, Allah provided revelations for the guidance of men. The Koran is the transcending revelation of Allah that cannot be contradicted by any other revelations of Allah. Still, Muslims recognize other revelations, which include the Jewish and Christian holy scriptures, as well as the Zoroastrian texts.

Muslims believe in the angels (*malaika*), who are the servants of Allah. Angels were not given the free will that Allah granted to humans. Their duties include recording all human deeds, ensouling the fetus at 120 days of gestation (although some Islamic scholars believe ensoulment occurs on the 40th or 80th day), watching over and caring for creation, gathering souls at death, and much more.

All Muslims also believe in the Day of Judgment and in the Resurrection (*qiyama*), when Allah will return to judge all of humanity, Muslim and non-Muslim, including the dead. After the Resurrection, every human is held accountable for his or her deeds. The deeds of each individual are judged by Allah and weighed on a scale. If the good outweighs the evil, then the individual gains entrance into paradise. If the evil outweighs the good, the individual spends eternity in hell.

In the pre-Islamic era, referred to as the *jahiliyya* or time of barbarity, people believed entirely in preordination. Islam rejects this passivity because people possess free will and can thus choose to do good or evil and are held accountable for their decisions. At the same time, it is difficult to retain faith in the face of tragedy, poverty, or disaster. The Muslim belief in the omnipotence of God, his transcendence and simultaneous immanence, is meant to solace the believer.

The application of reason, in the form of Hellenic philosophical arguments to theology, philosophy, and the sciences, was prominent in the Golden Age of Islam. Reacting to the philosophers and those who used logical reasoning (*kalam*) were Traditionists, the scholars who focused on *hadith* to determine the *sunnah* and rejected the methodology of logical reasoning. Multiple Sunni traditions, or schools of law and theology, arose over time. Not all survive today. These schools share the basic theology described above and assert the primacy of the Koranic revelation, but there are notable differences.

Sunni Islamic law is based on the Koran and the *sunnah*, as nuanced by the particular *hadith* collector and his interpretation. Different scholars using different assumptions, reasoning, hermeneutics (guiding interpretive principles), and source materials arrived at different applications of Islamic law, which were organized into schools known as *madhahib*. Muslims assert that Sharia never changes but that the understanding and application of it into jurisprudence (*fiqh*) does change, since jurisprudence is carried out by human beings. Muslims generally seek to avoid illicit innovation (*bidah*), but many "innovations"

have to be considered. Thus, the Koran predates the telegraph. Thus, the application of *fiqh* to adjudicate the use of the telegraph was a matter of interpretation. In addition to the usual sources of law, jurists took into account *maslaha*, public benefit or the common good, in considering new technology. There are four surviving major schools of law in Sunni Islam. The various schools predominate in different regions. These dominant Sunni schools of law are Hanbali, Hanafi, Maliki, and Shafi, and all use the Koran as their primary source.

Hanbali law is the strictest tradition and was practiced by Muslims in Saudi Arabia, Qatar, Syria, Palestine, and elsewhere; with the growth of *salafism* and *neosalafism*, it has expanded. It was founded by Ahmad ibn Hanbal and is the dominant tradition on the Arabian Peninsula, although it has adherents in Iraq, Syria, Jerusalem, and Egypt as well. The Hanafi *madhhab* may be the largest school. It was founded by Abu Hanifa and encompasses 30 percent of Sunnis. Its adherents are mainly in Turkey, Central Asia, the Balkans, Iraq, Afghanistan, Pakistan, India, Bangladesh, lower Egypt, and in former states of the Soviet Union. Both the Mongol Empire and the Ottoman Empire promoted the Hanafi tradition. When the Ottoman sultan Selim the Grim (1512–1520) captured Palestine, he imposed Hanafi law on the region. The official judicial traditions and systems in contemporary Syria, Jordan, and Palestine are derived from the Hanafi tradition.

The Maliki school has approximately 15 percent of Sunnis as adherents. It was founded by Malik ibn Anas and has adherents in North Africa and West Africa, particularly upper Egypt, Algeria, Tunisia, Morocco, Mauritania, and Libya, as well as in the Sudan, Kuwait, Dubai, and Abu Dhabi. The Maliki school derives its *fiqh* through consensus more than do any of the other traditions. The Maliki system of lawmaking is built on the Koran and the *hadith*, supplemented by an interpretation of *ijma* (consensus), as being the consensus or agreed opinion of the People of Medina, and analogy (*qiyas*). In addition, Malik considered the statements of the Prophet's companions and referred to the public good (*maslahah*), customary law (*urf*), common practice (*adat*), and several other legal principles.

The Shafi school was founded by Muhammad ibn Idris al-Shafi and has adherents in the southern Arabian Peninsula, the Hijaz, Palestine, Indonesia, Malaysia, Thailand, Cambodia, parts of India, the Philippines, Sudan, Ethiopia, Somalia, North Yemen, Kurdistan, Sri Lanka, and lower Egypt. The Shafi school utilizes the *usul al-fiqh* (roots of lawmaking) in a way that places *ijma* ahead of analogy.

Historically, there were many Sunni schools and trends in theology. Among the important or well-known trends were the Mutazila, whose doctrine was abandoned, and the Ashariyyah, Maturidiyyah, and Salafism (which has at least two versions).

The Mutazila school was established in Iraq by Wasil bin Ata (699–749). Abbasid caliph al-Mamun (813–827) made Mutazila theology the state religion and persecuted all dissenters. At the time, Muslims had debated the uncreatedness versus the created (manmade) nature of the Koran and many other theological questions. Mutazilites rejected the doctrine of the uncreated Koran, but with their downfall Muslims accepted precisely that doctrine. The Mutazila's name came from their intermediate position on the question of sin: they asserted that Muslims who commit grave sins and die without repentance cannot be treated as nonbelievers,

but judgment must be withheld until the resurrection. The Mutazilites rejected anthropomorphic interpretations of God. For instance, the phrase "hand of God" might refer symbolically to God's power to the Mutazila, whereas their opponents would insist it meant the actual hand of God.

The Ashariyyah school was founded by Abu al-Hasan al-Ashari (873–935) and became the dominant Sunni theology in that era. It emphasizes divine revelation and stresses the understanding of that revelation through the application of human reasoning.

The Maturidiyyah was founded by Abu Mansur al-Maturidi (d. 944). Maturidis believe that the existence of Allah as understood in Islam can be derived through reason alone and that such is true of major concepts of good and evil, legal and illegal.

Salafism, a reform movement in Islam, actually developed in two different contexts in 18th-century Arabia and in 19th-century Egypt and Ottoman Empire. The 19th-century to early 20th-century reformers Jamal al-Din al-Afghani, Muhammad Abduh, Qasim Amin, and Rashid Rida initiated a discussion about the decline of the Muslim world and the reforms it should carry out to overcome the negative influence of Western colonialism and imperialism. While Afghani looked for an Islamic ruler who would stand up to the West and believed that Pan-Islam could solve the problem, Muhammad Abduh, an Egyptian jurist, recommended reform of Islamic education and the methodology of Islamic law in which blind imitation of the past would cease. He thought that Sunni Muslims should consider a return to *ijtihad* (a Shia methodology of lawmaking) to meet contemporary requirements, and he wanted Western sciences introduced into the educational curriculum. Qasim Amin argued for an end to enforced marriages, female seclusion, and lack of education for women, while Rashid Rida pursued a somewhat stricter and more Islamist approach to the proper way of life for Muslims.

Earlier, Muhammad abd al-Wahhab in Arabia promoted a strict monotheism, which he claimed would cleanse Islam of many syncretic traditions that constituted *shirk*, or polytheism. This tradition is referred to by his enemies as Wahhabism, which is the general term used today in the West. The *muwahiddun*, or Unitarians as they call themselves, or Wahhabists who fought as warriors for the Saud tribe, were known as the Ikhwan (brethren). In general, the *muwahiddun* are considered *salafis*, because they wanted to cleanse Islamic practice and society of un-Islamic accretions and innovations (*bida*) that had arisen through cultural synthesis. However, this cleansing is a matter of gradation, so not all Wahhabis, as the West calls them, are either violent purists or ardent *salafists*. The Wahhabis adhere to the Hanbali school of law, although some modern *salafis* speak of rejecting all legal tradition and utilizing only the Koran and the *sunnah*. The *salafis* were anti-Ottoman, anti-Shia, and anti-Sufi, and opposed such practices as Sufi ceremonies and visiting tombs, even at Mecca. These *salafis* called for jihad in its active form with which they, in alliance with the Saud family, drove out first the Ottomans and then, in a later historical period, the Rashids and the Hashimites.

Terrorist and Al-Qaeda leader Osama bin Laden was a *neosalafi* and a Wahhabi. He believed that the Saudi Arabian royal family does not strictly uphold Wahhabi or *salafi* values and should be militantly opposed for its alliance with the West. Other *salafis* have been part of the resistance to U.S. occupation and the new Iraqi government in post-2003 Iraq.

Some *salafis* consider the Shia to be renegades (this refers to a specific denigrating legal epithet given them during the civil wars in Islamic history) or apostates, apostasy being a capital crime in Islam. The Shia had come to fear and hate the Wahhabis because of their raids on Shia areas historically, but this animosity is not true of all Sunnis and Shia who, in general, lived peacefully alongside each other in prewar Iraq. Some charge that the United States and Israel, as well as certain Arab countries, are heightening fears in the region of a Shia crescent of influence, running from Iran to the Shia of Iraq and the Gulf States, and then to the Shia of Lebanon. Such discourse could create more problems among Muslims in the region. Therefore, King Abdullah of Saudi Arabia has spoken out against sectarian discord. Elsewhere leaders such as at al-Azhar try to represent the Jafari *madhhab* as a legitimate legal school of Islam.

Richard M. Edwards and Sherifa Zuhur

See also: Al-Qaeda; Bin Laden, Osama; Hezbollah (Party of God); Islamic Radicalism; Shia Islam

Further Reading

Armstrong, Karen. *Islam: A Short History*. New York: Modern Library, 2002.

Esposito, John L. *The Oxford History of Islam*. New York: Oxford University Press, 2000.

Fuller, Graham E., and Rend Rahim Francke. *The Arab Shi'a: The Forgotten Muslims*. Hampshire, UK: Palgrave Macmillan, 2001.

Gregorian, Vartan. *Islam: A Mosaic, Not a Monolith*. Baltimore: Brookings Institute Press, 2004.

Swift Project

Within weeks of the events of September 11, 2001, the George W. Bush administration launched a secret program to trace the financial records of people suspected of having ties to Al-Qaeda. This secret project is called the Swift Project, named after the Brussels banking consortium, Society for Worldwide Interbank Financial Telecommunication (SWIFT). The SWIFT serves as a gatekeeper for electronic transactions between 7,800 international institutions, and it is owned by a cooperative with more than 2,200 organizations. Every major commercial bank, brokerage house, fund manager, and stock exchange has used its services.

The Bush administration entrusted the Central Intelligence Agency (CIA) and the U.S. Treasury Department to set up and run the Swift Project. Legal justification for the implementation of this project was the president's emergency economic powers. American agents used computer programs to wade through huge amounts of sensitive data from the transactions of SWIFT. Treasury officials have maintained then and now that the Swift Project was exempt from American laws restricting government access to private financial records because the cooperative was classified as a messaging service, not a bank or financial institution. This allowed the U.S. government to track money from a Saudi bank account of a suspected terrorist to a source in the United States, or elsewhere in the world. Evidently it was information of this type that allowed American officials to locate and capture Riduan Isamuddin Hambali, the operations chief of the Indonesian terrorist group Jemaah Islamiyah, in Thailand.

News of the Swift Project became public in 2006 and became identified with the surveillance of American citizens by the U.S. government. Despite considerable negative publicity, the Bush administration and, later, the Barack Obama administration, continued to use the Swift Project to track the financial records of organizations and people suspected of giving money to Al Qaeda. Additonally, in 2013, disclosures by former National Security Agency contractor Edward Snowden alleged the NSA was systematically undermining the SWIFT-agreement. No démenti was issued by the American side, and the European Parliament voted to suspend the agreement.

Stephen E. Atkins

See also: Bush Administration; Central Intelligence Agency; Obama Administration

Further Reading

Bender, Bryan. "Terrorist Funds-Tracking No Secret, Some Say." *Boston Globe*, June 28, 2006.

Bilefsky, Dan. "Bank Consortium Faces Outcry on Data Transfer." *International Herald Tribune*, June 29, 2006, 4.

Lichtblau, Eric, and James Risen. "Bank Data Sifted in Secret by U.S. to Block Terror." *New York Times*, June 23, 2006.

Meyer, Josh, and Greg Miller. "U.S. Secretly Tracks Global Bank Data." *Los Angeles Times*, June 23, 2006.

Stolberg, Sheryl Gay, and Eric Lichtblau. "Cheney Assails Press on Report on Bank Data." *New York Times*, June 24, 2006.

T

Taliban

The first casualty of the American reaction to the September 11, 2001, attacks was the Taliban regime in Afghanistan. Mohammed Omar had founded the Taliban in the spring of 1994, and he remained its head until the Northern Alliance, with the assistance of the United States and other coalition nations, overthrew the Taliban regime in late 2001. It was Omar's alliance with Osama bin Laden and the sponsorship of Al-Qaeda training camps that led to the overthrow of the Taliban.

Omar founded the Taliban in reaction to the feuding among Afghan warlords. He was born in 1959 into a poor Pashtun family in the small village of Nodeh near Kandahar, Afghanistan. His father was a landless peasant belonging to the Pashtun Hotak tribe of the Ghilzia branch of the Pashtuns. His early death left Omar in the hands of relatives. Omar studied at an Islamic school in Kandahar but never graduated from it. This failure to graduate did not prevent him from opening a madrassa (religious school) in Singhesar, a village near Kandahar.

Shortly after fighting broke out between the Soviet army and the Afghans, Omar joined the mujahideen. He served in the ranks of the Younis Khalis' Brigade of the Islamic Party. Omar was in the middle of heavy fighting, and he suffered four wounds, including a shrapnel wound that caused the loss of his right eye. His combat experience and his wound increased his prestige among the Afghan Islamists because it proved he had suffered for the Muslim cause. After the end of the war in 1989, Omar returned to his religious school.

Omar remained at his school until he became enraged by the conduct of an oppressive warlord who had raped two young women. He gathered a group of religious students (*taliban*), and they hanged the warlord. Pakistani authorities in the Pakistani Inter-Services Intelligence (ISI) noted Omar's growing popularity among the Pashtuns after this act. They decided to give military aid to Omar and his Taliban forces. In the March 1996 council of Afghanistan's religious leaders at Kandahar, Omar was selected to be the head of the Taliban, or Commander of the Faithful. Using this religious authority, along with financial and military aid from Pakistan and Saudi Arabia, Omar and his Taliban forces were strong enough militarily on September 27, 1996, to seize Kabul and control most of Afghanistan.

After the triumph of the Taliban, Omar's strict interpretation of the Koran led him to institute severe religious restrictions on the Afghan population. The Taliban had difficulty ruling Afghanistan because its members preferred to focus on religion rather than politics or ways to run a government. Consequently, it was easy to turn to the

Members of the Taliban pose with AK-47 assault rifles and rocket-propelled grenades in Zabul province, south of Kabul, Afghanistan, in October 2006. (AP Photo/Allauddin Khan)

Koran to rule. The Taliban regime issued a series of rules. Men were subjected to compulsory praying, and they were required to grow beards and wear turbans. With only a few exceptions, women lost all rights to hold jobs outside the home, and they could appear in public only when completely covered from head to foot and in the company of a male relative. Art, dancing, music, and television were forbidden. All secular education ended immediately, and boys were required to attend religious schools. Schooling for girls ended entirely. Criminals faced execution or mutilation for their crimes following the laws laid down in the Koran.

Omar had his Islamist Taliban regime firmly in control of most of Afghanistan, but his forces were still trying to defeat the anti-Taliban coalition of the Northern Alliance in the northern area of Afghanistan. For this the Taliban needed an ally, and bin Laden and Al-Qaeda were avail-

able. Bin Laden had settled in Afghanistan in May 1996 after leaving Sudan, and his Al-Qaeda network had been placed at the disposal of the Taliban regime. To consolidate his relationship with the Taliban, bin Laden swore an oath of allegiance (*bayat*) to Mullah Omar. Al-Qaeda forces fought alongside Taliban forces in the war against the Northern Alliance. In return, the Taliban allowed bin Laden to build training camps to train Al-Qaeda operatives.

Omar refused requests by the United States to hand bin Laden over after the September 11 attacks. In response, the United States and its North Atlantic Treaty Organization (NATO) allies joined with the Northern Alliance in fighting against the Taliban. During the struggle, many local pro-Taliban leaders switched sides. Despite losing its most important military leader in the assassination of General Ahmed Shah Massoud by Al-Qaeda, the Northern Alliance was able to overthrow the Taliban regime. Taliban forces retreated from Kabul on November 12, from Jalalabad on November 13, and from Kandahar by early December. Omar and his followers fled to neighboring Pakistan, where they found support among various tribal groups. Since that time, the name Taliban has been used to refer to both Omar's original group and, more generally, the other factions fighting alongside the exiled regime.

Although U.S. and coalition forces easily toppled the Taliban regime, they have not been able to eradicate its members or establish lasting stability in the region. Taliban forces continue to engage in an ever-worsening guerrilla war that by October 2010 had claimed the lives of more than 750 U.S. troops and wounded thousands of others. Coalition forces have countered these attacks with targeted missile strikes aimed at Taliban leaders and strongholds and carried out by special operations forces or unmanned Predator drones. Rising numbers of civilian casualties from these air strikes, as well as the destruction of opium poppy fields (a major funding source for the Taliban but also the economic livelihood of many rural farmers in Afghanistan), have led to a resurgence in support for the Taliban.

In late 2009, President Barack Obama announced that the United States would begin a troop surge in Afghanistan similar to that used in Iraq, with the goal of definitively ending the Taliban and Al-Qaeda insurgency. The surge ended in late 2012, but was not successful in curbing Taliban/Al Qaeda violence. In January 2010, Taliban leaders suggested that the group was ready to break with Al-Qaeda in order to bring about peace in Afghanistan. However, this pledge was belied within months when the group took responsibility for simultaneous bombings in Kandahar that killed at least 35 people and wounded 57. The attack set the stage for subsequent strikes and assassinations throughout 2010 and 2011, including one audacious raid against the U.S. embassy in Kabul (September 2011). Although at the time of this writing, communication channels had been reopened via a Taliban office in Doha, Qatar, both the situation in Afghanistan and the final fate of the Taliban remain uncertain. According to the United Nations, the Taliban and their allies were responsible for 75 percent of Afghan civilian casualties in 2010, 80 percent in 2011, and 80 percent in 2012. During 2013 and into early 2014, violence that included civilian casualties increased even more.

Stephen E. Atkins

See also: Al-Qaeda; Bin Laden, Osama; Enduring Freedom, Operation; Zawahiri, Ayman al-

Further Reading

Atwan, Abdel Bari. *The Secret History of Al Qaeda*. Berkeley: University of California Press, 2006.

Gohari, M. *The Taliban: Ascent to Power*. Oxford: Oxford University Press, 1999.

Marsden, Peter. *The Taliban: War and Religion in Afghanistan*. Rev. ed. London: Zed Books, 2002.

Rashid, Ahmed. *Taliban: Islam, Oil and the New Great Game in Central Asia*. London: Tauris, 2002.

Taliban, Destruction of Bamiyan and Pre-Islamic Artifacts

The Taliban's decision to sanction the destruction of Afghanistan's cultural heritage, including the world's tallest-standing Buddhas—the Buddhas of Bamiyan—

shocked and outraged many Afghans and international observers alike. The Taliban regime, which traced it origins to the early 1990s, was a right-wing Sunni Islamic fundamentalist movement that effectively ruled Afghanistan from late 1995 until late 2001. Following a campaign to crack down on un-Islamic segments of Afghan society by conservative Islamic clerics, the Supreme Court of the Islamic Emirate of Afghanistan issued a fatwa on March 1, 2001. This fatwa sanctioned the destruction of all pre-Islamic statues and idols in Afghanistan. Almost immediately, members of the Department for the Promotion of Virtue and the Prevention of Vice set about destroying many of the cultural treasures of Afghanistan's long and storied history.

Situated at the crossroads of ancient civilizations, Afghanistan experienced successive waves of migrating peoples, each leaving its religious and cultural imprint on the Afghan landscape. As trade along the Silk Road spread, Buddhist culture spread throughout Afghanistan and came to dominate political and religious life there until the 9th century. In consequence, Buddhist architecture and iconography dotted the landscape of Afghanistan. As Islam gradually displaced Buddhism in Afghanistan, Buddhist statues and paintings were ignored because Muslims are enjoined not to recognize idols or encourage idol worship. Afghanistan's cultural history remained undiscovered until the early 20th century, when archaeologists uncovered and brought to light some of the ancient cities along the Silk Road.

Following its rise to power in September 1995, the Taliban sought to create a state based on its religious interpretation of Islamic governance. In accordance with its interpretation of sharia (Islamic law), the Taliban implemented a ban on all forms of imagery, including television, music, and sports. The first steps in destroying Afghanistan's cultural heritage began with the systematic looting of archaeological sites under Taliban control. At the Greek city of Ai Khanoum in a remote area of northeastern Takhar Province, the plunderers, under financial agreements with ruling Taliban commanders, gouged out the surface with bulldozers and probed deeply through long tunnels. Beginning in 1996, attempts were also made to destroy ancient statues housed in the National Museum in Kabul as well as pre-Islamic artifacts stored in the Ministry of Information and Culture.

In 1997, a Taliban commander trying to seize the Bamiyan Valley declared that the Bamiyan Buddhas would be destroyed as soon as the valley fell into his hands. The resulting international outcry caused the Taliban leadership to prohibit the Buddhas' destruction and to promise that the cultural heritage of Afghanistan would be protected. In 1998, however, the smaller Buddha's head and part of the shoulders were blown off, and the face of the larger Buddha was blackened by burning tires.

It was not until the United Nations (UN) Security Council imposed economic sanctions on the Taliban in December 2000 that the Taliban decided to destroy the Bamiyan Buddhas altogether. In January and February 2001, the Taliban stepped up its efforts at destroying all pre-Islamic artifacts in Afghanistan. Invoking the Islamic prohibition against the depiction of living things, the Taliban destroyed more than a dozen Greco-Buddhist statues in the National Museum. On February 26, 2001, Taliban ruler Mullah Mohammed Omar announced that all pre-Islamic statues in the Taliban-controlled areas of Afghanistan were to be destroyed, and on March 9, 2001, members of the Taliban blew up the Buddhas of Bamiyan. A few months later, smaller Buddha statues in Falodi and Kakrak were also destroyed. The destruction of the Buddhas of Bamiyan especially drew international ire because of their immense size and cultural importance; also driving global outrage at the Taliban's actions was the coverage of the destruction on television that was seen across the globe.

Keith A. Leitich

See also: Cultural Imperialism, U.S.; Democratization and the Global War on Terror; Martyrdom; Sunni Islam; Taliban

Further Reading

Marsden, Peter. *The Taliban: War and Religion in Afghanistan*. London: Zed Books, 2002.

Nojumi, Neamatollah. *The Rise of the Taliban in Afghanistan: Mass Mobilization, Civil War and the Future of the Region*. Basingstoke, UK: Palgrave, 2002.

Targeted Killing. *See* Kill List

Television, Middle Eastern

Television is one of the major sources of information in the modern world. Television stations in the Middle East have played a significant role through the broadcasting and transmitting of information, not just to the nations in that region but to the rest of the world. As in the West, television stations in the Middle East are regulated by governments, but there is more extensive control of it by government under state-centrism or state socialism. Still, a wide variety of programs can be found on television, especially with the advent of ca-

ble and satellite TV. These have brought about an explosion of new stations and viewpoints.

Television has played an important role in the major wars in the Middle East: the ongoing war between the Palestinians and the Israelis; Israeli wars in Lebanon (1978, 1982, 1993, 1996, 2006); the Lebanese civil war (1975–1990); relentless civil war in Sudan; and the Iran-Iraq War of 1980–1988. Additionally, the 1991 Persian Gulf War, the 2001 war against the Taliban in Afghanistan, and the 2003 Iraq War have all unfolded before television cameras.

In recent decades, technological developments and the expansion in global communications, together with the establishment of cable/satellite television, have made television in the Middle East a transnational phenomenon. This expansion has been best associated with the outbreak of the Persian Gulf War in 1991. Since then, a wide range of local and regional channels has been available by subscription in the Middle East. A major example is the Qatar satellite television channel Al Jazeera, which was launched in 1996 with a $150 million grant from the emir of Qatar. In the late 1990s, Al Jazeera became very popular in the Arab world yet was oddly ignored in the West. Al Jazeera set out to counter the formula of state-supported television and its one-sided news reportage. It built a reputation for exciting debates and strong disagreements in interviews and panels.

After September 11, 2001, Al Jazeera earned the ire of the U.S. government, when the Al Jazeera formula of endeavoring to present all sides of an issue came under fire as supporting terrorism. This occurred when Al Jazeera reported atrocities in Iraq and broadcast video statements of Osama bin Laden and other Al-Qaeda leaders. In contrast to Al Jazeera, the Saudi

TV channel al-Arabiyya was established on March 3, 2003, and based in the United Arab Emirates (UAE). Its primary focus is lighter entertainment, music, and dance videos. Its news coverage is influenced by the Western-allied UAE government. Alongside Al Jazeera and al-Arabiyya, there are several other Arab television channels that have facilitated a significant change in the media in relation to the Middle East. The most notable are: the LBCI (Lebanon), Future TV (Lebanon), Manar TV (Lebanon), Nile TV International (Egypt), Syria Satellite Channel (Syria), and Abu Dhabi TV (UAE).

There is now a wide range of Arab television stations broadcasting from the Middle East to other parts of the region and to the entire world. The importance of television is also seen in the coverage of the Middle East during wartime. Many Middle East channels compete to be among the first to broadcast from war zones and to send new and exclusive information to their audience. Moreover, continuously running news tickers became another way to broadcast the news around the clock, which allows an audience to follow news stories at any time. Beyond that, breaking news provides important supplements to a story when a war or a crisis is underway. More recently, Middle Eastern television has played a pivotal role in covering the so-called Arab Spring, which began in late 2010. That movement resulted in regime changes in Tunisia, Egypt, Libya, and Yemen and sparked violence and unrest in Bahrain, Syria, Algeria, Morocco, and Sudan, among other nations in the region. In places like Syria, however, heavy government censorship of the Internet and the press have made it more difficult for Middle Eastern television outlets to cover the continuing civil war there.

One of the problems of Middle Eastern television is that satellite television channels do not necessarily reach various sectarian communities equally. Viewers may choose to watch other channels or not to subscribe at all. During the summer 2006 Israeli-Hezbollah War in Lebanon, for example, there was another war underway between Arab satellite channels, which were essentially taking sides in their coverage of the conflict. Some Arab satellite stations have also clearly reflected their own politics, and some have shown biases both for and against the West. Al-Arabiyya has repeatedly sought to create undercurrents of bias during times of war. In this way, the Arabic television stations reflect the tendencies that Americans view on FOX television or, at the opposite extreme, on MSNBC.

Rami Y. Siklawi

See also: War Correspondents

Further Reading

Sakr, Naomi. *Satellite Realms: Transnational Television, Globalization & the Middle East.* London: I. B. Tauris, 2001.

Taylor, Philip M. *War and the Media: Propaganda and Persuasion in the Gulf War.* Manchester, UK: Manchester University Press, 1992.

Weisenborn, Ray, ed. *Media in the Midst of War: Cairo Reporting to the Global Village.* Cairo: Adham Center for Television, 1992.

Tenet, George

(1953–)

George Tenet was the head of the Central Intelligence Agency (CIA) from 1997 until 2004, during the period leading up to

Director of the Central Intelligence Agency George Tenet testifies on March 24, 2002, before the federal panel reviewing the September 11, 2001, terrorist attacks. Tenet resigned on July 11, 2004, shortly before the release of the 9/11 Commission report, which was critical of the CIA and its intelligence-gathering abilities. (AP Photo/J. Scott Applewhite)

and including September 11, 2001. He was appointed head of the CIA by President Bill Clinton, and his mission had been to revitalize the organization. The CIA had experienced limited success with its two previous heads, leading to low morale and several key retirements. Tenet's background in congressional circles made him a good choice to repair damaged relations between the CIA and Congress.

Most of Tenet's professional life has been in government service. His first job was as the research director of the American Hellenic Institute. After three years there, he found a position working for Senator John Heinz of Pennsylvania. His next job was as a staff member of the Senate Select Committee on Intelligence (SSCI),

and he then served as its staff director. It was his experience on the SSCI that led president-elect Bill Clinton to select him as a member of the national security transition team. After Clinton became president, Tenet was appointed senior director of intelligence programs at the National Security Council. He held this post from 1993 to 1995.

The Clinton administration decided that Tenet's next position should be in the CIA. Tenet was appointed deputy director of central intelligence in July 1995. He served in this post until the abrupt resignation of John Deutch in 1996. During most of 1996, until the U.S. Senate confirmed him as the director of central intelligence on July 1997, he served as the acting director. Tenet was a compromise candidate after President Clinton's first choice was rejected. The CIA was in disarray with budget cuts from Congress leading to severe personnel cuts. CIA personnel welcomed Tenet because it was known that he was an effective political operator, and the CIA needed to improve its image with Congress and other outsiders. Besides restoring relations with Congress and building morale, Tenet placed counterterrorism high on the CIA's agenda. He did so because of his increasing concern about the growing influence of Osama bin Laden and Al-Qaeda.

Tenet's relationship with President Clinton was always tenuous. By the time Tenet was head of the CIA, Clinton was in serious trouble with the Republicans in Congress on a range of foreign policy and domestic issues. Intelligence matters were considered important but were low on the agenda. Tenet rarely saw Clinton to give him briefings. Clinton relied on written intelligence summaries from the CIA. The terrorist incidents in 1998 and 1999 allowed Tenet to win President Clinton's attention, but Clinton still had reservations about trusting the CIA's intelligence. Steve Coll characterized Tenet's strength as his ability to "synthesize and organize the views of others." Clinton was more comfortable with intellectuals. At this time, Tenet's attention was divided between two concerns—the proliferation of weapons of mass destruction and terrorism—with terrorism further down on his agenda.

When George W. Bush's term began, Tenet was a holdover from a Democratic administration. In a briefing a week before Bush's inauguration, Tenet was able to establish a positive relationship with Bush with a series of intelligence briefings. He was able to impress the incoming president enough that he was retained as director of the CIA. In addition, George H. W. Bush recommended that his son retain Tenet. The younger Bush and Tenet developed a strong professional relationship based on mutual respect.

Every morning Tenet traveled to the White House to give President Bush an intelligence briefing. The CIA's presidential briefer on the occasions when Tenet was unavailable or when President Bush traveled was Mike Morell, whose presence ensured that CIA intelligence briefings to President Bush could continue wherever the president was at any given time. In his and Morell's briefings, Tenet warned President Bush at least 40 times about the possible danger from an Al-Qaeda operation. Bush's reaction was that "the Clinton administration's response to bin Laden only confirmed that the U.S. would do little to go after him." Tenet's positive relationship with the president allowed him to survive the political fallout over the failure of the CIA to gather intelligence on the September 11 plot. With regard to September 11, Tenet was as surprised as the rest of the intelligence community, and he confessed as much in later remarks.

On the morning of September 11, 2001, Tenet was in Washington, D.C., having breakfast at the St. Regis Hotel with his friend and mentor, former senator David Boren, when he first learned of the events at the World Trade Center complex. His first comment to Boren was that this was probably a bin Laden–Al Qaeda operation. He immediately launched an investigation into the hijackers. When the CIA began its investigation, there were some objections from the bureaucracy over privacy issues, but with some pressure the CIA was able to find out the names of the hijackers in short order.

After September 11, Tenet revamped the CIA's counterterrorism efforts. The

Counterterrorism Center's staff increased from 340 to 1,500. Every lead about an Al-Qaeda terrorist threat was followed up, and around 1,500 suspected Al-Qaeda operatives were rounded up around the world in the next two years. President Bush gave Tenet a blank check in the pursuit of terrorists. They became even closer as Bush realized that Tenet's CIA was the only government agency that had any intelligence on bin Laden and Al-Qaeda. This information was especially useful because Bush wanted to end bin Laden's sanctuary in Afghanistan even if this meant the overthrow of the Taliban regime. To this end, Bush defended the CIA from critics attacking it for its intelligence failures.

Tenet continued to be in President Bush's favor until the debacle over Iraq's alleged possession of weapons of mass destruction (WMDs). Although Tenet believed the March 2003 invasion of Iraq was a mistaken policy, he went along after President Bush informed him in the fall of 2002 that war was inevitable. Despite his misgivings, prior to the invasion of Iraq by American and its allies, the CIA presented to President Bush evidence that Iraq had weapons of mass destruction—biological agents such as mustard gas and sarin. Tenet briefed Colin Powell, then secretary of state, on these weapons before Powell's speech before the United Nations (UN) on February 5, 2002. The failure to find weapons of mass destruction in Iraq was considered another intelligence blunder by the CIA. This time Tenet was seriously weakened because of the intelligence failure. Tenet remained head of the CIA until June 2, 2004, when President Bush accepted his resignation. The official reason for his resignation was a heart condition. His replacement was Porter Goss, former Republican congressman from Florida.

Both statements made by Goss and his initial appointments made it clear that Goss came to the CIA determined to make it loyal to the Bush administration.

Tenet's seven-year term as CIA director was the second longest in American history. President Bush awarded Tenet the Presidential Medal of Freedom on December 14, 2004. His 2007 book, *At the Center of the Storm*, gives his defense of his tenure at the CIA. Tenet has also attacked the 2005 CIA inspector general's report on his responsibilities for the CIA's deficiencies before September 11. Tenet sits on a number of corporate and organization boards, including the investment bank Allen & Company; a biometric identity software provider L-1 Identity Solutions; and a leadership program working to involve students in public affairs, the Next Generation Initiative.

Stephen E. Atkins

See also: Bush Administration; Clinton Administration; Central Intelligence Agency

Further Reading

Coll, Steve. *Ghost Wars: The Secret History of the CIA, Afghanistan, and Bin Laden, from the Soviet Invasion to September 10, 2001.* New York: Penguin, 2004.

Drumheller, Tyler, and Elaine Monaghan. *On the Brink: An Insider's Account of How the White House Compromised American Intelligence.* New York: Carroll and Graf, 2006.

Kessler, Ronald. *The CIA at War: Inside the Secret Campaign against Terror.* New York: St. Martin's Griffin, 2003.

Risen, James. *State of War: The Secret History of the CIA and the Bush Administration.* New York: Free Press, 2006.

Tenet, George, and Bill Harlow. *At the Center of the Storm: My Years at the CIA.* New York: HarperCollins, 2007.

Woodward, Bob. *State of Denial.* New York: Simon and Schuster, 2006.

Terrorism

There is no settled definition of the word "terrorism." Most scholars and defense analysts believe that terrorism is a tactic rather than a philosophy or set ideology. History has shown that groups may employ terrorism at some times and not at others. There is an active debate about whether terrorism is the appropriate term solely for violence by nonstate entities, or whether state terrorism must also be included.

Some consider terrorism to be acts or threats of violence, directed against noncombatants, to shock or achieve a change in a political status quo by indirect means. However, others label some actions against military or governmental personnel to be terrorist in nature when they do not comply with international law. Still others write about terrorism as a pathology wherein violence is the motivating force and not merely a means to an end. This approach is problematic as it could apply to individual pathological acts of violence as in recent cases of school shootings in Western countries. Terrorism may be employed for a wide variety of ideological, religious, or economic reasons.

Terrorism is also a tool in asymmetric conflict and a force magnifier. The impact of a small number of individuals committing terrorist actions can be huge, and even a large paramilitary or military force may seem ineffective in combating it, particularly if success is measured by the complete eradication of such incidents.

Numerous academic and governmental experts recognize the arguments over what constitutes terrorism and thus do not employ the term. Certainly there has been reaction to the U.S. government's application of the term in the global war on terror. "Violent extremism" has been used for many years in place of "Islamic terrorism" in the Muslim world and has begun to be used in the West in the last few years. Here, the focus is on the use, or relinquishment, of violence, rather than the movement employing it.

Some analysts date modern terrorism to the Russian anarchist organization Narodnaya Volya (People's Will) of the 19th century, which attempted, through assassinations, to overthrow the czarist regime. Their methods were adopted by anarchists throughout the world, and the decades leading up to World War I were marked by frequent assassinations, including that of U.S. President William McKinley in 1901. The assassinations of Austrian archduke Franz Ferdinand and his wife, Sophie, in Sarajevo in June 1914 were the result of a terrorist attack, and precipitated the outbreak of World War I.

Terrorist activities occurred in the Middle East prior to World War I, but in most cases the group responsible for terrorist activities was either a state-controlled force that claimed to be acting in the interests of

Prominent Terrorist Organizations in the Middle East

Name	Date Founded
al-Aqsa Martyrs Brigade	2000
Al-Qaeda	1988
al-Zarqawi Network	2003
Fatah	1974
Hamas	1987
Hezbollah	1982
Kahane Chai	1994
Mahdi Army	2003
Palestine Liberation Front (PLF)	1959
Popular Front for the Liberation of Palestine	1967

state security or engaged in war, or a militia or force fighting against the state or another organization. Examples include the genocide perpetrated by Turkish authorities against the Armenians and subsequent actions in recent years by Kurds against Turks in Turkey. Yet atrocities committed by Israeli forces in 1948 against Palestinians have often been excused as legitimate acts of war.

In numerous instances, colonial powers have been confronted by indigenous peoples employing asymmetric warfare tactics, and both have resorted to terrorism. For instance, in the conflict between Algerian nationalist groups and the French government and military, both sides engaged in acts of terrorism. The nationalist Front de Liberation Nationale (National Liberation Front, FLN) bombed crowded civilian locations frequented by Westerners as well as Algerians, and the French bombed residences in the Arab-inhabited *casbah* of Algiers and resorted to the torture of suspects in retaliation.

Terrorism by both Arabs and Jews against each other and by Jewish forces against the British mandate power occurred in Palestine in the 1930s. Following Israel's creation in 1948, Palestinian groups, some supported by neighboring Arab governments, began to launch military attacks against Israel. After Israel's victory in the 1967 Six-Day War and the rise of the Popular Movement in the refugee camps, Palestinian groups organized a wave of terrorist activities during 1969–1973. The political leadership of the movement then determined that these tactics brought too heavy an Israeli response and were detrimental to their cause, although they had served a purpose in focusing world attention on the plight of the Palestinians. In these same years, radi-

cal left-wing organizations in the United States such as the Weathermen and the Red Army in Europe and beyond (Japan) also engaged in acts of terrorism. Terrorism continued to be a major aspect of the Israeli-Palestinian confrontation and the inability to conclude an Arab-Israeli peace treaty but also as a response to Israeli military actions employing collective punishment against Palestinians or Palestinian communities.

Terrorist actions also appeared in Saudi Arabia. After the 1991 Persian Gulf War, extremists began preaching against U.S. military forces in Saudi Arabia, claiming that it was unconscionable for the Saudi government to allow Christian forces to determine the political responses of the Saudi government toward other Muslim governments and to operate from the peninsula where the holy cities of Mecca and Medina are located. Their objection was chiefly regarding the presence of Western military forces; however, Saudi Arabia has long been home to a large expatriate community in its oil industry, and some extremists objected to their presence on Saudi soil as well.

On November 13, 1993, the Office of the Program Manager/Saudi Arabian National Guard (OPM/SANG) was badly damaged by a car bomb. Four Saudi nationals confessed and were executed on May 31, 1996. According to their confessions, they were veterans of jihads in Afghanistan, Bosnia, and Chechnya; they claimed that the Saudi rulers were apostates; and they were inspired by Islamic law to commit the attacks.

One month later, the Khobar Towers in Dhahran, Saudi Arabia, were destroyed by a truck bomb, killing 19 U.S. servicemen in a plot carried out by Saudi Hezbollah. In 1996 and again in 1998, Al-Qaeda leader

Osama bin Laden announced a fatwa declaring that Muslims should attack U.S. personnel and interests around the world, drive U.S. forces from Saudi Arabia, remove the Saudi royal family and other apostate Arab regimes from power, and liberate Palestine. Of these goals, the most vital, and yet most unattainable, for bin Laden was the removal of the Saudi royal family, and in fact his campaign against the United States was based on his analysis of U.S. government support for the Saudi royal family's hold on power. Bin Laden moved to various locations—Pakistan, Afghanistan, the Sudan, and then back again to Afghanistan—to plan his campaign.

The current war on terror began with Operation Enduring Freedom in Afghanistan, a month after the devastating September 11 attacks on the United States carried out by Al-Qaeda. Objectives of the operation included removing the Taliban from power, destroying Al-Qaeda's training camps, and killing or capturing its operatives. In 2002, the Taliban was partially defeated, but many Al-Qaeda and Taliban members escaped and new recruits soon appeared, drawn from Afghanistan and the religiously conservative northwest region of Pakistan. These groups continue to attack North Atlantic Treaty Organization (NATO) troops, Afghan government officials, and civilians. Suicide bombings, never before utilized in Afghanistan, became a regular occurrence. Taliban and Al-Qaeda operatives (including bin Laden) operated with relative freedom in the northwest reaches of Pakistan and could easily slip back across the border into Afghanistan.

In 2003, Operation Iraqi Freedom spearheaded by the United States removed Saddam Hussein and his regime from power and liberated Iraq. However, more than 40 different groups of Sunni Muslims as well as some Shiite militias opposed and began to fight the coalition forces. These included such groups as Al-Qaeda in Mesopotamia, Ansar al-Islam, and others. They engaged in regular fighting but also used terrorist attacks, mainly suicide bombings, against U.S., coalition, and Iraqi forces and civilians in attempts to destabilize the country so that they might drive the United States and its allies from Iraq and take power.

Between 2003 and 2005, more than 500 suicide car bombings and vest attacks occurred. Targets included refineries, electrical stations, police stations, open-air markets, and even mosques. The insurgents' intent was to undermine the public's confidence that the government would ever be able to provide essential services and security. However, in 2006, Sunni sheikhs, with strong financial incentives from both Saudi Arabia and the coalition, formed alliances to fight against Al-Qaeda in Mesopotamia and other violent Islamist groups. This strategy accompanied the Western insistence on a coalition troop surge that began in early 2007. Yet acts of terrorism increased in the spring of 2009 and targeted the sheikhs who had cooperated with the coalition forces. After coalition forces withdrew from Iraq in late 2011, sectarian violence and terrorism sponsored by Al-Qaeda as well as Shiite and Sunni militias spiked, and by early 2014 the country was perched on the edge of a civil war. Meanwhile, terror attacks against civilians had increased exponentially. Other acts of terrorism with suicide and truck bombings continue to plague Afghanistan and now, increasingly, Pakistan as well. In the summer of 2013, it was revealed that the United States Intelligence Community spent over $22 billion annually just to combat terrorism.

Donald R. Dunne and Elliot Paul Chodoff

See also: Al-Qaeda; Al-Qaeda in Iraq; Bin Laden, Osama; Counterterrorism Strategy; Democratization and the Global War on Terror; Global War on Terror; Hezbollah (Party of God); Taliban

Further Reading

Crenshaw, Martha, ed. *Terrorism in Context.* University Park: Pennsylvania State University Press, 1995.

Dershowitz, Alan. *The Case for Israel.* New York: Wiley, 2003.

Gettleman, Marvin, and Stuart Schaar, eds. *The Middle East and Islamic World Reader.* New York: Grove, 2003.

Gunaratna, Rohan. *Inside Al Qaeda: Global Network of Terror.* New York: Berkley Publishing Group, 2003.

Harel, Amos, and Avi Issacharoff. *34 Days: Israel, Hezbollah and the War in Lebanon.* New York: Palgrave Macmillan, 2008.

Times Square Bomb Plot

On May 1, 2010, a U.S. citizen of Pakistani descent attempted to carry out a car bombing in the center of Times Square, New York City. Although the device had been primed, it failed to detonate and was disabled after a policeman saw smoke being emitted from the vehicle. There were no casualties. Two days later authorities arrested Faisal Shahzad, a 30-year-old resident of Bridgeport, Connecticut, after he was identified on video surveillance footage from near the scene of the incident. He was charged with trying to use weapons of mass destruction and at his trial admitted to wanting to destroy buildings and kill and injure as many people as possible.

Shahzad became a U.S. citizen in April 2009. Soon thereafter, he left for Pakistan and spent six months with his family in Peshawar. In December, he and a friend traveled to Waziristan, where they joined up with the Tehrik-e-Taliban (TTP) and over a period of 40 days received bomb-making training. During this period, Shahzad apparently developed his plot to attack Times Square and allegedly received the endorsement of the TTP to proceed.

Shahzad returned to the United States in February 2010 with $8,000 in cash, half of which had come from the TTP. He used the money to acquire the various components required for the bomb and a 1993 blue Nissan Pathfinder sport-utility vehicle (SUV). The device was assembled at his house in Bridgeport and packed into the SUV. Authorities later determined that the bomb was made up of four parts, combining firecrackers, gasoline, propane, and fertilizer. It was to have been triggered using a cell phone and digital wristwatch.

At about 6:30 p.m. Shahzad drove the SUV to Times Square and parked it on a tourist-crowded block at the eastern corner of 1 Astor Plaza near the entrance of the Minskoff Theater. He exited the vehicle and later testified that he set the bomb to go off after a five-minute delay. The detonation system malfunctioned, however, and merely started a small fire that failed to ignite the firecrackers as intended. Two nearby street vendors noticed smoke coming from the vehicle's interior and notified the authorities. An ordnance-disposal team was quickly dispatched, which after using a remote-controlled robot to explore the SUV's interior rendered the bomb safe. According to New York Police Department Commissioner Raymond Kelly, had the explosion occurred, it would have caused a huge fireball and sent shrapnel that would likely have killed many people.

At his trial, Shahzad said he had been inspired by the teachings of Anwar al-

Awlaki, a radical Islamist based in Yemen and the main ideologue for Al-Qaeda in the Arabian Peninsula (AQAP). He pled guilty to all charges, justifying his actions as a legitimate response to the U.S. wars in Iraq and Afghanistan and the repeated use of drones to attack Muslims in Somalia and Yemen. He also claimed that had the attack been successful, he intended to target four other high-profile venues in the New York area, including the Rockefeller Center, the Grand Central Terminal, the World Financial Center, and the corporate headquarters of Sikorsky, a Connecticut-based company that manufactures helicopters for the U.S. military. Shahzad was sentenced to life imprisonment without the chance of parole on October 5, 2010.

Peter Chalk

See also: Abdel-Rahman, Omar (aka the Blind Sheikh); Al-Qaeda in the Arabian Peninsula; New York City Landmarks Bombing Conspiracy; New York Stock Exchange Bomb Plot; Reid, Richard; Terrorism

Further Reading

Berger, Joseph. "Pakistani Taliban behind Times Sq. Plot, Holder Says." *New York Times*, May 9, 2010.

"Faizal Shahzad Had Contact with Anwar Awalki, Taliban and Mumbai Massacre Mastermind—Officials Say." *ABC News*, May 6, 2010. http://abcnews.go.com/Blotter/faisal-shahzad-contact-awlaki-taliban-mumbai-massacre-mastermind/story?id=10575061&page=2.

Hennsessey, Kathleen. "N.Y. Bomber Has al-Qaeda Tie, White House Says." *Los Angeles Times*, May 10, 2010.

Hodge, Amanda. "From Harmless Tenant to Terror Plot Accused." *The Australian*, May 6, 2010.

Norington, Brad. "I Received Training in Pakistan, Admits Charged U.S. Bomb Suspect." *The Australian*, May 6, 2010.

Weiser, Benjamin. "A Guilty Plea in Plot to Bomb Times Square." *New York Times*, June 22, 2010.

TIPOFF

TIPOFF is a U.S. State Department watch list, already in existence prior to September 11, 2001, designed to keep terrorists from obtaining visas to enter the United States. It also provided a way to tip off intelligence and law enforcement agencies about potential terrorists already in the United States. This watch list was established in 1987 by John Arriza, a U.S. State Department civil servant. Any agent of an American agency could send a name or a group of names to the State Department's Bureau of Intelligence and Research for inclusion on this list.

Before September 11, the U.S. State Department was the most active in contributing names to this list. In 2001 it had contributed more than 2,000 names. The second most active in contributing names was the Central Intelligence Agency (CIA), with more than 1,500 names. Other agencies added to the list, but the least active was the Federal Bureau of Investigation (FBI). In 2001, the FBI added only 60 names to the list. By September 2001, there were approximately 60,000 names on the TIPOFF list.

The biggest weakness of TIPOFF was that the Federal Aviation Administration (FAA) did not participate because the airline industry opposed it. The FAA maintained a much smaller watch list: there were fewer than 20 names on it on September 11, 2001. The FAA's leadership maintained that it did not want to burden the commercial airline industry with having to deal with the huge TIPOFF watch list, which would cause delays, inconvenience travelers, and cost money.

Stephen E. Atkins

See also: Federal Emergency Management Agency (FEMA); U.S. Department of Homeland Security

Further Reading

Goldman, Jan. *Words of Intelligence: A Lexicon for Foreign and Domestic Intelligence Professionals.* Lanham, MD: Rowman and Littlefield, 2010.

Strasser, Steven, ed. *The 9/11 Investigations.* New York: Public Affairs, 2004.

Torture of Prisoners

Torture is generally defined as the deliberate infliction of pain, whether physical or psychological, on a victim or a prisoner for a variety of purposes. In wartime, torture has historically been most commonly used as an interrogation technique to extract intelligence information from prisoners of war (POWs) in a rapid fashion. Otherwise, it has been used as a punishment and method of dehumanization. This has been particularly true in the various recent Middle East wars. Torture has also been routinely employed to achieve propaganda advantage, as in securing confessions or testimonials denouncing the policies of their own government.

Torture is banned by international law as a fundamental violation of human rights, whether inflicted on enemies or one's own population. It is specifically banned by the Third and Fourth Geneva Conventions (1929 and 1949), as well as the United Nations Convention against Torture (1987). Torture nonetheless remains a disturbingly common aspect of contemporary conflicts, and not only in the Middle East. Beyond

wartime, the United Nations Convention against Torture regards capital punishment as well as many of the sanctioned legal punishments in Iran, Saudi Arabia, Libya, Pakistan, and under the Taliban to be torture.

Torture was long an established part of judicial procedure to extract confessions and was regularly employed, for example, during the Spanish Inquisition. Only in the past two centuries have there been concerted efforts to ban torture and establish penalties for its use.

There is an ongoing debate over what constitutes torture by nations that do not conform to international standards. Some nations have regularly employed drugs to extract information from prisoners and interrogators have routinely used sleep deprivation, enforced positions, light and sound bombardment, harassment, beatings, waterboarding, removal of teeth and fingernails, confinement in extremely small spaces, severe cold, and electric shocks to secure what they seek. In the United States, some police departments and law enforcement agencies had, even prior to September 11, 2001, assaulted detainees.

Amnesty International reported that more than 150 nations routinely employed torture in the period 1997 to 2000. Clearly, it remains a prominent human rights issue into the 21st century.

In the Middle East, a region that contains numerous totalitarian regimes as well as religious strife, torture has played a role in internal security, warfare, and in struggles between political movements. Israel has long used assault, sleep deprivation, enforced bodily positions, electric shock (more recently forbidden), and other "coercive interrogation" methods when questioning suspected Palestinian terrorists. Although the Israeli Supreme Court ruled that all torture was illegal, allegations of degrading and inhuman treatment of Palestinian detainees continue to be leveled against Israeli authorities. Likewise, the government of Saudi Arabia claims that torture is against Islamic law, but there is ample evidence that the Saudi regime continues to employ torture, particularly against domestic prisoners. In addition, the punishments of lashing, beheading, and amputation are considered torture by the United Nations (UN), but Saudi Arabia does not accept this position. Similar evidence of the routine use of torture in interrogations of suspects has been documented in Egypt, Iran, Iraq, Jordan, Lebanon, and Syria.

During the Israeli-Arab War of 1948–1949, the 1967 Six-Day War, and the 1973 Yom Kippur (Ramadan) War, each side accused the other of torturing POWs. There is strong evidence that prisoners were subjected to physical beatings and other forms of punishment to discover useful information and that many were killed. During the Iran-Iraq War (1980–1988), both belligerents were accused of torturing prisoners. Sometimes, the torture was designed to elicit information for tactical use on the battlefield; more often, however, the torture was for purely sadistic reasons, to punish an enemy.

In the 1991 Persian Gulf War (Operation Desert Storm), captured coalition pilots were paraded before international news cameras showing signs of physical injuries. Upon their release, American pilots reported that they had been beaten by their Iraqi captors, who demanded that they renounce their religious beliefs in favor of Islam and that they sign statements admitting to war crimes.

During the U.S.-led global war on terror (from 2001), American military forces have been repeatedly accused of torturing suspected terrorists to obtain information about planned attacks on U.S. targets. In particular, human rights advocates have accused U.S. authorities of employing inhumane and degrading treatment against detainees at the Guantánamo Bay Naval Base in Cuba. This included severe beatings, waterboarding, sleep deprivation, and sensory deprivation. The detainees also claimed that they received threats of bodily harm and were humiliated sexually and forced to remain in uncomfortable positions for prolonged periods. Despite international condemnation, the United States has refused to release the majority of the prisoners held at Guantánamo Bay, has yet to charge them with a particular crime, and has not opened the facility to international observers or the media. After his administration took office in January 2009, President Barack Obama directed that the Guantánamo Bay facility be closed within a year. However, as of January 2014 it remains open, and its closure does not seem imminent.

In 2003, after the U.S.-led Operation Iraqi Freedom began, allegations of torture perpetrated by U.S. military personnel began to surface. These first concerned the infamous Abu Ghraib prison in Baghdad. Abu Ghraib had served as a major detention facility under the dictatorship of Saddam Hussein, and unspeakable offenses had been committed there against opponents of the regime and other prisoners. After U.S. forces took Baghdad in April 2003, they began using the prison to hold suspected terrorists and members of the Iraqi military. In April 2004, the prison came to the public's attention when photographs of naked prisoners, some hooded and attached to electrical wires, were published in a variety of media sources. An internal U.S. Army investigation determined that some guard personnel, led by Army Specialist Charles Graner, had instigated the mistreatment of prisoners without official sanction. A number of the individuals were charged and brought to trial. Others, such as those in authority, saw their military careers ended because of the scandal.

By mid-2005, there was mounting evidence that the United States had indeed engaged in torture in Afghanistan, Iraq, and Guantánamo, and rumors circulated concerning torture at the secret detention facilities believed to be in Jordan, Morocco, Eastern Europe, and elsewhere. This prompted a public outcry as well as protests from Human Rights Watch, Amnesty International, and even the UN. On December 30, 2005, President George W. Bush signed legislation passed by Congress that banned the torture of detainees, although critics pointed out that the president can still approve such tactics by using the broad powers of commander in chief. The law was enacted after an acrimonious fight between the Bush administration and many members of Congress, at the time controlled by Bush's own Republican Party.

On June 12, 2008, the U.S. Supreme Court dealt the Bush administration a severe blow when it declared that suspected terrorist detainees at Guantánamo Bay may petition U.S. civilian courts to release them. The *Boumediene v. Bush* case essentially gave enemy combatants the right to file a writ of habeas corpus in a U.S. court. Just a few weeks later, on June 23, a federal appeals court struck down the Bush administration's classification of detainees

at Guantánamo as "enemy combatants." Many argued for the closing of the Guantánamo detention facility, including some within the Bush administration, and the decision to do this by the Obama administration received the endorsement of the commander of the U.S. Central Command (CENTCOM), General David Petraeus. The disposition of the prisoners at Guantánamo remains the principal stumbling block. Thus, some claim that the Yemeni prisoners, who constitute a large number of those held there, should not be returned to Yemen. The concern is that an indigenous movement linked to Al-Qaeda is known to be active there.

Paul Joseph Springer

See also: Abu Ghraib; Coercive Interrogation Techniques; Guantánamo Bay Detainment Camp; Iraqi Freedom, Operation

Further Reading

Danner, Mark. *Torture and Truth: America, Abu Ghraib, and the War on Terror*. New York: New York Review Books, 2004.

Friedman, Lori, ed. *How Should the United States Treat Prisoners in the War on Terror?* Farmington Hills, MI: Greenhaven, 2005.

Hersh, Seymour. *Chain of Command: The Road from 9/11 to Abu Ghraib*. New York: HarperCollins, 2004.

Meeropol, Rachel, and Reed Brody. *America's Disappeared: Secret Imprisonment, Detainees, and the "War on Terror."* New York: Seven Stories, 2005.

Sampson, William. *Confessions of an Innocent Man: Torture and Survival in a Saudi Prison*. Toronto: McClelland and Stewart, 2005.

U

United Airlines Flight 93

United Airlines Flight 93's Boeing 757-222 was the fourth aircraft hijacked by Al-Qaeda hijackers on September 11, 2001. It took off from Newark International Airport at 8:43 a.m. bound for San Francisco International Airport. Normal flight time was six hours. The flight was nearly 45 minutes late for its scheduled takeoff time of 8:01 a.m. On board were two pilots, Captain Jason M. Dahl and First Officer LeRoy Homer; a crew of five flight attendants; and 37 passengers (including the four hijackers). The plane held 11,489 gallons of aviation fuel.

The hijack team had little difficulty passing security. Security checkpoints at Newark International Airport were operated by Argenbright Security under contract to United Airlines. Only two of the four hijackers had luggage and only one of them triggered the CAPPS (Computer-Assisted Passenger Prescreening System) process—Ahmed al-Haznawi's luggage was checked for explosives.

This hijack team was the smallest of the four. Ziyad al-Jarrah was the team leader and designated pilot. He sat in first-class seat 1B, nearest the cockpit door. Other members of the team, Saeed al-Ghamdi, Ahmed al-Haznawi, and Ahmed al-Na'ami, were in seats 3C, 3D, and 6B, respectively. The hijackers seized control of the aircraft at 9:28 a.m., just minutes after the pilot received a warning about possible cockpit invasions on the cockpit computer device ACARS (Aircraft Communications and Reporting System). The cockpit door was no obstacle, taking only about 150 pounds of pressure to knock down. In addition, the flight attendants had keys to the cockpit door—another means of access to the cockpit.

Exactly how the hijackers gained access to the cockpit will never be known, but they took control relatively easily. They probably took a key to the cockpit from the flight attendant in first class. Within minutes of the assault, the hijackers had complete control of the aircraft. Both pilots were down—either killed or seriously incapacitated. Ahmed al-Haznawi, Saeed al-Ghamdi, and Ahmed al-Na'ami took turns controlling the 33 passengers and five flight attendants. Matters were complicated by having about a dozen passengers in the first-class section, with the rest seated in the back of the plane. Unlike the other teams, these hijackers were lenient on passenger discipline. After injuring one of the passengers, the hijackers controlled the others and the crew by threatening them with a bomb. To keep discontent down, they encouraged passengers and crew to contact their families by cell phone. Passengers made more than two dozen phone calls. This relaxed style came back to haunt the hijackers, for passengers who contacted family members learned that three other aircraft had been

FBI investigators comb the crater left by United Airlines Flight 93, a Boeing 757, near Shanksville, Pennsylvania, about 80 miles southeast of Pittsburgh; more than 200 federal investigators were on the scene. (AP Photo/Gene J. Puskar)

hijacked and had been turned into flying bombs.

As passengers began to realize there was no possibility of survival, plans circulated among some of the more aggressive men on board to attack the hijackers and regain control of the aircraft. By this time, the passengers suspected that the hijackers had no bomb. About a dozen of them had experience in action sports, including football, rugby, and judo. Todd Beamer, Mark Bingham, Tom Burnett, Jeremy Glick, and several others decided to wait until the aircraft cleared populated areas to begin their attack. They were under no illusion about their probable fate, and showed extraordinary courage and compassion for others by waiting for the aircraft to fly over a rural area. They had other allies in CeeCee Ross-Lyles, one of the flight attendants, who was a former police officer; Rich Guadago, an enforcement officer with the California

Fish and Wildlife Service; Linda Gronlund, a lawyer who had a brown belt in karate; and William Cashman, a former paratrooper with the 101st Airborne. Finally, Don Greene, vice president of Safe Flight Instrument Group, was a pilot with experience in single-engine aircraft, who could follow instructions to land the aircraft.

The passengers waited for their opportunity. In the meantime, flight attendant Sandy Bradshaw started boiling water to be used against the hijackers. Sometime around 10:00 a.m., the passengers attacked the hijackers using a food tray container to smash into the cockpit area. Earlier, the hijackers had all retreated into the cockpit area. A voice recording from the black box (cockpit data recorder) indicated the fierce nature of the struggle. For the next seven minutes the outcome was in doubt.

Jarrah was the pilot, and his contingency plan was to crash the aircraft if it seemed as though the hijackers would lose control of the plane. Evidently this is what happened, for the aircraft crashed upside down at a 45-degree angle, creating a crater 30 feet or more in diameter. The plane crashed in a reclaimed mining area, where the ground was relatively soft, and plunged deep into the ground.

The fuel tanks exploded, leaving a blackened crater. Smoke from the explosion allowed local volunteer authorities to find the site soon after the crash. The crash was reported by numerous witnesses, and a visual inspection from a passing unarmed Air National Guard C-130H cargo jet on a mission from Washington, D.C., to Minnesota confirmed the crash site.

The violence of the crash left no survivors. The black box was excavated 15 feet into the crater, and the cockpit voice recorder was found 25 feet down. Only body parts were recovered. Sixty percent of the recovered remains were identified by a combination of fingerprint verification, dental records, and DNA analysis.

In commercial air disasters, the National Transportation Safety Board (NTSB) handles investigations, but because this was a case of air piracy, the Federal Bureau of Investigation (FBI) assumed control, although the Bureau of Alcohol, Tobacco, Firearms and Explosives (ATF); the NTSB; and the Pennsylvania State Police also assisted. Nothing could be done at the site, however, without the permission of the FBI. Early in the investigation, 2,000 people worked at the site daily.

The probable target of Flight 93 was the U.S. Capitol. Earlier meetings by Al-Qaeda leaders had determined that the White House would present navigational problems. They had preferred that the White House be the target, but the Capitol was a target more easily recognized by inexperienced navigators.

Stephen E. Atkins

See also: American Airlines Flight 11; American Airlines Flight 77; Pentagon Attack; United Airlines Flight 175; World Trade Center, September 11, 2001

Further Reading

Aust, Stefan, et al. *Inside 9/11: What Really Happened.* New York: St. Martin's, 2001.

Beamer, Lisa, and Ken Abraham. *Let's Roll! Ordinary People, Extraordinary Courage.* Wheaton, IL: Tyndale House, 2002.

Kashuba, Glenn J. *Quiet Courage: The Definitive Account of Flight 93 and Its Aftermath.* Somerset, PA: SAJ, 2006.

Longman, Jere. *Among the Heroes: United Flight 93 and the Passengers and Crew Who Fought Back.* New York: Perennial, 2003.

9/11 Commission. *The 9/11 Commission Report: Final Report of the National Commission on Terrorist Attacks upon the United States.* New York: Norton, 2004.

Trento, Susan B., and Joseph J. Trento. *Unsafe at Any Altitude: Failed Terrorism Investigations, Scapegoating 9/11, and the Shocking Truth about Aviation Security Today.* Hanover, NH: Steerforth, 2006.

United Airlines Flight 175

Terrorists gained control of the Boeing 767-222 of United Airlines Fight 175 on September 11, 2001, and crashed it into the South Tower of the World Trade Center in New York City. Although this flight was scheduled to leave at 7:59 a.m., it left Logan International Airport at 8:15 a.m., with Los Angeles International Airport its destination. The pilot was Captain Victor Saracini, a 51-year-old U.S. Navy veteran pilot, and the first officer was Michael Horrocks. On board with the two pilots were seven flight attendants and 56 passengers. The plane held 23,980 gallons of aviation fuel. Shortly after takeoff, traffic controllers asked Saracini whether he could see American Airlines Flight 11. After he replied affirmatively, the pilots were ordered to maintain distance from the hijacked aircraft.

Among the 56 passengers on board were five members of an Al-Qaeda terrorist team. The leader of this hijack team and its pilot was Marwan al-Shehhi. Other members of the team were Fayez Rashid Ahmed Hassan al-Qadi Banihammad, Ahmed al-Ghamdi, Hamza al-Ghamdi, and Mohand al-Shehri. The hijackers had little difficulty passing through security. The security checkpoint at Logan International Airport for United Airlines was staffed by personnel from Huntleigh USA. The hijackers had purchased tickets in the first-class section to be close to the cockpit. Much as in the takeover of American Airlines Flight 11, the terrorists organized themselves into sections: two were near the cockpit (in seats 2A and 2B), pilot al-Shehhi was in seat 6C, and the other two sat near the passenger section (in seats 9C and 9D).

The hijackers seized control of the aircraft sometime around 8:47 a.m. They used knives and mace to subdue the pilots and crew, and then killed the pilots and at least one flight attendant. The hijackers then herded the crew and passengers toward the rear of the aircraft, assuring them everything would be okay. They lulled the passengers into thinking that the plane would land someplace safely and that the hijackers would use them as hostages in negotiations. Not all passengers believed this. One passenger, Peter Hanson, called his father in Easton, Connecticut, and reported the hijackers' takeover. One of the flight attendants also reported the hijack-

ing to the United Airlines office in San Francisco.

Al-Shehhi turned the aircraft around and headed it toward the New York City area; air traffic controllers lost contact with the plane. The passengers became concerned because of the aircraft's jerky movements. At this point some of the passengers considered storming the cockpit to regain control of the plane, but they did not have enough time. At 9:03 a.m. United Airlines Flight 175 slammed into the South Tower of the World Trade Center complex. The aircraft hit between floors 78 and 84. Because the aircraft hit at greater speed than American Airlines Flight 11 had hit the North Tower, the South Tower was more severely damaged than the North Tower had been. Consequently, the South Tower collapsed before the North Tower. There were no survivors on United Flight 175.

Stephen E. Atkins

See also: American Airlines Flight 11; American Airlines Flight 77; Pentagon Attack; United Airlines Flight 93; World Trade Center, September 11, 2001

Further Reading

Aust, Stefan, et al. *Inside 9/11: What Really Happened*. New York: St. Martin's, 2001.

9/11 Commission. *The 9/11 Commission Report: Final Report of the National Commission on Terrorist Attacks Upon the United States*. New York: Norton, 2004.

Unmanned Aerial Vehicles

Unmanned aircraft (drones) flown by remote control and formerly known as remotely piloted vehicles (RPVs), unmanned aerial vehicles (UAVs) have evolved into powerful aerial reconnaissance, surveil-

A U.S. Air Force RQ-1 Predator unmanned aerial vehicle takes off from the Rafael Hernandez Airport outside Aguadilla, Puerto Rico, for a mission in support of Operation Unified Response, on January 28, 2010. (U.S. Department of Defense)

lance, and strike platforms. Although the U.S. Air Force employed AQM-34 Drones for high-risk aerial reconnaissance missions during the Vietnam War, those units were quickly retired after the conflict, and postwar funding cuts prevented any new unmanned aerial reconnaissance systems entering service. Israel subsequently pioneered RPV development, and the U.S. government became interested in using RPVs by the late 1980s. Now RPVs are an integral part of the battlefield environment.

The success of Israeli UAV operations over Lebanon in the early 1980s convinced the U.S. Navy to examine unmanned aircraft for artillery spotting and to provide a UAV capability for the U.S. Marine Corps. Pioneer RPVs were then acquired and embarked first aboard the Iowa-class battleship *Iowa*. Pioneer short-range UAVs saw their first operational employment during Operations Desert Shield and Desert Storm from the Iowa-class battleships and

amphibious warfare ships when they flew more than 300 combat reconnaissance missions. The best-known instance of their use came when the battleship *Missouri* used its Pioneer to direct devastatingly accurate fire from its 16-inch guns against the Iraqi defenses of Faylaka Island near Kuwait City. When the battleship *Wisconsin* sent its Pioneer over the island shortly thereafter, the defenders used handkerchiefs, undershirts, and other objects to signal their surrender. Desert Storm demonstrated the advantages of an RPV over aircraft and space-based reconnaissance systems. The foremost of these was their ability to linger over a target, providing comparatively long-term surveillance of the area. They were also cheaper than aircraft, and their loss to accident or enemy fire did not imperil a pilot and aircrew. Over the next decade, Pioneers flew some 14,000 flights and supported every major U.S. military operation.

Buoyed by the success of RPVs in Operation Desert Storm, America's intelligence agencies and military services accelerated the development of far more capable unmanned aerial platforms. As these entered operational testing, their greater capabilities and expense drove their sponsors to introduce the designation UAV to distinguish them from their earlier, more primitive counterparts. The primary difference was in the control system. RPVs are radio-controlled from within line of sight of the vehicle, while UAVs can be programmed to fly autonomously along a planned route, utilize satellite links that enable their operators to control them from thousands of miles away, or perform a mix of manual and autonomous operations. Stealthy and equipped to provide instantaneous and nearly continuous transmission of their collected information, UAVs have been a critical component of all major U.S. military operations since 1994 but most especially during the global war on terror.

All U.S. military services now operate UAVs, and their missions have expanded from reconnaissance and strike to communications relay and even tactical logistics support to units in the field. The Pioneer RPV, which entered service in 1985, has now been supplanted by a vast array of UAVs ranging from the long-range Global Hawk to the hand-launched RQ-11 Raven. The RQ-1 Predator is the best known of the UAVs in service during America's later Middle Eastern conflicts. First entering service in 1995, the Predator has a 40-hour endurance and is equipped to provide near-real reporting from a wide variety of sensor packages, including electro-optical, infrared, and radar imaging and electronic signals (ELINT) monitoring. Flying at an operational altitude above 26,000 feet, its

sensors can monitor an area the size of New York City.

The Predator is most famous for its use in Hellfire missile strikes on terrorist leaders, their compounds, and entourages as part of the global war on terror. Developed in 2002 to ensure the rapid engagement of terrorists as opportunities arise, each strike-configured Predator carries two Hellfire air-to-surface missiles. The Predator can maintain station for 24 hours over an area 500 nautical miles from its launch point. The latest version of the Predator, the MQ-1, has a more extensive sensor suite, greater range and endurance, and higher operating ceiling. Media claims suggest that Predator strikes have killed hundreds of Taliban and Al-Qaeda operatives from November 2001 into 2010 and that the number of these strikes is increasing.

Less well known but more extensively employed are the U.S. Army's FQM-151 Pointer and RQ-1 Raven short-range tactical UAVs. Weighing in at nine and four and a half pounds, respectively, the Pointer and RQ-1 enable special operations units and tactical ground commanders to scout the route ahead for enemy forces and improvised explosive devices (IEDs) and look behind or over buildings and blocking terrain features. The Pointer entered service with Special Forces Command in 1989 and first saw action in Desert Storm. It has a 90-minute endurance, is hand launched, and can be controlled by an operator using a laptop. Essentially a scaled-down Pointer, the Raven has an 80-minute endurance, but microminiaturization enables it to have similar sensor capabilities. More importantly, it can be carried in a standard army backpack. Employed extensively in Iraq and Afghanistan, it is credited with saving hundreds of soldiers' lives by exposing insurgent ambushes, IEDs, and other dangers. Both UAVs cruise at 40–50 miles per hour (mph), employ autonomous and manual flight control, and link infrared or electro-optical imagery back to the operator. The Pointer's better high-altitude performance has led to its extensive use in Afghanistan.

The RQ-5 Hunter Joint Tactical UAV entered service in 1993 and conducts reconnaissance for army divisions and corps. Employed alone, it can conduct surveillance up to 120 miles (200 kilometers) from its ground-control station. That can be extended to 165 miles (300 kilometers) if a second Hunter is used to relay the link signals. It cruises at 118 mph and has a two-hour endurance at 75 miles (125 kilometers) from its launch point. The BQM-147A Dragon drone fulfills a similar function for expeditionary warfare units such as the U.S. Marine Corps Expeditionary Forces and the U.S. Army's 82nd Airborne and 101st Air Assault divisions. The 89-pound Dragon entered service in 1993 and has a two-and-a-half-hour endurance. As with the RQ-5, it operates at an altitude of 3,000–5,000 feet and can be controlled manually, can operate autonomously, or can use autopilot with manual override.

America's longest-ranged UAV is the RQ-4 Global Hawk, which has intercontinental range, operates at altitudes above 50,000 feet, and can remain in the air for more than 42 hours. It carries electronic signal monitoring and infrared, electro-optical, and radar-imaging sensors. The Global Hawk entered service in 2002 and is operated by the U.S. Air Force's 11th and 15th Strategic Reconnaissance wings. All of its collected information can be disseminated in real time via satellite links. It can be flown manually or autonomously or via autopilot with manual override. Its operators use satellite links to maintain contact with the UAV, but it can be programmed to return to base or divert fields if it loses contact.

UAVs now constitute an integral component of all U.S. security operations from the military through to the Coast Guard and Border Patrol. The U.S. Navy is testing the use of UAVs from submarines, including those that are submerged, and aircraft carriers down to patrol craft. Microminiaturization and high-tech data links and computer systems promise to give the smallest tactical units reconnaissance capabilities beyond that imagined for major field forces 100 years ago. Newer systems coming online include the MQ-8B Fire Scout, which entered service in 2010, and UAVs even smaller than the Raven were in service by 2010. The use of drones, particularly in Afghanistan, the border regions of Pakistan, and in African locales (notably Yemen and Somalia) has increased significantly under the Barack Obama administration, which took office in 2009. This policy has resulted in the killing of a number of high-level Al-Qaeda operatives and other terrorists, but it has also come under fire because a number of civilians have been inadvertently killed or wounded in drone attacks.

Carl Otis Schuster

See also: Al-Qaeda; Enduring Freedom, Operation; Global War on Terror; Iraqi Freedom, Operation; Persian Gulf War; Predator

Further Reading

Department of Defense, Office of the Under Secretary of Defense for Acquisition, Technology, and Logistics. *Unmanned Aerial Vehicles (UAVs): Roadmap, 2002–2027.*

Washington, DC: Progressive Management, 2008.

Munson, Kenneth. *Jane's Unmanned Aerial Vehicles and Targets, 1995–1996.* London: Jane's, 1996.

Munson, Kenneth. *World Unmanned Aircraft.* London: Jane's, 1988.

Taylor, John William Ransom. *Jane's Pocket Book of Remotely Piloted Vehicles.* New York: Collier, 1977.

USA PATRIOT Act

One of the first post–September 11 legislative outcomes was adoption of the USA PATRIOT (Uniting and Strengthening America by Providing Appropriate Tools Required to Intercept and Obstruct Terrorism) Act. The intent of this legislation was to plug holes in domestic intelligence gathering that were considered to have developed over the previous decades. The legislation was controversial because it dropped many of the safeguards that Americans had come to rely on for protection against government interference in their private affairs.

The USA PATRIOT Act moved through Congress to the White House in a hurry. In an immediate reaction to the events of September 11, the USA PATRIOT Act was approved in the Senate on October 11, 2001, by a vote of 96 to 1. On October 12, 2001, the House of Representatives approved it with a vote of 337 to 79. The act became law when President George W. Bush signed it on October 26, 2001. Rarely has legislation moved through Congress and been signed into law with such speed. Critics have charged that the adoption was too hasty, allowing the Department of Justice, under Attorney General John Ashcroft, to throw provisions defeated during the Clinton administration into a package that was passed with few members of Congress understanding it thoroughly.

Provisions of the original act were controversial for having greatly expanded the power of government, with few checks and balances. The act expanded the range of crimes that could be tracked by government agencies using electronic surveillance. Federal authorities were granted authority to use "roving wiretaps" on any phone that a suspected terrorist might be expected to use. Law enforcement officers could now conduct searches of suspects without notifying them until later, a tactic that became known as a "sneak-and-peek" operation. This particular type of search had previously been used against organized crime figures and major drug dealers. Now Federal Bureau of Investigation (FBI) agents could obtain secret court orders to search such personal records as business, medical, library, and other files without probable cause in potential terrorism cases. The act made it a federal crime to harbor a terrorist. It also increased criminal penalties for a laundry list of offenses, ranging from conspiracy to commit terrorism to interference with a flight crew. Search warrants became easy to obtain in terrorist-related investigations. The attorney general was authorized to detain foreign terrorism suspects for a full week without initiating any type of legal proceeding or having to show cause. Finally, the law provided for new financial and legal tools to end international money laundering. The only restriction on this law was that its surveillance and wiretap provisions were required to be renewed in 2005.

Critics of the USA PATRIOT Act have come from two ends of the political spectrum. Among the leading critics has been the American Civil Liberties Union (ACLU). From the other end of the spectrum, a second leading critic has been the oldest conservative grassroots lobbying organization in the country, the American Conservative Union (ACU). The ACLU's opposition is based on the argument that the law violates rights to privacy. In contrast, the ACU's opposition stems from its belief in the need to limit federal authority. Both organizations are hesitant about the use of antiterrorism investigations to charge American citizens with crimes unrelated to terrorism. The PATRIOT Act has been used to investigate everything from murder to child pornography. Together, the ACLU and ACU have lobbied to amend the USA PATRIOT Act to ensure protection for civil liberties.

Two other critics of the USA PATRIOT Act have been business interests and librarians. Business interests object to the act's anti–money-laundering provisions. These provisions were intended to prevent, detect, and prosecute money laundering and the financing of terrorism, and they required banks and other financial institutions to establish programs to monitor financial activities. Fines and prison sentences are the penalties for noncompliance with money-laundering restrictions, and representatives of financial institutions have complained about the cost of compliance.

Librarians have challenged the right of FBI investigators to inspect library records, with the American Library Association having initiated several lawsuits against this provision. Besides objecting to the access given the FBI to inspect individuals' library records, librarians also oppose the act's prohibition on informing patrons that their records are the subject of a search. Most court fights to defeat the issuance of National Security Letters (the subpoenas for records, which do not require a judge's

approval) have been unsuccessful, but the public's negative opinion of the practice has deterred the FBI from using it, except in rare cases.

Supporters of the USA PATRIOT Act have maintained that its restrictions are necessary to fight the war against terrorism, and they favor even greater restrictions if they prevent terror operations on American soil. The act is required to be periodically renewed, and supporters consider it a necessity as long as terrorist threats continue.

Despite opposition to several of its provisions, the USA PATRIOT Act was renewed on March 7, 2006. With amendments to address a few objections to it, the act was approved in the Senate by a vote of 95 to 4, and in the House by 280 to 138. One amendment excluded libraries that function in a "traditional capacity" from having to furnish the records sought in a National Security Letter. Another amendment gave persons subpoenaed by the Foreign Intelligence Surveillance Act (FISA) Court the right to challenge the nondisclosure, or gag order, requirement of the subpoena. Finally, two of the act's provisions—the FBI's authority to conduct roving wiretaps and the government's power to seize business records with the FISA Court's approval—were constrained by a sunset requirement and were set to expire on December 31, 2009. In February 2010, however, the House of Representatives and Senate approved a one-year extension of these provisions, as well as a third that allowed for surveillance of non-U.S. citizens engaged in terrorism but not part of a recognized terrorist organization. On February 27, President Barack Obama signed the extensions into law. On May 26, 2011, Obama signed the Sunsets Extension Act of 2011, which provided for another four-year extension of the legislation.

The PATRIOT Act still remains highly controversial, particularly among civil liberty advocates. In 2013, press reports, some of which covering the leaks from the Edward Snowden affair, raised new concerns about the scope and purview of the PATRIOT Act. Those reports revealed that the National Security Agency (NSA) had been snooping on American citizens at home and abroad by monitoring Internet activity and collecting data of telephone calls made and received by American citizens. Many Americans, including those in Congress who had supported the PATRIOT Act and its amendments and extensions, now believed that the government was going too far in the name of national security.

In January 2014, President Obama announced a series of changes that would be made to mitigate snooping on innocent American citizens, but it remains to be seen how these changes would be implemented and how far they would go to protect civil liberties. Many critics of the NSA claimed that the announced changes did not go far enough.

Stephen E. Atkins

See also: Al-Qaeda; Bush Administration; Global War on Terror; National Security Agency; Obama Administration; Pentagon Attacks; Taliban; World Trade Center, September 11, 2001

Further Reading

Babington, Charles. "Congress Votes to Renew PATRIOT Act, with Changes." *Washington Post*, March 8, 2006.

Baker, Stewart. *Patriot Debates: Experts Debate the USA PATRIOT Act.* New York: American Bar Association, 2005.

Ball, Howard, and Mildred Vasan, eds. *The USA PATRIOT Act: A Future Reading Handbook.* Santa Barbara, CA: ABC-CLIO, 2004.

Etzioni, Amitai. *How Patriotic Is the PATRIOT Act?* New York: Routledge, 2004.

Leone, Richard, and Greg Anriq, eds. *The War on Our Freedoms: Civil Liberties in the Age of Terrorism.* New York: PublicAffairs, 2003.

Yoo, John. *War by Other Means: An Insider's Account of the War on Terror.* New York: Atlantic Monthly Press, 2006.

U.S. Central Command

One of 10 unified U.S. combatant commands responsible for U.S. military planning regarding 27 nations, stretching from the Horn of Africa through the Persian Gulf states to Central Asia. The U.S. Central Command (CENTCOM) has its primary headquarters at MacDill Air Force Base in Tampa, Florida, and a forward headquarters at Camp al Sayliyah, Qatar, to handle the demands of operations in Iraq and the Middle East.

The Ronald Reagan administration established CENTCOM on January 1, 1983, to deal with growing instability in the Middle East following the Islamic Revolution in Iran and the Soviet invasion of Afghanistan, both in 1979. Policy makers were worried that the Soviet Union or one of its client states would invade oil-producing nations and deprive the Western powers of access to this vital resource. CENTCOM was built from the assets of the Rapid Deployment Joint Task Force (RDJTF). Its first commander was General Robert C. Kingston. The original intent was that CENTCOM would not be based in the region, but instead rely on political allies to provide facilities on an as-needed basis. As such, CENTCOM to this day is not assigned combat units but instead consists of five component commands that are assigned forces from their parent service as the mission requires. These include the U.S. Army Forces Central Command (ARCENT), U.S. Central Command Air Forces (USCENTAF), U.S. Marine Forces Central Command (US-MARCENT), U.S. Naval Forces Central Command (USNAVCENT), and U.S. Special Operations Command Central (SOCCENT).

CENTCOM engaged in its first combat mission in August 1990, when Iraqi president Saddam Hussein ordered his armed forces to invade Kuwait. In Operation, CENTCOM commander General H. Norman Schwarzkopf supervised the deployment of forces to Saudi Arabia to deter Hussein from advancing into Saudi Arabia. With a broad international consensus and the assistance of Saudi Arabia's logistics facilities, in Operation Desert Storm, CENTCOM led the invasion of Kuwait and Iraq in February 1991 with a nine-division multinational force. The Iraqi Army was ejected from Kuwait in short order, but President George H. W. Bush decided to terminate the war without toppling the Hussein regime. For the next 12 years, CENTCOM contained Hussein's power by maintaining a permanent ground presence to the south of Iraq and enforcing no-fly zones in the north and south of the country.

Since the terror attacks of September 11, 2001, CENTCOM has become the central front in the Global War on Terror. In the late autumn of 2001, CENTCOM successfully toppled the Taliban government in Afghanistan as part of Operation Enduring Freedom to destroy the Al-Qaeda organization. Two years later, in March 2003, CENTCOM launched Operation Iraqi Freedom and ended the rule of Saddam Hussein. To support further stabilization and counterterrorism operations in these countries and the region as a whole, CENTCOM has operated several joint and multinational subordinate commands: Multi-National Force–Iraq (MNF-I), Multi-National Security Transition Command–Iraq (MNSTC-I), Combined Forces Command Afghanistan, Combined Joint Task Force–Horn of Africa, and Joint Task Force Lebanon. MNF-I and MNSTC-I both ended by late 2011, with the withdrawal of U.S. and coalition forces from Iraq.

On February 7, 2007, the U.S. Army announced that a U.S. Africa Command (US-AFRICOM) would be organized and take responsibility for CENTCOM's African portfolio, which had included Djibouti, except for Egypt. Almost all of Africa had been under European Command (EUCOM), however. EUCOM retained both Israel and Turkey.

Among CENTCOM's more notable commanders have been U.S. Army general Schwarzkopf (November 1988–August 1991), Marine Corps general Anthony Zinni (August 1997–July 2000), U.S. Army general Tommy R. Franks (July 2000–July 2003), and U.S. Army general John P. Abizaid (July 2003–March 2007). In March 2007, Admiral William Fallon assumed command, the first naval officer to hold that position. He resigned in March 2008, following public remarks that were seen as critical of the George W. Bush administration's position regarding possible hostilities with Iran. Fallon was replaced by acting commander army lieutenant general Martin Dempsey. In October 2008, General David Petraeus became permanent CENTCOM commander, a post he held until June 2010. Following Petraeus were Marine Corps lieutenant general John R. Allen (June 30–August 10, 2010); Army general James Mattis (August 11, 2010–March 22, 2013); and Army general Lloyd Austin (March 22, 2013–present).

James E. Shircliffe, Jr.

See also: Al-Qaeda; Enduring Freedom, Operation; Global War on Terror; Iraqi Freedom, Operation; Persian Gulf War; Petraeus, David Howell

Further Reading

DeLong, Michael, with Noah Lukeman. *Inside CENTCOM: The Unvarnished Truth about the Wars in Afghanistan and Iraq.* Washington, DC: Regnery, 2004.

Eshel, David. *The U.S. Rapid Deployment Forces.* New York: Arco, 1985.

U.S. Department of Homeland Security

The Department of Homeland Security (DHS) is a federal cabinet-level agency established on November 25, 2002, with the passage of the Homeland Security Act of 2002. Created in the aftermath of the September 11, 2001, terrorist attacks, it marked the largest restructuring of the federal government since the end of World War II. The DHS commenced operations on January 24, 2003, and brought together approximately 180,000 federal employees and 22 agencies into a cabinet-level department. The DHS was created to prevent terrorist attacks within the United States, reduce the vulnerability of the United States to terrorism, and minimize the damage from, and speed the recovery after, terrorist attacks.

Homeland security within the United States was traditionally viewed as a state concern, interpreted by the Constitution as related to public health and safety. The federal government historically focused on national security while leaving local and state governments responsible for these types of domestic concerns. However, as federal power has increased in relation to the states, so has the role of the federal government in homeland security matters.

Until the war years of the 20th century, the federal government largely took a secondary role to state governments in homeland security issues. One notable exception to this trend rests with the U.S. Army Corps of Engineers. This organization was tasked with providing flood protection for the nation through such legislation as the Flood Control Act of 1936, in addition to a range of other disaster-related roles. During the Cold War, homeland security took on a truly national role with the creation of the Office of Civil and Defense Mobilization in the early 1950s. Commonly referred to as the Civil Defense Agency, this body gave the federal government a major role in preparing the domestic population for nuclear attack. Other notable federal interventions into domestic homeland security include the Office of Emergency Preparedness, established in 1961, and the Federal Emergency Management Agency (FEMA), established in 1979.

With the end of the Cold War, the federal government increasingly focused on homeland security. The rising threat of weapons of mass destruction (WMDs) and terrorism prompted the national government to take on an even greater role in homeland security. Presidential Decision Directive/National Security Council (PDD/NSC) document 39 of June 21, 1995, and PDD/NSC 63 of May 22, 1998, both reflected the increased federal focus in protecting domestic populations and resources from terrorist attacks. The National Defense Panel of 1997 called for the federal government to reform homeland security. The panel's recommendations included the need to incorporate all levels of government into managing the consequences of a WMD attack or terrorist activities. Similar findings were made by the Hart-Rudman Commission (the U.S. Commission on National Security/ Twenty-First Century) in January 2001. The commission recommended a cabinet-level agency to combat terrorism.

After the September 11, 2001, terrorist attacks, the George W. Bush administration undertook significant reforms to promulgate the earlier recommendations. Bush established the Office of Homeland Security (OHS) under the direction of former Pennsylvania governor Tom Ridge on October 8, 2001, through Executive Order 13228. The goals of the OHS involved coordinating homeland security efforts among the various federal, state, and local government agencies, and the development of a comprehensive homeland security strategy. However, the new body had no real budgetary or oversight authority, and its ability to accomplish its goals was limited. The principal strategy for DHS was developed in the July 2002 National Strategy for Homeland Security White Paper and the earlier October 24, 2001, USA PATRIOT Act. Legislative authority was granted for the formation of DHS on November 25, 2002, through the Homeland Security Act.

Headquartered in Washington, D.C., DHS became the 15th cabinet department within the federal government. It was tasked to serve as the coordinating body for the 87,000 different jurisdictions within the United States. The DHS consists of four major directorates: Border and Transportation Security, Emergency Preparedness and Response, Science and Technology, and Information Analysis and Infrastructure Protection.

In the area of border and transportation security, the U.S. Customs and Border Protection agency and the U.S. Immigration and Customs Enforcement service were established. Other agencies transferred into this directorate include the Federal Protective Service, Animal and Plant Health Inspection Service, Transportation Security Administration, and the Federal Law Enforcement Training Center. The Emergency Preparedness and Response section was created when the Homeland Security Act transferred the following agencies into the DHS: FEMA; the Strategic National Stockpile, Office of Emergency Preparedness, Metropolitan Medical Response System, and the National Disaster Medical System, all transferred from the Department of Health and Human Services; Domestic Emergency Support Team, from the Department of Justice; National Domestic Preparedness Office, from the Federal Bureau of Investigation (FBI); and the Integrated Hazard Information System, from the National Oceanic and Atmospheric Administration (NOAA). In addition, the Department of Energy's Nuclear Incident Response Team can operate from DHS during emergencies. To facilitate Information Analysis and Infrastructure Protection, the act transferred to the DHS the Critical Infrastructure Assurance Office, from the Department of Commerce; the Federal Computer Incident Response Center; the National Communications System, from the Department of Defense; the National Infrastructure Protection Center, from the FBI; and the National Infrastructure Simulation and Analysis Center, including the energy security and assurance program, from the Department of Energy. To deal with science and technology issues, the Homeland Security Act transferred from the Department of Energy various programs relating to the nonproliferation of chemical, biological, and nuclear weapons and research; the Environmental Measurements Laboratory; and the Lawrence Livermore National Laboratory. All functions relating to the Department of Defense's National Bio-Weapons Defense Analysis Center and the Plum Island Animal Disease Center were also transferred to the DHS.

In addition, the U.S. Coast Guard and the U.S. Secret Service were transferred into DHS. The Coast Guard is the primary agency for maritime safety and security. In addition, the Coast Guard's long history of interdiction and antismuggling operations bolstered the ability of the DHS to protect the nation's maritime boundaries. The Secret Service is the lead agency in protecting senior executive personnel and the U.S. currency and financial infrastructure. Under the DHS, the U.S. Citizenship and Immigration Services was formed to replace the Immigration and Naturalization Service. A fifth directorate, Management, is responsible for budget, facilities, and human resource issues.

In addition to the key directorates and agencies, DHS operates a number of other offices. The Office of State and Local Government Coordination serves as the primary point of contact for programs and for exchanging information between DHS and local and state agencies. The Office for Domestic Preparedness assists state and local authorities to prevent, plan for, and respond to acts of terrorism. The Office of the Private Sector facilitates communication between DHS and the business community. The Privacy Office of the U.S. Department of Homeland Security minimizes the dangers to, and safeguards, the rights to privacy of U.S. citizens in the mission of homeland security. The Office for Civil Rights and Civil Liberties provides policy and legal guidance on civil rights and civil liberties issues. These agencies were created to allay the fears and concerns of civil libertarians and ensure that the DHS does not violate the nation's civil liberties. The National Infrastructure Advisory Council provides advice to security agencies on protecting critical information systems. The Interagency Coordinating Council on Emergency Preparedness and Individuals with Disabilities ensures the consideration of disabled citizens in disaster planning.

DHS relies on other branches of government to fulfill its mission of protecting the U.S. homeland. Tasked with a largely preventive role, investigative responsibility continues to primarily rest with local, state, and federal law enforcement agencies, including the FBI. While DHS employs many of its own analysts, the majority of its intelligence-collection efforts are conducted outside of the department by other members of the intelligence community. Some called for the DHS to incorporate the FBI and the Central Intelligence Agency (CIA) into a single intelligence clearinghouse within the department. However, the two were left as autonomous entities. In order to aid states, the DHS provides funding in the form of grants and targeted expenditures to states, localities, and private bodies, including research centers.

The military also maintains a role in homeland security, chiefly through its Northern Command. The Northern Command plays a role in homeland defense as well as domestic airway security. The military currently maintains the largest capability for chemical, biological, and nuclear incident response, as well as personnel augmentation during domestic emergencies, most notably through federalization of the National Guard. One example of this type of federalization occurred with the deployment of the National Guard to bolster airport security following the September 11, 2001, terrorist attacks.

Former governor of Pennsylvania Tom Ridge was appointed the first secretary of Homeland Security and oversaw the creation of the OHS and its conversion into a cabinet-level department. By 2004, the DHS had grown to 183,000 employees with an annual budget of $36.5 billion. Ridge resigned on November 30, 2004, to pursue a career in private industry. He was replaced by Michael Chertoff on February 15, 2005. Chertoff was succeeded by Janet Napolitano on January 21, 2009; she was succeeded by Jeh Johnson on December 23, 2013. By the end of 2013, DHS had more than 225,000 employees, and its yearly budget was approximately $100 billion. DHS has reportedly given over $40 billion in grants since 2003 to state and local governments for homeland security and to improve their ability to find and protect against terrorists.

Tom Lansford

See also: Bush Administration; Global War on Terror; Pentagon Attack; Terrorism; Weapons of Mass Destruction; World Trade Center, September 11, 2001

Further Reading

Daalder, Ivo H., I. M. Destler, James M. Lindsay, Paul C. Light, Robert E. Litan, Michael E. O'Hanlon, Peter R. Orszag, and James B. Steinberg. *Assessing the Department of Homeland Security.* Washington, DC: Brookings Institution Press, 2002.

Kettl, Donald F. *The Department of Homeland Security's First Year: A Report Card.* New York: Century Fund, 2004.

White, Jonathan. *Defending the Homeland: Domestic Intelligence, Law Enforcement and Security.* Belmont, CA: Wadsworth, 2003.

U.S. Embassy (Athens) Rocket Attack

On January 12, 2007, members of the Epanastatikos Agonas (EA, or Revolutionary Struggle) fired a small antitank rocket at the heavily fortified U.S. embassy in Athens. The attack, which occurred at 5:58 a.m., shattered windows but caused no injuries. Dozens of police cars immediately surrounded the building and cordoned off all roads in the area, including a major boulevard in front of the mission.

Greek officials doubted the attack was the work of foreign or Islamic terrorists and instead pinned the likely responsibility on extreme left-wing radicals seeking to hit a highly iconic target: the huge American seal on the front of the embassy. The round narrowly missed the symbol, punching through a window a few feet above and landing in a bathroom on the building's third story.

Shortly after the attack, a call was made to Greek authorities claiming credit for the strike in the name of EA. According to a subsequent statement sent to the weekly Pontiki, the group said the action had been carried out to protest U.S. policy in Iraq and the Middle East. In response, Panayiotis Stathis, a spokesman for the Greek Public Order Ministry, said the attack was a violent act aimed to provoke public opinion and disturb the government's relations with Washington.

Terrorism expert Maria Bossis went further, asserting that the attack was a deliberate attempt by EA to assert itself as the "boss" among the plethora of left-wing terrorist entities that had emerged following the demise of the Epanastatiki Organosi 17 Noemvri (EO17N, or Revolutionary Organization 17 November) in 2003.

EA first surfaced in 2003 with a minor bombing outside an Athens courthouse. The group made headlines again with a triple bombing on a police station, again in the capital, that took place just three months before the city hosted the 2004 Olympic Games. Subsequent actions included an attempted assassination of the minister of culture (and former minister of public order) Giorgos Voulgarakis on May 30, 2006 (he was not injured); the bombing of the U.S. embassy in 2007; and a shooting attack on police guarding the Ministry of Culture building in Athens on January 5, 2009 (critically wounding one). The weapon used in the second incident was linked to two previous acts of violence against law enforcement, one on April 30, 2007, that targeted another police station and one on December 23, 2008, on a bus transporting members of the riot squad. The European Union added EA to its list of designated terrorist organizations. Two years later, the United States formally designated the group as a foreign terrorist organization.

Donna Bassett

See also: Global War on Terror; Terrorism

Further Reading

"Explosion Reported at U.S. Embassy in Athens." *International Herald Tribune*, January 12, 2007. http://www.nytimes.com/2007/01/12/world/europe/12iht-web.0112athens.4180082.html.

"Rocket Fired at U.S. Embassy in Greece: Police." *CBC News*, January 12, 2007. http://www.cbc.ca/news/world/story/2007/01/12/blast-embassy.html.

U.S. Embassy (Beirut) Bombing

On April 18, 1983, Shia fundamentalists bombed the U.S. embassy in Beirut, killing 63 people and injuring more than 100. It was the deadliest strike on an American diplomatic mission up to that time and would be followed later that year with a devastating attack on the headquarters of the U.S. Marine Corps, which had been deployed as part of the Multi-National Force (MNF) in Lebanon. The two events are widely considered as the reason for President Ronald Reagan's decision to withdraw all U.S. forces from the country and are often portrayed as a clear-cut example of the coercive "success" of suicide terrorism.

The attack took place at around 1 p.m. A dark-colored delivery van packed with 2,000 pounds (916 kilograms) of explosives drove into the embassy car park and parked under the portico at the front of the mission. The driver then detonated his payload, collapsing virtually the entire seven-story building. Seventeen Americans died in the bombing, eight of whom were employees of the Central Intelligence Agency (CIA). Among the fatalities were Station Chief Kenneth Haas and the CIA's top Middle East analyst, Robert Ames.

A pro-Iranian group calling itself the Islamic Jihad Organization (IJO) telephoned a local news agency immediately after the blast and took responsibility. The anonymous caller justified the bombing as a legitimate response to the "imperialist presence in Lebanon" and warned that future attacks would be forthcoming, including strikes on the MNF. Just over six months later, on October 23, another group known as Islamic Jihad made good on the threat by carrying out simultaneous attacks on the American and French components of the MNF in Beirut, killing a total of 299 servicemen.

Subsequent investigations tied both the April and October bombings to Hezbollah, although there has not been consensus on the identity of the perpetrators since the group announced its existence only in 1985. The U.S. government believes that elements that would eventually coalesce into Hezbollah planned and carried out the bombings with the financial and logistic support of Iran and Syria. All three have consistently denied any involvement—although Hezbollah has acknowledged and defended the attacks as if they were its own.

One of the most enduring ramifications of the April and October 1983 bombings was that they precipitated the full-scale withdrawal of the MNF from Lebanon, a tacit admission that this style of attack not only had rendered all known counterterrorist measures essentially useless but in so doing had also acted as a highly effective force equalizer. As President Ronald Reagan later explained in his memoirs, "The price we had to pay in Beirut was so great, the tragedy at the barracks so enormous. . . . We had to pull out. . . . We couldn't stay there and run the risk of another suicide attack on the Marines."

Following the April attack, Washington moved its embassy to a supposedly more secure location in East Beirut. However, on September 20, 1984, Shia extremists managed to gain access to the annex of the new compound, where they detonated a Chevrolet van packed with 2,000 pounds of explosives. This bombing killed 22 people (20 of whom were Lebanese) and injured more than 30.

Paul Joseph Springer

See also: Hezbollah (Party of God); Marine Corps Barracks (Beirut) Bombing; Suicide Bombings; Terrorism

Further Reading

Blanford, Nicholas. "The Lasting Impact of the 1983 Beirut Attacks." *Christian Science Monitor*, October 24, 2008.

Chalk, Peter, and Bruce Hoffman. *The Dynamics of Suicide Terrorism: Four Case Studies of Terrorist Movements*. Santa Monica, CA: RAND, 2005.

"Iran Denies Any Involvement in Bombing of U.S. Embassy." *New York Times*, May 20, 1983.

"U.S. Embassy in Lebanon Devastated by Bomb Blast; Dozens Killed, Pro-Iranian Group Named." *Facts on File World News Digest*, April 22, 1983.

U.S. Embassy (Sana'a) Attack

At 9:15 a.m. on September 17, 2008, gunmen wearing military uniforms attacked the U.S. embassy in Sana'a, Yemen, with rocket-propelled grenades and automatic weapons after detonating two vehicle-borne improvised explosive devices (VBIEDs) at the main gate. The 20-minute incident left 19 people dead and 16 wounded, and was the most serious incident involving U.S. interests in Yemen since the suicide bombing of the USS *Cole* at the Port of Aden in 2000 (which killed 17 American sailors and wounded 32).

Among the casualties were six terrorists, six Yemeni policemen, and eight civilians. Among the toll was Susan Elbaneh, a Yemeni American from New York who had celebrated a traditional arranged marriage less than a month earlier. She was also a cousin of Jaber Elbaneh, then on the Federal Bureau of Investigation's (FBI) most wanted terrorist list.

The assault itself was well planned and coordinated, involving sniper fire, rocket-propelled grenades, and VBIEDs. It would have been even deadlier had a car bomb breached the second security ring of concrete blocks within the compound. Overall, up to five explosions may have occurred during the entire incident.

Yemeni authorities quickly tied affiliates of Osama bin Laden's global terrorist movement to the attack. On November 1, 2008, the government announced that the six dead had all trained in Al-Qaeda camps located in the provinces of Hadramaut and Marib and that three of them had also fought against coalition troops in Iraq.

This was the second attack against the U.S. embassy in six months. In the previous incident, on March 18, 2008, a mortar meant for the diplomatic mission missed and instead hit a nearby girls' school. Six children, as well as Yemeni workers protecting the embassy, were injured. Islamic Jihad of Yemen, an Al-Qaeda affiliate, claimed responsibility for both strikes.

On September 18, 2008, Yemeni authorities arrested another 30 suspects in the country who were allegedly connected to Al-Qaeda. Foreign Minister Abou Bakr al-Qurbi said that the 2008 attack on the embassy was in retaliation for measures taken by the Sana'a government to fight terrorism.

Donna Bassett

See also: Al-Qaeda; Al-Qaeda in the Arabian Peninsula; Islamic Radicalism; USS *Cole* Bombing

Further Reading

Dorman, Shawn. *Inside a U.S. Embassy: Diplomacy at Work, The Essential Guide to the Foreign Service.* Dulles, VA: Potomac Books, 2011.

Johnsen, Gregory D. *The Last Refuge: Yemen, al-Qaeda, and America's War in Arabia.* New York: W. W. Norton & Company, 2012.

U.S. Embassy (Tehran) Hostage Crisis

On November 4, 1979, 63 people were abducted at the U.S. embassy in Tehran, with three more staffers found and seized soon afterward. After the release of 13 captives, 52 remained for the duration of the crisis, from November 4, 1979, to January 20, 1981 (444 days). The hostage takers were Islamist students from a group calling itself the Muslim Student Followers of the Imam's Line. Led by Ebrahim Asgharzadeh, they hoped their actions would support the Iranian Revolution that had led to overthrow of the American-backed shah, Mohammad Reza Pahlavi. The crisis eventually ended with an agreement between Iran and the U.S. government and the release of the hostages.

The group began by monitoring the embassy from nearby neighborhood rooftops about two weeks prior to the attack. At 6:30 a.m. on November 4, Asgharzadeh and his co-leaders gathered several hundred students they had chosen to participate in the takeover. One female was sent to cut the locks off the mission's gates, opening the way for the remainder of the group to storm the complex. They quickly overpowered the building's guards, who were then blindfolded and forced in front of photographers. During the first week of the crisis those who had escaped or not

This photo taken on the first day of occupation of the U.S. embassy in Tehran shows American hostages being paraded by their militant Iranian captors on November 4, 1979. (Bettmann/Corbis)

been present when the attack occurred were rounded up and taken back to the mission as hostages. However, six U.S. diplomats managed to get to the Canadian and Swiss embassies.

Although Ayatollah Khomeini did not know of the plans beforehand, the student group did receive his full backing, with the new Iranian leader lauding their actions as a "second revolution" against "a den of spies." Khomeini's support prolonged the takeover as he took control over the conditions of release.

At first the Muslim Student Followers intended to hold the embassy for only a short time and to demand the return of the shah (who was receiving medical treatment in the United States) for trial and execution. However, as the takeover gained popularity in the country, the terrorists

changed their demands and announced they would keep their hostages as part of a prolonged fight to battle American imperialism. Some have blamed the U.S. president Jimmy Carter for allowing the crisis to escalate in this fashion, criticizing him for not threatening Iran at the very outset of the crisis.

Several attempts were made to bring the affair to an end through negotiation. In early February 1980, a clandestine meeting between Iran's foreign minister, Sadegh Ghotbzadeh, and Hamilton Jordan, an aide to President Carter, took place in Paris. This resulted in an agreement to end the takeover. However, when details of the accord leaked on February 19, 1980, Khomeini announced that a decision on releasing the hostages would only be made in the Iranian parliament.

In April 1980, a second attempt to gain the captives' release was similarly unsuccessful. In this instance, the plan called for Washington to agree against sanctioning Iran and for the hostages to be transferred first to government officials in Tehran and then to the United States. Despite last-minute additions to the agreement by Abulhassan Bani-Sadr, Iran's president, Carter agreed. However, Khomeini again voiced disagreement with the accord, which subsequently fell through.

Following this failure an effort to rescue the captives by military means was made. Known as Operation Eagle Claw and instituted on April 24, 1980, the operation had to be aborted, however, after the helicopters that were flying American Delta Force commandos to the embassy malfunctioned during a sandstorm. On their return, one crashed into a C-130 transport plane, killing eight U.S. servicemen. As a result of the attempt, which was lambasted as a disaster for the United States, the hostages were split up and held in several locations around Tehran to make any further raids impossible.

As Carter's term was coming to a close and after Pahlavi died on July 27, 1980, an agreement was finally brokered by Algeria. Among other things, this guaranteed that the United States would not pursue any legal claims against Tehran, provided for the release of billions of dollars of Iranian assets from American banks, and committed Washington to issuing an official apology for its historical interference in Iranian affairs. The final details of what came to be known as the Algerian Accords were finalized on January 19, 1981. The hostages were released the next day, which also marked the end of Carter's presidency and the beginning of the Ronald Reagan presidency.

For Iran, the hostage crisis had both positive and negative implications. While the country lost international support in the West, it was able to consolidate considerable national backing for what was to become a characteristic anti-American stance. In the United States, the crisis was overwhelmingly viewed as a humiliating defeat and a major black mark on the Carter administration's record.

Ezekiel Fraint

See also: Carter Doctrine; Eagle Claw, Operation; Terrorism

Further Reading

Bowden, Mark. *Guests of the Ayatollah.* New York: Atlantic Monthly Press, 2006.

Ebtekar, Massoumeh (as told to Fred A. Reed). *Takeover in Teheran: The Inside Story of the 1970 U.S. Embassy Capture.* Vancouver, BC, Canada: Talonbooks, 2000.

Farber, David. *Taken Hostage.* Princeton, NJ: Princeton University Press, 2005.

Skow, John. "The Long Ordeal of the Hostages." *Time,* January 26, 1981.

U.S. European Command

One of 10 U.S. unified combatant commands and authority offices established on August 1, 1952. Located in Stuttgart, Republic of Germany, it oversees all of the U.S. military forces in Europe. EUCOM consists of U.S. Army Europe (USAREUR), U.S. Air Forces Europe (USAFE), U.S. Naval Forces Europe (NAVEUR), U.S. Marine Forces Europe (MARFOREUR), and U.S. Special Operations Command Europe (SOCEUR). Currently EUCOM's area of responsibility covers more than 20 million square miles and more than 50 countries, including all European states as well as Iceland, Turkey, and Israel. It was the lead command for actual and potential operations during the Cold War and the conflict in Kosovo in the late 1990s. It was also the chief command for U.S. air forces flying in operations during the 1991 Persian Gulf War and the enforcement of the northern no-fly zone in Iraq (1997–2003) leading up to the U.S. invasion of Iraq in March 2003. In addition to commanding all U.S. military forces in Europe, the commander of EUCOM also serves as the Supreme Allied Commander, Europe (SACEUR) for the North Atlantic Treaty Organization (NATO).

The combat power of EUCOM is formed around the U.S. Seventh Army, the U.S. 6th Fleet, and the U.S. Third Air Force. Headquartered in Heidelberg, Germany, the Seventh Army makes up the ground component of EUCOM. The naval component, the 6th Fleet, patrols the Mediterranean Sea, covers Europe and NATO's southern flank, and provides protection to shipping in the Mediterranean Sea. The Third Air Force is based at Ramstein Air Base. The Southern European Task Force and its 173rd Airborne Brigade based in Vicenza, Italy, were until recently USAREUR's principal combat force south of the Alps. In December 2008, the Southern European Task Force (SETAF) became the army component of U.S. Africa Command.

EUCOM's special operations component, SOCEUR, is headquartered at Patch Barracks in Stuttgart-Vaihingen, Germany. Forces under SOCEUR include the 352nd Special Operations Group of the U.S. Air Force, based at Royal Air Force Mildenhall in the United Kingdom; the 10th Special Forces Group, a U.S. Navy SEALs unit; Naval Special Warfare Unit 2 in Germany; and other U.S. Army Special Forces elements. EUCOM also has command and control over American nuclear forces in Europe.

The first U.S. commander in chief Europe (USCINCEUR) was General Matthew B. Ridgway, former commander of the U.S. Eighth Army and the U.S. Far East Command during the Korean War (1950–1953). In 1954, EUCOM moved to a French army base (Camp des Loges) west of Paris and then to Patch Barracks, Stuttgart, Germany, in 1967, where it remains today. The troop strength of EUCOM has varied greatly over the years and has depended on the current world politico-military situation. In the 1950s and 1960s, U.S. military personnel in Europe went from 120,000 to more than 400,000 at the peak during the Cold War. Likewise, U.S. Air Forces in Europe grew from 35,000 to 136,000 personnel, and the 6th Fleet went from 20 ships to more than 40.

After the Cold War ended, EUCOM took its airborne command post off alert. In 1990–1991, the command began to provide forces to CENTCOM for Operation Desert Storm (the Persian Gulf War). It also provided forces for operations in the Balkans as well as support against terrorist attacks in its theater after the attacks of September 11, 2001, as part of the global war on terror (2001–present). EUCOM has furnished forces and logistical support to the war in Afghanistan as part of Operation Enduring Freedom (beginning in October 2001) and in 2003 for Operation Iraqi Freedom.

Richard B. Verrone

See also: Enduring Freedom, Operation; Global War on Terror; Iraqi Freedom, Operation; U.S. Central Command

Further Reading

Bolt, Paul J., Damon V. Coletta, and Collins G. Shackelford Jr., eds. *American Defense*

Policy. Baltimore: Johns Hopkins University Press, 2005.

Gregory, Shaun R. *Nuclear Command and Control in NATO: Nuclear Weapons Operations and the Strategy of Flexible Response.* New York: Palgrave Macmillan, 1996.

Lindley-French, Julien. *A Chronology of European Security and Defence, 1945–2006.* New York: Oxford University Press, 2008.

USS *Cole* Bombing

The attack on the USS *Cole* in Yemen on October 12, 2000, marked the first time a modern U.S. Navy warship was successfully targeted by terrorists. On October 12, 2000, the 8,600-ton displacement (full load), 506-foot-long Arleigh-Burke class destroyer *Cole* (DDG-67) was docked in the Yemeni port of Aden for a refueling stop. At 11:18 a.m. local time, two suicide bombers in a small harbor skiff pulled alongside the anchored ship and detonated a 500–700-pound (227–317 kilogram) shaped charge composed of TNT and C4. The ensuing blast killed both bombers and 17 members of the *Cole*'s crew; another 39 were injured. The operation allegedly cost $500,000 and took three years to plan.

Although the attack did not sink the *Cole*, it ripped a gaping hole in the vessel's hull that measured 43 feet high and 36 feet long. Crew members aboard the *Cole* clearly recollect having seen the two men as they approached the ship. The bombers, however, made no untoward moves, and indeed appeared friendly; apparently some of the sailors believed that the attackers worked for the harbor services and were collecting trash or performing some other kind of routine task.

Three days after the bombing, the stricken destroyer was taken aboard the Norwegian ship *Blue Marlin* off Yemen and transported to the United States. It reached its home port of Norfolk, Virginia, in December and continued on to Pascagoula, Mississippi, for extensive renovations. Repairs took approximately one year and cost more than $240 million.

U.S. and Yemeni officials stated on the day after the bombing that key suspects in the affair had fled to safety in Afghanistan. There was no immediate credible claim of responsibility, but American officials made Al-Qaeda and Osama bin Laden the focus of their investigation. Still, however, some military and national security officials faulted the Bill Clinton and George W. Bush administrations for failing to take appropriate retaliatory measures after the bombing.

The *Cole* bombing prompted an investigation into the ease with which the attackers had been able to approach the ship. An initial Pentagon inquiry found that the commanding officer had acted reasonably and that the facts did not warrant any punitive action against him or any other members of the *Cole*'s crew.

Coordination between U.S. and Yemeni officials investigating the incident was aided by a counterterrorism agreement signed by Yemen and the United States in 1998, and the trial of 12 suspects formally commenced in June 2004. In late September 2004, Abd al-Rahim al-Nashiri and Jamal Mohammed al-Badawi both received the death penalty for their participation in the terrorist act. Four other participants were sentenced to 5 to 10 years in jail.

Paul G. Pierpaoli, Jr.

See also: Al-Qaeda; Bin Laden, Osama; Nashiri, Abd al-Rahim al-; Terrorism

Further Reading

Blomquist, Brian. "Suspected Mastermind of the USS *Cole* Bombing Arrested." *New York Post*, November 26, 2003.

Raghavan, Sudarsan, and Jonathan Landay. "Advance Information on *Cole*'s Yemen Stop under Scrutiny." *Stars and Stripes*, November 1, 2000.

Risen, James. "Pakistan Nabs al-Qaeda Planner." *New York Times*, May 1, 2003.

Rodgers, Walter, and Terry Frieden. "USS *Cole* Probe Seeks Evidence of Conspiracy." *CNN.com*, October 20, 2000. http://transcripts.cnn.com/2000/us/10/20/cole.evidence/.

Schmidt, Susan. "Two Al-Qaeda Suspects Charged in *Cole* Attack." *Washington Post*, May 16, 2003.

U.S. Special Operations Command

Unified command responsible for the conduct of all unconventional warfare missions undertaken by the U.S. military. U.S. Special Operations Command (USSOCOM) was activated on June 1, 1987, and is headquartered at MacDill Air Force Base, Florida. It is one of the 10 unified commands in the U.S. military structure.

USSOCOM was established in response to the failure of Operation Eagle Claw, the 1980 attempt to free Americans taken hostage from the U.S. embassy in Tehran by Iranian revolutionaries. The preparations for and execution of Eagle Claw were impeded by serious problems with cross-service command and control, coordination, funding, and training. Action analysis of the failed operation led to the establishment of the Special Operations Advisory panel and the 1st Special Operations Command in 1982. In 1983, further movement to consolidate Special Operations Forces (SOF) was led by Senator Barry Goldwater (R-AZ). By 1984, the U.S. Congress created the Joint Special Operations Agency, but it had no operational control. Over the next two years, Congress studied the uses and funding of SOF. Senators Nunn and Cohen introduced a bill calling for a joint military operation for SOF and an office within the Department of Defense to oversee it. This organization was to be commanded by a four-star general. The Nunn-Cohen Act was signed into law in October 1986. With the dissolution of the U.S. Readiness Command, USSOCOM was created and approved for operations by President Ronald Reagan on April 13, 1987.

USSOCOM draws its manpower from all branches of the U.S. Armed Forces. Its two original members were the U.S. Army and the U.S. Navy. Army elements include the 75th Ranger Regiment, U.S. Army Special Forces, 160th Special Operations Aviation Regiment, 4th Psychological Operations Group (Airborne), 95th Civil Affairs Battalion (Airborne), and Special Operations Support Command (Airborne). Navy elements include SEALs, Special Warfare Combatant-Craft Crewman, and Seal Delivery Vehicle Teams. The U.S. Air Force special operations units came under USSOCOM in 1990, including the 1st Special Operations Wing, the 27th Special Operations Wing, the 352nd Special Operations Group, the 353rd Special Operations Group, the 919th Special Operations Wing (U.S. Air Force Reserve), and the 193rd Special Operations Wing (Air National Guard). In 2005, the Pentagon authorized the addition of U.S. Marine Corps elements to USSOCOM, which included the Marine Special Operations Battalion, Marine Special Operations Advisory Group, and Marine Special Operations Support Group.

To handle highly classified missions requiring swift action, possible hostage rescue, and counterterrorism, USSOCOM also contains the Joint Special Operations

Command consisting of 1st Special Forces Operational Detachment–Delta, Naval Special Warfare Development Group, Intelligence Support Activity, and 24th Special Tactics Squadron. Each service maintains its own command and training regime.

Since its inception, USSOCOM has played a major role in U.S. military actions. It provided forces for the safe navigation of the Persian Gulf (Operation Earnest Will) and the capture of Panamanian president Manuel Noriega (Operation Just Cause). As world attention shifted more to the Middle East, USSOCOM again was asked to lead the way. For Operation Desert Storm, SOF led the invasion of Iraq with strategic intelligence and by locating Scud missile sites. In the global war on terror, SOF and USSOCOM have won more battles, ranging from overthrowing the Taliban in Afghanistan in late 2001 to leading the search for Al-Qaeda leader Osama bin Laden, to providing counterterrorism operations in Iraq.

Shawn Livingston

See also: Al-Qaeda; Bin Laden, Osama; Eagle Claw, Operation; Enduring Freedom, Operation; Global War on Terror; Iraqi Freedom, Operation; Persian Gulf War

Further Reading

Clancy, Tom, Carl Stiner, and Tony Koltz. *Shadow Warriors: Inside the Special Forces.* New York: Berkley Books, 2003.

U.S. Special Operations Command. *United States Special Operations Command History: 20 (1987–2007) Proven in the Past, Vigilant Today, Prepared for the Future.* MacDill Air Force Base, FL: U.S. Special Operations Command, 2007.

Zimmerman, Dwight Jon, and John Gresham. *Beyond Hell and Back: How America's Special Operations Forces Became the World's Greatest Fighting Unit.* New York: St. Martin's, 2007.

W

War Correspondents

The history of news reporters covering combat operations dates back at least to the Crimean War (1853–1856) waged by Great Britain, France, and Turkey against Imperial Russia. William Howard Russell, who covered that war for the *Times*, is generally considered the world's first war correspondent. Since that time, correspondents have covered virtually every major conflict throughout the world. During the 20th century, war correspondents brought the realities of combat "up close and personal" to the readers and viewers in their respective countries in major wars, such as World War I, World War II, the Korean War, and the Vietnam War, and in countless lesser conflicts throughout the world. Yet inevitably, the presence of civilian reporters on the battlefield creates an unavoidable tension between the correspondents, whose only job is to report the facts as they witness them, and the military officers and government officials whose principal duty is to win the war they are fighting. Increasingly, this tension centers on the degree of access to the wars' combat zones that governments grant to war correspondents. While reporters—driven by deadlines and the need to produce ratings-garnering headlines—consistently demand unrestricted free access, government officials and military officers seek to keep war correspondents' access limited to what they judge as "reasonable." The recent wars in the Middle East serve as prime examples of this issue.

In the modern Middle East, three recent or ongoing conflicts—the 1991 Persian Gulf War, the Afghanistan War (October 7, 2001–present), and the Iraq War (March 20, 2003–present)—have led to dramatic developments in the history of war correspondence. These include the growing prominence of media giants such as Cable News Network (CNN), MSNBC, and Fox News, news briefings by high-ranking military officers, news pools attached to military units, and journalists embedded with fighting forces. All of these developments have exposed news media to accusations of government and corporate control, however. An attempt to counter this alleged censorship has led to a proliferation of chiefly Internet-based alternative news sites. Moreover, the rising casualty rates among journalists in Afghanistan and particularly Iraq have highlighted the inherent risks of war correspondence. No longer viewed as neutral observers, journalists are increasingly targeted for their alleged political or sectarian affiliations.

The roots of increasing governmental and military control over journalistic reporting go back to the Vietnam War, the Falklands War, and the U.S. invasions of Grenada (1983) and Panama (1989). U.S. supporters of the Vietnam War and many Vietnam War combat veterans alleged that negative journalistic reports were largely responsible for the erosion of American support for the war, in particular, coverage of the 1968 Tet Offensive. The general lack of the largely Saigon-based Vietnam War reporters' "up front" credibility and the perception of inaccurate reporting during Tet and the Vietnam War in general resulted in virtually an entire generation of military officers distrusting the media's accuracy and even their motives.

This distrust of media methods, accuracy, and motives has had a profound impact on U.S. government attitudes and policies regarding reporters' access to combat operations when they are in progress. When many of the Vietnam-generation military officers assumed high command in the Persian Gulf War and the Afghanistan and Iraq conflicts, their perception of media bias in the past greatly influenced the U.S. government decision to forego a policy of unrestricted access for journalists in the later conflicts in the Middle East.

During the 1982 Falklands War, the British government sought to control press coverage. British governmental and military officials assigned no more than 29 correspondents and photographers to pools that accompanied the Falklands invasion force. Various reporters later complained of direct censorship. Following the British cue, American government and military officials largely excluded the media from Operation Urgent Fury, the 1983 invasion of Grenada. The 15 reporters finally allowed on Grenada found their movements severely curtailed. Similarly, Operation Just Cause, the 1989 invasion of Panama to overthrow President Manuel Noriega, deployed a very select pool of journalists who complained that they were barely briefed and kept well away from military action.

Persian Gulf War

Although U.S. government and military officials aimed at creating more transparency during the Persian Gulf War, the inevitable accusations of censorship and disinformation abounded since the government did not permit reporters unrestricted access. Following governmental cues, the American media demonized Iraqi president Saddam Hussein, some echoing President George H. W. Bush's characterization of him as a "new Hitler," and representing the war as inevitable. Opposition to the war, which at any rate was slight and disorganized, was mainly ignored except for a few high-profile incidents. Although Iraqi forces committed sufficient outrages during their occupation of Kuwait to fill numerous news reports, charges of propaganda were raised when it was discovered that many of these were Kuwaiti public relations fabrications—such as reports of Iraqi soldiers throwing Kuwaiti babies out of incubators.

Seventeen members of the national media pool arrived in Saudi Arabia on August 13, well before Operation Desert Storm was launched on January 17, 1991, and were closely monitored during Operation Desert Shield. Headed by Michael Sherman, six government public affairs officers were to handle Persian Gulf media. These officials set up the main military briefing rooms and television studios in Dhahran and Riyadh, Saudi Arabia, and organized "media response teams," a pool system whose members were sometimes permitted to accompany select military units. An intense competition among journalists ensued, but reporters were largely denied access to actual combat. A number of disgruntled journalists affiliated with small media organizations filed a legal brief, claiming that the pool system violated their First Amendment right of free expression. The war ended, however, before courts ruled on the matter.

So-called unilaterals or freelancers also found their movements hampered. By mid-February 1991, some 20 had been detained or threatened with detention. Similarly, television correspondents Peter Arnett of CNN, John Simpson of the BBC, and Brent Sadler of Independent Television News (ITN) evoked criticism for reporting the first stage of the war from Baghdad. Their vivid film of initial air attacks garnered high viewer ratings and helped fuel the soaring popularity of major news networks. Nevertheless, U.S. government officials objected to the correspondents' presence in an enemy capital. In particular, reports of the bombing of a deep military command and control bunker in the Amariyah district of Baghdad—the upper levels of which were also being used as a civilian air raid shelter—that killed 408 civilians deeply embarrassed coalition officials and provided the Saddam Hussein regime with useful propaganda.

Prompted by governmental and military spokespersons and backed by correspondents from major news media, a sanitized version of combat emerged from coverage of the Persian Gulf War. Critics cited the U.S. government's portrayals of the success of weapons systems such as smart bombs, Tomahawk cruise missiles, and the Patriot antimissile system as grossly exaggerated, charges generally confirmed by postwar analysis. Criticism was far from limited to weapons systems, however. Charges abounded that unrestricted free press access had prevented reporters from independently verifying official information provided regarding the extent of U.S. friendly fire casualties, the true number of Iraqi military and civilian deaths resulting from coalition ground and air combat actions, and the amount of oil pollution caused by coalition bombing (versus that caused by Iraqi sabotage). Barry Zorthian's statement to the National Press Club on March 19, 1991, may well summarize the judgment of many war correspondents who felt shut out by Department of Defense press restrictions during the Persian Gulf War: "The Gulf War is over and the press lost."

Afghanistan War

As in the Persian Gulf War, war correspondents in the ongoing conflict in Afghanistan, which began as Operation Enduring Freedom on October 7, 2001, have been targeted by appeals to patriotism and national security. For instance, shortly after the war began, major U.S. networks agreed to have any statements from Al-Qaeda leader Osama bin Laden screened and edited by the government. The Arab-language television network Al Jazeera soon was targeted for broadcasting a release from bin Laden on the eve of the first air strike on Afghanistan. On November 13, 2001, Al Jazeera's office in Kabul was struck by a U.S. missile, which officials claimed was intended to hit a well-known Al-Qaeda facility. A second attack, again claimed to be mistaken, targeted Al Jazeera's Baghdad office on April 8, 2003, killing a reporter and wounding a cameraman.

From the outset of Operation Enduring Freedom, U.S. defense secretary Donald Rumsfeld warned the media to expect little Pentagon cooperation. When the aerial bombardment began on October 7, 2001, no Western journalists were within the three-quarters of the country controlled by the Taliban, for reporters had gathered in Pakistan and territory held by the anti-Taliban Northern Alliance. By November 10, seven journalists had been killed as they spread out to areas abandoned by the Taliban, whose forces had arrested *Sunday Express* reporter Yvonne Ridley on September 28. Several months later, the Pentagon unveiled plans to establish three coalition press information centers, in Mazar-e Sharif and Bagram, and at the Qandahar Airport. Staff members would be charged with helping journalists get photographs and interviews. Still, Assistant Secretary of Defense Victoria Clarke encouraged journalists to remain in Bahrain for the best access to war coverage. These procedures led to questions about how much uncensored news was reaching Western readers or viewers. As early as 2002, for instance, *Daily Mirror* correspondent John Pilger claimed that about 5,000 civilian deaths had resulted from bombing raids in Afghanistan, almost double the toll of the September 11, 2001, terrorist attacks on New York.

Yet the dangers of reporters' unrestricted access to war zones is clearly shown in Afghanistan. Faced with problems of access, an inhospitable terrain, language barriers, and the danger of ambush, journalists complain that they face a hidden war in Afghanistan. Particularly in the south of the country, correspondents have encountered difficulties in hiring local "fixers" willing to risk Taliban retribution. On March 4, 2007, for instance, Taliban forces abducted *La Republica* reporter Daniele Mastrogiacomo along with Afghan journalist Ajmal Nakshbandi and their driver, Sayed Agha, in Helmand Province. While Mastrogiacomo was later released in a prisoner exchange, both Afghans were beheaded. This incident followed the killing of two German *Deutsche Welle* journalists in October 2006.

Iraq War

Operation Iraqi Freedom, an ongoing conflict that began with the invasion of Iraq on March 20, 2003, accomplished a new twist in the pool system that had been practiced in the Persian Gulf War and, to some extent, in Afghanistan. At the commencement of the campaign, such major news syndicates as CNN had announced huge budgets for war coverage, planning to devote 24 hours a day to the conflict. However, much to the disappointment of reporters demanding unrestricted free access to combat operations, the Department of Defense chose only to use reporters embedded with combat units. "Embeds" would receive basic training and accompany their assigned units through combat. Embeds were allowed to report what they wished so long as they revealed no information that the enemy could use.

While supporters saw the embed system as restoring "up front" credibility to reporters, whom they had perceived as being aloof and unsympathetic to the real problems faced by troops engaged in waging war, critics of the embed system claimed that it resulted in a loss of objectivity among correspondents—who soon discovered that they identified with troops in their assigned units. A few correspondents, including CNN's Christiane Amanpour (who became a media celebrity through her reporting of the Persian Gulf War and Bosnian conflict), objected to the restrictions; however, Amanpour was warned that she had to abide by the rules.

More than in the 1991 Persian Gulf War, journalists found that dry, colorless government media briefings offered them little material to produce the dramatic headlines that garner top ratings in the highly competitive news business. Moreover, increasingly international television viewers have become the media giants' target audience, and correspondents often found their reports hampered by syndicate expectations. Yet, despite the claims that access was unduly restricted, war correspondents were instrumental in exposing such incidents as Abu Ghraib prisoner abuse, the overhyped Jessica Lynch "rescue" operation, and the extent of Iraqi civilian casualties due to coalition bombing, such as during the Second Battle of Fallujah, in November 2004.

In short, the war in Iraq suggests that correspondents, unlike during the Persian Gulf War, became more critical, a mood that reflected and even fueled the growing public opposition to the war. Statistics also suggest that Iraq became the world's most dangerous location for journalists between 2003 and 2011. The conservative estimates of the Committee to Protect Journalists indicate that violence in Iraq claimed the lives of 32 journalists in 2006, the highest number that the organization had recorded to date. Between 2003 and the end of 2011, the Committee to Protect Journalists reported that at least 150 journalists died in Iraq, while 54 additional media workers (nonjournalists) died. The conflicts in Kuwait, Afghanistan, and Iraq reveal that war correspondence is becoming an increasingly risky enterprise, whether "pooled," "embedded," or acting independently.

Anna M. Wittmann

See also: Abu Ghraib; Al-Qaeda; "Axis of Evil"; Counterinsurgency; Counterterrorism Center; Enduring Freedom, Operation; Ground Zero Mosque Controversy; Iraqi Freedom, Operation; Persian Gulf War; Terrorism

Further Reading

Allan, Stuart, and Barbie Zelizer, eds. *Reporting War: Journalism in Wartime*. New York: Routledge, 2004.

Fisk, Robert. *The Great War for Civilization: The Conquest of the Middle East*. New York: Vintage Books, 2007.

Knightley, Phillip. *The First Casualty: The War Correspondent as Hero and Myth-Maker from the Crimea to Iraq*. Baltimore: Johns Hopkins University Press, 2004.

McLaughlin, Greg. *The War Correspondent*. London: Pluto, 2002.

Tumber, Howard, and Frank Webster. *Journalists under Fire: Information War and Journalistic Practices*. London: Sage, 2006.

Warlords, Afghanistan

In Afghanistan, warlords traditionally have been military leaders who often served as the de facto government of provinces and cities, usually organized by ethnic or tribal affiliation, but sometimes by ideology, as with the mujahideen and Taliban. A warlord system has variously comprised the collection of taxes and customs duties, the maintenance of private armies and fiefdoms, and the exploitation of the criminal, or underground, economy.

Historically, Afghanistan has been the meeting point of the Indian subcontinent, Central Asia, and the Middle East. Over the course of numerous invasions, it evolved into a nation comprising numerous ethnic groups. These include Persian, Pashai, Baluch, Chahar, Tajik, Turkmen, Aimak, Pashtun, Uzbek, Arab, Nuristani, Kirghiz, and Hazara. Of these groups, the Pashtun emerged as the most dominant both numerically and politically. They represent about 50 percent of the total population; politically, they have constituted the royal family and have often held power. The Tajiks are the second largest ethnic group, comprising some 25 percent of the population.

Afghan warlords emerged following the end of the British protectorate in 1919. In the aftermath of the Bolshevik Revolution in Russia in 1917, the king of Afghanistan, Amanullah, who ascended the throne in 1919, marked the country's independence by signing a treaty of aid and friendship with Russian revolutionary Vladimir Lenin and declaring war on Britain. In response, the British Royal Air Force bombed the Afghan capital of Kabul, and the British government conspired with conservative religious groups and land-owning communities who had grown contemptuous of Amanullah's attempts at secularization and reform. This gave birth to the warlords.

In 1929, Amanullah abdicated following an uprising and civil unrest, and the warlords then competed in earnest for power. The turn of events that led to the abdication of Amanullah marked the first, but not final, instance in which disgruntled religious and land-owning factions would collaborate with Western or Soviet powers to achieve change in Afghanistan.

Afghanistan's new king, Muhammad Nadir Shah, commenced an ill-fated reign that was cut short four years later with his assassination in 1933. Muhammad Zahir Shah succeeded to the throne. He ruled for 40 years before he was deposed by his cousin, Mohammad Daoud Khan, in 1973, whereupon Afghanistan was formerly declared a republic. In the meantime, warlords played a sizable role in Afghanistan, especially at the provincial and municipal levels.

From the early 20th century on, the significant role of the warlords in determining the political and religious orientation of Afghanistan indicates not only the deep-rooted nature of warlordism in the country, but also an enduring determination to vie for power both internally and with external intervening powers. Nevertheless, warlords of both the mujahideen, beginning in the 1980s, and the Taliban in the 1990s have demonstrated a willingness to court both Western and Soviet powers to serve national and personal interests. While the "Great Game" in the late 19th century had rendered Afghanistan a buffer between British and Russian interests, the end of the 20th century brought a proactive mobilization of the warlords.

The most recent contingent of warlords flourished during the ongoing civil war and Soviet occupation (1979–2001) and amidst the ensuing breakdown of central authority. As young military commanders usurped traditional governance structures and bodies of authority, such as the village *shura* or *jirga*, the warlords provided rudimentary public services while exhibiting predatory behavior toward local communities.

Despite the seemingly negative implications that have arisen from the assimilation of Taliban warlords into the Afghan state, their involvement has been endorsed by the international community, most notably the United States, which has favored the formation of alliances with regional commanders to preserve security and stability until the Afghan National Security Forces (ANSF) are trained and equipped.

Nevertheless, the strategy of placing warlords in government has so far lacked the degree of success that had been anticipated by both Afghanistan and international observers. A significant obstacle has been ongoing competition between the warlords. Between 2002 and 2003, the forces of Rashid Dostum, the leader of the predominantly Uzbek political group *Junbish-e Milli-ye-Islami*, and Ustad Atta Mohammed, a key figure in the Tajik-dominated *Jamaat-e-Islami*, clashed in northern Afghanistan, despite the fact that both Dostum and Mohammad were prominent allies of the government. While the hostilities between the two groups had been quelled through the intervention of the central government and international community, skirmishes continue to persist. In October 2006, fighting between two Pashtun clans in Herat killed 32 people and injured many more.

The integration of warlords into the Afghan government has also borne negative security implications. Just as warlords are able to stand in elections, they also find other avenues of political influence open to them. For example, the parliament's standing committees are being dominated by former jihadi commanders, often to the detriment of more qualified individuals. Moreover, the warlords have gained further protection since the passing of a motion on February 1, 2007, which guaranteed immunity to all Afghans who had fought in the civil war, thereby preventing further prosecution of commanders for their involvement in war crimes.

K. Luisa Gandolfo

See also: Al-Qaeda in Iraq; Enduring Freedom, operation; Global War on Terror

Further Reading

Dorronsoro, Gilles. *Afghanistan: Revolution Unending, 1979–2002*. London: C. Hurst, 2003.

Hodes, Cyrus, and Mark Sedra. *The Search for Security in Post-Taliban Afghanistan*. Adelphi Paper 391. Abingdon, UK: Routledge for the International Institute for Strategic Studies, 2007.

Tanner, Stephen. *Afghanistan: A Military History from Alexander the Great to the Fall of the Taliban*. New York: Da Capo, 2003.

War on Terror. *See* Global War on Terror

War Powers Act

A joint resolution of the U.S. Congress, enacted on November 7, 1973, the War Powers Act limits the authority of the president to deploy U.S. troops and/or wage war without the express consent of Congress. It has influenced nearly every major American military deployment in the Middle East since its passing. The act became law over then-president Richard M. Nixon's veto following the withdrawal of U.S. combat forces from the Republic of Vietnam (South Vietnam) during the Vietnam War. It was designed to assure that the president and Congress would share responsibility in making decisions that might lead the United States into a war. Its passage was prompted by the highly unpopular Vietnam War, during which both the Lyndon Johnson and Richard Nixon administrations enmeshed the United States in a major war while bypassing the constitutional provision that grants Congress the power to declare war (Article I, Section 8).

Under the War Powers Act, the president is required to notify and consult with Congress prior to deploying U.S. troops into hostile situations and to consult regularly with Congress once troops have been deployed. If within 60 days of introducing troops Congress has not declared war or approved of the military deployment, the president must withdraw the troops unless he certifies to Congress an "unavoidable military necessity" that requires an additional 30 days to remove the troops. Although every president, Democrat and Republican, has claimed the War Powers Act to be an unconstitutional violation of the president's authority as commander in chief, presidents have been careful nevertheless to notify Congress of their decision to deploy U.S. forces.

According to the Congressional Research Service, since the passage of the War Powers Resolution in 1973, U.S. presidents have submitted over 100 such reports to Congress. On April 24, 1980, following the failed attempt to rescue American hostages in Iran, President Jimmy Carter submitted a report to Congress. Some members of Congress objected to Carter's failure to consult with Congress before executing the operation. Carter, however, claimed that because the mission depended on complete secrecy, consultation was not possible; moreover, the White House argued that a rescue operation did not constitute an act of aggression or force.

On September 29, 1983, Congress invoked the resolution to authorize the deployment of U.S. Marines to Lebanon for 18 months as part of a United Nations (UN) peacekeeping mission there. Following several years of growing tensions with Libya and skirmishes between both countries, on April 14, 1986, President Ronald W. Reagan ordered air strikes on Libya for its involvement in a terrorist bombing in a West Berlin discotheque that killed two U.S. soldiers. Reagan informed Congress of the attack, but because the operation was short-lived the question of congressional approval was essentially moot.

In January 1991, President George H. W. Bush secured congressional authorization to use force to compel Iraq to withdraw from Kuwait per a UN mandate. After the end of the Persian Gulf War on February 28, 1991, the War Powers Act again became a potential issue regarding

the situation in the Middle East. President Bill Clinton launched several air attacks against Iraqi targets in an effort to compel Iraqi dictator Saddam Hussein's compliance with UN resolutions. In 1998, Clinton also ordered cruise-missile attacks on targets in Afghanistan and Sudan in retaliation for two deadly bombings involving U.S. embassies, likely carried out by Al-Qaeda. Clinton did not invoke the War Powers Act because of the brief and secretive nature of the operations, however.

Following the September 11, 2001, terrorist attacks on the United States, President George W. Bush secured congressional authorization a week later to use whatever force necessary against those responsible for the attacks. Based on this authorization, in October 2001, the U.S. attacked and invaded Afghanistan to overthrow the Taliban regime that had given sanctuary to Osama bin Laden and Al-Qaeda.

In 2002, the Bush administration sought another congressional approval to wage a potential war against Iraq to compel it to cooperate with the United Nations resolution that had called for the disarming of Iraq and the declaration of all weapons of mass destruction (WMDs). On October 16, 2002, Bush signed into law the joint congressional resolution, which enjoyed wide bipartisan support, empowering him to wage war against the regime of Iraqi dictator Saddam Hussein. The October 2002 authorization of military force against Iraq obviated presidential compliance with the War Powers Act.

Although Congress authorized the use of force against Iraq, the March 2003 invasion of Iraq and subsequent war and insurgency there called into question not only the effectiveness of the War Powers Act but also, and more importantly, Congress's role in foreign policy and decisions involving war. The failure to find any weapons of mass destruction, the principal reason cited by Bush for the invasion of Iraq, led critics of the war to question not only the president's responsibility to both Congress and the public, but also the role of Congress in declaring war and, specifically, as the War Powers Act intended, checking or overseeing the president's war-making powers.

Regardless of which administration holds the White House, tension over the exercise of war powers undoubtedly will continue between the executive and legislative branches of government. Presidents, Democrat and Republican, will still seek to implement U.S. foreign policy through the unrestricted use of all elements of national power—economic, political, and military—while Congress, through its legislative powers, will continue to exercise its vital role of providing the necessary "checks and balances" to ensure that executive branch power does not become "unrestricted." Given the volatile situation in the Middle East, the region will likely continue to be the focal point for future confrontations between president and Congress over war powers.

Stefan M. Brooks

See also: Al-Qaeda; Bin Laden, Osama; Bush Administration; Clinton Administration; Enduring Freedom, Operation; Global War on Terror; Iraqi Freedom, Operation; Persian Gulf War

Further Reading

Bobbit, Phillip. "War Powers: An Essay on John Hart Ely's *War and Responsibility: Constitutional Lessons of Vietnam and Its Aftermath*." *Michigan Law Quarterly* 92, no. 6 (May 1994): 1364–400.

Irons, Peter. *War Powers: How the Imperial Presidency Hijacked the Constitution*. New York: Metropolitan Books, 2005.

Yoo, John. *The Powers of War and Peace: The Constitution and Foreign Affairs after 9/11*. Chicago: University of Chicago Press, 2005.

Weapons of Mass Destruction

The term "weapons of mass destruction" (WMDs) refers to biological, chemical, and nuclear weapons capable of inflicting mass casualties. Use of these weapons is viewed as not only immoral but also contrary to international law and the laws of war because WMDs have the ability to kill indiscriminately large numbers of human beings and inflict extensive damage to man-made structures beyond combatants or military assets. During the Cold War, fears about nuclear weapons and their use was commonplace. Nevertheless, these weapons were under tight control, and neither side dared employ them for fear of the total destruction that a retaliatory strike would bring. With the end of the Cold War, however, nuclear proliferation has become a significant problem, and the likelihood of a rogue state or terrorist group attaining WMDs, including nuclear weapons, has increased substantially.

During his trial for war crimes in December 2006, Iraqi dictator Saddam Hussein publicly admitted that during the Iran-Iraq War (1980–1988), Iraq had employed chemical weapons against Iranian troops. It remains in dispute whether Iran employed them as well. In 1988, as part of an operation to suppress a revolt by Iraqi Kurds, the Hussein government unleashed a chemical attack on the north-

United Nations weapons inspectors carry equipment to their jeep prior to leaving Baghdad UN headquarters on March 6, 1998. The men were part of a group of UN weapons inspection teams that conducted spot tours of suspected weapons sites. (AP Photo/Peter Dejong)

ern Iraqi town of Halabja, killing at least 5,000 people in the first recorded event of such weapons being used against civilians after the Japanese use of chemical weapons against the Chinese during the Second Sino-Japanese War of 1937–1945.

Since the terror attacks of September 11, 2001, the fear of and danger posed by WMDs have increased significantly, owing to the desire of terrorist groups such as Al-Qaeda and their affiliates to acquire and employ such weapons against the United States and other countries. The September 11 terrorist attacks on the United States and the 2004 Madrid and 2005 London bombings clearly demonstrated the ability and willingness of Al-Qaeda to engage in terrorism to inflict mass casualties, leaving no doubt about their willingness to use WMDs in future terrorist attacks. Al-Qaeda is believed to

have been responsible for a series of terrorist attacks in March and April 2006 in Iraq, in which chlorine gas killed dozens and sickened hundreds.

Because of the instability and recurrence of war and conflict in the Middle East, the presence of WMDs has only heightened the arms race between Arab states and Israel and also among Arab states themselves. Egypt, Syria, Algeria, and Iran are all believed to have significant stockpiles of biological and chemical weapons. In 2003, seeking to normalize relations with the United States and Europe and end its international isolation and reputation as a sponsor of terrorism, Libya announced that it was abandoning its WMD programs. Observers have suggested that President George W. Bush's decision to invade Iraq in 2003, ostensibly to rid it of WMDs, and Libya's failure to end its isolation and convince the United Nations (UN) to lift its sanctions prompted this change of behavior.

Syria possesses extensive chemical weapons stockpiles and delivery systems and had been seeking to develop a similarly robust biological weapons program. In 2013, during the ongoing Syrian civil war that began in 2011, the United States and Russia brokered a deal, which was subsequently sanctioned by Syrian president Bashar al-Assad, in which the Syrian government agreed to rid itself of its chemical weapons arsenal under international supervision. This agreement was reached after evidence surfaced that chemical weapons had been employed during the civil war and to forestall military action against Syria by a multilateral military coalition. Egypt was the first country in the Middle East to develop chemical weapons, which may have been prompted, at least in part, by Israel's construction of a nuclear reactor in 1958. The size of Egypt's chemical weapons arsenal is thought to be perhaps as extensive as Iraq's prior to the 1991 Persian Gulf War, although the end of hostilities between Egypt and Israel since the 1978 Camp David Accords may have obviated the need for maintaining the same quantities of such weapons.

In 1993, as part of the Arab campaign against Israel's nuclear weapons program, Egypt and Syria (along with Iraq) refused to sign the Chemical Weapons Convention (CWC), which bans the acquisition, development, stockpiling, transfer, retention, and use of chemical weapons. These states also refused to sign the Biological Weapons Convention (BWC) of 1975, which prohibits the development, production, acquisition, transfer, retention, stockpiling, and use of biological and toxin weapons. Iraq later signed the BWC, and

it signed the CWC after Hussein's ouster. The extent of Egypt's biological weapons program is unknown, but it clearly has the ability to develop such weapons if it already does not have weaponized stockpiles.

Israel has repeatedly shown its willingness to use force to maintain its suspected Middle East nuclear monopoly and deny any Arab state the ability to acquire or develop nuclear weapons. In 1981, the Israeli air force destroyed an Iraqi nuclear reactor site under construction at Osiraq, Iraq. In September 2007, Israeli warplanes carried out an attack against a suspected nuclear facility in Syria. Iran is currently enriching uranium for what it claims are peaceful purposes, but the United States and much of Western Europe have accused Iran of aspiring to build nuclear weapons. That state's refusal to cooperate with the IAEA led the United Nations to impose sanctions on Iran in December 2006 and March 2007 as punishment for its defiance of the UN. After that, the West pressed for more sanctions, but in late 2013 those sanctions, combined with a change in administration in Iran, seemed to be paying dividends. Iran by then had tentatively agreed to abide by certain international prescriptions regarding its nuclear program, including limiting enrichment efforts and allowing international inspectors into the country to monitor compliance. In turn, some sanctions against Iran were lifted. Only time will tell, however, if Iran will fully abide by the agreements it has made.

Of particular international concern in 2009 were Pakistan in southern Asia and the Democratic People's Republic of Korea (DPRK, North Korea) in East Asia. Pakistan had successfully conducted underground nuclear tests in May 1998 and is believed to possess a number of atomic bombs. Abdul Qadeer Kahn, widely regarded as the chief scientist in the development of Pakistan's atomic bomb, confessed in January 2004 to having been involved in a clandestine network of nuclear proliferation from Pakistan to Libya, Iran, and North Korea (which in October 2006 successfully conducted its first underground nuclear test). Pakistani president General Pervez Musharraf then announced that he had pardoned Kahn, who is regarded by many Pakistanis as a national hero, despite the fact that the technology transfer is thought to have made possible North Korea's acquisition of the atomic bomb.

Beginning in the spring of 2009, however, major fighting erupted between Pakistani government forces and the Taliban, who controlled the Swat Valley in the northwestern part of the country, along the Afghani border. The stability of Pakistani's government and the security of its nuclear arsenal remains in question.

Stefan M. Brooks

See also: Al-Qaeda; Iraqi Freedom, Operation; Persian Gulf War; Taliban; Terrorism

Further Reading

Hamel-Green, Michael. *Regional Initiatives on Nuclear- and WMD-Free Zones: Cooperative Approaches to Arms Control and Non-Proliferation.* New York: United Nations Publication, 2006.

Katona, Peter, et al. *Countering Terrorism and WMD: Creating a Global Counter-Terrorism Network.* New York: Routledge, 2006.

Mauroni, Albert. *Where Are the WMDs? The Reality of Chem-Bio Threats on the Home Front and on the Battlefield.* Annapolis, MD: Naval Institute Press, 2006.

Schneider, Barry. *Avoiding the Abyss: Progress, Shortfalls, and the Way Ahead in Combating the WMD Threat.* Westport, CT: Praeger Publishing, 2006.

Whistleblowers. *See* Rowley, Coleen

Woodward, Robert Upshur

(March 26, 1943–)

American journalist, acclaimed investigative reporter, and chronicler of the George W. Bush administration following the September 11, 2001, terror attacks on the United States, Robert (Bob) Upshur Woodward was born in Geneva, Illinois, on March 26, 1943, but spent his childhood in nearby Wheaton, Illinois. He graduated from Yale University in 1965 and was commissioned a lieutenant in the U.S. Navy. He left the navy in 1970.

Instead of attending law school as his father wished, Woodward went to work as a reporter for the *Montgomery Sentinel* before moving on to the much more prestigious *Washington Post* in 1971. The investigative work by Woodward and fellow *Washington Post* reporter Carl Bernstein on the June 1972 Watergate break-in ultimately led to revelations about President Richard M. Nixon's use of slush funds, obstruction of justice, and various dirty tricks that resulted in congressional investigations and the president's resignation in August 1974.

The Watergate Scandal made Woodward a household name and one of the most sought-after investigative reporters in the nation. He and Bernstein later wrote *All the President's Men*, which was made into a movie starring Robert Redford and Dustin Hoffman, and *The Final Days*, covering their Watergate reporting. Woodward's work on the Watergate story garnered him a Pulitzer Prize. In 1979, the *Washington Post* promoted him to assistant managing editor of the Metro section, and in 1982, he became assistant managing editor for investigative news. Woodward received a second Pulitzer Prize for his reporting on the attacks of September 11, 2001, and their aftermath.

Woodward's books are written in the voice of an omniscient narrator and are compiled from in-depth research, but they rely most heavily on extensive interviews with crucial principals. Most often, the subjects of these works have a natural interest in cooperating with Woodward. Without their input, they are more likely to be portrayed poorly in the product. All of Woodward's books have received criticism from some commentators, who usually point to inconsistencies or contest the factuality of the interviews.

Woodward's *The Commanders* (1991) covered the George H. W. Bush administration's handling of the December 1989–January 1990 Panama invasion and the Persian Gulf War of 1991. In *The Agenda* (1994), Woodward examined the passing of President Bill Clinton's first budget. In *The Choice* (1996), Woodward covered the 1996 presidential election contest. In *Shadow* (1999), he examined how the legacy of Watergate has affected how five presidents have dealt with scandal since 1974. In 2000's *Maestro*, he analyzed the Federal Reserve Board; its chairman, Alan Greenspan; and the American economy. In 2005, following the death of Marc Felt, the anonymous source "Deep Throat" from Watergate, Woodward and Bernstein wrote *Secret Man*, giving new revelations about their Watergate experience.

Woodward has also written four books on the George W. Bush administration following the terrorist attacks of September 11, 2001: *Bush at War* (2002), *Plan of At-*tack (2004), *State of Denial* (2006), and *The War Within: A Secret White House History, 2006–2008* (2008). Woodward received criticism for being allegedly excessively friendly to Bush and his agenda after the publication of both *Bush at War* and *Plan of Attack*. The third and fourth books, however, were far more critical of the Bush administration and its failings in the Iraq War. All of the books illustrate well the divisions within the White House and the Pentagon and the manner in which decisions were made within the Bush administration.

Woodward's *Plan of Attack* chronicles the Bush administration's reaction to September 11, the opening salvos in the global war on terror, and the planning and implementation of Operation Enduring Freedom, which saw U.S. and coalition forces topple the Taliban regime in Afghanistan. *Plan of Attack*, on the other hand, takes a more controversial slant by examining how, when, and why Bush decided to go to war against Iraq in 2003 and remove Saddam Hussein from power. Woodward's main contention is that the Bush administration had planned on regime change in Iraq just weeks after the September 11, 2001, attacks, even though there was no evidence linking Hussein to these. In *State of Denial*, the journalist chronicled the many missteps, mistakes, and gaffes that turned the 2003 war in Iraq into an embarrassing quagmire. The book also showed how many members of the administration were in denial about their role in the debacle and refused to see the seriousness of the situation. The book came out less than a month before the November 2006 congressional elections, which swept the Republicans from power in both houses and brought about the forced resignation of Secretary of Defense Donald Rumsfeld.

In 2008, Woodward published *The War Within*, his fourth book on the Bush presidency. Woodward's conclusions were damning, claiming that Bush was detached and divorced from reality vis-à-vis the Iraq War and that he had left management of the conflict to his generals. Bush's troop surge strategy was purportedly postponed until after the 2006 midterm elections because the president did not want to hamper the Republicans' chances at the voting booth.

Woodward published a book about the Barack Obama administration in 2010. Entitled *Obama's Wars*, the book focuses on the internal debates and ensuing struggles over U.S. policy in both the Iraq and Afghanistan wars. Not as critical as some of his books on the Bush White House, the work was generally well received. Then–White House press secretary Robert Gibbs commented soon after the book's publication that the Obama administration believed the book to have accurately portrayed the decisions made regarding Iraq and Afghanistan, particularly the decision to pursue a troop surge strategy in Afghanistan beginning in 2010.

Michael K. Beauchamp and
Paul G. Pierpaoli, Jr.

See also: Bush Administration; Enduring Freedom, Operation; Iraqi Freedom, Operation; Obama Administration; Rumsfeld, Donald Henry

Further Reading

Shephard, Alicia P. *Woodward and Bernstein: Life in the Shadow of Watergate*. Indianapolis: Wiley, 2006.

Woodward, Bob. *The War Within: A Secret White House History, 2006–2008*. New York: Simon and Schuster, 2008.

Woodward, Bob. *State of Denial: Bush at War, Part III*. New York: Simon and Schuster, 2006.

Woodward, Bob. *Plan of Attack*. New York: Simon and Schuster, 2004.

Woodward, Bob. *Bush at War*. New York: Simon and Schuster, 2002.

World Trade Center Bombing

(1993)

This was the first attempt by Islamist terrorists to destroy the World Trade Center complex, which failed to seriously damage the structure. At 12:18 p.m. on Friday, February 26, 1993, Islamist terrorists exploded a bomb in the underground garage, level B-2, of One World Trade Center (North Tower). They employed a yellow Ford Econoline Ryder rental truck filled with 1,500 pounds of explosives. The bomb was built using a mix of fuel oil and fertilizer with a nitroglycerin booster.

The conspirators were militant Islamists led by Ramzi Ahmed Yousef, who was of Kuwaiti and Pakistani descent with connections to the Al-Qaeda terrorist organization. Yousef confessed to American authorities after his capture that they had selected the World Trade Center complex because it was "an overweening symbol of American arrogance." Other participants were Mohammed Salameh, Nidal Ayyad, Mahmud Abuhalima, and, to a lesser extent, the cleric Omar Abdel-Rahman.

Beginning in January 1993, Yousef and his fellow conspirators began to locate and buy the ingredients for the bomb. They required everything from a safe place to work to storage lockers, tools, chemicals, plastic tubs, fertilizer, and lengths of rubber tubing. It took about $20,000 to build the bomb, although Yousef had wanted more money so that he could build an even bigger bomb. Most of the funds were raised in the United States, but some money came from abroad. Yousef's uncle, Khalid Sheikh Mohammed, had sent him $600 dollars for the bomb. It was Yousef's intention for the explosion to bring down the North Tower of the World Trade Center complex; its impact on the South Tower, he hoped, would bring it down also. This expectation was too high, however, as the North Tower shook in the explosion but withstood its force without major structural damage.

Despite the force of the explosion, casualties were relatively low. The bomb produced a crater 22 feet wide and five stories deep within the garage structure. The force of the explosion came close to breaching the so-called bathtub, a structure that prevented water from the Hudson River from pouring into the underground areas of the complex and into the subway system. If this breach had occurred, the resulting catastrophic loss of life would likely have eclipsed the losses from the subsequent attacks on September 11, 2001. Six people—John DiGiovanni, Bob Kirk-Patrick, Steve Knapp, Bill Backo, Wilfredo Mercado, and Monica Rodriguez-Smith—were killed in the attack, and more than 1,000 were injured.

The New York City Fire Department responded with 775 firefighters from 135 companies, but they arrived too late to do anything but tend to the wounded and carry away the dead. It took nearly 10 hours to get everyone out because the elevators shorted out in the explosion and power to the staircases failed. Evacuations took place in the dark and in the midst of heavy smoke. The tower was repaired at a cost of $510 million, and the complex reopened in less than one month. The bombing was significant in revealing how vulnerable the

World Trade Center complex was to terrorist attacks.

At first, investigators believed that a transformer had blown up, but once they began examining the site it became obvious that a large bomb had detonated. Within five hours, the Federal Bureau of Investigation (FBI) and the New York City Police Department had confirmed that the explosion had been caused by a bomb. The next question was determining responsibility for the blast. There had been 20 calls to the police claiming responsibility, but this was not unusual. At first it was believed that the deed was the work of Balkan extremists upset with U.S. policy there, but the investigation was just beginning.

Within weeks, the investigating team of 700 FBI agents had identified or arrested all of the World Trade Center bombers. What broke the case was the discovery of a unique vehicle identification number on the frame of the Ryder truck. From that number they learned that Salameh had rented the van; he had reported the van stolen, and was trying to recover the $400 deposit. Salameh was arrested while trying to collect the deposit. Investigators then turned to identification of his fellow conspirators, and Yousef was finally determined to be the leader of the plot.

By the time authorities had identified Yousef as the leader and maker of the bomb, he was already in Pakistan planning other operations. Ultimately, a Central Intelligence Agency (CIA) and FBI team captured him there, but not before he had initiated several other plots. Yousef had always been a freelancer, but there was evidence that he had connections with Al-Qaeda operatives before and after the World Trade Center bombing. Following a series of trials, the participants in the bomb plot were found guilty and received life sentences. Yousef was sentenced to 240 years in solitary confinement.

Stephen E. Atkins

See also: Mohammed, Khalid Sheikh; World Trade Center, September 11, 2001; Yousef, Ramzi Ahmed

Further Reading

Bell, J. Bowyer. *Murders on the Nile: The World Trade Center and Global Terror.* San Francisco: Encounter Books, 2003.

Caram, Peter. *The 1993 World Trade Center Bombing: Foresight and Warning.* London: Janus, 2001.

Davis, Mike. *Duda's Wagon: A Brief History of the Car Bomb.* London: Verso, 2007.

Lance, Peter. *1000 Years for Revenge: International Terrorism and the FBI, the Untold Story.* New York: Regan Books, 2003.

Reeve, Simon. *The New Jackals: Ramzi Yousef, Osama bin Laden, and the Future of Terrorism.* Boston: Northeastern University Press, 1999.

World Trade Center, September 11, 2001

On September 11, 2001, the day started normally in the World Trade Center. In the Twin Towers, the usual number of employees was 14,154. Approximately 14,000 people were present at the time the first commercial aircraft hit the North Tower. American Airlines Flight 11 crashed into the North Tower at 8:46:40 a.m. The aircraft cut a swath through eight floors—from the 93rd to the 100th—as it hit at about 450 miles an hour.

The force of the impact and the resulting fire from aviation fuel destroyed most elevators and most staircases above the 100th and below the 93rd floors. Nearly 1,000 people were trapped on the upper floors of the North Tower, the majority of whom worked for Cantor Fitzgerald brokerage company. At least 60 people jumped from the North Tower rather than burn to death. A firefighter was killed after being hit by one of the jumpers.

An emergency call went out to the Fire Department City of New York (FDNY). More than 1,000 firefighters from 225 units showed up at the World Trade Centre complex. There were so many vehicles that parking became a problem. Immediately, FDNY commanders realized that they could not extinguish the growing fire in the North Tower, so they concentrated on evacuating people. Because of lack of water, only a few firefighters were engaged in trying to put out the fire. Operators for the 911 system told people to stay put, and assured them that firefighters would be coming to rescue them. For those on the top floors of the North Tower, the

Moments before United Flight 175 hit the South Tower of the World Trade Center, on September 11, 2001. (AP Photo/Carmen Taylor)

deteriorating conditions made it imperative that help come soon. Some tried to make it to the roof, but the FDNY had decided after the 1993 World Trade Center bombing to lock the heavy doors leading to the building's sole roof exit. This decision had been made because rooftop rescues by helicopters were a safety risk.

Events at the North Tower caused concern among those in the South Tower. Many of those in the South Tower decided to evacuate the building. Those who tried to evacuate the South Tower were told to return to their offices. This was because the standard firefighting philosophy in high-rise fires was to "stay put, stand by." An announcement broadcast over the intercom at 8:55 a.m. stated that there was no need to evacuate the South Tower. This announcement directly contradicted a decision by Sergeant Al DeVona, ranking Port Authority police officer on the scene, who had ordered that both the North Tower and the South Tower be evacuated within minutes of the first crash. DeVona reordered the evacuations at 8:59 a.m. Captain Anthony Whitaker, commander of the Port Authority Police, confirmed this order shortly thereafter. Faulty communications equipment made these decisions difficult to implement. Because of the communication problems, the 911 operators could not be informed of the deteriorating situation and they continued to give outdated advice to people to stay where they were.

The difficulty in evacuating the towers was compounded by their structural defects. Decisions made during construction made it difficult for people to evacuate, there being only three staircases. Changes in building codes in 1968 had reduced both the number of staircases and the level of fire protection required for high-rise buildings. These changes allowed more rentable space, but meant that the staircases were built for only a few hundred people at a time to walk three or four stories, not for mass evacuation. The location of the three staircases in the center of the building, rather than being dispersed, turned the upper floors of both towers.

To a large extent, the World Trade Center is a disaster that could be as much a result of its fundamental design as was the *Titanic*. The plane hit the South Tower and distributed the burning fuel throughout. The temperature of the fire was such that steel was stretched throughout. The steel trusses that held the weight of the corrugated steel and the three inches of concrete that formed the floor stretched. The weight of the floor was shifted to the interior columns, all 47 of them around the elevators and stairs, but those stretched and weakened columns could not withstand such a burden. The trusses on the fire floors separated from the exterior walls, almost all of them simultaneously, and the exterior walls buckled. Since the weight of the floor was no longer sustained by the exterior wall connections and no longer held by the interior columns, the floor collapsed. But it did not collapse partially; it collapsed fully in a pancaked layer to the floor below. The floor below could not sustain the dynamic weight of a uniform falling body, and it, too, collapsed, to the next floor, and to the next, and to the next, until moving at 120 miles per hour, the building fell in 12 seconds.

The buildings were turned into death traps because the planes crashed into both structures and cut off access to the staircases. With inferior fireproofing, there was nothing to prevent the spread of the fires. The New York City building codes were not to blame because the builder, the Port

Authority of New York and New Jersey, as a regional entity was not required to follow building codes.

The Twin Towers had been able to sustain the impact of the two airliners, but the fires endangered the structures. Later reports indicated that the high temperature of the fire, caused by the ignition of the aviation fuel and intensified by the burning office furniture and paper, caused the worst damage. Another factor was that the World Trade Center complex buildings had been constructed with 37 pounds of steel per square foot, in contrast to the normal high-rise buildings of that era, which were built with 75 pounds of steel per square foot. This type of construction saved millions of dollars during construction and increased the square footage of rental space, making the buildings more profitable. Since steel begins to degrade at 300 degrees and continues to degrade by 50 percent at 1,000 degrees, the high-temperature fire, combined with the reduced amount of steel supporting the buildings, led to weakening of the structure of the buildings.

The South Tower collapsed first. United Airlines Flight 175 hit at higher speed than did American Airlines Flight 11. This higher speed and the resulting explosion and fire in the South Tower caused it to collapse in a heap.

Total deaths at the World Trade Center numbered 2,749. Of this total, 147 were passengers and crew of the two aircraft. Another 412 of the dead were rescue workers killed when the two towers collapsed. The remaining 2,190 dead succumbed either to the plane crashes or the collapse of the towers. Without the actions of key individuals and the firefighters, the casualties could have been much higher. Except in the case of those trapped in the Twin Towers above where the planes hit, there was no discernable reason for some people to have died while others survived.

Besides attacking the physical structures of the towers, the hijackers also affected the financial health of the United States. Many companies simply went out of business in New York City. Many others struggled to regain financial viability. Layoffs in the period between September 12 and January 21, 2002, related to September 11 were calculated at 1,054,653. The attack on the airline industry was an indirect financial blow in that it accounted for about 9 percent of the total gross domestic product of the United States, and because around 11 million jobs are directly related to commercial aviation.

Stephen E. Atkins

See also: Al-Quds Mosque; Atta, Mohamed el-Amir Awad el-Sayed; Bin Laden, Osama; Hamburg Cell; Pilot Training for September 11 Attacks; World Trade Center Bombing; Mohammed, Khalid Sheikh; North American Aerospace Defense Command

Further Reading

Bernstein, Richard. *Out of the Blue: The Story of September 11, 2001, from Jihad to Ground Zero*. New York: Times Books, 2002.

Dwyer, Jim. "Errors and Lack of Information in New York's Response to Sept. 11." *New York Times*, May 19, 2004, B8.

Dwyer, Jim, and Kevin Flynn. *102 Minutes: The Untold Story of the Fight to Survive Inside the Twin Towers*. New York: Times Books, 2005.

Smith, Dennis. *Report from Ground Zero: The Story of the Rescue Efforts at the World Trade Center*. New York: Viking, 2002.

Y

Yahya, Abu al-Libi

Abu Yahya al-Libi was an Islamist terrorist and high-ranking member of Al-Qaeda. International authorities also believed him to be a member of the Libyan Islamic Fighting Group. He is best known for producing a series of propaganda videos advancing the cause of Al Qaeda and other Islamist terrorist groups' activities.

Abu Yahya al-Libi was born Mohamed Hassan Qaid in 1963 in Libya. Little is known about his early life. It is believed that al-Libi went to Afghanistan in the early 1990s, where he met Osama bin Laden and became familiar with his ideological views. He then spent some years studying Islam in Mauritania, later returning to Afghanistan. During this time, he became associated with the Taliban and preached jihad against the West. After the 2001 U.S.-led invasion of Afghanistan, al-Libi was captured by North Atlantic Treaty Organization (NATO) forces in 2002. He was held in extrajudicial detention in the U.S. Bagram interim detention facility in the Parwan Province of Afghanistan. At that time, U.S. counterterrorism analysts found that al-Libi was a member of Al-Qaeda. He was reportedly the heir apparent to Osama bin Laden and reportedly served on Al-Qaeda's Shariah Committee. Al-Libi was one of several high-profile Bagram captives who escaped on the night of July 10, 2005.

On November 4, 2005, al-Libi appeared in a Ramadan video on the Arabic television station al-Arabiya. In this broadcast, he mentioned that he had escaped from the Bagram detention facility. He was then re-listed as an escapee by U.S. authorities. In October 2006, he was listed among the U.S. Department of Defense's "Most Wanted." A Terrorist Recognition Card used by NATO personnel repeated the earlier claim that he was one of the four escapees from Bagram.

After his escape, al-Libi produced a series of propaganda videos. On May 30, 2007, a 45-minute video featuring al-Libi was released. On June 22, 2008, al-Libi released a 19-minute video urging Somalis to resist United Nations (UN) forces in Somalia. Al-Libi also appeared in a July 2009 video from al-Sahab, *Swat: Victory or Martyrdom*, about the Pakistani military's campaign against Pashtun militias and jihadist groups in the Swat Valley in Pakistan. On March 12, 2011, al-Libi urged Libyans to overthrow Muammar Gaddafi's regime and establish Islamic rule. This was an attempt at expanding the terror network's attempts while capitalizing on the wave of unrest sweeping the region during the Arab Spring.

Given his international notoriety as an Islamic scholar popular for his appearances in various propaganda videos protesting Western military actions and calling for violence against NATO forces, a $1 million bounty was placed on him. The United States targeted him with a drone strike on June 4, 2012, in Mir Ali, where he was killed. On June 5, 2012, U.S. officials confirmed that Libi was among 15 militants killed the previous day when a U.S. drone fired four missiles at a compound in Mir Ali, North Waziristan. His death was later confirmed by Al-Qaeda leader Ayman al-Zawahiri in a video released in September 2012 to coincide with the anniversary of the September 11, 2001, terrorist attacks.

Jan Goldman

See also: Al-Qaeda; Counterterrorism Center; Global War on Terror; Impact of 9/11 on U.S. Foreign Policy; Unmanned Aerial Vehicles

Further Reading

Anonymous. *Terrorist Hunter: The Extraordinary Story of a Woman Who Went Undercover to Infiltrate the Radical Islamic Groups.* New York: Ecco, 2003.

IntelCenter. *Words of Abu Yahya al-Libi.* Alexandria, VA: Tempest Publishing, LLC, 2009.

White, Jonathan R. *Terrorism and Homeland Security.* Independence, KY. Cengage Learning, 2013.

Yemen Hotel Bombings

(December 29, 1992)

The bombing of two hotels in Aden, Yemen, on December 29, 1992, attributed to the terrorist organization Al-Qaeda in Yemen. Long before the events of September 11, 2001, the Al-Qaeda group centered in Afghanistan and Pakistan was well known to intelligence experts. It carried out or was linked to a number of attacks on Western interests, including the bombings of the World Trade Center in February 1993, the U.S. embassies in East Africa in August 1998, and USS *Cole* in Yemen in October 2000. Al-Qaeda in Yemen, a separate organization, has also been active within that country. One of its least-known and earliest plots unfolded in December 1992, aimed at Western hotels in Yemen.

The hotel bombings came at the end of a year that had witnessed considerable terrorist activity in the country. In April, the Yemeni justice minister was seriously wounded by a gunman while driving in the capital city, Sana'a. In June, the brother of Yemeni prime minister Haydar Abu Bakr al-Attas was assassinated in the city of Mukalla. In a separate incident the same month, an adviser to the minister of defense was killed by unknown assailants. Throughout the spring and summer of 1992, several top officers in the Yemeni military were also assassinated or mysteriously killed. That August and September, bombs went off at homes and offices of leading Yemeni government officials.

Westerners were also targeted in the terror spree. In September and again in November 1992, small bombs detonated near the U.S. embassy, while another exploded just outside the German embassy in October. Yemeni officials released little information on the incidents to the world press, just as other countries such as Egypt and Saudi Arabia had not readily admitted opposition activity. Members of the Yemeni Islamic Jihad were eventually arrested for some of the attacks. The larger attacks came on December 29, 1992, when bombs went off at two major hotels in the city of Aden. One exploded at the Gold Mohur Hotel, frequented by foreigners. A second bomb went off in the parking lot of the Aden Movenpick Hotel, adjacent to where U.S. military personnel were staying en route to assist with relief operations in Somalia. It is believed that the attacks were in protest of American soldiers being billeted in Yemen and the perceived Westernization of Aden, a major international port and the economic capital of the country. Two people—an Austrian tourist and a Yemeni hotel worker—died in the first attack. Several dozen were wounded, including two suspected terrorists involved in the second attack. They turned out to be Yemenis trained in Afghanistan, where Al-Qaeda had camps for an international network of operatives. There were no casualties from the second bombing. In response to the incidents, U.S. forces stationed in Aden were withdrawn by December 31.

Six men were eventually arrested in connection with the bombings, but all managed to escape from jail in July 1993. This development led to allegations that Yemeni government officials had connections to the terrorists and had aided in their escape. Two of the terrorist bombers involved in the hotel bombings later took part in other terrorist plots, including the attack on USS *Cole* that killed 17 U.S. sailors.

Arne Kislenko

See also: Al-Qaeda; Bin Laden, Osama; USS *Cole* Bombing; Terrorism; World Trade Center Bombing

Further Reading

Rotberg, Robert I. *Battling Terrorism in the Horn of Africa.* Washington, DC: Brookings Institution Press, 2005.

Shai, Shaul. *The Red Sea Terror Triangle: Sudan, Somalia, Yemen, and Islamic Terror.* New Brunswick, NJ: Transaction Publishers, 2005.

West, Deborah L. *Combating Terrorism in the Horn of Africa and Yemen.* Cambridge, MA: World Peace Foundation, 2005.

Yousef, Ramzi Ahmed

Ramzi Ahmed Yousef, the mastermind of the February 26, 1993, World Trade Center bombing, was born Abd al-Basit Mahmud Abd al-Karim on April 27, 1968, in Fuhayil, Kuwait, the son of a middle-class engineer. He was raised in a strict Wahhabist environment. His uncle Khalid Sheikh Mohammed was a major figure in the September 11, 2001, terror attacks. In 1986, Yousef went to Great Britain to study English and engineering; from there he went to Afghanistan in 1988, ostensibly to help fight with the mujahideen against Soviet forces. Instead, he spent most of his time in Peshawar, the site of an Al-Qaeda training camp. He attended a university in Afghanistan and became a member of a local Muslim Brotherhood cell. Yousef went to Kuwait, probably in late 1989, and took a job with the Kuwaiti government. But Iraq's invasion of Kuwait in August 1990 forced him to leave the country, and he subsequently settled in Quetta, Pakistan.

Sometime soon after he relocated to Pakistan, Yousef decided to focus his efforts on waging jihad against the West. Despite his father's strict Wahhabism, he was not very religious. He was, however, upset over the plight of the Palestinians. In 1990–1991, Yousef attended another Al-Qaeda training camp and began to plot terrorist acts against Israel. Realizing that pulling off a successful terrorist assault in Israel would be very difficult, he instead turned his sights on the United States. His first target was to be the New York World Trade Center, which he hoped to destroy with a massive truck bomb.

In early 1992, Yousef traveled to the United States. Lacking a proper visa, he filed for religious asylum with the Immigration and Naturalization Service (INS). When his request was denied, he was briefly arrested but then released on his own recognizance. His INS hearing was scheduled for December 1992, but he never appeared. Although he was then in the United States illegally, no efforts were made to track him down.

Within days, Yousef became associated with other extremist Muslims in New York's al-Kifah Refugee Center in Brooklyn. There, according to the Federal Bureau of Investigation (FBI), he came under the influence of Sheikh Omar Abdel-Rahman, who was preaching in Brooklyn and was alleged to have been planning terrorist attacks in the United States. While at the Refugee Center, Yousef recruited likeminded militants, including Mahmud Abu Abouhalima, his chief co-conspirator, to help him plan and execute the bombing of the World Trade Center, with the goal of destroying the complex and killing as many as 250,000 Americans.

Yousef was unable, however, to finance a bomb that would cause the damage he sought, so he settled on a 1,500-pound bomb hidden in a rented van, which would be driven into an underground parking garage and detonated. His accomplices were successful in getting the explosives-laden truck into the garage, and it detonated on the morning of February 26, 1993. The attack killed 6 people, wounded more than 1,000 others, and caused $510 million in damage.

When the bomb went off, Yousef had already fled the United States for Pakistan. Once there, he began to plot more attacks, including flying bomb-laden planes into the Pentagon and other U.S. government buildings. Allegedly, his uncle Khalid Sheikh Mohammed met with Al-Qaeda leader Osama bin Laden in 1996 and detailed his nephew's plans to him. Meanwhile, Yousef helped carry out terror attacks in Pakistan, Iran, and Thailand. Sometime in 1994, Yousef moved to the Philippines, where he hatched plots to assassinate Pope John Paul II and U.S. president Bill Clinton (both of which were part of the so-called Operation Bojinka).

An ingenious bomb maker, Yousef attempted—and almost succeeded in—blowing up several jetliners, including an American aircraft, in 1994 and 1995. After Filipino intelligence uncovered the Bojinka plot, Yousef fled the country and returned to Pakistan. In his hasty departure, he left behind a computer, which Filipino authorities used to link him to various terrorist attacks. That also led them to detain one of Yousef's lieutenants, who later detailed his chief's involvement in the 1993 World Trade Center bombing.

In February 1995, Yousef was arrested in a hotel in Islamabad. The Pakistani government immediately turned him over to U.S. authorities, who extradited him to the United States. Yousef was tried twice: once for his attempts to blow up American jetliners and once for his role in the World Trade Center bombing. In September 1996, he was found guilty in the jetliner conspiracy and was sentenced to life in prison without the possibility of parole. In February 1997, he was convicted on all counts for his involvement in the World Trade Center bombing. A judge sentenced him to 247 years in prison and a $4.5 million fine and also placed strict limits on his prison visits.

There has been much speculation about how much direct involvement Yousef had with Al-Qaeda. The best guess is that he operated largely on his own, and although he had more than coincidental connections to Al-Qaeda, it seems unlikely that he received funding from the organization.

Edward F. Mickolus and
Paul G. Pierpaoli, Jr.

See also: Al-Qaeda; Bin Laden, Osama; Mohammed, Khalid Sheikh; World Trade Center Bombing

Further Reading

Boyer Bell, J. *Murders on the Nile: The World Trade Center and Global Terror*. San Francisco: Encounter Books, 2003.

Reeve, Simon. *The New Jackals: Ramzi Yousef, Osama bin Laden and the Future of Terrorism*. Boston: Northeastern University Press, 1999.

Z

Zammar, Muhammad Heydar

Muhammad Heydar Zammar was an Al-Qaeda operative who recruited the key leader of the September 11 conspiracy. In the late 1990s, he was able to convince the members of the Hamburg Cell to train in Afghanistan rather than travel to Chechnya to fight with the Chechen rebels. Once they returned from the training camps, Zammar kept track of them for Al-Qaeda.

Zammar had extensive experience as a fighter for Islamist causes. He was born in 1961 in Aleppo, Syria. At age 10, he moved with his family to West Germany. After high school, he attended a metal-working vocational school, and his goal was to work for Mercedes-Benz. Zammar traveled to Saudi Arabia, where he worked for a time as a translator. After returning to Germany, he found a job as a truck driver in Hamburg. His strong religious views led him to abandon truck driving in 1991 and travel to Afghanistan, where he underwent Al-Qaeda training. Upon returning to Germany, Zammar spent all of his time as a freelance mechanic and traveled around Europe and the Middle East. He volunteered to fight in Bosnia in 1995. After leaving Bosnia in 1996, Zammar visited Afghanistan, where Osama bin Laden invited him to join Al-Qaeda.

On his return to Hamburg, Germany, Zammar became a full-time recruiter for Al-Qaeda, sustaining his wife and six children on welfare payments. He traveled around Germany making speeches praising bin Laden and other jihadist leaders. His association with the Muslim missionary organization Tabligh afforded him some cover, but German police began watching him.

It was at the al-Quds mosque that Zammar came into contact with the members of what would subsequently become the Hamburg Cell. He first met and became friends with Mohamed Atta in 1998. He persuaded Atta, Marwan al-Shehhi, Ramzi bin al-Shibh, and Ziad Jarrah to train at Al-Qaeda camps in Afghanistan for important missions. Zammar continued as the Al-Qaeda contact person for the Hamburg Cell until its key leaders left for the United States.

Zammar continued to act as an Al-Qaeda recruiter until his arrest. Many other Muslims in Germany were willing recruits for Al-Qaeda, and Zammar was Al-Qaeda's principal contact in Germany. German authorities left him alone, but they watched his activities with interest. American intelligence was also displaying concern about Zammar's connections with Al-Qaeda. In July 2001, Zammar was briefly detained in Jordan but was released after a short interrogation. After September 11, German police questioned Zammar, but released him because they believed they had too little evidence to charge him with a crime.

On October 27, 2001, Zammar traveled to Morocco to divorce his second wife;

while there, he was arrested by Moroccan security forces. The Moroccans sent Zammar to Syria, where he has undergone extensive interrogation at the notorious Far Falastin Detention Center in Damascus. Zammar remains in Syrian custody, but American officials have learned much about the September 11 plot from him through answers to questions sent through the Syrians. There is evidence that Zammar has undergone torture at the hands of the Syrians, and this has led international organizations to protest. Regardless of how he is treated by the Syrians, Zammar knew the central players in the September 11 attack and had a general knowledge of the plot, and so he has proven to be a valuable resource. In June 2007, the UN Working Group on Arbitrary Detention stated that Muhammad Haydar Zammar was detained arbitrarily and called upon the Syrian authorities to "remedy the situation." His exact whereabouts remain unknown.

Stephen E. Atkins

See also: Al-Qaeda; al-Quds Mosque; Atta, Mohamed el-Amir Awad el-Sayed; Hamburg Cell

Further Reading

Finn, Peter. "Al Qaeda Recruiter Reportedly Tortured." *Washington Post*, January 31, 2003.

Finn, Peter. "German at Center of Sept. 11 Inquiry." *Washington Post*, June 12, 2002.

McDermott, Terry. *Perfect Soldiers: The 9/11 Hijackers: Who They Were, Why They Did It*. New York: HarperCollins, 2005.

Zawahiri, Ayman al-

Prior to 2011, Ayman al-Zawahiri was the second most important leader of Al-Qaeda, behind Osama bin Laden. As the former leader of the Egyptian terrorism group Islamic Jihad (EIJ), he had considerable influence over bin Laden. Al-Zawahiri merged his group into Al-Qaeda in the late 1990s, making his contingent of Egyptians influential in the operations of Al-Qaeda.

Al-Zawahiri came from a prominent Egyptian family of medical doctors and religious leaders. He was born on June 9, 1951, in al-Sharqiyah, Egypt. Both sides of his family have roots going back to Saudi Arabia, and his mother's family claims descent from the Prophet Muhammad. His father was a professor at Cairo University's medical school. At an early age, al-Zawahiri joined the Muslim Brotherhood; he was first arrested by the Egyptian police in 1966, at the age of 15. After studying medicine at the Cairo University, al-Zawahiri qualified as a physician in

Ayman al-Zawahiri, an Egyptian linked to the Al-Qaeda network in Afghanistan. This photo was taken two months after the attacks on September 11, 2001. (Reuters/Corbis)

1974 and then received a master's degree in surgical medicine in 1978.

Al-Zawahiri left medicine to engage in political agitation against the Egyptian government of President Anwar Sadat. Inspiring his conversion to Islamic militancy were the writings of Sayyid Qutb, the ideological and spiritual leader of the Muslim Brotherhood. He was shocked by Qutb's execution in 1965 by the Nasser regime—enough that he considered forming a clandestine Islamist group. While still in medical school, al-Zawahiri was instrumental in founding the terrorist group Islamic Jihad in 1973. This group's mission was to direct armed struggle against the Egyptian state. It did not take the Egyptian government long to ban the activities of the EIJ.

In the aftermath of the 1981 assassination of Sadat, Egyptian authorities arrested al-Zawahiri. He had learned of the plot against Sadat only a few hours before it went into operation. He had advised against proceeding because the plot was premature and destined to fail. Al-Zawahiri has claimed that prison authorities treated him brutally. After being tried and acquitted for his role in the assassination plot, al-Zawahiri served a three-year prison sentence for illegal possession of arms. His stay in prison only increased his militancy. It was in prison that al-Zawahiri and Sheikh Omar Abdel-Rahman shared their views. Under torture, al-Zawahiri assisted the police in capturing some of his associates in the Islamic Jihad.

After his release from prison, al-Zawahiri resumed his antigovernment activities. In 1984, he assumed the leadership of EIJ after its former head, Lieutenant Colonel Abbud al-Zumar, was arrested by the Egyptian police. Al-Zawahiri fled Egypt for Jeddah, Saudi Arabia, in 1985 in the middle of President Hosni Mubarak's purge of Egyptian dissidents. There he worked in a medical dispensary. Al-Zawahiri first met bin Laden in Jeddah in 1986. The ongoing war against the Soviets in Afghanistan attracted al-Zawahiri, and he decided to move to Pakistan.

Soon after arriving in Pakistan, al-Zawahiri started coordinating plans between EIJ and the Afghan Arabs fighting against Soviet forces in Afghanistan. He served as the chief advisor to bin Laden in the creation of the Al-Qaeda network in 1988. Al-Zawahiri also engaged in a campaign to undermine bin Laden's relationship with Abdullah Azzam. Azzam's assassination benefited al-Zawahiri, but there is no concrete evidence that he played any role in it. The Pakistani security service concluded that six associates of al-Zawahiri carried out the assassination.

For the next several years in the early 1990s, al-Zawahiri played a dual role as a member of Al-Qaeda and a leader of the EIJ. Al-Zawahiri left Pakistan and moved to Sudan with bin Laden in 1992. His closeness to Egypt allowed him to plot against the Egyptian government of President Mubarak. Al-Zawahiri's goal from the beginning was the overthrow of the Egyptian government and its replacement with an Islamic state. As head of the EIJ, he planned the unsuccessful assassination attempt against Mubarak during his visit to Addis Ababa on June 25, 1995. This failure led the Sudanese government to expel him and his followers from Sudan.

His activities for Al-Qaeda kept him traveling around the world. Bin Laden sent al-Zawahiri to Somalia to aid the opposition to American intervention there. Then he was active in building support for the Bosnian Muslims in their separatist war against Yugoslavia. Next, he coordinated aid for Albanian Muslims in the Kosovo War. Finally, al-Zawahiri received the assignment to set up terrorist operations in Europe and the United States. He visited the United States in 1996 to inspect sites for possible terrorist operations there. His conclusion was that major terrorist activities could be undertaken against American targets in the United States.

Al-Zawahiri returned to Afghanistan to join bin Laden. He decided to merge EIJ into Al-Qaeda in 1998 for a combination of political, financial, and operational reasons. In 1997, al-Zawahiri had been implicated in his group's participation in the terrorist massacre of 58 European tourists and four Egyptian security guards at Luxor, Egypt. This terrorist act was so brutal that it caused a backlash both in Egyptian public opinion and among the leadership of the EIJ. It led to a schism within its leadership, with a significant number of the leaders concluding a cease-fire with the Egyptian government. Al-Zawahiri opposed the cease-fire with what he considered to be an apostate government. He led a much-weakened EIJ into an alliance with Al-Qaeda.

Al-Zawahiri's influence over bin Laden had grown over the years. Bin Laden was neither as intellectual nor as militant as al-Zawahiri. Al-Zawahiri's views were expressed in the tract *Knights under the Prophet's Banner*. In this work al-Zawahiri justified the use of violence as the only way to match the brute military force of the West led by the United States. For this reason it is necessary to target American targets, the tract posits, and the most effective way to do this is by the use of human bombs. The proposed strategy is to inflict enough damage to the United States that its citizens will demand that their govern-

ment change policies toward Israel and the Arab world. This treatise was written before the September 11 attacks, but such attacks were obviously in its author's mind.

In his position as number two in Al-Qaeda, al-Zawahiri served as the chief advisor to bin Laden. Because of his more radical religious views, al-Zawahiri pushed bin Laden toward more radical positions. Al-Zawahiri was aware of the September 11 plot from the beginning but stayed in the background. The subsequent loss of Afghanistan as a staging area for Al-Qaeda made al-Zawahiri go into hiding along with bin Laden. Although the two kept in contact, they stayed in separate areas to avoid the possibility of Al-Qaeda's chief leaders being wiped out in a single attack by the Americans and their allies. On August 1, 2008, CBS News speculated that al-Zawahiri may have been seriously injured or even killed during a July 28 missile strike on a village in South Waziristan. This conjecture was based on an intercepted letter dated July 29 that urgently called for a doctor to treat al-Zawahiri. On August 2, however, senior Taliban commander Maulvi Omar dismissed the report as false.

Al-Zawahiri assumed the leadership of Al-Qaeda following the 2011 killing of bin Laden in Abbottabad, Pakistan. In June 2013, al-Zawahiri argued against the merger of the Islamic State of Iraq with the Syrian-based Jabhat al-Nusra into Islamic State of Iraq and the Levant as was declared in April by Abu Bakr al-Baghdadi. The U.S. State Department has offered a $25 million reward for information leading to al-Zawahiri's apprehension. He is under worldwide sanctions by the United Nations Security Council 1267 Committee as a member or affiliate of Al-Qaeda.

Stephen E. Atkins

See also: Al-Qaeda; Atta, Mohamed el-Amir Awad el-Sayed; Bin Laden, Osama; Mohammed, Khalid Sheikh

Further Reading

Atwan, Abdel Bari. *The Secret History of Al Qaeda*. Berkeley: University of California Press, 2006.

Boyer Bell, J. *Murders on the Nile: The World Trade Center and Global Terror*. San Francisco: Encounter Books, 2003.

Kepel, Gilles. *The War for Muslim Minds: Islam and the West*. Cambridge, MA: Belknap Press, 2004.

Wright, Lawrence. *The Looming Tower: Al-Qaeda and the Road to 9/11*. New York: Knopf, 2006.

Zinni, Anthony Charles

(September 17, 1943–)

U.S. Marine Corps general, commander of U.S. Central Command (CENTCOM), and special envoy for the United States to Israel and the Palestinian National Authority (PNA), Anthony Charles Zinni was born to Italian immigrant parents in Philadelphia, Pennsylvania, on September 17, 1943. In 1965, he graduated from Villanova University with a degree in economics and was commissioned in the U.S. Marine Corps. In 1967, he served in Vietnam as an infantry battalion adviser to a South Vietnamese marine unit. In 1970, he returned to Vietnam as an infantry company commander. He was seriously wounded that November and was medically evacuated. Thereafter Zinni held a variety of command, administrative, and teaching positions, including at the Marine Corps Command and Staff College at Quantico, Virginia.

In 1991, as a brigadier general, Zinni was the chief of staff and deputy commanding general of the Combined Joint Task Force (CJTF) for Operation Provide Comfort, the Kurdish relief effort in Turkey and Iraq. In 1992–1993, he was the director of operations for Operation Restore Hope in Somalia. As a lieutenant general, he commanded the I Marine Expeditionary Force (I MEF) from 1994 to 1996. In September 1996, as a full general, he became deputy commanding general of the CENTCOM, the U.S. military combatant command responsible for most of the Middle East. He served as commanding general of CENTCOM from August 1997 until his retirement from the military in September 2000.

Upon leaving the military, Zinni participated in a number of different diplomatic initiatives. In late 2001, at the request of his old friend Colin L. Powell, then secretary of state, Zinni became the special envoy for the United States to Israel and the PNA.

Zinni arrived in Israel on November 25, 2001. He conducted several negotiating sessions with Prime Minister Ariel Sharon and PNA president Yasser Arafat individually but never with the two together. On December 12, the Palestinian suicide bombing of a bus near the settlement of Emmanuel effectively cut off all dialogue between the two sides. Zinni returned to the United States on December 17.

Zinni made his second short trip to the region during January 3–7, 2002. While he was conducting a meeting with Arafat, the Israelis intercepted and captured an illegal Palestinian arms ship in the Red Sea. The *Karine A* was carrying some 50 tons of weapons ordered by the PNA from Iran, a direct violation of the Oslo Accords.

Zinni returned to the region for the last time on March 12, 2002. While he believed that he was starting to make some headway, on March 27, a Palestinian suicide bomber struck a Passover Seder being held at an Israeli hotel. The Israelis launched a massive military retaliation against the Palestinians and severed all ties with Arafat. Zinni departed the region on April 15.

Although Zinni resigned his position as a special envoy, he continued to serve as an unofficial consultant. On August 5, 2003, he spent several hours in Washington, D.C., briefing Major General David T. Zabecki, incoming senior security adviser of the newly established U.S. Coordinating and Monitoring Mission. In an address Zinni gave at Harvard's Kennedy School of Government on December 8, 2004, he stressed that resuming the peace process between Israel and the Palestinians was the single most important step the United States could take to restore its stature in the world. But interestingly enough, he noted that it would be a mistake to assign more high-profile special envoys to the mission. He favored the presence of professional negotiators. Following his retirement from the military, Zinni held visiting appointments at several U.S. universities and in May 2005, he became the president of international operations for M.C.I. Industries, Inc.

An initial supporter of the George W. Bush administration and its foreign policy, Zinni quickly became one of the highest-profile military critics of the war in Iraq after he retired from CENTCOM. Distinguishing Afghanistan from Iraq, Zinni continued to believe that the invasion of Afghanistan to oust the Taliban regime and deprive Al-Qaeda of its operating base was the right thing to do. Iraq was a totally different case. Although Saddam Hussein was a regional nuisance, Zinni believed his regime was totally contained and was no real strategic threat. Zinni was also certain that the case for weapons of mass destruction (WMDs) was vastly overstated, remembering well the intelligence picture he had monitored daily while at CENTCOM.

While Zinni was still at CENTCOM in early 1999 immediately following the air strikes of Operation Desert Fox, intelligence indicators and diplomatic reporting painted a picture of Hussein's regime as badly shaken and destabilized. In anticipation of the possible requirement for CENTCOM to have to lead an occupation of Iraq should Hussein fall, Zinni ordered the preparation of a comprehensive operations plan (OPLAN). Code-named Desert Crossing, it called for a robust civilian occupation authority with offices in each of Iraq's 18 provinces. The Desert Crossing plan was a dramatic contrast to what eventually played out under the anemic Coalition Provisional Authority, which for almost the first year of its existence had very little presence outside Baghdad.

During the run-up to the invasion of Iraq, Zinni became increasingly concerned about the quality of the planning, especially the post-hostilities phase. Queries to old contacts still at CENTCOM confirmed that OPLAN Desert Crossing had all but been forgotten. Zinni came to believe that the United States was being plunged headlong into an unnecessary war by political ideologues who had no understanding of the region. True to the promise he made to himself when he was wounded in Vietnam, Zinni became one of the first senior American figures to speak out against what he saw as "lack of planning, underestimating the task, and buying into a flawed strategy." Zinni soon found himself one of the most influential critics of the Bush administration's handling of the war in Iraq. In 2008, Zinni joined the teaching faculty at Duke University's Sanford Institute of Public Policy.

David T. Zabecki

See also: Arab-Israeli Conflict, Overview; Bush Administration; Iraqi Freedom, Operation

Further Reading

Clancy, Tom, with Anthony Zinni and Tony Kolz. *Battle Ready.* New York: Putnam, 2004.

Leverett, Flynt, ed. *The Road Ahead: Middle East Policy in the Bush Administration's Second Term.* Washington, DC: Brookings Institution, 2005.

Zinni, Anthony, and Tony Koltz. *The Battle for Peace: A Frontline Vision of America's Power and Purpose.* London: Palgrave, Macmillan, 2006.

Zubaydah, Abu

Abu Zubaydah was Al-Qaeda's chief of operations and number three in its hierarchy until his capture in March 2002. His position put him in charge of the Al-Qaeda training camps that selected the personnel for the September 11 plot. Zubaydah was originally a member of Ayman al-Zawahiri's Egyptian Islamic Jihad (EIJ), but with al-Zawahiri he made the transition from that group to Al-Qaeda in 1996.

Zubaydah has engaged in extremist Islamist activities since his youth. He was born on March 12, 1971, in Saudi Arabia. His original name was Zayn al-Abidin Mohamed Husayn, but he adopted the name Zubaydah early in his career as a radical Islamist. Although born a Saudi, he grew up among the Palestinians in a refugee camp in the Gaza Strip of Palestine. His first political association was with Hamas. Al-Zawahiri recruited him from Hamas to the EIJ. When al-Zawahiri moved to Pakistan, Zubaydah went with him. As a teenager, he fought with the Afghan Arabs in military operations against the Soviets. In one of these engagements in Afghanistan, Zubaydah lost an eye. His abilities allowed him to move up in the hierarchy of Al-Qaeda until he became Al-Qaeda's chief of operations.

As chief of operations, Zubaydah played a role in all of Al-Qaeda's military operations. Zubaydah selected Mohamed Atta for an important future martyrdom mission while Atta was in training at Khaldan camp in 1998. He was also active in planning the failed millennium plots in Jordan and the United States. After the failed plots in Jordan and the United States, he became field commander for the attack on the USS *Cole* on October 12, 2000. Khalid Sheikh Mohammed was the operational chief for the September 11 attacks, but Zubaydah participated in the final draft of the plan and was also active in post–September 11 plots. American authorities decided that Zubaydah was important enough to either capture or eliminate. What made Zubaydah important in Al-Qaeda was his role in keeping all members' files and in assigning individuals to specific tasks and operations.

In a joint operation, Pakistani security personnel, American special forces, and a Federal Bureau of Investigation (FBI) special weapons and tactics (SWAT) unit arrested Zubaydah in a suburb of Faisalabad, a town in western Pakistan, on March 28, 2002. From intercepted Al-Qaeda communications, the National Security Agency (NSA) learned that Zubaydah might be at a two-story house owned by a leader of the Pakistani militant extremist group Lashkar-e-Taiba (LeT). In the subsequent assault 35 Pakistanis and 27 Muslims from other countries were arrested. Among the captured was Zubaydah. He had been seriously wounded, with gunshots to the stomach, groin, and thigh. A medical unit determined that

Zubaydah would survive, and he was taken into American custody.

Zubaydah has been held in American custody at various locations since his capture. The Americans decided to interrogate him by pretending to employ Saudis as interrogators. Instead of being frightened, Zubaydah asked his phony "Saudi" interrogators to contact a senior member of the Saudi royal family—Prince Ahmed bin Salman bin Abdul-Aziz—who would save him from the Americans. This claim stunned the interrogators. They returned later to confront him for lying. Zubaydah instead gave more details about agreements between Al-Qaeda and high-level Pakistani and Saudi government leaders. He went so far as to indicate that certain Pakistani and Saudi leaders knew about September 11 before the attack occurred. According to him, these officials did not have the details and did not want them, but they knew the general outlines of the plot. After Zubaydah learned that the "Saudi" interrogators were really Americans, he tried to commit suicide. This attempt failed, and Zubaydah no longer volunteered information and denied what he had said earlier.

American investigators quizzed the Saudi government about Zubaydah's comments. Representatives of the Saudi government called his information false and malicious. In a series of strange coincidences, three of the Saudis named by Zubaydah died in a series of incidents in the months after the inquiries—Prince Ahmed died of a heart attack at age 41, Prince Sultan bin Faisal bin Turki al-Said died in an automobile accident, and Prince Fahd bin Turki bin Saud al-Kabir died of thirst while traveling in the Saudi summer at the age of 25. The supposed Pakistani contact, Air Marshal Ali Mir, was killed in an airplane crash on February 20, 2003, with his wife and 15 senior officers.

Zubaydah remains in American custody, his eventual fate unknown. Because American interrogators tricked him into talking, he has refused to provide further information about Al-Qaeda or the September 11 plot. In September 2006, he was transferred to the Guantánamo Bay Detainment Camp. In 2006, Ron Suskind published the book *One Percent Doctrine*, which claimed that Zubaydah was not nearly so important in Al-Qaeda as had been thought. Suskind claimed that Zubaydah was mentally ill and was only a minor figure in Al-Qaeda. Suskind's assertions have been countered by numerous others, including former Al-Qaeda operatives. Regardless of the controversy, Zubaydah appeared before a Combatant Status Review Tribunal in Guantánamo on March 27, 2007. There, he downplayed his role in Al-Qaeda but still claimed some authority.

Zubaydah has also become part of another controversy because he was extensively tortured by Central Intelligence Agency (CIA) operatives. A May 30, 2005, CIA memorandum states that Zubaydah was subjected to waterboarding 83 times. A report completed by the International Committee of the Red Cross (ICRC) in February 2007 and released to the public on April 7, 2009, found that Zubaydah had been subjected to 11 other forms of torture in addition to waterboarding. These included sleep deprivation, confinement in a small box, food deprivation, and exposure to extreme cold. Videotapes showing the interrogation and torture of Zubaydah and another detainee, however, were destroyed by the CIA in November 2005.

In September 2009, in a statement filed at Zubaydah's hearing for the reinstatement of habeas corpus protections, the U.S. government changed its position, claiming it no longer believed Zubaydah was a member of Al-Qaeda or had played any role in the African embassy bombings or the September 11 attacks. Despite this, in 2014, Zubaydah remained in U.S. custody.

Stephen E. Atkins

See also: Al-Qaeda; Coercive Interrogation Techniques; Dar es Salaam, U.S. Embassy Bombing; Guantánamo Bay Detainment Camp; Nairobi, Kenya, Bombing of U.S. Embassy; Zawahiri, Ayman al-

Further Reading

Corbin, Jane. *Al-Qaeda: The Terror Network That Threatens the World.* New York: Thunder's Mouth, 2002.

Posner, Gerald. *Why America Slept: The Failure to Prevent 9/11.* New York: Ballantine Books, 2003.

Suskind, Ron. *One Percent Doctrine.* New York: Simon and Schuster, 2006.

Timeline: Events, Actions, and Decisions Related to the United States and Terrorism

1787: The inability of America under the Articles of Confederation to deal with the North African pirates is one of the factors leading to the Constitutional Convention in Philadelphia.

1794: March 27, Congress establishes the U.S. Navy with a bill authorizing the construction of six frigates to provide protection to American merchant shipping from the North African pirates.

1795–1797: Algiers, Tripoli, and Tunis sign treaties to cease piracy in their coastal waters.

1801: May 10, U.S. president Thomas Jefferson dispatches a naval squadron of three frigates and a schooner under the command of Commodore Richard Dale.

1803: October 31, the U.S. frigate *Philadelphia* runs aground near Tripoli while pursuing a Tripolitan ship and is captured with its crew by gunboats sent out from Tripoli. The Tripolitans begin work to convert the *Philadelphia* for their use as a warship.

1815: July 5, In the Barbary War of 1815, Captain Stephen Decatur, Jr., sails to Algiers with a powerful squadron and captures two Algerine warships before that state learns of the U.S. Navy presence, and speedily concludes a peace treaty with Algiers.

1920: September 16, in New York City, a TNT bomb planted in an unattended horse-drawn wagon explodes on Wall Street opposite House of Morgan, killing 35 people and injuring hundreds more. Bolshevist or anarchist terrorists believed responsible.

1945–1949: Emergence of a bipolar Cold War pitting the United States and its allies against the Soviet Union and its allies. Meanwhile, there is growing dependence among Western nations on Middle Eastern oil.

1948: May 14, Israel declares its independence and is immediately recognized by the United States and the Soviet Union. The declaration immediately brings invasions by neighboring Arab states, initiating the First Arab-Israeli War (1948–1949), also known as the Israeli War of Independence.

1950: September 30, U.S. president Harry Truman signs National Security Council Report 68 (NSC-68), formally committing the United States to a policy of containing communism wherever it might threaten throughout the world. The global commitment of the containment policy ensures that the Middle East will be drawn into the Cold War maneuvering between the superpowers as each side attempts to expand its influence in the region.

1958: July 14, a coup in Iraq supported by Egypt and Syria overthrows the pro-Western Iraqi monarchy.

1972: September 5, the Black September terrorist group massacres members of the Israeli Olympic team in Munich. Israel then launches a major manhunt for the assassins.

1975: January 24, in New York City a bomb set off in historic Fraunces Tavern killed 4 and injured more than 50 people. A Puerto Rican nationalist group (FALN) claimed responsibility.

1976: June 27, Entebbe hostage crisis occurs in Uganda; **September 10,** TWA hijacking occurs in the United States.

1978: October 25, President Jimmy Carter signs the Foreign Intelligence Surveillance Act, which allows investigations of foreign persons who are engaged in espionage or international terrorism.

1978: March 16, Moro (Aldo) kidnapping and assassination occurs in Italy.

1979: January 16, Mohammad Reza Shah Pahlavi of Iran, a staunch ally of the United States, bows to increased internal opposition to his pro-U.S. stance, uneven reforms, and considerable corruption and leaves Iran; **March 26,** Egyptian-Israeli Peace Treaty signed in Washington, D.C.; **November 4,** Iranian students, with the support of Ayatollah Ruhollah Khomeini, seize the U.S. embassy in Teheran, taking the 52 Americans there hostage and holding them for 444 days; **December 24,** having provided major military support to several Afghan regimes but now seeing the communist regime there threatened and acting under the Brezhnev Doctrine (to defend communism wherever it is established in power), the Soviet Union invades Afghanistan and occupies it, employing as many as 115,000 troops and providing considerable military and economic aid to the Afghan regime. Osama bin Laden, from a prominent wealthy family in Saudi Arabia, travels to Afghanistan to assist the resistance to the Soviets, now known as the mujahideen. Extensive but classified U.S. assistance to the resistance also comes in the form of training and equipping Afghan rebels in Pakistan.

1980: April 24, President Jimmy Carter orders Operation Eagle Claw, an attempt to rescue the embassy hostages in Iran. The mission fails when eight U.S. military personnel are killed and four are wounded when aircraft collide at the Desert One landing site.

1981: January 20, following protracted negotiations, Iran frees the U.S. embassy hostages only minutes after Ronald Reagan is sworn in as U.S. president.

1982–1991: In Lebanon, 30 U.S. and other Western hostages are kidnapped by Hezbollah. Some are killed, some die in captivity, and some are eventually released. Terry Anderson is held for 2,454 days.

1982: February 1, the U.S. government removes Iraq from its list of terrorist nations; **September 14,** Bashir Gemayel assassination occurs in Lebanon.

1983: Israel invades Lebanon to subdue terrorist attacks on northern Israel from Lebanon; **April 18,** U.S. embassy (Beirut) suicide bombing in Lebanon kills 63 people, including 17 Americans. The Islamic Jihad claims responsibility; **October 23,** a suicide truck bomber attacks the poorly defended U.S. Marine Corps barracks at Beirut airport, killing 241 marines and wounding more than 100. President Ronald Reagan soon withdraws U.S. military forces from Lebanon; **December 3,** in Beirut, Lebanon, a Kuwait Airways Flight 221, from Kuwait to Pakistan, is hijacked and diverted to Tehran. Two Americans are killed; **December 12,** in Kuwait City, Kuwait, Shiite truck bombers attack the U.S. embassy and other targets, killing 5 and injuring 80; **December 17,** Harrods Department Store bombing occurs in the United Kingdom.

1984: September 20, a truck bomb explodes outside the U.S. embassy annex northeast of Beirut, Lebanon, killing 24 people, including 2 U.S. military personnel; **October 31,** Indira Gandhi assassination occurs in India.

1985: April 12, in Madrid, Spain, a bombing at a restaurant frequented by U.S. soldiers kills 18 Spaniards and injures 82; **June 14,** in Beirut, Lebanon, TWA Flight 847 en route from Athens to Rome is hijacked to Beirut by Hezbollah terrorists and held for 17 days. A U.S. Navy diver is executed; **October 7,** in the Mediterranean Sea, gunmen attack an Italian cruise ship, the *Achille Lauro*. One U.S. tourist is killed. The hijacking is linked to Libya; **December 18,** in Rome, Italy, and Vienna, Austria, airports are bombed, killing 20 people, 5 of whom are Americans. The bombing is linked to Libya.

1986: January 17, the Ronald Reagan administration authorizes shipment of 4,000 anti-aircraft missiles to Iran, to be shipped through Israel. This is part of what becomes the Iran-Contra Affair, the sale of U.S. military equipment to Iran, the proceeds from which are used to support Contra insurgents fighting the communist Sandinista regime in Nicaragua; **April 2,** in Athens, Greece, a bomb explodes aboard TWA Flight 840 en route from Rome to Athens, killing four Americans and injuring nine; **April 5,** in West Berlin, Germany, Libyans bomb a disco frequented by U.S. servicemen, killing two and injuring hundreds.

1987: January–March, the United States reflags Kuwaiti tankers to protect them from Iranian attack in the Persian Gulf; **mid-March,** U.S. president Ronald Reagan admits illegal sales to Iran to finance Contra operations in Nicaragua; **May 18,** an Iraqi Exocet aircraft-launched missile strikes the U.S. Navy frigate *Stark* in the Persian Gulf, killing 37 sailors. The attack is declared accidental, a consequence of the continuing Iran-Iraq War.

1988: August 11, Osama bin Laden and Sheikh Abdullah Azzam start the Al-Qaeda organization in Afghanistan; **November 24,** an unknown group assassinates Islamist leader Sheikh Abdullah Azzam in Peshawar, Pakistan, with a car bomb, leaving Osama bin Laden in control of Al-Qaeda; **December 21,** in Lockerbie, Scotland, a New York–bound Pan-Am Boeing 747 explodes in flight from a terrorist bomb and crashes into a Scottish village, killing all 259 aboard and 11 on the ground. Passengers include 35 Syracuse University students and many U.S. military personnel. Libya formally admits responsibility 15 years later (August 2003) and offers $2.7 billion in compensation to victims' families.

1989: February 15, the last Soviet forces depart Afghanistan. This frees the Islamic fundamentalist Taliban to begin a slow conquest of Afghanistan, aided by Osama bin Laden's Al-Qaeda terrorist organization. Al-Qaeda thereby gains a secure base for its operations in Taliban-dominated Afghanistan; **March 2–7,** the U.S. Central Command (CENTCOM) at MacDill Air Force Base has responsibility for military operations in the Middle East and develops a plan to send 200,000 American troops to defend Saudi Arabia from an Iraqi attack should military aid be requested; **March 8,** American fighter aircraft begin arriving in Saudi Arabia in Operation Desert Shield. The Iraqi government formally declares Kuwait to be Iraq's 19th province.

1990: November 5, El Sayyid Nosair assassinates Rabbi Meir Kahane in New York City.

1991: February 7, Downing Street mortar attack occurs in the United Kingdom; **May 22,** Rajiv Gandhi assassination occurs in India.

1992: March 17, Israeli embassy (Buenos Aires) bombing occurs in Argentina.

1993: February 26, the World Trade Center (New York City) bombing by an Islamist terrorist team led by Ramzi Ahmed Yousef kills 6 and wounds 1,042; **March 4,** the Federal Bureau of Investigation (FBI) discovers the VIN number of the Ryder van used in the World Trade Center bombing, leading to the arrest of some of those involved.

1994: March 4, three of the World Trade Center bombers are convicted; **April 9,** the Saudi government revokes Osama bin Laden's Saudi citizenship; **December 11,** Ramzi Ahmed Yousef plants a bomb on Philippine Air Lines Flight 434 that kills a Japanese engineer.

1995: January 6, Bojinka operation occurs in Philippines; Ramzi Ahmed Yousef accidentally causes a fire in a Manila apartment that exposes his plot to assassinate the pope; **January 20,** Abdul Hakim Murad confesses to a plot to fly a small plane into Central Intelligence Agency (CIA) headquarters in Langley, Virginia; **February 7,** Pakistani authorities arrest Ramzi Ahmed Yousef, the head of the 1993 World Trade Center bombing, in Islamabad, Pakistan; **March 20,** Tokyo subway sarin attack occurs in Japan; **April 19,** Oklahoma City bombing occurs in the United States; **November 13,** in Riyadh, Saudi Arabia, a car bomb explodes at U.S. military headquarters, killing five U.S. military servicemen.

1996: January 17, Sheikh Abdel-Rahman receives a life sentence for his role in planning the bombing of New York City landmarks; **May 18,** Osama bin Laden, leader of the Al-Qaeda terrorist organization, returns to Afghanistan from Sudan. The Bill Clinton administration misses the opportunity to place bin Laden in custody; **June 25,** the Khobar Towers bombing occurs in Saudi Arabia, in which a truck bomb explodes outside Khobar Towers, home to half the U.S. force of 5,000 military personnel in Saudi Arabia. The blast kills 19 Americans and injures another 240. The U.S. government links the attack to Al-Qaeda; **July 17,** an explosion downs TWA Flight 800 near Long Island, New York; **July 27,** the Centennial Olympic Park bombing occurs in United States; **August 23,** Osama bin Laden, leader of the Al-Qaeda terrorist organization, issues a call for jihad against the United States for its continued military presence in Saudi Arabia.

1997: May 26, the Saudi government is the first to recognize the Taliban government in Afghanistan.

1998: January 8, Ramzi Ahmed Yousef receives a sentence of 240 years for his role in the World Trade Center bombing in 1993; **February 23,** Al-Qaeda leader Osama bin Laden issues a fatwa against the enemies of Islam; topping his list is the United States, which he claims is the "root of all evil"; **August 7,** in Nairobi, Kenya, and Dar es Salaam, Tanzania, truck bombs explode almost simultaneously near two U.S. embassies, killing 224 (213 in Kenya and 11 in Tanzania) and injuring about 4,500. Four men connected with Al-Qaeda, two of whom had received training at Al-Qaeda camps inside Afghanistan, were convicted of the killings in May 2001 and later sentenced to life in prison; **October 8,** the Federal Aviation Administration (FAA) warns U.S. airports and airlines of Al-Qaeda's threat to U.S. civil aviation; **November 1,** Mohamed Atta, Said Bahaji, and Ramzi bin al-Shibh move into 54 Marienstrasse in the Harburg area of Hamburg, beginning the Hamburg Cell; **October 18,** the Vail ski resort bombing occurs in the United States; **December 1,** U.S. intelligence makes the assessment that Osama bin Laden has been planning attacks inside the United States.

1999: June 7, the FBI puts Osama bin Laden on its 10 Most Wanted list; **October,** the creation of the special intelligence unit Able Danger; **December 15,** millennium plots occur in the United States.

2000: January–February, the special intelligence unit Able Danger identifies Mohamed Atta and three associates as possible Al-Qaeda agents; Pentagon lawyers block Able Danger reporting to FBI three times during the year; **January 5–8,** Al-Qaeda holds a summit conference in Kuala Lumpur, Malaysia, where plans for the September 11 attacks are discussed; early **July,** Mohamed Atta and Marwan al-Shehhi begin flying lessons at Huffman Aviation in Venice, Florida; **July–August,** Defense Intelligence Agency (DIA) employees destroy evidence gathered by Able Danger; **August 12,** Italian intelligence wiretaps an Al-Qaeda terrorist cell in Milan, Italy, whose members talk about a massive strike involving aircraft; **October 12,** while anchored off the Yemeni port of Aden, the USS *Cole* comes under attack by a small boat laden with explosives. The suicide bombers, linked to the Al-Qaeda terrorist organization, detonate the craft next to the ship. The explosion rips a large hole in the side of the ship and kills 17 sailors; 39 others are injured; **October 24–26,** an emergency drill is held at the Pentagon on the possibility of a hijacked airliner crashing into the building; **December 20,** Richard Clarke proposes a plan to attack Al-Qaeda, but it is postponed and later rejected by the new George W. Bush administration; **December 21,** Mohamed Atta and Marwan al-Shehhi receive their pilot's licenses; **December 26,** Mohamed Atta and Marwan al-Shehhi abandon a rented plane on the taxiway of Miami Airport after the plane's engine fails during takeoff; **December 24,** Christmas Eve bombings occurs in Indonesia.

2001: Early January, Lieutenant Colonel Anthony Shaffer, a member of Able Danger, briefs General Hugh Shelton on the group's findings; **February 23,** Zacarias Moussaoui arrives in the United States; **March 7,** government leaders discuss a plan to fight Al-Qaeda, but there is no urgency to proceed; late **March,** the Able Danger program is terminated; **April 1,** Oklahoma police give a speeding ticket to Nawaf al-Hazmi; **April 16,** Mohamed Atta receives a traffic ticket for driving without a license; **April 18,** the FAA warns airlines about possible Middle Eastern hijackers; **April 30,** Deputy Defense Secretary Paul Wolfowitz downplays the importance of Osama bin Laden at a meeting on terrorism; **May 10,** Attorney General John Ashcroft omits counterterrorism from a list of goals of the Justice Department; **May 15,** the CIA refuses to share information with the FBI about the Al-Qaeda meeting in Malaysia in January 2000; **June 10,** the CIA notifies all its station chiefs of a possible Al-Qaeda suicide attack on U.S. targets over the next few days; **June 11,** a CIA analyst and FBI agents have a shouting match over sharing terrorists' identification information; **June 20,** FBI agent Robert Wright sends a memo that charges the FBI of not trying to catch known terrorists living in the United States; **June 21,** Osama bin Laden tells a Muslim journalist that an attack on the United States is imminent; **June 28,** CIA director George Tenet issues a warning of an imminent Al-Qaeda attack; **July 2,** the FBI warns of possible Al-Qaeda attacks abroad, but also possibly in the United States; **July 5,** Richard Clarke briefs senior security officials on the Al-Qaeda threat at the White House and tells them Al-Qaeda is planning a major attack; **July 8–19,** Mohamed Atta, Ramzi bin al-Shibh, and Marwan al-Shehhi travel to Spain to finalize attack plans; **July 10,** FBI agent Ken Williams sends a memo about the large number of Middle Eastern men taking flight training lessons in Arizona; CIA director George Tenet briefs Condoleezza Rice and warns of the possibility of an Al-Qaeda attack in the United States; **July 17,** Mohamed Atta and Marwan al-Shehhi meet with Al-Qaeda leaders in Taragona, Spain, to make final plans for the September 11 attacks; **July 18,** both the FBI and FAA issue warnings about possible terrorist activity; **August 6,** President Bush receives a briefing titled "Bin Laden

Determined to Strike in U.S." at his Crawford, Texas, ranch; **August 15,** FBI agents in Minneapolis request a FISA search warrant for Zacarias Moussaoui; **August 16,** Zacarias Moussaoui is arrested by Harry Samit in Minneapolis for visa violation; **August 19,** the FBI's top Al-Qaeda expert, John O'Neill, resigns from the FBI under pressure; **August 20,** Harry Samit sends a memo to FBI headquarters in Washington, D.C., citing Zacarias Moussaoui as a terrorist threat for an aircraft hijacking; **August 23,** the FBI adds two of the September 11 conspirators, Nawaf al-Hazmi and Khalid al-Mihdhar, to the Terrorist Watch List; Israel's Mossad gives the CIA a list of terrorists living in the United States, on which are named four of the 9/11 hijackers; **August 24,** Khalid al-Mihdhar buys his 9/11 ticket; **August 25,** Nawaf al-Hazmi buys his 9/11 ticket; **August 28,** the FBI's New York office requests to open a criminal investigation of Khalid al-Mihdhar, but FBI headquarters turns down the request; Mohamed Atta buys his 9/11 ticket; **August 29,** Khalid Sheikh Mohammed gives the go-ahead for the September 11 attacks in a call from Afghanistan; Mohamed Atta tells Ramzi bin al-Shibh the date of the attack in code; **September 4,** cabinet-level advisers approve of Richard Clarke's plan, proposed eight months earlier, to attack Al-Qaeda; **September 9,** Maryland police give Ziad Jarrah a ticket for speeding; **September 10,** Attorney General John Ashcroft turns down an increase of $58 million for the FBI's counterterrorism budget; **September 11,** 19 Al-Qaeda suicide terrorists board four U.S. domestic aircraft flights in Boston, Newark, and Dulles Airport outside Washington, D.C. They hijack the planes in flight. One flight hits the North Tower of the World Trade Center in New York City at 8:46 a.m., another strikes the South Tower at 9:03 a.m., and the third slams into the Pentagon in northern Virginia at 10:03 a.m. The fourth plane, targeted for the White House or the U.S. Capitol building, crashes in western Pennsylvania after passengers overwhelm the hijackers but fail to control the aircraft. All 19 terrorists and 246 passengers and crew die, along with 2,603 in the collapse of the Twin Towers in New York and 125 at the Pentagon. Emergency personnel respond to the attacks, resulting in the deaths of 411 New York firefighters, police, and paramedics. Another 24 people thought to have been at the crash sites are missing, and there are serious injuries to rescue personnel and civilians near the attack areas. Both World Trade Center towers are completely destroyed, and seven nearby structures suffer complete destruction or severe damage. The Pentagon also sustains extensive structural damage.

Following is the day's timeline of the assault on World Trade Center and the Pentagon:

12:45 a.m. Willie Brown, the mayor of San Francisco, receives a call from security at San Francisco International Airport warning him about air travel on September 11.

6:45 a.m. Two workers at the instant messaging company Odigo, an Israeli-owned company based in Herzilya Pituah, near Tel Aviv, reportedly received messages warning of a possible attack on the World Trade Center.

6:50 a.m. Mohamed Atta and Abdulaziz al-Omari's flight from Portland, Maine, arrives at Boston Logan International Airport.

7:45 a.m. Mohammed Atta and Abdulaziz al-Omari board American Airlines Flight 11.

7:59 a.m. American Airlines Flight 11 leaves Boston Logan Airport, headed for Los Angeles.

8:13:31 a.m. Last routine radio communication from American Airlines Flight 11; the aircraft begins climbing to 35,000 feet.

8:14 a.m. United Airlines Flight 175 leaves Boston Logan Airport, headed for Los Angeles, after a 16-minute delay.

8:17 a.m. Daniel Lewin, former member of Sayeret Matkal, the counterterrorist unit of the Israel Defense Forces (IDF), is killed.

8:20 a.m. American Airlines Flight 77 leaves Washington, D.C., headed for Los Angeles.

8:21 a.m. The transponder in American Airlines Flight 11 stops transmitting identification.

Flight attendant Betty Ong, on American Airlines Flight 11, notifies American Airlines of the hijacking.

8:25 a.m. The Boston air traffic control center becomes aware of the hijacking of American Airlines Flight 11 and notifies several air traffic control centers that a hijacking is in progress.

8:26 a.m. American Airlines Flight 11 makes a 100-degree turn to the south, toward New York City.

8:37:08 a.m. Boston flight control asks the pilots of United Airlines Flight 175 whether they can see American Airlines Flight 11, and they answer in the affirmative.

8:38 a.m. The Boston air traffic control center notifies North American Aerospace Defense Command (NORAD) of the hijacking of American Airlines Flight 11.

8:40 a.m. The FAA notifies NORAD of the American Airlines Flight 11 hijacking.

8:42 a.m. Last radio communication from United Airlines Flight 175 with New York air traffic control; afterward, the transponder is inactive.

8:43 a.m. The FAA notifies NORAD of the United Airlines Flight 175 hijacking.

United Airlines Flight 93 takes off from Newark International Airport, headed for San Francisco after a 41-minute delay.

8:46 a.m. NORAD scrambles fighter jets from Otis Air National Guard Base in search of American Airlines Flight 11.

The transponder signal from United Airlines Flight 175 stops transmitting.

8:46:40 a.m. American Airlines Flight 11 crashes into the North Tower of the World Trade Center in New York City.

8:47 a.m. NORAD learns about American Airlines Flight 11 striking the World Trade Center.

8:49 a.m. United Airlines Flight 175 deviates from its assigned flight path.

8:50 a.m. A female flight attendant from United Airlines Flight 175 reports to a San Francisco mechanic that the flight had been hijacked.

8:50:51 a.m. Last radio communication from American Airlines Flight 77.

8:52 a.m. A flight attendant on United Airlines Flight 175 notifies United Airlines of hijacking.

8:53 a.m. Otis Air National Guard Base fighter jets become airborne.

8:54 a.m. American Airlines Flight 77 makes an unauthorized turn south.

8:55 a.m. Barbara Olson, a passenger on American Airlines Flight 77, notifies her husband, Solicitor General Theodore Olson, at the Justice Department that her aircraft has been hijacked.

8:56 a.m. The transponder on American Airlines Flight 77 stops sending signals.

American Airlines Flight 77 begins making a 180-degree turn over southern Ohio and heads back to the Washington, D.C., area.

8:57 a.m. The FAA formally informs the military about the crash of American Airlines Flight 11 into the World Trade Center.

9:00 a.m. The FAA starts contacting all airliners to warn them of the hijackings.

9:01 a.m. An aide informs President Bush of the crash of American Airlines Flight 11 into the World Trade Center at Emma E. Booker Elementary School in Sarasota, Florida.

9:02:54 a.m. United Airlines Flight 175 crashes into the South Tower of the World Trade Center in New York City.

9:03 a.m. Boston air traffic control center halts traffic from its airports to all New York area airspace.

9:05 a.m. American Airlines becomes aware that American Airlines Flight 77 has been hijacked.

An aide informs President Bush about the second plane hitting the World Trade Center, and he understands that the United States is under attack.

9:06 a.m. The FAA formally informs the military that United Airlines Flight 175 has been hijacked.

9:08 a.m. The FAA orders all aircraft to leave New York airspace and orders all New York–bound aircraft nationwide to stay on the ground.

9:11 a.m. Two F-15 Eagles from Otis Air National Guard Base arrive over New York City airspace.

9:15 a.m. The New York air traffic control center advises NORAD that United Airlines Flight 175 has also crashed into the World Trade Center.

9:16 a.m. American Airlines becomes aware that American Airlines Flight 11 has crashed into the World Trade Center.

9:17 a.m. The FAA shuts down all New York City area airports.

9:20 a.m. United Airlines headquarters becomes aware that United Airlines Flight 175 has crashed into the World Trade Center.

9:21 a.m. The Port Authority of New York and New Jersey orders all bridges and tunnels in the New York area closed.

9:24 a.m. The FAA informs NORAD that American Airlines Flight 77 has been hijacked.

NORAD scrambles fighter jets from Langley Air Force Base to search for American Airlines Flight 77.

United Airlines Flight 93 receives a warning from United Airlines about possible cockpit intrusion by terrorists.

9:25 a.m. Herndon Command Center orders the nationwide grounding of all commercial and civilian aircraft.

9:26 a.m. Barbara Olson calls her husband again to give him details about the hijacking.

9:27 a.m. Last routine radio communication from United Airlines Flight 93.

9:28 a.m. Likely takeover of United Airlines Flight 93 by terrorists.

9:29 a.m. Jeremy Glick, a passenger on United Airlines Flight 93, calls his wife, who informs him about the attacks in New York City.

9:30 a.m. President Bush states in an informal address at the elementary school in Sarasota, Florida, that the country has suffered an apparent terrorist attack.

F-16 Fighting Falcons take off from Langley Air Force Base and head toward New York City until redirected to Washington, D.C.

9:32 a.m. Dulles Tower observes the approach of a fast-moving aircraft on radar.

Secret Service agents take Vice President Dick Cheney to the underground bunker in the White House basement.

9:34 a.m. The FAA advises NORAD that American Airlines Flight 77's whereabouts are unknown.

Herndon Command Center advises FAA headquarters that United Airlines 93 has been hijacked.

9:35 a.m. United Airlines Flight 93 begins making a 135-degree turn near Cleveland, Ohio, and heads for the Washington, D.C., area.

9:36 a.m. A flight attendant on United Airlines Flight 93 notifies United Airlines of hijacking.

Ronald Reagan Washington National Airport asks a military C-130 aircraft that has just departed Andrews Air Force Base to locate American Airlines Flight 77, and it answers that a 767 was moving low and very fast.

9:37:46 a.m. American Airlines Flight 77 crashes into the Pentagon.

9:40 a.m. Transportation Secretary Norman Y. Mineta orders the FAA to ground all 4,546 airplanes currently in the air.

9:41 a.m. The transponder on United Airlines Flight 93 stops functioning.

9:42 a.m. Mark Bingham, a passenger on United Airlines Flight 93, calls his mother and reports the hijacking.

9:45 a.m. The White House evacuates all personnel.

President Bush leaves the elementary school in Sarasota, Florida, to board Air Force One.

Todd Beamer, a passenger on United Flight 93, tells a Verizon supervisor that the passengers have voted to storm the hijackers.

9:47 a.m. Military commanders worldwide are ordered to raise their threat alert status to the highest level to defend the United States.

9:49 a.m. The F-16s arrive over the Washington, D.C., area.

9:57 a.m. The passenger revolt begins on United Airlines Flight 93.

President Bush departs from Florida.

9:58 a.m. After receiving authorization from President Bush, Vice President Cheney gives instructions to engage United Airlines Flight 93 as it approaches the Washington, D.C., area.

10:03:11 a.m. United Airlines Flight 93 crashes in a field in Shanksville, Pennsylvania.

10:05 a.m. The South Tower of the World Trade Center collapses.

10:07 a.m. The Cleveland air traffic control center advises NORAD of the United Airlines 93 hijacking.

10:10 a.m. A portion of the Pentagon collapses.

10:15 a.m. United Airlines headquarters becomes aware that Flight 93 has crashed in Pennsylvania.

The Washington air traffic control center advises Northeast Air Defense Sector (NEADS) that Flight 93 has crashed in Pennsylvania.

10:24 a.m. The FAA orders that all inbound transatlantic aircraft flying into the United States be diverted to Canada.

10:28:31 a.m. The North Tower of the World Trade Center collapses.

10:30 a.m. American Airlines headquarters confirms that American Airlines Flight 77 has crashed into the Pentagon.

10:31 a.m. Presidential authorization to shoot down hijacked aircraft reaches NORAD.

10:32 a.m. Vice President Cheney tells President Bush that a threat against Air Force One has been received.

10:50 a.m. Five stories of the Pentagon collapse due to the blast and fire.

11:02 a.m. New York City mayor Rudolph Giuliani asks New Yorkers to stay home and orders an evacuation of the area south of Canal Street.

11:40 a.m. Air Force One lands at Barksdale Air Force Base in Louisiana.

12:04 p.m. Los Angeles International Airport is evacuated and shut down.

12:15 p.m. San Francisco International Airport is evacuated and shut down.

1:04 p.m. President Bush, speaking from Barksdale Air Force Base in Louisiana, announces that all appropriate security measures are being taken and all U.S. military has been put on high alert worldwide.

1:48 p.m. President Bush flies to Offutt Air Force Base in Nebraska.

2:00 p.m. Senior FBI sources tell CNN that they are assuming that the aircraft hijackings are part of a terrorist attack.

4:10 p.m. Reports surface that Building Seven of the World Trade Center complex is on fire.

4:30 p.m. President Bush leaves Offutt Air Force Base to return to Washington, D.C.

5:20:33 p.m. The 47-story Building Seven of the World Trade Center collapses.

6:00 p.m. Northern Alliance launches a bombing campaign against the Taliban in Kabul, Afghanistan.

6:54 p.m. President Bush arrives at the White House in Washington, D.C.

8:30 p.m. President Bush addresses the nation about the events of the day.

September 14, U.S. deputy secretary of defense Paul Wolfowitz declares that the global war on terror must go beyond seeking out and destroying terrorist groups and must also punish nations that support terrorist activities; **September 18,** the first of several anthrax-infected letters is sent through the U.S. mail. In all, 5 individuals will die and 17 more will become infected. Public fears that these attacks are being perpetrated by Al-Qaeda prove groundless; however, **September 20,** before a televised joint session of Congress, U.S. president George W. Bush introduces the term "global war on terror," blames the 9/11 attacks on the Al-Qaeda terrorist organization based in Afghanistan, and demands that the Taliban government turn Al-Qaeda leader Osama bin Laden over to the United States. Afghanistan refuses the demand. British and U.S. aircraft attack an Iraqi air defense in-stallation in southern Iraq. Iraq denies any connection to September 11; **September 21,** the George W. Bush administration claims a close connection between Saddam Hussein's Iraq and Al-Qaeda, including training that supposedly took place on a model Boeing 707 aircraft at Salman Pak in Iraq; **September 22,** the Air Transportation Safety and System Stabilization Act is signed into law. The act creates the September 11th Victim Compen-sation Fund, which will eventually award some $7 billion to survivors and family mem-bers of victims of the 9/11 attacks in exchange for agreeing not to file lawsuits against the airline companies involved; **September 23,** Pakistan is the only country that continues to recognize the Taliban as the legitimate government in Afghanistan; Saudi Arabia and the United Arab Emirates had previously withdrawn recognition; **October–February,** Khalid Sheikh Mohammed plans a series of airline hijackings similar to those of 9/11 that will target West Coast buildings such as the Library Tower in Los Angeles; his plan fails after one recruit is arrested and others drop out; **October 5,** anthrax attacks occur in United States; **October 7,** the Taliban government of Afghanistan offers to try Osama bin Laden in an Islamic court. The United States rejects this and, along with the United Kingdom, begins bombing Afghanistan. This is the official opening of Operation Enduring Freedom. Cruise missiles from American and British submarines and aircraft from two American aircraft carriers strike targets that include Kabul, Kandahar, and Jalalabad; **October 14,** the Taliban government of Afghanistan offers to turn Al-Qaeda leader Osama bin Laden over to a third nation for trial if the bombing ceases and the United States presents evidence of Al-Qaeda involvement in the September 11 attack; **October 21,** Osama bin Laden gives his justification for the 9/11 attacks in an interview with an Al Jazeera journalist; **October 25,** the Senate passes the USA PATRIOT Act; **October 24,** the House of Representatives passes the USA PATRIOT Act; **October 26,** President Bush signs the USA PATRIOT Act; **October–November,** continuation of air attacks and Special Forces actions to destroy Afghan government communications, command, and control capabilities. Regional Afghan groups, such as the Northern Alliance, join the fight against Taliban forces. Meanwhile, thousands of Pashtun militia from Pakistan join the struggle on the side of the Taliban. Suspecting that Osama bin Laden and the Taliban leadership have moved into the Tora Bora mountains near the Afghan-Pakistani border, the United States employs Boeing B-52 Stratofortress bombers to strike suspected hiding places; **November 9,** a ground offensive in Afghanistan begins against Taliban and Al-Qaeda forces in the Mazar-e Sharif area, a key concentration area for Taliban forces. Carpet bombing of the Chesmay Gorge at the entrance to Mazar-e Sharif allows forces of the Northern Alliance, supported by the United States, to sweep into the city; **November 10,** the fall of Mazar-e Sharif permits forces of the Northern Alliance to take control of five northern provinces of Afghanistan; **November 12,** the Taliban evacuates the Afghan capital of Kabul; **November 13,** Al-Qaeda and Taliban forces concentrate in the rugged Tora Bora region, utilizing the extensive cave complexes there; **November 15,** a U.S. Hellfire missile targets Al-Qaeda leaders near Gardez and kills several, including Muhammad Atef. Al-Qaeda leader Osama bin Laden, however, remains elusive; **November 16,** continuation of bombardment of the Tora Bora mountain region and Special Forces operations. The United States undertakes the payment of Afghan militias to fight the Taliban and Al-Qaeda. The siege of Kunduz begins; **November 19,** the Aviation and Transportation Security Act is signed into law. The act creates the Transportation Security Administration (TSA), which will be responsible for ensuring security in all modes of transportation, particularly air travel; **November 25–26,** the Afghan city of Kunduz falls to Northern Alliance forces after heavy bombardment by U.S. aircraft. Up to 5,000 Taliban and Al-Qaeda fighters relocate across the border into northwestern Pakistan. U.S. and Afghan allies take hundreds of captives to Ala-i-Janghi near Mazar-e Sharif, where 300 rise up and attempt to take over the compound. The rebellion is quelled by allied ground forces and Lockheed AC-130 Spectre gunships. U.S. Central Intelligence Agency (CIA) officer Johnny Michael Spann, there to question prisoners, is killed, becoming the first American casualty of the Afghanistan War; **December 5,** Afghan leaders opposed to the Taliban agree in the course of a meeting in Bonn, Germany, to form an interim government after the defeat of the Taliban; **December 7,** Taliban leader Mullah Mohammed Omar orders the evacuation of the city of Kandahar, the last major Taliban stronghold in Afghanistan. This follows intensive bombardment and ground attacks and includes several hundred U.S. marines, the first major American ground forces involved in the war. The Taliban also surrenders Spin Boldak on the Pakistani border; **December 17,** U.S., British, and allied Afghan forces overrun much of the Tora Bora mountain area. About 200 Taliban and Al-Qaeda are killed in the fighting. Mullah Mohammed Omar and Osama bin Laden evade capture along with other Taliban and Al-Qaeda leaders and an unknown number of fighters; **December 22,** Richard Reid, who later claims to be a follower of Osama bin Laden, is arrested after attempting to blow up American Airlines Flight 63 with a shoe bomb that fails to detonate; **December 26,** Osama bin Laden issues a statement of homage to the 19 martyrs of September 11.

2002: January 9, some 4,500 foreign peacekeepers under British leadership begin deployment in Afghanistan to support the interim government. The major focus will be security in the capital of Kabul; **January 29,** during his State of the Union address, U.S. president George W. Bush declares Iraq part of the "axis of evil" that also includes Iran and North Korea, all of whom, he claims, are trying to develop weapons of mass destruction (WMDs); **March–May,** United Nations (UN) secretary-general Kofi Annan tries unsuccessfully to persuade Iraq to allow the return of weapons inspectors; **June 14,** a bomb explodes outside American consulate in Karachi, Pakistan, killing 12; the explosion is linked to Al-Qaeda; **July 5–6,** after the failure of his efforts in early 2002 to secure the renewal of United Nations (UN) weapons inspections, UN secretary-general Kofi Annan enters into personal talks with Iraqi foreign minister Naji Sabri. The negotiations fail; **July 25,** the Iraqi government declares that arms inspections must be accompanied by the lifting of sanctions against Iraq and an end to the northern and southern no-fly zones; **September 12,** U.S. president George W. Bush addresses a special session of the United Nations (UN) and declares the need for a coordinated plan of action against Iraq. Iraq rejects this and states that it will not engage in discussions about weapons inspections unless the United States promises not to sponsor any more punitive resolutions against Iraq; **September 22,** the British government releases information, later proved to be erroneous, indicating that Iraq has significant weapons of mass destruction (WMDs); **October 12,** suicide bombers kill more than 200 people, including 7 Americans, at two discotheques and outside the U.S. consulate in Bali. Osama bin Laden claims that the attacks were committed in retaliation for the involvement by the United States and Australia in the war on terror; **November,** the Homeland Security Act, which creates the Department of Homeland Security (DHS) and grants it sweeping powers, is signed into law; **November 15,** the National Commission on Terrorist Attacks upon the United States (the 9/11 Commission) is chartered over the objection of President Bush; **December 12,** the *Washington Post* runs a front-page article by Barton Gellman entitled, "U.S. Suspects Al-Qaeda Got

Nerve Agent from Iraqis"; although unfounded, it helps reinforce the commonly held misconception among Americans that Iraqi president Saddam Hussein is closely tied to Al-Qaeda and the 9/11 attacks; **December 20,** the *Final Report of the Senate Select Committee on Intelligence and the House of Representatives Permanent Select Committee on Intelligence Joint Inquiry into the Terrorist Attacks of September 11* is issued.

2003: February 5, armed with what is later revealed as a deeply flawed intelligence estimate, U.S. secretary of state Colin Powell addresses the United Nations (UN) Security Council plenary session charging that Iraq has or is developing weapons of mass destruction. Powell argues unsuccessfully in favor of UN-sanctioned international military action against Iraq; **March 18,** the U.S. government unveils the so-called "coalition of the willing," 30 nations agreeing to associate themselves with the United States in military action against Iraq; 15 more nations will provide support; **March 20,** U.S.-led invasion of Iraq begins; **May 1,** Brooklyn Bridge bomb plot occurs in the United States; **May 12,** in Riyadh, Saudi Arabia, suicide bombers kill 34, including 8 Americans, at housing compounds for Westerners; Al-Qaeda is suspected; **May 16,** the U.S. military characterizes the resistance in Iraq as a "classic guerrilla-type campaign"; **May 19,** Iraqi insurgents bomb the United Nations (UN) compound in Baghdad, leaving at least 20 people dead. Among those killed is the top UN envoy in Iraq, Brazilian native Sergio Vieira de Mello; **October 27,** International Red Cross (ICRC) headquarters (Baghdad) bombing occurs in Iraq; **December 13,** U.S. forces capture deposed Iraqi dictator Saddam Hussein.

2004: March 11, terrorists in Madrid, Spain, launch a series of coordinated bombings against the Cercanias (commuter train) system in the Spanish capital. Known as the Madrid Train Bombings, 3/11, and in Spanish as 11-M, the bombings kill 191 people and wound 1,800. The bombings occur three days before the Spanish general elections. An official Spanish investigation determines that the attacks were committed by a Spanish Al-Qaeda terrorist cell; **March 31,** insurgents kill four security contractors employed by Blackwater, Inc., in Fallujah. They drag the bodies through the streets and then hang them on a bridge over the Euphrates River; **April 4,** an attack by the Mahdi militia organized by Muqtada al-Sadr on Najaf and Karbala signals the organized resistance of Iraqi Shias to the national government and the U.S. occupation; **May 4,** U.S. Army major general Antonio Taguba announces results of an investigation ordered on January 24, 2004, confirming prisoner abuses at Abu Ghraib Prison by members of the 800th Military Police Brigade; **May 29–31,** in Riyadh, Saudi Arabia, terrorists attack the offices of a Saudi oil company in Khobar, Saudi Arabia, and take foreign oil workers hostage in a nearby residential compound, leaving 22 people dead, including 1 American; **June 11–19,** terrorists kidnap and execute Paul Johnson, Jr., an American, in Riyadh, Saudi Arabia. Two other Americans and BBC cameraman killed by gun attacks; **June 26–28,** opening weekend of filmmaker Michael Moore's controversial documentary *Fahrenheit 9/11,* which is highly critical of the Bush administration. The film pulls in more than $20 million in these three days, instantly becoming the highest-grossing documentary; **July 22,** the final report of the 9/11 Commission is issued; **December 6,** in Jeddah, Saudi

Arabia, terrorists storm the U.S. consulate, killing five consulate employees. Four terrorists are killed by Saudi security.

2005: January 30, some 60 percent of eligible voters participate in Iraq's first free elections since Saddam Hussein came to power. Turnout for the parliamentary elections is heaviest among Shia Muslims and Kurds; Sunni participation is lower; **February 9,** the Madrid Convention Center bombing occurs in Spain; **May 20,** the *New York Times* reports abuse of prisoners by U.S. military forces at detention centers in Afghanistan; **July 7,** in the London Underground bombings, four Al-Qaeda–affiliated suicide bombers attack three subway trains and one double-decker bus in London, killing more than 50 people; **July 21,** London Underground bombings are attempted in the United Kingdom; **August 17,** Lieutenant Colonel Anthony Shaffer, a member of Able Danger, issues a public statement about the identification of Mohamed Atta and others as Al-Qaeda agents by Able Danger as early as 2000; **September 21,** the Senate Judiciary Committee holds a hearing on Able Danger, but the Defense Department prohibits Able Danger officers from participating in the hearings; **November 9,** in Amman, Jordan, suicide bombers hit three American hotels, the Radisson, Grand Hyatt, and Days Inn, in Amman, Jordan, killing 57. Al-Qaeda claims responsibility.

2006: February 9, Hangu (Hanga) bombing occurs in Pakistan; **March 9,** President Bush reauthorizes the USA PATRIOT Act; **April 17,** Mayor Falafel restaurant bombing occurs in Israel; **April 24,** Dahab bombings occur in Egypt; **May 3,** Zacarias Moussaoui is sentenced to life in prison without the possibility of parole for conspiring to commit acts of terrorism in conjunction with the September 11 attacks; **June 2,** Toronto 18 plot occurs in Canada; **June 7,** a U.S. air strike near Baquba, Iraq, kills Abu Musab al-Zarqawi, leader of Al-Qaeda in Iraq; **June 22,** the Sears Tower bomb plot occurs in the United States; **July 31,** Giessen commuter train plot occurs in Germany; **August 10,** Heathrow liquid bomb plot occurs in the United Kingdom; **August 31,** Yala bank bombings occur in Thailand; **September 13,** in Damascus, Syria, an attack by four gunmen on the American embassy is foiled; **November 5,** an Iraqi court convicts former president Saddam Hussein of crimes against humanity and sentences him to death by hanging; **December 30,** the Madrid airport bombing occurs in Spain.

2007: January 12, in Athens, Greece, the U.S. embassy is fired on by an antitank missile, causing damage but no injuries; **March,** at Guantánamo Bay Detainment Camp, Khalid Sheikh Mohammed confesses to masterminding the September 11 attacks and the 2002 Bali bombings; **May 7,** the Fort Dix plot occurs in the United States; **May 13,** United Nations (UN) and Afghan forces kill Mullah Dadullah, senior Taliban military commander in Afghanistan; **June 2,** JFK International Airport bomb plot occurs in United States.

2008: March 11, insurgent attacks in Iraq decline significantly. U.S. authorities announce that there were only 60 in January 2008, compared with 180 the preceding July; **March 18,** the U.S. embassy (Sana'a) attack occurs in Yemen; **May 26,** in Iraq, a suicide bomber on a motorcycle kills six U.S. soldiers and wounds 18 others in Tarmiya; **June 12,** in

Afghanistan, four American servicemen are killed when a roadside bomb explodes near a U.S. military vehicle in Farah Province; **June 15,** Afghan president Hamid Karzai declares the intention of sending Afghan forces to attack Pakistani border areas if Pakistan does not subdue Taliban and Al-Qaeda forces there; **June 24,** in Iraq, a suicide bomber kills at least 20 people, including three U.S. Marines, at a meeting between sheiks and Americans in Karmah, a town west of Baghdad; **July 13,** in Afghanistan, nine U.S. soldiers and at least 15 NATO troops die when Taliban militants boldly attack an American base in Kunar Province, which borders Pakistan. It is the most deadly attack against U.S. troops in three years; **August 18–19,** in Afghanistan, as many as 15 suicide bombers backed by about 30 militants attack a U.S. military base, Camp Salerno, in Bamiyan. Fighting between U.S. troops and members of the Taliban rages overnight. No U.S. troops are killed; **September 16,** a car bomb and a rocket strike the U.S. embassy in Yemen as staff arrive at work, killing 16 people, including 4 civilians. At least 25 suspected Al-Qaeda militants are arrested for the attack; **November 26,** in India, a series of attacks occur on several of Mumbai's landmarks and commercial hubs that are popular with Americans and other foreign tourists, including at least two five-star hotels, a hospital, a train station, and a cinema. About 300 people are wounded and nearly 190 people die, including at least 5 Americans; **December 27,** Benazir Bhutto is assassinated in Pakistan.

2009: February 9, in Iraq, a suicide bomber kills four American soldiers and their Iraqi translator near a police checkpoint; **April 10,** in Iraq, a suicide attack kills five American soldiers and two Iraqi policemen; **June 1,** in Little Rock, Arkansas, Abdulhakim Muhammed, a Muslim convert from Memphis, Tennessee, is charged with shooting two soldiers outside a military recruiting center. One is killed and the other is wounded. In a January 2010 letter to the judge hearing his case, Muhammed asked to change his plea from not guilty to guilty, claimed ties to Al-Qaeda, and called the shooting a jihadi attack "to fight those who wage war on Islam and Muslims"; **May 20,** New York City bomb plots occur in the United States; **September 24,** the Dallas skyscraper bomb plot occurs in the United States; **October 17,** following a series of suicide bomb attacks mounted by the Taliban against both civilian and top security targets in Pakistan, the Pakistani Army begins a major offensive against the Al-Qaeda terrorist organization; **October 25,** in the deadliest bomb blasts since 2007, two massive synchronized truck bombs explode in Baghdad, killing at least 155 people and wounding more than 500; **December 1,** U.S. president Barack Obama announces that he will send 30,000 additional U.S. forces to Afghanistan to allow the beginning of a drawdown in American forces; **December 25,** Umar Farouk Abdulmutallab, a 22-year-old Nigerian, attempts to blow up Northwest Flight 253 from Amsterdam as it begins its descent into Detroit, Michigan. The explosive device is hidden in his underpants, which he removes and tries to ignite in his seat. This is the same explosive utilized by so-called shoe bomber Richard Reid in 2001 when he attempted to blow up another transatlantic flight with explosives hidden in his shoe; **December 30,** in Iraq, a suicide bomber kills eight Americans civilians, seven of them CIA agents, at a base in Afghanistan. It is the deadliest attack on the agency since 9/11. The attacker is reportedly a double agent from Jordan who was acting on behalf of Al-Qaeda.

2010: May 1, Times Square bomb attack attempt occurs in the United States: Pakistani-born Faisal Shahzad plants a car bomb at Times Square in New York City, but the bomb is detected and defused before it can be detonated. Government officials suggest that Shahzad was acting in conjunction with a terrorist organization closely allied with Al-Qaeda; **May 10,** plans to build a Muslim community center, dubbed the "Ground Zero Mosque," several blocks from the World Trade Center sparks nationwide controversy; in Jacksonville, Florida, a pipe bomb explodes while approximately 60 Muslims are praying in a mosque. The attack causes no injuries; **September 23,** Iranian president Mahmoud Ahmadinejad delivers a speech before the United Nations (UN) General Assembly in which he claims that while most American politicians advance the idea that September 11 was carried out by Al-Qaeda, most Americans believe that the terrorist attacks were in fact orchestrated by the U.S. government for economic and political gain. Ahmadinejad's comments trigger a mass walkout at the UN, and political leaders around the world criticize his speech.

2011: January 17, in Spokane, Washington, a pipe bomb is discovered along the route of the Martin Luther King, Jr., memorial march. The bomb, a "viable device" set up to spray marchers with shrapnel and to cause multiple casualties, is defused without any injuries; **May 1,** President Obama announces that U.S. special forces, acting on intelligence gathered by the CIA over the last few months, have conducted a successful raid on a large compound in Abbottabad, Pakistan, where they shot and killed bin Laden. Spontaneous celebrations erupt across the United States; **September 13,** U.S. embassy/United Nations headquarters (Kabul) attacks occur in Afghanistan.

2012: May 13, a pair of U.S. drone strikes kills 11 suspected Al-Qaeda militants in Yemen's Mareb province, part of a continuing air campaign targeting the terror organization; **June 4,** Abu Yahya al-Libi, the number two man in Al-Qaeda and a longtime public face of the terrorist network, is killed in a U.S. drone strike; **September 11,** in the deadly attack on the U.S. consulate in Benghazi, Libya, militants armed with antiaircraft weapons and rocket-propelled grenades fire upon the American consulate, killing U.S. ambassador to Libya Christopher Stevens and three other embassy officials; **October 5,** five terror suspects, including the radical cleric Abu Hamza al-Masri, are on their way to face charges in the United States after extradition from the UK; **December 13,** the European Court of Human Rights rules in favor of Khaled El-Masri, a German man, who says the CIA illegally kidnapped him and took him to a secret prison in Afghanistan in 2003. It said the government of Macedonia violated El-Masri's rights repeatedly and ordered it to pay €60,000 in damages.

2013: February 1, in Ankara, Turkey, Ecevit Sanli detonates a bomb near a gate at the U.S. Embassy. Sanli dies after detonating the bomb. One Turkish guard is also killed. Didem Tuncay, a respected television journalist, is injured in the blast. Unlike the bombing at the embassy in Benghazi the previous September, the U.S. government immediately calls the bombing a terrorist attack. According to Turkish officials, the attack is from the Revolutionary People's Liberation Party, which has been labeled a terrorist organization by the United States and other nations; **February 27,** in Ireland, Ali Charaf Damache is arrested while leaving a courthouse. He had just walked free after three years in prison when detectives acting on an American extradition warrant rearrest and escort him, handcuffed, to an unmarked police car. The FBI and the U.S. Justice Department accuse Damache of being the ringleader behind an unrealized 2009 conspiracy to target artist Lars Vilks in Sweden over his series of drawings depicting the Muslim prophet Muhammad as a dog; **February 28,** Sulaiman Abu Ghaith, the son-in-law of Osama bin Laden, is captured by the FBI in Jordan as he is being deported to Kuwait from Turkey. On **March 9,** he pleads not guilty in federal court in New York to conspiring to kill Americans; **March 27,** Eric Harroun of Phoenix, Arizona, is arrested upon returning to the United States from Turkey, where he had described to FBI agents his bizarre journey to the front lines of Syria's civil war with fighters from the al-Nusra Front, a designated terrorist organization also referred to as Al-Qaeda in Iraq. Harroun served in the U.S. Army from 2000 to 2003; **April 15,** two bombs are detonated near the finish line of the Boston Marathon, killing 3 people and leaving more than 170 others injured. Dzhokar Tsarnaev and his older brother Tamerlan Tsarnaev are identified as the main suspects; **April 19,** Tamerlan is killed during a shootout with police in Watertown, Massachusetts, in the early hours of the morning, and Dzhokar is arrested about 18 hours later. The two are also suspected of fatally shooting a police officer prior to the police chase; **September 21,** masked gunmen storm into a crowded mall, in Nairobi, Kenya, and shoot dead at least 70 people and wound more than 150 people. Al-Shabaab, an Islamist militant group based in Somalia, takes responsibility for the attack, saying it was revenge for Kenya's military operations in Somalia. Viewing the deadly siege at a shopping mall in Kenya as a direct threat to its security, the United States deploys dozens of FBI agents. For years, the FBI has been closely watching Al-Shabaab, which has recruited numerous Americans to fight and die—sometimes as suicide bombers—for its cause. **October 5,** Nazih Abdul-Hamed al-Ruqai is captured by U.S. Special Forces in Libya for his role the 1998 bombings of the U.S. embassies in Tanzania and Kenya; on the same day in Somalia, a Navy SEAL team exchanges gunfire with militants at the home of a senior leader of the Al-Shabaab, the Somali militant group. The raid is in response to the massacre for which Al-Shabaab claimed responsibility two weeks earlier at a Nairobi, Kenya, shopping mall. The SEAL team withdraws before it can confirm that it had killed the Al-Shabaab leader. **December 20,** the Food and Drug Administration proposes to require major food producers to develop a plan to prevent intentional attempts to contaminate the food supply. Under the rule, companies would need plans to address vulnerabilities in production processes, particularly to acts of terrorism and they would have three years to comply. **December 31,** a federal judge orders a "compassionate release" for Lynne Stewart, the former defense lawyer convicted of assisting terrorism who is dying from cancer in a federal prison in Texas. Ms. Stewart, 74, was convicted in 2005. She is best known for her defense of Sheikh Omar Abdel-Rahman, the blind Egyptian cleric who was convicted in 1995 of conspiring to blow up landmarks in New York City. She was later tried and convicted of smuggling messages from Abdel-Rahman in prison to his violent followers in Egypt, and was sentenced to 10 years in prison.

2014: January 30, six suspected members of Islamic State of Iraq and the Levant (ISIS) seize control of a government building in Baghdad. The attackers kill nine hostages when the Iraqi army take control of the building and four of the attackers detonate suicide explosive vests throughout the building. The final toll of this attack stands at 24 dead and 50 wounded; **May 27,** Obama announces plans to end U.S. troop presence in Afghanistan by 2016; **June 8,** in Las Vegas, Nevada, two lone wolf white supremacists kill two police officers as they are eating lunch, they then enter a nearby Walmart and kill a shopper before both killing themselves; **June 14,** ISIS claims to have executed 1,700 Iraq soldiers and civilians in northern Iraq; **June 15,** the mastermind behind the Benghazi attack, Ahmed Abu Khatallah, is captured and brought to the United States to face charges for his role in the attack.

Bibliography

Aboul-Enein, Youssef H., and Sherifa Zuhur. *Islamic Rulings on Warfare*. Carlisle Barracks, PA: Strategic Studies Institute, 2004.

Abuza, Zachary. *Militant Islam in Southeast Asia: Crucible of Terror*. Boulder, CO: Lynne Rienner, 2003.

Acheson, Dean. *Present at the Creation: My Years at the State Department*. New York: Norton, 1969.

Alagha, Joseph. *Hezbollah's Documents: From the 1985 Open Letter to the 2009 Manifesto*. Amsterdam: Pallas, 2001.

Allan, Stuart, and Barbie Zelizer, eds. *Reporting War: Journalism in Wartime*. New York: Routledge, 2004.

Al-Rasheed, Madawi. *Contesting the Saudi State: Islamic Voices from a New Generation*. Cambridge: Cambridge University Press, 2006.

Anonymous. *Imperial Hubris: Why the West Is Losing the War on Terror*. New York: Brassey's, 2004.

Armstrong, Karen. *Islam: A Short History*. New York: Modern Library, 2002.

Associated Press. "In Motley Array of Iraqi Foes, Why Does U.S. Spotlight al-Qaida?" *International Herald Tribune*, June 8, 2007.

Atkinson, Rick. *In the Company of Soldiers: A Chronicle of Combat*. New York: Henry Holt, 2005.

Atran, Scott. *Talking to the Enemy: Faith, Brotherhood, and the (Un)Making of Terrorists*. New York: HarperCollins, 2010.

Atwan, Abdel Bari. *The Secret History of Al Qaeda*. Berkeley: University of California Press, 2006.

Aust, Stefan, et al. *Inside 9/11: What Really Happened*. New York: St. Martin's, 2001.

Ayoub, Mahmoud M. *Redemptive Suffering in Islam: A Study of the Devotional Aspects of "Ashura" in Twelver Shi'ism*. The Hague: Brill, 1978.

Babington, Charles. "Congress Votes to Renew Patriot Act, with Changes." *Washington Post*, March 8, 2006.

Bacevich, Andrew J. *The New American Militarism: How Americans Are Seduced by War*. New York: Oxford University Press, 2005.

Baird-Windle, Patricia, and Eleanor J. Bader. *Targets of Hatred: Anti-Abortion Terrorism*. New York: St. Martin's, 2001.

Baker, Peter. "Obama Says Al Qaeda in Yemen Planned Bombing Plot, and He Vows Retribution." *New York Times*, January 3, 2010.

Baker, Stewart. *Patriot Debates: Experts Debate the USA PATRIOT Act*. New York: American Bar Association, 2005.

Ball, Howard. *Bush, the Detainees, and the Constitution: The Battle over Presidential Power in the War on Terror*. Lawrence: University Press of Kansas, 2007.

Ball, Howard, and Mildred Vasan, eds. *The USA PATRIOT Act: A Further Reading Handbook*. Santa Barbara, CA: ABC-CLIO, 2004.

Ball, Simon J. *The Cold War: An International History, 1947–1991*. New York: St. Martin's, 1998.

Bamford, James. *Body of Secrets: Anatomy of the Ultra Secret National Security Agency.* New York: Anchor, 2002.

Banks, William C., Renee de Nevers, and Mitchell B. Wallenstein. *Combatting Terrorism: Strategies and Approaches.* Washington, DC: CQ Press, 2008.

Barker, A. J. *Arab-Israeli Wars.* New York: Hippocrene, 1980.

Barnett, Thomas P. M. "The Man between War and Peace." *Esquire*, March 11, 2008, 1–4.

Barno, David W. "Fighting 'The Other War': Counterinsurgency Strategy in Afghanistan, 2003–2005." *Military Review* (September–October 2007): 32–44.

Barret, Devlin. "Mosque Debate Isn't Going Away." *Wall Street Journal*, August 3, 2010.

Barsky, Robert F. *Noam Chomsky: A Life of Dissent.* Cambridge, MA: MIT Press, 1997.

Beck, Richard A. "Remote Sensing and GIS as Counterterrorism Tools in the Afghanistan War: A Case Study of the Zhawar Kili Region." *Professional Geographer* 55, no. 2 (May 2003): 170–79.

Beckwith, Charlie A., and Donald Knox. *Delta Force: The Army's Elite Counterterrorist Unit.* New York: Avon, 2000.

Bell, J. Bowyer. *Murders on the Nile: The World Trade Center and Global Terror.* San Francisco: Encounter Books, 2003.

Bellamy, Alex J. "No Pain, No Gain? Torture and Ethics in the War on Terror." *International Affairs* 82 (2006): 121–48.

Belluck, Pam. "Unrepentant Shoe Bomber Is Given a Life Sentence for Trying to Blow Up Jet." *New York Times*, January 21, 2003.

Bender, Bryan. "Terrorist Funds-Tracking No Secret, Some Say." *Boston Globe*, June 28, 2006.

Benjamin, Daniel, and Steven Simon. *The Next Attack: The Failure of the War on Terror and a Strategy for Getting It Right.* New York: Times Books, 2005.

Benjamin, Daniel, and Steven Simon. *The Age of Sacred Terror.* New York: Random House, 2002.

Bennett, Brian, and Douglas Waller. "Thwarting the Airline Plot: Inside the Investigation." *Time*, August 10, 2006.

Bergen, Peter L. *Manhunt: The Ten-Year Search for Bin Laden: From 9/11 to Abbottabad.* New York: Random House, 2012.

Bergen, Peter L. *The Osama bin Laden I Know: An Oral History of al Qaeda's Leader.* New York: Free Press, 2006.

Bergen, Peter L. *Holy War Inc.: Inside the Secret World of Osama bin Laden.* New York: Touchstone, 2002.

Bergesen, Albert. *The Sayyid Qutb Reader: Selected Writings on Politics, Religion and Society.* New York: Routledge, 2007.

Bernstein, Richard. *Out of the Blue: The Story of September 11, 2001, from Jihad to Ground Zero.* New York: Times Books, 2002.

Berntsen, Garry. *Human Intelligence, Counterterrorism, and National Leadership: A Practical Guide.* Washington, DC: Potomac Books, 2008.

Berton, Hal, Mike Carter, David Heath, and James Neff. "The Terrorist Within." *Seattle Times*, July 2, 2002.

Beschloss, Micahel R., and Strobe Talbott. *At the Highest Levels: The Inside Story of the End of the Cold War.* Boston: Little, Brown, 1993.

Biddle, Stephen. *Afghanistan and the Future of Warfare: Implications for Army and Defense Policy.* Carlisle, PA: Strategic Studies Institute, 2002.

Bigelow, Bruce V. "Predator, Part II: Spy Plane's New Version Is Bigger, Better, More Capable." *San Diego Union-Tribune*, August 27, 2002.

Bilefsky, Dan. "Bank Consortium Faces Outcry on Data Transfer." *International Herald Tribune*, June 29, 2006.

Bjelopera, Jerome, and Mark Randol. *American Jihadist Terrorism: Combating a Complex Threat.* Congressional Research Service (CRS) Report for Congress R41416. Washington, DC: Congressional Research Service, November 15, 2011. Accessed February 18, 2012. http://www.fas.org/sgp/crs/terror/R41416.pdf.

Blackburn, Robin, and Oliver Kamm. "For and against Chomsky." *Prospect* (London), October 20, 2005.

Blanchard, Christopher. *Libya: Background and U.S. Relations*. Washington, DC: Congressional Research Service, 2007. Accessed February 16, 2012. http://www.opencrs.com.

Blanford, Nicholas. *Killing Mr. Lebanon: The Assassination of Rafik Hariri and Its Impact on the Middle East*. New York: I. B. Tauris, 2006.

Blomquist, Brian. "Suspected Mastermind of the USS *Cole* Bombing Arrested." *New York Post*, November 26, 2003.

Blumenkrantz, Zhoar, and Yoav Stern. "Scores Dead in Three Amman Hotel Bombings; Israelis Evacuated before Attack." *Haaretz*, November 10, 2005. http://www.haaretz.com/print-edition/news/scores-dead-in-three-amman-hotel-bombings-israelis-evacuated-before-attack-1.173770.

Bobbit, Phillip. "War Powers: An Essay on John Hart Ely's *War and Responsibility: Constitutional Lessons of Vietnam and Its Aftermath.*" *Michigan Law Quarterly* 92, no. 6 (May 1994): 1364–400.

Bohn, Michael K. *The Achille Lauro Hijacking: Lessons in the Politics and Prejudice of Terrorism*. Dulles, VA: Potomac Books, 2004.

Bolt, Paul J., Damon V. Coletta, and Collins G. Shackelford Jr., eds. *American Defense Policy*. 8th ed. Baltimore: Johns Hopkins University Press, 2005.

Bonner, Raymond. "Echoes of Early Design to Use Chemicals to Blow Up Airlines." *New York Times*, August 11, 2006.

Booth, William. "*Fahrenheit 9/11* Too Hot for Disney?" *Washington Post*, May 6, 2004, C1.

Borzou, Daragahi. "Bin Laden Takes Responsibility for Christmas Day Bombing Attempt." *New York Times*, January 24, 2010.

Bowman, Karlyn. "Public Opinion on the War with Iraq." American Enterprise Institute, AEI Public Opinion Studies. Updated March 19, 2009. http://www.aei.org/publicopinion2.

Boyer Bell, J. *Murders on the Nile: The World Trade Center and Global Terror*. San Francisco: Encounter Books, 2003.

Braddon, Derek. *Exploding the Myth? The Peace Dividend, Regions and Market Adjustment*. Amsterdam: Oversees Publishers Association, 2000.

Brisard, Jean-Charles, in collaboration with Damien Martinez. *Zarqawi: The New Face of al-Qaeda*. New York: Other Press, 2005.

Brzezinski, Zbigniew. *Power and Principle: Memoirs of the National Security Adviser, 1977–1981*. New York: Farrar, Straus and Giroux, 1985.

Buckley, Mary E., and Robert Singh. *The Bush Doctrine and the War on Terrorism: Global Responses, Global Consequences*. London: Routledge, 2006.

Bumiller, Elisabeth, and Mark Massetti. "General Steps from Shadow." *New York Times*, May 13, 2009.

Burns, John. "Separatists Halt Violence to Advance Basque Goals." *New York Times*, October 21, 2011.

Burton, James G. *The Pentagon Wars*. Annapolis, MD: Naval Institute Press, 1993.

Buzzell, Colby. *My War: Killing Time in Iraq*. New York: Putnam, 2005.

Calabresi, Massimo. "Prosecuting KSM: Harder Than You Think." *Time*, November 13, 2009.

Calvert, John. *Sayyid Qutb and the Origins of Radical Islamism*. Chichester, NY: Columbia University Press, 2010.

Caram, Peter. *The 1993 World Trade Center Bombing: Foresight and Warning*. London: Janus, 2001.

Carlisle, David. "Dhiren Barot: Was He an Al Qaeda Mastermind or Merely a Hapless Plotter?" *Studies in Conflict and Terrorism* 30, no. 12 (2007): 1057–71.

Carter, Barry E. *International Economic Sanctions*. Cambridge: Cambridge University Press, 1988.

Carter, Jimmy. *Keeping Faith: Memoirs of a President*. Fayetteville: University of Arkansas Press, 1982.

Cassese, Antonio. *Terrorism, Politics and Law: The Achille Lauro Affair*. Princeton, NJ: Princeton University Press, 1989.

Cha, Victor D. "Korea's Place in the Axis." *Foreign Affairs* 81, no. 3 (May/June 2002): 79–92.

Chalk, Peter, and Bruce Hoffman. *The Dynamics of Suicide Terrorism: Four Case Studies of Terrorist Movements*. Santa Monica, CA: RAND, 2005.

Chalk, Peter, Angel Rabasa, William Rosenau, and Leanne Piggott. *The Evolving Terrorist Threat to Southeast Asia: A Net Assessment*. Santa Monica, CA: RAND, 2009.

Chandrasekaran, Rajiv. "Car Bombs Kill at Least 35 in Baghdad." *Washington Post*, October 28, 2003.

Chen, David W. "More Get 9/11 Aid, but Distrust of U.S. Effort Lingers." *New York Times*, August 27, 2002, B1.

Chernus, Ira. *Monsters to Destroy: The Neoconservative War on Terror and Sin*. Boulder, CO: Paradigm Publishers, 2006.

Chomsky, Noam. *9/11*. New York: Seven Stories, 2001.

Choueri, Youssef. *Islamic Fundamentalism*. New York: Continuum Publishing Group, 2002.

Clancy, Tom, Carl Stiner, and Tony Koltz. *Shadow Warriors: Inside the Special Forces*. New York: Berkley Books, 2003.

Clancy, Tom, with Anthony Zinni and Tony Kolz. *Battle Ready*. New York: Putnam, 2004.

Clarke, Richard A. *Against All Enemies: Inside America's War on Terror*. New York: Free Press, 2004.

Clarke, Walter S., and Herbst Jeffrey Ira. *Learning from Somalia: The Lessons of Armed Humanitarian Intervention*. Boulder, CO: Westview, 1997.

Clinton, Bill. *My Life*. New York: Vintage Books, 2005.

Cockburn, Patrick. *The Occupation: War and Resistance in Iraq*. New York: Verso, 2007.

Cogan, Charles. "Desert One and Its Disorders." *Journal of Military History* 67 (2003): 273–96.

Coll, Steve. *Ghost Wars: The Secret History of the CIA, Afghanistan, and Bin Laden, from the Soviet Invasion to September 10, 2001*. New York: Penguin, 2004.

Combat Studies Institute Contemporary Operations Study Group. *A Different Kind of War: The United States Army Operation Enduring Freedom (OEF), September 2001–September 2005*. Fort Leavenworth, KS: Combat Studies Institute Press, 2009.

Congressional Research Service, Report to Congress. *Iraq: Post-Saddam Governance and Security, September 6, 2007*. Washington, DC: U.S. Government Printing Office, 2007.

Cook, David. *Paradigmatic Jihadi Movements*. West Point, NY: Combating Terrorism Center, 2006. Accessed February 10, 2012. http://www.ctc.usma.edu/posts/paradigmatic-jihadi-movements.

Corbin, Jane. *Al-Qaeda: The Terror Network That Threatens the World*. New York: Thunder's Mouth, 2002.

Cordesman, Anthony H., and Nawaf Obaid. *Al-Qaeda in Saudi Arabia: Asymmetric Threats and Islamist Extremists*. Washington, DC: Center for Strategic and International Studies, 2005.

Cornelia Beyer, *Violent Globalisms: Conflict in Response to Empire*. Burlington, VT: Ashgate, 2008.

Couch, Dick. *Down Range: Navy SEALs in the War on Terrorism*. New York: Three Rivers, 2006.

Coughlin, Con. *American Ally: Tony Blair and the War on Terror*. New York: Ecco, 2006.

Craig, Olga. "At 8:46 a.m., the World Changed in a Moment." *Sunday Telegraph* (London), September 16, 2001, 14.

Crenshaw, Martha, ed. *Terrorism in Context*. University Park: Pennsylvania State University Press, 1995.

Crippen, James B. *Improvised Explosive Devices (IED)*. New York: CRC Press, 2007.

Cullison, Alan, and Andrew Higgins. "Account of Spy Trip on Kabul PC Matches Travels of Richard Reid." *Wall Street Journal*, January 16, 2002.

Daalder, Ivo H., I. M. Destler, James M. Lindsay, Paul C. Light, Robert E. Litan, Michael E. O'Hanlon, Peter R. Orszag, and James B. Steinberg. *Assessing the Department of Homeland Security.* Washington, DC: Brookings Institution Press, 2002.

Danner, Mark. *Torture and Truth: America, Abu Ghraib, and the War on Terror.* New York: New York Review Books, 2004.

Davis, Brian. *Qaddafi, Terrorism, and the Origins of the U.S. Attack on Libya.* New York: Praeger, 1990.

Davis, Mike. *Buda's Wagon: A Brief History of the Car Bomb.* New York: Verso Books, 2007.

Day, Thomas L. *Along the Tigris: The 101st Airborne Division in Operation Iraqi Freedom: February 2003–March 2004.* Atglen, PA: Schiffer, 2007.

DeForest, M. J. *Principles of Improvised Explosive Devices.* Boulder, CO: Paladin, 1984.

DeLong, Michael, with Noah Lukeman. *Inside CENTCOM: The Unvarnished Truth about the Wars in Afghanistan and Iraq.* Washington, DC: Regnery, 2004.

DeMers, Michael. *Fundamentals of GIS.* 3rd ed. Hoboken, NJ: Wiley, 2004.

Denby, David. "Michael Moore's Viciously Funny Attack on the Bush Administration." *New Yorker*, June 28, 2004, 108.

Department of Defense, Office of the Under Secretary of Defense for Acquisition, Technology, and Logistics. *Unmanned Aerial Vehicles (UAVs): Roadmap, 2002–2027.* Washington, DC: Progressive Management, 2008.

Department of Transport Air Accidents Investigation Branch. *Aircraft Accident Report 2/90.* London: Royal Aerospace Establishment, 1990. Accessed February 16, 2012. http://www.aaib.gov.uk/home/index.cfm.

Dershowitz, Alan. *The Case for Israel.* New York: Wiley, 2003.

Dershowitz, Alan M. *Is There a Right to Remain Silent?: Coercive Interrogation and the Fifth Amendment after 9/11.* Oxford: Oxford University Press, 2008.

DeYoung, Karen. *Soldier: The Life of Colin Powell.* New York: Knopf, 2006.

Dobson, Christopher. *Black September: Its Short, Violent History.* London: Robert Hale, 1975.

Dockery, Kevin. *Navy SEALs: A Complete History from World War II to the Present.* New York: Berkley Books, 2004.

Dolan, Chris J. *In War We Trust: The Bush Doctrine and the Pursuit of Just War.* Burlington, VT: Ashgate, 2005.

Donegan, Lawrence, and Paul Harris. "American Right Vows to Settle Score as Bush's Nemesis Turns Up the Heat." *Observer* (London), June 27, 2004, 18.

Dorronsoro, Gilles. *Afghanistan: Revolution Unending, 1979–2002.* London: C. Hurst, 2003.

Doty, John M. "Geospatial Intelligence: An Emerging Discipline in National Intelligence with an Important Security Assistance Role." *DISAM Journal* 27, no. 3 (Spring 2005): 1–14.

Doyle, Michael W. "Liberalism and World Politics." *American Political Science Review* 80 (December 1986): 1151–69.

Draper, Robert. *Dead Certain: The Presidency of George W. Bush.* New York: Free Press, 2008.

Drumheller, Tyler, and Elaine Monaghan. *On the Brink: An Insider's Account of How the White House Compromised American Intelligence.* New York: Carroll and Graf, 2006.

Dumbrell, John. *A Special Relationship: Anglo-American Relations from the Cold War to Iraq.* New York: Palgrave Macmillan, 2006.

Dwyer, Jim, and Kevin Flynn. *102 Minutes: The Untold Story of the Fight to Survive Inside the Twin Towers.* New York: Times Books, 2005.

Dwyer, Jim. "Errors and Lack of Information in New York's Response to Sept. 11." *New York Times*, May 19, 2004, B8.

Eckes, Alfred, and Thomas Zeiler. *Globalization and the American Century.* Cambridge: Cambridge University Press, 2003.

Eggen, Dan. "Agent Claims FBI Supervisor Thwarted Probe." *Washington Post*, May 27, 2002.

Eisenhower Research Project, Brown University. "Estimated Cost of Post-9/11 Wars: 225,000 Lives, up to $4 Trillion." Accessed June 20, 2014. http://news.brown.edu/pressreleases/2011/06/warcosts.

Elliott, Michael. "The Shoe Bomber's World." *Time*, February 16, 2002.

Emerson, Steven. *Jihad Incorporated: A Guide to Militant Islam in the U.S.* Foreword by Peter Hoekstra. Amherst, NY: Prometheus Books, 2006.

Engbrecht, Shawn. *America's Covert Warriors: Inside the World of Private Military Contractors*. Dulles, VA: Potomac Books, 2010.

Eshel, David. *The U.S. Rapid Deployment Forces*. New York: Arco, 1985.

Esposito, John. *What Everyone Needs to Know about Islam*. New York: Oxford University Press, 2002.

Esposito, John L. *The Oxford History of Islam*. New York: Oxford University Press, 2000.

Etzioni, Amitai. *How Patriotic Is the PATRIOT Act?* New York: Routledge, 2004.

Ezzo, Matthew V., and Amos N. Guiora. "A Critical Decision Point on the Battlefield—Friend, Foe, or Innocent Bystander." *University of Utah Legal Studies Paper* 8, no. 3 (2008).

Fair, Christine C. "Antecedents and Implications of the November 2008 Lashkar-e-Taiba (LeT) Attack upon Several Targets in the Indian Mega-City of Mumbai." *Testimony Given before the House Homeland Security Committee, Subcommittee on Transportation and Infrastructure*, March 11, 2009. http://home.comcast.net/~christine_fair/pubs/CT-320_Christine_Fair.pdf.

Farren, Mick. *CIA: Secrets of "The Company."* New York: Barnes and Noble, 2003.

Fearon, James D., and David D. Laitin. "Ethnicity, Insurgency, and Civil War." *American Political Science Review* 97 (2003): 75–76.

Feith, Douglas. *War and Decision: Inside the Pentagon at the Dawn of the War on Terrorism*. New York: Harper, 2008.

Ferguson, Amanda. *The Attack against the U.S. Embassies in Kenya and Tanzania*. New York: Rosen Publication Group, 2003.

Filkins, Dexter, and Alex Berenson. "Suicide Bombers in Baghdad Kill at Least 34." *New York Times*, October 28, 2003.

Finkelstein, Claire, and Jens David Ohlin. *Targeted Killings: Law and Morality in an Asymmetrical World*. Oxford: Oxford University Press, 2012.

Finn, Peter. "Al Qaeda Recruiter Reportedly Tortured." *Washington Post*, January 31, 2003.

Finn, Peter. "German at Center of Sept. 11 Inquiry." *Washington Post*, June 12, 2002.

Finn, Peter, and Anne E. Kornblut. "Opposition to U.S. Trial Likely to Keep Mastermind of 9/11 Attacks in Detention." *Washington Post*, November 13, 2010.

Firdaus, Irwan. "Indonesia Executes Bali Bombers." *Jakarta Post*, November 9, 2008.

Fisher, Louis. "Bush and the War Power: A Critique from the Outside." In *Testing the Limits: George W. Bush and the Imperial Presidency*, edited by Mark J. Rozell and Gleaves Whitney, 157–76. Lanham, MD: Rowman and Littlefield, 2009.

Fisher, Louis. *Military Tribunals and Presidential Power: American Revolution to the War on Terrorism*. Lawrence: University Press of Kansas, 2005.

Fisher, Louis. *Presidential War Power*. Lawrence: University Press of Kansas, 2004.

Fisk, Robert. *The Great War for Civilization: The Conquest of the Middle East*. New York: Vintage Books, 2007.

Fisk, Robert. *Pity the Nation: The Abduction of Lebanon*. New York: Touchstone, Simon & Schuster, 1990.

Fontaine, Andre. *History of the Cold War, 1917–1966*. 2 vols. New York: Pantheon, 1968.

Fontenot, Gregory, et al. *On Point: The United States Army in Iraqi Freedom*. Annapolis, MD: Naval Institute Press, 2005.

Forest, James, ed. *Teaching Terror: Strategic and Tactical Learning in the Terrorist World*. Lanham, MD: Rowman & Littlefield, 2006.

Forrest, James J. F. *Countering Terrorism and Insurgency in the 21st Century*. 3 vols. Westport, CT: Praeger Security International, 2007.

Fouda, Yosri, and Nick Fielding. *Masterminds of Terror: The Truth behind the Most Devastating Terrorist Attack the World Has Ever Seen*. New York: Arcade, 2003.

Freedman, George. *America's Secret War: Inside the Worldwide Struggle between America and Its Enemies*. New York: Broadway Books, 2004.

Friedman, Lauri S. *What Motivates Suicide Bombers?* Farmington Hills, MI: Greenhaven, 2004.

Friedman, Lori, ed. *How Should the United States Treat Prisoners in the War on Terror?* Farmington Hills, MI: Greenhaven, 2005.

Friedman, Norman. *The Naval Institute Guide to U.S. Amphibious Ships and Craft: An Illustrated Design History*. Annapolis, MD: Naval Institute Press, 2002.

Friman, H. Richard. *Narcodiplomacy: Exporting the U.S. War on Drugs*. Ithaca, NY: Cornell University Press, 1996.

Frum, David. *The Right Man: The Surprise Presidency of George W. Bush*. New York: Random House, 2003.

Frum, David, and Richard Perle. *An End to Evil: How to Win the War on Terror*. New York: Random House, 2003.

Fuentes, Gidget. "The Search for SEALs—Changes to Special-Warfare Recruiting, Training, Practices Shows Promise to Growing Unit." *Navy Times* (April 26, 2007): 18.

Fukuyama, Francis. *The End of History and the Last Man*. New York: Free Press, 1992.

Fuller, Graham E., and Rend Rahim Francke. *The Arab Shi'a: The Forgotten Muslims*. Hampshire, UK: Palgrave Macmillan, 2001.

Gaddis, John Lewis. *The Cold War: A New History*. New York: Penguin, 2005.

Gaddis, John Lewis. *The Long Peace: Inquiries into the History of the Cold War*. New York: Oxford University Press, 1989.

Gaddis, John Lewis. *Strategies of Containment: A Critical Appraisal of Postwar American National Security Policy*. New York: Oxford University Press, 1982.

Gambetta, Diego, ed. *Making Sense of Suicide Missions*. Oxford: Oxford University Press, 2005.

Gates, Robert M. *Understanding the New U.S. Defense Policy through the Speeches of Robert M. Gates, Secretary of Defense*. Rockville, MD: Arc Manor, 2008.

Gates, Robert M. *From the Shadows: The Ultimate Insider's Story of Five Presidents and How They Won the Cold War*. New York: Simon and Schuster, 1996.

Gatsiounis, Ioannis. "Somali Terror Group Curtailed." *Washington Times*, July 10, 2011.

Gettleman, Marvin, and Stuart Schaar, eds. *The Middle East and Islamic World Reader*. New York: Grove, 2003.

Ghosh, Bobby. "Mosque Controversy: Does America Have a Muslim Problem?" *Time*, August 19, 2010.

Gillibrand, Senator Kristen, Senator Frank Lautenberg, Senator Robert Menendez, and Senator Charles Schumer. *Justice Undone: The Release of the Lockerbie Bomber*. Washington, DC: U.S. Senate, 2010. Accessed February 16, 2012. http://www.hsdl.org.

Goh, Evelyn. "Hegemonic Constraints: The Implications of 11 September for American Power." *Australian Journal of International Affairs* 57, no. 1 (April 2003): 77–97.

Gohari, M. *The Taliban: Ascent to Power*. Oxford: Oxford University Press, 1999.

Goldberg, Alfred, et al. *Pentagon 9/11*. Washington, DC: Historical Office, Office of the Secretary of Defense, 2007.

Goldenberg, Suzanne. "Agents Who Led Bin Laden Hunt Criticises CIA." *Guardian* (London) (July 8, 2006), 14.

Gonzales, Daniel. *Network-Centric Operations Case Study: The Stryker Brigade*

Combat Team. Santa Monica, CA: RAND Corporation, 2005.

Goodman, Amy, and Juan Gonzalez. "'Aspirational Rather than Operational'—7 Arrested in Miami Terrorism Plot." *Democracy Now*, June 26, 2006. Accessed February 18, 2012. http://www.democracynow.org/2006/6/26/aspirational_rather_than_operational_7_arrested.

Gordon, Greg. "Ex-CIA Official: Bush Plays into Al Qaeda's Hands." *Sacramento Bee*, November 20, 2004, A12.

Gordon, Greg. "Rowley Explains Criticisms." *Star Tribune* (Minneapolis), June 7, 2002.

Gordon, Michael R., and General Bernard E. Trainor. *Cobra II: The Inside Story of the Invasion and Occupation of Iraq*. New York: Pantheon Books, 2006.

Gordon, Michael R., and General Bernard E. Trainor. *The Generals' War: The Inside Story of the Conflict in the Gulf*. New York: Little, Brown, 1995.

Graham, Bob. *Intelligence Matters: The CIA, the FBI, Saudi Arabia, and the Failure of America's War on Terror*. New York: Random House, 2004.

Graham, Bradley. *By His Own Rules: The Ambitions, Successes, and Ultimate Failures of Donald Rumsfeld*. New York: PublicAffairs, 2009.

Grant, Rebecca. "Air Warfare in Transition." *Air Force Magazine* 87, no. 12 (December 2004): 120–32.

Graveline, Christopher, and Michael Clemens. *The Secrets of Abu Ghraib Revealed*. Dulles, VA: Potomac Books, 2010.

Greenberg, Karen J., and Joshua L. Dratel, eds. *The Torture Papers: The Road to Abu Ghraib*. Cambridge: Cambridge University Press, 2005.

Greenberg, Karen J., and Stephen Holmes. *The Torture Debate in America*. Cambridge, MA: Cambridge University Press, 2006.

Gregorian, Vartan. *Islam: A Mosaic, Not a Monolith*. Baltimore: Brookings Institute Press, 2004.

Gregory, Shaun R. *Nuclear Command and Control in NATO: Nuclear Weapons Operations and the Strategy of Flexible Response*. New York: Palgrave Macmillan, 1996.

Grey, Sten, and Ian Cobain. "From Secret Prisons to Turning a Blind Eye: Europe's Role in Rendition." *Guardian* (London), June 7, 2006, 1.

Griffiths, Katherine. "U.S. Airline Industry in Tailspin to Disaster." *Independent* (London), September 10, 2004, 46.

Gross, Emmanuel. "Use of Civilians as Human Shields: What Legal and Moral Restrictions Pertain to a War Waged by a Democratic State Against Terrorism?" *Emory International Law Review* 16 (2002): 445–524.

Guiora, Amos N. *Constitutional Limits on Coercive Interrogation*. New York: Oxford University Press, 2008,

Guiora, Amos N. *Global Perspectives on Counterterrorism*. New York: Aspen Publishers, 2007.

Gunaratna, Rohan. *Inside Al Qaeda: Global Network of Terror*. New York: Berkley Publishing Group, 2003.

Gurtov, Melvin. *Superpower on Crusade: The Bush Doctrine in U.S. Foreign Policy*. Boulder, CO: Lynne Rienner, 2006.

Hafez, Mohammed. *Suicide Bombers in Iraq: The Strategy and Ideology of Martyrdom*. Washington, DC: U.S. Institute of Peace Press, 2007.

Hamel-Green, Michael. *Regional Initiatives on Nuclear- and WMD-Free Zones: Cooperative Approaches to Arms Control and Non-Proliferation*. New York: United Nations Publication, 2006.

Hammel, Eric. *Six Days in June: How Israeli Won the 1967 Arab-Israeli War*. New York: Scribner, 1992.

Hansen, Andrew, and Lauren Vriens. "Al-Qaeda in the Islamic Maghreb (AQIM) or L'Organisation Al-Qaïda au Maghreb Islamique (Formerly Salafist Group for Preaching and Combat or Groupe Salafiste pour la Prédication et le Combat)." *Council on Foreign Relations, Backgrounder*. Updated July 31, 2008. Available online at www.cfr.org/publication/12717.

Hanson, Victor Davis. *Between War and Peace: Lessons from Afghanistan to Iraq.* New York: Random House, 2004.

Harding, Jim. *After Iraq: War, Imperialism and Democracy.* Black Point, NS: Fernwood, 2004.

Harel, Amos, and Avi Issacharoff. *34 Days: Israel, Hezbollah and the War in Lebanon.* New York: Palgrave Macmillan, 2008.

Harnden, Toby. "Sect Inspired 'Leader of Sears Tower Plot.'" *Daily Telegraph* (UK), June 25, 2006. http://www.telegraph.co.uk/news/worldnews/northamerica/usa/1522288/Sect-inspired-leader-of-Sears-Tower-plot.html.

Harris, Paul. "Newburgh Four: Poor, Black, and Jailed under FBI 'Entrapment' Tactics." *The Guardian* (UK), December 12, 2011. http://www.guardian.co.uk/world/2011/dec/12/newburgh-four-fbi-entrapment-terror.

Hastings, Max. *Yoni, Hero of Entebbe.* New York: Bantam Books, 1979.

Hedges, Michael. "Workers at Pentagon Recount Horrific Scene." *Houston Chronicle,* September 12, 2001, A22.

Hegarty, Shane. "Lighthouse of the Left." *Irish Times* (Dublin), January 14, 2006, 5.

Heisbourg, François. "Work in Progress: The Bush Doctrine and Its Consequences." *Washington Quarterly* 6, no. 22 (Spring 2003): 75–88.

Hennessey, Kathleen. "N.Y. Bomber Has al-Qaeda Tie, White House Says." *Los Angeles Times,* May 10, 2010.

Hernandez, Javier C. "Vote Endorses Muslim Center Near Ground Zero." *New York Times,* May 25, 2010.

Hersh, Seymour. *Chain of Command: The Road from 9/11 to Abu Ghraib.* New York: HarperCollins, 2004.

Herzog, Chaim. *Heroes of Israel: Profiles of Jewish Courage.* London: Little, Brown, 1989.

Hillard, Robert L., and Michael C. Keith. *Waves of Rancor: Tuning in the Radical Right.* New York: M. E. Sharpe, 1999.

Hironaka, Ann. *Neverending Wars: The International Community, Weak States, and the Perpetuation of Civil War.* Cambridge, MA: Harvard University Press, 2005.

Hirschman, David. "I Didn't See Evil." *Atlanta Journal-Constitution,* January 27, 2002.

Hirsh, Michael. "Bush and the World." *Foreign Affairs* 82, no. 5 (September–October 2002): 18–43.

History Office. *History of the Air Armament Center, 1 October 2006–30 September 2007.* Eglin Air Force Base, FL: Air Armament Center, 2008.

Hixson, Walter. *George F. Kennan: Cold War Iconoclast.* New York: Columbia University Press, 1989.

Hodes, Cyrus, and Mark Sedra. *The Search for Security in Post-Taliban Afghanistan.* Adelphi Paper 391. Abingdon, UK: Routledge for the International Institute for Strategic Studies, 2007.

Hodge, Amanda. "From Harmless Tenant to Terror Plot Accused." *The Australian,* May 6, 2010.

Hogan, Michael J., ed. *The End of the Cold War: Its Meaning and Implications.* New York: Cambridge University Press, 1992.

Horowitz, Craig. "Anatomy of a Foiled Terrorist Plot: Two Would-Be Bombers of the Herald Square Subway Station Find That Three Is a Crowd." *New York Magazine,* May 21, 2005. http://nymag.com/nymetro/news/features/10559/.

Huband, Mark, and Mark Odell. "Unmanned Weapon Makes Its Mark in Yemeni Sea of Sand." *Financial Times* (London), November 6, 2002, 24.

Hueston, Harry R., and B. Vizzin. *Terrorism 101.* 2nd ed. Ann Arbor, MI: XanEdu, 2004.

Human Rights First. *Getting to Ground Truth: Investigating U.S. Abuses in the "War on Terror."* Washington, DC: Human Rights First, 2004.

Hunt, Emily. "Islamist Terrorism in Northwestern Africa: A 'Thorn in the Neck' of the United States?" Washington, DC: The Washington Institute for Near East Policy, Policy Focus #65, February 2007. www.washingtoninstitute.org/templateC04.php?CID=266.

Hutto, Jonathan W., Sr. *Antiwar Soldier: How to Dissent within the Ranks of the Military.* New York: Nation Books, 2008.

Ibrahim, Raymond. *The Al Qaeda Reader: The Essential Texts of Osama bin Laden's Terrorist Organization.* New York: Broadway Books, 2007.

International Crisis Group. *Terrorism in Indonesia: Noordin's Networks.* Asia Report no. 114, May 5, 2006.

International Crisis Group. *Jordan's 9/11: Dealing with Jihadi Islamism.* Middle East Report no. 47, November 23, 2005.

Iraq Veterans against the War and Aaron Glantz. *Winter Soldier Iraq and Afghanistan: Eyewitness Accounts of the Occupations.* Chicago: Haymarket Books, 2008.

Irons, Peter. *War Powers: How the Imperial Presidency Hijacked the Constitution.* New York: Metropolitan Books, 2005.

Jackson, Brian, John Baker, Kim Cragin, John Parachini, Horacio Trujillo, and Peter Chalk. *Aptitude for Destruction.* Vol. 2, *Case Studies of Organizational Learning in Five Terrorist Groups.* Santa Monica, CA: RAND, 2005.

Jackson, Michael. *Hezbollah: Organizational Development, Ideological Evolution, and a Relevant Threat Model.* Washington, DC: Georgetown University Press, 2009.

Jalali, Ali A. "The Future of Afghanistan." *Parameters* (Spring 2006): 4–19.

James, Scott C. "The Evolution of the Presidency: Between the Promise and the Fear." In *Institutions of American Democracy: The Executive Branch*, edited by Joel P. Aberbach and Mark A Peterson, 3–40. New York: Oxford University Press, 2005.

Jervis, Robert. *American Foreign Policy in a New Era.* New York: Routledge, 2005.

Johnson, Chalmers. *The Sorrows of Empire: Militarism, Secrecy, and the End of the Republic.* New York: Metropolitan Books, 2004.

Joint Inquiry into Intelligence Community Activities before and after the Terrorist Attacks of September 11, 2001. *Hearings before the Select Committee on Intelligence U.S. Senate and the Permanent Select Committee on Intelligence House of Representatives.* Vol. 2. Washington, DC: U.S. Government Printing Office, 2004.

Jones, Seth G. "The Rise of Afghanistan's Insurgency: State Failure and Jihad." *International Security* 32 (2008): 7–40.

Jordan, Hamilton. *Crisis: The Last Year of the Carter Presidency.* New York: Putnam, 1982.

Kagan, Frederick. *Finding the Target: The Transformation of American Military Policy.* New York: Encounter Books, 2006.

Kalkan, Kerem, and Yu-Sung Su. "A Change in Attitudes toward Muslims? A Bayesian Investigation of Pre and Post 9/11 Public Opinion." Paper presented at the annual meeting of the MPSA Annual National Conference, Chicago, IL, April 3, 2008. http://citation.allacademic.com/meta/p266549_index.html.

Kant, Immanuel. *Perpetual Peace, and Other Essays on Politics, History, and Morals.* Translated by Ted Humphrey. Indianapolis: Hackett, 1983.

Kashurba, Glenn J. *Quiet Courage: The Definitive Account of Flight 93 and Its Aftermath.* Somerset, PA: SAJ Publishing, 2006.

Katona, Peter, et al. *Countering Terrorism and WMD: Creating a Global Counter-Terrorism Network.* New York: Routledge, 2006.

Kawar, Mark. "9/11 Shock Didn't Bring Bears to Stock Market." *Omaha World Herald*, September 17, 2002, 1D.

Kean, Thomas H., Lee H. Hamilton, and Benjamin Rhodes. *Without Precedent: The Inside Story of the 9/11 Commission.* New York: Knopf, 2006.

Keegan, John. *The Iraq War: The Military Offensive, from Victory in 21 Days to the Insurgent Aftermath.* New York: Vintage, 2005.

Keegan, William, Jr., with Bart Davis. *Closure: The Untold Story of the Ground Zero Recovery Mission.* New York: Touchstone Books, 2006.

Keeley, Graham. "ETA Car Bomb Targets BAA Owner in Madrid." *The Times* (London), February 9, 2009.

Kennan, George F. *Memoirs, 1925–1950.* Boston: Little, Brown, 1967.

Kepel, Gilles. *The War for Muslim Minds: Islam and the West.* Cambridge, MA: Belknap Press, 2004.

Kepel, Gilles, and Jean-Pierre Milelli, eds. *Al Qaeda in Its Own Words.* Cambridge, MA: Harvard University Press, 2008.

Kertcher, Chen. *The Search for Peace—or for a State: UN Intervention in Somalia, 1992–95.* Jerusalem: Harry S. Truman Research Institute for the Advancement of Peace, 2003.

Kessler, Ronald. *The CIA at War: Inside the Secret Campaign against Terror.* New York: St. Martin's Griffin, 2003.

Kettl, Donald F. *The Department of Homeland Security's First Year: A Report Card.* New York: Century Fund, 2004.

Khosrokhavar, Farhad. *Suicide Bombers: Allah's New Martyrs.* Translated by David Macey. London: Pluto, 2005.

Kitson, Frank. *Low Intensity Operations: Subversion, Insurgency and Peacekeeping.* London: Faber and Faber, 1971.

Knightley, Phillip. *The First Casualty: The War Correspondent as Hero and Myth-Maker from the Crimea to Iraq.* Baltimore: Johns Hopkins University Press, 2004.

Korn, David A. *Assassination in Khartoum.* Bloomington: Indiana University Press, 1993.

Kreimer, Nancy Fuchs. "Proposed Muslim Community Center Near Ground Zero: 'A Slap in the Face' or 'Repairing the Breach?'" *Huffington Post,* May 21, 2010.

Kyle, James, and John Eidson. *The Guts to Try: The Untold Story of the Iran Hostage Rescue Mission by the On-Scene Desert Commander.* New York: Orion Books, 1990.

Labbe, Theola, and Keith B. Richburg. "Decades of Good Deeds Provide No Armor; Red Cross Reassesses Its Presence in Iraq." *Washington Post,* October 28, 2003.

Labévière, Richard. *Dollars for Terror: The United States and Islam.* New York: Algora Publishing, 2000.

Lafeber, Walter. *America, Russia and the Cold War, 1945–2002.* Updated 9th ed. New York: McGraw-Hill, 2004.

Lambeth, Benjamin S. *Air Power against Terror: America's Conduct of Operation Enduring Freedom.* Santa Monica, CA: RAND Corporation, 2005.

Lance, Peter. *Triple Cross: How Bin Laden's Master Spy Penetrated the CIA, the Green Berets, and the FBI—and Why Patrick Fitzgerald Failed to Stop Him.* New York: ReganBooks, 2006.

Lance, Peter. *1000 Years for Revenge: International Terrorism and the FBI.* New York: Harper-Collins, 2003.

Lauffer, Peter. *Mission Rejected: U.S. Soldiers Who Say No to Iraq.* White River Junction, VT: Chelsea Green, 2006.

Lawrence, Bruce. *Messages to the World: The Statements of Osama bin Laden.* London: Verso, 2005.

Leone, Richard, and Greg Anriq, eds. *The War on Our Freedoms: Civil Liberties in the Age of Terrorism.* New York: PublicAffairs, 2003.

Leverett, Flynt, ed. *The Road Ahead: Middle East Policy in the Bush Administration's Second Term.* Washington, DC: Brookings Institution, 2005.

Levis, Alexander H., John C. Bedford, and Sandra Davis, eds. *The Limitless Sky: Air Force Science and Technology Contributions to the Nation.* Washington, DC: Air Force History and Museums Program, 2004.

Levitt, Matthew. "Hezbollah Finances: Funding the Party of God." In Jeanne Giraldo and Harold Trinkunas, eds., *Terrorism Financing and State Responses: A Comparative Perspective,* 134–51. Stanford, CA: Stanford University Press, 2007.

Levy, Robert. "Jose Padilla: No Charges and No Trial, Just Trial." *CATO Institute,* Washington D.C., August 11, 2003. Accessed September 16, 2011. http://www.cato.org/pub_display.php?pub_id=3208.

Lewis, Bernard. *The Crisis of Islam: Holy War and Unholy Terror.* New York: Random House, 2003.

Lewis, Bernard. *What Went Wrong? The Clash between Islam and Modernity in the Middle East.* New York: Oxford University Press, 2002.

Lichtblau, Eric, and James Risen. "Bank Data Sifted in Secret by U.S. to Block Terror." *New York Times,* June 23, 2006.

Lindley-French, Julien. *A Chronology of European Security and Defence, 1945–2006.* New York: Oxford University Press, 2008.

"Lockerbie Verdict, *Her Majesty's Advocate v Abdelbaset Ali Mohmed Al Megrahi and Al Amin Khalifa Fhimah, Prisoners in the Prison of Zeist, Camp Zeist (Kamp van Zeist), the Netherlands,* 2001." February 16, 2012. http://www.lawphil.net/international/int_cases/lockerbie_verdict.html.

Loeb, Vernon. "Planned Jan. 2000 Attacks Failed or Were Thwarted; Plot Targeted U.S., Jordan, American Warship, Official Says." *Washington Post,* December 24, 2000.

Luttrell, Marcus, with Patrick Robinson. *Lone Survivor: The Eyewitness Account of Operation Redwing and the Lost Heroes of SEAL-10.* Boston: Little, Brown, 2007.

Macfarquhar, Neil. "In Jail or Out, Sheik Preaches Views of Islam." *New York Times,* October 2, 1995.

Mahajan, Rahul. *The New Crusade: America's War on Terrorism.* New York: Monthly Review, 2002.

Maley, William. *The Afghanistan Wars.* New York: Palgrave Macmillan, 2002.

Malloy, Michael P. *United States Economic Sanctions: Theory and Practice.* Netherlands: Kluwer Law International, 2001.

Mango, Caroline, Paul Gitau, and Cyrus Ombati. "Top al-Qaeda Man Now Back in Africa." *Africa Press International,* August 4, 2008. http://africanpress.me/2008/08/04/top-al-qaeda-man-now-back-in-kenya/.

Mansfield, Edward D., and Jack Snyder. *Electing to Fight: Why Emerging Democracies Go to War.* Cambridge, MA: MIT Press, 2005.

Margasak, Larry, Lara Jakes, and Jim Irwin. "Man Cites Orders from al-Qaeda in Failed Bid to Blow Up Plane." *Globe and Mail* (Canada), December 26, 2011.

Markusen, Ann, Peter Hall, Scott Campbell, and Sabrina Deitrick. *The Rise of the Gunbelt: The Military Remapping of Industrial America.* New York: Oxford University Press, 1991.

Marolda, Edward, and Robert Schneller. *Shield and Sword: The United States Navy and the Persian Gulf War.* Annapolis, MD: U.S. Naval Institute Press, 2001.

Marsden, Peter. *The Taliban: War and Religion in Afghanistan.* London: Zed Books, 2002.

Mauroni, Albert. *Where Are the WMDs? The Reality of Chem-Bio Threats on the Home Front and on the Battlefield.* Annapolis, MD: Naval Institute Press, 2006.

May, Ernest R., ed. *The 9/11 Report with Related Documents.* Boston: Bedford, 2007.

McCarthy, Andrew C. "It's Time to Investigate Able Danger and the 9/11 Commission." *National Review* (December 8, 2005): 1.

McCormick, Thomas J. *America's Half-Century: United States Foreign Policy in the Cold War and After.* Baltimore: Johns Hopkins University Press, 1995.

McDermott, Terry. *Perfect Soldiers: The 9/11 Hijackers: Who They Were, Why They Did It.* New York: HarperCollins, 2005.

McGregor, Andrew. "Strike First." *The World Today* 58, no. 12 (2002).

McKinley, James. "Suspected Bombing Leader Indicted on Broader Charges." *New York Times,* April 1, 1995. http://www.nytimes.com/1995/04/14/nyregion/suspected-bombing-leader-indicted-on-broader-charges.html.

McLaughlin, Greg. *The War Correspondent.* London: Pluto, 2002.

Meason, James E. "The Foreign Intelligence Surveillance Act: Time for Reappraisal." *International Lawyer* 24 (Winter 1990): 1043.

Meeropol, Rachel, and Reed Brody. *America's Disappeared: Secret Imprisonment, Detainees, and the "War on Terror."* New York: Seven Stories, 2005.

Melman, Yossi. *The Master Terrorist: The True Story of Abu-Nidal*. New York: Adama, 1986.

Melzer, Nils. *Targeted Killing in International Law*. New York: Oxford University Press, 2009.

Mendelsohn, Sarah E. *Closing Guantanamo: From Bumper Sticker to Blueprint*. Washington, DC: Center for Security and International Studies, 2008.

Menkhaus, Kenneth. *Somalia: State Collapse and the Threat of Terrorism*. Oxford: Oxford University Press, 2004.

Meyer, Josh, and Greg Miller. "U.S. Secretly Tracks Global Bank Data." *Los Angeles Times*, June 23, 2006.

Michael, George. "The Legend and Legacy of Abu Musab al-Zarqawi." *Defence Studies* 7, no. 3 (September 2007).

Mickolus, Edward, Todd Sandler, and Jean M. Murdock. *International Terrorism in the 1980s: A Chronology of Events*. Vol. 2, *1984–1987*. Ames: Iowa State University Press, 1989.

Miller, Frederic. *2008 Indian Embassy Bombing in Kabul*. Mauritius: Vdm, 2010.

Miller, John, Michael Stone, and Chris Mitchell. *The Cell: Inside the 9/11 Plot and Why the FBI and CIA Failed to Stop It*. New York: Hyperion, 2002.

Milligan, Susan. "FBI Whistle-Blower." *Boston Globe*, June 7, 2002, A33.

Milton-Edwards, Beverly. *Islamic Fundamentalism since 1945*. New York: Routledge, 2002.

Mitchell, Kirsten B. "Government Trying to Decide FEMA's Fate." *Tampa Tribune*, August 7, 2002, 1.

Morin, Richard, and Claudia Deane. "Poll: Strong Backing for Bush, War: Few Americans See Easy End to Conflict." *Washington Post*, March 11, 2002, A1.

Morrow, Stacy, and Elvira Sakmari. "FBI Arrests Man in Dallas Skyscraper Bomb Plot." *NBC News*, September 25, 2009. http://www.nbcdfw.com/news/local-beat/FBI-Arrests-Man-Accused-in-Skyscraper-Bomb-Plot—61272512.html.

Moussaoui, Abd Samar, with Florence Bouquillat. *Zacarias, My Brother: The Making of a Terrorist*. New York: Seven Stories, 2003.

Mueller, John, ed. "Case 5: Barot and the Financial Buildings." *Terrorism since 9/11: The American Cases*. Columbus: Ohio State University Press, 2012. Accessed January 30, 2012. http://pswbe.sbs.ohio-state.edu/faculty/jmueller/since.pdf.

Mulgrew, Ian. "Ressam Gets 22 Years in Prison." *The Gazette* (Canada), July 28, 2011.

Munson, Kenneth. *Jane's Unmanned Aerial Vehicles and Targets, 1995–1996*. London: Jane's, 1996.

Murphy, Caryle. "Saudi Arabia Indicts 991 Suspected Al Qaeda Militants." *Christian Science Monitor*, October 22, 2008.

Murphy, Jack, and Brandon Webb. *Benghazi: The Definitive Report*. New York: HarperCollins, 2013.

Murray, Williamson, and Robert H. Scales, Jr. *The Iraq War: A Military History*. Cambridge, MA: Belknap, 2005.

Musallam, Adnan. *From Secularism to Jihad: Sayyid Qutb and the Foundations of Radical Islam*. Westport, CT: Praeger, 2005.

Naftali, Timothy. *Blind Spot: The Secret History of American Counterterrorism*. New York: Basic Books, 2005.

Nagl, John A. *Learning to Eat Soup with a Knife: Counterinsurgency Lessons from Malaya and Vietnam*. Chicago: University of Chicago Press, 2005.

Naughtie, James. *The Accidental American: Tony Blair and the Presidency*. New York: PublicAffairs, 2004.

Netanyahu, Iddo. *Yoni's Last Battle: The Rescue at Entebbe*. Jerusalem: Gefen Books, 1976.

Nichols, John. *The Rise and Rise of Richard B. Cheney: Unlocking the Mysteries of the Most Powerful Vice President in American History*. New York: New Press, 2005.

9/11 Commission. *The 9/11 Commission Report: Final Report of the National Commission on Terrorist Attacks Upon the United States*. New York: Norton, 2004.

Noftsinger, John B., Jr., Kenneth F. Newbold, Jr., and Jack K. Wheeler. *Understanding Homeland Security: Policy, Perspectives, and Paradoxes.* New York: Palgrave Macmillan, 2007.

Nojumi, Neamatollah. *The Rise of the Taliban in Afghanistan: Mass Mobilization, Civil War and the Future of the Region.* Basingstoke, UK: Palgrave, 2002.

Norington, Brad. "I Received Training in Pakistan, Admits Charged U.S. Bomb Suspect." *The Australian,* May 6, 2010.

Norton, Augustus Richard. *Hezbollah: A Short History.* Princeton, NJ: Princeton University Press, 2007.

Nugent, Paul. *Africa since Independence: A Comparative History.* New York: Palgrave Macmillan, 2004.

Oakley, Robert B., and John I. Hirsch. *Somalia and Operation Restore Hope: Reflections on Peacemaking and Peacekeeping.* Washington, DC: United States Institute of Peace Press, 1995.

Obwogo, Subiri. *The Bombs That Shook Nairobi & Dar es Salaam: A Story of Pain and Betrayal.* Nairobi: Obwogo and Family, 1999.

Oliphant, Thomas. *Utter Incompetents: Ego and Ideology in the Age of Bush.* New York: Thomas Dunne Books, 2007.

Oliver, Anne Marie, and Paul Steinberg. *The Road to Martyrs' Square: A Journey into the World of the Suicide Bomber.* Oxford: Oxford University Press, 2005.

Omar, Hamsa. "Somali Soldier Who Killed al-Qaeda Leader Is Injured in Retaliatory Attack." *Bloomberg News,* August 17, 2011. http://www.bloomberg.com/news/2011-08-17/somali-soldier-who-killed-al-qaeda-leader-is-shot-in-retaliation.html.

O'Neill, Sean, and Daniel McGrory. *The Suicide Factory.* London: Harper Collins, 2006.

Oren, Michael B. *Power, Faith, and Fantasy: America in the Middle East 1776 to the Present.* New York: W. W. Norton, 2007.

Oren, Michael B. *Six Days of War: June 1967 and the Making of the Modern Middle East.* Novato, CA: Presidio, 2003.

Owen, John M., IV. *Liberal Peace, Liberal War: American Politics and International Security.* Ithaca, NY: Cornell University Press, 1997.

Painter, David S. *The Cold War: An International History.* New York: Routledge, 1999.

Pape, Robert A. *Dying to Win: The Strategic Logic of Suicide Terrorism.* New York: Random House, 2005.

Parker, Richard B. *The Politics of Miscalculation in the Middle East.* Bloomington: Indiana University Press, 1993.

Patterson, Thomas G., et al. *A History of American Foreign Relations since 1895.* Boston: Houghton Mifflin, 2005.

Peltz, Eric. *Speed and Power: Toward and Expeditionary Army.* Santa Monica, CA: RAND Corporation, 2003.

Pfiffner, James P. *Power Play: The Bush Presidency and the Constitution.* Washington, DC: Brookings Institution Press, 2008.

Philipps, Thomas. "The Dozier Kidnapping: Confronting the Red Brigades." *Air and Space Power Journal,* February 7, 2002. http://www.airpower.maxwell.af.mil/airchronicles/cc/philipps.html.

Phillips, James. "Zarqawi's Amman Bombings: Jordan's 9/11." *Heritage Foundation,* Washington D.C., November 18, 2005. Accessed January 31, 2012. http://www.heritage.org/research/reports/2005/11/zarqawis-amman-bombings-jordans-9-11.

Pinedo, Emma. "Suspected ETA Bomb Explodes in Madrid." Reuters, February 9, 2009. http://www.reuters.com/article/cdUSTRES1825120090209.

Pirnie, Bruce, and Edward O'Connell. *Counterinsurgency in Iraq (2003–2006) RAND Counterinsurgency Study.* Vol. 2. Santa Monica, CA: RAND, 2008.

Polgreen, Lydia. "Study Confirms 9/11 Impact on New York City Economy." *New York Times,* June 30, 2004, B6.

Polmar, Norman. *The Naval Institute Guide to the Ships and Aircraft of the U.S. Fleet.* 18th ed. Annapolis, MD: Naval Institute Press, 2005.

Posner, Eric A., and Adrian Vermeule. *Terror in the Balance? Security, Liberty, and the Courts*. New York: Oxford University Press, 2007.

Posner, Gerald. *Why America Slept: The Failure to Prevent 9/11*. New York: Ballantine Books, 2003.

Powell, Colin, and Joseph E. Persico. *My American Journey*. New York: Ballantine, 2003.

Powers, Richard Gid. *Broken: The Troubled Past and Uncertain Future of the FBI*. New York: Free Press, 2004.

Prestholdt, Jeremy. "Phantom of the Forever War: Fazul Abdullah Mohammed and the Terrorist Imaginary." *Public Culture* 21, no. 3 (Fall 2009).

Priest, Dana. "Former Chief of CIA's Bin Laden Unit Leaves." *Washington Post* (November 12, 2004), A4.

Puniyani, Ram. *Terrorism: Facts versus Myths*. New Delhi: Pharos Media, 2007.

Qutb, Sayyid. *In the Shade of the Quran*. Falls Church, VA: WAMY International, 1995.

Rabasa, Angel. *Radical Islam in East Africa*. Santa Monica, CA: RAND, 2009.

Rabasa, Angel, Peter Chalk, Kim Cragin, Sara A. Daly, Heather S. Gregg, Theodore W. Karasik, Kevin A. O'Brien, and William Rosenau. *Beyond al-Qaeda Part 1: The Global Jihadist Movement*. Santa Monica, CA: RAND, 2006.

Raghavan, Sudarsan, and Jonathan Landay. "Advance Information on *Cole*'s Yemen Stop under Scrutiny." *Stars and Stripes*, November 1, 2000.

Rajan, Karim, and Fred Mukinda. "Two Arrested as Top Terror Suspect Flees." *Daily Nation* (Kenya), August 30, 2008. http://www.nation.co.ke/News/-/1056/446582/-/tj2yrs/-/index.html.

Randal, Jonathan. *Osama: The Making of a Terrorist*. New York: Knopf, 2004.

Raphaeli, Nimrod. *'The Sheikh of the Slaughterers': Abu Mus'ab Al-Zarqawi and the Al-Qaeda Connection*. Inquiry and Analysis Series Report no. 23, July 1, 2005. Washington, DC: The Middle East Media Research Institute.

Rasanayagam, Angelo. *Afghanistan: A Modern History*. London: I. B. Tauris, 2005.

Rashbaum, William. "In Tapes of Subway Plot Suspect, a Disjointed Torrent of Hatred." *New York Times*, April 26, 2006.

Rashid, Ahmed. *Taliban: Islam, Oil and the New Great Game in Central Asia*. London: Tauris, 2002.

Rauf, Feisal Abdul. "Building on Faith." *New York Times*, September 7, 2010.

Reagan, Timothy. *National Security Case Studies Special Case-Management Challenges*. Washington, DC: Federal Judicial Center, 2010. Accessed February 16, 2012. http://www.fjc.gov/public/pdf.nsf/lookup/ts100222.pdf/$file/ts100222.pdf.

Reardon, Mark, and Jeffery Charlston. *From Transformation to Combat: The First Stryker Brigade at War*. Washington, DC: Center of Military History, 2007.

Reeve, Simon. *The New Jackals: Ramzi Yousef, Osama bin Laden and the Future of Terrorism*. Boston: Northeastern University Press, 1999.

Ressa, Maria. "Philippines: U.S. Missed 9/11 Clues Years Ago." *CNN.com*, July 26, 2003. http://www.cnn.com/2003/WORLD/asiapcf/southeast/07/26/khalid.confession/index.html.

Rhine, Staci L., Stephen Bennett, and Richard Flickinger. "After 9/11: Television Viewers, Newspaper Readers and Public Opinion about Terrorism's Consequences." Paper presented at the annual meeting of the American Political Science Association, Boston Marriott Copley Place, Sheraton Boston & Hynes Convention Center, Boston, MA, August 28, 2002. http://fs.huntingdon.edu/jlewis/Terror/FlickingerAPSA02ppr.pdf.

Richelson, Jeffrey T. *The U.S. Intelligence Community*. 4th ed. Boulder, CO: Westview, 1999.

Ricks, Thomas E. *Fiasco: The American Military Adventure in Iraq*. New York: Penguin, 2006.

Riedel, Bruce, and Bilal Y. Saab. "Al Qaeda's Third Front: Saudi Arabia." *Washington Quarterly* 21 (2008): 33–46.

Riley, Mark. "Arsonists Sabotage Top Ski Resort." *Sydney Morning Herald* (Australia), October 24, 1998.

Risen, James. *State of War: The Secret History of the CIA and the Bush Administration.* New York: Free Press, 2006.

Risen, James. "Pakistan Nabs al-Qaeda Planner." *New York Times*, May 1, 2003.

Roberts, Brad. "Conclusion." In *Hype or Reality? The 'New Terrorism' and Mass Casualty Attacks,* edited by Brad Roberts, 220–35. Alexandria, VA: Chemical and Biological Arms Control Institute, 2000.

Roberts, Pat, ed. *Report on U.S. Intelligence Community's Prewar Intelligence Assessments on Iraq: Conclusions.* Washington, DC: Diane Publishing, 2004.

Rodgers, Walter, and Terry Frieden. "USS *Cole* Probe Seeks Evidence of Conspiracy." *CNN.com*, October 20, 2000. http://transcripts.cnn.com/2000/us/10/20/cole.evidence/.

Rosebraugh, Craig. *Burning Rage of a Dying Planet: Speaking for the Earth Liberation Front.* New York: Lantern Books, 2004.

Rosen, James. "Able Danger Operatives Sue Pentagon." *News Tribune* (Tacoma, WA), March 4, 2006, 6.

Rosenthal, Franz. "On Suicide in Islam." *Journal of the American Oriental Society* 66 (1946): 239–59.

Rotberg, Robert I. *Battling Terrorism in the Horn of Africa.* Washington, DC: Brookings Institution Press, 2005.

Rotberg, Robert I., ed. *When States Fail: Causes and Consequences.* Princeton, NJ: Princeton University Press, 2003.

Roth, David. *Sacred Honor: Colin Powell: The Inside Account of His Life and Triumphs.* New York: HarperCollins, 1995.

Roth, Margaret. "Recent Conflicts Mark Turning Point for SEALs, Other Special Ops Forces." *Seapower* (February 2005): 14–16.

Rubin, Barry, and Judith Colp Rubin, eds. *Anti-American Terrorism and the Middle East: A Documentary Reader.* New York: Oxford University Press, 2002.

Russo, Robert. "FBI Likened to Little Shop of Horrors." *Gazette* (Montreal), June 7, 2002, B1.

Ryan, Paul. *The Iranian Rescue Mission.* Annapolis, MD: Naval Institute.

Saar, Erik, and Viveca Novak. *Inside the Wire: A Military Intelligence Soldier's Eyewitness Account of Life at Guantanamo.* New York: Penguin, 2005.

Sageman, Marc. *Understanding Terror Networks.* Philadelphia: University of Pennsylvania Press, 2004.

Said, Edward. *Culture and Imperialism.* New York: Knopf, 1999.

Sakr, Naomi. *Satellite Realms: Transnational Television, Globalization & the Middle East.* London: I. B. Tauris, 2001.

Sampson, William. *Confessions of an Innocent Man: Torture and Survival in a Saudi Prison.* Toronto: McClelland and Stewart, 2005.

Saunders, Stephen, ed. *Jane's Fighting Ships, 2006–2007.* Coulsdon, UK: Jane's Information Group, 2006.

Savage, Charlie. "Nigerian Indicted in Terrorist Plot." *New York Times*, January 6, 2010.

Savage, Charlie. "Accused 9/11 Mastermind to Face Civilian Trial in N.Y." *New York Times*, November 13, 2009.

Scahill, Jeremy. *Dirty Wars: The World is a Battlefield.* New York: Nation Books, 2013.

Scales, Robert H. *Certain Victory: The U.S. Army in the Gulf War.* Washington, DC: Brassey's, 1994.

Scarborough, Rowan. *Rumsfeld's War: The Untold Story of America's Anti-Terrorist Commander.* Washington, DC: Regnery, 2004.

Schafer, Chelsea E., and Grey M. Shaw. "The Polls Trends: Tolerance in the United States." *Public Opinion Quarterly* 73, no. 2 (Summer 2009): 404–31.

Schanzer, Jonathan. "Behind the French Tanker Bombing: Yemen's Ongoing Problems with Islamist Terrorism." *Columbia International Affairs Online*, October 21, 2002. Accessed January 31, 2012. http://www.ciaonet.org/pbei/winep/policy_2002/2002_670.html.

Scheuer, Michael. *Through Our Enemies' Eyes: Osama bin Laden, Radical Islam and the Future of America*. Dulles, VA: Brassey's, 2006.

Scheuer, Michael. "A Fine Rendition." *New York Times*, March 11, 2005, A23.

Scheuer, Michael. *Imperial Hubris: Why the West Is Losing the War on Terror*. Washington, DC: Potomac Books, 2004.

Schiller, Herbert. *Communication and Cultural Domination*. New York: M. E. Sharpe, 1976.

Schlesinger, Arthur M. *War and the American Presidency*. New York: Norton, 2004.

Schmidt, Susan. "Two Al-Qaeda Suspects Charged in Cole Attack." *Washington Post*, May 16, 2003.

Schmitt, Eric, and Carolyn Marshall. "In Secret Unit's 'Black Room,' a Grim Portrait of U.S. Abuse." *New York Times*, March 19, 2006.

Schmitt, Gary. "Constitutional Spying: The Solution to the FISA Problem." *Weekly Standard* 11, no. 16 (January 2–January 9, 2006): 1–2.

Schneider, Barry. *Avoiding the Abyss: Progress, Shortfalls, and the Way Ahead in Combating the WMD Threat*. Westport, CT: Praeger Publishing, 2006.

Schuster, Henry. *Hunting Eric Rudolph*. New York: Penguin, 2005.

Schwab, Peter. *Africa: A Continent Self-Destructs*. New York: Palgrave Macmillan, 2001.

Schwartz, John. "Appeals Court Throws Out Sentence in Bombing Plot, Calling It Too Light." *New York Times*, February 2, 2010.

Sciolino, Elaine. "Separatists Admit to Madrid Airport Attack but Stand by Cease-Fire." *New York Times*, January 10, 2007.

Seale, Patrick. *Abu Nidal, a Gun for Hire: The Secret Life of the World's Most Notorious Arab Terrorist*. New York: Random House, 1992.

Serrano, Richard A. "Release of Lindh Again Urged." *Los Angeles Times*, April 5, 2007.

Shai, Shaul. *The Red Sea Terror Triangle: Sudan, Somalia, Yemen, and Islamic Terror*. New Brunswick, NJ: Transaction Publishers, 2005.

Sharansky, Natan, and Ron Dermer. *The Case for Democracy: The Power of Freedom to Overcome Tyranny and Terror*. New York: PublicAffairs, 2004.

Sharockman, Aaron. "9/11 Hijackers Practiced Here." *St. Petersburg Times*, March 31, 2006.

Shawcross, William. *Allies: The U.S., Britain, and Europe in the Aftermath of the Iraq War*. New York: PublicAffairs, 2005.

Shay, Shaul. *The Shahids: Islam and Suicide Attacks*. New Brunswick, NJ: Transaction Publishers, 2004.

Shephard, Alicia P. *Woodward and Bernstein: Life in the Shadow of Watergate*. Indianapolis: Wiley, 2006.

Shepherd, Michelle. "Dossier Reveals Secrets of Forming al-Qaeda Cell." *Toronto Star* (Canada), April 25, 2011.

Shukovsky, Paul. "Terrorist Ahmed Ressam Is Sentenced but U.S. Judge Lashes Out." *Seattle Post-Intelligencer*, July 28, 2005.

Sidahmed, Abdel Salam. *Islamic Fundamentalism*. Boulder, CO: Westview, 1996.

Sidel, John. *Riots, Pogroms, Jihad: Religious Violence in Indonesia*. Ithaca, NY: Cornell University Press, 2006.

Silber, Mitchell D., and Arvin Bhatt. *Radicalization in the West: The Homegrown Threat*. New York: New York Police Department Intelligence Division, 2007.

Skaine, Rosemarie. *Female Suicide Bombers*. Jefferson, NC: McFarland, 2006.

Skerker, Michael. "Just War Criteria and the New Face of War: Human Shields, Manufactured Martyrs, and Little Boys with Stones." *Journal of Military Ethics* 3, no. 1 (2004): 27–39.

Smith, Dennis. *Report from Ground Zero: The Story of the Rescue Efforts at the World Trade Center*. New York: Viking, 2002.

Smith, Gavin. "Michael Moore Gives Much More." *New Statesman*, July 19, 2004, 1.

Smith, Jane I., and Yvonne Haddad. *The Islamic Understanding of Death and Resurrection*. Albany: State University of New York Press, 1981.

Smith, Paul. *The Terrorism Ahead: Confronting Transnational Violence in the Twenty-First Century*. Armonk, NY: M. E. Sharpe, 2008.

Snow, Donald M. *Distant Thunder: Third World Conflict and the New International Order*. New York: St. Martin's, 1993.

Sobhani, Ayatollah Jafar, and Reza Shah Kazemi. *Doctrines of Shi'i Islam: A Compendium of Imami Beliefs and Practices*. London: I. B. Tauris, 2001.

Spaeth, Anthony. "Rumbles in the Jungle." *Time*, March 4, 2002.

Spires, David N. *Beyond Horizons: A Half Century of Air Force Space Leadership*. 2nd ed. Honolulu: University Press of the Pacific, 2002.

Stanik, Joseph T. *El Dorado Canyon: Reagan's Undeclared War with Quddafi*. Annapolis, MD: Naval Institute Press, 2003.

Stevenson, William. *90 Minutes at Entebbe*. New York: Bantam, 1976.

Stewart, Richard W. *The United States Army in Afghanistan: Operation Enduring Freedom, October 2001–March 2002*. Washington, DC: U.S. Government Printing Office, 2003.

Stolberg, Sheryl Gay, and Eric Lichtblau. "Cheney Assails Press on Report on Bank Data." *New York Times*, June 24, 2006.

Stora, Benjamin. *Algeria: A Short History*. Ithaca, NY: Cornell University Press, 2004.

Strasser, Steven, ed. *The Abu Ghraib Investigations: The Official Independent Panel and Pentagon Reports on the Shocking Prisoner Abuse in Iraq*. New York: Public Affairs, 2004.

Strasser, Steven, ed. *The 9/11 Investigations; Staff Reports of the 9/11 Commission; Excerpts from the House-Senate Joint Inquiry Report on 9/11 Testimony from 14 Key Witnesses, Including Richard Clarke, George Tenet, and Condoleezza Rice*. New York: PublicAffairs, 2004.

Sundquist, Leah R. *NATO in Afghanistan: A Progress Report*. Carlisle Barracks, PA: U.S. Army War College, 2008.

Suskind, Ron. *One Percent Doctrine*. New York: Simon and Schuster, 2006.

Tankel, Stephen. "Lashkar-e-Taiba: From 9/11 to Mumbai." International Center for the Study of Radicalisation and Political Violence, London, April/May 2009. Accessed January 1, 2011. http://www.iscr.info/news/attachments/12408469161SRTTankelReport.pdf.

Tanner, Stephen. *Afghanistan: A Military History from Alexander the Great to the Fall of the Taliban*. New York: Da Capo, 2003.

Tarazona-Sevillano, Gabriela. *Sendero Luminoso and the Threat of Narcoterrorism*. New York: Praeger, 1990.

Tatham, Steve. *Losing Arab Hearts and Minds: The Coalition, Al-Jazeera and Muslim Public Opinion*. London: Hurst, 2006.

Taylor, Alan R. *The Superpowers and the Middle East*. Syracuse, NY: Syracuse University Press, 1991.

Taylor, Philip M. *War and the Media: Propaganda and Persuasion in the Gulf War*. Manchester, UK: Manchester University Press, 1992.

Temple-Raston, Dina. *The Jihad Next Door: The Lackawanna Six and Rough Justice in the Age of Terror*. New York: Perseus Books, 2007.

Tenet, George, and Bill Harlow. *At the Center of the Storm: My Years at the CIA*. New York: HarperCollins, 2007.

Tibi, Bassam. *Arab Nationalism: Between Islam and the Nation-State*. New York: St. Martin's, 2007.

Tibi, Bassam. *The Challenge of Fundamentalism: Political Islam and the New World Disorder*. Berkeley: University of California Press, 1998.

Tiboni, Frank. "Information Becomes Weapon." *Federal Computer Week*, February 13, 2006, 10–13.

Trento, Susan B., and Joseph J. Trento. *Unsafe at Any Altitude: Failed Terrorism Investigations, Scapegoating 9/11, and the Shocking Truth about Aviation Security Today*. Hanover, NH: Steerforth, 2006.

Tucker, Stephen. *Terrorist Explosive Sourcebook: Countering Terrorist Use of Improvised Explosive Devices*. Boulder, CO: Paladin, 2005.

Tumber, Howard, and Frank Webster. *Journalists under Fire: Information War and Journalistic Practices*. London: Sage, 2006.

Turnbull, Wayne. "A Tangled Web of Southeast Asian Islamic Terrorism: The Jemaah Islamiya Terrorist Network." Monterey, CA: Monterey Institute of International Studies, July 31, 2003.

Tyler, Patrick. *A World of Trouble: The White House and the Middle East—from the Cold War to the War on Terror.* New York: Farrar Straus Giroux, 2009.

Tyler, Patrick. "British Charge 8 with Conspiracy in a Terror Plot." *New York Times*, August 18, 2004.

United States Department of Defense. "Summary of Evidence for Combatant Status Review Tribunal—Al Nashiri, Abd Al Rahim Hussein Mohammad," March 14, 2007. http://www.defenselink.mil/news/ISN10015.pdf#1.

United States of America v. John Philip Walker Lindh. U.S. District Court for the Eastern District of Virginia, Alexandria Division, January 15, 2002. http://www.usdoj.gov/ag/criminalcomplaint1.htm.

United States Department of Defense. *21st Century Complete Guide to American Intelligence Agencies*. Washington, DC: U.S. Government Printing Office, 2002.

U.S. Congress. *Private Security Firms: Standards, Cooperation, and Coordination on the Battlefield*; Congressional Hearing. Darby, PA: Diane Publishing, 2007.

U.S. Senate. *Report of the Select Committee on Intelligence on the U.S. Intelligence Community's Prewar Assessments on Iraq.* Washington, DC: U.S. Government Printing Office, 2004.

U.S. Senate, Committee on Foreign Relations. *The Nomination of Hon. John D. Negroponte to be U.S. Ambassador to Iraq, April 27, 2004.* Washington, DC: U.S. Government Printing Office, 2004.

Valentine, Douglas. *The Strength of the Wolf: The Secret History of America's War on Drugs*. London: Verso, 2004.

Vance, Cyrus. *Hard Choices: Critical Years in America's Foreign Policy.* New York: Simon and Schuster, 1983.

Vidino, Lorenzo. *Al Qaeda in Europe: The New Battleground of International Jihad.* Amherst, NY: Prometheus Books, 2006.

Von Hippel, Karin. *Europe Confronts Terrorism*. New York: Palgrave Macmillan, 2005.

Weisenborn, Ray, ed. *Media in the Midst of War: Cairo Reporting to the Global Village.* Cairo: Adham Center for Television, 1992.

Weiser, Benjamin. "A Guilty Plea in Plot to Bomb Times Square." *New York Times*, June 22, 2010.

Weiser, Benjamin. "A Jury Torn and Fearful in 2001 Terrorism Trial." *New York Times*, January 5, 2003.

Weiser, Benjamin. "Going on Trial: U.S. Accusations of a Global Plot; Embassy Bombings Case." *New York Times*, February 4, 2001, 29.

West, Deborah L. *Combating Terrorism in the Horn of Africa and Yemen*. Cambridge, MA: World Peace Foundation, 2005.

White, Jonathan. *Defending the Homeland: Domestic Intelligence, Law Enforcement and Security.* Belmont, CA: Wadsworth, 2003.

Whitlock, Craig. "In Letter, Radical Cleric Details CIA Abduction, Egyptian Torture." *Washington Post*, November 10, 2006.

Wilkinson, Tracy. "Details Emerge in Cleric's Abduction." *Los Angeles Times*, January 10, 2007.

Wilson, George. "Kidnapped Officer Seen as a 'Soldier's Soldier.'" *Washington Post*, December 18, 1981, A52.

Woodward, Bob. *State of Denial: Bush at War, Part III*. New York: Simon and Schuster, 2006.

Woodward, Bob. *Plan of Attack*. New York: Simon and Schuster, 2004.

Woodward, Bob. *Bush at War*. New York: Simon and Schuster, 2002.

Wright, Lawrence. *The Looming Tower: Al Qaeda and the Road to 9/11*. New York: Knopf, 2006.

Wright, Robin. *Sacred Rage: The Wrath of Militant Islam*. New York: Touchstone Books, Simon & Schuster, 2001.

Yee, John. *War by Other Means: An Insider's Account of the War on Terror*. New York: Atlantic Monthly, 2006.

Yergin, Daniel H. *Shattered Peace: The Origins of the Cold War*. New York: Penguin, 1990.

Yoo, John. *War by Other Means: An Insider's Account of the War on Terror*. New York: Atlantic Monthly Press, 2006.

Yoo, John. *The Powers of War and Peace: The Constitution and Foreign Affairs after 9/11*. Chicago: University of Chicago Press, 2005.

Zabecki, David T. "Landpower in History: Strategists Must Regain an Understanding of the Role of Ground Forces." *Armed Forces Journal* (August 2002): 40–42.

Zimmerman, Dwight Jon, and John Gresham. *Beyond Hell and Back: How America's Special Operations Forces Became the World's Greatest Fighting Unit*. New York: St. Martin's, 2007.

Zisser, Eyal. "Hezbollah in Iran: At the Cross-Roads." *Terrorism and Political Violence* 8, no. 2 (Summer 1996): 146–65.

Zuhur, Sherifa. "Decreasing Violence in Saudi Arabia and Beyond." In *Home Grown Terrorism: Understanding and Addressing the Root Causes of Radicalisation among Groups with an Immigrant Heritage in Europe*, Vol. 60, edited by Thamas M. Pick, Anne Speckard, and B. Jacuch, 74–98. NATO Science for Peace and Security Series. Amsterdam: IOS Press, 2010.

Zuhur, Sherifa. *A Hundred Osamas: Islamist Threats and the Future of Counterinsurgency*. Carlisle Barracks, PA: Strategic Studies Institute, U.S. Army War College, 2006.

About the Editor and Contributors

Editor

Dr. Jan Goldman has worked and taught in the U.S. Intelligence Community for over 30 years. He is the founding editor of the *International Journal of Intelligence and Ethics* (Rowman and Littlefield Publishers), and an adjunct professor at the McCourt School of Public Policy and the Georgetown Global Education Institute, both at Georgetown University. He is the author or editor of several publications on intelligence, including *The Central Intelligence Agency: An Encyclopedia of Covert Operations, Intelligence Gathering, and Spies*, 2 vols. (ABC-CLIO, 2014); *Words of Intelligence: An Intelligence Professional's Lexicon for Domestic and Foreign Threats* (Roman and Littlefield, 2010), and *Ethics of Spying*, volumes 1 & 2 (Rowman and Littlefield, 2006 and 2010).

Contributors

Kristian P. Alexander
Independent Researcher

Christopher Anzalone
Independent Scholar

James Arnold
Independent Scholar

Ojan Aryanfard
Independent Scholar

Stephen E. Atkins
Adjunct Professor of History
Texas A&M University

Donna Bassett
Senior Manager
The Information Project

Dr. Robert F. Baumann
Professor of History
U.S. Army Command & General Staff
  College

Michael K. Beauchamp
Texas A&M University

Robert G. Berschinski
Independent Scholar

Amy Hackney Blackwell
Independent Scholar

Walter Boyne
Independent Scholar

Ben Brandt
Director
Lime Consultancy, UAE

Jessica Britt
Independent Scholar

Dr. Stefan M. Brooks
Assistant Professor of Political Science
Lindsey Wilson College

Stephanie Caravias
Georgetown University

Peter Carey
Georgetown University

Dr. Peter Chalk
Senior Analyst
RAND Corporation

Elliot Paul Chodoff
University of Haifa
Israel

Dr. Dylan A. Cyr
Department of History
University of Western Ontario

Marcel A. Derosier
Independent Scholar

Dr. Karl R. DeRouen
Professor and Director of the International
    Studies Program
University of Alabama

Scott R. DiMarco
Director of Library and Information
    Resources
Mansfield University of Pennsylvania

Dr. Paul W. Doerr
Associate Professor
Acadia University
Canada

Colonel Donald R. Dunne
U.S. Army

Dr. Richard M. Edwards
Senior Lecturer
University of Wisconsin Colleges

James O. Ellis III
Senior Fellow
Memorial Institute for the Prevention of
    Terrorism

Chuck Fahrer
Assistant Professor of Geography
Georgia College

Ezekiel Fraint
Georgetown University

Dr. K. Luisa Gandolfo
University of Exeter
United Kingdom

Greg Hannah
Senior Political Scientist
RAND Corporation, Cambridge, UK

Eric Harris
Independent Scholar

Dr. Arthur M. Holst
MPA Program Faculty
Widener University

Dr. Charles Francis Howlett
Associate Professor
Molloy College

Dr. Harry Raymond Hueston II
Independent Scholar

Dr. Donna R. Jackson
Wolfson College, Cambridge

Dr. Robert B. Kane
Adjunct Professor of History
Troy University

Elinor Kasting
Georgetown University

Paul Kemppainen
Georgetown University

Daniel Katz
Analyst
Defense Industry

Chen Kertcher
School of History
Tel Aviv University

Dr. Arne Kislenko
Ryerson University
Canada

Daniel W. Kuthy
Georgia State University

Jeffrey Lamonica
Assistant Professor of History
Delaware County Community College

Dr. Tom Lansford
Academic Dean, College of Arts and Letters
Professor of Political Science
University of Southern Mississippi

Keith A. Leitich
Independent Scholar

Shawn Livingston
Public Service Librarian
University of Kentucky

Julie Manning
Georgetown University

Paul Martin
Southern Illinois University

Mitchell McNaylor
Independent Scholar

Abraham O. Mendoza
Defense Researcher

Dr. Edward F. Mickolus
President
Vinyard Software

Dr. Jerry D. Morelock
Colonel, U.S. Army, Retired
Editor in Chief, *Armchair General*
    Magazine

Gregory Wayne Morgan
Independent Scholar

Dr. Lisa Marie Mundey
Assistant Professor
University of St. Thomas

Dr. Keith Murphy
Associate Dean
Fort Valley State University

Benjamin P. Nickels
Independent Scholar

Terri Nichols
Independent Scholar

Dr. Paul G. Pierpaoli, Jr.
Fellow
Military History, ABC-CLIO, Inc.

Dr. Peter J. Rainow
Independent Scholar

Captain Carl Otis Schuster (retired)
U.S. Navy
Hawaii Pacific University

Dr. Jeff R. Schutts
Instructor
Douglas College

Dr. Frank Shanty
Director of Research
Cobra Institute in Maryland

Nate Shestak
Georgetown University

James E. Shircliffe, Jr.
Principal Research Analyst
CENTRA Technology, Inc.

Dr. Rami Y. Siklawi
University of Exeter
United Kingdom

Dr. Ranjit Singh
Assistant Professor of Political Science
    and International Affairs
University of Mary Washington

Dr. Paul Smith
Professor
Naval War College, Rhode Island, NY

Dr. Paul Joseph Springer
Associate Professor of Comparative
    Military Studies
Air Command and Staff College
Maxwell Air Force Base, Alabama

Horacio Trujillo
Security Consultant
Los Angeles, California

Dr. Spencer C. Tucker
Senior Fellow
Military History, ABC-CLIO, Inc.

Dr. Richard B. Verrone
Texas Tech University

Richard Warnes
Senior Political Scientist
RAND Corporation, Cambridge, UK

Lori Weathers
Independent Scholar

Dr. Wyndham E. Whynot
Assistant Professor of History
Livingstone College

Dr. Anna M. Wittmann
University of Alberta

Taryn Wolf
Georgetown University

Dr. Clarence R. Wyatt
Pottinger Professor of History
Centre College, Kentucky

Gregory Wyatt
Georgetown University

Dr. Joseph K. Young
Assistant Professor
Southern Illinois University

Yara Zogheib
Georgetown University

David T. Zabecki
Major General, US Army (Retired)

Dr. Sherifa Zuhur
Visiting Professor of National Security
    Affairs
Regional Strategy and Planning
    Department
Strategic Studies Institute

Index

Page numbers in **bold** indicate main entries.